GB

The Great Ideas

Man
Mathematics
Matter
Mechanics
Medicine
Memory and Imagination
Metaphysics
Mind
Monarchy
Nature
Necessity and Contingency
Oligarchy
One and Many
Opinion
Opposition
Philosophy
Physics
Pleasure and Pain
Poetry
Principle
Progress
Prophecy
Prudence
Punishment
Quality
Quantity

Reasoning
Relation
Religion
Revolution
Rhetoric
Same and Other
Science
Sense
Sign and Symbol
Sin
Slavery
Soul
Space
State
Temperance
Theology
Time
Truth
Tyranny
Universal and Particular
Virtue and Vice
War and Peace
Wealth
Will
Wisdom
World

The
Great Ideas
Today

1985

Encyclopædia Britannica, Inc.

CHICAGO

AUCKLAND • GENEVA • LONDON • MANILA • PARIS • ROME • SEOUL • SYDNEY • TOKYO • TORONTO

"The Inefficacy of the Good: On Reading Thucydides," by Douglas Allanbrook, is from
The St. John's Review, Spring 1984. Reprinted by permission of the author.

"The Bhagavad Gita," translated by Eliot Deutsch, was first printed by Holt, Rinehart and
Winston. Copyright 1968 by Eliot Deutsch. Reprinted by permission of the translator.

Library of Congress Catalog Card Number: 61-65561
International Standard Book Number: 0-85229-431-X
International Standard Serial Number: 0072-7288
Printed in the U.S.A.

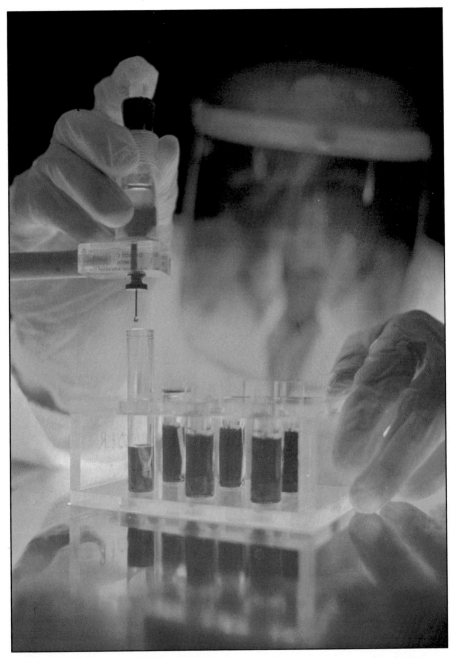

Scientists have found that many complex molecular relationships can be demonstrated in the single-celled organism *E. coli.* One drop of the dissolved and centrifuged *E. coli* cells shown here contains trillions of bits of replicating DNA.

A NOTE ON REFERENCE STYLE

In the following pages, passages in *Great Books of the Western World* are referred to by the initials '*GBWW*,' followed by volume, page number, and page section. Thus, '*GBWW*, Vol. 39, p. 210b' refers to page 210 in Adam Smith's *The Wealth of Nations*, which is Volume 39 in *Great Books of the Western World*. The small letter 'b' indicates the page section. In books printed in single column, 'a' and 'b' refer to the upper and lower halves of the page. In books printed in double column, 'a' and 'b' refer to the upper and lower halves of the left column, 'c' and 'd' to the upper and lower halves of the right column. For example, 'Vol. 53, p. 210b' refers to the lower half of page 210, since Volume 53, James's *Principles of Psychology*, is printed in single column. On the other hand, 'Vol. 7, p. 210b' refers to the lower left quarter of the page, since Volume 7, Plato's *Dialogues*, is printed in double column.

Gateway to the Great Books is referred to by the initials '*GGB*,' followed by volume and page number. Thus, '*GGB*, Vol. 10, pp. 39–57' refers to pages 39 through 57 of Volume 10 of *Gateway to the Great Books*, which is James's essay, "The Will to Believe."

The Great Ideas Today is referred to by the initials '*GIT*,' followed by the year and page number. Thus '*GIT* 1968, p. 210' refers to page 210 of the 1968 edition of *The Great Ideas Today*.

Contents

Preface

This is the twenty-fifth issue of *The Great Ideas Today* to appear since 1961—which makes this year our twenty-fifth anniversary. We grope for some appropriate remarks, hoping the occasion will seem remarkable. Unhappily, such a milestone suggests mellowness and middle age, with a good deal of white about the head and a certain portliness of figure—all of which may apply, in a metaphorical sense, to what the book has become, although the editors believe, not without a wistful glance at some of the achievements of the past, that on balance it is a better publication now than it was when it began. But that is what middle-aged people always say, and the young merely smile. To which we can respond that at least we have got this far, have managed to keep the enterprise going all this time, and that, like a lasting marriage, it deserves acknowledgment, if not a pair of silver candlesticks.

The real achievement is that of *Great Books of the Western World*, of course, the set of books which *The Great Ideas Today* was designed to accompany, and does. *GBWW*, as we say for short, has been in print for more than thirty years and, judging by the sharply increased sales it has lately had, it is likely to be around a good deal longer. Why that is so is hard to explain, except on its merits, which are perhaps sufficient reason, although one cannot help thinking of other deserving sets of books, and other editions of distinguished titles, which have not survived as long. Such longevity would seem at any rate to affirm that the writings *GBWW* includes really are great books. For these, in the definition of the editors of the set, are the kind of books that, as they transcend their historic origins, do not date, remain continuously current.

This is true also, it seems fair to claim, of the *Syntopicon*, the index to *GBWW* that provides a survey of its contents arranged according to the ideas that occur oftenest in the works the set contains, notwithstanding variations in their meaning owing to different authors in different ages writing in different languages. Of course, while the ideas do not date, what is said about them in the summaries the *Syntopicon* provides might well have lost its pertinence—might betray some mind-set of mid-century from which it came. But the interesting fact is that it does not. The summaries still manifest the neutral spirit in which they were composed, the impartiality, as between one author and another, and one argument and another, that was the only ground on which they could be trusted as a guide. Impartiality is not equivalent to indifference. Truth is a matter of concern in the *Syntopicon* summaries, only they do not undertake to say, while giving the reader directions as to where it may be located, what they believe it is. That is why *they* have survived, too, like the books of which they speak, and are still useful.

The Great Ideas Today owes whatever endurance it can boast to this example, and to the conviction that underlies it. The conviction is that there exist ideas in the first place, about which arguments can be made and reflections offered, but which remain constant while that is going on. We have this originally from Plato, who maintained, *contra* the Sophists, that ideas are more than the sum of what we think about them, that (as we might say nowadays) their pursuit involves something greater than the presentation of a point of view. Most argument is content to rest on the latter assumption, and learning for the most part exemplifies it.

The Great Ideas Today is devoted to the opposite belief. It presents, year after year, articles and essays upon ideas and topics of fundamental importance, on the assumption that these exist independently of us, that there is always room for fresh grasp and insight of their nature, and that it is by examining this that we realize ourselves. No doubt the volume could do its job better than it does. But what it does is in the interest of this undertaking, and no issue has ever claimed more or less for itself than to have served that end.

The twenty-fifth volume seems typical as we survey it, except that its contributors have been especially good at going about their tasks. Such is the case with the two reviews of the arts and sciences we have been able to include. Once is by Stephen Spender, who under the title of "Post-Political and Elegiac Poetry" surveys recent works by various figures in English poetry, English being understood as the common language, not the exclusive nationality, of poets many of whom in fact are American or Irish. Mr. Spender is himself one of the celebrated poets of the age, and his criticism of the current scene is thus professional, a fact that readers will appreciate as they reflect upon it, and the more so if they know something of the political strain in his own verse.

The other review of a discipline in this year's issue is by Theodore Puck, who last appeared in these pages nearly twenty years ago, and who now considers the implications of current genetic and biological research with respect to medicine, the field in which he specializes. Readers will see that Dr. Puck there discerns the outline of what he thinks may be an entirely new science.

In furtherance of our aim to help owners of the set of *GBWW* read the writings it contains, and by way of pursuing also the issues they raise, we include three discussions of Great Books. One is by Maurice Cranston, who has twice been a contributor previously, and who here offers with his customary thoroughness and elegance a comprehensive reading of Rousseau's two most important treatises—the one that is called *Discourse on the Origin of Inequality,* and the other known as *Of the Social Contract.* A second discussion, by our contributing editor, Otto Bird, is devoted to Montaigne. This writer is usually regarded, notably on the basis of his longest *essai,* "Apology for Raimond de Sebonde," as a skeptic in religion, but Mr. Bird maintains that that view is incorrect as he wonderfully evokes Montaigne's presence. The third piece, originally a lecture given at St. John's College, Annapolis, Maryland, by Douglas Allanbrook, a tutor there, is devoted to Thucydides, and considers how unavailing were the best of human purposes and achievements in the war that destroyed the Athenian Empire, how grave the implications must be for mankind in any future circumstances of a similar sort.

There are also three "Special Features" in this year's issue. First in order is an account by Curtis Wilson of Newton's coming to the controlling idea of the *Principia Mathematica*—the idea of universal gravitation. Mr. Wilson takes issue with the traditional view of this, which is that Newton had worked the theory out some twenty years before he actually published mathematical demonstrations. Second is a piece by Charles Van Doren on the computer, a subject he has discussed before in these pages. Here he concedes the limitations of computers as compared with human minds, but ascribes such limitations to a different cause from the one that is usually offered, and suggests a different cure. Third is a discussion by George Anastaplo—whose essay on the *Analects* of Confucius appeared in last year's *Great Ideas Today*—of the *Bhagavad Gītā,* the poem that constitutes one of the Hindu sacred scriptures. Again, Mr. Anastaplo asks what a Western reader can make of a work written for a different and in many ways alien culture, and suggests how it can be grasped.

To go with this last essay, we have included among the year's "Additions to the Great Books Library" a translation of the *Gītā* itself, done by Professor Eliot Deutsch of the University of Hawaii, Manoa. Readers will thus have an opportunity to compare their own view of the poem with the one that Professor Anastaplo offers. Other "Additions" in this year's issue are three essays by Josiah Royce, the Harvard philosopher who was a contemporary of William James at the turn of the century and whose reputation has faded while that of James has continued to grow since his death, but who can still be read with both pleasure and profit. And we publish also a reprint of Gotthold Ephraim Lessing's *Laocoon,* a classic eighteenth-century essay on the difference between painting and poetry that really should be in the library of every owner of *GBWW* and will now at least belong to those who have subscribed to *The Great Ideas Today.*

PART ONE

Current Developments in the Arts and Sciences

Post-Political and Elegiac Poetry

Stephen Spender

Stephen Spender first achieved recognition as a member of a group of young Oxford poets—he had graduated from University College there in 1930—noted for including social and political commentary in their verse. Since then he has contributed much to English and American literature as a poet, critic, editor, translator, and lecturer. Coeditor of the influential literary journal *Horizon* and a founder of *Encounter* magazine, he has taught at several American universities. He has also delivered the Clark Lectures at Cambridge University, the Northcliffe Lectures at the University of London, and the Andrew W. Mellon Lectures in Washington. Among his many books are *Collected Poems* (1955), an autobiography called *World Within World* (1951), and various collections of critical essays: *The Creative Element* (1953), *The Making of a Poem* (1955), and *The Struggle of the Modern* (1963), to name a few. In recognition of his service to English letters, Mr. Spender was made a Commander of the British Empire (1962) and was knighted in 1983. Among his more recent writings are *The Thirties and After* (1978), a book of essays, and *Chinese Journal,* an account of a trip to China (1982).

It is perhaps inevitable that, in the last two decades of the century, we should find ourselves much given to thinking that an age of giants has passed; and it is tempting to suppose that we are now living in an age of dwarfs. With painting, when we count over the names of dead great painters—Picasso, Braque, Matisse, Léger, Bonnard, Pollock, Rothko— this seems obvious. The list of dead poets is also formidable; at the beginning of the century, Yeats, Hardy, Pound, Eliot, Stevens, Frost, Marianne Moore; and in the second half, Auden, Lowell, Roethke, Berryman, MacNeice, and, most recently, Empson.

Yet perhaps, with poetry, the disappearance of great masters is not so much a judgment on its condition as with the other arts. The distinction between "major" and "minor" poets may be a misleading one. What is arguably the most beautiful poem in the language ("They flee from me, that sometime did me seek") is by Sir Thomas Wyatt, a poet who cannot possibly be judged other than "minor."

A "minor poet" may write "great" poetry, and a poet like Tennyson, who is undoubtedly a "great" poet may write very few poems whose claim to be great poetry seems incontestable. T. S. Eliot made the point that William Blake wrote great poetry without being a great poet. Lytton Strachey compared certain passages of Blake to the symphonies of Beethoven.

"Great poet" is a category on its own and sometimes goes with the great ambitions of the poet. These may be so obvious that the ego of the poet, willing his poetry's greatness, shows through the poetry. This is the quality in Wordsworth which Keats characterized as the "egotistical sublime" and to which, in spite of his admiration for that poet, he objected. To be a "great poet" is partly a matter of sense of vocation. The poet who wishes to be a "great poet"—as distinct from him who wishes simply to write poetry—wants to use a vehicle of poetry that is the equivalent of his idea of poetic greatness. Traditionally such a vehicle is the epic. We recognize that Spenser, Milton, Wordsworth, Tennyson, Browning, and Yeats all had the ambition to write epics. For this very reason, all of them—with Virgil thrown in for good measure— were disliked by Robert Graves, who thought that poets should be like artisans or craftsmen belonging to a guild. They should write poems for other poets only, taking in each other's works as certain islanders take in each other's washing. Graves detested the roar of the claim to greatness which he discerned in the later poetry of Yeats, "a minor poet who wrote memorable poems until he decided to blow himself up like a bullfrog," he once said to me. Of course one suspects here the voice of envy, but one sees the point he implicitly made about Auden, and which he would doubtless also have made about Lowell, Roethke, and Berryman. Auden was evidently conscious of the distinction between "poet" and "great poet" when, as an Oxford undergraduate, he told his tutor, Nevill Coghill—who had found out that Auden wrote poetry and told him that doing so would help him in his studies of English literature—"You don't seem to understand. I want to be a great poet."

Before the eighteenth century and the Age of Patronage, English poets thought of writing poetry as one of the accomplishments of a gentleman. The aristocrat, the statesman, the churchman, the officer, in addition to his professional activities, also wrote poetry—some of the best in the language. The professional poet was such either because he was a playwright, and writing poetry for the stage, or because he considered himself to be in a tradition going back to antiquity—prophet, bard, or writer of epics. In the Age of Patronage the position of the poet came to be that of one who was attached to the aristocrat to whom he dedicated his poems. He was, as it were, a vocational guest (and often a humiliated one) at the great man's table.

During the nineteenth century, in the full flow of the Industrial Revolution, with Darwinism and the breakdown of religious belief, the poet became a kind of displaced person in the society of bourgeois values. The minor poet became an amateur, a clergyman, schoolmaster, or officer who wrote in his spare time. The poet who wished to be only or principally poet was forced into the position of having to become a professional, in the modern sense of *not* amateur, and in token of this he had to make claims for himself as a "great poet." He was thus representative of large numbers of middle-class people for whom he expressed the dilemma of wanting to believe in the spiritual values of religion and art, while living in a society dominated by materialism. Tennyson, Browning, Matthew Arnold were forced into the role of great poet because there was no other role for them in the society which would be recognized. Indirectly, Arnold was asserting this claim when he wrote that at bottom poetry was "a criticism of life," and that it would ultimately replace religion. The position then of the poet was that he had to choose between making extraordinary claims or accepting a minor role. There was nothing in between.

All the same, the idea of the poet as a source of religious and moral wisdom superior to the rest of society proved to be a fallible one, preposterous even, when Tennyson made assertions such as "Vex not the poet, with thy shallow wit." The moment the Victorian poet took himself seriously as a prophet of religion in a world of little faith, hollowness showed through his portentousness. The poets of the Victorian era who wrote great poetry were those who made no claims to be great poets: Thomas Hardy and Gerard Manley Hopkins.

Looking back now, it seems that the greatness of their poetry lies not in their fitting into any category of "great" or "minor," but in their acceptance of their alienation from the society in which they lived. Hopkins wrote out of one kind of despair, that of the religious in an age of irreligion; Hardy wrote out of another, that of the traditionally minded who could no longer believe in the church. But neither poet set up for himself a position that fit the standards of bourgeois society, that was either "great" or "minor."

English poets at the turn of the century, the so-called Georgian poets, accepted the position of being minor. There were excellent poets among them, but they had retreated, as it were, into cubbyholes of romanticized nature or romantic dream which left them singularly irrelevant as Arnoldian critics of life. They chose instead a kind of half-life, aptly named in the case of the youthful Yeats, "The Celtic Twilight."

It is significant that of poets who met the challenge of writing poetry in a modern idiom about modern urban civilization, the foremost were both Americans, T. S. Eliot and Ezra Pound. However, while attacking their English contemporaries for their poeticisms, their "weekender's" attitude toward writing poetry, their lack of rigorous critical standards, their unreflecting attitude toward technique, Pound and Eliot also regarded America as a cultural desert whose sands they had shaken from their feet. What they were escaping from in America was the lack of any tradition they could find useful to them in writing their poetry: and what they were seeking in England was to enter far more deeply into the past than the English poets of their time, who mostly took for granted that they were, and should be, followers of their Victorian predecessors.

There are English poets writing today (notably Philip Larkin and Donald Davie) who claim that the influence of these Americans on the development of English poetry was an aberration, the real continuity of the English tradition being provided by the poetry of Hardy. According to Larkin, all the poetry that Auden wrote after he left England in 1939 and went to America is inferior to the poetry he wrote in England up till 1939. One should not conclude from this that Larkin and Davie recommend that English poetry today should revert to the bucolicism, dreaminess, and tweediness of much Georgian poetry. Both these poets are extremely conscious technicians. The peculiar pleasure which Larkin's poetry provides is that of work in which supremely conscious art coincides with his observation of minute particulars of nature and feeling.

In the 1980s there seems something of affectation about the little-Englandism of these self-consciously English poets who never want to think about life outside England. It is often expressed with a

Ezra Pound

tongue-in-cheek insistence that seems perverse. However, a profound reason for it may be due to a return of the English to a traditional view of the unobtrusive role of the ego of the poet in his poem and a reaction against the egotism in their poetry of American poets of the generation of Lowell, Berryman, Jarrell, Roethke—and Ginsberg.

All in all, even today the English poet fits, however awkwardly and complainingly, into the great broad family of the English middle class. He may indeed find this all too cozy. One of the reasons Auden would give for leaving England was that he wished to break away from the cliquey English literary family. He wanted to live in America because there as a poet he was alone. If the English poet comes from the working class he may resent finding that all his colleagues and readers are middle class or have middle-class attitudes, while he has no working-class readers. D. H. Lawrence felt like this, and so, today, does one of the most brilliant young English poets, Tony Harrison.

The American poet has never had the feeling that he belongs to a section of society which is representative of the whole of America. Exceptions to this were perhaps certain Southern poets, in the 1930s, at the time of the Southern Agrarian movement; but viewed from the standpoint of the whole of America, the Southern gentleman poet was slightly absurd. The Bostonian gentleman today seems also a survival. Allen Tate and Robert Lowell as gentlemen seemed to represent a past tradition at odds with their modernist poetry.

Essentially, the American poet feels that he belongs to a thinly spread elite which, in relation to the whole of America, is about the size of Martha's Vineyard. American poets from Delmore Schwartz to Randall

T. S. Eliot

Jarrell have complained in bitter essays against the isolation of the American poet. Their feelings have been echoed by almost all American poets up to the present day.

To the English poet who travels to America in order to reach an audience larger than he is likely ever to meet in his own country, these complaints may seem puzzling. The reasons for them though are clear. The English poet, insofar as he has a traditional position in the society, accepts it, though he may wish to extend it. His status, as I have pointed out, classes him but does not isolate him. The American has status of a kind which, even though it may be numerically more extensive than that of his English colleague, limits his public to the academy. Beyond the academy, his poetry is scarcely read, and he has no public image.

Writing this in 1985 certain events illustrate my argument. All over England there is a certain subdued excitement, as at some minor sporting event, at the appointment of Ted Hughes as Poet Laureate. This means little, but it does mean that people have been comparing the merits of the work of the two favorites for this appointment: Hughes and Philip Larkin. It also means that Hughes will be asked to read his poems on the BBC so that people can judge the merit of his work. One cannot imagine there being a comparable event on a national scale in America (though there might be in the Soviet Union and in almost any Latin-American or Spanish-speaking country).

At the same time poetry, which is somehow associated by politicians with Ideals, receives unctuous lip service in America. While this debate about the candidates for Laureate was being carried on in England, I was in America and happened to attend a prestigious banquet held in

Ted Hughes

Washington on the occasion of the presentation of the 1985 Kennedy Center Honors to five American artists for their lifelong contributions to American culture through the performing arts. They were Arthur Miller, Isaac Stern, Lena Horne, Gian-Carlo Menotti, and Danny Kaye. Although no American poet seems to have been asked to this festivity (I was invited because I was a friend of one of the award winners), two of the distinguished speakers (who included the secretary of state, Mr. Shultz, and a famous senator) went out of their way to say that the noblest ideals of American life were embodied in poetry which expressed the highest reaches of American public thought. To demonstrate the point, the first speaker quoted some lines from an English poetaster of the early part of this century called Sir William Watson; the second quoted lines from an American poet of equal banality, Sara Teasdale. For a moment I could enter into the feelings of colleagues from a country which has produced some of the greatest poets of the present century. American poets seem to be unacknowledged non-legislators.

The American poet has in America only the university elite and other intellectuals, some of them also poets, to fall back on as his constituency. With a few exceptions, such as Longfellow and Emerson, this has really always been the case, and the reaction of poets to the situation in which they find themselves has been various. Over the past hundred years or so, certainly, there seemed three possible choices for them to make. One was to accept that he belonged to this elite; another was, like Henry James, Eliot, and Pound, to leave America and go to Europe; the third alternative was to throw himself upon the whole

Allen Ginsberg

of America—the vitality of its people, its geographical immensity, its originality—as contrasted with European decrepitude, the Europe of great traditions and achievements honored and respected, which was— as Walt Whitman put it—a corpse lying in the funeral parlor, whose vital offspring had migrated to America.

Several American poets of the fifties and sixties came to see the figure of Whitman as providing the classic example of the American poet dealing with the problem of being one. The American poet could no longer look to Europe as the source of the tradition of which America was the extension and which he could reenter. Nor could he take shelter in the academy in America. He had to be born anew by immersing himself in the life of the new continent. He had to cultivate his own ego as that self in his poetry which would merge into all other American selves, insofar as these were alive as he was.

The Beats in particular have dramatized an updated Whitmanesque American self in their poetry. But the free verse "turned on" style of Ginsberg and other Beat poets (Creeley, Ferlinghetti, Corso), while utterly different from the technically accomplished scholarly writing of poets such as Lowell, Berryman, Jarrell, Kunitz, and others, should not be allowed to obscure the fact that both have in common the cultivation of the self as American poet in their poetry. The Beat makes a great point of planting the poetic self in his instinctual unconscious life and his physical body. The rebellious self of Ginsberg in *Howl* is the voice not just of Ginsberg but of all his mind-and-body colleagues. The reader of *Howl* is implicitly invited by the poet to come in and join Ginsberg and friends in the verbal orgy ending in tragedy which is also the real-life

9

orgy. This is at the extreme from Lowell, Jarrell, Berryman, and the others who assert their superiority to the reader through the power of their intellects. Nevertheless, with their stricken psyches they belong also to the world of Ginsberg, and they are not afraid or ashamed to say so. Nietzsche remarked of Wagner's characters that they all live within a hundred yards of the hospital, and the same might be said of all poets and all really involved readers of this American generation, except that the hospital is the insane asylum. Both kinds of poet seem to fuse into one in the Bacchante-like poetry of Sylvia Plath.

In the course of a talk given at a literary conference held at Kenyon College in the early fifties, which I attended, Lowell, quoting Philip Rahv's distinction, divided this generation of poets into the Redskins and the Palefaces, the Redskins being the Beats, the Palefaces the intellectual poets who were established on the campuses of universities as teachers of poetry, professors of creative writing. But Berryman, Jarrell, Roethke, and Lowell himself, all of whom taught at American universities, were individualist rebels on the campus. Some of them were only tolerated there because they brought prestige to the university. The word *creative* had a magic which kept the university authorities at bay.

We have to remember that the fifties and sixties were the America of McCarthyism and Vietnam. These were events that reached far beyond the area of everyday politics and aroused feelings of moral outrage in the minds and imaginations of men and women usually little interested in them. Some readers in such situations are disposed to look to the poets as guardians of the imagination and to expect them to express for them their own feelings of outrage. The poets were in the exceptional situation of finding themselves called on to be leaders, even if those who called were for the most part the same students they taught on the campuses. Robert Lowell, with his patriarchal Bostonian background, felt strongly the force of this appeal. He also felt very aware of the fact that his poetic indignation had not the slightest effect on government. In the late sixties I once heard Lowell remark to the Russian poet Andrey Voznesensky that he could almost envy Russian dissident poets who were persecuted in Russia, because this at least showed that the men in the Kremlin took poets seriously enough to wish to silence them.

The American poets of the fifties and sixties, whether Paleface or Redskin, were as one in being poets of protest. Today there is still protest poetry, but instead of being united in defense of the same freedoms (freedom of speech, freedom to refuse to be conscripted in a war that was seen as immoral) protest is now fragmented into support of sectional causes: Women's Rights, Black Rights, Gay Rights, and so on. Protest of this kind represents some special interest, whereas that of a previous generation was aimed at the whole of materialist, power-mongering, mechanistic, political America on behalf of an America that stood for intellect, flesh, and psyche.

The best American poets of today, however, are not the poets of sectarian protest and do not write a kind of egotistic or self-obsessed poetry. Nor is it certain that this is an altogether bad thing. The poets of Lowell's generation can be said to have invested their egos too heavily in their poetry. They sought with their tragic lives and their sometimes violent deaths to punish America for its failure to acknowledge them as a moral force of national influence. If Auden, who stated positions dogmatically, was exaggerating when he wrote in his elegy on the death of W. B. Yeats that "poetry makes nothing happen," and even more when, later in life, he said that the political world would not be in the least different today if Dante, Shakespeare, and Goethe had never lived, this was perhaps better than for the poet to put himself in the position whereby his failure to influence the nation's politics through his poetry becomes his personal tragedy.

The American poet who today attracts the most critical attention, John Ashbery, does so through qualities which seem the opposite almost of those of Lowell and Berryman—a continual withdrawing of the poet's self from the poem, leaving a kind of space in language where we had come to expect the poet's projected persona. But before discussing Ashbery I shall turn to a monumental poem published in three volumes, the center of which is an elegy for W. H. Auden and other recently dead friends of James Merrill and his friend David Jackson. Around this nucleus of the recently dead—one of whom, Auden, is conceived as being gifted with language that can interpret heaven to earth—Merrill constructs a masque-like pageant in which the living (Merrill and Jackson) communicate with the dead, who, together with them, conduct a series of seminars or classes, describing the hierarchy of forces which govern the worlds of heaven and of earth.

The three volumes of *Divine Comedies*—the title of the complete trilogy—are *The Book of Ephraim, Mirabell,* and *Scripts for the Pageant.* As the title of the trilogy shows, Merrill regards Dante as his predecessor on such a journey in which a guide who is a senior poet (for Dante, Virgil; for Merrill, Auden) reveals to the poet who is still living in this world the nature of the life after death, and the divine laws which govern the universe. The ideology behind Dante's vision was derived from the *Summa Theologica* of Aquinas. Merrill's system, or science—in fact, the poem is best described as science fiction raised to the level of dialogue between the living and the dead—is achieved by messages dictated to Merrill and Jackson on their Ouija Board, sometimes in their house at Stonington, Connecticut, sometimes in their house in Athens, or wherever else they may be.

Auden did in fact have a theology and was regarded by Reinhold Niebuhr as a distingushed theologian, within the Anglican Church. But here he is made to renounce this in a rather striking passage which, pre-

Robert Lowell

sumably, would shock Anglicans and would scarcely please the Auden whom his friends knew in this world, where he despised astrology and spiritualism. However, on being asked by Merrill in "Mirabell: Book 1," whether these talks through the mediumship of the Ouija Board repel him, he replies:

> GREEN
> MY DEARS WITH ENVY   I COULD CURSE MY HIGH
> ANGLICAN PRINCIPLES   IN OXFORD DAYS
> THE TABLES TAPPED OUT MANY A SMART OR EERIE
> RHYTHM UNTIL OUR POLITICS TOOK OVER
> THEN THE ABSORBING LOVES & THEN THE DREARY
> WASH   CONFESSION DONT U SEE   THE CHURCH
> MY DEARS THE DREARY DREARY DEAD BANG WRONG
> CHURCH   & ALL THOSE YEARS I COULD HAVE HELD
> HANDS ON TEACUPS

which papers over rather awkwardly, if not outrageously, the gap between the objective nature of Auden's beliefs and what he would surely have regarded as a deceptive form of subjective self-communicating—the Ouija Board.

This passage also lays open the question of whether JM and DJ (as they are called in the poem) themselves believe that they were the recipients of messages coming from the outside universe of eternity, or that they were projecting through the medium of cup and board their own inner self-communings. Sometimes *Divine Comedies* has the look of a poem written to celebrate the platonic collaboration of JM and DJ, rather like the collaboration of Auden and his friend Chester Kallman in writing the libretto of *The Rake's Progress* for Stravinsky. For Auden and Kallman seem clearly to have felt the sense of being in touch with the divine, their relationship spiritualized within the music. And some of the most beautiful passages in *Divine Comedies* are also about music. This is a poem in which one feels the harmony of the spheres.

As excuse for the use of the Ouija Board, it may be said that today one cannot imagine any better convention of communication between the living and the dead. After reading a few pages of *Divine Comedies,* the reader, I think, accepts the conventions of the dialogue.

The dead with whom the mediums JM and DJ are in communication, are—apart from Auden—a rather distinguished Greek friend of theirs, daughter of a prime minister of Greece, Maria Mitsotáki; another Greek friend, George Cotzias; and an American, Robert Morse. Those were all friends of JM and DJ. Converse between the living and dead has the character of social intercourse between friends that is sometimes rather frivolous but has serious undertones. The idiom which is conducted is, for the most part, "high camp," as the example quoted from Auden above shows. Sometimes, however, it becomes, especially when Auden is speaking, that of poetic prophecy. The speakers include not only the humans, living and dead, but also angels, archangels, and God's most exalted representative, called here God B. B stands for Biology, the medium through which God himself (who does not appear) realizes his creative will and purpose. There are also Akhnaton, Homer, Montezuma, Nefertiti, and Plato, called here *The Five.* The matter of central concern is whether the invisible God, the creator, standing behind his functionary God B, will spare his experiment, the earth, from nuclear destruction. As a kind of miniature image of this, there is the question of the fate of those recently dead who are either reborn again or revert to the elements from which they derived—thus Auden must be sent back to his origins, the minerals (Auden's interest in geology is relevant to this).

The interchange between the living, the dead, and the angelic and immortal is carried on with such effect that, for the most part, it enchants the reader. Merrill humanizes the speech of the angels. When the subject matter or situation require this, he elevates the speeches of the dead to that of these immortals. Whether or not *Divine Comedies* convinces the reader as a vision, it triumphs as language channeled into forms commanded by the "young poet" (as Merrill is called by those in heaven) with extraordinary virtuosity. Apart from the many changing verse forms, there is a larger inclusive form, a visual shape imposed by the dramatic action, which seems vertical and which shows language moving from earth upward to heaven and from heaven downward to earth. The pronouncements of the angels, and of Auden, have an authority one can well believe to be divine. They go beyond personal expression, the egotistic sublime, the confessional. Auden, toward the end of "Mirabell: Book 9," pronounces on poetry, rejecting "doing your own thing:"

> THINK WHAT A MINOR
> PART THE SELF PLAYS IN A WORK OF ART
> COMPARED TO THOSE GREAT GIVENS   THE ROSEBRICK
>   MANOR
> ALL TOPIARY FORMS & METRICAL
> MOAT ARIPPLE! FROM ANTHOLOGIZED
> PERENNIALS TO HERB GARDENS OF CLICHES
> FROM LATIN-LABELLED HYBRIDS TO THE FAWN
> 4 LETTER FUNGI THAT ENRICH THE LAWN
> IS NOT ARCADIA TO DWELL AMONG
> GREENWOOD PERSPECTIVES OF THE MOTHER TONGUE
> ROOTSYSTEMS UNDERFOOT WHILE OVERHEAD
> THE SUN GOD SANG & SHADES OF MEANING SPREAD
> & FAR SNOWCAPPED ABSTRACTIONS GLITTERED NEAR
> OR FAIRLY MELTED INTO ATMOSPHERE?

Yet inevitably one has misgivings about the work of a poet who already in the title of his poem seems to challenge comparison with Dante. Dante conveys the multitudinousness of humanity, not just in his examples of individuals, but in his portrayals of vast crowds. JM and DJ, with their Ouija Board and their friends, some of whom die while these sessions are in progress, and whom they then get in touch with, cannot escape giving the impression that they enjoy heaven as a very exclusive club, a kind of unending cocktail party of the gifted and intelligent. Chester Kallman, who did have something plebeian about him, is put down by being sent to South Africa of apartheid to be reborn there as a black baby. Most readers, I feel, are unlikely to be able to read *Divine Comedies* without feeling that heaven is a place to which it is unlikely they will be invited, not so much on grounds of their damnation as from imperfect aesthetic sensibility. The list of those, drawn from all of history, who are given speaking parts (if only a line long) at the class which makes up the last volume of the trilogy is: the Architect of Ephesus, Marius Bewley, Maria Callas, Maya Deren, Kirsten Flagstad, Hans Lodeizen, Robert Lowell, Pythagoras, The Blessed Luca Spionari, Gertrude Stein, Wallace Stevens, Richard Strauss, Alice B. Toklas, Richard Wagner, W. B. Yeats. One cannot help feeling that if Dante had been writing in the late seventies he would have summoned Hitler, Stalin, Roosevelt, Churchill to *Inferno* or *Purgatorio* and given the readers the sense, as background to the time, of the concentration camps and the Holocaust.

There is little feeling in *Divine Comedies* of what Keats meant in "Hyperion: A Vision" when the prophetess Moneta who, in his poem,

embodies his own poetic conscience admonished the poet—Keats—who
had been a medical student in London and who also knew himself to
be dying of consumption, in these words:

> "None can usurp this height," return'd that shade,
> "But those to whom the miseries of the world
> "Are misery, and will not let them rest.
> "All else who find a haven in the world,
> "Where they may thoughtless sleep away their days,
> "If by a chance into this fane they come,
> "Rot on the pavement where thou rottedst half."

Moneta then goes on to throw the real suffering of the world at the
poet as if challenging him with his own death:

> "What benefit canst thou do, or all thy tribe,
> "To the great world? Thou art a dreaming thing,
> "A fever of thyself: think of the earth."

It is not of course that the inhabitants of Merrill's heaven and earth
do not know about suffering. Their dead have died with it, and JM
and DJ have cared for some who were dying. What is lacking, it seems
to me, is a feeling for the world of the simply and multitudinously human, including the untalented. That is a feeling which Auden certainly
had. Reviewing a volume of poems by the great Greek poet Cavafy,
he commented on one in which Cavafy recalled how many years ago
he had spent a night of squalor in a brothel together with a young
man, a memory in which he now rejoiced because it had enabled him
to write this poem. Auden wrote that he could very well understand
Cavafy's feelings about a past which had produced such a present, but
he could not help wondering what had happened to his companion,
the young man.

Nevertheless, Merrill has taken what is given to him, and what he
knows about, and made what is often wonderful poetry out of it.
Whether his epic reveals as great a humanity as Dante, or Proust, is
impossible to say at this time, so near to its publication. But undoubtedly it has the kind of magnetism which makes the reader want to turn
back to it again and again, sure that on each occasion when doing so,
he will discover new meanings. If the machinery of the Ouija Board
seems dubious, and if one doubts whether Auden would have approved
of it, there is one article of faith which he shared most certainly with
JM and DJ: that science provides descriptions of the laws that govern
nature, but that it does not explain the forces that lie behind those
laws, and that these are mysterious. If God B is Biology, he takes orders
from a further God, who is imagination. The world is governed by
mysterious forces.

Merrill's poem is immensely ambitious, but in it Merrill sees himself

James Merrill

not as the poetic self of a Whitman or a Lowell including all other selves that enter his poetry, but as transcriber of a vision communicated to him. With Ashbery, the self is even more elusive. It disappears and reappears like the Cheshire cat. Ashbery seems to exemplify what Keats called "negative sensibility," receiving impressions but not imposing his own stamp on them: receiving them as a sensitized plate or film in a camera receives them, precisely and passively, but without comment. His poems have titles, but these are hints at, rather than indications of, the subject.

In their impersonality—the casual, almost accidental, seeming way in which one image in a poem is set side by side with another—Ashbery's early poems show the influence of the early Auden. Auden when he wrote those poems was influenced by the black and white silent movies of the late twenties. What he got from them was not the continuity of a story which was provided by the captions, but rather a certain discontinuity, the abrupt shifting of scenes from one place to another—indoors, outdoors, etc.—conveyed by the photographic images and independent of the captions. This kind of disconnectedness of images and events, together with the implication of hidden or suppressed links, provided by an enclosing atmosphere—a certain grayness of the Nordic landscape, for example—is also to be found in some of Ashbery's poems.

Auden was trying at that time to write a depersonalized poetry of poems put together by the poet with the detachment of a chemist in a

John Ashbery

laboratory making up a formula. In making a poem out of fragments of his reading or his seeing or his feeling, and putting them together as synthetic artifacts, Auden thought that he was working in accordance with a program deduced from Eliot's critical writings: that poetry should not be an expression of the poet's personality but an escape from it. But in Ashbery's poetry—the substitution of a diffused personal sensibility is open to all surrounding impressions without, apparently, a central "I" which orders those impressions within its own conformities. Impersonality seems more an attitude to truth than an aesthetic principle—if one can make this distinction. It is as though he regards the "I" which arranges received impressions as a censor suppressing what it cannot bring within the unity of a subject.

Ashbery's poems record the invasion of the personal sensibility by the impersonal external world, and there is little room here for the imposing and arranging ego of the poet in his poem. The titles of his poems indicate not subjects concerning which conclusions are drawn in the writing but directions from starting points, trains of thought. His poems are journeys, and their tone is often that of language or thought as they occur to one midway between dreaming and waking, as in this passage from "Collective Dreams":

The old poems
In the book have changed value once again. Their black letter
Fools only themselves into ignoring their stiff, formal
    qualities, and they move

> Insatiably out of reach of bathos and the bad line
> Into a weird ether of forgotten dismemberments. Was it
> This rosebud? Who said that?

Such poetry seems to record the invasion of the inside world of the poet's sensibility by the outside world of impressions which are at the edge of larger impressions stretching to infinity. The sense of the imagery of inner worlds being set down at the very moment when they are dissolving in the ocean of a larger, enclosing world is felt. But there is no rigidity about this. Sometimes the experiences that force themselves upon Ashbery seem to put themselves forward as subjects, to take over poems, as it were. But this happens in life when, for example, the death of a friend usurps surrounding impressions for some time.

What Ashbery appears to be writing about is the way in which sensibility may entertain the outside world as a whole rather than rejecting or selecting from it. In this his poetry has affinities with the fiction of Virginia Woolf. It is to be noted that although he sometimes employs strict forms (the sestina even) with mastery, much of his work seems based on rhythms which are close to prose. Some poems are, as it were, prose nudged into verse: and these rhythms seem entirely appropriate to the kind of reverie which is the area of consciousness he explores. Significantly, he moves easily from writing in strict or free verse to the prose poem—some of the best prose poems I have read. The sensitivity shown in this poetry is very close to thought changing into music. What Ashbery has to say about music is to the point:

> What I like about music is its ability of being convincing, of carrying an argument through successfully to the finish, though the terms of this argument remain unknown quantities. What remains is the structure, the architecture of the argument, scene or story. I would like to do this in poetry.

In this poetry the poet is developing an argument which is going on at a deeper level than the arguments of explicatory consciousness. This lack of a self as persona at the center of the poem, patterning it into a message which is the subject, means that there is in Ashbery's work an openness to metaphors and images of great delicacy on the margin of both poet's and reader's attention. The reader feels "I hardly noticed that," in this passage from "Pyrography":

> One day we thought of painted furniture, of how
> It just slightly changes everything in the room
> And in the yard outside, and how, if we were going
> To be able to write the history of our time, starting with today,
> It would be necessary to model all these unimportant details
> So as to be able to include them; otherwise the narrative

Would have that flat, sandpapered look the sky gets
Out in the middle west toward the end of summer,
The look of wanting to back out before the argument
Has been resolved, and at the same time to save appearances
So that tomorrow will be pure.

The last six lines are like images which flash by in conversation, almost unnoticed, with the brilliance of the instantly forgotten. Such tenuous illuminations do not often find their way into poetry.

In his most recent volume, *A Wave,* there is the fragmentariness, the flotsam and jetsam of observation (like the objects one sees, or interprets into—scarcely believing one's eyes—the foreground of Turner's wonderful seascape, "The Slave Ship"). Ashbery implicitly claims that this haul of impressions seemingly relevant or seemingly irrelevant, netted in language, adds up to a life: or, one might say with equal truth, to a death (always imminent in his poetry, which is suffused with a great deal of pain). In the long title poem of the volume, indirections are related to this general direction, the sheer weight of events drifting toward oblivion.

The inner individual subjective life, that which calls itself "I," is seen to be a transparent film through which what is outside it and not arranged is viewed, the inexorable stream of things leading toward death:

No one came to take advantage of these early
Reverses, no doorbell rang;
Yet each day of the week, once it had arrived, seemed the threshold
Of love and desperation again. At night it sang
In the black trees: *my mindless, oh my mindless, oh.*
And it could be that it was Tuesday, with dark, restless clouds
And puffs of white smoke against them, and below, the wet streets
That seem so permanent, and all of a sudden the scene changes:
It's another idea, a new conception, something submitted
A long time ago, that only now seems about to work
To destroy at last the ancient network
Of letters, diaries, ads for civilization.
It passes through you, emerges on the other side
And is now a distant city, with all
The possibilities shrouded in a narrative moratorium.

Ashbery is often associated with other poets whose work is "open" and who are from New York: Frank O'Hara, Kenneth Koch, and, particularly, James Schuyler, with whom he has collaborated in a novel, *A Nest of Ninnies.*

Of these writers he is, I think, nearest to Schuyler, in his witty elusiveness, like that of a person who seems to be approaching the reader and withdrawing from him in the same gesture. Like Ashbery, Schuyler has a very civilized refinement, though he is less mysterious than Ashbery. The opening lines of "A Head" show something of his quality:

> A dead boy living among men as a man
> called an angel
> by me, for want of a word,
> spaniel-eyed: wet, with bits
> of gold deep in the eyeballs
> hidden, like a mysterious ingredient
> (c'est là, le mystère)
> fringed with black and with black
> thick-grown, delicately thumb-smudged eyebrows
> and brown cast on the face
> so the lips are an earth red
> and the rings or pouches under the eyes
> are dark.

O'Hara is very much himself: vivacious, sociable, welcoming, embracing whomever he meets in the street who has his candor—Whitmanesque—very much a New Yorker, but one of the elite, with a job at the Museum of Modern Art:

> I walk up the muggy street beginning to sun
> and have a hamburger and malted and buy
> an ugly NEW WORLD WRITING to see what the poets
> in Ghana are doing these days
>   I go on to the bank
> and Miss Stillwagon (first name Linda I once heard)
> doesn't even look up my balance for once in her life
> and in the GOLDEN GRIFFIN I get a little Verlaine
> for Patsy with drawings by Bonnard although I do
> think of Hesiod, trans. Richmond Lattimore or
> Brendan Behan's new play or *Le Balcon* or *Les Nègres*
> of Genet, but I don't, I stick with Verlaine
> after practically going to sleep with quandariness.

This, from "The Day Lady Died," is the world democracy including everything in radiant heat, also perhaps the poet whistling to keep his courage up.

The ego which has disappeared from Ashbery's poetry is cheerfully present in O'Hara's; and the poet as a man was felt by his friends to be both rare and populist, so that it struck them as bitterly ironic that he should be killed by being run over on Fire Island where there is customarily no traffic. He might have written a poem about this. His poems seem lengths cut off from a fabric of a life which wrote itself out every hour on ticker tape, in this respect resembling A. R. Ammons, essentially a "nature" poet as self-denyingly passive to his experiences of particular bits of nature as Ashbery is to more urban experiences.

One feels, reading O'Hara's poems, that it must have been delightful to know this poet who puts himself across in his poems as a colorful social personality. Although Ashbery is associated with these other New York poets, there is really an absolute difference between the quality of his work and theirs—as great, say, as that between Auden and the English poets associated with him in the thirties. In his poems Ashbery defines himself by negation, in withdrawing, as I have suggested, from the "I" in the poem and entering into the amorphousness of the surrounding world. His persona assumes the color of the weather.

*   *   *   *   *

Merrill, Ashbery, and the New York poets do not lend themselves to a political interpretation which would be helpful toward explaining their poetry. In this, as in the lack of a self-asserting ego in their work, they show a shift of sensibility in their writing as great as that among certain English poets from the American-influenced to a form of little-England-ism. What might be called social consciousness appears rather, as I have pointed out, in sectarian propagandist poets who advocate some such cause as Women's Lib, Black Lib, Gay Lib, etc. Examples of this rhetoric, which merges with confessional writing, impressive—especially in the case of Women's Lib—for its vituperativeness, confronts us with the question, What is poetry? I will not attempt to answer that here, but it may be helpful to point out that historically there has always been a difference between writing that aims at universality by reaching beyond the occasion from which the poetry arose, and the immediate, occasional, or propagandist poem written, when it concerns politics of any kind, to produce an immediate effect.

The position of the political-propagandist poet is that the wrongs with which he or she is concerned are so great, the causes he or she supports so pressing, that the poet cannot and should not aim at a public which has a preconceived idea of what makes a poem poetry, since this is certainly some artifact. The poet must urge upon the reader the necessity of taking immediate action about some cause. Expecting poetry, what the reader gets is a scream or an insult. The situation is further complicated by the fact that there exists a public that wants to hear this and will take such writing not really as a call to action but as a criticism of the effeteness of any "literary" mode of writing poetry.

A good deal of this writing gives the impression of the writer crashing into poetry like someone barging into a party, or an automobile running a roadblock. One is reminded sometimes of the anti-poetry written by some Polish poets after the experiences of the suppression of the Warsaw Ghetto uprising in 1943 by the Nazis with Stalin's connivance. These poets regarded poetry—all previous poetry—as a betrayal of humanity, because even when it is concerned with suffering it provides

Diane Wakoski

that pleasure which is the poet's—and which the reader shares—in converting personal suffering to literary pleasure. For according to the anti-poets, suffering at the extreme contains truth so profound that the attempt to render it pleasing through art is obscene.

Sometimes one has the impression that feminist poets would like to invent a language which had nothing to do with men, a kind of inter-women tribal version of English. And of course black writers are confronted by the fact that they do have their own kind of spoken "demotic" which makes all English and American literature, however idiomatic, foreign to them. Black protest poetry has, for this reason, a character quite different from white feminist poetry, however violent this may be. Compare, for example, lines of Diane Wakoski with some by Don L. Lee. Here is Wakoski, enraged:

> You ride a motorcycle
> past wintry trees
> and summer trees
> and never once
> think of me.
> but my friends are
> the falling branches
> that will tilt you
> and snap your neck one day.
> I dream of your thick body
> uprooted
> and torn by a storm
> on a motorcycle track.

This quotation, from "You, Letting the Trees Stand as My Betrayer," is forceful but, apart from the violence of the hatred for the male which it expresses, it does not as language reflect any exclusively female sensibility. If a man who felt betrayed by a lady-motorcyclist felt as bitterly, he might use the same language. But it is unthinkable that a white poet, resenting blacks, would use rhythm and vocabulary resembling Don L. Lee's in his poem about the black poet Gwendolyn Brooks:

> into the sixties
> a word was born. . . . . .BLACK
> & with black came poets
> & from the poet's ball points came:
> black doubleblack purpleblack blueblack beenblack was
> black daybeforeyesterday blackerthan ultrablack super
> black blackblack yellowblack niggerblack blackwhi-teman
> blackerthanyoueverbes ¼ black unblack coldblack clear
> black my momma's blackerthanyourmomma pimpleblack fall
> black so black we can't even see you black on black in
> black by black technically black mantanblack winter
> black coolblack 360degreesblack coalblack midnight
> black black when it's convenient rustyblack moonblack
> black starblack summerblack electronblack spaceman
> black shoeshineblack jimshoeblack underwearblack ugly
> black auntjimammablack, uncleben'srice black williebest
> black blackisbeautifulblack i justdiscoveredblack negro
> black unsubstanceblack.

As language and as rhythm this has accusatory hypnotic power. There is about it an arrogant possession of the vocabulary which a black poet can use as his right, but which is simply not available to the white poet. It immediately sets up a division between genteel effete white poetry and people's poetry, asserting the right of the black to speak the language of the people. Any white proleterian poetry, in whatever vernacular, would seem studied and self-conscious beside this. One is made by it to reflect on the future of English/American language and to wonder whether literary English/American will not be driven into the position of being a learned language for scholars and philosophers, like Latin in the Middle Ages, finally to be superseded by this very virulent indignant language of the people.

Such language thrives, though, like all the literature of protest and confession, on cultivated hysteria, and the hysterical always has the effect of making the unhysterical look tame, genteel, polite. Kenneth Koch, in his poem "Fresh Air," perhaps with tongue in cheek pokes fun at the poets of Academia, the New Criticism (now outdated), all the great names of Modern Poetry, and pleads the cause of Ignorance, Innocence, and Spontaneity (which, today, perhaps hardly needs defending).

>"Oh to be seventeen years old
>Once again," sang the red-haired man, "and not know that poetry
>Is ruled with the sceptre of the dumb, the deaf, and the creepy!"
>And the shouting persons battered his immortal body with stones
>And threw his primitive comedy into the sea
>From which it sang forth poems irrevocably blue.
>
>Who are the great poets of our time, and what are their names?
>Yeats of the baleful influence, Auden of the baleful influence,
>   Eliot of the baleful influence
>(Is Eliot a great poet? no one knows), Hardy, Stevens, Williams
>   (is Hardy of our time?).

This use of parenthesis is too reminiscent of Walt Whitman for us to have much confidence in Koch as a pointer to the new, the really new. Perhaps what is wrong is to think that a populist, low culture of protestors, makers of confessional statements, vers-librists, sectarians has to replace the high culture of learning, wit, technical virtuosity, and diversity of forms. The situation in which we live surely cries out that we should have both, Lowell's Redskins and Palefaces, the traditionalists who keep alive the forms and standards of past achievement while giving them new life, and the barbarians who let out their screams and break down the gates in order to draw attention to the injustices which past and present history have inflicted on them.

Perhaps that sounds too tolerant. But surely, in the arts, during the present century the worst intolerance was that of supporters of the modern movement, outstanding among them Pound and Williams, who declared that all poets and artists should write or paint in the modernist manner, however they defined this (and they themselves quarreled about definitions). One of the greatest *bêtises* of the century, among poets, must surely have been that of the young Ezra Pound in the early 1900s telling the young Robert Frost that he must modernize his style—only equalled by that of William Carlos Williams, in the 1920s, declaring that *The Waste Land* was an act of betrayal by Eliot of the aims of his fellow American poets. Almost as nonsensical, if considered as a program for all his fellow poets, and not just an approximate description of his own way of writing poetry, is Charles Olson's prescription for "projective verse."

The state of poetry reflects the fragmented state of civilization, but it does not follow from that that all poetry should be fragmented. What it does mean, surely, is that there will be many different tendencies—extremes of classicism and extremes of expressionism.

Nevertheless, different and even opposing tendencies should have some characteristic in common which we can distinguish as being poetry. The most general characteristic of poetry is, I should say, that the poet in his work distinguishes between two orders of reality: the material one which controls our lives and whose worldly values we all, to varying extents, conform to and live by and needs must deal with, and a quite other world of values which with our inner selves we recognize to be true, of love and justice and beauty. To the poet, the "real" life is that which he imagines as embodying the values of his own inner life—values which may well be derived, as they affect his poetry, from his reading of past literature. But they also, of course, include many other matters: things seen and heard and felt and loved and hated.

The objection to any kind of political poetry is that in order to write it the poet has to identify the life of the imagination—his own inner life—with an external political cause. He must believe that if and when that political cause triumphs over the existing political order and replaces it with the new order which he imagines, this new order will achieve the revolution as he has imagined it, a liberation of life forces without dictatorship or police, what the Marxists used to call "the withering away of the state." But although there may be political arrangements which are worse or better than others, politics is always to do with power. The poet finds always that supporting a political cause means putting his own inner imaginative life at the mercy of external power. The political poet attempts, in short, to celebrate revolution as the marriage of power with imagination, like those French students who in 1968 went marching down the Boulevardes of Paris, with their slogan *"L'imagination c'est la Revolution."* If he writes propaganda for political revolution by identifying it with his own inner vision, his poetry will seem unreal on the levels both of external social life and the inner life of the imagination: the kind of unreality which is disconcerting in Shelley's political visionary poetry.

Ashbery's poetry, which is not political, seems nevertheless to recognize this kind of danger insofar as it maintains that experience of the world outside the poet invades his interior self to a greater extent than he is able to order it within his own inner world. Instead of the "I" being center of its own self-image which it has crystallized, it is part of a much larger picture into which it is dissolved. The reality which is the inner life of the imagination recognizes its own limitations, but in doing so it imagines the rather fragmentary experiences which it cannot resolve into a unity. James Merrill sustains his own inner vision by grounding it on a combination of strong superstition and scientific truism. The superstition (superstition because it has never been scientifically proved) is the idea that there is survival after death, a reincarnation and communication of the living with the dead by means of the Ouija Board. The truism is that science provides descriptions of the laws that govern nature but does not attempt to explain what force, if any, directs these laws. That question is open to speculation, and scientists from Newton to Einstein have speculated about the God who manifests himself, in Merrill's poem, through the agency of God Biology.

Of course the poets of protest are necessarily concerned with politics. They have a strong sense of injustices embedded in the political systems in which they live, and which, they scream, should be removed. But there are other, and perhaps greater, poets writing now who accept politics as phenomena affecting the shape of the times in which they live, and who seem to avoid making political judgments about those times. Two of these are Derek Walcott and Seamus Heaney. Living in entirely different contexts, they seem to approach their situations with a similar detachment, as realizations of the tragic process of past history moving into modern times, where they have deep sympathies but do not take sides politically. I should perhaps add, having written this, that one may assume that as men, if not as poets, they conform to a liberal, anti-racist, freedom-loving consensus. They are humanists. But they do not press these views as any kind of message in their poetry.

Walcott is a Trinidadian, a half-caste. He is a most sophisticated writer. Indirectly, and sometimes directly, in his poetry he pays tribute to the excellent education he received under British colonial rule. This does not mean that he forgets his own origins. But the reader would be quite wrong to anticipate finding in his writing the proclaimed and insistent "blackness" found in the lines quoted above from Don L. Lee, or the former French-colonial African "negritude."

Walcott very consciously emerges from the geography of the Caribbean, but his knowledge embraces the history of the world. In some ways he seems, more than any other poet living in the West, a world poet. His greatness—for he has greatness—seems very much connected with the splendor and misery of his country, before and after independence—the before and the after providing bitter contrasts. His work has affinities with that of V. S. Naipaul (and perhaps even with that of Seamus Heaney in tragically divided Ireland) in conveying the decrepitude and corruption of colonial countries that have gained their noisily acclaimed freedom but have lost the order, efficiency, and ceremony of the occupying imperialist power, indeed its civilization. That power survives as a haunting greatness, like the "dream encounters with familiar ghosts" of Heaney's poem "Station Island." Much of Heaney's sequence is written in approximate Dantesque *terza rima;* and Walcott, at his most elegiac, writes a stanza with a last line which has the effect of a door being closed on what has gone before, as in a canto from Dante:

> There, at the year's horizon, he had stood,
> as if the pool's meridian were the line
> that doubled the burden of his solitude
> in either world; and, as one leaf fell,
> his echo rippled: "Why here, of all places,

a small, suburban tropical hotel,
its pool pitched to a Mediterranean blue,
its palms rusting in their concrete oasis?
Because to make my image flatters you."

This is from "The Hotel Normandie Pool," a haunt in Trinidad to which the poet has returned to be confronted by a visitor (or visitant) with "white towel, toga-slung, / foam hair repeated by the robe's frayed hem." He takes this man to be a Latin ghost who

magnifies the lines
of our small pool to that Ovidian
thunder of surf between the Baltic pines.

The position, though, of Ovid exiled among the barbarians is, in Walcott's case, reversed—he is exiled from St. Lucia, his island home-land, which has gained decolonial liberty of a kind which proves to be, in fact, petty dictatorship, reflecting the corruption of "Roman" civilization from which it is freed:

Our emerald sands
are stained with sewage from each tin-shacked Rome;
corruption, censorship, and arrogance
make exile seem a happier thought than home.
"Ah, for the calm proconsul with a voice
as just and level as this Roman pool,"
our house slaves sigh; the field slaves scream revenge;
one moves between the flatterer and the fool
yearning for the old bondage from both ends.

Politics offer only choices between evils, the old and the new corrup-tion, a petty tyranny superseding a great one, which is dead. If it comes to that, echoes of Dante, strong in Merrill, subdued in Walcott and Heaney, emphasize the postmortem preoccupations of all these poets: postmortem on Auden, on British rule in the Caribbean and in Ireland. One might define the attitude of Walcott and Heaney to public events as post-political.

Moving between his Roman exile and his provincial homeland, Wal-cott has a tone more Roman than provincial. His poems about America are more white—than black—American. The Caribbean element adds a richness to his vocabulary but does not pervade his consciousness which is, I have suggested, that of a citizen of the world. But he is so remarkably receptive to differences of cultural climate that his poetry, chameleon-like, seems to acquire the tone of whatever geographical area he visits or inhabits, while at the same time retaining its luxuriance. His New England (in *The Fortunate Traveller*) is on speaking terms with Robert Lowell's Boston:

> The hillside is still wounded by the spire
> of the white meetinghouse, the Indian trail
> trickles down it like the brown blood of the whale
> in rowanberries bubbling like the spoor
> on logs burnt black as Bibles by hellfire.
> The war whoop is coiled tight in the white owl,
> stone-feathered icon of the Indian soul,
> and railway lines are arrowing to the far
> mountainwide absence of the Iroquois.

Walcott understands better than many American writers who rail at America while, in the same breath, loving it, how to express this passionate contradiction, as in "Upstate":

> The spring hills are sun-freckled, the chaste white barns flash
> through screening trees the vigor of her dream,
> like a white plank bridge over a quarreling brook.
> Clear images! Direct as your daughters
> in the way their clear look returns your stare,
> unarguable and fatal—
> no, it is more sensual.
> I am falling in love with America.
>
> I must put the cold small pebbles from the spring
> upon my tongue to learn her language.

An American reader of these lines would surely feel that Walcott has, indeed, from putting "the cold small pebbles" on his tongue, learned America's language, though the very phrases in which he expresses this aspiration are in an English that has deeply read Spanish. Indeed, Walcott moves easily into a translated, or translatese, Spanish idiom, as in "Cantina Music":

> Hot, hot as ingots,
> music glows from the bars.
> They lean back like bandidos
> in the cantinas circling St. James;
> their fantasies
> shine like the rain's guitars;
> of generals whose names
> darken their iron stallions,
> against whose dusky faces the palms droop,
> morose mustaches of dead liberators.

As with so much poetry in English under powerful Hispanic influence, this reads rather like a translation, as if the poet were thinking in a language that is totally alien to that in which he is writing. Robert Bly's poetry is, when influenced by Spanish, a more extreme

Derek Walcott

example of the same tendency, for example in "Waking from Sleep," which begins:

> Inside the veins there are navies setting forth,
> Tiny explosions at the water lines,
> And seagulls weaving in the wind of the salty blood.

This has the air of English or American yearning to be translated back into the language which it came from, like a caged animal wanting to go back to the jungle. It is not just a matter of difference of language, but of ways of thinking and of mind and blood. The peculiar imagistic rhetoric of the Spanish is in the blood, its contact with things outside the body it inhabits, seizing on them and turning them into an idiomographic dictionary in which images mean what in another language would be abstract words. There is a sense in which we know that if it were written in another language (Spanish) we would believe the following (from "Evolution from the Fish"), but since it is written in English we don't:

> This grandson of fishes holds inside him
> A hundred thousand small black stones.

Fortunately Walcott's poetry does not often read like a translation. Its integrity lies in the assured truth, combined with the shock of surprise in recognizing such truth, of simile and metaphor. Lines such as the following (part of "From This Far") give the reader the pleasure of cut stone fitting into cut stone:

> The white almonds of a statue stare
> at almond branches wrestling off their shade
> like a girl from her dress—a gesture rarely made
> by abstract stone.

It is not just the idea expressed with the witty comment on abstract art at the end which delights here, but the way in which the poet directs the reader toward and makes him admit the justice of his beautiful simile of the shade and the girl pulling off her dress.

Another poem, "Hurucan," opens:

> Once branching light startles the hair of the coconuts,
> and on the villas' asphalt roofs, rain
> resonates like pebbles in a pan,
> and only the skirts of surf
> waltz round the abandoned bandstand,
> and we hear the telephone cables
> hallooing like fingers tapped over an Indian's mouth.

Walcott sends up similes like rockets. Seldom does the excess of the "exotic" tire the reader. On the contrary, what is so impressive about him is the dazzling instants of correspondence between things he sees and expresses with the human warmth peculiar to him. For his part, the reader feels at one and the same time that images or similes communicated are new to him, and yet that he has always known them. The impression of novelty concides with that of recognition.

Walcott himself seems very present in his poems, yet unobtrusive. The kind of thing he sees demonstrates his humanity in a rather general way. It does not insist on the poet's greatness. That is very different from the rhetoric of the poet who uses violent images to convey something about his own state of being—Yeats writing about his old age, for instance:

> An aged man is but a paltry thing,
> A tattered coat upon a stick, unless
> Soul clap its hands and sing, and louder sing
> For every tatter in its mortal dress.

This is magnificent, but it thrusts the soul of the poet forward upon the reader declaring his magnificence. "A tattered coat upon a stick" illustrates the poet's sense of what he has come to in his old age, but without any exactitude of correspondence which makes us see the simile as though it revealed something about old age which we had never seen before, but of which, being told, we immediately recognize the truth. It is, rather, as though Yeats, whose father was a painter, and who himself studied in art school, had painted such a garment, and seeing it in a gallery, and knowing that he was a septuagenarian when he painted it, we had sighed, "Ah, it is how he feels about himself." Yeats in general makes us see what he sees with the eye of his imagination—his own, inner life. He is always the egoist in his poetry, and the greatness of the poetry is that of the man.

Walcott's imagery seems to owe more to the thing outside himself, the phenomenon in nature, than to himself, except insofar as he transforms it into words that make us see it. The surprise is that the poet has seen the object which the reader has allowed to go unnoticed even though, on the margin of his consciousness, he was aware of it. These are effects of genius which we find frequently in Wordsworth. Walcott is perhaps a tropical Wordsworth, the Wordsworth who noticed things which when he sets them down, seem to ring bells of recognition in the reader. Thus, in the first book of "The Prelude," remembering scenes of village skating on the lake in his childhood:

> All shod with steel,
> We hissed along the polished ice in games
> Confederate, imitative of the chase
> And woodland pleasures,—the resounding horn,
> The pack loud chiming, and the hunted hare.
> So through the darkness and the cold we flew,
> And not a voice was idle; with the din
> Smitten, the precipices rang aloud;
> The leafless trees and every icy crag
> Tinkled like iron.

Genius of transforming into words that of which everyone was semi-consciously aware but had not brought forward into language lies in the words "tinkled like iron": what one might call the noticed gone unnoticed, the hidden memory summoned and instantly recognized as true when set down.

Another kind of truth—of one who, as it were, keeps his poetic nose to the ground—characterizes much of the poetry of Seamus Heaney. His work is sometimes compared with that of the early Yeats (perhaps because it is felt Ireland ought to have a Yeats), but in fact Heaney goes back to an Irish poet of a more realist intervening generation. Indeed the opening lines of Patrick Kavanagh's masterpiece, *The Great Hunger,* might be the prelude to the poetry of several young Irish poets (whether they are from the South or the North) writing since 1950:

> Clay is the word and clay is the flesh
> Where the potato-gatherers like mechanised scarecrows move
> Along the side-fall of the hill—Maguire and his men.
> If we watch them an hour is there anything we can prove

> Of life as it is broken-backed over the Book
> Of Death? Here crows gabble over worms and frogs
> And the gulls like old newspapers are blown clear of the hedges, luckily.

Yeats's early *Celtic Twilight* and his later magnificent rhetoric hide from us the extent to which the peasant and the poor fisherman (not Yeats's fisherman in Connemara tweed) enter into the Irish poetic tradition (see *The Faber Book of Irish Verse,* edited by John Montague). This tradition, extended into our own time by Kavanagh, forms, surely, the background to the poetry of several young Irish poets (they all seem to come from Ulster, but their sympathies are far from being Unionist): Seamus Heaney, Tom Paulin, Paul Muldoon, and John Montague himself. Whatever their politics or non-politics, they share a sense of bitter exile in their own country: a feeling not rare among the literary Irish since the eighteenth century, and dramatized by the fact that G. B. Shaw, W. B. Yeats, and James Joyce to differing degrees all felt themselves to be exiles. Possibly all these young Irish writers feel some part of their mentality portrayed in Joyce's Stephen Daedalus.

Of them all, perhaps the one who responds most bitterly to Yeats's description of Ireland as "great hatred, little room," is, in his recent poetry, Tom Paulin. In these poems that seem to conceal desperate signals, Paulin seems to concentrate all the bitternesses of disillusioning revolution and counterrevolution of recent world history and apply them with ferocity to the particular situation of Ireland today:

> So we break black bread
> in the provinces and can't be certain
> what it is we're missing, or what sacrament
> this might be, the loaf wrapped in a shirt-tail
> like a prisoner's secret or a caked ikon,
> that is sour and good, and has crossed over versts,
> kilometres, miles.

His most recent volume, *Liberty Tree,* ends with a poem, "To the Linen Hall," which, in striking contrast with much that has gone before, has a touching simplicity and evokes the fusion of poetry with traditional learning in a way that seems so salutary today, it deserves quotation in full simply for what it says and what it is:

> Here we have a form
> and a control
> that is our own,
> and on the stone steps
> of that eighteenth-century,
> reasoned library
> we catch the classic spore
> of Gibbon and new *ceps,*

> the busts and statues
> that might be stored
> under the squares.
> Our shaping brightness
> is a style and discipline
> that finds its tongue
> in the woody desk-dawns
> of fretting scholars
> who pray, invisibly,
> to taste the true vine
> and hum gently
> in holy sweetness.

The careers of the Ulster poets seem to follow similar patterns. Emerging from the countryside and comparative poverty, they win places at the university. Then, their works having been "discovered" by English editors, they go to America to make their living. Unlike Yeats and MacNeice, both of whom were educated in England, they become not so much Anglo-Irish as Irish-American, of the American campuses. "The More Man Has the More Man Wants," the longest poem in Muldoon's volume *Quoof,* is a freewheeling mock epic describing the hero's wild and mostly drunken adventures in America.

Perhaps the only sense in which Heaney might be said to resemble Yeats is in the impression he gives of a kind of tragic impartiality in his attitude, or the lack of it, toward events in Ireland. His early poems are the work of a poet who clings to the symbolic realities and mythology of the earth and stone of ancient places, worked upon and fought over, knowing that there is poetry above all in these. As it were, he digs into the landscape for poetry, finding a word for every spadeful of clay. In "Anahorish," for example:

> My 'place of clear water',
> the first hill in the world
> where springs washed into
> the shiny grass
>
> and darkened cobbles
> in the bed of the lane.
> *Anahorish,* soft gradient
> of consonant, vowel-meadow,
>
> after-image of lamps
> swung through the yards
> on winter evenings.

He also digs his way back into the archaeological past of the exhumed "Tollund Man":

> In the flat country nearby
> Where they dug him out,
> His last gruel of winter seeds
> Caked in his stomach.

Heaney follows poetry through landscape like an animal following the scent. His poetry is founded on things, but he is also one of the learned poets. He brings intellect and knowledge to bear on them. His Ireland, like that of the other Ulster poets, is enmeshed in past and present violence. Some words which Montague in the Introduction to his anthology of Irish verse quotes from Conor Cruise O'Brien apply to Irish poets of this generation:

> Irishness is not primarily a question of birth or blood or language; it is
> the condition of being involved in the Irish situation, and usually of
> being mauled by it.

For Heaney, present violence seems almost like the resurrection of past violence in the lives of the politically active who, today, are ghosts of the past, reenacting past history in his haunted poetry. In "An Ulster Twilight," he recalls from his childhood Eric Dawson, carpenter, a friend fifteen years his senior making a toy battleship for him. Many years later, the poet thinks that if Dawson and he were to meet again, they would doubtless talk "in a speech all toys and carpentry." The poem continues:

> A doorstep courtesy to shun
> Your father's uniform and gun,
> But—now that I have said it out—
> Maybe none the worse for that.

After his early poems about his childhood, his poetry becomes, as I have suggested here, haunted. His ambitious sequence "Station Island" is about the poet becoming aware of his vocation through a series of dream encounters with ghosts. Heaney explains that these encounters are

> set on Station Island on Lough Derg in County Donegal. The island is
> also known as Saint Patrick's Purgatory because of a tradition that Patrick
> was the first to establish the penitential vigil of fasting and praying
> which still constitutes the basis of the three-day pilgrimage.

The theme of Purgatory throughout this poem, in its Dantesque *terza rima*, also owes something to the use of approximate *terza rima* by T. S. Eliot, especially the passage in "Little Gidding" in which Eliot records an encounter during an air raid on London during the war, when he was fire-watching, with the "familiar compound ghost" of "some dead

Seamus Heaney

master." But perhaps the most successful of Heaney's cantos is that in which he follows most closely Dante's method of compressed narrative, those scenes in the *Purgatorio* or *Inferno* in which the poet meets a figure out of his past who narrates his unhappy story to him. Here Heaney records with poignant vividness meeting a spirit, companion of his youth, later a shopkeeper, who was murdered on his premises by armed intruders.

There is much violence too in *Sweeney Astray,* Heaney's vigorous rendering of legendary stories already beginning in the ninth century about *Buile Suibhne* (Sweeney), the wild and violent king (historically of the sixth century) deposed by the saintly Christian Ronan, who becomes miraculously transformed into a bird with a peculiarly savage nature who continues to taunt and torment his pious enemies. Again we are among scenes of violence, of primitive, volcanically imaginative energies in turbulent opposition to the sanctimonious order imposed upon the native culture by the invading proselytizing religious. *Sweeney Astray* is the most invigorating poetry Heaney has written, and the reader should not be put off by the fact that it goes as a translation. It is an entirely contemporary rendering of a world which does not lose, in the telling, the sense of its being of another age, half historic, half legendary, always fantastically alive. Sweeney is an archetype who, in Heaney's rendering, burns through the past into a situation always with us which divides the creative imaginative intelligences of any time into those that are orthodox and those that are heretical. Sweeney provides a flamboyant caricature of the Beat on the campus, of what, as I have mentioned above, Lowell called the Redskins and the Palefaces. But also in each alive and self-aware individual he is the unredeemed unconscious dream life taunting the sublimated super-ego. He is the drunken husband, son, or mother, in the conventional bourgeois household, for example, in Ibsen's *Ghosts*. Indeed, it might almost be said that no writer was more conscious of a character such as Sweeney than was Ibsen. Sweeney is about a pre-Christian Celtic Ireland and reminds us that there was always something primitively native about the Irish consciousness which felt invaded by whatever forces came from the outside.

The Irish poets whom I have discussed here begin their poetry with the poverty of the land, "the great hunger." With the exception sometimes of Muldoon, they are hardly concerned with the industrial proletariat. Two English poets, Tony Harrison and Craig Raine, are both extremely conscious of their working-class origins in the North of England. It would be wrong to describe the writing of either as autobiographical, yet both carry round with them an autobiographical load, an extreme awareness of their origins which weighs on them. In their very sophistication and display of learning (strikingly evident in both) there is a sense of the past like a burden only partly shed.

Another characteristic they have in common is that the past of each—in the form of parents, uncles and aunts, childhood friends— hardly recognizes their present. They appear not so much in the guise of home boy made good as changeling come out of his carapace of working-class childhood, sensational and brilliant as any dragonfly, with quivering shining rainbow-colored wings, from the chrysalis shed and falling back onto the soil of origin. At the same time, both are at pains to explain their origins as though they were explaining the inexplicably miraculous. How did *this* come out of *that*?

The sense of transformation, in disowning continuity, abolishes any sense of political class consciousness. Harrison and Raine show that they are in many ways proud of what might be called their Folk Origins. They give reasons for this which are cogent. They persuade us that their working-class homes were centers of a more warmly human love than bourgeois or aristocratic English homes, and we can readily be persuaded of this. But what they see as relating, or not relating, these origins to their poetry and themselves as poets, is disconnectedness. They are sentimentally attached to, and in every other way completely broken away from, a proletarian background that seems to have no future. In their writing no moral of historical inevitability, leading to the class from which they derive becoming the politically ruling class, pertains. Through the qualification of their exceptional talents they have moved, like D. H. Lawrence, from the morally superior class (the workers)—which, despite its superiority has no future that they recognize—into the morally inferior middle class which provides the circumstances in which talents shine. No conclusions are to be drawn from this, except that each individualist gifted changeling has found his corrupt fairy godmother—the bourgeoisie.

Harrison and Raine both write of their fathers, both of whom were extremely eccentric characters. Harrison makes ironic poetry out of a home where his parents and all his family knew nothing about poetry and, if they had done so, would have considered it a kind of affront. The lines in which he attempts to relate his birth to his vocation (from "Heredity") seem to bite deeper into metal or stone than all but the rarest epitaphs:

> How you became a poet's a mystery!
> Wherever did you get your talent from?
>
> *I say:* I had two uncles, Joe and Harry—
> one was a stammerer, the other dumb.

Harrison's father worked in a bakery, supervising its ovens. There was very little verbal communication between father and son. Their companionship grew to be that of two men who sit either side of the fireplace drinking beer and neither of them saying a word—real enough if there is affection between them. In a sequence of sixteen-line sonnets about his childhood in Newcastle, Harrison appears as epitome of the child not so much misunderstood as locked *incommunicado* in his childhood: a condition made ironic by the fact that his gift is, of course, communication. With that part of him which is poet he is shut off from his working-class home, and because he speaks in his parents' vocabulary and accent, he is also shut off at school from the English teacher. "Them & [uz]" begins:

> ay, ay! . . . stutterer Demosthenes
> gob full of pebbles outshouting seas—
>
> 4 words only of *mi 'art aches* and . . . "Mine's broken,
> you barbarian, T.W.!" *He* was nicely spoken.
> "Can't have our glorious heritage done to death!"

The irony of the Newcastle schoolteacher sneering at the schoolboy Harrison for his pronunciation is emphasized by the fact that Keats himself was derided in his lifetime by the *Edinburgh Review* as being of the "cockney school" of poets and perhaps himself spoke with a slight cockney accent (he came from a background not altogether dissimilar from that of Harrison).

The poem quoted above continues:

> I played the Drunken Porter in *Macbeth.*
>
> "Poetry's the speech of kings. You're one of those
> Shakespeare gives the comic bits to: prose!

> All poetry (even Cockney Keats?) you see
> 's been dubbed by [Λs] into RP,
> Received Pronunciation, please believe [Λs]
> your speech is in the hands of the Receivers."

The sequence of sixteen-line sonnets, called *Continuous*, is elegiac of many things: the death of the older generation, that of Harrison's parents, his own buried childhood, the end of a historic phase in the lives of people in the industrial North of England, bombed in the war and now with the identity of its working-class population largely blotted out by waves of Asian immigrants. Making poetry out of the lack of it in his family, Harrison employs a glaringly unpoetic idiom sometimes insulting to the reader—if that reader is a shade of his Newcastle English teacher—with phrases twisted like rods of iron into forced rhymes, the whole held together by a bitter, mocking, malignant but not unlovable if unloving humor (where perhaps in other countries the class self-hatred would have a nihilist destructive flavor, Harrison avoids this, and perhaps this is what makes his poetry peculiarly English, not transferable perhaps into terms of any other culture).

Harrison finds irony in his successes, of which he is nonetheless proud, as a playwright and translator whose works have been performed on Broadway—his name in lights. He is remembering such triumphs, and the fact that he has climbed out of his origins on ladders of dictionaries. He is aware of his resemblance to some Latin poet, perhaps a slave who has been given his freedom, who educates himself and travels in Roman African and East European provinces (just as he through his employment as teacher by the British Council has been to Africa, Prague, and other places). Seneca is a model for him, and lines of his Latin provide an epigraph for the poem "Newcastle is Peru."

"Marked with D.," a poem about the cremation of his father, who put bread in ovens, shows the quality of an imagination which forces burning metaphors out of an actual scene of burning:

> I thought of his cataracts ablaze with Heaven
> and radiant with the sight of his dead wife.

These are lines of extreme literalism of the imagination, extremely "unpoetic," pushed with great courage and audacity to where the ugliness of a fact becomes the beauty of the spirit in the impassioned affirmation of love. In this whole sequence of poems love for Harrison's parents, as for his own children and the woman he lives with, is affirmed against what for the most part is a singularly bleak and desolate background, made the more so through being connected with the decline of the North of England.

However, Harrison's family, which seems so unconcerned with poetry and shows so little understanding of the psychology and motives of the child who writes it, has traditions with roots reaching beyond the industrial North of England into the surrounding countryside, whose inhabitants were driven at the time of the Industrial Revolution to become the proletariat of the barrack-like slums in the great industrial Black-Country Towns. Harrison finds confirmation in his own ancestry of Richard Hoggart's thesis, in *The Uses of Literacy,* that more of the peasant culture and patterns of behavior of the country people than is generally recognized, by social historians, was transferred into the towns. Harrison has looked back to his own forebears, as, for example, in "Lines to My Grandfathers":

> Ploughed parallel as print the stony earth.
> The straight stone walls defy the steep grey slopes.
> The place's rightness for my mother's birth
>
> Exceeds the pilgrim grandson's wildest hopes—
>
> Wilkinson farmed Thrang Crag, Martindale.
>
> Horner was the Haworth signalman.
>
> Harrison kept a pub with home-brewed ale:
>
> Fell farmer, railwayman, and *publican.*

A photograph of the Harrison family grave at a hillside cemetery on Beeston Hill in Leeds, opposite Leeds University, is printed on the jacket of Tony Harrison's *Selected Poems.*

A traditional attitude carried over from the pre-industrial English village into the industrial towns, as much to Harrison's slum Leeds or Newcastle as to D. H. Lawrence's Nottingham, was a fierce puritanism, different from the middle-class puritanism that degenerated into gentility. The effects of this can be observed in Harrison's dislike of the inhibitions of his upbringing on his sexuality, in that very lewdness which some critics note in his early volume *The Loiners,* and in his satire on the sexual lives of the white occupiers of colonial Africa.

Here, and in his deep concern with his origins, Harrison has much in common with Raine, from whom he diverges, however, in refusing to push intellectual cleverness in his poetry to the point where it can only be shared by readers who are skilled in solving intellectual riddles.

It must be said though that in Raine's most recent volume, *Rich,* this, the centerpiece, a prose section containing an unforgettable description of Raine's father, is as accessible as Harrison when Harrison is writing about his father. It opens:

I was born in 1944. In the thirties, my father had been a painter and decorator, plumber, electrician, publican and boxer, but when I was growing up, he was a Spiritualist and a faith healer, talking about his negro spirit-guide, Massa, and explaining how he knew when people were cured because he felt burning coals in the palms of his hands.

Later we learn that during the war his father, who had worked in a munitions factory "in some undisclosed, remote part of Scotland" had been the victim of some terrible accident. This had resulted in his having to have five major operations on his brain, and having a silver plate inserted in his skull. With his cures, his gift as a storyteller, his fearlessly expressed socialist views, his boasting about his early achievements as boxer, football player, and his success as an amateur comedian, together with the fact that ever since the accident he was subject to epileptic fits, Raine's father was evidently eccentric on the scale of the hero of a Smollett novel. The title of Raine's volume reminds us that the rich common heritage of the English workers is the eccentricity of a few of them, a characteristic which Dickens exploited to great advantage in his novels.

Harrison and Raine are both learned poets. But whereas Harrison, while in no way writing down to his public, makes a virtue of avoiding obscurity, Raine is essentially a poet of wit, writing poems some of which are for the members of a highly educated elite. His imagery, apt, but often not immediately taken, forces the reader to see resemblances which are sometimes very amusing, in the manner more of a witty caricaturist than an observer of nature. "City Gent" opens:

> On my desk, a set of labels
> or a synopsis of leeks,
> blanched by the sun
> and trailing their roots
>
> like a watering can.
> Beyond and below,
> diminished by distance,
> a taxi shivers at the lights:
>
> a shining moorhen
> with an orange nodule
> set over the beak,
> taking a passenger
>
> under its wing.

The reader does not take in the similes of labels/leeks/roots/watering can with the immediate concurrence with which he feels illuminated inwardly by the things seen in a poem of Walcott. He assents to them, perhaps slowly, with his mind rather than his eye, and perhaps having mentally translated the language into visual cartoon. The whole effect of the lines quoted above is, indeed, rather like Walt Disney, whom one can well imagine drawing a taxi to look like a moorhen that takes a passenger under her wing.

I put forward the example of Disney because it may be helpful in approaching Raine's poetry; but if taken as suggesting that Raine is a crude though delightful caricaturist, it could be misleading. Readers of French poetry will probably find his poetry more accessible than those who only read English. A sonnet called "Arsehole" is based on one of the scabrous sonnets which Rimbaud wrote in collaboration with Verlaine in their love affair's mutuality of outrageousness. The effect is produced by the combination of the disgusting and the beautiful. The uniqueness of Raine's imagery does not derive from him seeing what everyone sees but has never before seen expressed, as with the lines of Wordsworth and of Walcott quoted above, but in a kind of originality which we think of as French, where French poetry combines poetic with painterly qualities. A poem called "Inca" offers these lines:

> Inca. Now is there only this.
> Since the past is past,
> the future is fiction:
> a garden with walls
> where I stand in another life,
>
> the luminous deckchair
> poised like a cricket
> in stifling moonlight.

As with the simile of the moorhen and the taxi, one sees this best if one sees the thing observed in nature as a painting rather than as immediately transmitted verbal observation, in the same way as I have suggested above that Yeats's metaphor of old age, "a tattered coat upon a stick," becomes more apparent if one thinks of the image as a painting—seen perhaps in a gallery—of a tattered coat, which suggests the old age of the painter. "The luminous deckchair / poised like a cricket / in stifling moonlight"—very beautiful if one, as it were, pauses to visualize it, to translate the words read, with deliberate effort, into the thing seen. The effect then is intellectual, not immediate like Wordsworth's "every icy crag / Tinkled like iron," or both surprising and instantly recognized like Walcott's "Once branching light startles the hair of the coconuts, / and on the villas' asphalt roofs, rain / resonates like pebbles in a pan."

The volume, *Rich*, which I have been discussing here is divided into three sections: "Rich" (poems), "A Silver Plate" (prose), and "Poor" (poems). The poems in the third section are more accessible than those in "Rich." There are also poems which refer to the Russian revolution and to the lives of Russian writers during the Stalinist period (Raine is married to Pasternak's niece).

In sum, then, the poems of Walcott, Heaney, Harrison, and Craig are haunted by the politics of this and preceding centuries like ghosts in the machine, without the writers appearing to take sides politically. The more obviously political writers in America and England today are, I have suggested above, sectarian, pleading special causes. Walcott is on the side of the blacks, I suppose, but that is almost taken for granted in his work. This generation of writers, while still conformist in supporting the good humanist cause, is aware of the greater disorder caused by the good cause's triumph. Walcott writes in "Port of Spain":

> The oven alleys stifle
> where mournful tailors peer over old machines
> stitching June and July together seamlessly,
> and one waits for lightning as the armed sentry
> hopes in boredom for the crack of a rifle—
> but I feed on its dust, its ordinariness,
> on the inertia that fills its exiles with horror.

And

> The terror
> is local, at least. Like the magnolia's whorish whiff.
> And the dog barks of the revolution crying wolf.

Heaney and Muldoon are, presumably, anti-Unionist Irish, yet they do not identify in their poetry with any Irish cause. Harrison's poems memorialize the poor in Newcastle slums but do not look forward to any kind of workers' state. Politics is there in the work of all these poets, but where, fifty years ago, they might have joyfully anticipated a future of peace and social justice, today there is a void. In large parts of the Western world, perhaps even in China, the Soviet Union has made the name of revolution the abyss, and nothing has taken its place. It should be pointed out, though, that the lack of illusions, political or of any other kind, is not a bad thing.

One English poet has a very well developed political awareness and social conscience. Just because he has these, the lack of a political program supported in his work, apart from the liberal humanism which is a state of mind rather than an ideology, is all the more significant. I am speaking of James Fenton. As a journalist, Fenton was in Vietnam and Cambodia in the late sixties and saw the horrors of the war there. When he began writing, he was much influenced by the early Auden of the thirties who wrote exhilarating poems about a symbolic landscape of spies, civil war, and revolution, projecting these into an England of neurotic reactionary upper-class aristocrats, generals, and nannies. However, lacking the inventive imagination of Auden, he is not at his strongest in poems of allegorical fantasy. He comes into his own when he is writing poetry of actual events, describing a real war-torn landscape. When he does this his poetry has the clarity of lines seen through a magnifying glass held over a map. A poem called "In a Notebook" shows the influence of Auden's poem "The Shield of Achilles": but it has a power of its own independent of that poem, and in a way a realization of it, because it is a description of the landscape in Cambodia:

> There was a river overhung with trees
> With wooden houses built along its shallows
> From which the morning sun drew up a haze
> And the gyrations of the early swallows
> Paid no attention to the gentle breeze
> Which spoke discreetly from the weeping willows.
> There was a jetty by the forest clearing
> Where a small boat was tugging at its mooring.

This is a poignant evocation of the Cambodian landscape so soon to be ravaged by war. In another poem, "Children in Exile," Fenton writes about a Cambodian family who have been adopted by American friends of his living in Tuscany. The subject of the poem is the way in which the children in their new and peaceful surroundings in Florence are haunted by the horrors they have survived and re-live them in dreams and in their behavior. In winter, the poet asks,

> And how would they survive the snows of Italy?
>   For the first weeks, impervious to relief,
> They huddled in dark rooms and feared the open air,
>   Caught in the tight security of grief.

America, cause of these children's misfortunes, as the poet believes, is very much on his mind. "For it is we, not they, who cannot forgive America," he writes, and yet the inference—which would seem inevitable if this poem were by, say, a Cuban poet—that these children should grow up in order to oppose America, is not drawn. Instead, the poet's American friends, together with the children whom they have adopted, have bestowed on them by him a kind of general blessing with good wishes for their future. The bonhomie seems almost Dickensian, a Christmas story conclusion, but it arises, surely, from terrible doubts concerning the validity of any political solution, the inability, honestly admitted, of the poet to draw a conclusion which would seem to accord with what twenty or thirty years ago would have been seen as "the logic of events." So, near the end of the poem, Fenton writes:

> My dear American friends, I can't say how much it means to me
>   To see this little family unfurl,
> To see them relax and learn, and learn about happiness,
>   The mother growing strong, the boys adept, the girl

43

> Confident in your care. They can never forget the past.
>   Let them remember, but let them not fear.
> Let them find their future is delightfully accomplished
>   And find perhaps America is here.

Here is a poet, deeply interested in politics, and feeling passionately about them, who ends his poem on a note of aspiration that cannot apply to politics in any historic situation, as we have experienced history. For it is impossible to believe that the kindness of an American family adopting a Cambodian family can be translated into the foreign policy of a superpower. In a way, what Fenton is expressing here is the powerlessness of poetry.

Perhaps "the logic of the times" in which we live points to the elegiac—Merrill about Auden and other friends, the Ulster poets about Ireland. The elements of mythmaking fantasy and journalistic realism in Fenton come together best in a sequence of poems called "A German Requiem," with which *Children in Exile* opens. This is about the terrible vacuum, a kind of blankness as to the destruction of the now rebuilt German cities and the moral evil of the Nazis, which is felt in post-1945 Germany today:

> It is not what they built. It is what they knocked down.
> It is not the houses. It is the spaces between the houses.
> It is not the streets that exist. It is the streets that no longer exist.

The force of this poem lies in its very negation; and in this it has something in common with Harrison writing about Newcastle, Walcott about the Caribbean, Heaney about Ireland.

But as for elegy, a magnificent poem which is elegiac on a monumental scale is Geoffrey Hill's "The Mystery of the Charity of Charles Péguy." Hill himself is emphatically a learned poet. His early poems are uncompromisingly severe, twisted sometimes, as though this poet regarded sentence structure as material which he could bend to the shape of his poems. These are like sculpture, the modern idiom contorted in order to make the poem an artifact placed among old things belonging to past history. Sentences are arranged so that the objects they contain are placed before the reader in the order in which the poet wishes him to see them. In "Requiem for the Plantagenet Kings" the poet without using archaic language seems to wrest the content of the poem out of our time and set it in another age: rather museum-like, as though we are looking at things from four centuries ago set out in order for our modern inspection. But the interest is not simply historic. The violence, which we see more clearly just because its instruments, its location, and its blood can be set out before us, reflects back on our gore, our power-mongering, our wickedness, our violence. Here is "Requiem for the Plantagenet Kings":

For whom the possessed sea littered, on both shores,
Ruinous arms; being fired, and for good,
To sound the constitution of just wars,
Men, in their eloquent fashion, understood.

Relieved of soul, the dropping-back of dust,
Their usage, pride, admitted within doors;
At home, under caved chantries, set in trust,
With well-dressed alabaster and proved spurs
They lie; they lie; secure in the decay
Of blood, blood-marks, crowns hacked and coveted,
Before the scouring fires of trial-day
Alight on men; before sleeked groin, gored head,
Budge through the clay and gravel, and the sea
Across daubed rock evacuates its dead.

The word-order, with verbs thrust to the end of sentences, seems Germanic, and the images suggest, as I have indicated above, sculpture or, what is close to this, Dürer's line engravings and woodcuts. There is though something perhaps a little too willed about this, as though the poet were compounding an archaic style all his own, not ancient and not modern.

Charley Péguy, of French peasant stock, born in 1873 and killed in the Battle of the Marne in September 1914, was nationalist, Catholic, and socialist. Hill celebrates him as being the last of those French of "*l'ancienne France*." The quotation from Péguy which the poet chooses as epigraph to his elegy may seem to look forward to the void of belief in the work of the poets discussed above (for I do not count the Ouija Board as any kind of belief). We are the "*après-derniers*." Speaking for the believers of his own generation, Péguy writes:

Nous sommes les derniers. Presque les après-derniers. Aussitôt après nous commence un autre âge, un tout autre monde, le monde de ceux qui ne croient plus à rien, qui s'en font gloire et orgueil.

Hill's poem is faithful to this prophecy. In it there seems to be a line drawn between the Europe of "*l'ancienne France*"—that Europe which eviscerated itself in the First World War—and all that followed. The bristling packed imagery is nostalgic rather than heroic, evoking that France of deep patriotism, religion, *gentillesse,* and intelligence which in his best poetry Paul Claudel portrays (for example in his play *L'annonce faite à Marie*). The France that Hill depicts in his dense and studied imagery lingers in old French cemeteries, in the pathos of First World War village epitaphs or memorials of the dead—for instance, a poilu in stone or bronze, equipped with helmet, pack, and gun, perhaps with an angel who is a village girl at his side, crowning him with a wreath, his stance a gesture of departure to war and, even more, of farewell, the whole scene created with a certain naiveté which comes from the heart of the sculptor and seems to embody the life of the village.

> Memory, Imagination, harvesters of those fields,
>
> our gifts are spoils, our virtues epitaphs,
> our substance is the grass upon the graves.
> 'Du calme, mon vieux, du calme.' How studiously
> one cultivates the sugars of decay,
>
> pâtisserie-tinklings of angels ''sieur-'dame',
> the smile of the dead novice in its plush frame,
> while greed and disaffection are ingrained
> like chalk-dust in the ranklings of the mind.

A merit of Hill's poem is that it provides information about Péguy and the times in which he lived, the things he believed in. The reader sees in his mind's eye this stubborn, contrarious, devout, courageous, *fidèle* pamphleteer. We are left to wonder whether words Péguy wrote led to some fanatic shooting and killing, such as that of the great socialist leader Jean Jaurès, with whom Péguy was in dispute. Reading Hill's wonderful elegy, one lives for a time in that time, and that France, as real here as the England in Gray's country churchyard, which at moments it seems to echo.

*　　*　　*　　*　　*

A paradox of modern poetry, and of much other modern art, is that it has been written against the opinion of critics who indicated that in our time of fragmented values and the breakdown of the standards of civilization the writing of great poetry had become impossible. Ever since Matthew Arnold wrote his famous essay on the state of poetry and the state of criticism, critics like T. E. Hulme, F. R. Leavis, and others have emphasized that today, owing to the absence of traditional values embodied in modern patterns of living, criticism, by establishing links with the past through upholding the standards of the works of the "great tradition," has become more important than poetry.

Great poems by Eliot, Yeats, and others seem to prove that this judgment is wrong. But the wrongness may have been a kind of rightness in that the critics, by putting forward the difficulties of creating great art, provoked the artists into producing miracles. The nature of the miracle is that the work of art embodies in the moment of creation critical awareness of the immense difficulty of creating it. Critical awareness included not only literary criticism but awareness of the fragmented values of the time and the breakdown of civilization as it had been understood in the past.

This complex critical/creative awareness implied that with changing times strategies would change. Early in the century, the strategy of Eliot was the suppression of the self, the poetic ego, in the poem: for the poet, in order to write his masterpiece, had to immerse himself in the past tradition, to objectify his creative/critical consciousness. This was at a time when the poet could see the surrounding civilization simply in terms of its decay, without a history in which he felt the need to participate. There followed, in the thirties and, in varying forms, up till the sixties, a period in which surrounding events as it were forced the poet back into history. For this reason, the self of the poet, as both writing his poem and participating in contemporary history, became important in his poetry. We see the consequences of such historic pressure in the poetry of Lowell, and his persona in his poetry.

I have suggested that the poetry of certain—though not all—poets considered in this essay represents a "post-political" phase, the consequence really of despair about the possibility of any kind of revolutionary politics transforming societies. Several poems I have considered here seem to show this. However, I am all too conscious that in discussing these examples I have not discussed poems and poets as important and interesting as those I have chosen. Even worse, I have missed the opportunity of writing about poets whose work is neglected, but which I consider important. I can at least now mention one of these. F. T. Prince, a South African poet who has lived most of his life in England, and who, until his retirement a few years ago, was for many years professor of English literature at Southampton University. Prince is one of the best poets now living writing in English. One poem of his, "Soldiers Bathing," is, I think, widely recognized as a modern classic (though I notice that neither this nor any other poem of his appears in *The Norton Anthology of Modern Poetry* which, incidentally, also omits another famous poem written during that war, Henry Reed's "Naming of Parts"). Prince's most recent work is a slim volume of three longish poems with a common theme which is conversation in speech or thought between friends when they are together or separated from one another. The first of the three describes the thoughts of the Chinese poet Po Chü-i (A.D. 772–846) about Yüan Chên, and another absent friend Han-Lang, when Po Chü-i was in exile; the second is about the thoughts of the dog, depicted in many paintings, who fed Saint Rock on his pilgrimage from Montpellier to Rome, in the fourteenth century, bringing him fragments of bread; the third is a conversation carried on in the present time between the spirits of Byron and Shelley on the Italian coast near Lerici, where Shelley was drowned.

These poems are very different from Prince's early work, which was almost classical in style, even Latinate ("Soldiers Bathing," a middle-period poem, is in a kind of free verse perhaps modeled on a mixture of eighteenth-century prose in the self-communing manner of Gibbon's *Autobiography* and the prose of Henry James's last novels). The poems are original in technique—light, airy, and in tone, Shelleyan, though without imitating Shelley's metrical patterns. In all three poems the language seems strangely floating, sky-like. It is controlled, yet on the loosest of reins. Prince's stanzas and images seem to enter realms of invisibility. Vast spaces seem traveled through by the thoughts of the Chinese poet, in short lines that have the delicacy of Chinese brush drawings. In the second poem, the short lines like little runs, growls, or barks are perfectly adapted to the thoughts of the dog about the saint, his master. Conversation between Byron and Shelley suggests in form and language, disembodiment. Perhaps the most immediately attractive of these poems is "His Dog and Pilgrim" with its imitativeness of a dog wagging and running and barking:

> —and rumbles, tumbles
> turns here to be shrewd
>
> panting importantly
> sitting down hastily
> to itch, then on
>
> to such collating
> snufflicating, dating
> what all they, every one
> gone said and done:
>
> 'sez he? said that, she did?
> indeed and wuz it and
> how could, who would
> so gabble?'

This poem has the charm of its originality. Like "The Yüan Chên Variations," with imagist touches of extreme lightness, it keeps close to the spiritual aspect of Prince's subject (he is a Catholic) as it appears in paintings of Saint Rock with the cicatrice on his thigh and his attendant dog:

> to shun society
> and walk in piety
> he carries all,
> and carries on his back
> a pilgrim's pack
>
> *
>
> was bearded, had
> eyes that were set
> wide and well back.

In short, this is a very careful word-painting from a dog's-eye point of view.

In the scene about Byron and Shelley, those two poets exchange ideas about their lives. Prince is penetrating about what is mysterious in the relationship of Byron the sensualist and man of action, and Shelley the idealist and ineffectual revolutionary. For the two poets had a deep respect for each other, despite the fact that there was so much in Shelley for Byron to deride, so much in Byron for Shelley to disapprove. The most beautiful poetry here is Byron's description of his Grecian journeys:

> Hellespont and Hero's lamp!
> —Yes, if in turn
> I look within to learn
> what might be peace,
> I must think, not of the camp
>
> at Missolonghi,
> but certainly of Greece.
> Wild, bathed in light,
> her beauty under blight,
> the unheroic, unfree
>
> wide murmuring sea—
> mountains and promontories,
> scarred columns in the sun,
> the wandering bee:
> when I was twenty-one,
>
> *milord* travelling alone,
> I found in these
> like nakedness, my own
> unknown or half-known
> famine and despair.

But it is Shelley who brings the reminiscing debate to a conclusion, sublimating Byron's passion within his own spiritualized eroticism, the fusion of soul, flesh, and landscape, closer perhaps to D. H. Lawrence's concept of "phallic consciousness" than Lawrence was capable of realizing.

> And why come, if not to cleave,
> not just to the old Italy
> and old feeling, by the same
> pinewoods and sea—
> but to erotic fury?

49

—as if the flame
imprisoned in the flame
might then be free—
melt glittering in that sleeve
of light by Lerici . . .

I began by remarking that we have the sense of the great poets and artists with the great names of this century having passed away. Part of my argument has been, though, that poetry is a special art in that great poetry can be written by poets who are not "great poets," just very good ones. I should end this essay by calling to mind some of the poets who are writing, some of the best poems being written today.

The Collected Poems of Peter Porter, who is Australian by birth, are lively, intelligent, witty, wonderfully varied in subject matter and form, exhilarating. They cover an immense range of the poet's interest in places, art, music, and other poetry. One has the impression, reading them, of a man who has lived and suffered, energetic, courageous, but who, as an observer, traveler, commentator, could afford to be more himself in his poems. His personal modesty, as it were, obtrudes.

It suffices merely to mention a few names to realize that a great deal of very distinguished and interesting poetry is being written. In America there are Robert Penn Warren, Richard Wilbur, Stanley Kunitz, Lincoln Kirstein, Anthony Hecht, William Meredith, Howard Nemerov, James Dickey, Robert Bly, Adrienne Rich, A. R. Ammons, Gary Snyder, John Hollander, to mention only a few of the most obvious; in England Philip Larkin, Ted Hughes (now poet laureate), Charles Causley, Peter Redgrove, Donald Davie, Charles Tomlinson, C. H. Sisson.

Particular attention should be drawn to two young American poets— Amy Clampitt, very aware in her work of previous poets meticulous in their observation of minute particlars of nature, but full of original insights of her own; and Gjertrud Schnackenberg, witty, learned, intellectually overwhelming, but also a poet of deep feeling and technical mastery.

For poets, a question about poetry is not so much whether it is being written as whether it is being read. But, while sympathizing with their impatience to be recognized and to earn money, I should point out that the question, though having very pressing relevance to the poet, is not so obviously relevant to the state of poetry. Whitman's dictum that "great poets need great audiences" seems to have a peculiarly American significance, but it is not necessarily true at all times and places. However else poetry is to be judged, it is scarcely to be estimated by the number of readers of a particular poet. In a sense, a poem, unless it is poetic drama, only has one reader at any time—the person who happens to be reading it. Poetry is a one-to-one relationship between poet and reader. "Many readers" means simply that there are many such one-to-ones. In his lifetime, Gerard Manley Hopkins had scarcely more than three readers of his poetry, the only effective one being his rather obtuse, though highly educated, friend, Robert Bridges. Early in the century, Ezra Pound wrote that a poet needed about thirty readers.

These truisms may seem hard on poets, but they are not necessarily so to poems, and the distinction should be borne in mind. If it is, we shall be less likely to feel that the condition of contemporary poetry is to be judged (apart from the welfare of poets) by counting readers (as the poet and critic Randall Jarrell seemed always to be doing).

A phenomenon to note in this century is the development of world poetry. The great poets of the time, especially those from Spain and Latin America—but also Russia, Greece, and Italy—less so, perhaps, France and Germany—are translated and are internationally known. Poets from all over the world attend international meetings and conferences where poets read their poems and exchange ideas about poetry. I have suggested here that there is a strong influence of Spanish on some recent American poetry, though I consider it a rather dangerous one. Auden and Lowell were both international poets in being influenced by their foreign contemporaries—Auden by Brecht, Rilke, Saint Jean Perse, Garcia Lorca, Cavafy, and probably others: Lowell by Russian poets and by Montale, the great Italian poet.

Modern poetry is very much alive. There is not much point in saying that the twentieth century will prove to be one of the greatest periods in the history of poetry all over the world. But it is probably true.

The New Biology and Its Human Implications

Theodore T. Puck

Dr. Theodore T. Puck is active in several areas of the sciences. He is a professor in the Department of Biochemistry, Biophysics, and Genetics, and at the same time a professor in the Department of Medicine at the University of Colorado Health Science Center. Dr. Puck also directs the Eleanor Roosevelt Institute for Cancer Research and serves on the Editorial Board of Encyclopædia Britannica, Inc. He was born in Chicago in 1916 and was educated at the University of Chicago, from which he received his Ph.D. in physical chemistry in 1940. Since then he has taught at various universities and has held visiting professorships at Stanford and Yale universities, as well as at the University of California. He has received several awards for biomedical research over the years, including the Lasker Award (1958), the Borden Award (1959), the Louisa Gross Horwitz Prize from Columbia University (1973), and recently the E. B. Wilson Medal from the American Society for Cell Biology (1984) and the Bonfils-Stanton Foundation Award in Science (1984).

Dr. Puck is the author or coauthor of more than 150 scientific articles dealing with prevention of airborne disease, bacterial and virus metabolism, mammalian cell growth, genetics, and radiobiology. He has held research grants from the National Foundation–March of Dimes, the National Institutes of Health, and the United States Public Health Service, which enabled him to undertake some of the studies described in this essay. A member of the National Academy of Sciences, as well as many other learned organizations, he lives in Denver, Colorado.

Introduction

During the last half of the current century, biomedical research has begun one of the greatest of scientific revolutions. A new biology is centered in the cell, the fundamental building block of all living organisms. New developments have for the first time illuminated structures and functions of the genetic and biochemical constituents of the cell and have yielded new concepts which seem to apply to all living organisms. These advances in understanding promise great new powers in human health. They also introduce new considerations affecting our conception of the nature of man and his unique powers and needs.

This paper attempts to explain some of these important new concepts and achievements and discusses some of their implications for the human condition.*

Early molecular advances in understanding cell structure and function

Each cell carries out many thousands of different chemical reactions which extract energy from energy-rich molecules and make use of it for the many operations of the life process. These operations include the building of enormous numbers of other large and small molecules, which carry out the essential chemical reactions that constitute living behavior. Such reactions include thousands of specific chemical transformations and usually are linked into reaction chains, exquisitely regulated and integrated with respect to each other. Taken together, these beautifully coordinated chemical reactions form a pattern constituting the unique living process for each organism as a whole, with each step in the process being made possible through the mediation of a different, specific protein molecule called an enzyme.

*Studies carried out in the author's laboratory referred to in this paper were supported by grants from the American Cancer Society, the National Institutes of Health PO1 HDO2080, R. J. Reynolds Industries, the Monsanto Company, and the Henry J. Kaiser Family Foundation.

Every cell in every living organism continually carries on the many thousands of different chemical reactions needed for its own individual life processes. In multicellular forms, all of the individual chemical steps in this complex array of reactions are modulated from millisecond to millisecond in accordance with changes in the environment of each cell and the needs of the body as a whole. In the mammalian organism each cell synthesizes the many thousands of different proteins it needs to keep these different reaction pathways proceeding at rates that are adjusted to fit both the needs imposed by external and internal molecular conditions and the overall needs and drives of the organism.

Thus, on the microscopic scale specific chains of reactions, brought about at every step by a specific enzyme (protein), are carried on in each cell, and these combine in macroscopic processes as diverse as the contractions of the heart, the excitation of nerves carrying complex messages back and forth between the nervous system and the parts of the body, the formation of specific antibodies in response to invasion by an infectious agent, and the synthesis of hemoglobin and other components of the blood.

Each protein molecule is made up of linear chains of smaller molecules called amino acids which are strung together like pearls on a

Figure 1. Shown here is the structure of the protein lysozyme, an enzyme found in human tears, that destroys invaders by hydrolyzing their cell walls. The indicated cross-links are formed by chemical bonds involving sulfur atoms and serve to fold the linear structure into a 3-dimensional configuration which is chemically active.

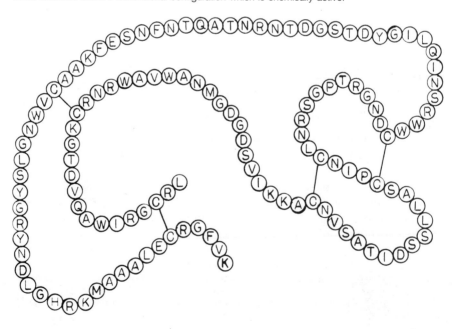

necklace. Several such chains can combine to form a complex protein (fig. 1). Other chemical moieties may become attached to such simple or complex chains. Some of these proteins form structural elements of cells, like the rigid microtubules which help give each body cell its characteristic shape (fig. 2). Others—the enzymes—serve to catalyze specific chemical reactions; some are universal and present in every cell while others are unique to cells of particular tissues. The twenty different amino acids from which all proteins are built can be arranged in an astronomically large number of different structures, since each different order of amino acids constitutes a different protein (table 1). Proteins can contain as few as 100 or as many as 100,000 amino acids.

How does each cell know which proteins to build? One of the great triumphs of the new molecular biology was the demonstration that the genes present in every living cell determine this. Each gene consists of a

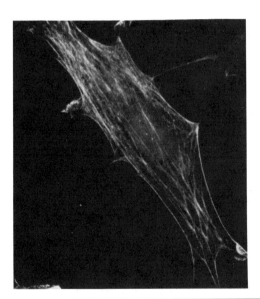

Figure 2 (left). The actin filaments of a Chinese hamster ovary cell (stained with antibody and a fluorescent dye) represent part of the cytoskeleton found in all cells. The cytoskeleton is made up of both rigid and contractile fibers that give each cell its characteristic shape and participate in a variety of functions. Table 1 (bottom) lists the 20 amino acids which make up the proteins of all living organisms on earth and gives their common abbreviations.

amino acid	abbr.	amino acid	abbr.
Alanine	A	Aspartic acid	D
Valine	V	Glutamic acid	E
Glycine	G	Threonine	T
Leucine	L	Asparagine	N
Isoleucine	I	Glutamine	O
Proline	P	Cysteine	C
Phenylalanine	F	Methionine	M
Tyrosine	Y	Histidine	H
Tryptophan	W	Lysine	K
Serine	S	Arginine	R

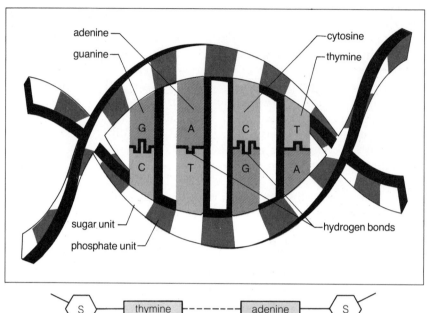

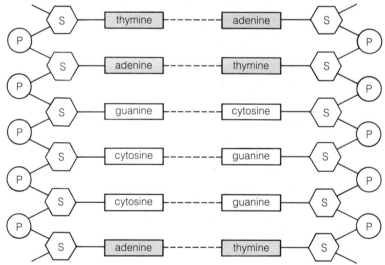

Figure 3. The double helix of DNA at top is composed of a ladder whose sidepieces are twisted into a helix, with crosspieces consisting of adenine-thymine (A—T) and guanine-cytosine (G—C) base pairs. Below, a segment of the structure is shown as though the helix had been straightened by unwinding. The sugar moities (S) and the phosphate residues (P) form a continuous backbone constituting the sidepieces of the ladder, and the organic base pairs form the crosspieces that hold the entire structure together. Three bases in appropriate order spell out each amino acid. When proteins are formed, the two strands separate. The six bases pictured in the left-hand strand, reading from the bottom up, would code for the amino acids threonine and aspartic acid.

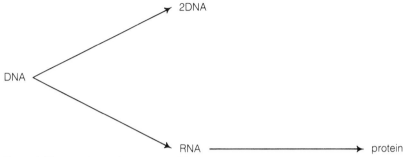

Figure 4. Diagram shows the dual role of DNA in achieving self-replication that initiates biological reproduction and produces RNA copies of itself. The RNA copies are then translated within the ribosomes into the specific protein encoded by the DNA.

molecule of deoxyribonucleic acid, or DNA (fig. 3). Each DNA molecule encodes the information that spells out the structure of a particular cell protein. The DNA itself is built up of repeating units arranged in linear order, each of which consists of a pair of organic bases joined up through sugar molecules linked to phosphate groups. A particular sequence of three such base pairs specifies the identity of each amino acid. Therefore, the sequence of the triplet base pairs in the linear DNA structure spells out the sequence of amino acids which form the structure of each protein (fig. 4). The linear sequences of base pairs of all the DNA molecules present in a cell constitute its total genetic structure, or genome, which embodies a prescription that spells out all of the different protein chains the cell can construct.

DNA has three fundamental functions in all living cells. It encodes the structure of specific proteins; it replicates itself, an act which constitutes the first step of the process of biological reproduction; and it can regulate the expression of the protein-coding DNA's. All of the DNA sequences of a cell are in linear order on a relatively small number of chromosomes, with the protein-coding sequences occasionally interspersed by other regulatory sequences. The chromosomes are contained within the nucleus of each cell.

The process by which a given protein-coding DNA causes the formation of the protein its structure spells out involves the following steps: First, an exact copy of the information contained in a specific molecular fragment of the large DNA chain is made in the form of a related structure called an RNA (ribonucleic acid) molecule. This RNA molecule constitutes an exact transcription of the sequence of the particular gene in question. It migrates away from the master DNA chain and eventually collides and attaches to cellular bodies called ribosomes. The ribosome is an ultramicroscopic factory that builds the particular proteins in accordance with the specific instructions contained in the RNA molecule.

Thus, each RNA is a working copy of the fundamental information repository of the appropriate DNA molecule present in the chromosome.

Many complex details of these processes have been elucidated and are available in other publications. The point essential for the purpose of the present discussion is that even in the simplest living cell, an incredibly complex orchestration of chemical events is continuously carried out. Each of these events is mediated by a specific protein enzyme which is synthesized in accordance with its particular formula, and this is built into the very structure of a fragment of the large DNA chain that constitutes the cell's genetic complement or genome.

Likewise, the synthesis of each protein is mediated by its own RNA molecule, which carries the information from the gene to the ribosomal assembly plant. The synthesis is regulated, at least in part, by DNA sequences that control the RNA formation from each gene in accordance with the needs of the cell at any moment. When a cell reproduces, all of its chromosomes replicate, so that each daughter cell in every generation inherits the same DNA complement, and hence the capacity to make the same proteins as the original cell. So we have, for the first time—putting everything together—a working model of the cell as a functional system. This has now replaced the mysterious "black box" of previous states of biological science.

We have more, of course, as well. Indeed, the following facts have been established as a result of these studies:

(1) Every living organism utilizes DNA, RNA, and proteins.

(2) Every living organism builds its proteins from the same twenty amino acids.

(3) Every living organism uses the same four organic bases, adenine, thymine, guanine, and cytosine, paired in the fashion shown in figure 3 to form its DNA.

(4) The code by which each amino acid is spelled out by a set of three ordered base pairs is identical in all living organisms.

(5) The same structures, the ribosomes, which actually fasten the amino acids together in accordance with the order dictated by the DNA and RNA are found in every living cell.

Thus, while on gross examination the various kinds of life on earth appear to exhibit a bewildering array of different forms, structures, life cycles, and functions, at the molecular level the elementary building blocks and their functions are the same throughout the vast extent of the living kingdom. From amoeba, to redwood trees, to man, the same kinds of molecular and chemical transformations recur in a universal pattern, although each species possesses individual variations on the common theme. It is difficult to deny the conclusion, when reflecting on this, that all life on earth forms a set of different modulations on the same basic molecular pattern and, therefore, that all living forms trace back to a single origin.

The difference between the simplest living cell (*E. coli*) and the cells of the mammalian body

The foregoing molecular relationships were first demonstrated in cells like those of the bacterium *E. coli*, which is an example of the simplest cell. The difference between *E. coli* and the cells of the mammalian body is enormous. Mammalian cells have a complexity many orders of magnitude beyond that exhibited by the relatively simple organization occurring in *E. coli*. Indeed, the structure, function, and interrelationships of the cells of the mammalian body are far from completely understood, and their elucidation constitutes the greatest and most immediate challenge of today's biology. The human cell alone has forty-six chromosomes instead of the single chromosome in *E. coli;* it has approximately 1,000 times as much DNA and, therefore, can synthesize many more proteins; and it exhibits many cell structures or organelles not found in *E. coli*.

E. coli is both a single cell and a whole organism. When a single *E. coli* divides, its daughter cells are identical to each other and to the original parent. All cells of *E. coli* contain the same DNA, manufacture the same proteins, and carry out identical biochemical reactions. If one permits multiplication to occur until thousands of billions of *E. coli* cells develop, they still constitute no more than a mass of identical cells, all carrying out the same biochemical reactions.

The mammalian body also begins as a single cell, i.e., the fertilized egg which results from the original act of conception. However, as cell reproduction proceeds, differentiation occurs and cells acquire different forms and functions. Although virtually all the cells of the body contain the same chromosomes and genes—which is to say, the same potential for differentiation—only specific portions of the DNA are active in each type of differentiated cell, while other portions are quiescent. Thus, as the differentiated cells multiply, they form discrete tissues and organs such as the brain, spleen, and liver. But the cells of these tissues, specialized as they are for performance of unique biochemical functions, are not without shared characteristics. For in each tissue two sets of genes are active: those that produce proteins common to all cells, and those that produce special proteins characteristic of a particular state of differentiation. The proteins common to all cells include those responsible for aspects of nutrient ingestion, the general machinery for protein synthesis and cell reproduction, and other functions, many of which are also exhibited by *E. coli*. The proteins unique to particular differentiated tissues are responsible for functions as diverse as muscular action, nerve conduction, and the various modalities of memory recording in the brain.

All in all, the mammalian body consists of approximately 10,000 billion cells. Powerful and complex communicative and integrative systems must exist so that all of the different cells, tissues, and organs in such a body will have their activities sufficiently coordinated. Only then can the resulting structure behave like a single organism instead of a random collection of metabolizing cells. Thus, a large part of the mammalian genetic structure must be specialized for communication and coordination activities of a kind for which there is no counterpart in *E. coli.*

Somatic cell genetics

When the role of DNA in the economy of the simplest living cell was understood, it became important to extend our knowledge to mammalian cells generally and human cells in particular. This required an understanding of mammalian genetics, and especially of human genetic structure and function. Such an understanding seemed for a long time to be impossible, except in the most general terms. Genetics seeks to identify the individual genes responsible for all of the specific characteristics which are transmitted from parents to offspring. Therefore it requires large numbers of reproductive events to be analyzed. In the classical genetic approach devised by Mendel, the reproductive events resulting from a large series of identical matings are collected and the distribution of particular characteristics among the resulting offspring is analyzed. From such data the identities and behavior of individual genes can be inferred. These operations are well-suited to living organisms like corn and the fruit fly. However, it is not possible to carry out human matings chosen so as to answer specific genetic questions. Moreover, the long generation time of man, approximately twenty-five years, lends further difficulty to genetic analysis. For these reasons then, it seemed as though application of the concepts of molecular genetics to human populations was destined to be long delayed.

A solution to this difficulty was found in our laboratory by the development of a new approach to genetic analysis in multicellular organisms. The basic concept involved study of genetics by means of individual mammalian cells instead of reproduction of the entire organism. Since each of the somatic (i.e., body) cells contains a nucleus that houses the chromosomes on which the genes are carried, it seemed reasonable to sample these cells, to grow them into large populations in glass vessels by the methods of tissue culture, and then to study the genetics of such cell populations as though each cell were an independent microorganism like *E. coli.* Development of this concept into a scientific discipline required the following achievements:

(1) Development of a method for taking samples of living cells from the skin (or any other organ) (fig. 5), and growing these cells into a

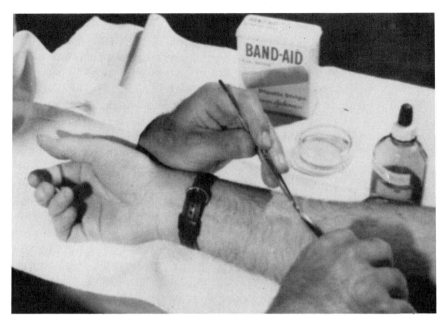

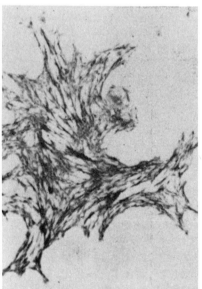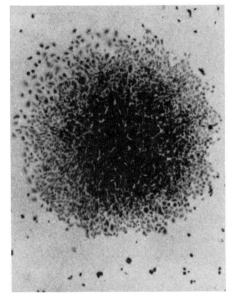

Figure 5 (top). A long-term culture of a subject's cells can be initiated by removing a tiny sample of skin. These cells each contain the characteristic chromosomes and genes of the person sampled, and permit genetic and biochemical studies of the constitution and function of his genetic structure. Figure 6. At bottom, left, a fibroblastic cell colony develops from the growth of a single cell in a glass dish. Shown at right is a similar colony from a cancer cell.

large population by methods of tissue culture in a process that would be simple, reliable, and inexpensive.

(2) Development of a means whereby single cells from such a culture could be deposited in a vessel and grown in the incubator under conditions such that each cell multiplying in isolation produces a large, visible colony. Such colonies arising from single cells are called clones and constitute a genetically uniform population (fig. 6). Since all the cells of a clone are identical, it becomes easily possible to recognize mutant clones and to isolate them to form new cell stocks. Such mutants are essential for genetic studies, because mutations furnish genetic markers which illuminate the operation of the genetic process.

(3) Identification of the human chromosomes. Until 1956, not even the correct number of the human chromosomes was known. These are the bodies in each cell nucleus which carry the human genes. Their exact identification is a necessary step to the building of a systematic human genetics. The identity of each of the human chromosomes was first established by means of cell growth in culture in 1958,[1] and the Denver System for classification of the human chromosomes was developed in 1960.[2] This classification system, achieved by a self-appointed study group meeting in Denver, Colorado, is still the one in use today and has made possible many fundamental discoveries in human genetics, as well as recognition of the chromosomal basis of many human diseases (fig. 7).

(4) Development of the single-cell survival curve by which the effects of any physical, chemical, or biological agent on the multiplication of mammalian cells could be quantitatively measured.[3] This methodology for the first time offered quantitative measurement of the effects of agents on the reproductive capacity of mammalian cells. For example, it greatly improved the power of radiotherapy by substituting accurate information about the amount of radiation needed to destroy tumors. It also made possible isolation and characterization of many kinds of mutants needed for a variety of genetic studies.

These four basic developments, which owe a considerable debt to earlier studies in tissue culture and to microbial genetic concepts, were carried out in our laboratory and initiated a new discipline of somatic cell genetics. Many other laboratories have joined in the study of somatic cell genetics.

One of the most important contributions to this science involved the phenomenon of cell hybridization whereby two or more cells could be fused together in the test tube to produce a single cell with chromosomal contributions from each of the parental cells. This technique, which was perfected into practicable form by Henry Harris, of Oxford University,[4] made it possible to carry out mating of somatic cells in the test tube and, therefore, allowed exploration of the effects of different combinations of chromosomes placed together in the same cell. More-

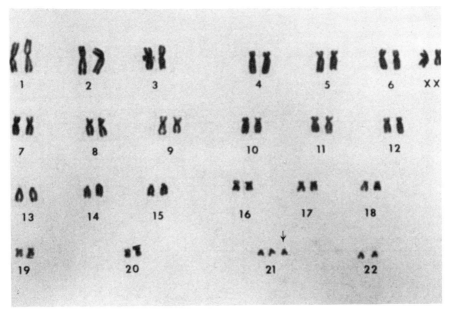

Figure 7. The somatic cell chromosomes of a human patient, arranged in accordance with the Denver Classification System, reveal the presence of an extra chromosome (arrow), so that three copies of this chromosome are present instead of two. The extra chromosome causes Down's syndrome, a disease that occurs approximately once in every 600 live births and involves mental retardation.

over, these techniques made possible new kinds of mating experiments that are impossible in conventional genetics, where mating can only be carried out between members of the same species. It is routine now to fuse cells so as to produce hybrids from organisms of widely different species. Thus, genetic markers can be brought together in the same cell from widely different organisms so that more powerful experimentation is possible. Figure 8 demonstrates a hybrid cell in which a single human chromosome has been incorporated into a Chinese hamster cell. By making such hybrids with different single human chromosomes, the genes on each such chromosome can be studied against the common background of the Chinese hamster cell chromosomes.

Recombinant DNA

A great milestone was reached with the introduction of a series of manipulative operations that are included in the general term, recombinant DNA. These methodologies permit the following procedures to be carried out on DNA and related molecules from any cell population:

(1) Interconversion of any DNA sequence into its corresponding RNA,

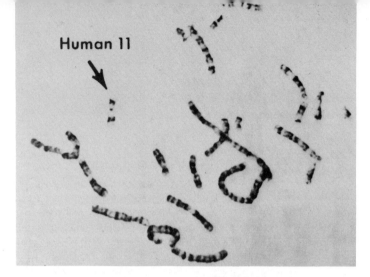

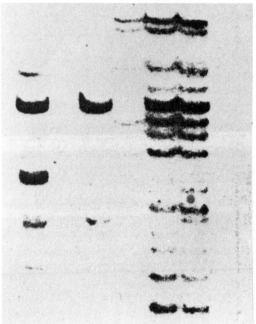

Figure 8 (top). A hybrid cell is formed by fusion of a Chinese hamster ovary cell with that of a human. The standard Chinese hamster somatic chromosomes have been retained plus a single human chromosome, number 11. Figure 9 (bottom). When DNA from a cell population is chopped into smaller pieces by an enzyme and then allowed to migrate in an electrical field on a strip of plastic, a DNA sequence can be detected from the resultant fragments. The fragments are sorted out, with the smaller sizes traveling to the bottom and the larger ones remaining at the top of the strip, and the probe containing the known sequence is made radioactive. It attaches only to points on the gel where it encounters its homologous sequence. A photographic film is then placed over the gel and the site of radioactive deposition is identified by production of the dark bands shown in the figure.

of any RNA sequence into its equivalent DNA, or of any RNA into its equivalent protein, can now be carried out routinely in the test tube. Also, the sequence of base pairs in a sample of DNA and the sequence of amino acids of any particular protein can be determined. Finally, the DNA molecule corresponding to a given protein structure can be synthesized. Thus, the major molecular protagonists of the genetic system can be structurally analyzed and can be interconverted in the test tube as needed.

(2) Long stretches of DNA can be chopped into defined smaller particles by appropriate enzymes called restriction enzymes, which cut the double helix only at particular, coded stretches of DNA. Thus, DNA from any cell can be cut up into identical smaller pieces, themselves reproducible, at specific cleavage points, so that easy comparison can be made between the pattern of fragments so obtained from different cells, or from the same cells of different individuals. This operation has become extremely important in finding differences between particular DNA samples from different individuals and makes possible effective diagnostic tests for a variety of genetic diseases.

(3) A population of DNA molecules can be applied to a plastic strip and sorted out by size by application of an electric current. The DNA particles migrate through the strip when an electric current is applied. The smaller, rapidly moving molecules end up at the bottom, while the larger, slowly moving ones remain near the top.

(4) Radioactive or colored probes of particular DNA sequences can be prepared and tests can be conducted to determine whether these particular sequences do, or do not, exist in any other DNA sample. If the sequence of the test probe is present in the sample of unknown DNA, the test probe will attach to the common sequence to form a band that can be readily visualized (fig. 9).

(5) The DNA from any cell can be cut up by restriction enzymes into pieces that can be singly inserted into bacteria or bacterial viruses. The resulting collection of microorganisms is allowed to multiply many millions-fold. Single-cell isolates can be made at any time and grown into new clonal populations from which large amounts of the particular DNA inserted can be isolated. The collection of these microorganisms, each carrying a single piece of DNA, is called a library. Such libraries can be rapidly analyzed, and particular kinds of DNA, of interest for particular purposes, can be rapidly isolated and prepared in large amounts.

(6) DNA segments can be incorporated into the genome of selected bacteria under conditions such that these bacteria will then synthesize large amounts of the proteins corresponding to the given DNA structure. This method is not only a powerful research tool; it makes possible preparation of pure human proteins for use in medicine, as in the use of human insulin and growth hormones.

(7) DNA sequences can also be introduced into mammalian cells so that they become functional genes, and their effect on the metabolism of the mammalian cell can then be investigated. In some cases, genetic defects of particular cells in the test tube have been cured.

(8) A computerized genetic data bank has been established such that all of the human (and other) DNA sequences that become analyzed are recorded in its memory banks. Many important questions can then be posted and answered by the computer about the human genome as well as that of other organisms.

(9) DNA molecules and fragments can be spliced together in any desired order to make a single linear chain of desired composition.

(10) The mapping of the human genes is proceeding apace. At the time of writing, more than eight hundred human genes have been assigned to specific chromosomes, and regional mapping and more highly detailed mapping has already been carried out for many of them. The rate at which mapping information accumulates is increasing steadily. Gene mapping data is essential for understanding the strategy utilized by cells in regulating gene activities, for diagnostic purposes in a variety of diseases, and for elucidation of the biochemical abnormalities underlying specific chromosomal lesions that is necessary for rational treatment to be developed.

These new powerful techniques are producing yet another revolution in mammalian genetics generally and human genetics specifically. Among the new advances which have raised fundamental new problems are the following findings:

(1) It has been demonstrated that the mammalian genome contains a very significant portion of its DNA—possibly as much as 50%, in the form of repetitive DNA sequences—that does not code for proteins and whose function is presumed to be regulatory, although the specific details of these actions are still a mystery.[5]

(2) The human genes are distributed among the chromosomes in a fashion whose logic has not yet been clarified. Many investigators believe that the particular order is of great importance and will someday reveal new kinds of regulatory phenomena.[6]

(3) Large numbers of so-called pseudogenes exist which are DNA sequences closely resembling other sequences that code for actual proteins but are unable themselves to make proteins because of certain distortions in the actual DNA sequence. Their function is as yet obscure.[7]

(4) Most human DNA's that spell out specific proteins are interrupted by several noncoding DNA stretches called introns. When the DNA structure is copied into the corresponding RNA, these strange intervals are also incorporated into the corresponding RNA. However, specific enzymes then are activated which excise the intron material leaving the pure protein-coding RNA. The function of the introns and the reason for this complexity is still a mystery.[8]

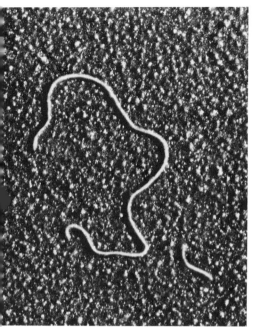

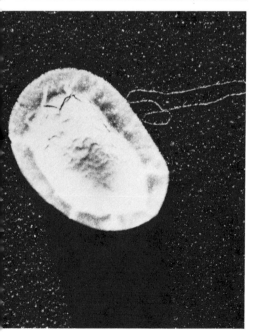

In a dramatic demonstration of a recombinant DNA technique, a ring of DNA is cut so that a foreign gene (in the lower right-hand corner of the photo, top left) can be inserted to form a new DNA molecule (photo at top, right). The new ring of DNA is about to enter an *E. coli* bacterium in the photo at left, endowing the organism with a capability it never before possessed.

(5) A series of genes called oncogenes has been identified. Such genes appear to be activated when cell growth or tissue regeneration is required, as when liver regeneration occurs after partial surgical ablation. When such genes are inappropriately activated, they can cause cancer. The specific nature of the regulatory processes affecting these genes has not yet been clarified.[9]

(6) The cytoskeleton, a structure of fibers within the cell, has been shown to regulate cell shape, locomotion, and ingestion of particles. However, an unexpected finding is that this structure exercises an important role in regulating gene exposure or sequestration within the mammalian cell nucleus, and that this reaction is also important in cancer. Specific genes affected by the state of the cytoskeleton have not yet been identified but are the subject of intensive study.[10]

(7) As a final example, it can be mentioned that many new insights have been attained and much new complexity has been revealed in the operation of the mammalian immune system. Aspects of cellular and molecular immunity have been shown to require regulatory mechanisms that are just beginning to be understood. However, one of the classical mysteries involved in antibody formation has now been clarified. Since each protein manufactured by the body presumably arises from a specific gene, and since there cannot be more than perhaps 50,000 different protein-coding genes in the mammalian genome, how is it that the body can make many millions of different protein antibodies against specific invaders? In a brilliant series of experiments, primarily carried out by Leroy Hood and his associates at Cal. Tech., it has been demonstrated that a specific set of antibody-forming genes can be made to undergo an enormously large number of recombinational events in which different parts of one DNA sequence are broken and recombined with parts of other DNA sequences. In this way, a tremendously amplified number of different proteins can be produced by these antibody-forming gene regions. The number seems more than large enough to account for the immunological potential of the mammalian body.[11]

New powers of protein analysis

While the fantastic increase in our ability to identify, isolate, and manipulate DNA and RNA molecules has made new understanding possible, a corresponding increase in the ease of recognizing and manipulating proteins has also evolved. This is especially important because, while the DNA is the master code that defines the cells' potentialities, the proteins that actually are made from this DNA determine the kinds of biochemical activities that each cell can carry out, and these in turn determine its biological functions.

Space does not permit mention of more than a few of these new powers in handling proteins. One of them is two-dimensional (2D) gel analysis.[12] In this procedure, all of the proteins of a cell population are separated by consecutive application of two electric fields so as to become distributed over a 2-dimensional sheet. Individual proteins can be recognized by their position on the sheet, which is determined by their individual sizes and electrical charges. The amount of each protein can be measured, and upon being taken from the sheet the chemical composition can be identified. Methods for carrying out the latter step have been developed resulting in a machine called a sequenator that establishes the exact order of amino acids in an incredibly small amount of a given protein.[13]

Clonal cell cultures can be established which manufacture so-called monoclonal antibodies.[14] These are antibodies of exactly the same protein composition that will recognize the particular chemical grouping of any protein. Such antibodies permit exquisitely specific recognition of different kinds of protein molecules. Also, complex proteins can be dissociated into their simple components and recombined into their more complex forms; the exact point in a cell life cycle at which particular proteins are manufactured or destroyed can be determined; and chemical modification of proteins in cells can be accurately measured, including changes by which pieces of protein chains are specifically removed, or particular groups like phosphate groups and sugar moities are added, profoundly affecting their biological behavior.

Many other powers of manipulation, identification, and analysis of the structure and functions of cellular proteins have been developed. But the examples cited are sufficient to establish the point: a great variety of new tools is available by which the many thousands of different proteins present in each cell can be studied. From the data so obtained it will be possible eventually to infer which part of the total gene complement has been expressed in cells of a particular state of differentiation, which proteins are being synthesized at each point in the cell's life cycle, the role of biochemical actions carried out by these molecules in the economy of the tissue to which the cell belongs, and how these features are altered in the presence of disease.

Complexity of the genetic structure and organization in man

Application of these powerful new tools to analysis of mammalian cell structure and function has produced new understanding of their operation but also has revealed complexity far greater than was previously suspected. For example, the nucleus in which the chromosomes are located houses thousands of different proteins which form an intricate scaffolding that appears to control the exposure of particular genes either (a), so that they may be used as templates for the synthesis of their corresponding RNA's which will then be used to make corresponding proteins, or (b), for replication of the gene in order to carry out cell reproduction.[15] To one of the bases of the gene structure, cytosine, a methyl group, is often attached by appropriate protein enzymes; this becomes a further element in its complex regulatory structure.[16] Parts of the DNA with a special sequence of bases can take up an altered spatial configuration without changing the order of their base pairs; the resulting so-called Z-DNA possesses an altered spatial configuration. Extra and fewer twists can be imparted to DNA chains by specific protein enzymes, and again these operations are presumed to play a part in the overall regulatory functions.[17] Mammalian DNA is wrapped around protein cores located ten base pairs apart whose exact function is still unknown.[18] Then there is the mysterious function of the repetitive sequences of DNA, which has already been mentioned. Finally, at the very last stage of the reproductive life cycle of the mammalian cell, the chromosomes become supercoiled so that their length is reduced approximately twenty thousand-fold, and their thickness becomes correspondingly increased until each chromosome is readily observed in the ordinary microscope, a phenomenon whose molecular dynamics are not yet understood in detail.

While vast areas of clarification remain to be achieved, most scientists are agreed on two points: (a) understanding of these phenomenona should yield up the secret of the process by which the fertilized egg grows and differentiates to produce all the different tissues of the body; and (b) it appears that the tools necessary for achieving this understanding are now largely in hand.

While many details remain to be filled in, a general picture of the living process at the molecular level has now been achieved. These developments have led to a new conceptual picture of the structure and operation of the mammalian cell which, in the minds of most investigators, has answered the frequently posed question as to whether biological phenomena are, indeed, bound by the laws of physics and chemistry. This question seemed reasonable as long as the cell remained a sealed black box of unknown constitution, capable of performing what seemed to be miraculous feats. Our present understanding of the mammalian cell makes it possible, at least in principle, to see how the almost unbelievably diverse phenomena of life in general and human life in particular can take place by means of interactions of the molecules which form the genetic structure and its associated molecular machinery.

These considerations lead inevitably to the basic unity of physics, chemistry, and biology. These once separate disciplines are now recognized to form a continuous region of molecular science. The principal difference between biology and other parts of this unity lies in the greater degree of orderly and directed molecular changes which characterize biology as opposed to the more random molecular interactions traditionally associated with physics and chemistry. The virtually miraculous manifestations of living organisms attest to the great powers contained in atoms and molecules when these are properly organized. Impressive as our present knowledge may seem, we have barely begun to understand the vast mysteries and their human implications for physical, mental, and moral achievements which lie still undiscovered in the universe of molecular behavior.

Applications to medicine

As might be expected, the first medical application of these advances has been to genetic diseases, where great understanding has been gained. Diseases clinically recognized for generations have been shown to be caused by the presence of either an extra or a missing fragment of a particular chromosome. Scores of other diseases, including a number of cancers, have been demonstrated to result from various chromosomal abnormalities. Many new diagnostic procedures have been devised based on the new somatic cell and molecular genetics, and these are now among the most secure diagnostic procedures known to medicine. In many cases, diagnosis of the fetus can be carried out *in utero* early in pregnancy, so that pregnancies certain to result in horribly deformed births can be terminated, or so that early counseling of the parents-to-be can be initiated. Moreover, elucidation of the underlying biochemical causes of such abnormalities now affords hope that we may in the future be able to restore biochemical integrity to a genetically distorted developmental situation. At some future date it may also be possible to introduce healthy genes to replace and overcome the effects of damaged ones in a fetus.

These fairly obvious applications of the new cellular and molecular genetics to problems of human health represent only a small part of the ultimate benefits which are expected. Full appreciation of what lies ahead requires more understanding of medical history.

Today's medicine has achieved unprecedented powers. The lengthening of the life span, the degree of freedom from infectious disease, and the general physical well-being of people who share our way of life represent phenomenal accomplishments. However, despite the many advances of the past, including immunization, antibiosis, and new developments in surgery and anesthesiology, our knowledge of health and disease processes still contains extremely large gaps.

The medicine of our time is still based, for the most part, on gross phenomena of the body as a whole—the manifestations of tissues and organs—rather than on understanding of the structure and function of the cellular and molecular constitutions of these entities. In this respect, the state of the science resembles that of physics before the structures of atoms and molecules were understood. Diseases are characterized mostly on the basis of symptoms, signs, and the results of relatively crude laboratory tests. Treatment is evaluated on the statistical basis of tabulating the outcomes of various procedures.

There now looms the possibility of adding to this largely empirical base a new conceptual structure based on the activities of the component cells of the body. Health or dysfunction of any tissue or organ ultimately depends on the activities of its component cells. Such activities in turn depend in large part on the biochemical functions of the cells' contained enzymes and other proteins. These functions in turn are regulated in large degree by the activities of the genes lodged in the chromosomes of each cell nucleus. Thus, except for situations like malnutrition or toxic insult, every cell function can be traced, at least in principle, to the presence of appropriate genes and to their normal regulatory responses. From this point of view, diseases that are not recognized as genetic (in the sense that the pathological condition itself is not directly inherited from the parents) can be genetically analyzed, and even genetically treated.

I have made a distinction between germ cell genetic disease and somatic cell genetic disease. In the former, a defective gene situation, inherited from the parents or induced by a mutation in the original fertilized egg, is transmitted to every cell of the body. Yet the defect may be expressed only in a single tissue if the gene in question normally operates only in one tissue, as for example, in the failure of the islet cells of the pancreas to manufacture insulin.

In somatic cell genetic disease, a genetic defect may be introduced into the cell of a given tissue after the developmental process has begun. Such an insult usually will not be transmitted to offspring of the affected individual, but it can produce defective function if the affected cell multiplies sufficiently so as to produce a clone of cells that are likewise damaged. The classic example would be a mutational event leading to cancer. In this case, a cell anywhere in the body suffering a mutation that damages its ability to regulate its reproduction can initiate uncontrolled growth that eventually threatens the integrity of the entire organism.

Obviously, defects can be introduced into aspects of the body's function without damage to particular genes. A variety of traumatic experiences can upset the biochemical equilibrium of the various organ and tissue systems. If these biochemical pathways were understood, it would be possible to prevent or restore damage in many instances by chemical adjustment through drugs, vitamins, and other factors. At the present time, it has been estimated that less than one-tenth of a percent

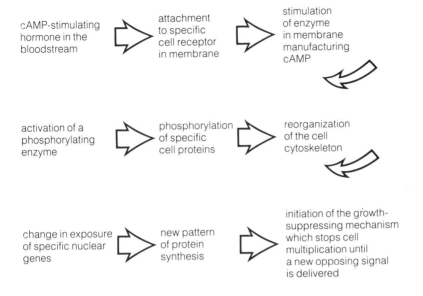

Figure 10. A proposed scheme demonstrates the metabolic pathway by which growth control is initiated in normal cells. If any step of this pathway is blocked, the growth control mechanism cannot operate, and the cell enters into a phase of unlimited reproduction. This is believed to happen in cancer through the abnormal activation of an oncogene that prevents initiation of the reproductive control pathway.

of the chemical pathways by which the body's functions are carried out have been delineated sufficiently so that such adjustment could be attempted. Thus, underlying processes like wound healing, antibody formation, and the biochemical events of normal differentiation are still largely unknown. However, the genetic-biochemical approach offers a means for uncovering these pathways. Such studies are now being carried out in various laboratories. A great era of increasing power in the diagnosis, treatment, and prevention of disease may be expected from such investigations. In these developments will be included the design and manufacture of large numbers of new drugs with much greater effectiveness and many fewer side effects than any we now have.

Extraordinary progress has been made in the use of molecular genetics to understand the nature of cancer. Normal tissue cells contain a biochemical pathway that leads to growth cessation when an appropriate number of cells of the given kind has developed. In cancer cells this pathway is blocked, usually by a change in the cellular genetic structure, so that the affected cell continues to multiply without limit and threatens the entire organism. As noted earlier, it has been demonstrated that inappropriate activation of a homologous oncogene or the introduction of a foreign one can cause a cell to become cancerous.

Further analysis of the biochemistry of oncogene action, in at least one situation that has been carefully studied, has shown that the oncogene causes abnormal addition of phosphoric acid moieties to critical and as yet unidentified proteins (a process called phosphorylation) within the mature cell, and that this prevents normal establishment of the cell cytoskeleton. Failure of the normal cytoskeletal structure to be achieved prevents initiation of the growth suppressive mechanism that all normal cells exhibit when their number has become sufficiently large to meet the body's needs. The crucial factor is cyclic AMP, an internal chemical messenger produced by each cell in response to an appropriate hormonal stimulus. Cyclic AMP produces a phosphorylation of cell proteins that promotes establishment of the normal cytoskeletal structure that initiates growth arrest (fig. 10).

It has been demonstrated that organization of the appropriate cytoskeleton under the influence of cyclic AMP results in a change in state of a fraction of the cellular genes, so that their DNA becomes more highly exposed to the action of particular chemical reagents. Soon it may be possible to identify the specific genes and their concomitant biochemical reactions involved in the chain of events leading to reproduction control in the body cells. Understanding of this pathway should make possible totally new approaches to the control of cancer.

The prevention of environmentally caused gene-related disease, and other health-related applications

There is increasing evidence that a substantial part of our incapacitating diseases are caused by externally applied genetic insults. A recent report by the American Cancer Society demonstrates that incidence of cancer is still increasing in this country. More than half of the beds in pediatric hospitals are housing patients with genetic disease. Recent developments in the asbestos industry demonstrate the enormously great effects on cancer incidence that can be exerted by one substance alone, and how inadequate are conventional methods of toxicology to detect substances that can cause so many thousands of tragedies.

The problem in the case of cancer is compounded by the fact that as much as twenty years may elapse before the malignant effects of a given exposure are revealed as symptoms in a patient. In the case of genetic disease, the effects of a toxic exposure may not become manifest until several generations have elapsed, but they can affect large numbers of people. Genetic diseases in particular can be devastating in the multiplicity of their effects on people and society. Down's syndrome alone now has an incidence of approximately one out of 600 live births. Persons born with such a disease can never become independent members of society. They will never contribute to society's economic needs but on the contrary will need care during the entire period of their lives. It has been estimated that the United States now spends several billions of dollars each year taking care of Down's syndrome patients now living. There is also the even greater tragedy, which cannot be estimated in dollars, in the loss of human potential in the victims and the terrible emotional cost to their families.

The danger is widespread. Our times have seen the largest introduction of women into the industrial work force in history. At the same time, new chemical compounds are being introduced into industrial processes. This means that workers of all kinds, but most significantly pregnant women, are being exposed to compounds about whose action we are largely ignorant, and for which adequate methods of estimating potential human risk are not available.

In attempting to devise new approaches to this situation, it would seem that the first step required is development of a means of measuring damage to cellular genetic structures. If protein structures are damaged, but the genome is intact, the possibility exists that the damaged proteins can be replaced by new biosynthesis. However, if the DNA itself is damaged, there would appear to be no possibility of regaining normal structure and function.

Somatic cell genetics has been applied to develop methods for detecting mutagenic situations in the environment. Early developments (i.e., developments which utilized the principle of Bruce Ames and his colleagues at the University of California, Berkeley, for tests with bacteria) were less than optimal, since they only detected a small fraction of the genetic lesions that can be introduced into mammalian cells by environmental agents. New developments have produced means for monitoring virtually all medically important genetic insults to body cells. They also make possible the actual measurement of mutation efficiency at the low levels to which humans may actually be exposed and offer the further possibility of understanding mutagenesis, carcinogenesis, and birth defects resulting from genetic damage. In short, new approaches now make it possible to avoid significant human exposures and to discover antimutagenic agents that may prevent, or at least ameliorate, the pathological consequences of such exposure.

Space does not permit detailed discussion of how the new science of somatic cell and molecular genetics is offering the possibility of revolutionizing food production in the world. The introduction of new genetic elements into plants offers hope of increasing the quantity and quality of their nutrient products and increasing their resistance to parasitic disease and other environmental stress. Similarly, genetic application to animal husbandry offers the hope of achieving substantial new advances. These developments are sorely needed in a world in which the majority of humans suffer from hunger. It appears highly possible that advances may well permit amelioration of crisis situations. However, no one is able to foresee any means of coping with hunger if human reproduction is permitted to proceed at its maximum possible levels. There is no indication that Malthus's pronouncements are not as true now as they were in his own time. Human reproduction appears to be able still to exceed any foreseeable increase in available supplies of food. The bitter experience is already available in which modern methods of disease control, introduced into a nonindustrialized society, have eliminated the natural check on human populations previously exercised by disease and early death. Starvation situations can then develop that may make the ultimate result of disease control an increase in human suffering. It will be a sad commentary on our species if with all our intellectual powers we cannot achieve a rational long-term solution to the problem of hunger.

Implications for the future

Recent developments have made it apparent that the number of classically identified hormones is only a small fraction of those that operate in the body. Molecules such as insulin, thyroxin, and testosterone were detected in early studies because they occur in relatively high concentrations in the body. The messenger molecules that are now coming to light are active in concentrations millions of times smaller than those of the hormones cited, and their dynamic analysis requires the full range of modern sophisticated molecular manipulation.

A combination of nervous system control and chemical messenger actions at the cellular level appears to be the ultimate regulatory apparatus by which the mammalian body achieves its integration. But, whereas man shares some aspects of such nervous and hormonal controls with many other living forms, the mind of man appears to be unique. Recent studies have uncovered a bewildering host of different chemical messengers operating in brain cells alone. Study of the genetic and biochemical dynamics of the brain, and of critical messenger molecules in states of mental health and disease, promises to reveal many functions of the human mind. We have as yet a most fragmentary and unsatisfactory understanding of these functions. The true possibilities latent in the human mind, its educability, and its reaction to experiences that either promote or thwart basic human needs and drives, still remain in large part to be explored. Significant advances in understanding are beginning through collaborative advances in many fields of which molecular biology is a part. The demonstration of the differential activities of the two hemispheres of the brain constitutes one of the most exciting advances in recent biology. It would appear as though half the human brain tends to act like a digital computer and the other half like an analog computer, so that both analytic and synthetic solutions to problems can be generated, with the results integrated for final decision making.

Man possesses general orienting and steering principles directing his thoughts and behavior, which in turn require coordination of all the components of the body. These steering principles are in part innate, consisting of genetic behavioral drives, and in part learned and stored in a truly fantastic and as yet mysterious set of memory storage systems. While all animals have genetic behavioral drives, that of man is unique in the great extent of its dependence on cultural inheritance, passed on from generation to generation, which is needed to fulfill the potentialities present in the DNA of the human genome. Intensive study of the interactions of these two kinds of inherited behavioral systems has only begun.

Perhaps the greatest tragedy of our time is that man has acquired the instruments for almost infinite destruction before achieving enough understanding of his own deepest needs sufficient to design a world at peace, with opportunities for fulfillment of individual potential for all. At present, peace is being enforced by threats. Far better if it were supported by the promise of new health achievements that modern biological science offers. Certainly, the realization of these achievements requires a world at peace. It would seem advisable that this fact be given wide circulation throughout the world, so that we may bring the new health benefits of modern biomedical science to all mankind.

---

[1]Tjio, J. H., and Puck, T. T., "The Somatic Chromosomes of Man," *P.N.A.S.* 44 (1959): pp. 1229–37.

[2]Book, J. A.; Chu, E. H. Y.; Ford, C. E.; Franccaro, M.; Harnden, D. G.; Hsu, T. C.; Hungerford, D. A.; Jacobs, P. A.; Lejeune, J.; Levan, A.; Makino, S.; Puck, T. T.; Robinson, A.; Tjio, J. H.; Catcheside, D. G.; Stern, C.; and Muller, H. J., "A Proposed Standard System of Nomenclature of Human Mitotic Chromosomes," *J.A.M.A.* 174 (1960): pp. 150–62.

[3]Puck, T. T., and Marcus, P. I., "Action of X-rays on Mammalian Cells," *J. Exp. Med.* 103 (1956): p. 653.

[4]Harris, H., *Cell Culture and Somatic Variation* (New York: Holt, Rinehart & Winston, 1970).

[5]Manuelidis, L., *Repeated DNA Sequences and Nuclear Structure in Genome Evolution*, Dover, G. A., and Flavell, R. B., eds. (New York: Academic, 1982), pp. 263–85.

[6]Bennett, M. D. *Nucleotypic Basis of the Spatial Ordering of Chromosomes in Eukaryotes and the Implications of the Order for Genome Evolution and Phenotypic Variation in Genome Evolution*, Dover, G. A., and Flavell, R. B., eds. (New York: Academic, 1982), pp. 239–61.

[7]Moos, M., and Gallwitz, D., "Structure of a Human B-actin Related Pseudogene Which Lacks Intervening Sequences," *Nuc. Acid. Res.* 10 (1982): pp. 7843–49.

[8]Chambon, P., "Split Genes," *Scientific American* 244 (May 1981): pp. 60–71.

[9]Duesberg, P. H., "Retroviral Transforming Genes in Normal Cells?" *Nature* 304 (1983): pp. 219–26.

[10]Ashall, F., and Puck, T. T., "Cytoskeletal Involvement in cAMP-induced Sensitization of Chromatin to Nuclease Digestion in Transformed Chinese Hamster Ovary K1 Cells," *P.N.A.S.* 81 (1984): pp. 5145–49.

[11]Perlmutter, R. M.; Crews, S. T.; Douglas, R.; Sorensen, G.; Johnson, N.; Nivera, N.; Gearhart, P. J.; and Hood, L., "The Generation of Diversity in Phosphorylcholine-Binding Antibodies," *Adv. Immunol.* 35 (1984): pp. 1–37.

[12]O'Farrell, P. H., "High Resolution Two-Dimensional Electrophoresis of Proteins," *J. Biol. Chem.* 250 (1975): pp. 4007–21.

[13]Hunkapiller, M.; Kent, S.; Caruthers, M.; Dreyer, W.; Firca, J.; Giffin, C.; Horvath, S.; Hunkapiller, T.; Tempst, P.; and Hood, L., "A Microchemical Facility for the Analysis and Synthesis of Genes and Proteins," *Nature* 310 (1984): pp. 105–11.

[14]Köhler, G., and Milstein, C., "Continuous Cultures of Fused Cells Secreting Antibody of Predefined Specificity," *Nature* 256 (1975): pp. 495–97.

[15]Ciejek, E. M.; Tsai, M.-J.; and O'Malley, B. W., "Actively Transcribed Genes are Associated with the Nuclear Matrix," *Nature* 306 (1983): pp. 607–9.

[16]Cooper, D. N., "Eukaryotic DNA Methylation," *Hum. Genet.* 64 (1983): pp. 315–33.

[17]Hamada, H.; Petrino, M. G.; and Kakunaga, T., "A Novel Repeated Element with Z-DNA-Forming Potential Is Widely Found in Evolutionarily Diverse Eukaryotic Genomes," *P.N.A.S.* 79 (1982): pp. 6465–69.

[18]Weisbrod, S., "Active Chromatin," *Nature* 297 (1982): pp. 289–95.

PART TWO

Reconsiderations of Great Books

The Social Contracts of Jean-Jacques Rousseau

Maurice Cranston

Maurice Cranston has taught at the London School of Economics since 1959. In 1968 he was elected to the chair of political science formerly held by Harold Laski and Michael Oakeshott. He was born in London in 1920 and was educated at Oxford, where, after his M.A., he received a B.Litt. for a thesis on the freedom of the will. This was later incorporated in his book *Freedom* (1953), which has since run into several editions and established his reputation as a political philosopher. In 1957 he published the definitive biography of John Locke, which won the James Tait Black Memorial Prize, among other literary awards. His other books include *The Mask of Politics* and *What Are Human Rights?* as well as a critical study of Sartre and translations of Rousseau's *Social Contract* and *Discourse on Inequality*. He has written a great deal for radio, notably *Political Dialogues*—imaginary conversations between political philosophers, later published in book form. Professor Cranston taught for four years at the European University Institute in Florence, Italy, and has several times been a visiting professor at Harvard, Dartmouth College, and the University of California in San Diego. He is currently completing a biographical study of Rousseau, of which the first volume, *Jean-Jacques,* was published by W. W. Norton in 1983.

Rousseau's name is always associated with the idea of a social contract—that is, with the idea of human societies coming into being as
a result of individuals pledging themselves to live together as members
of one civil community.[1] Not many such pacts are actually recorded
in history. There is a notable one in the Old Testament: the covenant
that was given by God to the people of Israel through Moses on
Mount Sinai; there was also the covenant of 1620 which united the
original colonists of New England in a body politic. Rousseau's social
contracts are less specifically historical events. Two quite distinct types
are in fact depicted in his writings: the first is the social contract which
"must have happened" generally at an early stage of human evolution;
the second is one which would need to take place if men are to live
together in freedom.

The idea of human societies being contractual in origin springs from
a recognition that human beings are not social beings in the way that
ants and bees, for example, are social; our instincts do not impel each
of us to do unreflectively what is advantageous for the group or tribe.
We may have, some of us more than others, altruistic feelings which
drive us to do for the community as much as, or more than, we do
for ourselves; but even that entails a process of reasoning, thinking out
what course of action would be best for society. There is no instinct
impelling each individual to perform an allotted social role, as there is
in the social insects. Each human being has to decide what part he is
to play, and where there is this freedom there is controversy. People
do not all agree as to what is to be done for the good of all, even if
all agree that the good of all should be promoted. Every human has a
mind of his own, and every human being's instincts are self-protective.
We are a race of individuals.

Rousseau believed more than most philosophers in the radical individualism of natural man; yet he also believed that man was, as Aristotle
said, a political animal, a *zoon politikon*. How can we reconcile these
beliefs? The answer lies perhaps in the ambiguity of a word which figures prominently in all eighteenth-century thought: *nature*. Nature, for
Rousseau, stood opposed to culture; natural man was original man as
he lived in the savage state under the rule of nature alone. But nature
was also a force that demanded the attention of man in the civilized

state. There its commands were of a different order and were often unheeded: unheeded to such an extent that Rousseau could even claim that modern man was alienated from nature and, as a result of this, that man had lost both his happiness and his freedom.

And yet Rousseau is in no sense a negative philosopher. He sets out to explain, first, how happiness and freedom have been lost, and next, how both can be recovered. This is what he undertakes in his two theories of the social contract. The first theory is expounded in his earlier writings, notably his *Discourse on the Origin of Inequality*[2] [*GBWW*, Vol. 38, pp. 323–66] and his *Essay on the Origin of Languages*.[3] The second theory is expounded in the book called *Of the Social Contract*[4] [*GBWW*, Vol. 38, pp. 387–439].

Discourse on the Origin of Inequality

It was in the fall of 1753 that the Academy of Dijon announced an essay competition on the question "What is the origin of inequality among men, and is it authorized by Natural Law?" Rousseau responded promptly: "If the Academy had the courage to raise such a question," he declared, "I would have the courage to answer it."[5] Rousseau did not, in his final treatment of the subject, have much to say about the second part of the question—as to whether inequality is authorized by natural law; what interested him was the problem of origins. He tells us that he went for long walks in the forest of St. Germain to reflect on what the life of man must have been before civilizations began: "I dared to strip man's nature naked, to follow the evolution of those times and things which have disfigured him; I compared man as he made himself with man as nature made him, and I discovered that his supposed improvements had generated all his miseries."[6]

The theme of apparent progress concealing actual regression was not a new one for Rousseau. He had expounded it in an earlier essay he had written for the Academy of Dijon, for which he won a prize: the *Discourse on the Sciences and the Arts* of 1750. There Rousseau had argued that the more science, industry, technology, and culture become developed and sophisticated, the more they carry human societies from decent simplicity toward moral corruption. Paradoxically, this discourse was a great success among the very people Rousseau attacked: the fashionable salons and scientific circles of Paris, which was also the milieu in which he himself at that time moved. What Rousseau said in his first discourse was not particularly original, for similar attacks on modern culture had been made by reactionary writers, both Catholic and Puritan. Rousseau's argument amazed the public because it came from a supposedly progressive author, one of the leading collaborators

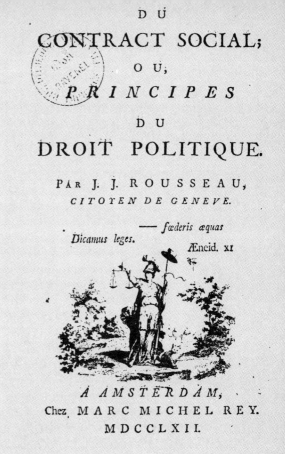

After his first and second treatises explained how man's happiness and freedom had been lost, Rousseau (above) revealed how both could be recovered in *Of the Social Contract*. Shown at right is the title page of the first edition, published in 1762.

of Diderot's great *Encyclopaedia,* an enterprise dedicated to the ideals of scientific progress and the improvement of knowledge. Some readers were left in doubt about the author's sincerity. But time was to prove that he really meant it. Progress, Rousseau insisted, was an illusion. The human race had taken a wrong turning, or more than one wrong turning. In the second discourse Rousseau wrote for the Academy of Dijon, on the *Origin of Inequality,* he carried his analysis much further back in time.

On this occasion, Rousseau did not succeed at Dijon, but the work was altogether more original and remarkable than the *Discourse on the Sciences and the Arts* which did win the prize. In less than a hundred pages Rousseau outlined a theory of human evolution which prefigured the discoveries of Darwin,[7] he revolutionized the study of anthropology and linguistics,[8] and he made a seminal contribution to political philosophy.[9] Even if his argument was distorted by his critics, and perhaps not always well understood by his readers, it altered people's ways of thinking about themselves and their world and even changed their ways of feeling.

Rousseau begins his inquiry by noting that there are two kinds of inequality among men. The first are natural inequalities, arising from differences in strength and intelligence, agility and so forth; the second are artificial inequalities, which derive from conventions that men themselves have introduced into society. Rousseau claims that it is because of these artificial inequalities that some men are richer than others, some more honored than others, and some obeyed by others. He takes the object of his inquiry to be to discover the origins of such artificial inequalities, since there would be no point in asking why nature had come to bestow its gifts unequally. He therefore sees his first task as that of distinguishing what is properly and originally natural to man from what man has made for himself. This Rousseau thinks can only be done by going back in time to ascertain what man was like before he had formed societies or groups. The way to learn about natural man was to rediscover original man. Although Rousseau did not advance the view later put forward by Darwin that man evolved from a cousin of the apes, he did suggest that man developed from a primitive biped, related to the orangutan, into the sophisticated creature of modernity, and that this evolution can be understood largely as a process of adaptation and struggle.[10]

Rousseau does not claim to be the first to try to explain human society by contrasting it with a pre-social state of nature; he simply argues that earlier writers, such as seventeenth-century English philosophers Thomas Hobbes and John Locke (whose works, with which he was at any rate partially familiar in French translations, had greatly impressed him), had failed in the attempt. "They have all felt it necessary to go back to the state of nature, but none of them has succeeded in getting there. . . . All these philosophers, talking ceaselessly of need, greed, oppression, desire, and pride, have transported into the state of nature concepts formed in society. They speak of savage man and they depict civilized man."[11]

The philosopher Rousseau has most in mind here is Hobbes [see *GBWW*, Vol. 23]. In Hobbes the state of nature is represented as one of war of each man against all men; human beings are seen as aggressive, avaricious, proud, selfish, and afraid; and on the basis of this analysis of natural man, Hobbes asserts that without the mortal solitude of an absolute sovereign to bind them together in the civil state, men's lives must be "solitary, poor, nasty, brutish, and short."[12] Rousseau argues, against Hobbes, that all the unpleasant characteristics of the human condition derive not from nature but from society, and that if we look far enough back in our search for the origins of man and reach the true state of nature, we shall find a being who is admittedly solitary (as Hobbes says) but otherwise healthy, happy, free, and good.

Rousseau envisages original man as being removed only to a small extent from the beast, "an animal less strong than some, less agile than others, but, taken as a whole, the most advantageously organized of all."[13] Natural man has an easy life. "I see him satisfying his hunger under an oak, quenching his thirst at the first stream, finding his bed under the same tree which provided his meal, and, behold, his needs are furnished."[14]

In Rousseau's state of nature there is no scarcity, and no ill health. He notes that the savages who still exist in the modern world are reported by explorers to have robust constitutions, to be free from the diseases which afflict men in Europe, where the rich are overfed and the poor underfed and everyone is harassed by the desires, anxieties, fatigues, excesses, passions, and sorrows which civilization generates.[15] Domesticated men, like domesticated animals, says Rousseau, grow soft, whereas in the state of nature they are fit, because they have to be fit in order to survive.

> Accustomed from infancy to the inclemencies of the weather, and the rigors of the seasons, used to fatigue, and forced to defend themselves and their prey naked and unarmed against other wild beasts or to escape from them by running faster than they, men develop a robust and almost immutable constitution. Children coming into the world with the excellent physique of their fathers, and strengthening it by the same exercise which produced it, thus acquire all the vigor of which the human race is capable. Nature treats them exactly as the law of Sparta treated the children of its citizens: it makes those who are well constituted strong and robust, and makes the others die.[16]

The reference to Sparta is significant here: for Sparta, as he understood it, was for Rousseau an ideal model of a republic; and one of the reasons why it was ideal is that it enabled men to recover something of what they lost when they left the state of nature.[17]

Now although Rousseau emphasizes the similarities between the life of original man and the life of a beast, he nevertheless depicts man as being, from the beginning, radically different from other animals in possessing two characteristics. These two characteristics do *not* include the one traditionally held to distinguish man from beast, the possession of reason. For Rousseau, what makes man unique among living creatures is first, his freedom, and second, his capacity for self-improvement. Here, whether Rousseau is right or wrong, he is arrestingly original.

Natural man is free for Rousseau in three senses of the word *freedom*. First he has free will. This is a crucial form of freedom for Rousseau. Hobbes and most of Rousseau's friends in the circle of the *Encyclopaedia* were determinists, believing that man was a "machine," albeit more complex than any other machine in nature, but subject to the same laws of cause and effect.[18] Rousseau was willing enough to use the metaphor of a machine, but he claimed that whereas among the beasts nature alone "operates the machine," in the case of human beings, the individual contributes to his own operations, in his capacity as an autonomous agent. "The one chooses or rejects by instinct; the other by an act of free will."[19]

This metaphysical freedom, or freedom of the will, is for Rousseau a defining characteristic of man, and as such it is possessed by all men in all conditions, whether of nature or society. But there are two other forms of freedom which he sees men as enjoying in the state of nature, but not necessarily having in society. One of these freedoms man could not possibly possess in civil society, and this is anarchic freedom— freedom from any kind of political rule. This would, of course, be absolute in the state of nature since the state of nature is by definition a condition in which there is no government and no positive law. The third freedom enjoyed by man in Rousseau's state of nature is personal freedom, the independence of a man who has no master, no employer, no superior, no one on whom he is in any way dependent. While Rousseau's remarks on anarchic feeedom are ambiguous, there is no uncertainty about the value and importance he attaches to personal freedom. This is the great advantage the savage has over the civilized man. In the civilized world, most men are enslaved; in the state of nature no one can enslave anyone else:

> Is there a man who is so much stronger than me, and who is, moreover, lazy enough and fierce enough to compel me to provide for his sustenance while he remains idle? He must resolve not to lose sight of me for a single moment . . . for fear I should escape or kill him.[20]

Besides *liberté* in these three senses, Rousseau's natural man differs from the beasts in possessing *perfectibilité*. Now this word must not be translated, as it often is, as 'perfectiblity'; because Rousseau did not assert in his *Discourse on Inequality,* or anywhere else, that man is per-fectible; all he claimed was that man has the capacity to better himself by his own efforts. Rousseau never suggested that man would ever be perfect, or even that man was on the road toward perfection.[21] The French verb *perfecter,* as he used it, means simply 'to improve'; and the capacity for *perfectibilité* which Rousseau attributed to human beings was nothing more than a *capacity for self-improvement.*

How men evolved

The story of human evolution as Rousseau unfolds it is in many ways a melancholy one, marked, in the first place, by man's loss of two of the three sorts of freedom he enjoyed in the state of nature and then by his misuse of his capacity for self-improvement to do things which have made him worse instead of better.

Original men, or "savages" as Rousseau sometimes chooses to call our forebears as they lived in the first state of nature, were simple beings, with no language, very little capacity for thought, few needs, and, in consequence, few passions. "Since savage man desires only the things which he knows and knows only those things of which possession is within his power or easily obtained, then nothing ought to be so tranquil as his soul or so limited as his mind."[22] For such a being, the exercise of will, desire, and fear will be the whole of his inner experience: even the fears of a savage are limited to apprehension of present danger. He can fear pain, but not death because he has no concept of death; anxiety, that disease of the imagination, is unknown to him.

Conceptual thinking, Rousseau suggests, developed only with speech; and in the early stages of life on earth, men needed no language.

> Having neither houses nor huts, nor any kind of property, everyone slept where he chanced to find himself, and often for one night only; as males and females united fortuitously, according to encounters, opportunities and desires, they required no speech to express what they had to say to one another, and they separated with the same ease.[23]

Here we have a denial of the view that the family is a natural society, and in a long footnote to the *Discourse on Inequality*, Rousseau offers a detailed criticism of Locke's argument that nature itself impels human males and females to unite on a settled basis to feed and shelter their young.[24] Rousseau agrees with Locke that a man may have a motive for remaining with a particular woman when she has a child, but he protests that Locke fails to prove that a man would have any motive for staying with a particular woman during the nine months of her pregnancy:

> For it is not a matter of knowing why the man should remain attached to the woman after the birth, but why he should become attached to her after the conception. His appetite satisfied, the man has no longer any need for a particular woman, nor the woman for a particular man. The man has not the least care about, nor perhaps the least idea of, the consequences of his action. One goes off in one direction, the other in another, and there is no likelihood that at the end of nine months either will remember having known the other.[25]

The point Rousseau is making here is that while it is undoubtedly advantageous to the human race that there should be permanent unions between males and females, it does not follow that such unions are "established by nature."[26] However, it will be noticed that in *Of the Social Contract*[27] and other later writings, Rousseau himself speaks of the family as a "natural society"; and in later pages of the *Discourse on Inequality* itself he speaks of a father being master of his child "by a law of nature." Is this a case of Rousseau contradicting himself? Perhaps not. For Rousseau, as we have noticed, uses the word *natural* in more than one sense: first for everything that belongs to the state of nature, and then, for what nature does to human beings once they leave the state of nature and start to live in society. Behavior which is not natural in the savage *becomes* natural in the civilized condition. Rousseau has a great deal to say about the transformation which man undergoes as he moves from the one state to the other. His reasoning looks less paradoxical if one follows his argument in detail.

A question Rousseau refuses to answer is: "which was more necessary, previously formed society for the institution of languages, or previously invented languages for the establishment of society?"[28] He limits himself in the *Discourse on Inequality* to saying that men's first words were natural cries. General ideas came into men's minds with the aid of abstract words, so that the development of language itself helped to create the difficulties with which civilized man torments himself. The savage, living by instinct, has no moral experience; he has no concept of right and wrong. In the state of nature man is good, but there is no question of his being virtuous or vicious. He is happy, free, innocent—and that is all: "One could say that savages are not wicked precisely because they do not know what it is to be good; for it is neither the development of intelligence nor the restraints of laws, but the calm of the passions and their ignorance of vice which prevents them from doing evil."[29]

There is here in Rousseau the germ of an idea developed more fully by his contemporary and friend David Hume, namely, the idea that all men's actions are prompted by passions and that while calm passions generate harmless behavior, violent passions drive men to do evil to themselves and others. Rousseau maintains that men's passions in the state of nature are both calm and few in number, and therefore innocuous, whereas in society their passions become so multiplied and intensified that the consequences are ruinous.

Man in the savage state has one sentiment or disposition which Rousseau speaks of as a "natural virtue," and that is compassion or pity. He suggests that this virtue can even be witnessed in animals, not only in the tenderness of mothers for their young, but in "the aversion of horses against trampling on any living body."[30] He goes on to argue that this natural feeling of pity is the source of all the most important social virtues, such as kindness, generosity, mercy, and humanity. He adds a characteristic comment on the corruption of this excellent sentiment among the men and women of today; because they are so removed from nature, they no longer feel pity. In "the state of reason," as Rousseau calls it, people cease to identify themselves with the suffering being, as they did in the state of nature; this is because reason "breeds pride . . . and turns man inward into himself."[31]

In the modern world, it is the least educated people, the ones in whom the power of reasoning is least developed, who exhibit toward their suffering fellowmen the most lively and sincere commiseration. Rousseau does not miss the opportunity here of pointing an accusing finger at his fellow philosophers:

It is philosophy which isolates a man, and prompts him to say in secret at the sight of another suffering: "Perish if you will; I am safe." No longer can anything but dangers to society in general disturb the tranquil sleep of the philosopher or drag him from his bed. A fellowman may with impunity be murdered under his window, for the philosopher has only to put his hands over his ears and argue a little with himself to prevent nature, which rebels inside him, from making him identify himself with the victim of the murder. The savage man entirely lacks this admirable talent.[32]

Nascent society

If Rousseau's state of nature has so few disadvantages, the reader is bound to ask, how did men ever come to leave it? Rousseau depicts this departure taking place by a series of stages. The first really important transformation of the human condition was the creation of what Rousseau calls "nascent society," a process he envisages as having evolved over a long stretch of time. He locates as the central feature of this development the institution of settled domiciles or "huts." Once men made homes for themselves, the prolonged cohabitation of males and females led to the introduction of the family; and it is this which marked—according to Rousseau's theory—man's departure from the true state of nature, where the individual was solitary and sexually promiscuous, into a condition where men formed the habit of living under the same roof with a mate and were therefore no longer alone.

Rousseau speaks of this passage of man from the state of nature to "nascent society" as the "epoch of a first revolution which established and differentiated families" and which introduced "property of a sort."[33] This "property of a sort" must, however, be distinguished from the full concept of property—that of lawful ownership—which emerges only after a further revolution. All that man has in "nascent society" is a feeling of possession of the hut he occupies. This feeling may have produced many quarrels, but Rousseau adds, "since the strongest men were probably the first to build themselves huts which they felt themselves able to defend, it is reasonable to believe that the weak found it quicker and safer to imitate them rather than try to dislodge them,"[34] and to have refrained from attempting to dispossess them from fear of blows rather than from any respect for ownership.

"Nascent society" is the period of human evolution which Rousseau regards as almost ideal: it is the Garden of Eden in his vision of the past.[35] Human beings had become gentler and more loving than they were in the savage state. No longer were men and women solitary and indifferent to the fate of others. Settled homes produced finer feelings. "The first movements of the heart were the effect of this new situation, which united in a common dwelling husbands and wives, fathers and children. The habit of living together gave birth to the noblest sentiments known to man, namely conjugal love and paternal love. Each family became a little society, all the better united because mutual affection and liberty were its only bond."[36]

Man in "nascent society" was no longer solitary, nor was he yet the enemy of his fellow creatures. Midway between "the stupidity of brutes" and "the disastrous enlightenment of civilized men," he was "restrained by natural pity from harming anyone."[37] It was the golden mean between the "indolence" of the primitive state of nature and the "petulant activity" of modern pride; it was the best time the human race had ever known, "the true youth of the world."[38]

Once more, the reader is bound to ask why, if the simple condition of "nascent society" was so delightful, did men ever quit it? In the *Essay on the Origin of Languages,* Rousseau suggests that primitive men were driven to organize more developed societies as a result of "natural disasters, such as floods, eruptions of volcanoes, earthquakes, or great fires";[39] as if only a miracle could explain their catastrophic passage to a condition of unhappiness. In the *Discourse on Inequality* he provides an alternative explanation for the development of organized society: economic shortage. As the number of persons on the earth increased, the natural abundance of provisions diminished; the individual could no longer feed himself and his family on the herbs he could find, so he had to start eating meat and to unite with his neighbors so as to hunt game in groups.

Thus associations larger than the family were formed; "nascent society" became "society"—although as yet still an anarchic or pre-political society. This development produced important moral and psychological changes in the individual. Ceasing in the context of the family to be a solitary person, he became in the context of society an egoistic person.

Even within the family, important changes took place. Individuals lost their independence. Women began to bear more children and so became less capable of providing for their nourishment and protecting them. They had to rely on their mates. Women became weaker in the context of the family home. Males and females were no longer equal as they had been in the state of nature. Differences between the sexes increased as women became sedentary in the house, and men became even more active as they roamed around, with male companions, looking for food and clothing and furnishings for their dwellings.

As men accumulated these more refined commodities, they began to develop 'needs"—that is, an attachment to things of which "the loss became more cruel than the possession was sweet."[40]

Language, too, developed with the demand for communication, first within the family, then between neighbors, and then as association between neighbors led to the formation of communities. It was at this point that inequality between one man and another originated: "People became accustomed to judging different objects and making comparisons; they gradually acquired ideas of merit and of beauty, which in turn produced feelings of preference."[41]

As ideas and sentiments were cultivated, the human race became sociable. People met in front of their huts or under a tree; singing and dancing became their amusements; and everyone looked at others, knowing that others looked at him. Each wanted to excel in his neighbors' eyes: "He who sang or danced the best, he who was the most handsome, the strongest, the most adroit or the most eloquent became the most highly regarded; and this was the first step towards inequality, and at the same time towards vice."[42]

Men began to base their conception of themselves on what other people thought of them. The idea of "consideration" entered their minds; each wanted respect and soon demanded respect as a right. The duties of civility emerged even among savages; a man who was wounded in his pride was even more offended than a man who was wounded in his body, and each "punished the contempt another showed him in proportion to the esteem he accorded himself."[43]

In society, says Rousseau, man becomes "denatured." His *amour de soi-même,* or self-love, an instinctive self-protective, self-regarding disposition derived from nature, was transformed in society into *amour-propre,* or pride, the desire to be superior to others and to be esteemed by them.

> One must not confuse self-love and pride: two passions very different in their nature and in their effects. Self-love is a natural sentiment which prompts every animal to watch over its own conservation and which, directed in man by reason and modified by pity, produces humanity and virtue. Pride is only a relative, artificial sentiment born in society, prompting each individual to attach more importance to himself than to anyone else and inspiring all the injuries men do to themselves and to others.[44]

Another important development took place in human experience at the stage of pre-political association. Sex became a destructive factor.[45] Rousseau claims that sexual desires are weak in the state of nature because they are like those of animals, directed to any available partner. In the social state sexual desires become strong as they come to be concentrated on a chosen person. In other words, there emerges not only conjugal love, but romantic love:

> As a result of seeing each other, people cannot do without seeing more of each other. A tender and sweet sentiment insinuates itself into the soul, and at the least obstacle becomes an inflamed fury; jealousy awakens with love; discord triumphs and the gentlest of passions receives the sacrifice of human blood.[46]

Sex, a trivial thing in the state of nature, serves from the earliest stages of civilization both to bring human beings together in love and to divide them in bitter rivalry. Romantic love has an evolutionary purpose, for while conjugal love keeps people within their own little family, romantic love carries them into a wider society.[47] It is a motor of community; but at the same time it undermines sociability by the bitter conflicts it provokes as a consequence of competition between suitors for a particular person's favors.

Love is seen by Rousseau as being even more important for women than it is for men. It is an instrument of their purposes. He asserts: "Love is cultivated by women with much skill and care in order to establish their empire over men, and so make dominant the sex that ought to obey."[48] How does this come about?

Rousseau's argument is that women, weakened as they are domesticated, and grown to be dependent on men to an extent that men are not dependent on women, have to use cunning to make men stay attached to them. Each woman must make some man love her enough to shelter, feed, and protect her, to choose her as his cherished mate. In order for women to make men as dependent on them as they are dependent on men, they must dominate men, and dominate them by devious maneuvers and manipulations, since they cannot dominate them by force.

Rousseau maintains that in order to understand sexual relationships in society it is necessary to stress the differences between male and female, and not to imagine, as feminists imagine, that the sexual equality which prevailed in the state of nature can prevail among the civilized.

Beginnings of political society

There are, however, some inequalities which Rousseau does deplore. The inequalities which he sees most inimical to freedom and to nature are those which arise from the division of labor:

> So long as they applied themselves only to work that one person could
> accomplish alone and to arts that did not require the collaboration of
> several hands, they lived as free, healthy, good, and happy men so far
> as they could be according to their nature, and they continued to enjoy
> among themselves the sweetness of independent intercourse; but from
> the instant one man needed the help of another, and it was found to be
> useful for one man to have provisions enough for two, equality
> disappeared, property was introduced, work became necessary, and vast
> forests were transformed into pleasant fields which had to be watered
> with the sweat of men, where slavery and misery were soon seen to
> germinate and flourish with the crops.[49]

Agriculture, then, together with metallurgy, led to those inequalities which Rousseau laments. "It is iron and wheat which first civilized men and ruined the human race."[50] As Rousseau reconstructs the past, the division of labor first took place between smiths, forging tools, and farmers, cultivating the land so as to produce food for both farmers and smiths. The cultivation of the land led to claims being made for rightful ownership of the piece of land which a particular farmer had worked; in other words, it introduced what Rousseau calls the "fatal" concept of property: "Things in this state might have remained equal if talents had been equal, and if, for example, the use of iron and the consumption of foodstuffs had always exactly balanced each other; but this equilibrium, which nothing maintained, was soon broken."[51] The difference between men's capacities and their circumstances produced even greater inequalities in men's possessions, which in turn led to a war between each and all.

At this point Rousseau's argument recalls that of Thomas Hobbes. And indeed while Rousseau rejects Hobbes's claim that the state of

A clergyman steals from the rich to give to the poor in this eighteenth-century artist's conception of the three orders of France. *"From the instant . . . it was found to be useful for one man to have provisions enough for two, equality disappeared. . . ."*

nature is a state of war between all men, he gives a Hobbesian picture of the state of society as it was before the introduction, by a "social contract," of the institutions of government and law. The great difference between Rousseau and Hobbes is that Rousseau argues in the *Discourse on Inequality* that a social condition, and not a state of nature, immediately preceded the introduction of government. Rousseau, as we have seen, claims that the state of nature was peaceful and innocent, and that it was only after the experience of living in society that men were led to introduce government—led to do so because conflicts over possessions arose with the division of labor. Nascent society "gave place to the most horrible state of war."[52]

This state of war in pre-political society is seen by Rousseau as having different causes from the state of war depicted by Hobbes. Hobbes speaks of a war between equals; Rousseau sees a war provoked by inequality, by what he calls "the usurpations of the rich and the brigandage of the poor."[53] War begins when the idea of property is born and one man claims as his own what another man's hunger prompts him to seize, when one man has to fight to get what he needs while another man must fight to keep what he has. For Hobbes, war sprang from natural aggressiveness; for Rousseau, war first began with the unequal division of possessions in the context of scarcity, coupled with the corruption of human passions which was the work of culture rather than of nature.

Both Hobbes and Rousseau envisage men finding the same remedy for the state of war between each and all; namely, by the institution, through common agreement, of a system of positive law which all must obey. But whereas Hobbes's social contract is a rational and just solution equally advantageous to all, Rousseau's social contract, as it is described in the *Discourse on Inequality,* is a fradulent contract imposed on the poor by the rich. In his later book *Of the Social Contract,* concerning which more will be said later in this essay, Rousseau describes an altogether different sort of social contract—a just covenant which would ensure liberty under the law for everyone. But that is something men must enter into with full knowledge of what they are doing. In the *Discourse on Inequality,* Rousseau is describing a contract which took place in the remote past, where men first emerged, most of them without much intelligence, from anarchic communities to political society.[54]

There Rousseau imagines the first founder of civil government as a wily rich man saying to the poor: "let us unite . . . let us institute rules of justice and peace . . . instead of directing our forces against each other, let us unite them together in one supreme power which shall govern us all according to wise laws."[55] The poor, who can see that peace is better than war for everybody, agree; they do not see that in setting up a system of positive law they are transforming existing possessions into permanent legal property and so perpetuating their own poverty as well as the wealth of the rich. And so, as Rousseau puts it, "all ran towards their chains, believing that they were securing their liberty."[56]

It should be noticed that in his account of the fraudulent social contract, Rousseau speaks of the rich dominating and deceiving the poor, not of the strong dominating and and intimidating the weak:

> The first man who, having enclosed a piece of land, thought of saying "This is mine" and found people simple enough to believe him was the true founder of civil society. How many crimes, wars, murders; how much misery and horror the human race would have been spared if someone had pulled up the stakes and filled in the ditch and cried out to his fellow men: "Beware of this impostor: you are lost if you forget that the fruits of the earth belong to everyone and that the earth itself belongs to no one."[57]

Of course Rousseau knew that the past could not be undone. He was not recommending that people should return to "nascent society" or primitive anarchism; if he deplored the choices that men once made, he nowhere suggested, as did some later socialist theorists, that communal ownership of the fruits of the earth could be introduced in modern times.[58] On the contrary, Rousseau insisted that he was writing of a past that was exceedingly remote; and he went on to argue that since the original foundation of governments, societies had gone through further stages of evolution.

Once civil societies had been instituted, the power conferred on rulers led to the division of men into the strong and the weak. In the next stage, legitimate power was converted into arbitrary power, and this divided men into masters and slaves. Although Rousseau does not go into detail, he obviously sees the degeneration of political systems from primitive law into absolute despotism as the reflection of the further degeneration of the human animal. Living under government did nothing, in Rousseau's view, to arrest the moral corruption of the individual. It ended the war of each against all to the advantage of the rich, but in the end it did little good to anyone, even the rich. It failed because civilized man cannot be happy. The savage, says Rousseau, has only to eat and he is at peace with nature "and the friend of all his fellow men."[59] But civil man is never satisfied: "First of all it is a matter of providing necessities, then providing the extras; afterwards come the luxuries, then riches, then subjects, then slaves—he does not have a moment's respite."[60] As men's needs become less natural, the desire to satisfy them becomes more impassioned, so that civil man is never content; he will "cut every throat until he is master of the whole universe."[61]

But Rousseau, in painting this charmless portrait of modern man, still denies that nature is responsible for man's defects: "Men are wicked;

melancholy and constant experience removes any need for proof; yet man is naturally good; I believe I have demonstrated it. What then can have depraved him?"[62] Rousseau's answer is: the changes that have come about in men's constitution as a result of the cultural factors they themselves have introduced into the world. Besides this, there are acquired defects of character in the individual.

Once again, Rousseau stresses the fatal role of *amour-propre* in the life of civil man; the role is not unlike the part played by pride and vainglory in Hobbes's account of natural man. For both philosophers, the psychological or moral causes of human conflict are much the same, the main difference being that Hobbes regards the egoism of man as a product of nature whereas Rousseau insists that it is a product of society. It is at once an outcome of men's progress and the cause of their discontent. "If this were the place to go into details," he writes,

> . . . I would observe to what extent this universal desire for reputation, honours, and promotion, which devours us all, exercises and compares talents and strengths, I would show how it excites and multiplies passions; and how, in turning all men into competitors, rivals or rather enemies, it causes every day failures and successes and catastrophes of every sort by making so many contenders run the same course; I would show that this burning desire to be talked about, this yearning for distinction . . . is responsible for what is best and what is worst among men, for our virtues and our vices, for our sciences and our mistakes; for our conquerors and our philosophers—that is to say, for a multitude of bad things and very few good things.[63]

The tragedy of modern man, as Rousseau sees it, is that he can no longer find happiness in the only way it can be found, and that is by living according to his nature. Natural man enjoys repose and freedom; civil man, on the contrary, is always active, always busy, always playing a part, sometimes bowing to greater men whom he hates, or to richer men, whom he scorns; always ready to do anything for honors, power, and reputation, and yet never having enough: "The savage lives within himself; social man lives always outside himself; he knows how to live only in the opinion of others and it is, so to speak, from their judgements alone that he derives the sense of his own existence."[64]

As an indictment of human civilization, Rousseau's *Discourse on Inequality* would seem to offer no possibility of redemption, no prospect for social man to recover freedom, happiness, or authenticity. But Rousseau's other writings are less discouraging; there we find indications of a way to salvation. The basis of hope is his belief that man is naturally good. If culture is responsible for all that has gone wrong, is not culture something that can be modified?

The ideal state

Rousseau's earlier discourse—the *Discourse on the Sciences and the Arts*[65]—had argued that only certain forms of culture were corrupting, not all forms of culture. And in the preface to his *Discourse on Inequality* there is a clear promise that a certain type of civil society can restore to men, even in the modern world, the freedom, happiness, and authenticity which the human race in general has lost in the course of its evolution.

The preface to the *Discourse on Inequality* takes the form of a dedication to the Republic of Geneva, and in those pages Rousseau holds up that republic as a model to the world: a civil society which has escaped the corruption of the rest. It is undoubtedly an idealized portrait of Geneva that he gives us. But the important thing is that it is there: it enables us to put down Rousseau's *Discourse on Inequality* without a feeling of total despair. Not so Voltaire, perhaps, who detested Rousseau, and who could find no redeeming feature in the *Discourse*. "I have received, Monsieur, your new book against the human race, and I thank you," he wrote to Rousseau after he had sent him a copy. "No one has employed so much intelligence to turn men into beasts. One starts wanting to walk on all fours after reading your book. However, in more than sixty years I have lost the habit."[66]

Voltaire had not the patience to try to understand what Rousseau had been attempting to do—to provide a genuinely scientific account of the facts of the human condition before developing a speculative theory which might point the way to improvement. Rousseau's image of Geneva was a central feature of that theory.

In dedicating his *Discourse on Inequality* to the citizens of Geneva he congratulates them on being "that people which, among all others, seems to me to possess the greatest advantages of society and to have guarded most successfully against the abuses of society."[67] Rousseau is proud to number himself among those citizens:

> Having had the good fortune to be born among you, how could I reflect on the equality which nature established among men and the inequality which they have instituted among themselves, without thinking of the profound wisdom with which the one and the other, happily combined in this Republic, contribute in the manner closest to natural law and most favourable to society, to the maintenance of public order and the well-being of individuals.[68]

The Republic of Geneva was a country unlike others, and Rousseau, who was born there in 1712, had been brought up to be an eager and uncritical patriot. It had been an independent city-state since the middle years of the sixteenth century, when its constitution was formulated—or reformulated—by a lawgiver of genius, Jean Calvin.[69] But the circumstances of its institution were not simple. Before it acquired

"*Rousseau holds up* [Geneva, where he was born in 1712] *as a model to the world.* . . ."

independence, sovereignty of the city was effectively divided between the Bishops of Geneva and the Dukes of Savoy, and the burghers, by playing one ruler against the other, had acquired for themselves an extensive range of civil rights. The bishops gave the burghers powers to use against the dukes, but the ungrateful burghers used those powers in turn against the bishops and rid themselves in time of both their sovereigns. They had not intended, however, to proclaim themselves a republic; they aspired only to seek incorporation as a canton in the Swiss confederation. This purpose was thwarted as a result of the Reformation, which divided the Swiss among themselves: the Genevans had counted on joining the confederation on the basis of existing alliances with Fribourg and Bern, but as Fribourg remained Catholic and Bern turned Protestant, Geneva could not please one canton without antagonizing the other. In any event, Bern proved more useful to the Genevans in turning out the duke and bishop, so the Genevans chose to become Protestant. By this step they alienated Fribourg and the other Catholic Swiss cantons, with the result that Geneva's entry into the Swiss confederation was vetoed until the nineteenth century.

Calvin enabled the Genevans to make a virtue of a necessity: denied membership of a larger nation, they learned from him how to construct a peaceful little nation of their own. They instituted an autonomous, independent city, where the people themselves were sovereign. Administration was placed in the hands of elected elders and the guidance of the people entrusted to the clergy of the national Calvinist church. The republican constitution was a skillful mixture of the democratic, the aristocratic, and the theocratic elements. Almost by a miracle, it survived as an independent city-state in an age of expanding kingdoms and empires. But not entirely by a miracle. In Calvin's lifetime, Swiss troops from the friendly Protestant canton of Bern surrounded Geneva's frontiers and after Calvin's death, when Geneva became a center of international banking, the rulers of Europe's larger powers preserved Geneva's neutrality in order to protect their own financial interests. And so, despite having no credible national defenses, the city-state of Geneva kept its autonomy and republican constitution at a time when the other small republics of Europe—Florence, for example, or Siena or Lucca—fell into the hands of monarchs.

Rousseau had been brought up by his ardently patriotic father to think of Geneva as the one state in the modern world which had recovered the glory of the ancient republics.[70] He read as a child the works of Plutarch and could boast, "I was a Roman at the age of twelve."[71] In his *Confessions,* Rousseau says that admiration for ancient Rome "helped to create in me that free and republican spirit, that proud and strong character, impatient of any yoke or servitude, which has tormented me all my life in situations where it has been least appropriate."[72]

In the dedication of his *Discourse on Inequality,* Rousseau explains why he considers Geneva the nearest to an ideal state to be found on this earth. It is small; with a population of only several thousand, every citizen can be acquainted with all his fellow citizens and everyone's life is open to the gaze of others; it is a state where everyone's private interest coincides with the public interest, where no one is subject to any law except the law he has made and imposed on himself, where the constitution has stood the test of time, where military virtues are cultivated but wars are not engaged in, where the magistrates are chosen by all but vested with undisputed authority, where democracy is "wisely tempered."

This is not at all an accurate description of Geneva as it had become in the middle of the eighteenth century, but it is what Calvin had designed Geneva to be, what Geneva should have been, and what the rulers of Geneva in all their public pronouncements claimed that Geneva was. To the author of the *Discourse on Inequality* the myth of Geneva was more important than the reality of Geneva. For it is that myth which holds out the possibility of what might be called the renegotiation of the social contract. The old fraudulent social contract which had marked the introduction of government into human experience could be reenacted as a genuine social contract. A revolution could end all those centuries of servitude and men could come together, as the Genevans had come together under the guidance of Calvin in the sixteenth century, and make a civil covenant which would not be a device by which the rich would cheat the poor but a means of combining liberty and law.

Geneva, which Rousseau visited for several months after he had written the *Discourse on Inequality,* was something of a disappointment to him. He came to realize that it was far from being the "wisely tempered democracy" he had described in his dedication. But he did not forsake the idea of an authentic social contract as a means of reconciling liberty and law. He did not falter in his republicanism. This is what inspired his next most important essay in political theory, the book he called *Of the Social Contract,* which was published in 1762, some seven years after the *Discourse on Inequality.*

Of the Social Contract

The *Discourse on Inequality* was coldly received by the authorities of Geneva; *Of the Social Contract* was actually banned, burned on the orders of the censors and a warrant issued for the author's arrest. And yet Rousseau could say, with complete sincerity, that in *Of the Social Contract* he had presented Geneva as an example to all governments: "People were pleased to relegate *Of the Social Contract* with the *Republic* of Plato to the realm of illusions: but I depicted an existing object. . . . My book . . . proposed one state as a model, and in just that one state it has been burned!"[73]

Thomas Hobbes was in Rousseau's mind when he wrote *Of the Social Contract* just as he had been when he wrote the *Discourse on Inequality.* Even if his knowledge of Hobbes was imperfect, he had read enough of his work, either in French translation or in Hobbes's own Latin, to be excited by him, and to regard his theory as a challenge that had to be answered.

Hobbes, as Rousseau understood him, argued that men had to choose between law and liberty, between being governed and being free. For Hobbes, freedom meant the absence of opposition:[74] the liberties of subjects "depend on the silence of the law."[75] Freedom went with anarchy: law, to be effective, meant the rule of an absolute and individual sovereign. Men loved freedom, but the consequences of anarchy were so appalling that any sort of government was better than no government at all. Hobbes's social contract was a covenant made between men to collectively surrender their natural rights to a sovereign in return for the peace and security of a civil order which that sovereign could secure by holding all men in awe.

Common hangmen burned copies of Rousseau's *Of the Social Contract* in the streets of Geneva in 1763. The Genevan authorities rejected his theories.

Rousseau did not agree that freedom was antithetical to the constraints of government. Freedom was not the absence of opposition but the exercise of ruling oneself. He believed it was possible to combine liberty and law, by instituting a regime which would enable men to rule themselves. Such an arrangement would entail, as Hobbes's system did, a covenant being made between individuals to surrender their natural rights to a sovereign: but that sovereign should be none other than the people themselves, united in one legislative corps.

Rousseau not only rejects Hobbes's idea that men must choose between being free and being ruled, he asserts that it is only through ruling themselves that men can recover freedom. In the *Discourse on Inequality* Rousseau speaks of the three kinds of freedom men enjoy in the state of nature, one and perhaps two of which they lose on entering society. In *Of the Social Contract* he speaks of another kind of freedom which men can experience only in society: political freedom. And this is something altogether superior to mere independence.

In *Of the Social Contract,* Rousseau speaks less of the innocence of savage man and more of his brutishness. Man in the state of nature is described as a "stupid and unimaginative animal" who becomes "an intelligent being and a man" only as a result of entering civil society. Assuredly, as a result of the development of the passions and sophistry which society breeds, men have generally grown worse with the passage of time; but that is because culture, instead of improving men, has corrupted them—the theme of Rousseau's early *Discourse on the Sciences and the Arts,* to which he returned again and again. Culture is bound to change men, and if it does not make them better, it will make them worse.

In the state of nature, a man cannot, by definition, be a citizen. But once he has quit the state of nature and entered society, man's nature can only be realized if he becomes a citizen. In this sense Rousseau accepts Aristotle's definition of man as a *zoon politikon.* Here again we meet the two senses of "nature" in Rousseau's argument. Just as the family, unnatural in the state of nature, becomes natural in society, so does political freedom, logically impossible for the savage, become natural for the civilized man.

The answer to Hobbes

In a way, Rousseau's response to the challenge of Hobbes is wonderfully simple. Clearly, men can be at the same time ruled and free if they rule themselves. For then the obligation to obey will be combined with the desire to obey; everyone in obeying the law will only be acting in obedience to his own will. In saying this, Rousseau was going a good deal further than liberal theorists such as John Locke, who associated freedom with the people's consent to obey a constitutional monarch in whom they have invested sovereignty. For Rousseau there is no investment or transfer of sovereignty: sovereignty not only originates in the people, it stays there.

Rousseau's solution to the problem of being at the same time ruled and free might plausibly be expressed as "democracy." But this is a word he seldom uses, and even then his use of it looks paradoxical. We have noted that in the dedication of the *Discourse on Inequality* he praises the republic of Geneva as a "democracy well tempered," but in *Of The Social Contract,* he writes: "If there were a nation of Gods, it would govern itself democratically. A government so perfect is not suited to men."[76] There is in fact no contradiction here, in view of the particular use Rousseau makes of the word *government.* He carefully separates government, as administration, from sovereignty, as legislation. He maintains that legislation must be democratic, in the sense that every citizen should participate in it and participate in person. This is the democratic element in the constitution of Geneva which Rousseau has in mind when he speaks of that state as a "democracy well tempered." At the same time, Rousseau rejects—as unsuited to men— democratic administration. The participation by all the citizens in the administration, or executive government, of the state, he considers altogether too impractical and utopian an arrangement to be desirable in practice. Executive government, he argues, must be entrusted to duly elected magistrates or ministers.

In the dedication to his *Discourse on Inequality,* Rousseau declares "I would have fled from a republic, as necessarily ill-governed, where the people . . . foolishly kept in their own hands the administration of civil affairs and the execution of their laws."[77] He stresses the need for a state to have "chiefs" (*chefs*). "I would have chosen a republic where the individuals, content with sanctioning the laws and making decisions in assemblies on proposals from the chiefs on the most important public business . . . elected year by year the most capable and upright of their fellow citizens to administer justice and govern the state."[78]

The point Rousseau dwells on is that superiority in public office shall correspond to superiority of capability and rectitude. Such a system he can call "aristocratic" in the true classical sense of that word: government by the best. This is clearly the sense he has in mind when in *Of the Social Contract* he speaks of an elective aristocracy as "the best form of government";[79] and in doing so he does not contradict the preference expressed in the *Discourse on Inequality* for "democratic government, wisely tempered"—for what he means there is democratic legislation, wisely tempered by an aristocratic administration, democratically elected. He contrasts this sort of aristocracy with an aristocracy based on heredity, characteristic of feudal regimes: "the worst form of government."[80]

In *Of the Social Contract* Rousseau draws attention to the dangers inherent in a system which separates the executive, the aristocratic body, from the legislative, the democratic body. He points out that while it is desirable for the business of administration to be entrusted to magistrates or chiefs, those magistrates will naturally tend with the passage of time to encroach on the sacred territory of legislation, and thus to invade the sovereignty of the people, and finally to destroy the republican nature of the state. "This is the inherent and inescapable vice which, from the birth of the body politic, tends relentlessly to destroy it, just as old age and death destroy the body of a man."[81]

Rousseau says nothing about this "vice" in his dedication to Geneva of his *Discourse on Inequality.* One can suggest a reason for this. He did not realize, when he wrote that dedication, the extent to which the magistrates of Geneva had invaded the sphere of democratic sovereignty, but by the time he wrote *Of the Social Contract* he had woken up to the reality of the political situation of his supposedly ideal city-state.

The republican constitution of Geneva had not changed since Calvin established—or reestablished—it in the 1530s, but much had altered behind the facade. The main institutions of the republic were the General Council, the Council of Two Hundred, and the Council of Twenty-Five. The General Council was the democratic body to which every male citizen over the age of twenty-five belonged, and which had the power to enact laws, to elect the principal magistrates, and to approve or reject proposals concerning defenses, alliances, taxation, and so forth. Its members had the vote, but no right to speak, or initiate legislation. The Council of Two Hundred was in effect the debating forum, and the Council of Twenty-Five the instrument of executive government.

What had happened in the two centuries since Calvin's time was that the Council of Twenty-Five had progressively taken over control of the state, dominating the Council of Two Hundred, summoning the General Council as seldom as possible and then only to give mute assent to the magistrates' proposals for legislation and their list of candidates for executive office. What is more, the members of the Council of Twenty-Five had come to be drawn from an ever narrower circle of Genevan society, a group of patrician families which contrived to keep all the offices of state for themselves and their nominees. In effect, a hereditary nobility had grown up in Geneva—not an open avowed patriciate like that of Bern, but one which clothed itself in all the forms and rhetoric of classical republican ideology.

At the same time the citizen class shrank progressively. In the sixteenth century, the majority of adult males in Geneva were enrolled as burgesses and citizens. By the end of the seventeenth century those citizens constituted a minority, a middle class of about 1,500 adult males in a population of 25,000. Below them was a disfranchised lower class, not only excluded from the voting register, but denied access to the more lucrative trades of the city.[82]

Rousseau was born into a family of equivocal social standing. His paternal grandfather was a superior artisan and burgess who had been engaged in political activity on behalf of citizens' rights against the patrician magistrates—a "liberal," we might call him, anachronistically. Rousseau's father seems to have been more of a "conservative." He had married a woman of superior social status, not quite in the patrician class, but in the upper academic class, and living among the *élite* at the fashionable center of town. Rousseau was born in one of the smartest houses; and although his mother died soon after his birth, and Rousseau had to move down the hill to live in humble quarters, he was brought up by his father to think of himself as a superior person and to take an uncritical view of the political arrangements of his native city-state. Writing about Geneva many years later, Rousseau recalled a military festivity he had witnessed as a child with his father:

> My father, embracing me, was thrilled in a way that I can still feel and share. "Jean-Jacques," he said to me, "love your country. Look at these good Genevans: they are all friends; they are all brothers: joy and harmony reigns among them. You are a Genevan. One day you will see other nations, . . . but you will never find any people to match your own."[83]

Rousseau ran away from Geneva when he was sixteen because he was wretchedly unhappy in his work as an engraver's apprentice, and he did not return to the city for any length of time until the age of forty-two—just after he had written the *Discourse on Inequality*. When he wrote *Of the Social Contract* he had learned rather more about the way things were in Geneva, and one cannot doubt that his warnings about the tendency of the executive government to invade the rights of the legislative were based on this newly acquired awareness of what had happened over several generations of Genevan history.

Perhaps we should not be surprised that *Of the Social Contract* was banned and burned in Geneva. Rousseau could well protest that he had provided in his pages an advertisement for Geneva: "I took your constitution as my model for political institutions."[84] But at the same time he showed how such a constitution came to be undermined; in fact, there was no hiding the implication that the constitution of Geneva had been undermined in just that way. There were other features of Rousseau's argument that were bound to be offensive to people who proclaimed themselves not only good republicans but good Christians.

For Rousseau, although he distances himself from that universally detested atheist and materialist Thomas Hobbes, does so only to align himself with a political philosopher of equally ill repute, Niccolò Machiavelli [*GBWW*, Vol. 23]. Rousseau saw in Machiavelli, not the supposed champion of monarchy who wrote *Il principe,* but the ideologue of republicanism who wrote the *Discorsi.* Like Machiavelli, Rousseau was in love with the political system of antiquity: that is what he meant when he said "I was a Roman at the age of twelve."[85] In time he came to prefer Sparta to Rome, but only because he thought it remained more perfectly republican.

Rousseau does not tell the whole truth when he says that in writing *Of the Social Contract,* "I took your constitution (of Geneva) as my model," for he also took another constitution as his model. At the end of his exploration of the idea of what a civil society must look like if it is successfully to combine liberty and law, we find Calvin's Geneva fortified with further institutions and practices derived from Sparta.

Rousseau insists that citizens can only be free—can only be citizens in the true sense of the word—if they make in person the rules under which they live. The idea of representation or delegation is wholly unacceptable to him. He writes very critically of the parliamentary system of legislation by elected deputies. "The English people believes itself to be free; it is gravely mistaken; it is free only during the election of Members of Parliament; as soon as the Members are elected, the people is enslaved, it is nothing."[86]

Here again we must note the special meaning Rousseau attaches to freedom. Political freedom entails participation in legislation—as distinct from the unimpeded enjoyment of rights. It is freedom as it was understood in Sparta: freedom expressed in active citizenship. And like the Spartans, Rousseau limits citizenship to adult males. There is only one kind of representation in his system: the head of the family represents the women and children.

Exclusion of women

Genevan women had always been excluded from the citizens' roll, and in his dedication to the *Discourse on Inequality,* Rousseau proposes that the women of Geneva should "command" only in the context of the family. "The destiny of your sex will always be to govern ours," he tells the women of Geneva. "Happy are we so long as your chaste power, exerted solely within the marriage bond, makes itself felt only for the glory of the state and the well-being of the public! It was thus that the women commanded at Sparta and thus that you deserve to command in Geneva."[87]

The difference between male and female is an important feature of Rousseau's political theory.[88] He had once worked as a research assistant to an earlier pioneer of feminism, Mme Dupin, and he had no patience with her kind of argument for equal rights.[89] Instead of equality between the sexes, Rousseau proclaims a sort of equilibrium between them: men should rule the world, and women should rule men. One of Rousseau's criticisms of the modern world—of which France is his prime example (and from which Geneva is held to be an exception)—is that women have acquired an undue predominance. How had this come about? Rousseau had already explained in tracing the history of "nascent society" how women, becoming dependent on men in the context of domestic life, have to strive to make men correspondingly dependent on them. Since sexual desire is (according to Rousseau) less intense in the male than in the female, females have to stimulate it, and they do this by hiding their sexual charms, making themselves mysterious and playing hard to get. In a word, they acquire modesty.

This strategy is advantageous to everyone. When women are hard to get, men are not only spared the ordeal of being devoured by women's voracious sexual appetites, they are also "civilized," that is, trained in the art of pleasing women. Once the male's sexual desire has been elevated to a ruling passion, and once the female refuses to satisfy that desire unless the male does a great many tricks to earn his reward, then it becomes as important for men to study how to please women as it is for women to study how to please men.

One of the reasons why male sexual desire is weak in the state of nature is that there are plenty of females in the forest and no limits to the mating season. The situation is reversed in society by the introduction of female modesty, a somewhat bogus virtue as Rousseau describes it, but one very necessary to the female if she is to transform the male's weak lust into a strong passionate love.

Modesty is not natural (in a way it goes against nature), but it is suggested to women by nature, together with shame, "to arm the weak in order that they shall enslave the strong."[90] Here again we meet the two senses of "nature" in Rousseau's writings. By original nature, women are immodest and shameless; in the social context, nature propels them, for their own protection, toward shame and modesty. The ambiguity of the situation is reflected in women's actual behavior. It is pride which enables women to triumph over themselves and become chaste, but the same pride makes them want to have the whole world at their feet.

Rousseau deplores the fact that in modernity, women have been able to satisfy this extravagant desire. He believes it is right that women should rule men privately, but that it is men's task to rule the world publicly. This again is part of his republican ideology; it is as a republican that he attacks the sexual arrangements which prevail in the decadent kingdom of France. There he discerns a deplorable form of sexual uniformity in which men have come to resemble women by becoming equally effeminate; they have been reduced to being the foppish slaves of women in society and of a despot in the state.

In Sparta things were different; there austerity, manliness, and military virtues prevailed, and Rousseau is eager for Geneva to keep Sparta in mind as a model. The women of Sparta knew that their duty was to rear citizens, not to aspire to be citizens themselves. Rousseau sees no place for women in legislative activity because his conception of the citizen is that of a citizen-soldier, and women cannot be asked to bear arms (they are too frail and too precious as mothers of future soldiers), nor can a good wife and mother be relied upon always to put the interests of the state before the interests of her own family, as a good citizen must. Women's skill lies in the use of hidden, personal, devious power; whereas public politics requires impersonal, rational legislation and open forthright utterance, for which men are suited by nature. The abilities of each sex, as Rousseau sees them, are distinct; man is the "arm," and woman the "eye" of the partnership. If everything is in its place, there will be no confusion of roles; privately women will rule men, and publicly men will rule the state.

The general will

Rousseau's *Of the Social Contract* begins with a sensational opening sentence: "Man was born free, but he is everywhere in chains."[91] But the argument of the book is that men need not be in chains. When a state is based on a genuine social contract (as opposed to the fraudulent social contract depicted in the *Discourse on Inequality*), men receive in exchange for their independence a better kind of freedom, true political freedom or republican freedom. In entering a civil society based on the right kind of social contract, man loses his "natural liberty and his absolute right to anything that tempts him," but he gains "civil liberty and the legal right of property in what he possesses";[92] to this is added the moral liberty which makes a man master of himself, "for to be governed by appetite alone is slavery, while obedience to a law one prescribes to oneself is liberty."[93]

In this formulation of Rousseau's argument we confront a serious problem. It is easy to understand that an individual can be said to be free if he prescribes to himself the rules he obeys in his life, but how can a group of people be said to be free in prescribing for themselves the rules they obey? An individual is a person with a single will, but a group of people is a number of persons each with his own will. How can a group of persons have *a* will, in obedience to which all its members will be free? For it clearly must have such a single will, if any sense is to be made of Rousseau's proposition.

Rousseau's reponse to the problem is to define his civil society as an "artificial person" so that people become *a* people, a people with a single will, which he calls *la volonté générale* or general will. The social contract which brings the civil society into being is itself a pledge, and the civil society remains in being as a pledged group. Ernest Renan, the dissident French theologian, defined the nation as a "plebiscite renewed every day"; and this is exactly Rousseau's conception: the republic is the creation of will, of a will that never falters, in each and every member, to further the public, the common, the national interest—even though it might sometimes compete with personal interest. Of course, no one can be expected to cease to desire his own good; but as each individual is transformed into a citizen, he acquires besides his private will a public or general will.

Rousseau sounds very much like Hobbes when he says that under the pact by which men enter civil society, everyone makes a "total alienation of himself and all his rights to the whole community."[94] However, it must be understood that Rousseau represents this alienation as a form of exchange—men give up natural rights in return for civil rights; the total alienation is followed by a total restitution, and the bargain is a good one because what men surrender are rights of dubious value, unsupported by anything but an individual's own powers, rights which are precarious and without a moral basis, while what they receive in return are rights that are legitimate and enforced. The rights men alienate are rights based on might; the rights they acquire are rights based on law.

There is no more haunting paragraph in the whole book *Of the Social Contract* than that in which Rousseau speaks of forcing a man to be free.[95] But it would be wrong to put too much weight on these words, in the manner of those who consider Rousseau a forerunner of modern totalitarianism. He is "authoritarian" in the sense that he favors authority, but his authority is carefully distinguished from mere power and is offered as something wholly consistent with liberty, being based on the expressed assent and credence of those who follow it. Rousseau does not say that *men* may be forced to be free, in the sense of a whole community being forced to be free; he says that *a* man may be forced to be free, and Rousseau is thinking here of the occasional individual who, as a result of being enslaved by his passions, disobeys the voice of law, or of the general will, within him. The general will is something inside each man as well as in society generally, so that the man who is coerced by the community for a breach of that law is, in Rousseau's view of things, being brought back to an awareness of his own true will. Thus in penalizing a lawbreaker, society is literally correcting him, restoring him to his own authentic purposes. Legal penalties are a device for helping the individual in his struggle against his own passions, as well as a device for protecting society against the antisocial depredations of lawbreakers. This explains the curious footnote wherein Rousseau writes: "In Genoa the word *Libertas* may be seen on the doors of all the prisons and on the fetters of her galleys. This use of the motto is excellent and just."[96]

For Rousseau there is a radical dichotomy between true law and actual law. Actual law is what he describes in the *Discourse on Inequality* and again in *Émile,* where he writes: "The universal spirit of laws in all countries is to favor the stronger against the weaker, and those who have against those who have nothing."[97] True law, which is what he describes in *Of the Social Contract,* is different. It is just law, and what assures its being just is that its rules are made by a people in its capacity as sovereign and obeyed by the same people in its capacity as subject. Rousseau is confident that such laws cannot be oppressive on the grounds that no people would forge fetters for itself.

The distinction between true law and actual law corresponds to the distinction Rousseau draws between the general will and the will of all. The general will is a normative concept, its rightness is part of its definition. The will of all is an empirical will: the only test of the will of all is to ascertain that all actually do will. Rousseau takes care to note the logical distinction between "right" and "fact."

Why should I abide by the decision of the majority? Because by the deed of the social contract itself, to which everyone must subscribe and pledge (there is no question of a majority decision here: you either pledge or you are out of civil society altogether), each contractant agrees to accept the decision of the majority in the formulation of the laws. It is also understood that the members of the majority, whose decision is accepted as binding, do not will as a majority but simply as interpreters of the general will—so that it is a majority interpretation of the general will which is binding, not a majority will. This is how it becomes morally obligatory for the minority to accept those decisions.

However, Rousseau is troubled by the fact that the majority of citizens is not necessarily the most intelligent. Indeed, he agrees with Plato that most people are rather stupid. The "general will is always rightful" but it is sometimes mistaken.[98] Hence the need for a lawgiver, to draw up, for the people and on behalf of the people, the constitution or system of laws under which that people is to live.

One of the most striking chapters in *Of the Social Contract* is that in which Rousseau writes "to discover the rules of society that are best suited to nations, there would need to exist a superior intelligence,"[99] and he then goes on to invoke the names of such supermen as Lycurgus, Calvin,[100] and Moses.[101] Rousseau not only praises these great founders; he notes their techinque, which is that of claiming that they have received their constitutions from a supernatural source. Rousseau quotes Machiavelli on this point, printing—admittedly in Italian—the following paragraph from Machiavelli's *Discorsi*.

> The truth is that there has never been a lawgiver who in introducing extraordinary laws to a people did not have recourse to God, for otherwise his laws would not have been accepted.[102]

Rousseau does not suggest here that the lawgiver should really have God's authority, only that he should *pretend* to; the lawgiver "puts his own laws into the mouth of the immortals, thus compelling by divine authority persons who cannot be moved by human prudence."[103]

This passage is all the more remarkable in view of Rousseau's insistence in so many of his writings on the importance of sincerity. In his *Letter to Monsieur d'Alembert* for example, he attacks the profession of the stage at great length, arguing that the art of acting is one of "counterfeit, . . . the art of assuming a personality which is not one's own, of simulating passions one does not feel, saying things one does not believe."[104] Rousseau contrasts the actor's role with that of the political orator, who "speaks only in his own name, and says nothing other than what he thinks, so that the man and the *persona* are identical."[105] It is strange therefore that Rousseau should advise the most important orator of all, the lawgiver, to have recourse to dissimulation, and to suggest to the crowd that the proposals he has thought out himself have been given to him by the deity.

The civil religion

The Machiavellian element in Rousseau's thinking comes out even more conspicuously in the chapter in *Of the Social Contract* where he discusses "The Civil Religion": this was a chapter which caused particular shock and indignation in Geneva, and it is only surprising that Rousseau did not expect it to do so. It forms the very last chapter of the book, and its argument is asserted aggressively: Christianity is the true religion, but it is worse than useless as a civil religion [*GBWW*, Vol. 38, pp. 435–39].

> Christianity is a wholly spiritual religion, concerned solely with the things of heaven; the Christian's homeland is not of this world. The Christian does his duty, it is true, but he does it with profound indifference towards the good or ill success of his deeds. . . . The essential thing is to go to paradise, and resignation is but one more means to that end. . . . [In war] all will do their duty, but they will do it without passion for victory; they know better how to die than to conquer.[106]

In this chapter Rousseau does not quote Machiavelli by name, but he repeats Machiavelli's arguments against Christianity, that it teaches monkish virtues of humility and submission instead of the manly virtues a republic needs—courage, virility, patriotism, love of glory, and the service of the state. Rousseau agrees with Machiavelli: there can be no such thing as a Christian republic, "for each of these terms contradicts the other."[107] What is needed as a civil religion is a neo-pagan cult. Rousseau does not go so far as Machiavelli in proposing a revival of bloodthirsty pagan rituals, but he does propose a civil religion with minimal theological content which will fortify and not impede (as Christianity impedes) the cultivation of republican virtue.

It is understandable that the authorities of Geneva, profoundly convinced that the national church of their republic was at the same time a truly Christian church and a nursery of patriotism, should consider Rousseau's arguments both subversive and heretical. Rousseau's insistence on the need for a non-Christian civil religion is the measure of the extent to which his own ideal of a republic went beyond the model of Calvin's Geneva. Assuredly Calvin had himself banished what had been traditionally understood as Christianity by abolishing the Catholic Church in Geneva and setting up his own Protestant national church in its place; but Calvin, of course, considered this reform as the institution of an authentic form of Gospel Christianity. Rousseau in his private religion claimed to do something similar, to subscribe to the true teaching of Christ which all the churches, Protestant as well as Catholic, had betrayed. But Rousseau's public religion—the civil religion described in *Of the Social Contract*—is unequivocally anti-Christian, and he makes no attempt to disguise that fact.

In short, pagan Sparta, to an even greater extent than Christian Geneva, appears as Rousseau's model in the later chapters in *Of the Social Contract*. This was spotted by one of Rousseau's earliest and—to my mind—most cogent critics, Benjamin Constant.[108] A native of Lausanne, and an inhabitant of the neighboring canton of Vaud, Constant knew Geneva well and was familiar with the myth which Rousseau shared with so many of his compatriots that this city-state had revived in a modern state the best republican features of the ancient world. Constant saw in Rousseau's *Of the Social Contract* an attempt to treat this myth as a reality. He argued that the ancient city-state could not be revived in the modern world, first, because the large-scale kingdom had become the standard form of the nation; and second, because the ancient republics were not so desirable anyway—Sparta in particular being no better than a "warrior's monastery."

Constant focused his attack on Rousseau's endeavor to revolutionize men's conception of freedom, to replace the idea of "modern liberty"—something which men could and should enjoy at the present time—with the idea of "ancient liberty"—something which had its place only in the lost world of antiquity.[109] Invited to surrender "modern liberty" for the sake of "ancient liberty," men were being offered a meretricious illusion in place of a practicable and realistic objective.

"Ancient liberty," as Constant explained it, meant "direct personal participation in the government of one's own state"; it was "whatever ensured citizens the largest share in exercising political power."[110] By contrast, "modern liberty" was "whatever guarantees the independence of citizens from their government."[111] In the ancient republics, a man believed himself to be free to the extent that he exercised his political power. In the modern world, Constant suggested, men found their freedom in doing what they chose to do, enjoying the rights to express opinions, to come and go, to assemble and worship as they pleased, and to dispose of property. Modern liberty was largely a matter of freedom *from* interference in the pursuit of one's own lawful ends.

Constant, who lived long enough to see Rousseau's concept of "ancient liberty" invoked by Robespierre and others to justify some of the worst excesses of the French Revolution as expressions of popular sovereignty, was sharply critical of Rousseau's argument. But he was not entirely hostile. He suggested that some element of "ancient liberty" should be added to "modern liberty" to give it a more positive content:[112] He believed that everyone's liberty should include, besides the right to be left alone, "the right to exert influence on the administration of government, either through the election of some or all of its public functionaries or through petitions, remonstrances and demands."[113]

In effect Constant was the first to draw from Rousseau what the world as a whole came in time to learn from him: namely, the need to add a democratic dimension to its understanding of freedom. In response to this demand, representative governments since the late eighteenth century have been progressively democratized. The United States led the way; other states have followed. Universal suffrage has become the norm, even under those régimes where "parliamentary" or "legislative" assemblies are powerless. Even in its best and most authentic form, democratized representative government is not what Rousseau understood by "democracy." But his plea for *his* kind of democracy, for *his* kind of "ancient freedom" was so eloquent that it impelled men's thoughts toward the mprovement of "modern freedom." Rousseau did not become a "legislator for mankind": but he stirred the imagination of men, first with his disturbing picture of what had happened to them in the course of their evolution, and second with his exhilarating picture of what they might become if they were to remake the institutions under which they lived. There was both an optimistic and a pessimistic side to Rousseau's political theory. It was the optimistic side which captured most attention and which has earned him the right to be remembered as one of the great prophets of revolution.

Abbreviations used in notes

Annales	*Annales de la Société Jean-Jacques Rousseau.* Geneva, 1905–.
C.C.	*Correspondance complète de J.-J. Rousseau.* Edited by R. A. Leigh. Geneva, Banbury, and Oxford, 1965–.
D.I.	*J.-J. Rousseau: A Discourse on Inequality.* Trans. M. Cranston. New York and London, 1984.
J.J.	Maurice Cranston. *Jean-Jacques: The Early Life and Work of Jean-Jacques Rousseau.* New York and London, 1983.
O.C.	*Oeuvres complètes de J.-J. Rousseau.* Edited for the Bibliothèque de la Pléiade by B. Gagnebin, M. Raymond, *et al.* Paris, 1959–.
Reappraisals	*Reappraisals of Rousseau.* Simon Harvey *et al.*, eds. Manchester, 1980.
S.C.	J.-J. Rousseau. *The Social Contract.* Trans. M. Cranston. Baltimore and Harmondsworth, 1968.

---

[1]The idea of a social contract can be traced to the Bible and to philosophers of classical antiquity. (*See*, for example, J. W. Gough, *The Social Contract, a critical study of its development*, Oxford and New York, 2nd ed., 1957, and Simone Goyard-Fabre, *L'interminable querelle du contrat social*, Ottawa, 1983). However, it did not become in any way central to political and legal philosophy until the late medieval and Renaissance period. We may well ascribe an ideological motive to this, in the sense that it was a philosophical concept developed for a political objective. The rise of the idea of a social contract coincided with the rise of absolutism in the sphere of government, and it was developed by champions of constitutional, or limited, sovereignty as an alternative to the patriarchal theory invoked by apologists of absolutism.

The absolutist case rested in part on the teaching of Aristotle that man is a "social animal," partly on an appeal to texts of Holy Scripture where there are intimations that man is a "family creature" by God's design. On the basis of this view, the absolutist philosophers argued that just as God is the head of the whole human race, and a father the head of his family, so is a king the head of the nation, deriving his authority from God and exercising it by the same right that a father has over his family. This was the doctrine of patriarchalism, which became known in the seventeenth century—the high peak of European absolutist monarchies—as the Divine Right of Kings.

The idea of a social contract played a central role in theories which opposed the patriarchal thesis. They rejected the argument that a nation, or kingdom, is a natural association of human beings on the model of a family and maintained instead that such societies were contractual unions of individuals, who had come together for their mutual defense and advantage and were held together by an implied covenant or contract. Civil societies were pledged societies, not natural societies.

This concept of a social contract as expounded by most of its early modern theorists can be seen to have involved a double contract. First, there was assumed to have taken place at the origin of societies a "pact of association," a *Gesellschaftsvertrag;* that is to say, a compact made by a number of persons to unite together in a society; in the jargon of sociology, this marked the transformation of a *series* of individuals (each with his isolated purposes and interests) into a *group* (with a common purpose and a common interest). Evidence of such events having actually taken place was, in the nature of things, not forthcoming; but the experience of the Pilgrim Fathers in Massachusetts in November 1620 provided an instance of a social contract which its subsequent theorists exploited to the full.

The second contract which formed part of the social contract theory was the "pact of submission" or *Herrschaftsvertrag.* This was conceived in several ways, but for the most part it took the form of an agreement between a group of persons, on the one side, and a candidate for sovereignty on the other, to vest government in the hands of the latter on condition that he agree to rule the people according to commonly recognized laws. By the terms of this contract, they become subjects and he becomes monarch (a monarch being defined as a lawful prince); in standard formulations, this "contract of submission" commits the people to allegiance not only to the first prince who is party to the contract, but to all his heirs; and he, and his heirs, are committed in turn always to rule according to the law.

This second element in the idea of a double social contract played an important part in the political disputes of Western Europe for several generations. In kingdoms such as France and England, the actual contract or *Herrschaftsvertrag* was believed by many people—and argued in detail by theorists of constitutional government—to have been enacted at a certain moment in the past between the people and their prince, that is to say, between members of the feudal nobility as representatives of the people and the founding member of the ruling dynasty as representative to his house; and the coronation oaths taken by the kings of France and England signaled their acceptance of the terms of the contract.

Even if these constitutional foundations were "lost in the mists of time" they were widely believed to have existed. Such belief was the basis of the case presented by lawyers to justify the exclusion of James II from the throne of England in 1689 and the execution of Louis XVI in France after his flight to Varennes. We are, of course, dealing here with a highly controversial area; there are, nevertheless, good grounds for thinking that there can be no answer to despotism unless one insists on imposing obligations on a sovereign at the same time as they are imposed on the citizen: this is the most telling argument in favor of the theory of the *Herrschaftsvertrag.* Indeed, whenever constitutional government, whether republican or monarchical, is introduced, a contractual element must be introduced with it. On entering into his functions, a president of the United States is called upon to take an oath, and it became manifestly evident during the later months of Nixon's term of office that the nation will insist on such pledges being kept: they are *not* an empty formula. During the brief reign of Edward VIII in England, it became equally clear that the nation would require its monarch to respect the terms of the "contract of submission" even before the king had actually taken the coronation oath. The obligation to respect the contract is equally laid upon the citizen even though native-born inhabitants of any given state are seldom called upon actually to take an oath of allegiance to their constitution. It is natural for the citizen to feel bound, so to speak, by the unspoken pledge that is implied by the privilege (or right) of citizenship.

Thomas Hobbes is unique among political philosophers in setting out a social contract theory in which the double contract of traditional theory is compressed into one single contract. For Hobbes the social contract—or covenant, as he calls it—serves at the same time to bring isolated, nonsocial men together in a society and to unite them in obedience to a sovereign. The pact of association and the pact of submission are, for Hobbes, one single exercise. There is no contract between the people and the ruler to determine the terms on which the ruler shall rule. There is simply a pact between the individuals to submit, one and all, to the ruler they severally and mutually agree to obey. The compact imposes on the ruler one duty and one duty only: to rule—to hold society together under his single and absolute will and to protect it from its enemies. That, for Hobbes, is what "sovereignty" means: and so long as he does the job, the sovereign is the sovereign and every member of society is obligated by his pledge (the social contract or covenant) to obey him in all things.

One remarkable feature of Hobbes's theory is that he employs the social contract idea to uphold absolutism, while all the other social contract theorists had used it as an instrument against absolutism. Hobbes regarded the Aristotelian notion of man as a social animal as false and the patriarchal theory of the kingdom as a family writ large as ruinously unscientific. He believed that absolute government was the only alternative to anarchy, and he tried to develop a case in defense of it on the basis of what he considered a truly scientific conception of man as an egoistic aggressive individual. The unified social contract, which fused the *Gesellschaftsvertrag* and the *Herrschaftsvertrag* into one single covenant, was Hobbes's answer to the problem.

Locke, as Hobbes's most distinguished successor in the history of political philosophy, restored the social contract to its former place as a keystone in the theoretical edifice of constitutionalism. He did so by refuting Hobbes's notion of a single social contract involving both association and submission, and he restated, with more sophisticated arguments, the case for a double contract. Locke maintained that individuals formed societies by mutual agreement to live together—and that they then had a fairly prolonged experience of living together in these anarchic societies before they introduced the second social contract, which instituted civil government, sovereignty, for Locke, being a *trust* invested in a prince, who was closely circumscribed by the terms of that trust to secure the defense of the lives, liberties, and properties of individuals, rights which the people had already possessed in the state of nature.

Rousseau's use of the social contract argument was, as is argued in the text of this essay, more complicated; and the book which he called *Of the Social Contract* contains only one part of his treatment of the subject. If the concept of a social contract meant something different for Locke from what it meant for Hobbes, Rousseau's use of the concept is different from both.

Critics of the social contract theory, at one time most prominent among champions of absolutist and patriarchal government, began to appear, from the time of Hobbes onward, among theorists whose arguments were more strictly philosophical, no longer ideologically motivated. Montesquieu, Diderot, and Hume, among philosophers of the Enlightenment, revived Aristotle's notion of man as a social animal against the radical individualism of Hobbes, Locke, and Rousseau. In nineteenth-century philosophy the "social" conception of man was dominant in almost all schools of thought. The social contract theory has, however, come into prominence again in twentieth-century theory, adopted, in one form or another, by philosophers as diverse as John Rawls, Jean-Paul Sartre, and Robert Nozick. It is fashionable once more.

It is also subject once again to criticism. Mortimer J. Adler in *Ten Philosophical Mistakes* (New York and London, 1985) names the social contract as "the most important of the modern philosophical mistakes about society." Dr. Adler argues first that all the evidence refutes the notion that human beings once lived in isolation from one another: "this," he writes, "should be manifest to everyone in the light of the incontrovertible fact that the human species could not have survived without the existence of families for the preservation of infants"; secondly Dr. Adler argues that it is a logical error to assume that civil societies may not be *both* natural and contractual in character; the one, he claims, does not preclude the other.

There can be no denying that as arguments based on an appeal to history and to logic, Adler's criticisms are overwhelming. But they apply to some formulations of the social contract more directly than to others. They apply with particular force to the theories of Hobbes and Locke. I think they are less relevant to Rousseau, who, indeed, defended himself against them in advance by saying that he was going to "set aside the facts." What Rousseau offers is a kind of philosophical anthropology concerning a time so remote that historical methods cannot be applied.

What he offers is myth, but a myth of a particular significance, forming part of what Professor Ronald Grimsley has called Rousseau's "religious quest." He challenges Christian orthodoxy, but his work remains profoundly influenced by Calvinist teaching. The *Discourse on the Origin of Inequality,* as the story of man's pre-history and his fall from innocence, is Rousseau's Old Testament; his *Of the Social Contract,* with its vision of man's redemption, is Rousseau's New Testament. Each, to be understood, must be read in relation to the other.

[2]The full title of this work is *Discours sur l'origine et les fondements de l'inégalité parmi les hommes,* and it was first published in 1755 by Marc-Michel Rey, a Genevan bookseller operating in exile in Amsterdam, where the press was free, in marked contrast to the strict censorship which prevailed in Geneva. The manuscript of this discourse has disappeared, but some fragments have been traced. *See* R. A. Leigh, "Manuscrits disparus de Jean-Jacques Rousseau," *Annales* XXXIV (1956–58) and the commentary by Jean Starobinski in *O.C.* III, pp. 1285–1389.

[3]Rousseau's *Essai sur l'origine de langues* was not published in his lifetime, and it is not clear when he wrote it. There are, however, good reasons for believing that he began it in the 1750s, when he was concentrating on the theory of music, and returned to it in the 1760s. *See* Charles Porset, "L'Inquiétante étrangeté de l'Essai," and Robert Wokler, "L'Essai en tant que fragment du *Discours sur l'Inequalite*" in M. Launay, ed., *Rousseau et Voltaire en 1978* (Geneva, 1981), pp. 145–69. An English translation is available in *On the Origin of Language: Two Essays by J.-J. Rousseau and J. G. Herder,* translated by John H. Moran and Alexander Gode (New York, 1966). The best edition of Rousseau's original text is that of Porset, published in Bordeaux and Paris, 1970.

[4]*Du contrat social: Ou, principes du droit politique par J.-J. Rousseau* was first published by Marc-Michel Rey in Amsterdam in 1762. The whereabouts of the manuscript used by Rey are unknown. In the Public and University Library in Geneva there is the manuscript of an earlier draft of the work, and other fragments can be seen in the Municipal Library, Neuchâtel. *See* Albert Schinz, *Jean-Jacques Rousseau et le libraire-imprimeur Marc-Michel Rey* (Geneva, 1916), and *C.C.* III, pp. 49–136.

[5]*O.C.* I, p. 388.

[6]*O.C.* I, p. 389.

[7]*See* Hiram B. Glass, ed., *Forerunners of Darwin* (Baltimore, 1968); Émile Guyénot, *L'évolution de la pensée scientifique, les Sciences de la vie aux XVIIᵉ et XVIIIᵉ siècles* (Paris, 1941).

[8]*See* C. Lévi-Strauss, "J.J. Rousseau, *fondateur* des science de l'homme" in J.-J. *Rousseau* (Neuchâtel, 1962), pp. 240 ff.; Jacques Derrida, *De la grammatologie* (Paris, 1967), pp. 149–202; Michèle Duchet, *Anthropologie et histoire au siècle des lumières* (Paris, 1971); Wokler, "The *Discours sur les sciences et les arts* and its offspring" in *Reappraisals,* pp. 250–78.

[9]*See* Roger Masters, *The Political Philosophy of Rousseau* (Princeton, 1968); Jean Starobinski, *J.-J. Rousseau: la transparence et l'obstacle* (Paris, 1971); John Charvet, *The Social Problem in the Philosophy of Rousseau* (Cambridge, 1974); Raymond Polin, *La politique de la solitude* (Paris, 1971); and the special number of *Daedalus* magazine, vol. 107, no. 3 (Summer, 1978): "Rousseau for Our Time."

[10]The most thoroughgoing supporter of Rousseau's theory about the relationship between man and the orangutan was Lord Monboddo. *See* his *Of the Origin and Progress of Language,* 6 vols. (Edinburgh, 1774–92). *See also* A. O. Lovejoy, "Monboddo and Rousseau" in his *Essays in the History of Ideas* (Baltimore, 1948) and Wokler, "The Ape Debates in Enlightenment Anthropology" in *Studies on Voltaire and the Eighteenth Century,* vol. CXCLL (1980), pp. 1164–75.

[11]*O.C.* III, p. 132; *D.I.,* p. 78.

[12]Thomas Hobbes, *Leviathan* I, 13, § 11 [*GBWW,* Vol. 23, p. 85c].

[13]*O.C.* III, pp. 134–35; *D.I.*, p. 81.

[14]Ibid.

[15]Rousseau drew on the authority of such explorers and travelers as Peter Kolben, Father du Tetre, Olfert Dapper, Jerome Merolla, Andrew Battel, and others whose reports were published in *Samuel Purchas, his Pilgrimages,* four volumes (London, 1625) and A. F. Prévost, *Histoire générale des voyages,* 20 vols. (Paris, 1746–89). These writers were largely responsible for promoting the idea of the "noble savage," which is often associated exclusively with Rousseau's name but which was widely entertained in the eighteenth century. Rousseau never used the expression "noble savage," but his close friend Diderot provided a notably idealized picture of what he called the "noble, sacred character" of the savage in his *Supplément au voyage de Bougainville.* (See *Oeuvres complètes de Diderot,* J. Assézat and M. Tourneux, eds. [Paris, 1875], vol. II, p. 203.)

[16]*O.C.* III, p. 135; *D.I.*, p. 82.

[17]A veneration for the republics of antiquity was as common among the philosophers of the Enlightenment as it was among those of the Renaissance. On Rousseau's particular attachment to Sparta, *see* Denise Leduc-Fayette, *J.-J. Rousseau et le mythe de l'Antiquité* (Paris, 1974). The more disagreeable features of the Spartan regime—its oppression of subject peoples, for example, and the systematic extermination of helots—to which modern historians draw our attention, were unknown to Rousseau, who as a self-educated man had, in any case, a very imperfect knowledge of ancient history, even by eighteenth-century standards.

[18]*See* Norman Hampson, *The Enlightenment* (New York and Harmondsworth, 1968), pp. 73–96.

[19]*O.C.* III, p. 141; *D.I.*, p. 87.

[20]*O.C.* III, p. 161; *D.I.*, p. 106.

[21]Most philosophers of the French Enlightenment, from Voltaire onward, were eager adherents of the doctrine that man was destined to progress from a dark past toward a golden future, a progress which had only been hindered by the superstitions of the Middle Ages. *See* Robert Nisbet, *History of the Idea of Progress* (New York, 1980).

[22]*O.C.* III, p. 214; *D.I.*, p. 161.

[23]*O.C.* III, p. 147; *D.I.*, p. 93.

[24]Rousseau refers here to Locke's *Two Treatises of Government,* bk. III, chap. vii [*GBWW*, Vol. 35, p. 42b, f.]. He read the book in David Mazel's French translation, published in Amsterdam in 1691 and again in Geneva in 1724 as *Du Gouvernement civil.* Rousseau probably derived a more extensive knowledge of Locke's philosophy from his friend the Abbé de Condillac, who was Locke's chief French disciple. (See *J.J.,* pp. 218–19.)

[25]*O.C.* III, p. 217; *D.I.*, p. 165.

[26]*O.C.* III, p. 216; *D.I.*, p. 163.

[27]"The oldest of all societies, and the only natural one, is that of the family" (*O.C.* III, p. 325; *S.C.*, p. 50).

[28]*O.C.* III, p. 151; *D.I.*, p. 96.

[29]*O.C.* III, p. 154; *D.I.*, p. 99. In this passage Rousseau seeks to refute an assertion he ascribes to Hobbes that man is naturally wicked. He is presumably thinking here of *De Cive,* chap. X, sec. 1, where Hobbes argues that in the state of nature brigandage is continual, passions reign, and barbarism, ignorance, and brutality deprive men of the sweetness of life. Rousseau could have read *De Cive* in the French translation of Samuel Sorbière, first published in 1649 in Amsterdam. But he seems to have owed much of his (admittedly limited) knowledge of Hobbes's philosophy to conversation with Diderot, who read English. *See* Wokler in *Studies on Voltaire and the Eighteenth Century,* CXXXII (1975), pp. 52–112; and Arthur Wilson, *Diderot,* 2 vols. (New York, 1957–72).

[30]*O.C.* III, p. 154; *D.I.*, p. 99.

[31]*O.C.* III, pp. 155–56; *D.I.*, p. 101.

[32]*O.C.* III, p. 156; *D.I.*, p. 101. In his *Confessions* (*O.C.* I, p. 389) he says, in a footnote, that he took from Diderot this remark about the philosopher putting his hands over his ears to harden his heart against the cries of a man being murdered. But Rousseau himself had written something very similar several years earlier in the preface to his play *Narcisse:* "The taste for philosophy slackens all bonds of sympathy and goodwill which join a man to society." (*O.C.* II, p. 967) When Rousseau wrote the *Discourse on Inequality* in 1754 he was a close friend of Diderot and had been since he had made his acquaintance as a

fellow aspirant to literary fame in Paris more than ten years earlier. But soon after the publication of the *Discourse on Inequality* the friendship cooled and in time turned to bitter hostility. At one stage, Rousseau accused Diderot of giving him bad advice when he was preparing the *Discourse;* later he accused him of having actually inserted bits of text. *See* Jean Morel, "Recherches sur les sources du *Discours de l'Inégalité*" in *Annales,* V (1909), pp. 124–98; and S. R. Havens, "Diderot, Rousseau and the *Discours sur l'inégalité*" in *Diderot Studies,* III (Geneva, 1961), pp. 155–213.

[33]*O.C.* III, p. 167; *D.I.,* p. 112.

[34]Ibid.

[35]On Rousseau's vision of an earthly paradise *see* Ronald Grimsley, *Rousseau and the Religious Quest* (Oxford, 1968), pp. 87–107.

[36]*O.C.* III, p. 168; *D.I.,* p. 112.

[37]*O.C.* III, p. 170; *D.I.,* p. 115.

[38]*O.C.* III, p. 171; *D.I.,* p. 115.

[39]*Essai sur l'origine des langues,* Charles Porset, ed. (Bordeaux and Paris, 1970), p. 113. See also Polin, *La politique de la solitude,* pp. 1–34.

[40]*O.C.* III, p. 168; *D.I.,* p. 113.

[41]*O.C.* III, p. 169; *D.I.,* p. 114.

[42]Ibid.

[43]*O.C.* III, p. 170; *D.I.,* p. 114.

[44]*O.C.* III, p. 219; *D.I.,* p. 167.

[45]*See* Joel Schwartz, *The Sexual Politics of Jean-Jacques Rousseau* (Chicago and London, 1984), pp. 10–40.

[46]*O.C.* III, p. 169; *D.I.,* p. 114.

[47]Schwartz, *op. cit.,* p. 27.

[48]*O.C.* III, p. 158; *D.I.,* p. 103.

[49]*O.C.* III, p. 171; *D.I.,* p. 116.

[50]Ibid.

[51]*O.C.* III, p. 174; *D.I.,* p. 118.

[52]*O.C.* III, p. 176; *D.I.,* p. 120.

[53]Ibid.

[54]On the temporal aspects of Rousseau's evolutionary theory *see* William Pickles, "The Notion of Time in Rousseau's Political Thought" in M. Cranston and R. S. Peters, eds., *Hobbes and Rousseau* (New York, 1972), pp. 366–400.

[55]*O.C.* III, p. 177; *D.I.,* p. 121.

[56]Ibid.

[57]*O.C.* III, p. 164; *D.I.,* p. 109.

[58]For the argument that Rousseau is a forerunner of Marx, *see* Galvano della Volpe, *Rousseau and Marx,* trans. John Fraser (London, 1978). Another commentator who sees Rousseau as a man of the left is Michel Launay, *Jean-Jacques Rousseau, écrivain politique* (Cannes, 1971). For commentaries which draw attention to Rousseau's conservatism *see* C. E. Vaughan, ed., *The Political Writings of Jean Jacques Rousseau,* vol. I (Cambridge, 1915); Starobinski's notes in *O.C.* III, pp. 1285–1389; and the contributions of Bertrand de Jouvenel, John McManners, and William Pickles to Cranston and Peters, eds., *Hobbes and Rousseau* (New York, 1972).

[59]*O.C.* III, p. 203; *D.I.,* p. 148.

[60]Ibid.

[61]*O.C.* III, p. 203; *D.I.,* p. 149.

[62]*O.C.* III, p. 202; *D.I.,* p. 147.

[63]*O.C.* III, pp. 188–89; *D.I.,* pp. 132–33.

[64]*O.C.* III, p. 193; *D.I.,* p. 136.

[65]*Discours sur cette question . . . : si le rétablissement des Sciences et des Arts a contribué à épurer les moeurs* (*O.C.* III, pp. 1–96, with notes by François Bouchardy, pp. 1237–82). For the circumstances in which Rousseau wrote this prize-winning essay see *J.J.,* pp. 230–70. The best translation is by Roger and Judith Masters in *J.J. Rousseau: First and Second Discourses* (New York, 1964).

[66]Voltaire to Rousseau, 30 August 1755 (*O.C.* III, pp. 1379–81).

[67]*O.C.* III, p. 111; *D.I.,* p. 57.

[68]Ibid.

[69]In *Of the Social Contract* Rousseau speaks of Calvin as a lawgiver like Lycurgus, but in a fragmentary *History of Geneva* which he wrote soon afterward, he speaks of Geneva having a constitution whose origin was "lost in the night of time" and he names an earlier Genevan "lawgiver" than Calvin, one Bishop Adémarus Fabri, who in 1387 gave the city "the charter of its rights and liberties" (Michel Launay, ed., *Oeuvres complètes de Rousseau* [Paris, 1971], vol. III, p. 384).

[70]See *J.J.*, pp. 21–29.

[71]*C.C.* V, p. 242.

[72]*O.C.* I, p. 9.

[73]*O.C.* III, p. 810.

[74]Hobbes, *Leviathan,* chap. xxi [*GBWW,* Vol. 23, p. 112d].

[75]Ibid, chap. xxi [*GBWW,* Vol. 23, p. 116a].

[76]*O.C.* III, p. 406; *S.C.,* p. 114.

[77]*O.C.* III, p. 114; *D.I.,* p. 60.

[78]Ibid.

[79]*O.C.* III, p. 406; *S.C.,* p. 115.

[80]Ibid.

[81]*O.C.* III, p. 421; *S.C.,* p. 131.

[82]For up-to-date accounts of Genevan history *see* Louis Binz, *Brève histoire de Genève* (Geneva, 1981); R. Guerdan, *Histoire de Genève* (Paris, 1981); and the collective work, *Histoire de Genève des origines à 1798,* published by the Société d'histoire et d'archéologie de Genève (1951).

[83]*Lettre à Monsieur d'Alembert,* ed. M. Fuchs (Lille, 1948), pp. 181–82; *J.J.,* p. 26.

[84]*O.C.* III, p. 809.

[85]*C.C.* V, p. 242.

[86]*O.C.* III, p. 430; *S.C.,* p. 141.

[87]*O.C.* III, p. 119; *D.I.,* p. 65.

[88]Schwartz, *op. cit.,* pp. 10–65.

[89]*J.J.,* pp. 205–7.

[90]*Émile,* trans. A. Bloom (New York, 1979), p. 358.

[91]*O.C.* III, p. 351; *S.C.,* p. 49.

[92]*O.C.* III, p. 364; *S.C.,* p. 65.

[93]*O.C.* III, p. 365; *S.C.,* p. 65.

[94]*O.C.* III, p. 360; *S.C.,* p. 60.

[95]*O.C.* III, p. 364; *S.C.,* p. 64.

[96]*O.C.* III, p. 440; *S.C.,* p. 153.

[97]*Émile* (Paris, 1924) p. 270.

[98]*O.C.* III, p. 371; *S.C.,* p. 72. Rousseau goes on to say: "We always want what is advantageous, but we do not always discern it."

[99]*O.C.* III, p. 381; *S.C.,* p. 84.

[100]*See* note 69 above.

[101]*See* B. Baczko, "*Moïse, législateur*" in *Reappraisals,* pp. 111–31.

[102]The quotation comes from Machiavelli's *Discorsi,* bk. 1, chap. 11 § 4.

[103]*O.C.* III, p. 384; *S.C.,* p. 87.

[104]*Lettre à Monsieur d'Alembert* (Amsterdam, 1758), p. 143.

[105]Ibid.

[106]*O.C.* III, p. 466; *S.C.,* pp. 183–84.

[107]*O.C.* III, p. 467; *S.C.,* p. 184.

[108]*See* Constant, *Cours de politique constitutionelle,* ed. E. Laboulaye, two volumes (Paris, 1872).

[109]*See* Stephen Holmes, *Benjamin Constant and the Making of Modern Liberalism* (New Haven, 1984), pp. 28–103.

[110]Constant, *op. cit.,* vol. II, p. 554.

[111]Ibid., p. 541.

[112]Ibid., p. 556.

[113]Ibid., p. 558.

The Christian Skepticism of Montaigne

Otto Bird

Born and raised in Ann Arbor, Michigan, Otto Bird attended the university there, graduating in 1935 with honors in English. He added a master's degree in comparative literature the following year. He took his doctorate in philosophy and literature at the University of Toronto in 1939.

From 1947 to 1950 he served as associate editor of the *Syntopicon,* for *Great Books of the Western World,* working with Mortimer Adler. In the latter year he joined the faculty at the University of Notre Dame, where he was director of the General Program of Liberal Studies until 1963. He was executive editor of *The Great Ideas Today* from 1964 to 1970, when he was appointed university professor of arts and letters at Notre Dame, from which he retired in 1977.

He has written four books, *The Canzoné d'Amore of Guido Cavalcanti with the Commentary of Dino del Garbo* (1942), *Syllogistic Logic and Its Extensions* (1964), *The Idea of Justice* (1967), and *Cultures in Conflict* (1976), besides articles on the history and theory of the liberal arts. In addition, he was a major contributor to the *Propædia,* or Outline of Knowledge, of the current (fifteenth) edition of the *Encyclopædia Britannica.*

Mr. Bird now spends much of the year in Shoals, Indiana, where he has built a house and grows grapes for making wine. He continues to be active in editorial projects of Encyclopædia Britannica, Inc., and remains consulting editor of *The Great Ideas Today.* He has contributed to many of our volumes. His essay on *Don Quixote* appeared last year.

One of the properties that makes a book great is its power to transcend the age in which it was written and to speak to readers living in other times and places, to catch and hold their interest, and to enlighten their minds. Unlike many a best-seller, a great book remains new. Nevertheless, any book is a product of its time and cannot help being influenced to some extent by the intellectual currents that were running during the time it was written. Hence new and deeper insights into even what might be called its perennial value can often be gained by reading the book in light of the intellectual context in which it was written. That this is so becomes especially evident from two recent studies devoted to the *Essays* of Michel de Montaigne.

One of these, the work of the professor of French language and literature at University College, London, M. A. Screech, entitled *Montaigne & Melancholy*, investigates the Renaissance theory of human temperament for the light that it can throw upon "the wisdom of the *Essays*," which is the subtitle of the book. The other is a book by Antoine Compagnon, a professor at the University of Paris, entitled *Nous, Michel de Montaigne* (i.e., *We, Michel de Montaigne*), which places the *Essays* within the context of philosophical nominalism, a scholastic doctrine that remained one of the leading schools in the sixteenth century.

The two books, although disparate in subject, share a common concern to show, if not the sources, at least the influences that contributed to Montaigne's rejection of rationalism with its conviction that human reason can discover and reveal all the truth about reality. In fact, Screech acknowledges that Compagnon's work "overlaps some of the preoccupations" of his own book. But besides the interest and value inherent in the subjects of their special study, the investigations of these two writers can also contribute greatly to the understanding of the vexed question concerning the relation of Montaigne's skepticism to the Catholic Christian faith that he professed, especially as it is given expression in his longest essay, the "Apology for Raimond de Sebonde." This question is a vexed one inasmuch as his readers have found him at one extreme a staunch and sincere apologist for the religion he professed and at the other a scoffer and a thoroughgoing skeptic in religion as well as in philosophy, and, if Catholic at all, certainly not a Christian. Although it is not a primary purpose of either writer, their investigations go a long way to show how his skepticism can both accompany and also serve as a support for the Christian religion.

Montaigne and melancholy

An easy and quick way to see how knowledge of the theory of melancholy can aid the understanding of Montaigne is to see what light it can throw upon the reading of a particular text. For that purpose I propose to consider the final pages of the essay with which Montaigne concludes his whole book, and which for that very reason is an important text.

In this text Montaigne extols the union of soul and body in man by claiming that the body has its rights every bit as much as the soul and condemning those who would attempt to divorce soul from body as being of little worth. Instead, he writes, we should confirm that union "by mutual offices; let the mind [*esprit*] rouse and quicken the heaviness of the body, and the body stay and fix the levity of the soul [*esprit*]" (III.13; *GBWW*, Vol. 25, p. 542b). He even takes to task his beloved Socrates, whom he calls his master, for preferring the pleasures of the mind over those of the body as having greater dignity. His intention is that "in this present that God has made us, there is nothing unworthy [*indigne*] our care; we stand accountable, even to a hair; and 'tis no slight commission to man, to conduct man according to his condition; 'tis express, plain, and the principal injunction of all, and the Creator has seriously and strictly enjoined it" (ibid.).

Montaigne has harsh criticism for any effort to separate soul from body, even though the results be "the ecstasies [*ravissements*] of Archimedes" that led to his great discoveries. He finds such "transcendental humours" frightening and declares that "nothing is hard for me to digest in the life of Socrates but his ecstasies and communication with demons." In the efforts of those who "would put themselves out of themselves," he sees only "folly." The consequence is that "instead of transforming themselves into angels, they transform themselves into beasts; instead of elevating, they lay themselves lower" (III.13, 542c–d).

In this entire text there is not a single mention of "melancholy." Yet Screech shows convincingly that Montaigne's argument draws heavily upon the Renaissance theory of melancholy. Knowledge of this theory was widespread, manifesting itself both in Dürer's engraving of *Melancholia* and in Robert Burton's *Anatomy of Melancholy*, the longest work in English on the subject (although posterior to Montaigne's work). Montaigne could have been acquainted with the doctrine from the works of such Renaissance writers as Ficino and Melanchthon, as well as from its ultimate source in a work of Aristotle.

This is the work entitled *Problems*, and although no longer accepted as genuine, it was considered such in classical times as well as in the Renaissance.* The work is divided into thirty-eight short books dealing

---

*A translation of the appropriate passages from a Latin version such as Montaigne may have read is provided in an appendix to the present essay.

Michel de Montaigne

with a number of more or less related questions. Book XXX is devoted to "problems connected with prudence, intelligence, and wisdom." Its first chapter raises the question, "Why is it that we find that men who excelled by genius in philosophical studies, in administering the republic, in composing songs, or in the arts were all melancholic?" and the few pages dealing with this problem, according to Screech, "have influenced the interpretation of human genius as much as anything ever written." Among geniuses who were of melancholic temperament Aristotle names Hercules and other ancient heroes, Empedocles, Socrates, Plato, numerous other well-known men, and "also most of the poets." But besides attributing genius to a preponderance of black bile (i.e., *melancholia*), Aristotle also claimed that it could result in madness and other diseases, such as epilepsy, which puts its subjects out of their minds. Hence "melancholy" serves to name not only a certain type of character but also a disease.

The theory is based on the ancient medical doctrine of the four humors or fluids identified in the body as phlegm, bile (or *choler*), blood (*sanguis*), and black bile (*melancholia* in Greek, *atra bilis* in Latin). The temperament or mixture of these four humors was supposed to determine a person's character, the excess of one over the others making one phlegmatic, choleric, sanguine, or melancholic; and although such bodily fluids are no longer accepted as causes, the names are still used to denote certain definite traits of character.

That Montaigne knew of the theory is evident from his use of it in his writings. The inception of the *Essays* he attributes to a "melancholic humour" that resulted in his "foolish attempt," but claims that such was "a humour very much an enemy to my natural complexion, engendered by the pensiveness of the solitude into which for some years past I have retired myself, that first put into my head this idle fancy [*resverie*] of writing" (II.8, 183c). *Resverie* is misleadingly translated here as merely "fancy," for, as Screech observes, in the French of the time "it means not vague dreaming but mad frenzy." In short, Montaigne had some fear that his enterprise may by taken by others, if not by himself, as a work of madness.

He knew well that Aristotle had associated madness with melancholy and cites him to that effect in the essay on drunkenness, which Aristotle had described as an instance of being "out of oneself."

> Aristotle says that no excellent soul is exempt from a mixture of madness
> [*folie*]; and he has reason to call all transports [*eslancement*], how
> commendable soever, that surpass our own judgment and understanding,
> madness; forasmuch as wisdom is a regular government of the soul,
> which is carried on with measure and proportion, and for which she is to
> herself responsible. (II.2, 166d)

Montaigne describes his own as a "complexion betwixt jovial and melancholic, moderately sanguine and hot" (II.17, 312a), and for this reason he could claim that the melancholic temperament as such was foreign to him. And such a mixture as his which combined the melancholic with the sanguine, as Screech notes, was supposed to avoid madness while still making for genius. By temperament then Montaigne is saying that he is averse not only to madness and drunkenness but also to any "transcendental humour" that would take one out of oneself, as though separating soul from body.

Yet in the final text that concludes the *Essays* there is a passage that admits one kind of ecstasy as favorable, although only as a privileged case. Because of its importance for the interpretation of Montaigne's attitude toward religion it deserves quoting in full:

> I do not here speak of, nor mix with the rabble of us ordinary men, and
> the vanity of the thoughts and desires that divert us, those venerable
> souls, elevated by the ardour of devotion and religion, to a constant and
> conscientious meditation of divine things, who, by the energy of vivid

Knowledge of the Renaissance theory of melancholy was widespread, as evidenced both by Dürer's engraving *Melancholia*, shown here, and by Robert Burton's treatise *Anatomy of Melancholy*.

and vehement hope, prepossessing the use of the eternal nourishment, the final aim and last step of Christian desires, the sole, constant, and incorruptible pleasure, disdain to apply themselves to our necessitous, fluid, and ambiguous conveniences, and easily resign to the body the care and use of sensual and temporal pasture: 'tis a privileged study. Between ourselves [*entre nous*], I have ever observed supercelestial opinions and subterranean manners to be of singular accord. (III.13, 542c)

This "privileged study" of separating soul from body is allowed to the venerable souls of the saintly Christian ascetics who, fed by the eternal nourishment of divine grace, are lifted above themselves. However, the interpretation of Montaigne's own attitude toward this exceptional case depends, as Screech well points out, on the way the *entre nous* at the beginning of the final sentence is understood. Taken as a snide "between you and me," it has been interpreted, Screech writes, "as though it were a bitter gibe, a sneer, demolishing what has just been said, aimed at Christians—especially the clergy—for using sublime spirituality as a cloak for lechery." But such a reading, he goes on to claim, "does unnecessary violence to the coherence of Montaigne's argument. It is read into his text, not found in it." In short, such an interpretation amounts to eisegesis, not exegesis. Instead of a sneer, the words are setting us and most of mankind ("the rabble of us ordinary men") off and apart from the few exceptional and privileged souls. Hence the phrase *entre nous* is better and more accurately translated, Screech declares, as "among people like you, me, or, say, Archimedes."

Screech develops this interpretation at some length, giving careful and detailed attention to Montaigne's language—much more attention than can be summarized here. However, perhaps the most compelling confirmation of this interpretation is contained in an earlier essay of Montaigne, in which he again makes an exception of a privileged case. It occurs in the text that concludes the long "Apology for Raimond de Sebonde." After quoting the Stoic philosopher Seneca to the effect that man is a vile and abject thing "if he do not raise himself above humanity," Montaigne comments:

'Tis a good word, and a profitable desire, but withal absurd; for to make the handful bigger than the hand, and the armful larger than the arm, and to hope to stride further than our legs can reach, is impossible and monstrous; or that man should rise above himself and humanity: for he cannot see but with his eyes, nor seize but with his power. He shall rise . . . by abandoning and renouncing his own proper means, and by suffering himself to be raised and elevated by means purely celestial. It belongs to our Christian faith, and not to his stoical virtue, to pretend to that divine and miraculous metamorphosis. (II.12, 294a–b)

This is another important text for understanding Montaigne's attitude toward religion and, for this reason, one that there will be occasion to consider again. Here it suffices to note that it confirms his suspicions, voiced in the previous text, of any pretense that man by his own power can transcend his natural condition of soul-in-body while on this earth—short, that is, of the exceptional and extraordinary help of divine grace. This same distrust, supported by still other reasons, shows up again when Montaigne is read in the light of the influence of nominalism upon his writing—the pioneer investigation of which has been done by Professor Antoine Compagnon.

Montaigne and nominalism

Montaigne is neither a technical nor a school philosopher. He claims to know nothing of theology (II.12, 209a), not to understand "scholastic lessons" (III.13, 523a), and to prefer a natural to "an artificial and scholastic way" (III.8, 448b). Yet from such protestations as these it would be mistaken to think that he was entirely ignorant of the scholastic theology and philosophy that still reigned in the universities of his day. We know from his own words that, at his father's instigation, he translated from Latin into French the *Natural Theology* of Raimond de Sebonde, which is a thousand-page book of scholastic theology and, in the opinion of a learned acquaintance of his, is "some abstract [*quinte essence*—fifth essence] drawn from Saint Thomas Aquinas" (II.12, 209a). Furthermore, his tutors at the College of Guienne were Nicholas Grouchy, the author of a work on dialectic, and William Guerente, who wrote a commentary upon Aristotle (I.25 [26], 78b).* Yet it remains a fact that Montaigne almost never refers to the scholastic writers by name, only to Saint Thomas Aquinas twice, and not at all to William of Ockham, the greatest proponent if not the founder of scholastic nominalism. How then can it be claimed that nominalism is an important influence in the *Essays*? The investigations of Compagnon have demonstrated how very profitable it is to read Montaigne in the context of the philosophical controversies of his time, where the position taken by Ockham was still maintained. But first a word is in order with regard to the basic division that separated all the main positions that were contended for.

---

*Editions of the *Essays* based upon the posthumous publication of 1595 differ from those based on the editions overseen by Montaigne himself in the numbering of the chapters between I.14 and I.40. The 1595 edition, which is cited here, is one number shorter than that found in the earlier editions as a result of transferring the 14th to the 40th place. Thus I.14 here appears as I.15 in the other. But this holds true only through I.40; thereafter the chapter enumeration is the same for both. Where there is a difference I will provide references to both, as above.

The customary, and perhaps also the simplest, way of describing the controversy is by identifying as the crucial question that of the nature and existence of the universal, that is to say of the referent of a general term such as "man." At one extreme is the position known as realism, which maintains that the universal has a real existence outside the mind. At the other extreme is the position that denies that the universal has any existence whatsoever outside the mind; this is called nominalism, for holding that the universal is nothing but a name used for referring to individuals. In between these two is the position of conceptualism, which admits that the universal exists as such only as a concept in the mind, yet maintains that it also has a basis in reality outside the mind.

Such a way of identifying the controversy is not wrong as long as it is realized that it is by no means limited to a question of logic and language; as will be seen, it also has major implications for metaphysics and theology, and especially for the way the relation between faith and reason is understood. In any case, once the controversy is taken into account, then, as Compagnon observes, the tension between nominalism and realism can be found appearing throughout the *Essays*.

Thus, for a precise statement of the nominalist position there is, for example, the beginning of the chapter on glory, in which Montaigne declares:

> There is the name and the thing: the name is a voice which denotes [*remerque*] and signifies the thing; the name is no part of the thing, nor of the substance; 'tis a foreign piece joined to the thing, and outside it. (II.16, 300c)

To call it a voice recalls the famous nominalist description of the universal as only a *flatus vocis,* a breathed voice. Thus the name "man," for example, does not name the very substance that makes a man to be man and that all humans share in common. It is only a mark or label put upon individuals from the outside.

On the other hand, Montaigne can also identify himself with the position of realism, as when he writes:

> Every man carries the entire form of the human condition. Authors communicate themselves to the people by some especial and extrinsic [*particuliere et estrangere*] mark; I, the first of any, by my universal being; as Michel de Montaigne. (III.2, 389a)*

But if the entire form of man can be found in every individual man, and if in writing about himself he is presenting a universal being, then

---

*Following Montaigne's own recommendation, I leave proper names in their original and do not translate them: thus "Michel," not "Michael" (I.46, 134d).

he has adopted the position of the realists that there is something really one and the same in the many.

This apparent paradox is the problem that Compagnon poses and resolves in his book, and it is interesting, indeed, fascinating to follow his complex and subtle argument. For the general reader the results he has achieved can greatly aid the reading of Montaigne. As an illustration I propose to consider in some detail the interpretation of Chapter 46 of Book I.

Of names

The chapter begins with an opening statement in which Montaigne declares that he intends to make in his consideration of names "a hodge-podge [*galimafrée*] of divers articles" in the same way that a great variety of greens are mixed together and enveloped under the one name of salad (I.46, 133d). In short, he is going to make a classification such as that in which the name "salad" serves as a genus of which the herbs entering into it serve as so many distinct species.

He then proceeds to develop his thesis more or less according to the model of a scholastic disputation. First, he lists a series of arguments or doubts, articulating them by introducing each one after the first by an "item" (although some translations omit one or more of the six that Montaigne wrote). He then closes the first part of the essay with a long paragraph, beginning with the words, "to conclude" (134a–d).

The second part turns from names to a consideration of glory or renown, a move more clearly appropriate in French, as from *nom* to *renom*. This part is again carefully divided into two parts, signaled by the words *firstly* and *secondly* (again, unfortunately omitted in some translations) (135c–d). The conclusion to the whole essay is a Latin quotation from the Roman satirist Juvenal, introduced by the word *however* (*toutesfois*) (136b).

Montaigne is sometimes accused of showing little respect for logic or order in writing his *Essays*. Such, however, is certainly not the case in this essay. Furthermore, the argument within it is tight as well as subtle and complex. To the unraveling of it Compagnon devotes at least 70 of his book's 230 pages—certainly far more than can be dealt with here at all adequately. We will have to limit ourselves to touching only the high spots, and especially those that reveal Montaigne's nominalism, although no attempt will be made to follow the analysis into the main sources of the doctrine in the logic of Ockham, as Compagnon does.

In his consideration of names Montaigne takes the proper name as a paradigm. By doing so, he can more readily, even blatantly, expose and ridicule the idea that the universal has any basis in reality. For in the first arguments he at once shows that even a proper name can readily become a common name and apply not just to one but to many individuals, thereby raising the question regarding what that common element might be, that one-in-many.

Thus he notes first that "every nation has certain names, that . . . are taken in no good sense" (*en mauvaise part,* i.e., ill-repute), such as in the France of his time the names Jehan, Guillaume, Benoit (I.46, 133d–34a). Although he claims not to know why, he thus suggests that the common element underlying the many Frenchmen named Benoit is some ill-repute.

The second argument, introduced by the first "item," observes that "in the genealogy of princes, also, there seem to be certain names fatally affected, as the Ptolemies of Egypt, the Henrys in England, the Charleses in France," etc., thereby implying that the shared common-ness is some fatal affect (134a).

The next two arguments are more humorous in citing cases of division based upon language alone. One tells of the division of the nobility that was made at a great feast at which those attending were assigned to troops according to the resemblance (*ressemblance*) of their names, with the result, for instance, that one hundred and ten knights were seated at the same table simply because they all bore the name "Guillaume" (134a). Another argument, the most "frivolous," relates the anecdote of the emperor who distributed the several courses of his meals according to the first letter of the names of the food to be eaten "so that those that began with B, were served up together, as brawn, beef, bream, bustards, beccaficos; and so of the others" (134b). As Compagnon remarks, these two stories are parodies of classification and reduce to ridicule the notion that such an undertaking is based on anything other than caprice, especially in this last case, where the only resemblance is the initial letter of the name. In short, a class is a nominal entity only, not a real or natural one.

Having considered how one name can apply to many individuals, Montaigne next moves to show how one individual can have many names and, in doing so, deals with the topic of the change of names. But first he draws a distinction that still further detracts from the value of the name by reducing it to merely a matter of sound: "There is a saying," he writes, "that it is a good thing to have a good name [*bon nom*], that is to say, credit and a good repute: but, besides this, it is really convenient to have a well-sounding name [*nom beau*], such as is easy of pronunciation and easy to be remembered" (134b).

As examples of the "vocal and auricular" value of a name, he notes that masters and kings more frequently call upon those whose names are easy to pronounce and remember, and he cites the case of Henry II, who called one of the maids of honor by the name of her race, since her own family name was so difficult, which provides a case of change of name. Two further anecdotes emphasize that merely the sound is sometimes sufficient to produce a conversion: how the sound of the name "Marie" converted a young man from his dissolute ways; and how Pythagoras could alter the intentions of a drunken party by having the singer change from wanton airs to a "solemn, grave, and spondaic music" (134b–c).

The next example of name-changing is more extensive in that it concerns not just individuals but whole communities. It involves the change in name preferences wrought by the Reformation in his own time. Thus Montaigne writes, certainly not without irony, that this change "not only combatted errors and vices, and filled the world with devotion, humility, obedience, [and] peace," but it has also quarreled with the "ancient baptismal names of Charles, Louis, Francis, to fill the world with Methuselahs, Ezekiels, and Malachis, names of a more spiritual sound [*sentans de la foy*]"—redolent of the faith (134c). From this it would appear that one is to combat errors and vices by combating names, which in effect amounts to reducing the religious wars to wars about words. That such a reading is not unlikely is supported, as Compagnon points out, by Montaigne's claim made in the "Apology" that "Grammar is that which creates most disturbance in the world. . . . How many quarrels, and those of how great importance, has the doubt of the meaning of this syllable *Hoc* created in the world?" where he is referring to the controversy over the interpretation of the first word in the consecration of the host in the Latin Mass (II.12, 253d).

With his observation concerning the effect of the Reform Montaigne has introduced the question of the import of time on the changing of names, as he makes explicit in the next anecdote: that of a neighbor of his, "a great admirer of antiquity," who loved to "dwell upon the lofty [*fierté*—fierceness] and magnificent sound of the gentlemen's names of those days, Don Grumedan, Quedregan, Agesilan, which but to hear named he conceived to denote other kind of men than Pierre, Guillot, and Michel," where the last three are those of his father, his race, and his own baptismal name (134d).

Montaigne began his discussion by noting the variation of names in space—"each nation has certain names"—and he now emphasizes their variation through time. But the change of things through space and time constitutes, according to Compagnon, "the two main arguments of nominalism against the reality of abstractions" and against the possibility of "a nontemporal and universal truth." The name may lack any universal truth, but it can have an individual and historical truth. For this reason Montaigne next praises Amyot, the French translator of Plutarch, for retaining the Latin names of persons mentioned in an oration of his and not translating them into another language than their original, thereby "metamorphosing names" until "we know not where we are" (134d). It is a historical fact, for example, that Montaigne's first name was Michel, and not Michael; and as he declared at length in his final essay, on experience, he preferred facts to abstractions, a trait again that is characteristic of nominalist thinkers.

However, there remains a still greater cause of the instability of names than any of those mentioned so far. That is the practice "of very ill consequence . . . to call everyone by the name of his manor or seigneury" (134d). This practice is found particularly among royal families but also holds for Montaigne himself. For his surname derives from the estate he owned, which his great-grandfather, Ramon Eyquem, had bought in 1477 from another family, and which eventually passed to still another family on the death of the essayist, since he died without male heirs. " 'Tis the thing in the world," he writes, "that most prejudices and confounds families and descents," and that has as a consequence that "the original of the family is totally lost" (134d–35a).

Although this complaint does confirm the variability and instability of names, it also raises a doubt about the thesis that in reality outside the mind there is no such thing as a one-in-many. For what is the family line that Montaigne is praising but something that somehow remains one in all members of the family; and the question of paternity, as Compagnon remarks, posed a thorny problem for nominalism.

Hence, Montaigne does not hesitate to imply that there is such a thing as a true name. Indeed, he attacks as a "falsification" the change of surnames and the making of new genealogies among royalty and the nobility (135a). Then in an anecdote that mocks the ambition to link one's genealogy with a royal line in pride of place he reports the person making the criticism as declaring: "Let us, in God's name, satisfy ourselves with what our fathers were contented with, with what we are," thereby reaffirming the continuity and so the unity of the paternal line (135b).

The final paragraph of this first part of the essay notes that coats of arms "have no more security than surnames," since both pass with the transfer of property, and the essayist's arms like those of his surname lack any "privilege to continue particularly" in his paternal line. In this, as in all the other cases cited since the start of his discussion, he finds "there is nothing wherein there is more change and confusion" (135c).

Summarizing Montaigne's accomplishment in this first part of the essay, Compagnon explains that in effect the essayist has been investigating what it is that warrants the attribution of a name to an individual. Logically, for a real and true relation between the two the name should be coextensive and essential. However, as Montaigne has shown, "the name does not have the same extension as the individual, since one sole name can belong to several subjects; it is not essential, since several names can have but one subject, and when the name changes . . . the new name is no more exact than the old." Since names have here

The Montaigne surname was derived from this château near Bordeaux, in France. *"A still greater cause of the instability of names . . . is the practice 'of very ill consequence . . . to call everyone by the name of his manor or seigneury.'"*

served as labels for classes or universals, his destructive criticism of nomenclature amounts to a denial of their reality by the disclosure that "there is nothing wherein there is more change and confusion."

From name to renown

Montaigne opens the second part of the essay by declaring that his consideration of names "leads [him], perforce, into another subject," that namely of examining "upon what foundation we erect this glory and reputation for which the world is turned topsy-turvy: wherein do we place this renown [*renommée*] that we hunt after with so much pains?" (135c).

The connection between the two parts is a tight one and justifies his saying that he is led "perforce." In making earlier the distinction between a *bon nom* and a *nom beau,* he had already noted the close relation between name and reputation, between *nom* and *renom*. But it is only at this place in the text that he directly addresses the question thus raised. The connection becomes still tighter when he identifies the foundation of glory, reputation, and renown: "It is, in the end, Pierre or Guillaume that carries it, takes it into his possession, and whom it only concerns. . . . And this Pierre or Guillaume, what is it but a sound when all is done?" (135c). The full force of that claim lies in this final phrase, which reads in the original "qu'est-ce, qu'une voix pour tous potages," and, as Compagnon notes, if the phrase is taken literally as "a *voix* for any soup or comestible," rather than idiomatically for "in all" or "when all is done," a tie is made with the very opening reference to herbs and salads. But it is *voix,* that is, voice or sound, that is the crucial word, for this at once makes it unmistakeably clear that it is the name "Pierre" or "Guillaume," and not the individuals so named, that Montaigne is identifying as the foundation of renown: and it also recalls the nominalist definition of the universal as a *flatus vocis,* as has already been noted.

The logic joining the two parts of this essay can now be simply stated. The first part considers the name as attribute, i.e., the attribution of names to individuals. The second concerns the name as subject, i.e., the name identified as the foundation of renown, since it is the name that has the fame. Fame rests on the name and the name's being repeated over and over: *nom* to *renom*. And since the name has been dismissed as nothing but change and confusion, the same must hold for renown.

Moreover, Montaigne has still more serious charges to direct against renown. Examining it "pour Dieu," he accuses the desire and search for it as presumption, a usurpation of qualities that belong to God alone: "that in a mortal subject, and in a moment, makes nothing of usurping infinity, immensity, eternity," all of which are attributes proper to God alone (135c).

So far the consideration of names has been limited to their "vocal and auricular" aspect as sounds. But henceforth to the end of the essay Montaigne considers names in their written form. To do so he follows the reverse of the procedure he followed in the first part, for he considers first how there can be many written names for one and the same person, and then how one and the same written name may be held by many individuals, both considerations aimed at showing the emptiness of fame or renown.

Thus he notes "premierement" that "three or four dashes with a pen" by altering the spelling of a name can throw into doubt "to whom is to be attributed the glory of so many victories, to Guesquin, to Glesquin, or to Gueaquin . . . which of these letters is to be rewarded for so many sieges, battles, wounds, imprisonments, and services done to the crown of France by this famous constable" (135d). And we meet again the old nominalist question, how can three be but one, or how can one be at the same time many?

The adoption of pen names or pseudonyms provides still another way that names can be multiplied. One way is by retaining the letters of the proper name but rearranging them in an anagram; so Nicholas Denisot won renown for the Count d'Alsinois to whom he attributed the "glory of his poetry and painting." Another way of forming a pen name is by change of meaning, as Suetonius, the Latin historian, abandoned his family surname of "Lenis" (meaning soft or gentle) for "Tranquillus," who thus became the "successor to the reputation of his writings" (135d).

After noting the case of pen names, Montaigne adds the names of two more military heroes, who owe their fame to another name than that of their family, one being known by two other names, the other by three. In all he provides five examples of fame through change of name. But as Compagnon notices, there is a constant logic in the progression from one to another: "the substitution of one letter, permutation of all the letters, pseudonym, double name, and finally triple name."

"Secondly," a few "dashes of the pen" can provide one name for many individuals. Many members of the same family bear the same names, but so too do members of wholly different families spread throughout space and time:

> History tells us [*a cognu*—has known] three Socrates, five Platos, eight
> Aristotles, seven Xenophons, twenty Demetrius, twenty Theodores; and
> how many more she was not acquainted with we may imagine.
> (Cf. 136a.)

It is misleading to translate the beginning of this sentence as history tells us of "three of the name of Socrates," etc. For to do so is to specify that Montaigne is here talking only about the name, whereas much of the paradox he is concerned with throughout the entire essay lies precisely in leaving open whether it is the name or the individual named that is the object of his concern.

"History" here is, of course, written history, the memory that supplies the repository of fame. How fickle and vain then is that fame when it depends upon a name that many different individuals can bear:

> Who hinders my groom from calling himself Pompey the Great? But
> after all, what virtue, what authority, or what secret springs are there
> that fix upon my deceased groom, or the other Pompey, who had his
> head cut off in Egypt, this glorious renown, and these so much honoured
> flourishes of the pen, so as to be of any advantage to them? (136a)

With the three Latin quotations closing the essay Montaigne reaffirms the vanity of fame: "the fine phrases" which the living are incited by "jealousy and desire" to flatter themselves into believing will one day be written of them, since, as the satirist Juvenal wrote, "so much greater is the thirst for fame than the thirst for virtue" (136d).

The Apology

The "Apology for Raimond de Sebonde" is the longest of the 107 essays; in a French edition of 1,086 pages it occupies no less than 174 of them, or a little less than a sixth of the entire volume. Screech calls it "delightfully paradoxical" and observes that it "gives full scope to his Catholic skepticism," whereas Compagnon finds that it along with the final essay on experience contains Montaigne's "most purely nominalist statements." Neither scholar considers the essay in detail for itself, but both cite and analyze it mainly as it can contribute to their own particular concerns. Yet because of the crucial importance of the essay for understanding Montaigne, especially with regard to the relation between skepticism and religious faith, that is a task eminently worth undertaking. Such will be the concern of the remainder of this paper in which the aim will be to show how the results of their investigation can help to determine at least the main lines of the "Apology."

This essay is indeed paradoxical. It is an apology for an apology in that it is a defense of Sebonde's book, which is itself a defense of the Christian faith. For Sebonde's purpose, as Montaigne describes it, is "by human and natural reasons, to establish and make good [*verifier*] against the atheists all the articles of the Christian religion" (II.12, 208d). But Montaigne's defense of that effort against rational objections to it is to attack, belittle, and denigrate the power of reason on its own to reach any certain truth whatsoever, and thus turn reason against itself.

The overall structure of the essay is determined by the "two principal objections" that he claims are directed against Sebonde:

> The first thing they reprehend in his work is, that Christians are to
> blame to repose upon human reasons their belief, which is only
> conceived by faith and the particular inspiration of divine grace. (209a)

> The second objection is that "his arguments are weak and unfit to make
> good [*verifier*] what he proposes." (213a)

To answer the first objection Montaigne's procedure is in effect to show how Sebonde's book is to be read. To this end he begins by declaring that the truth of the Christian religion so far transcends the reach of human reason that we could never know it at all if God did not "lend us His assistance, by extraordinary privilege and favour, to conceive and imprint it in our understandings" (209b). Yet he goes on to add immediately that just because it is by "faith alone" that we know the mysteries of the Christian religion we should not think that "it is not a brave and a very laudable attempt to accommodate the natural and human capabilities that God has endowed us with to the service of our faith . . . and accompany our faith with all the reason we have" (209b–c).

But to accomplish this purpose, or to do so properly and profitably, there are two conditions to be met. The first is "not to fancy [*estimer*] that it is upon us that it depends, nor that our arguments and endeavours can arrive at so supernatural and divine a knowledge." The second is that the service must be done "by the mediation of a lively [*vive*— living] faith" (209b). Montaigne is here distinguishing between a living and a dead faith, based on the passage in the *Epistle of James* claiming (in the Vulgate translation) that "faith without works is dead" (*James* 2:20), where a living faith is one that is inspired by charity and takes effect in action. He then proceeds for several pages to castigate Christians for their lack of a living faith, a lack that is manifest in both their words and works being so greatly at variance with the faith they profess.

Once these conditions are met, the reading of Sebonde is based on solid ground. For once "our heart and soul being governed and commanded by faith, 'tis but reason that they should muster all our other faculties [*pieces*], for as much as they are able to perform, to the service and assistance of their design" (212b). It is the presence of the grace of God that is the essential element. Appealing to the Aristotelian doctrine that things are a composite of matter and form, Montaigne compares human reason and discourse to so much "sterile and undigested matter" to which the grace of God is the form that "gives to it fashion and value" (212c). Sebonde's arguments thus presuppose the Christian faith and must be read in its light:

> They have a kind of body, but it is an inform mass, without fashion and without light, if faith and God's grace be not added to it. Faith coming to tint and illustrate Sebonde's arguments, renders them firm and solid, so that they are capable of serving for direction and first guide to a learner to put him into the way of this knowledge: they, in some measure, form him to and render him capable of the grace of God, by means whereof he afterwards completes and perfects himself in . . . belief. (212c–d)

Montaigne, as Screech notes, is here basing his defense of Sebonde upon a traditional distinction in the theology of grace. Since faith is a gift of God, its reception supposes a "prevenient grace" that inclines the will so as to make it capable of freely accepting that faith. (Pascal, incidentally, has much to say about prevenient grace in *The Provincial Letters; GBWW*, Vol. 33.) Hence, if Sebonde's arguments are read with a prior faith in the Christian mysteries, they become capable of further enlightening and developing the understanding of them. Montaigne's defense of Sebonde thus at bottom rests upon the traditional Augustinian and Anselmian principle: *Credo ut intelligam*—I believe in order that I may understand. What is needed for reading Sebonde correctly then is not a willing suspension of disbelief but rather a willing dependence upon belief.

The attack on reason

To meet the second objection, that Sebonde's arguments are weak, invalid, and inconclusive, Montaigne adopts a different method. Instead of showing how Sebonde is to be read, he will show that his arguments are "as solid and firm as any others of the same class." Not that he will cite particular objections and expose their weakness one by one; he chooses rather to attack reason itself so as to see if it be in man "to arrive at any certainty by argument and reason [*discours*]" (213b). He acknowledges that such is "an extreme remedy; 'tis a desperate thrust, wherein you are to quit your own arms to make your adversary abandon his" (270a); for to use reason and discourse against themselves is also to deprive oneself of their use.

His method here is the inverse of the one he followed to meet the first objection. There he insisted that in reading Sebonde reason must not be separated from faith. Now to meet the objections allegedly made in the name of reason he insists that reason must be considered entirely on its own and completely separate from any reliance on faith:

> Let us then now consider a man alone, without foreign assistance, armed only with his own proper arms, and unfurnished of the divine grace and wisdom . . . ; let us see what certainty [*tenue*—constancy] he has in this fine equipment. (213d)

The conclusion that he reaches after his long consideration of what unaided human reason claims to be able to accomplish on its own is the skeptical one that the claims are without foundation:

> Finally, there is no constant existence, either of the objects' being nor of our own; both we and our judgment, and all mortal things, are evermore incessantly running and rolling, and, consequently, nothing certain can be established from the one to the other, both the judging and the judge being in a continual motion and mutation. (292d)

To reach this skeptical conclusion that dismisses the pretension of reason, Montaigne's argument, according to Compagnon's analysis of it, goes through three stages: In the first, through the long comparison of man with other animals, he seeks to destroy the notion that there is a human species. In the second he shows the incoherence of human knowledge through his criticism of both reason and sense. Finally, in the third, he argues that not even an individual is one and the same through time so that there is no more subsistent reality to an individual than there is to a species. The single principle underlying all three stages is that there is nothing that remains one in the many so as to provide a stable foundation for certain knowledge. This, as we have noted, is the abiding principle of the nominalist denial of the reality of the universal, except that Montaigne goes even further by applying the same principle to deny any stability to the individual.

The logic that grounds Montaigne's attack upon the reality of the human species is that there is nothing that is one and the same in all human beings such as to really differentiate them from all other animals. In other words, there is no *differentia* that combined with animal as genus would define man as one distinct species. He is frankly a partisan of difference rather than of similarity when he looks at men and maintains that "there is more difference betwixt such and such a man, than betwixt such a man and such a beast" (222a). Hence the long and fascinating collection of incidents and anecdotes, fabulous as well as historical, in which he seeks to show the many differences among human beings, but also their lack of difference from other animals, and in some cases their superiority over some men. The claim that there is a real difference of man from all other animals such as to establish a more than nominal species is based, he claims, not upon knowledge but upon man's presumption and vanity: "that he equals himself to God, attributes to himself divine qualities, withdraws and separates himself from the crowd of other creatures, cuts out the shares of animals his fellows and companions, and distributes to them portions of faculties and force as himself thinks fit" (215b).

After thus dismissing the claim that there is any real species, man, to be known, Montaigne in the second stage of his argument attacks as pretense the claim to certain knowledge through either reason or sense and, thus in effect, argues that even if there were a real species man would not be able to know it. His criticism of rational knowledge consists in the main of consideration of what the most eminent thinkers using reason alone, as seen in the work of the ancient pagan thinkers, have concluded about subjects of greatest concern, such as God, man, the soul, immortality, and the laws by which to govern. As a criterion by which to judge the value of thought, Montaigne takes that of agreement and universal consent, on the ground that if there were any sound and certain knowledge on these subjects there would be unity and agreement about it. But everywhere he looks he finds only disagreement and "infinite confusion of opinions and determinations" (260c). Even mathematics, which supposedly enjoys the greatest certainty, he dismisses as irrelevant, not because there is no agreement about its conclusions, but because they depend upon principles that are postulated, as in axiomatic geometry, and hence are based only upon "the consent and approbation we allow them" (260d); and principles are presupposed, not known as certain. Hence those who profess, as the critics of Sebonde do, "not to admit or approve of anything but by the way of reason," have nothing to stand on, for "certainly, 'tis a test full of falsity, error, weakness, and defect" (261c).

Montaigne finds even stronger evidence for skepticism when he considers the claims of sense knowledge. He notes that "all knowledge is conveyed to us by the senses; . . . science begins by them, and is resolved into them," and can then argue that if the senses too are fallacious, there is even less reason for trusting any knowledge (285d). He marshals the evidence against their soundness and again finds nothing but "error and uncertainty" (288b); for there is no more agreement about sense than about reason: "We receive things variously, according as we are and as they appear to us" and have no way of knowing whether that is the way they are in fact. Hence the conclusion, "this foundation being shaken, all the knowledge in the world must of necessity fall to pieces" (291c).

Having failed to find any stability either in the idea of man as a real species or in the achievements of reason and sense, Montaigne considers as a last resort whether the individual can provide a sure foundation for knowledge. Here he comes up against a thesis dear to the nominalists, for although they distrusted the reality of abstractions, they maintained that in knowledge of the individual we do get a hold on reality. Montaigne, however, finds no basis for believing that even in the individual there is anything that remains one and the same:

> And that it is so let this be the proof; if we are always one and the same,
> how comes it then to pass, that we are now pleased with one thing, and
> by and by with another? how comes it to pass that we love or hate
> contrary things, that we praise or condemn them? how comes it to pass
> that we have different affections, and no more retain the same sentiment
> in the same thought? For it is not likely that without mutation we should
> assume other passions; and that which suffers mutation does not remain
> the same, and if it be not the same, it is not at all. (293c)

Thus Montaigne notes of himself and of his writing: "I do not paint its being, I paint its passage" (III.2, 388d). But if there is no permanence, nothing that remains one and the same, not even in the individual, then reason is deceived in its claim to have reached any sound knowledge, and Sebonde's critics in basing their objections on reason alone have no ground to stand on.

The primacy of faith

This skeptical conclusion that reason has "no communication with Being" (292d) does not mean, however, that there is no being that truly is, untouched by mutability and time. The affirmation that there is such a being has been anticipated many times during the course of the "Apology," and the text just quoted leads directly to the closing assertion:

> that God only is, not according to any measure of time, but according to an immutable and motionless eternity, not measured by time, nor subject to any declension; before whom nothing was, and after whom nothing shall be, either more new or more recent, but a real Being, that with one sole Now fills the forever, and there is nothing that truly is, but He alone, without one being able to say, He has been, or shall be, without beginning, and without end. (294a)

In the final lines of the essay Montaigne returns to his contention in the first part that it is not by reason but by faith alone and the grace of God that man can "pretend to that divine and miraculous metamorphosis" by which he can attain to a knowledge of God—a text we met above in Screech's interpretation of it.

Montaigne maintains that it is absurd and pretentious of men to think that they can reach God by their own reason. To do so, "we must make the divinity pass through our sieve," and reduce the divine to the human level (254b); whereas in fact "nothing about us can, in any sort, be compared or likened unto the divine nature that will not blemish and tarnish it with so much imperfection" (251c). Only God can know himself, and, if we can know anything about Him, it is only because He has interpreted His works to us "in our language," through His revelation to us (239a). Hence, according to Montaigne, it is not possible by reason alone to prove either the existence of God or His unicity, let alone any of His attributes. With this he has dismissed as impossible any natural, i.e., purely rational, theology—admittedly a somewhat paradoxical position for an essay which is a defense of Sebonde, whose work is primarily just such a theology. Yet in taking such a position Montaigne is entirely in accord with the nominalists and their master Ockham.

So too "of all human and ancient opinions concerning religion," Montaigne singles out as "the most likely and most excusable" that which identifies God as "an incomprehensible power" (246b); while the worst conception is that which "bound God to destiny, . . . enslaved Him to necessity" (254c). Both assertions are identical with those of Ockham on the subject, since he maintained that the most effective way of repudiating any limitation upon the freedom of God is to think of Him primarily as *potentia absoluta*—absolute power irreducibly separate from all His creation.

Thus, at least in matters of religion, Montaigne is left with an extreme and exclusive dependence upon faith, the belief that God has made Himself known to men, and best and most thoroughly, he thought, through the Roman Catholic Church—a position that has come to be known as fideism. He is even willing to maintain that the admission of ignorance and simplicity on our part toward God is "the best wisdom" and to find good in the presence of an incredible thing as offering "an occasion . . . to believe" (238d).

Montaigne's defense of Sebonde is thus in the end essentially a defense of faith. Yet it is a defense that may seem paradoxical in its marriage of faith with skepticism. For if religion rests entirely upon belief and acceptance, how is it any different from mathematics, which, as we have seen, Montaigne belittles as having no other basis than the human acceptance of its primary postulates? Even to answer in response that religious faith has a higher source than man and his reason in coming from God, there must be reasons for believing and accepting this very article. An attack on the power and validity of reason would thus appear to be also an attack on the reasons for believing. So how good a defense is this manner of arguing?

Doubt about its strength appeared even among members of Montaigne's own church, although in this case it was slow in coming. The first reception was highly favorable to it as an apology for the Catholic faith. During his long journey to Italy in 1580–81, Montaigne had to have the *Essays* (in their first edition, consisting of Books I and II) scrutinized by a papal censor. He found little to criticize, and Montaigne wrote in his travel journal that "[he] urged me to help the Church by my eloquence." So too the first complete and posthumous edition of 1595 (prepared by his executrix and adopted daughter, Mlle. de Gournay, whom Montaigne highly praised in II.17, 322a) was dedicated to Cardinal Richelieu as an eloquent defense of the faith.

Yet, some years later, Pascal, although a great reader of the *Essays* and much influenced by them, accuses Montaigne of turning men away from religion (*Pensées*, No. 63; *GBWW*, Vol. 33, p. 180a). Then in 1676 the *Essays* were officially placed upon the Index of Prohibited Books and Catholics forbidden to read them under pain of sin without ecclesiastical permission. So far from being a help to the faith, they were then declared to be an obstacle. Other readers refused to take Montaigne seriously in the declarations about his faith. Voltaire viewed him as one of his own and read his work as an attack on the church. Sainte-Beuve, the great 19th-century critic, biographer of Pascal and the Port-Royal movement, declared that if Montaigne was Catholic, he certainly was not Christian. The marriage between faith and skepticism proclaimed in the *Essays* was denied, and Montaigne's skepticism was turned against his faith.

Such an interpretation presupposes that Montaigne is not sincere when he writes about faith, and in turn entails that credence should not be given to the protestations that he makes about his love of truth and abomination of "counterfeiting and dissembling," in the essay on presumption in which he takes stock of his strengths and weaknesses

(II.17, 315a–b). As an exegetical principle such a position rests on very shaky ground. For it opens itself to the same mode of arguing that Montaigne uses in his defense of Sebonde. The alleged weakness of Sebonde's reason is countered by showing the wholesale debility of reason itself. So too if Montaigne is lying in his remarks about faith, why should he not also be lying about everything else he writes, including his skepticism? Montaigne may even be said to have anticipated this skeptical exegetical principle when he wrote in the *Apology* itself:

> Men willingly wrest the sayings of others to favour their own prejudicated opinions; to an atheist all writings tend to atheism; he corrupts the most innocent matter with his own venom. (213a)

So, rather than follow such a devious route, it may be safer to see whether there is a way of reconciling the Christian faith with skepticism. And for this task Professors Compagnon and Screech can offer considerable help.

Christian skepticism

By placing Montaigne's work in the intellectual context of its time they show very clearly that there is nothing especially unique in the joining of faith with skepticism. The nominalists were highly skeptical of reason's claim to reach any truths about God, yet many of them remained staunch believers in matters of religious faith. So too there were others besides Montaigne in the Renaissance who followed the ancient skeptical tradition in philosophy without finding it a threat to their belief. In fact, both skeptics and nominalists were in accord in maintaining that their way provided the best and strongest support for traditional values. Montaigne's own words, however, contain the best evidence for the reconcilability of faith and skepticism in his own work. They also reveal some mitigation of his own nominalist tendencies.

From the essay on names we have already detected a suspicion that the truest name is that of the paternal family. And it is in his consideration of paternity and of his relation to his own father that Montaigne comes to find a real resemblance, a one-in-many founded in extra-mental reality and, hence, a basis for a stand against nominalism.

Montaigne wrote two essays about fathers and several times tells of the love and respect he had for his own father. In them he shows himself to be less a partisan of difference (as he claimed to be) than of similarity. One of these is entitled "Of the affection of fathers to their children" (II.8), the other "Of the resemblance of children to their fathers" (II.37). The latter is the concluding essay of Book II and thus formed the close of the first edition of the *Essays;* its very last lines contain another strong assertion of Montaigne's belief in the predominance of diversity: "There never were, in the world, two opinions alike, no more than two hairs, or two grains: the most universal quality is diversity," which in effect is to deny the universal (379c). Yet in the same final paragraph he can also claim that his hatred and distrust of medicine and its practitioners (to which much of the essay is devoted) is a trait that he inherited from his ancestors and thus is not "a mere stupid and inconsiderate aversion, but [has] a little more form" (379a).

The previous essay contains a still stronger assertion of similarity, and it is one that is again based on paternity:

> If there be any law truly natural, that is to say, any instinct that is seen universally and perpetually imprinted in both beasts and men (which is not without controversy), I can say, that in my opinion, next to the care every animal has of its own preservation, and to avoid that which may hurt him, the affection that the begetter bears to his offspring holds the second place in this rank. (II.8, 184a).

In the parenthetical remark that the subject is a controverted one, Montaigne reveals his own acquaintance with philosophical arguments about it, among which those of the nominalists were the most prominent. Yet on this occasion he does not hesitate to side with their opponents.

As he grew older Montaigne discovered still further evidence of resemblance between himself and his father. He began to suffer from the same disease that had killed his father: a stone in the bladder, he calls it, or what would be a kidney stone. In writing about this fact and ruminating about its implications, he develops, as Compagnon well shows, his strongest argument against nominalism. He does so by pondering the similarity of names, and for this reason we must have recourse to Montaigne's French. His father was named Pierre, but "pierre" in French is the word for stone, and hence also for kidney stone, so that he can describe his infirmity as a *qualité pierreuse* (stony quality). But the French for stumbling block is *pierre d'achoppement,* and paternity was always a stone that blocked the path of nominalism. Montaigne too avails himself of it in writing:

> 'Tis to be believed that I derive this infirmity (*qualité pierreuse*) from my father, for he died wonderfully tormented with a great stone in his bladder. . . . I was born above five and twenty years before his disease seized him, and in the time of his most flourishing and healthful state of body, his third child in order of birth: where could his propension to this malady lie lurking all that while? And he being then so far from the infirmity, how could that small part of his substance wherewith he made me, carry away so great an impression for its share? and how so concealed, that till five and forty years after, I did not begin to be sensible of it? being the only one to this hour, amongst so many brothers and sisters, and all by one mother, that was ever troubled with it. (II.37, 367d–68a)

Montaigne does not hesitate to claim that paternity provides a basis in reality for a similarity that continues one and the same through generations. He remarks on "what a wonderful thing it is that the drop of seed from which we are produced should carry in itself the impression not only of the bodily form, but even of the thoughts and inclinations of our fathers! Where can that drop of fluid matter contain that infinite number of forms?" (367c). It is highly significant that Montaigne uses the word *form* here. In the Aristotelian terminology that is the technical term for the principle that makes a thing to be what it is. Thus, according to the realists, it is the real basis for the universal, and hence also the reason for maintaining that classes can be real and not merely nominal. As we have learned from the essay on names, Montaigne there ridicules the notion that there are any such classes. Yet here he is asserting that there is at least one natural class, namely that established through biological generation, which Montaigne believed to be principally the work of the father, and which consequently makes his the only "true" name.

Montaigne himself, however, failed to leave a surviving son to succeed him; he left a daughter, but daughters fail to retain the paternal name. If then the only real basis for continuity is through the male line, and he left no son to succeed him, how could he achieve a continuing real existence? The question appears to have bothered him, for he finally devised an answer. He had no natural son, but perhaps there are other kinds of offspring that would do as well, if not better. That he found in a "son" that was the fruit, not of his loins, but of his brain; not a man-child, but a book, the *Essays* that he produced through his writing. From his conviction of this follows the seemingly extravagant claims that Montaigne makes for himself in relation to his book, assertions that continue to bear upon the struggle between nominalism and realism.

Thus in the essay on repentance he could declare, as we have already seen, that "every man carries the entire form of [the] human condition," but that he is the first of any author to communicate himself, not by "some especial and extrinsic mark [*marque particuliere et estrangere*]," but by his "universal being; as Michel de Montaigne, not as a grammarian, a poet, or a lawyer" (III.2, 389a). In other words, he has discovered in himself as an individual the universal, man. Furthermore, he has so expressed his discovery in his book that he and his book cannot be separated: "My book and I go hand in hand together . . . who touches the one, touches the other" (389b). He exposes himself entire, writing not "my own acts, but myself and my essence" (II.6, 181b). But if his "essence," then a universal that he has grasped in himself as an individual and produced in his book with the result that "'Tis a book consubstantial with the author, of a peculiar design, a member of my life . . . a lasting record" (II.18, 323a–b). In making such an assertion,

Montaigne is now claiming that he has found qualities in his book that he had denied in the essay on names. His book is essential with him— "consubstantial with its author"—as belonging exclusively to him; and coextensive in that it makes a "lasting record" that identifies him throughout history.

With this much said, the ground is prepared for the boldest, most extravagant, claim of all. In the essay on the affection of fathers for their children Montaigne notes that parents have "this simple reason for loving our children, that we have begot them, therefore calling them our second selves [*autres nous memes*—our other selves]." But an author stands in an even closer relation to his written production:

> For that which we engender by the soul, the issue of our understanding
> [*l'esprit*], courage, and abilities, springs from nobler parts than those
> of the body, and that are much more our own: we are both father and
> mother in this generation. (II.8, 191c)

In thus affirming a closer and nobler relation to his writings than that of bodily parents to their offspring, Montaigne may well also be finding a closer resemblance to God, as Compagnon suggests, and remembering that the name Michel, in its Hebrew original, means "who is like God."

Granted that by this argument Montaigne mitigates his nominalism, and to that extent his skepticism about the reach of human reason, how is this of any help in validating his declarations about faith? Professor Screech's analysis of Montaigne's position regarding the relation between body and soul in man serves to point a way. On this subject Montaigne accepted the centuries-old teaching that man is a composite of body and soul, each different from the other, in some ways even opposed, yet both necessary and essential. But in addition he is also especially emphatic in asserting the dignity of the body and in repudiating any attempt to divorce the two. He holds that between body and soul there is not only a close and brotherly correspondence but also "a very convenient marriage of pleasure with necessity" (III.13, 542a). Further:

> They who go about to disunite and separate our two principal parts from
> one another are to blame; we must, on the contrary, reunite and rejoin
> them. We must command the soul not to withdraw and entertain itself
> apart, not to despise and abandon the body (neither can [it] do [so] but
> by some apish counterfeit), but to unite [itself] close to it, to embrace,
> cherish, assist, govern, and advise it, and to bring it back and set it into
> the true way when it wanders; in sum, to espouse and be a husband
> to it. (II. 17, 311a)

He then adds immediately as further support that "Christians have a particular instruction concerning this connection, "for in their doctrine of the resurrection of the body, "they know that the Divine justice embraces this society and juncture of body and soul, even to the making the body capable of eternal rewards" (ibid.). His argument for the marriage of body and soul thus rests, on the one hand, on the natural condition of man as a composite of the two and, on the other, on its reaffirmation and confirmation through faith.

Reason and faith are thus joined in the defense of his attitude toward the relation of body and soul. But Montaigne's defense of Sebonde rests on the same union of faith and reason, and the repudiation of any effort to separate the two. In short, marriage as the image of the relation between soul and body can very well serve also as the image for the relation between faith and reason in Montaigne's understanding of it, and they should no more be separated than the other two. His reason is a skeptical one, his faith supernatural as divinely given.

If then his faith is sound and sincere, and religion, as he himself writes, "the most important subject that can be" (II. 12, 281b), why, it may be asked, when he is so very fond of citing and quoting the words of others, does he so rarely quote Sacred Scripture and the saints? He has answered this question himself in the essay on prayers where he declares that he proposes "fancies merely human and merely my own; . . . matter of opinion, not matter of faith; . . . after a laical, not clerical, and yet always after a very religious manner" (I.56, 155b–c). In fact, he thinks that "the divine doctrine, as queen and regent of the rest, better keeps her state apart" (155a).

Another reason for this lack lies in the character of the essays as *assaying,* not resolving, "always learning and making trial" (III.2, 388d). Thus Montaigne is consciously distancing his writing from divine revelation and restricting his citations for the most part to the ancient pagan writings, not only because of his admiration for them, but also because they were written before the advent of Christianity. In this respect there was in his own century the example of Sir Thomas More, who wrote the whole of his *Utopia* [*GIT* 1965, pp. 373–437] without quoting the Bible or the Christian saints. In the Middle Ages Saint Anselm had adopted the same practice in his *Monologium,* as had Boethius in late antiquity in his *Consolation of Philosophy* [*GIT* 1982, pp. 297–379]. Even Montaigne's skepticism as an ally of the Christian faith had its predecessors among the earliest Christian apologists. As Gilson has noted in his *History of Christian Philosophy in the Middle Ages,* the third-century Latin apologist Arnobius sounds some of the main themes that Montaigne himself does, stressing the existence of problems that the human mind has to face and yet cannot answer and belittling man while exalting animals. In joining skepticism about the reach of reason with the Christian faith, Arnobius initiated a "genuinely Christian family" of thinkers. And of this family it can certainly be said without exaggeration that Montaigne is its most eminent member.

Documentation

The Essays of Michel Eyquem de Montaigne have been cited according to the translation of Charles Cotton as revised by W. Carew Hazlitt, contained in *Great Books of the Western World,* Volume 25.

The French text has been cited according to that of the *Oeuvres Complètes* in the Bibliothèque de la Pléiade, Bruges, Éditions Gallimard, 1962.

Antoine Compagnon, *Nous, Michel de Montaigne,* Paris, Éditions du Seuil, 1980.

M. A. Screech, *Montaigne & Melancholy: The Wisdom of the Essays,* London, Duckworth, 1983.

Appendix

Aristotle: *Problems* 30.1 (abridged) from the Latin version by Theodore Gaza (Paris, 1629), published in M. A. Screech, *Montaigne & Melancholy,* Appendix B, pp. 171–72, translated by O.A.B.

(953a10) Why is it that we find that men who excelled by genius in philosophical studies, in administering the republic, in composing songs, or in the arts were all melancholic? And that some also were infected by diseases from black bile, as among the heroes is related of Hercules? For he was thought to have been of such a nature, and the sacred disease (epilepsy) was first called after him Herculean. This also explains his madness against his children and the eruption of sores that somewhat preceded his death; for this is often caused by black bile. Lysander the Lacedaemonian shortly before his death had the same kind of sores. Add also Ajax and Bellerophon, one of whom became completely insane, while the other sought out desert places, of whom Homer writes "when Bellerophon came to be hated by all the gods, he wandered all desolate and dismayed upon the Alean plain, gnawing at his own heart, and shunning the path of man" (*Iliad* VI.200–202; *GBWW*, Vol. 4, p. 42b).

Also many others among the heroes were found to suffer from the same disease. In more recent years we know that Empedocles, Socrates, Plato, and many other eminent men were of this habit, as were also most of the poets. For diseases from such a corporeal temperament afflict many of this kind of men, and some clearly by nature are inclined to them: For almost all of them, as has been said, have just such a nature.

The cause of this may be found if first we take the example of the effect of wine. For the immoderate use of wine seems to make men just such as we affirm the melancholic to be and induces various characteristics, when drunk, so as to make them irritable, humane, merciful, rash, none of which can be produced by honey, or water, or milk, or anything similar. One can clearly understand how it makes men various if one observes how it gradually changes those drinking it. For wine takes a man cold and taciturn from sobriety and with a little drink warms him up and excites his words, while a larger drink makes him full of words, eloquent, and bold. In the process of drinking still more, he is made rash with a propensity for action; and with still more he turns to insolence and petulance; and then almost to insanity; still afterward he collapses from too much drink and becomes stupid like those who have labored under epilepsy from childhood, or like those who contain an excess of black bile (953b5–54a22).

If black bile exceeds the measure, it makes a man apoplectic, tortured, anxious, or terrified; but if it becomes overheated, it produces carelessness, singing, mental alienation, the eruption of sores, and other things of this sort. In most men, being abundant from their daily food, it does not change their characters, but only creates the melancholic disease. But those who by nature have such a temperament immediately develop many different kinds of habits in accord with their various temperaments. For example, those in whom there is much cold black bile are stolid and dull; those in whom there is much hot black bile are impetuous, ingenious, loving, quick to anger and lust, while some also become more verbose. Many too because the heat is close to the seat of the mind become affected by the disease of insanity or burst forth in a frenzied possession; such gives rise to the Sibyls, the Bacchantes, and all who are thought to be instigated by divine inspiration, when it is due not to disease, but to natural temperament. Maracus the Syracusan was also a more excellent poet when he was out of his mind. But those in whom the heat is less and dies down to a mean are indeed melancholic, but also much more prudent and although part exceed less, many are in other matters far superior to all others, some in literary studies, others in the arts, others in politics (954b3–55a29).

Melancholic men are different and unequal because the black bile is different and unequal and can make one very hot or very cold. And since it has the power to establish characters (for heat and cold more than anything else in our body builds our character), it affects and forms the quality of our characters, and just as wine interfuses and mixes more or less in the body, it makes different characters. For both wine and black bile are full of breath. Since it is possible for a portion to be tempered even in an inequable order and the breath integral, the character can respond as hotter or colder because of an excess of the quality, hence it is that all melancholics are of singular genius, not from disease, but from nature (955a40).

The Inefficacy of the Good:
On Reading Thucydides

Douglas Allanbrook

Douglas Allanbrook is a composer and tutor at St. John's College, Annapolis, Maryland. His interest in music started early, at the age of eight, and at twelve he had already begun composing. Subsequently he studied at the Longy School of Music in Cambridge with Nadia Boulanger. After spending three years in the army, he returned to study at Harvard with Walter Piston, and then went abroad as a traveling fellow of the school in order to study at the Conservatoire in Paris. He spent two additional years in Italy, studying harpsichord and early keyboard music as a Fulbright scholar with Ruggero Gerlin in Naples.

Since then, Mr. Allanbrook has composed a great deal of music—seven symphonies, four string quartets, two operas, and many other pieces, some commissioned by various music groups. His works have been performed by the National Symphony, the Baltimore Orchestra, the Stuttgart Philharmonic, and the Munich and Berlin Radio orchestras. He has received awards from both the American Society of Composers, Authors, and Publishers and the American Academy and Institute of Arts and Letters.

The following article was originally a formal lecture delivered at St. John's College in the fall of 1983. Among other published lectures Mr. Allanbrook has given at the college are ones on Homer, on Pascal, and on the Risorgimento.

The field upon which political actions are played is one of moral desolation. If certain men or cities stand high and brilliant above this field, are remembered and praised in future generations by their countrymen or by the world, this praise, these many political encomia, almost never arise out of the goodness or true virtue of the subject; they are service rendered by words and memory to power, fame, and empire. Caesar's name lives on in the very titles of power and empire— the Kaiser, the Czar of all the Russias—while Cato's suicide is cherished in the memory of a few as a proper failure, and he himself is most marvelously enshrined on the lowest slope of Purgatory as Dante leaves Hell and begins to go up. It is apposite in this consideration to remember Thucydides' words concerning poor Nicias when his life comes to an end at the end of the Syracusan adventure, as recounted almost at the very end of Book VII of the histories. You will recall Nicias's actions against the demagogue Cleon, whom Thucydides detests, and his opposition to Alcibiades in front of the assembly which was to decide upon the Sicilian expedition. He attempted to deter the Athenians from the venture by calling to their attention the enormity of the cost and the vastness of the armaments required. Of course the effect of his speech on the assembly was the opposite of what he had expected, "for it seemed to them that he had given good advice, and that now certainly there would be abundant security."* And soon, "upon all alike there fell an eager desire [*eros*] to sail" (VI: XXIV, 2–3) [Cf. *GBWW*, Vol. 6, p. 516a].

The Spartans in the Pylos affair knew that Nicias was for peace, and indeed the period of relative calm in the midst of the long war was known as the Peace of Nicias. He was a very rich and pious man, and it is a terrible irony that this very piety fatally delayed a possible retreat for the Athenians in the last awful month in front of Syracuse. He knew that the Spartans trusted him,

> and it was not least on that account that he trusted in Gylippus [the
> Spartan general] and surrendered himself to him. But it was said that some
> of the Syracusans were afraid, seeing that they had been in communication

---

*The translations of Thucydides are Charles Foster Smith's, published in the Loeb Classical Library, unless otherwise indicated.

with him, lest, if he were subjected to torture on that account, he might make trouble for them in the midst of their success; and others, especially the Corinthians, were afraid, lest, as he was wealthy, he might by means of bribes make his escape and cause them fresh difficulties; they therefore persuaded their allies and put him to death. For this reason, then, or for a reason very near to this, Nicias was put to death—a man who, of all the Hellenes of my time, least deserved to meet with such a calamity, because of his course of life that had been wholly regulated in accordance with virtue. (VII: LXXXVI, 4–5) [Cf. *GBWW*, 6, pp. 562d–63a.]

Many years ago from this platform I lectured on the Spanish Civil War, and I employed a lengthy simile in an attempt to catch the nature of what was revealed in that and perhaps in all civil wars. It struck me in my younger years that the Spanish War crystallized the conscience of the age, and revealed the more enormous civil war that is the perennial fact of our political life. My simile was drawn from Geology. Our landscapes, from sea to shining sea, with their fields of grain and their snowy Rockies, have their origins in vulcanism, in eruptions, in lava flows, in revolutions and the grinding of tectonic plates. The intent of the simile was to focus the attention of students upon the gleaming surface of our republics, empires, and cities, and to have them note how fragile, temporary, and full of illusion is any appearance of stability. The reality underneath is the force and power of human ambitions, fears, hopes, and desires for fame. In light of this simile any place that lasts for generations with both splendor and decency should be looked at with particular attention. God knows what blood was behind Rome; it still remains a fact that this empire lasted as a place of law for an enormous stretch of time. Saint Paul, a Jew from Tarsus, demanded his rights as a Roman citizen and hence was not tortured. The thousand years of the Most Serene Republic of Venice stand in front of us as a monument of probity and sagacity. It was certainly for an enormous stretch of time the best place to live and work in, and the best place to look at. It was the hub of a commercial empire, as was Athens. Both the Parthenon and Saint Mark's Square are the most spendid and shining things to see and to visit. They are long-lived memorials, though the increasing pollution of time has eroded their surfaces. Can the look of them tell us of Venice's long life and Athens' brief glory? As memorials they affect us more than words and seem to speak to something apart from both them and us, a vision of a place to be cherished. In this they resemble the funeral oration of Pericles. Thucydides, however, puts us on guard against reading too much into such appearances in the famous passage in Book I:

For if the city of Lacedaemonians should be deserted, and nothing should be left of it but its temples and the foundations of its other buildings, posterity would, I think, after a long lapse of time, be very loath to believe that their power was as great as their renown. (And yet they occupy two-fifths of the Peloponnesus and have the hegemony of the whole, as well as of their many allies outside; but still, as Sparta is not compactly built as a city and has not provided itself with costly temples and other edifices, but is inhabited village-fashion in the old Hellenic style, its power would appear less than it is.) Whereas, if Athens should suffer the same fate, its power would, I think, from what appeared of the city's ruins, be conjectured double what it is. (I: X, 2–3) [Cf. *GBWW*, 6, p. 351c.]

My geological simile came to me in the course of reading Thucydides' account of the revolution, or more properly, the civil war that occurred on Corcyra, the deeds committed in that island's internal eruption bearing every resemblance to the deeds committed in the Spanish War. In his account of the happenings on Corcyra Thucydides regards the larger more general war between Athens and Sparta as the catalyst which releases the convulsions of party and faction. Every city has within it democrats and oligarchs, but now the democrats can call upon Athens and the oligarchs upon Sparta. This fact brings to the surface something which Thucydides dares call human nature:

And so there fell upon the cities on account of revolutions many grievous calamities, such as happen and always will happen while human nature is the same, but which are severer or milder, and different in their manifestations, according as the variations in circumstances present themselves in each case. (III: LXXXII, 2) [Cf. *GBWW*, 6, p. 437a.]

This sentence has the chilling precision of a scientific appraisal of phenomena, presenting a general rule which may be applied to the variables of the given case. Thucydides then applies it in detail to the particular situation on Corcyra:

The ordinary acceptation of words in their relation to things was changed as men thought fit. Reckless audacity came to be regarded as courageous loyalty to party, prudent hesitation as specious cowardice, moderation as a cloak for unmanly weakness. (III: LXXXII, 4) [Cf. *GBWW*, 6, p. 437b.]

Words given as oaths lost all coinage, and under the banners of "political equality under law for the many" and "temperate aristocracy" everyone marched to his own tune. People who joined neither party were immediately under suspicion "either because they would not make common cause with them, or through mere jealousy that they should survive." Another universal statement about human nature occurs almost at the end of this section on Corcyra:

At this crisis, when the life of the city had been thrown into utter confusion, human nature, now triumphant over the laws, and accustomed even in spite of the laws to do wrong, took delight in showing that its passions were ungovernable, that it was stronger than justice and an enemy to all superiority. (III: LXXXIV, 2) [Cf. *GBWW*, 6, p. 438a.]

The section concludes with words which the author later puts into the mouths of the Melians in their famous fictive dialogue with the Athenians:

Indeed, men do not hesitate, when they seek to avenge themselves upon others, to abrogate in advance the common principles observed in such cases—those principles upon which depends every man's own hope of salvation should he himself be overtaken by misfortune—thus failing to leave them in force against the time when perchance a man in peril shall have need of some one of them. (III: LXXXIV, 3) [Cf. *GBWW*, 6, p. 438a–b.]

This lecture cannot have the brashness and passion inspired by an event which roused my conscience in high school, and which I found reflected in my experience as a soldier in Italy during the second world war. In Italy again, when I learned to see clearly, there was a civil war going on under my nose, a country torn internally with horrors being committed under the banners of party, and the whole of the mess fusing and coming to the fore under the catalyst of the great world war between the Germans and the Allies. Instead this lecture is about the book, or rather the memorial, which puts such contemporary events into focus for me. Thucydides states that this indeed was his intention in writing such a history:

But whoever shall wish to have a clear view both of the events which have happened and of those which will some day, in all human probability, happen again in the same or a similar way—for these to adjudge my history profitable will be enough for me. And, indeed, it has been composed, not as a prize essay to be heard for the moment, but as a possession for all time. (I: XXII, 4) [Cf. *GBWW*, 6, p. 354c–d.]

Such a book and such an attempt intend to make memory for the future. All battlefields and all wars want monuments. It is unbearable to think of all that blood shed and forgotten. Speeches after a battle on a battlefield must assert the worth and the fame of what has been accomplished by the dead. Only too often they are half-lies about the fatherland, or an invocation to the God of Battles for help in the future or a praise to him for the victory. At their best they call on Providence to help in binding up the wounds so unhesitatingly opened. Thucydides' whole enormous book is a discourse intended to memorialize. It is a landscape with no gods or God or Providence either in the sky above or under the earth in some law court in Hell. The author is enormously fussy about facts, but the book is no chronicle. Certain events are looked at with a particular intensity in view of the purpose of the memorial, and so that the book may be, if not the education of Greece, an aid to the clear seeing of all who read it. About the speeches in the book Thucydides says the following:

> As to the speeches that were made by different men, either when they were about to begin the war or when they were already engaged therein, it has been difficult to recall with strict accuracy the words actually spoken, both for me as regards that which I myself heard, and for those who from various other sources have brought me reports. Therefore the speeches are given in the language in which, as it seemed to me, the several speakers would express, on the subjects under consideration, the sentiments most befitting the occasion, though at the same time I have adhered as closely as possible to the general sense of what was actually said. (I: XXII, 1) [Cf. *GBWW*, 6, p. 354b–c.]

In this book which lays claim to being a "possession for all time" we must ask ourselves why the speeches are present—what part they play in the artful composition of this book. It is clear that spoken words are of crucial importance to Thucydides when the words are public, when they are directed toward future action, and when they issue from the mouths of certain men. Sometimes, however, the speakers are nameless; they are designated merely as "the Athenians," or "the Corinthians." And once in the book the speeches are part of a fictive dialogue between the people of Melos and these nameless "Athenians." It will be helpful, and it is easy enough, following Aristotle, to divide speeches in general into three types. There are speeches addressed to people who are judging concerning the future; such would be speeches made before a deliberative assembly. There are speeches made before people who are judging concerning the past; such would be speeches made in a court of law by a lawyer in front of a judge or a jury. Finally there are speeches mainly concerned with the present, eulogies perhaps, where the judges often are critics or appreciators of the speaker's words. These three types are formally spoken of as deliberative, forensic, and epideictic rhetoric. The business of deliberative speeches is to exhort and persuade concerning future actions, and the reason for the talking, the end at which it is aiming in its persuasion, is the expedient or the harmful. Will it further the ends of the Athenian state to slaughter the entire population of Mytilene or not? Thucydides gives us two speeches on this matter, one from the mouth of Cleon, a demagogue, which argues for the killing, and one from the mouth of Diodotus, an otherwise unknown man in the histories, which argues against the killing. Both speeches argue from expediency and as such fall precisely within the definition of a deliberative speech as rhetoric aimed at the useful or the harmful. While we may lament the lack of any talk of justice in the speeches of Cleon and Diodotus, Diodotus's speech saves the lives of the people of Mytilene. It is intended by the author that we take careful note that the best speech on expediency saves the population of an entire city.

The business of forensic rhetoric is to accuse or defend, its time the past, its end the just and the unjust. Was Alcibiades guilty of impiety in the scandal of the desecration of the Hermes? If this were not cleared up, the doubt would spoil his efficacy in the minds of the assembly however much they had been moved by his speech concerning their future. Did Mr. Nixon do the right thing in lying? That again was judged, and the outcome had much to do later with the future. What I mean to say here is that though speeches concerning past actions, which have to do with justice, are distinct from deliberations concerning the future, which have to do with expediency, we all wear two hats in such matters. If in our judgment Joe did lie or did, in fact, steal, we are not going to listen to him with any particular confidence when he advises us concerning the future, however prudently he may speak. Justice counts for something. The business of the epideictic is praise or blame, and it is most generally concerned with the present; its end is the noble or the disgraceful. At the end of this lecture we will examine the most famous of all epideictic speeches, Pericles' Funeral Oration.

In deliberative speeches the judges are immediately concerned with the subject at hand. It is, after all, their lives, their wealth, their fears, and their honor which are at stake in an assembly which is debating a future action. One would expect them to be more critical and suspicious given this fact. Given this frame of mind, the personal character of the speaker assumes a much greater importance than it does in forensic pleading. Who and what kind of a man Pericles is, has much to do with his persuasiveness. At the conclusion of Pericles' third speech in Book II Thucydides states this with perfect clarity:

> And the reason for this was that Pericles, who owed his influence to his recognized standing and ability, and had proved himself clearly incorruptible in the highest degree, restrained the multitude while respecting their liberties, and led them rather than was led by them, because he did not resort to flattery, seeking power by dishonest means, but was able on the strength of his high reputation to oppose them and even provoke their wrath. (II: LXV, 8) [Cf. *GBWW*, 6, p. 404b–c.]

The same holds true, however, for Alcibiades; character counts, both for and against. Once the enthusiasm for his youth and brilliance have had time to cool off, doubts of his virtue enter the assembly's mind, and he is relieved of his command. As a result the disastrous Sicilian campaign begins its downward plunge. Part of the study of power and politics, of things as they are, is the study of how people are persuaded to action. What rhetoric does is part of the truth of the way things are.

The very first speech in the histories begins with the word *dikaion*—it is fair or just. You may remember the situation. The Corinthians are trying to prevent the Athenian fleet from joining that of Corcyra, as this would hamper them in settling the war as they wish to settle it. An assembly is called, and first the Corcyraeans and then the Corinthians speak. The first sentence of the Corcyraeans, which, as we have noted, begins with the expression "it is fair," is a most complex sentence:

> It is but fair, citizens of Athens, that those who, without any previous claim on the score of important service rendered or of an existing alliance, come to their neighbors to ask aid, as we do now, should show in the first place, if possible, that what they ask is advantageous, or at least that it is not hurtful, and, in the second place, that their gratitude can be depended on; but in case they establish neither of these things clearly, they should not be angry if unsuccessful. (I: XXXII, 1) [Cf. *GBWW,* 6, p. 357a–b.]

The intent of the Corcyraeans, which governs the device they employ in this sentence, is to establish the reasonableness of what they want. Facts must be faced, and dismissed if they prove to be a hindrance. The fact is that the Corcyraeans have no existing alliance with, nor have they rendered any important service to, Athens; in fact they are a colony of Corinth, hence the opening section of the sentence. Given this embarrassing fact, it must be shown that what is asked is *xumphora*—advantageous, or at least not harmful—and that the gratitude of the Corcyraeans might even offer a certain security. The final reasonable appeal is that if none of the above can be established, no one's feelings are to be hurt. It is clear, even if it is not just, that the important persuasive word must be *advantage,* and that other things that might bind a political action, such as an alliance or ties of blood with the motherland, must be glossed over in light of the claims of "advantage." The speech continues with an insistence upon the changed fact of the Corcyraeans' isolation in foreign policy. What had been formerly considered discretion is now viewed as unwise and a cause of weakness. They then hold out to the Athenians the pleasing package of both honor and advantage, honor in helping one who is wronged, and advantage in having as an ally a great sea power. They argue that the Spartans through fear are eager for war, and that the Corinthians are abetting this fear. They then brush aside the illegality of an alliance with them (the Spartans and the Athenians are at this point allied, as you may recall), with a legal argument that has a certain petty rigor, and finally end their speech with the strongest set of appeals to expediency that they can muster. First, they argue that if they have more strength the Spartans will be still more afraid of breaking the truce; second, they appeal to the commercial and imperial passions of Athens by pointing out the convenience of Corcyra, situated as it is so conveniently for a voyage to Italy and Sicily; and third, they tote up a calculus of the naval power of Greece. There are three major navies, Athens, Corinth, and Corcyra. Two is more than one. Don't be stuck with only your own.

The Corinthians in their rebuttal take up one by one the arguments of the Corcyraeans. They argue that the contingency of a war in which the Corinthians fight with the Athenians is still most uncertain, and that to be stampeded by such fear will be to make a real enemy of the Corinthians; this then will be a fact and not a contingency. Also, and most pointedly, the Athenians of all people should not tamper with colonies and allies; the whole life of their city depends on its network of rule abroad. After the two speeches the Athenians in a second session of the assembly go along with the Corcyraeans, though all during the first assembly they are for Corinth. They make, however, a defensive alliance only, promising mutually to aid each other in case of attack. The Athenians believe that the war has to be faced and do not want to give up the navy of the Corcyraeans. Also they have done a calculus— or gambled on a probability—that the two navies, of the Corinthians and the Corcyraeans, will wear each other out, and hence Corinth will be weaker when war comes. And too the island does indeed seem so beautifully situated for a voyage to Italy and Sicily.

Both speeches are made before an assembly of judges who are debating a course of action future to them. The principal word in the vocabulary is certainly expedience as regards future benefits, and this is always contrasted with the harm that would result from not calculating on proper self-interest. Fairness and honor, fear and anger, figure also in this vocabulary, and each person in the assembly must be consulting his own desires and hopes and fears for the future. For us, the readers, these speeches are very different in meaning. We know, as did Thucydides, that the war will go on for more than a generation, that Athens will lose, that the society and world of the Greek cities will be debased by the war, that words having to do with probity, honor, and justice will be tarnished. We are also perfectly aware that it will not be the end of the world, as can so easily happen to our world right now, but that it will be the end of a kind of world in which certain cherished things somehow maintained themselves by tradition, luck, and guts against the desolation of the barbarian periphery. In other words, for us they are not deliberative speeches in that they refer to a future which we the judges do not know. We judge them not from their expediency or harmfulness to us, but as judges judging a past event. We are concerned with the just and the unjust, the good and the bad, and we accuse or defend the Athenians or the people of Melos, the Spartans or the noble defenders of Plataea, as we look back and down upon their speeches, knowing what their future is to be. They are for us writing samples open to our inspection; we are critics or appreciators or unabashed admirers.

Later in Book I the Athenians give a speech which we the readers must closely examine. The occasion is a general council of the allies in Sparta after the hostilities up at Potidaea have been going on for quite a time. The Corinthians have been hard at work in a preceding speech, stirring up the Spartans, inciting them to war. In their speech they have praised the Athenians' resourcefulness and derided the Spartans' old-fashioned habits. They have even put forth a general rule, stating it categorically and introducing it with the word *necessity* (*anangke*): "it is necessary that things coming after other things prevail." A more vivid translation would be "The new must by the nature of things take over." In our role as onlookers and critics of the speech it is easy enough for us to appreciate the reason the Corinthians have for saying this, and even the effectiveness of stating it as a law. The Spartans are stick-in-the-muds and have to be brought to their senses in a world that has changed and that is more quick in its wits than they. If we, as readers, are more than appreciators, we must ask ourselves if the proposition is true; does it have any validity as a law, or persuasive power, because we think it's scientific? On another level of meaning we are aware that Corinth is in many ways the same kind of place as Athens, commercial, rich, a port, and ancient.

The Athenians, who according to Thucydides happened by chance to be present, asked for permission to speak. They wanted to slow down the Spartans and to show the great power of their city, reminding the older men of what they knew, and telling the younger ones what they didn't know, believing that their words would direct the Spartans toward peace rather than war. Their opening sentences should put us, the readers, on guard as to what is being done. The Athenians submit that they are not going to answer any charges, or speak to the Spartans as if the Spartans were a jury deciding on matters of justice or injustice, but are only going to speak to them in order to dissuade them from making a wrong decision regarding the future. The record, on the other hand, still must be set straight. "As for all the words against us, we want to show that we have what we have in a manner that is not unseemly and that our city is worthy of being talked about." The next paragraph in their speech brings up the great event of fifty years ago, the Persian War. There is one acid sentence in this paragraph, which employs the perennial pair, actions and words, *erga* and *logoi*. The sentence may be rendered as follows: "When we did these things [the Athenians are speaking of their part in defeating the Persians], they were risked for the sake of a common benefit, and since you had a piece of the action, we will not be deprived of the words that give us credit, if indeed there is any benefit in that" [author's translations; cf. *GBWW*, 6, p. 367b–c]. The sentence revolves like a snake about the word *benefit*. A freer translation might be as follows: "We did these things and suffered danger for a common good; since you received a share of that work, we will not be deprived of the account of what we did, if indeed there is any good or profit in an account." The word *logos,* "account," at the end of this sentence is delivered with cutting irony. Its meaning might be rendered as "lip service"—the homage that words pay to action. Of course the actions the Athenians are talking about are gone into in detail in the next part of the speech. They are the glorious triumphs at Marathon and Salamis, events which we memorialize as model triumphs of civilization over barbarism, triumphs which the Athenians point to as being a benefit to the Spartans as well as to themselves.

The next paragraph then asks the question of worthiness. "Are we then deserving of hatred and jealousy merely because of empire, or rule?" This is the crucial fact to be dealt with in any dealing with the Spartans. Thucydides has given as the underlying cause of the war the fear the Spartans had of Athens' rule or empire, and now the Athenians must speak to this fact of empire and rule; they must demonstrate that it is natural and inevitable, and hence not blameworthy. They begin by arguing that it was according to the necessity of the work itself that they were driven to extend their rule, and that they were under the push exerted by fear, honor, and lastly self-interest. To quote exactly: "It was under the compulsion of circumstances that we were driven at first to advance our empire to its present state, influenced chiefly by fear, then by honor also, and lastly by self-interest as well." Later in the paragraph they say "No man is to be blamed for making the most of his advantages when it is a question of the gravest dangers." The argument here might be stated as follows: if anyone in the world would behave in a certain way given the appropriate circumstances, no blame follows for an individual who does behave in such a way. Certainly a very familiar and only slightly sleazy inference. The argument then turns to the named individual in a way we are all accustomed to, saying that "you," namely the Spartans, would have done the thing as we had if you had been in our shoes. The next stage is to pull in normalcy of behavior under a more telling name, "human nature." "Thus there is nothing remarkable or inconsistent with human nature in what we also have done, just because we accepted an empire when it was offered us and then, yielding to the strongest motives—honor, fear, and self-interest [the list now begins with honor and not fear, you will note]—declined to give it up." The next step is to move from normalcy of behavior to a general law, hence the next sentence: "Nor, again, are we the first who have entered upon such a course, but it has always been laid down that the weaker are hemmed in by the stronger" [author's translation]. The adverb in the argument has moved from "usually" to "always." We have now not an observation of normal behavior but a binding law of universal action.

The next job to be done in this most central of all paragraphs is to eliminate any principle or universal idea which will conflict with the principle of the strong lording it over the weak. This is done slyly and personally, with the intention of shaming any listener who clings to such notions.

> We [the nameless Athenians say] thought ourselves worthy to rule, and you shared that opinion, until you began toting up and calculating your own interests, and, just as you are doing now, began resorting to talk of justice [τό δικαιό λογό], which no one in his right mind ever put in front of force and advantage when opportunity gave him the chance of getting something by sheer strength. [Author's translation; cf. *GBWW*, 6, p. 368b–c.]

The grand reversal from blame to praise now follows, encompassing all that has been said, and carefully placing the small hand of justice into the muscular grasp of power:

> They are worthy of praise who, being subject to human nature as ruling over us, are more just than they might have been, considering their possession of power. We believe that anyone else, seeing our power, would demonstrate most clearly, as to whether we are walking a moderate path; in our case, however, from the very fact of our reasonableness, blame rather than praise arises in a most unfitting manner. [Author's translation; cf. *GBWW*, 6, p. 368c.]

This passage in this speech is of crucial importance to the whole book. The Athenians are explicating their power and rule. Their speech is an apology for empire and contains an argument based on what is claimed to be a universal law, a law present in human nature, namely that the strong rule the weak. In the immediate context of Book I the speech is unsuccessful. The Spartans decide that the treaty is broken, and that the Athenians are to be blamed, and decide to go to war with Athens. There is some doubt that the speech was ever made; it seems clear that Thucydides placed it here and composed it as part of his explication and memorial of the war. Its propositions are present in the words of Pericles in later speeches in the book. They are very much present in the terrifying debate on the fate of the population of Mytilene. They are the substance of the Athenian talk in the so-called Melian Dialogue.

Meaning, in even the simplest of contexts and situations, has as many layers as an onion. This is in no way intended to imply that the situation or the context determines the meaning, but rather that the context or the situation is the occasion for meaning. Who is talking and why? Is it Pericles or Cleon or Alcibiades or Nicias talking, and why do they say what they say about the war or about an expedition to Sicily? What kind of men are they—noble, ambitious, brilliant, or moderate? Are they talking to a popular assembly, or to a gathering of aristocrats? What kind of relation have they to the assembly, or the soldiers, or the aristocratic gathering, or their neighbors? What are they up to? Why does Pericles want the war? It can hardly be for the same reasons that Cleon or Alcibiades are driven by, though both might use the same arguments concerning power and justice. Are any of the sentences true statements of the way things are? In the case of this invented speech we have just examined there are still further layers of meaning for us. We are an audience separated by an enormous gulf of time from the author. Why he has the Athenians say what they say when they say it, and whether what they say is true or not, must be part of the meaning to us. It would be only too easy to nod one's head and, calling a spade a spade, assent to the propositions concerning power and human nature, the strong ruling the weak, and the weakness of the good. Is it that our very nodding our heads in assent to such propositions is part of the truth of the propositions? Does it reveal something of what we are when we do assent to them? Does rhetoric reveal the other side of being, the dark side, the shabby side, the reverse side of the coin? Is part of this dilemma embodied in that famous red-herring of a term, *human nature*? I have heard persons of good character sagely affirm that the Melians were wrong in not knuckling under to the Athenians. It is a fact that they were all slain and their city extirpated, and the ground it stood on plowed under. The truth is that their deaths only demonstrate the weakness of the good, not that they were wrong. I take this to be Thucydides' meaning, and it is with the darkest irony that he puts into the Athenians' mouths in the speech we have just looked at the harsh reference to just discourse (*dikaios logos*), their attempt being to shame the Spartans for resorting to such talk, to taunt them for their lack of manliness. I will read the sentence again:

> And at the same time we thought ourselves worthy to rule, and you shared that opinion, until you began toting up and calculating your own interests, and, just as you are doing now, began resorting to talk of justice, which no one in his right mind ever put in front of force and advantage when opportunity gave him the chance of getting something by sheer strength. [Author's translation; cf. *GBWW*, 6, p. 368b–c.]

If we can be bamboozled by shame into knuckling under to these propositions about force and power, then the propositions become operationally true.

It is very popular in all ages to dismiss just discourse, and you may recall Aristophanes' bitter satire in the *Clouds,* where just and unjust discourse parade their arguments in front of the audience of Athenian citizens, an audience full of the presence of the endless Peloponnesian War.

Pericles' Funeral Oration in Book II of the histories is the world's most famous speech, and it is in praise of the world's most memorable city. This speech is carefully positioned in front of the most famous description of a disease in literature, the great Plague of Athens. It is so carefully positioned in the structure of the histories that a former tutor, with his customary irony, used to insist that the Plague never happened. By this I gather he meant that it was too patently plotted into the literary scheme of the histories. Terrible and terrifying pairs are placed in front of us, a juxtaposition of light, life, and freedom under law next to darkness, death, and anarchy. Both the Funeral Oration and the account of the Plague have been imitated or copied. You will recall Lucretius's Plague, and we are all most familiar with the countless statesmen-like speeches which employ Pericles' oration as a model.

There are in addition two other speeches of Pericles in the book which frame the meaning of the Funeral Oration. The first one is in Book I, a speech in which he urges the assembly to war. The other occurs after the war has begun, and the city has suffered the Plague. It is because of the political aftermath of these events that Pericles finds it necessary to give this speech, a speech in which he urges the assembly to hold firm in its pursuance of the war. These two framing speeches are, of course, deliberative speeches, delivered before the assembly. They urge and advise concerning the future course of action to be taken by the assembly, in contrast to the Funeral Oration, which is a eulogy of the present and shining spectacle of Athens.

The first paragraph of the first speech contains the essence of practical decision-making and, as such, comments ironically on a future which we, the readers, know:

> I, O men of Athens, hold to the same judgment as always, namely that we must not yield to the Spartans, although I well know that once engaged in the actual work of warfare men are not actuated by the same passionate temper as they are when being persuaded to go to war, but change their judgments according to what happens. I also see that I must give you the same or nearly the same advice I used to give you, and I insist that those of you who are persuaded shall support the common decision, even if we should fail, or, in the case of success, claim no share in the good judgment shown. For it is perfectly possible for the course of events to unfold irrationally and dumbly as it is for the calculations of men; it is for this very reason that we lay the blame on fortune for what turns out contrary to our calculations. [Author's translation; cf. *GBWW,* 6, p. 384c.]

We never deliberate about what we know, but about what we don't know, and we don't know the future, and especially the future of a war. We may hope for a felicitous future, but hope is wishing for what rationally cannot be counted on. There is a piercing logic in the classification of hope as a theological virtue, an excellence beyond nature; for Thucydides, however, the word carries with it an ever-present irony. A political decision is always about the future and aspires to be a contract. It can't be a contract, however, for who will make it stick? What is the binding rule, and if the rule is binding, who will be the judge? It may be just as well that this is so, for if the decision is for war, sticking to the decision may bleed the city to death, or at the very least debase the spirit and counterfeit the moral coinage.

Later in the speech Pericles goes on to insist that the slightest concession to the Spartans will be read by them as fear, whereas a downright refusal of their demands means that they will treat the Athenians as equals. This is a kind of argumentation that numbs us every day in the discussions of deterrence and equal megatonnage. Pericles throws this at the assembly as an imperative:

> So make up your minds, here and now, either to take their orders before any damage is done you, or, if we mean to go to war—as to me at least seems best—do so with the determination not to yield on any pretext, great or small, and not to hold our possessions in fear. For it means enslavement just the same when either the greatest or the least claim is imposed by equals upon their neighbors, not by an appeal to justice but by dictation. (I: CXLI, 1) [Cf. *GBWW,* 6, pp. 384d–85a.]

You will note the force of the word *enslavement* in the last sentence, though there is no clear logical path to be followed from claiming that between equals the slightest concession means slavery rather than injustice. It is certainly a normal phenomenon that neighboring states hate each other. The nearer they are the greater the hate seems to be, in a kind of inverse-force law whose terms are hate and proximity. In Greece one has only to think of Thebes and Plataea, Sparta and Argos, Athens and Corinth, Athens and Thebes, or Athens and its even nearer neighbors (regarded with even more intense hatred), Megara and Aegina. This is one of the perpetual and damning observations which Dante makes as he looks at all the cities of Tuscany consuming each other in a wrath which he can only describe in bestial terms. In our own age we have only to cast our eyes on any part of the globe to observe this phenomenon: Poland and Russia, India and Pakistan, Iran and Arabia, Bolivia and Paraguay, Chile and Ecuador, Russia and China, Vietnam and Cambodia, England and Ireland. Often the hatred between neighbors grows up between states that are somehow united— this happened between the North and the South in our own United States, and the anguish of Lebanon presents a spectacle of hatred and blood between every tribe and every sect of a variety of religions.

These hatreds are nearly ineradicable and are a part of the calculus of power. They are present all through the events of the history we are reading, but they are never the cause of a major war. This is left to the fear that exists between equals. While it was under the aegis of the greater war that the Thebans had finally the satisfaction of seeing their nearest neighbors slaughtered one by one, that greater war arose from a fear between equals. Sparta and Athens are not near neighbors, and they are enormously different, one from the other. They don't know or understand each other enough to be able to hate. It is the fear between equals and the humiliation of being treated as an underling by someone who is the same height as you are that is behind Pericles' statement. This is the heart of his appeal, and the goad to the assembly's manliness. As Thucydides states over and over again, a man or a state is more humiliated at being treated unjustly by an equal than at being beaten or cowed physically by someone patently bigger or stronger. We ourselves for the past thirty years have seen an obscene proliferation of nuclear arms spring like mushrooms from the ground of fear between equals.

Any hope for the mere existence of the world lies in an untangling of, or an accommodation to, this grotesque calculus. And since the snarls caused by fear between equals have never been untangled in the political affairs of men, to hope for their dissolution may be irrational, and even naive. Given the presence of fear and power, reason staggers and redefines itself. It becomes a calculus, a rationalization arising out of the presence of fear and power, and the word *irrational* comes to mean "imperfectly calculated." It is for this reason that Hobbes, the translator of Thucydides, must redefine the meaning of words and base all meaning in the new and mechanical psychology with its roots in the fear of war and the presence of power. If I am driven, the forces that drive me must be analyzed, and a machine built to contain their energy and to ensure my life. In talking of Thucydides, who is no systemizer, we must limit ourselves to noting that in his gravest passages, when he discusses and notes the events and writes down the speeches concerning the considerations we have been pointing to, he employs the phrase *human nature.*

In the next part of his speech Pericles totes up the power and money of the Athenians. He notes their ability to act quickly, and to decide things with resilience by means of their popular assembly. This he contrasts with the complicated allied command structure of Sparta. The Athenians' navy will be their security and should be their hope, as it was at Salamis, and with it they need not fear for their land holdings; their strength lies in their power, their commerce, and their drachmas. Given all of these assets, he hopes that Athens will prove superior. This will only happen, he warns, if they do not attempt to extend their empire while they are waging a war, or weigh themselves down with other dangers of their own making—"for I fear more our own domestic mistakes than the calculations of the enemy" [author's translation].

We, the readers, are well aware of the prophecy implied in this sentence, and after Pericles' third speech Thucydides takes pains to point out the disasters that followed Pericles' death. He lived only two years and six months into the war, and without him Athens foundered, just as under him it was great and glorious and entered the path of war. The speech concludes by urging the assembly to adjust in a strictly legal way their affairs with the Spartans, but to do nothing upon dictation:

> This answer is just and fitting for the city—but it behooves us to know that the war is going to happen, and that the more willing we show ourselves to accept it, the less eager will our enemies be to attack us, and also that from the greater dangers the greater honors accrue both to a private man and to a state. [Author's translation; cf. *GBWW*, 6, p. 386c.]

At the conclusion to the conclusion Pericles appeals to the memory of their fathers, who withstood the Persians, and who with a courage greater than their strength beat back the barbarian and advanced their fortunes to their present state. Thucydides comments, "The Athenians thinking he was advising them for the best voted as he told them to" [author's translation].

It may be that a statesman has to act as if war were inevitable and see to it that the state is prepared. But Pericles' argument to the assembly—that not only is war inevitable but that the more we show ourselves prepared to accept war, the less eager will our enemies be to accept it—is specious. To an enemy such as Sparta, an equal in pride and strength, greater acceptance and preparedness on the part of the Athenians will mean greater fear on the part of the Spartans, and thus greater precautions. Out of that fear and preparedness will grow further armament and further marshalling of allies, finally ensuring the truth of the proposition that war is inevitable. It is apt to the point of slyness that the completion of Pericles' complex sentence contains the appeal to the honor and excellence that accrue to a man and a city from great dangers. He proceeds to buttress this by appealing to the memory of the great patriotic war waged against the Persian barbarians. This rhetorical induction from one war to another is false, as a war between Greeks and barbarian invaders has not the same nature as a war between Greeks. It would be like arguing in this century from the nature of the First World War of 1914, which in no way was worth the price of its blood, to a position which would deny the moral necessity of the war against Nazi Germany. An argument closer to the present generation would contain the faulty inference that since the Second World War was honorable to the nation, the war in Vietnam was also and hence should be pursued with vigor and moral certainty.

After the first speech of Pericles in Book I the war begins. The Spartans invade the land of Attica. Pericles' strategy has been to pull all of the population within the walls, to abandon the countryside to the devastation of the invading Spartans, and to trust in the navy, the empire, and the wealth of the city. Athens and Attica had been inhabited continuously for a length of time that seemed mythical to its inhabitants. They were proud of having been indigenous and co-eternal, as it were, with the soil of Attica. Their habits and mores were attached to the countryside, to their estates. The city of Athens, though the center of Attica politically, was the traditional center of this long-enduring and ancient countryside and had no existence apart from the land about. Pericles' strategy changed all of this, and the whole countryside crowded within the walls, squatting even within sacred places. The Funeral Oration takes place during the winter which closes the first year of war and the first invasion of the land of Attica. The next summer the Spartans invaded the countryside again, and before they had been many days in Attica, the Plague broke out. I shall quote from Thucydides' account:

> It is said, indeed, to have broken out before in many places, both in Lemnos and elsewhere, though no pestilence of such extent nor any scourge so destructive of human lives is on record anywhere. For neither were physicians able to cope with the disease, since they at first had to treat it without knowing its nature, the mortality among them being greatest because they were most exposed to it, nor did any other human art avail. And the supplications made at sanctuaries, or appeals to oracles and the like, were all futile, and at last men desisted from them, overcome by the calamity. (II: XLVII, 4) [Cf. *GBWW*, 6, p. 399b.]

Thucydides then proceeds to inform the reader as to how he will treat of this natural disaster:

> Now anyone, whether physician or layman, may, each according to his personal opinion, speak about its probable origin and state the causes which, in his view, were sufficient to have produced so great a departure from normal conditions; but I shall describe its actual course, explaining the symptoms, from the study of which a person should be best able, having knowledge of it beforehand, to recognize it if it should ever break out again. For I had the disease myself and saw others sick of it. (II: XLVIII, 3) [Cf. *GBWW*, 6, p. 399c.]

This passage cannot help suggesting to us, the readers, that Thucydides intends to write about the Plague in the same way that he writes about the war. He had the disease and saw others sick of it just as analogously he was an admiral in the war, was exiled, and examined it then from a distance. He next describes in detail the physical nature of the Plague, and finally turns to the moral desolation which resulted from it:

> And no one was eager to practice self-denial in prospect of what was esteemed honor, because everyone thought that it was doubtful whether he would live to attain it, but the pleasure of the moment and whatever was in any way conducive to it came to be regarded as at once honorable and expedient. No fear of gods or law of men restrained; for, on the one hand, seeing that all men were perishing alike, they judged that piety and impiety came to the same thing, and, on the other, no one expected that he

> would live to be called to account and pay the penalty of his misdeeds.
> (II: LIII, 3–4) [Cf. *GBWW*, 6, p. 401a.]

It is difficult not to compare this passage with the one which details the horror of the civil war on Corcyra, which Thucydides so clinically describes both as to its symptoms and to its progress. The attempt is to describe something so that it may be recognized if encountered again. In comparing the Plague with the civil war that broke out everywhere in Hellas there are differences to be noted—the Plague may have been carried by rats, a natural cause, whereas the civil war arose from human causes. Are human causes a branch of the natural, and are we obligated to employ the term *human nature?* If both are diseases, justice becomes medicine, assuming the meaning so common to it in the dialogues of Plato.

The Athenians now suffered a change of feelings. They blamed Pericles for having persuaded them to go to war. Their land had been invaded for the second time; the Plague had decimated the population. The Athenians even sent envoys to the Spartans pleading for peace but accomplished nothing. "Being altogether at their wits' end, they assailed Pericles. . . . He called a meeting of the assembly—for he was still general—wishing to reassure them, and by ridding their minds of resentment to bring them to a milder and less timorous mood." Pericles' third speech is then framed to meet this occasion. For us, the readers, it may be the saddest of his speeches. The war which he had argued for has begun. The glorious city which had reached its zenith under his leadership has just suffered the Plague. The anger and fear of the people have to be faced down, and the peace movement quelled. He has to ride the back of his tiger and find words to fit the situation. He begins by saying that he has expected this anger and will show them that they have no reason to be angry with him, or to give way to their misfortunes. A man's private misfortunes are worsened by the state's disasters, so it would be folly to sacrifice the state's security because of troubles at home. You're blaming both me and yourselves, he says, who voted after all for the war. I am as competent a man as you'll find, free from influence of money, and a good patriot. If you believed me once, believe me now.

Next he waves in front of their eyes the banner of near infinite rule and power, something, as he says, he had been loath to do before, as it is almost unseemly and boastful to do so. Seeing them so cast down, however, he will raise their spirits.

> You think that it is only over your allies that your empire extends, but I declare that of two divisions of the world which lie open to man's use, the land and the sea, you hold the absolute mastery over the whole of one,

only to the extent to which you now exercise it, but also to whatever fuller extent you may choose; and there is no one, either the Great King or any nation of those on the earth, who will block your path as you sail the seas with such a naval armament as you now possess. (II: LXII, 2) [Cf. *GBWW*, 6, p. 403a.]

That is, of course, Pericles speaking, not Alcibiades urging the conquest of Sicily.

You can go forth [he says] to meet your enemies not only with confidence but with contempt. For contempt belongs properly to the man who is persuaded by his own judgment that he is superior to his opponent. Such is our case. . . . Fortune being equal, this intelligent scorn renders courage more secure, in that it doesn't trust so much in *hope,* which is strongest when you're at a loss, as in well-founded opinion, opinion founded on the facts of the case, which is a lot surer as far as the future is concerned. [Author's translation; cf. *GBWW*, 6, p. 403b.]

These words of Pericles' find their final home in the mouths of the nameless Athenians as they present their view in the fictive dialogue with the Melians:

Hope is indeed a solace in danger, and for those who have other resources in abundance, though she may injure, she does not ruin them; but for those who stake their all on a single throw—hope being by nature prodigal— it is only when disaster has befallen that her true nature is recognized, and when at last she is known, she leaves the victim no resource wherewith to take precautions against her in future. (V: CIII) [Cf. *GBWW*, 6, p. 506a–b.]

They later butcher the people of Melos and existentially demonstrate the truth of their words.

The next words of Pericles follow a kind of scenario that might be summed up as follows: look at the truth, the facts, shiver, and then gird up your loins; don't be so fatuous as to play at being good, rather become famous. Everyone hates you because of the empire, but "it is far too late to back off, even if someone in the present hour of danger wants to play the 'good man' by shrinking from public actions" [author's translation]. The verb in this sentence which carries the weight of the scorn is *andragathídzetai*—from *anèr* and *agathos*—"play the good or honest man." Pericles continues:

The empire you possess is a tyranny, which it may seem unjust to have taken on, but which certainly would be dangerous to let go of. Such good and honest men would ruin a state either right here, if they could persuade others of their point of view, or if they went to found another city all of their own—men of peace who refrain from politics preserve nothing unless they are accompanied by men of action; it is no benefit in a ruling city but only in a vassal state, to submit for the sake of safety. [Author's translation; cf. *GBWW*, 6, p. 403b–c.]

169

The speech ends with an exordium to the assembly to act heroically. They are men, and Homer was their mentor:

> Anyone who has aspired to rule over others has been hated; but anyone who, aiming high, accepts this hate, is well advised. [Author's translation; cf. *GBWW*, 6, p. 403d.]

The Greek adverb in this sentence is *orthós*, "getting things straight." The author then comments: "Speaking in this way Pericles tried to purge the Athenians of their anger towards him and to channel their minds away from the present evils" [author's translation].

We, the readers, have now to attempt to step back and test the meaning of this speech from our numbing distance of over 2,000 years, a span approaching the everlasting memory Pericles speaks of to the Athenians. The speech is enshrined in this book designed by the author as a possession for all times. Are there true propositions, bona fide laws, stated in this or in other speeches in this book, laws which stand and hold as universal laws of power and politics? Or are the statements exposed to our attention by Thucydides merely the sort of thing which is always said and always will be said in order to persuade an assembly or a senate or a prince when he is deliberating concerning a future course of action? Is it true that the stronger rule the weaker, and that he who rules will be hated? If it's true, must Pericles say it to the assembly? If he does say it to the assembly as a means of rousing them to continued warfare, will they then act in such a way as to bring it about that they are hated even if they weren't before? Do words aimed at the heart and passions of a people sink in to such an extent that they become the mainsprings of their actions and become to all intents and purposes true? If Pericles, certainly as good a politican as one will ever get, finds it necessary to speak scathingly about men wanting to be good and hence not paying attention either to their own or to the state's benefit, what manly man will choose to be "good"? The later shadow of the *Gorgias* and the hero Callicles loom large in our minds as we read these speeches. If at the end of the *Gorgias* justice and right obtain only in the dark underworld court of Rhadamanthus, it is because the good and right do not rule in the desolation of the landscape of power. It would be a shameless naiveté to conceive of any of Plato's political works as arising from any ground other than one of the blackest pessimism regarding human affairs. It is true that he wrote after the Peloponnesian War, but that war does not, in itself, account for what he said any more than it accounts for what Thucydides said. The war was an occasion, first for Thucydides and then for Plato, for observing, for reflecting, and for setting things straight. In both of them one feels the ache for, and the absence of, an efficacious good, and while Socrates may speak of himself as the only true citizen of Athens, Thucydides the Athenian has put into the mouths of his Athenians words that fix forever in our memory the inexorable grind of power, time, and moral decline.

It remains now to speak of the most famous speech, the Funeral Oration. As is so with many very famous things, it turns out to be quite peculiar in many of its features. The occasion for the speech is that "the Athenians, following the custom of their fathers, celebrated at the public expense the funeral rites of the first who had fallen in this war . . . [and] a man chosen by the state, who is regarded as best endowed with wisdom and is foremost in public esteem, delivers over them an appropriate eulogy."

Pericles begins his speech with the usual disclaimer made by speakers on such occasions—who am I to praise such men? Actions speak louder than words. The speaker then attempts to give the best damn speech ever heard. In this case he succeeds. After the customary opening the speech takes on a rather sour note. The gist of what follows is that those who know the dead and what they did will think that scant justice is being done them by the speaker, and those who did not know them and their actions will think, out of envy, that the speaker has committed a gross exaggeration. Despite all this, he says, he will say what he has to say.

Again, as is familiar and customary upon such occasions, the forefathers and the past are mentioned; again the peculiarity is that, despite the enormous age and the weight of custom and tradition in such an ancient city as Athens, the forefathers are quickly passed over in favor of the immediate past, the fathers of those in the audience who acquired the empire, and those alive today who, in the prime of their life, further strengthened this empire so that it is well provided for both in peace and in war. The speech then immediately turns to the City itself and becomes the most famous eulogy of the most famous city. First the polity is praised; it is a democracy where all are equal under the law in the settlement of disputes, but where those who are distinguished are honored regardless of class and wealth. Pericles then praises the liberality of the town, its freedom from resentment and backbiting, the vigor and pizzazz of its talk. It is also a place with all kinds of relaxations, games and sacrifices, fine buildings and proper houses, and it is so rich and big that all the products of the earth flow into it. The city is stronger now because it is freer in its training and abhors secrecy. The citizen takes an interest at once in both private and public things: "we are lovers of beauty with the proper ends in mind, and lovers of wisdom without softness" [author's translation].

What is of particular interest to us as we reflect on the speeches is the next statement of Pericles, where he praises the Athenians as being the most daring in action and at the same time as believing that debate is not a hindrance to action; for most people boldness means ignorance and reasoning causes delay. "In respect of virtue," he says, "we differ from the many—for we acquire our friends not by receiving good from them but by doing good. We alone confer benefits not by calculating our own advantage so much as trusting in our own free and liberal habits" [author's translation].

If we pause for a moment in the midst of the praise we realize that this speech is of course to be classified, if we follow Aristotle's division, as a speech having to do with the present; its business is to praise or blame, and its aim is the noble or the disgraceful. All the other speeches we have considered, the speeches of the Corcyraeans and the Corinthians, the Athenians' speech to the Spartans, and the two flanking speeches of Pericles, had to do with deliberation about future events, and the propositions embedded in them had all to do with the exigencies of rule and power as applied to the benefit of the state.

When we read the glowing praise of Athens' freedom and liberality in this speech of praise, a facile judgment might tend toward cynicism. After all, men of good sense are always wary of exalted speeches, especially when they issue from the mouths of statesmen on solemn occasions. A part of prudence must always agree with Dr. Johnson's dictum that patriotism is the last refuge of a scoundrel. In this century the very name "fatherland" sounds as a nightmare when the memory of what was perpetrated in its name crosses our consciousness.

What is our judgment now, and what are our feelings as the speech continues? One statement rings so in our memory as nearly to preclude judgment. Pericles says, "Putting all this together I say to you that our whole city is the education of Greece." (A more euphonious translation speaks of the "School of Hellas.") The sentence that contains this statement continues, however, as follows:

And it seems to me that every single man amongst us could in his own person, with the greatest grace and versatility, prove himself self-sufficient in the most varied kinds of activity. Many are the proofs given of our power and we do not lack witnesses, and we shall be the wonder not only of men of today but of men of after-times. . . . We shall need no Homer to sing our praise nor any other poet whose verses may perhaps delight for the moment but whose presentation of the facts will be discredited by the truth. [Author's translation; cf. *GBWW*, 6, p. 397c–d.]

This is of course true, as we do all remember Athens 2,500 years later.

Pericles then turns to the remains of the dead, and says that it was for such a place that these men died.

Don't believe, he says, the advantages of such courage by the mere words of a speaker when you yourselves know as well as the speaker what is to be gained by warding off the enemy. Rather you must when you are about your daily work, fix your gaze upon the power of Athens and become lovers of her, and when she appears great to you, consider that all this has been gained by courage. [Author's translation; cf. *GBWW*, 6, p. 398b.]

This is soon followed by another sentence so beautiful that it is hard to look at it:

The whole world is the sepulchre of famous men, and it is not the epitaph upon monuments set up in their own land that alone commemorates them, but also in lands not their own there abides in each breast an unwritten memorial of them, planted in the heart rather than graven on stone. (II: XLIII, 3) [Cf. *GBWW*, 6, p. 398b–c.]

The eulogy becomes exhortation, and its charge may be paraphrased as follows: "you have more to lose, hence be unsparing of your lives, as the difference between your present beloved splendor and a disaster is enormous. The more you have to love, the harder you should fight; ordinary folk have no place they passionately love, as you do, a place so splendid, which shines in its might and beauty." The speech, whose occasion was the customary eulogy over the first to die in battle, becomes the eulogy of the city, not the city as a repository of old tradition and habit, but the present city, replete with power and beauty, standing in front of the citizen's eyes like the Parthenon on the hill, a love object of incomparable worth, worth so much that there can be no hesitation in fighting for her, as she is worth the price. The adoration of her power becomes the heart of the matter. Beauty and power are exhibited to the citizens, held up to them as love objects. Eros and Ares, Venus and Mars, are linked, and the hope of immortal fame standing beyond the inevitable future blood stirs them to heroic action. They have all been brought up on Homer. The implicit argument may be summed up as follows: major premise—lovers are famous; minor premise—patriots are lovers; conclusion—fight.

And fight they did. After Pericles' third speech Thucydides carefully notes:

And yet, after they had met with disaster in Sicily, where they lost not only their army but also the greater part of their fleet, and by this time had come to be in a state of sedition at home, they nevertheless held out ten years not only against the enemies they had before but also against the Sicilians, who were now combined with them, and, besides, against most of their allies, who were now in revolt, and, later on, against Cyrus, son of the King, who joined the Peloponnesians and furnished them with money for their fleet; and they did not finally succumb until they had in their private quarrels fallen upon one another and been brought to ruin. Such abundant grounds had Pericles at that time for his own forecast that Athens might quite easily have triumphed in this war over the Peloponnesians alone. (II: LXV, 12–13) [Cf. *GBWW*, 6, p. 404c–d.]

The fact remains that they lost, and in that long swath of wartime the words and arguments which we have examined, which in peacetime might have remained underground, in wartime came to the surface and became fixed and inexorable. They were used in the assembly which debated the fate of the population of Mytilene; they were present in the hearts of the Spartans as they led out the courageous citizens of Plataea and slaughtered them one by one; they were dramatically composed into the Athenians' dialogue with the Melians before that population was eliminated. In this same swath of time civil war erupted all over Greece, the paradigm of it being the horror on Corcyra, where words changed their meanings, and people became faceless, and words became masks behind which the anarchy of the passions paraded. The habits and customs of the past, the only safeguard to be counted upon, crumbled, and the pure present showed its face like the Gorgon's head.

Can the pure present of power and beauty waved like a banner in the faces of the Assembly in the Funeral Oration inflame nobly? Is the vision seen worthy, and worth such travail as the long years shift and pass? Patriotism is infinitely more difficult for all of us who inhabit these enormous modern nation-states; there's nothing to look at. To be a patriot now one has to love a principle and be willing to die for it, which is so different from gazing upon a place, bounded by its fields, beautiful to look upon, rich and marvelously racy to live in, full of ingenious and sharp-tongued people; a place where clearly one lives a better life than one would anywhere else.

Can the present vision of a shining and glorious city, the love object presented by Pericles, counter that other present vision, the immediate anarchy and horror present both in the Plague and in the civil war on Corcyra? Did Nicias see the same thing as Pericles? Does Thucydides the Athenian see the same thing as Pericles? Perhaps he does, but he frames the Funeral Oration with the two speeches we have considered and places it, in his composition, directly in front of his account of the Plague. He also praises Nicias, dying far from Athens, a failure at the end of a disaster, as the man who "least deserved to meet with such a calamity, because of his course of life that had been wholly regulated in accordance with virtue."

Some students with whom I read these speeches last year felt that the study of them and of this book led to cynicism. This is to read what is intended as irony wrongly. If no solution in human affairs is possible, it is because nothing of heartfelt concern is a problem that can be solved. If no solution is possible, human excellence calls for courage and shrewdness to walk hand in hand with decency and compassion. They don't walk hand in hand usually, and the best you can get is their mutual awareness, one of the other. I was struck recently by a documentary which I saw on television; it seemed to me like an allegory of power and the good. In it two women of extraordinary toughness and calculation were exhibited to us, the viewers. The documentary was about Mother Teresa, and the scene which stuck in my memory was filmed in the grand audience chamber in New Delhi. Mrs. Gandhi, that shrewd, tough, and resilient power broker, gave a medal honoring Mother Teresa to that shrewd, tough, and resilient nun. Mrs. Gandhi is the ruler of the most populous democracy in the world, a nation-state that came into being in the midst of one of those bloodbaths which our century is full of, an event of such terrifying barbarity and slaughter that ordinary descriptions of Hell seem painted in pastel, and Corcyra seems a tempest in a teapot, in comparison. For all that, the nation lurches on in its misery, guided and coaxed and dictated to by Mrs. Gandhi. Mother Teresa performs good works, and this is seen by any onlooker regardless of his faith or lack thereof. It is hard to conceive that either woman, so aware of the way things are, expects anything to change in this world she is so much in the midst of. Mrs. Gandhi, in addition to the parlous state of her enormous nation, lives under the shadow of the two monstrous powers with which she shares the continent, Russia and China. She lives also with the blood-hate of her nearest neighbor, Pakistan. Mother Teresa lives in the midst of the most utter poverty and human degradation in one of the great cities of the subcontinent. In the television encounter one could see the hard, clear glance of Mrs. Gandhi, but even more one could sense the calculation behind the nun's eyes: was the minister on the right good for a couple of ambulances, and was the fat and powerful man on the left to be counted on for a ton of medical supplies for the benefit of her hospital for incurables in the heart of that ultimate human city, Calcutta?

PART THREE

Special Features

Newton's Path to the *Principia*

Curtis Wilson

Curtis Wilson was born in Los Angeles in 1921 and attended the University of California there. Since 1948 he has been a tutor at St. John's College, Annapolis, Maryland, except for seven years spent as visiting associate professor, and then as professor, in the Department of History at the University of California, San Diego. He also served as dean of St. John's from 1958 to 1962 and again from 1973 to 1977. In 1952 he received a Ph.D. in the history of science from Columbia University, and since 1966 he has devoted much time to study of the history of astronomy in the seventeenth and eighteenth centuries.

Mr. Wilson has published articles on aspects of both Kepler and Newton in *Scientific American, Isis, Journal for the History of Ideas,* and other publications. At present, he is the editor of Volume 2 of *The General History of Astronomy,* a work of international scope with articles by many contributors, now being issued by the Cambridge University Press. He will also contribute the article on Newton to this work.

When and how did Newton come to conceive the central idea of his masterwork—the idea of universal gravitation? From the time of his death until very recently, the standard account was that he hit on this in 1665 or 1666, when he was twenty-two or twenty-three years of age, and that it came to him as a simple generalization: just as an apple falls toward the Earth, so falls the Moon as it moves in its orbit, for its orbital motion may be conceived as resulting from the compounding of the uniform rectilinear motion it would have if uninfluenced by other bodies and the attraction it undergoes because of the presence of the nearby Earth. The same kind of analysis can then be extended to the planets in their orbits about the Sun: their actual motions are the result of uniform rectilinear motions combined at each instant with a "fall" toward the central body, the Sun.

Today, this way of conceiving the matter is all too familiar; it is "old hat." And because that is so, we have no trouble imagining a bright young university student having such a conception in 1665 or 1666: if it is so obvious to us, why should it not have been obvious to him?

The fact is, however, that Newton did not have the idea of universal gravitation in 1665 or 1666, although in later years he was willing to let it be supposed that he did: that is one of the conclusions of the last quarter century of Newtonian research. It is possible that he first entertained this idea in the winter of 1679–80, but I shall argue that at this date there was strong evidence against it and that Newton did not conceive a compelling argument for universal gravitation before late 1684. Moreover, before 1679, Newton's thoughts about planetary motion and gravitation show no sign of ranging beyond the horizon set by the generally accepted views of his contemporaries: he assumed the existence of planetary vortices and, like Huygens, accepted the erroneous dynamics of circular motion that Descartes had introduced into the discussion of planetary motion. Newton also thought up additional aethereal mechanisms to account for gravity toward the Earth and the Sun. But there is no indication whatever of his having entertained during this period the hypothesis that the celestial bodies attract one another over the vast distances of interplanetary space.

In brief, Newton himself had to undergo the Newtonian revolution. His masterwork emerged from the sharp conflict of ideas. Some knowledge of this conflict can cast a fresh light on the *Principia* and help the reader to a clearer discernment of what it achieves.

To provide such a reader with a short account of the coming-to-be of this great book, stressing the logical relations of ideas to ideas and of ideas to facts, is the purpose of the present essay. It owes much to the work of a number of scholars, particularly D. T. Whiteside and R. S. Westfall, and makes no claims to originality of interpretation, although one scholar or another is likely to object to one or another of my formulations. References, reduced to a minimum, are given in abbreviated form; the full titles will be found at the end of the essay. A final bibliographical note will guide readers, should they be so inclined, to the sources on which I have depended.

Beginnings: the Trinity notebook

When Newton arrived in Cambridge in June of 1661—he was eighteen years of age—he acquired a small, leather-bound notebook, in which he proceeded to record systematic notes on his studies. The earliest notes are in Greek and pertain to Aristotelian and Neoplatonic readings. There are later notes on sixteenth- and seventeenth-century textbooks of Aristotelian and Scholastic branches of knowledge, from physics to rhetoric. But in late 1663 or early 1664 Newton began the reading of Walter Charleton's *Physiologia Epicuro-Gassendo-Charltoniana* (1654). This marks a turning point in his studies. On page 3 of Charleton's work Newton encountered a passage concerning rejectors of authority, "the Assertors of Philosophical Liberty," among whom Charleton lists, and goes on to celebrate,

> the heroical Tycho Brahe, the subtle Kepler, the most acute Galileo, the profound Scheinerus, the miraculous because universally learned Kircherus, the most perspicacious Harvey, and the epitome of all, Descartes. In honour of each of these heroes, we could wish (if the constitution of our times would bear it) a colossus of gold were erected at the public charge of students, and under each this inscription: *Amicus Plato, amicus Aristoteles, magis amica veritas.* [Plato is a friend, Aristotle is a friend, but truth is more a friend.]

Newton copied the proposed inscription into his notebook at the top of a blank page. Just below this he wrote *Quaestiones quaedam Philosophicae* (*Certain Philosophical Questions*), and the headings that follow, on this and succeeding pages, have to do, not with Aristotelian and Scholastic questions, but with questions raised by the new science of Galileo, Kepler, and Descartes.

The reading of Charleton's *Physiologia* sparked in Newton a lively interest in atomism. Charleton's book is largely based on writings of Pierre Gassendi (1592–1655), who did more than anyone else to reconcile Epicurean atomism, long stigmatized as atheistic, with Christian belief. Charleton follows Gassendi in attacking the dogmatism of Peripatetics and Cartesians alike, and in defending atomistic explanations of natural phenomena as more probable than the corresponding Aristotelian, Scholastic, or Cartesian explanations. Newton, in turn, followed Charleton in adopting the doctrine that the physical world is composed of material atoms and void. This doctrine formed the basis of his later inquiries in natural philosophy.

While writing the *Questions,* Newton began the study of Descartes's *Principles of Philosophy* (1644) and noted difficulties he found in the physical explanations given there. According to Descartes, the Sun's light is a pressure in the aether, directed outward from the Sun; also, according to Descartes, it is this same pressure in the aether, as directed inward toward the Sun, that keeps the planets (which are being carried about the Sun by vortices in the aether) from accelerating away from the Sun owing to the centrifugal force generated by their orbital motion. Newton objects:

> Light cannot be by pression, for then we should see in the night as well, or better, than in the day. We should see a bright light above us, because we are pressed downward. (*Trinity Notebook,* p. 381)

Newton doubts that the several functions that Descartes attributed to his postulated aether are compatible.

One of the headings in Newton's notebook, taken out of Charleton, was "Of Gravity and Levity," and Newton's disquisition under this heading presents an aethereal mechanism for gravity that, a decade later, he considered plausible enough to present to the Royal Society. His first account of it is curiously lacking in tentativeness. "The matter causing gravity," he says, "must pass through all the pores of a body." Newton is imagining a flux of aethereal matter which descends with great speed, bearing downward all bodies that it meets. Once inside the Earth, the aethereal particles collide with one another and form larger particles, which then ascend again, but more slowly, so as to yield from the surfaces of the bodies they meet with, and so as not to push these upward as much as the descending flux pushes them downward. Newton recognizes that the imagined mechanism might cause bodies of different internal structures to be accelerated downward with different degrees of acceleration. Speculating about this he writes:

> Try whether the weight of a body may be altered by heat or cold,
> dilation or condensation, beating, powdering, transferring to several places
> or several heights, or placing a hot or heavy body over it or under it, or

by magnetism. . . . Whether a plate flatways or edgeways is heaviest. Whether the rays of gravity may be stopped by reflecting or refracting them. If so a perpetual motion may be made in one of these two ways.

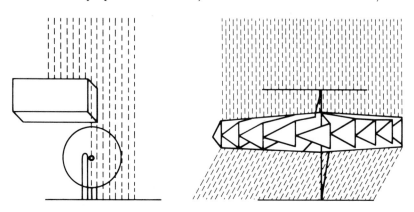

The gravity of bodies is as their solidity, because all bodies descend equal spaces in equal times, consideration being had to the resistance of the air. (*Trinity Notebook*, p. 431)

From this we see that, as the last sentence indicates, Newton was aware of the experimental result, mentioned by Charleton and also by Galileo (whose *Dialogo* Newton consulted at this time), that all bodies fall with equal speeds; and he knew this implies that their weights are as their "solidities," or amounts of matter. Was he aware of the inconsistency of his hypothesis about "altering" weights with the experimental result? We do not know. If he was, he may have considered the experiments insufficiently precise to exclude the possibility of slight differences in the acceleration of gravity to which different bodies might be subject, depending on their textures. In any case, this would prove to be a thought of crucial importance to Newton in 1684.

In the same notebook with *Certain Philosophical Questions* we encounter Newton's notes on Thomas Streete's *Astronomia Carolina* (1661), a book on the predictive astronomy of the planets and the Moon. It is from this work that Newton learned about Kepler's first and third laws of planetary motion.

Newton made detailed notes on Streete's use of Kepler's third law, according to which the squares of the planetary periods are as the cubes of their mean distances from the Sun. Here Streete does something not done before in any published work: he uses the observationally determined periods of the planets to compute their mean solar distances. In all previously published works the mean solar distances had been determined from observations of the planets together with observationally determined elements for the Earth's orbit.

Streete's source for the new way of proceeding was the manuscript of a work by Jeremiah Horrocks (1618?–41), *Venus in sole visa,* which was published in 1662. The Horrocksian procedure improves the accuracy of planetary theories, particularly those of Mercury and Venus, because of the precision with which the planetary periods can be determined. It was the procedure eventually recommended in the *Principia,* but before that work came to be written Newton was faced with claims of astronomers that forced him to question the strict exactitude of Kepler's third law.

In Streete, Newton also found a statement of Kepler's so-called first law, according to which the planets revolve in ellipses with the Sun at one focus. Neither here nor in the case of the third law does Streete offer confirmatory evidence.

As for the second law, the rule that the area swept out by the radius vector from Sun to planet is proportional to the time of description, Streete does not mention it. In its place, to determine the planet's motion in time, he gives a rule first published in 1657 by the French astronomer Ismael Boulliau (1605–94). In the accompanying diagram,

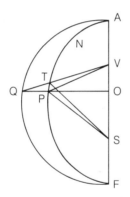

S is the Sun, and *V* the empty focus of the ellipse *ANF.* If the "mean motion" of the planet, that is, an angle increasing with the planet's mean angular rate about the Sun, is *AVP,* then to find the true place of the planet a perpendicular is dropped from *P* to the axis *AF* and prolonged in the other direction to the point *Q* where it meets the circumscribing circle; the planet will then be found at *T* where *QV* intersects the ellipse. This rule is not strictly equivalent to Kepler's areal rule; in the case of Mars, for instance, its predictions of heliocentric longitude (place of the planet as seen from the Sun) can differ from the Keplerian ones by as much as 2.5 minutes of arc. Yet in the 1660s such an error was not yet recognized as a glaring one, and Boulliau's rule was far more convenient to apply than was Kepler's.

Another such "modified equant" rule must have come into Newton's ken when, probably in the winter of 1664–65, he studied Vincent

Wing's *Harmonicon Coeleste* (1651). Wing's procedure for determining the motion of a planet was, like Boulliau's, checked against Tycho Brahe's observations of Mars. When it was that Newton learned of Kepler's areal rule we do not know, but it was certainly before 1676, by which year he had worked out an arithmetical series for applying it. Whenever it was, he would have had no reason to regard this rule as more accurate than the rules used by Streete or Wing, for Kepler had derived it from a hypothetical celestial dynamics that hardly anyone else accepted, and for its empirical warrant it had only the agreement with the very same Tychonic observations that other astronomers used as their touchstone.

Thus, contrary to what textbooks have often implied, I must insist that the strict accuracy of Kepler's laws was not a given for Newton; he could not take their exact truth for granted.

What else might Newton have gleaned from Streete's astronomy? Streete, like Descartes, taught that the planets are carried about the Sun in fluid vortices. As for comets, he followed Kepler in assuming their paths to be rectilinear:

> They are generated of planetary substance, but incompact and dissolvable . . . ; and according to the general consent of observations, their motions are (as Kepler defines them) in or near right lines. (Streete, p. 11)

Like Streete, and like most of the astronomical theorists of the day, Newton during the 1660s and 1670s accepted a vortex theory of planetary motion: we shall see the evidence for this shortly. As late as 1681 we shall find him concluding that the trajectories of comets are rectilinear, or nearly so, a conclusion directly contrary to the theory of universal gravitation.

Newton on dynamics and planetary motion in the 1660s

Newton's *Principia* is founded on dynamics, the laws of motion of bodies subject to the action of forces. In the 1660s these laws had been formulated only in part, and only with a considerable intermixture of error. Descartes had made a beginning in his *Principles of Philosophy*. In Part II of this work he attempted to formulate laws of motion and to apply them to collisions of bodies. Some of his assumptions were false, some of his inferences were invalid, some of his conclusions were contrary to what one could determine by experiment. To be sure, the Cartesian assumption that the universe is entirely full of matter implied that neither the laws of motion nor their consequences would be straightforwardly verifiable: the omnipresent matter would always interfere. To Newton the atomist, rejecting as he did Descartes's identification of matter with extension, and denying that space is everywhere full of matter, this result was neither satisfactory nor necessary. In his Waste Book, probably begun early in 1665, Newton entered upon the project of revising the Cartesian dynamics so as to give it consistency both with itself and with experimental findings.

The first law of motion in the *Principia* is the inertial principle: Every body continues in its state of rest, or of uniform motion, unless it is compelled to change that state by forces impressed upon it. Descartes was the first to enunciate this principle, and he gave it in two parts:

> (1) If [a body] is at rest we do not believe that it will ever begin to move unless it driven to do so by some external cause. Nor, if it is moving, is there any significant reason to think that it will ever cease to move of its own accord and without some other thing which impedes it. (Descartes, p. 59)
> (2) Each part of matter, considered individually, tends to continue its movement only along straight lines, and never along curved ones. (Descartes, p. 60)

Both parts of the principle derived, according to Descartes, from the "law" that "each thing, provided that it is simple and undivided, always remains in the same state as far as is in its power, and never changes except by external causes."

Newton in his formulation of the principle in the Waste Book follows an exactly parallel logical sequence. There can be no doubt that his articulation of the principle is drawn from Descartes's *Principles.*

In Newton's treatment of collision processes, it again appears that he is working from the *Principles.* Descartes starts from the assumption that no more action is required to produce motion in a body than is required to bring it to rest again by destroying this motion, the quantity of motion being understood as given by the quantity of matter and its velocity conjointly. Newton says the same:

> There is exactly required so much and no more force to reduce a body to rest as there was to put it upon motion: *et e contra.* (Herivel, p. 48)

In applying the principle, however, Newton quickly left Descartes behind, for Descartes's rules of impact, besides being new, were mostly wrong. Descartes had claimed that in a collision between a moving and a stationary body, the resting body's resistance to being moved could exceed the force of motion of the moving body, in which case, if the bodies were hard, the stationary body would remain at rest while the moving body would simply be reflected. If, on the other hand, the force of motion of the moving body exceeded the resting body's resistance to motion, the two would move on together, with conservation of the total quantity of motion.

Newton accepted from Descartes the principle of the conservation of total quantity of motion, but he realized that this total quantity must be calculated algebraically, account being taken of both the directions and the magnitudes of the motions of the bodies involved. Here he showed himself familiar with vector addition by means of the parallelogram of forces. In the case of perfectly elastic bodies he realized that the relative velocity of approach before impact must equal the relative velocity of separation after impact. With these assumptions he arrived at the correct rules for both inelastic and elastic impact, before these rules reached the public (in 1669) in writings of Christopher Wren, John Wallis, and Christiaan Huygens.

In presenting the rules of impact, Newton articulates the essence of the third law of motion as applied to collisions:

> If two bodies *p* and *r* meet the one the other, the resistance in both is the same for so much as *p* presses upon *r* so much *r* presses upon *p*. And therefore they must both suffer an equal mutation in their motion. (Herivel, p. 159)

Throughout his presentation Newton takes force to be proportional to quantity of motion (*mv*, or mass times velocity) created or destroyed. His usage is the same when he comes to formulate the second law of motion in the *Principia*.

There is one further respect in which Descartes's dynamics had a crucial influence on Newton: it is in the treatment of circular motion. According to Descartes,

> . . . any body which is moving in a circle constantly tends to move [directly] away from the center of the circle which it is describing. (Descartes, p. 61)

For illustration, Descartes cites the example of a stone whirled in a sling; the tendency of the stone to recede is experienced as a tug of the sling on one's hand. Actually Descartes recognizes more than one "endeavor" or *conatus* in the stone. He finds (1) an endeavor to move along the tangent to the circular path, and (2) an endeavor to recede from the center (*conatus recedendi a centro*). He appears to recognize that the endeavor from the center has its origin in the endeavor along the tangent, but nevertheless he treats the two as distinct. If, he points out, a tube containing a ball is rotated about one end, the ball is accelerated out of the tube. The example apparently persuaded him that the *conatus recedendi* was real.

Newton accepted from Descartes the reality of the *conatus recedendi a centro*. So he wrote in his Waste Book:

> . . . it appears that all bodies moved circularly have an endeavor from the center about which they move. (Herivel, p. 48)

As far as the evidence goes, before 1679 Newton never conceived the dynamics of circular motion differently, never became aware that the *conatus a centro* is only an apparent force, to be associated solely with a rotating frame of reference.

Yet within this questionable conceptualization, Newton derived, and went beyond Descartes in deriving, apparently by 1665 or 1666, a quantitative evaluation of the magnitude of the endeavor from the center, equivalent to our formula v^2/r. I will not here give Newton's derivation of this result in the Waste Book, but rather a derivation he devised toward the end of the decade, perhaps in 1669. In the accompanying diagram, *AB* is tangent to the circle at *A*, whence $AB^2 =$

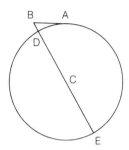

$BD \times BE$ (by Euclid's Proposition 36, Book III). If arc *AD* is considered infinitesimal, it can be equated with *AB*, and the difference between *BE* and *DE* will be negligible, so that $AD^2 = BD \times DE$. Here *BD* is the distance the revolving body would be carried away from the circle by the *conatus recedendi* in the time it takes for the body to move through arc *AD*. To find the distance *x* the body would be carried away from the circle during a complete revolution, Newton invokes Galileo's rule according to which the distances in uniformly accelerated motions are as the squares of the times. Then

$$x : BD :: (ADEA)^2 : (AD)^2 :: (ADEA)^2 : BD \times DE,$$

whence $x = (ADEA)^2/DE = (2\pi r)^2/2r = 2\pi^2 r$, where *r* is the radius.

"Hence," Newton concludes, "the endeavors from the centers of divers circles are as the diameters divided by the squares of the periodic times."

Of this result Newton makes a number of applications. The first is found in the Waste Book, and consists in a comparison of the acceleration of gravity with the *conatus recedendi a centro* of a body at the Earth's equator. By measuring the period of a simple pendulum, Newton determines that gravity would cause a body to fall 196 inches in the first second of descent—a very accurate value. The *conatus* of bodies to rise at the equator owing to the Earth's rotation, as calculated by Newton's formula, proves to be insignificant by comparison, and Newton concludes that the catastrophic consequences of the Earth's rotation imagined by anti-Copernicans would not occur.

In the manuscript of ca. 1669 from which we have extracted Newton's derivation of the measure of *conatus recedendi*, he applies his result to a comparison between the force of gravity at the surface of the Earth and the Moon's endeavor to recede from the Earth, using the *conatus recedendi* of an object at the Earth's equator as a middle term. Taking from Galileo's *Dialogo* the rather faulty value of 3,500 miles for the Earth's radius, he finds that the endeavor of a stone from the Earth's equator, due to the diurnal rotation, would cause it to traverse $5/9$ inch in the first second of motion. This he finds to be 12.5 times greater than the Moon's endeavor from the Earth, due to its orbital motion. Meanwhile, the acceleration of gravity at the Earth's equator is about 350 times greater than the *conatus recedendi* of the stone at the equator. "And so," Newton concludes, "the force of gravity is 4,000 and more times greater than the endeavor of the Moon to recede from the center of the Earth."

Years later (probably after 1712), in the context of priority disputes, Newton implied that he was here testing the inverse-square law of gravitation, and that the result "answered pretty nearly." Pemberton and Whiston, disciples of Newton who wrote in after years about his discoveries, say that he was then (in 1665 or 1666) somewhat disappointed and so turned his mind to other studies. Whiston adds that this disappointment "made Sir Isaac suspect that [the power restraining the Moon in her orbit] was partly that of gravity, and partly that of Cartesius's vortices. . . ."

It is not impossible to give this claim a meaning consistent with what else we know of Newton's thought in this period. We can do so if we suppose that Newton understood the Moon to be carried about the Earth in an aethereal vortex and was interested to test whether an additional flux of aether into the Earth, such as we have already seen him proposing in his Trinity notebook as an explanation for gravity, might not be responsible for counteracting the Moon's *conatus recedendi*. As we learn from a letter that Newton wrote Halley (i.e., Edmond Halley, the English astronomer and mathematician who first calculated the orbit of the comet later named for him) in 1686, Newton considered this aethereal hypothesis for gravity to be consonant with an inverse-square law. The notion of *universal* gravitation is not present.

In the manuscript of ca. 1669 I have been citing, Newton also applies his formula for evaluating *conatus recedendi* to the planets. The endeavor for any particular planet, assuming a circular orbit, will be as r/T^2, where r is the radius of the orbit and T the period. But by Kepler's third law, T^2 varies as r^3. Hence, the endeavors from the Sun or center will be as $1/r^2$. Here again the result is consonant with a theory combining an aethereal vortex about the Sun with an aethereal flux into the Sun—such a theory as we shall soon find Newton explicitly formulating. There is no evidence that Newton was here entertaining the idea of *universal* gravitation.

That Newton, in his thinking about planetary and lunar motion in the 1660s, assumed aethereal vortices, as his use of the Cartesian dynamics would suggest, is confirmed by notes he made on the endpapers of his copy of Vincent Wing's *Astronomia Britannica*, published in 1669. These notes also show him to be unsure of the exact truth of both the first and third Keplerian laws.

The mean solar distances of the planets as given by Wing had been determined from observations and differed from those implied by Kepler's third law. Newton remarks that Wing's tables would in most cases better agree with observations if the mean solar distances were derived from Kepler's rule, but he also shows signs of being uncertain of the strict exactitude of the rule.

For both the Moon and the planets, Newton proposes equant-style hypotheses in which a number of different parameters are to be fitted to observations in such a way that the shape of the orbit is allowed to vary from the elliptical. The lunar inequalities, he suggests, are due to the compression of the vortex that rotates about the Earth by the solar vortex that carries about with it both the Earth and the Moon. The terrestrial vortex will be more compressed, he believes, in winter, when the Earth is closer to the Sun, than in summer, when the Earth is farther away.

Newton's notes on Wing's *Astronomia Britannica* thus show that, in 1669 or 1670, Newton accepted the notion of solar and terrestrial vortices as at least a working hypothesis; there is no indication here that he has in mind a way of applying an inverse-square law of gravitation to the calculation of planetary orbits, or that he has ever entertained the idea of universal gravitation.

Philosophical underpinnings for natural philosophy: Newton's *De gravitatione* of ca. 1669

We have seen that Newton in his earliest writings on natural philosophy embraced atomism and was therefore opposed to the Cartesian doctrine, according to which empty space is a contradiction in terms. Early on, Newton became concerned with the theological and metaphysical underpinnings of his atomism. Between 1668 and 1670 he wrote some forty pages of an essay which we shall refer to as *De gravitatione,* and here in a long digression he sets forth his theological and epistemological beliefs as they relate to space, time, and body. These beliefs are essentially the same as those he later expressed in the General Scholium of the *Principia* (second and third editions). They furnish the framework and ultimate legitimation for his theories of matter, motion, and force. The essay is in large part a polemic against Descartes's philosophy, an attempt, as Newton puts it, "to dispose of his [Descartes's] fictions." At the same time, it supplies one more piece of evidence that Newton in the late 1660s still had no alternative or objection to the Cartesian analysis of circular motion, in terms of a *conatus recedendi a centro.*

Among the positions taken by Descartes in his *Principles of Philosophy* and addressed by Newton are the following. Descartes held to a traditional ontology according to which whatever is, is either substance or accident. A substance was something that existed independently of other things. Substances, Descartes contended, were either extended things or thinking things. What, then, was space—substance or accident? Descartes held that, in its essence, extension was not separable from the extended thing. Thus, it could not be substance; it was, rather, essential attribute.

It followed that there was no space unoccupied by body, all extension being the extension of some body. Were there nothing between the walls of a container, Descartes argued, the walls would be in contact; empty space was a contradiction in terms. Since the world is altogether full of matter, all motion entails the motion of matter in closed paths (vortices). All motion is relative to the surrounding bodies, for there is no independent or absolute space separable from body. Therefore, Descartes believed he could assert the Earth to be at rest, in accordance with the recent dictum of the Holy Office in the case of Galileo, for the Earth rests with respect to the aethereal vortex by which it is carried about the Sun.

To all these assertions Newton was vehemently opposed. Underlying his opposition is a theological premise; he believed in the biblical God, a God of power, lordship, dominion—an intelligent and active agent. Early and late, Newton always viewed any attempt to identify God with his perfections, or to locate Him outside space and time, or to describe his substance metaphysically, as a falsification of the biblical truth. God is a God who acts and is to be known by what He does. The human mind, Newton early decided, is incapable of having direct knowledge of substance or being, whether that of God or any other thing. It is a consequence of this tenet that human knowledge of nature must be grounded in sensible experience.

In opposing Descartes's views on space and motion, Newton drew on metaphysical and epistemological arguments he had met with in Charleton's *Physiologia*—arguments that Charleton, in turn, had come by in the writings of Gassendi. Following Gassendi and Charleton, Newton argued that space and time are neither substances nor defining accidents of substances. Rather, they are secondary attributes involved in the attribution of existence to any thing. Thus, Newton says in the *De gravitatione:*

Space is a disposition of being *qua* being. No being exists or can exist that is not related to space in some way. God is everywhere, created minds are somewhere, and body is in the space that it occupies; and whatever is neither everywhere nor anywhere does not exist. And hence it follows that space is an effect arising from the first existence of being, because when any being is postulated, space is postulated. (Hall, p. 136)

Analogous statements apply to time. Neither space nor time, Newton implied, has been created. Neither belongs to the essence of God. Rather, they are consequences or presuppositions of God's omnipresence and sempiternity. But this doctrine is not to be taken as implying that God is an extended spirit; in each instant and point of space, Newton evidently meant, God was to be understood as numerically the same.

It will be apparent from the foregoing that Newton had to deny the Cartesian identification of matter and extension, and, therefore, that he had metaphysical warrant for admitting void spaces or vacuums. He goes further in *De gravitatione,* elaborating a hypothesis as to the nature of corporeal things that makes the existence of each of them immediately dependent in each instant on the will of God:

If [God] should . . . cause some space projecting above the Earth, like a mountain or any other body, to be impervious to bodies and thus stop or reflect light and all impinging things, it seems impossible that we should not consider this space to be truly body from the evidence of our senses (which constitute our sole judges in this matter); for it will be tangible on account of its impenetrability, and visible, opaque and colored on account of the reflection of light, and it will resonate when struck because the adjacent air will be moved by the blow. . . . And I do not see that it would not equally operate upon our minds and in turn be operated upon, because it is nothing more than the product of the divine mind realized in a definite quantity of space. (Hall, p. 139)

The ontology here hypothesized remained Newton's to the end, and we should note that it liberated him in principle from the Cartesian restriction to explanations of natural phenomena solely in terms of matter in motion, with all transmission of motion by contact. Whereas Descartes had to suppose that matter was solely passive, Newton was free to hypothesize that it might be endowed by God with active powers that operate over distances. If "the mechanical philosophy" is understood—as Huygens, for instance, understood it—to require that all natural phenomena be accounted for in terms of the shapes, sizes, and motions of corpuscles of matter, with transmission of motion solely by contact, then we may doubt that Newton was ever a committed mechanist in this sense.

Another anti-Cartesian consequence of Newton's metaphysical position is that space and time are absolute, independent of the necessarily relative measure we may apply to them. Descartes's failure to recognize a spatiotemporal framework independent of matter, Newton argued, led him into self-contradiction. A body moving in a circle, Descartes maintained, has a *conatus* to recede from the center of the circle. According to Descartes also, motion is essentially relative, and so any body is moved with as many motions as there are other bodies with which to compare it. Hence, no one motion can be said to be true and absolute in preference to others. But, argues Newton,

> unless it is conceded that there can be a single physical motion of any body, and that the rest of its changes of relation and position with respect to other bodies are so many external designations, it follows that the Earth (for example) endeavors to recede from the center of the Sun on account of a motion relative to the fixed stars, and endeavors the less to recede on account of a lesser motion relative to Saturn and the aethereal orb in which it is carried, and still less relative to Jupiter and the swirling matter which occasions its orbit, and also less relative to Mars and its aethereal orb, and much less relative to other orbs of aethereal matter which, although not bearing planets, are closer to the annual orbit of the Earth; and indeed relative to its own orb it has no endeavor, because it does not move in it. Since all these endeavors and non-endeavors cannot absolutely agree, it is rather to be said that only the motion which causes the Earth to endeavor to recede from the Sun is to be declared the Earth's natural and absolute motion. (Hall, p. 127)

We here have the precursor of the rotating-bucket experiment in Newton's *Principia:* absolute motion manifests itself in rotations. On the one hand, Newton sees absolute space and time as necessary consequences of God's omnipresence and eternity; on the other hand, he views them as prerequisite to a coherent science of dynamics.

In agreement with Gassendi and in disagreement with Descartes, Newton rejected *a priori* proofs of the existence of God. Such proofs presuppose the intellectual apprehension of essences or substances, an act of which he believed the human mind to be incapable. All demonstrations of God's existence, Newton implied, must be *a posteriori,* founded on sensible appearances. Natural philosophy thus becomes a handmaiden of theology, and as Newton eventually said in the General Scholium he added to the second edition of the *Principia* (1713), it belongs to natural philosophy to discourse of God from the appearances. Whereas Cartesian science, in Newton's view, was fundamentally compatible with the atheistic idea of a nature and fate independent of God, he understood his own natural science as presupposing the being of an eternal, omnipresent God who actively rules the world. Thus, in his science he intended not merely to account for the phenomena of nature but to render Creator as well as creation so far intelligible as the limitations of human understanding permit.

Concerning the fundamental doctrines that Newton formulated in his *De gravitatione* of ca. 1669, his mind did not change.

Newton on gravitation and planetary motion during the 1670s

Twice during the 1670s Newton proposed aethereal hypotheses to account for gravitation, first in the "Hypothesis Explaining the Properties of Light" sent to the Royal Society in 1675, and again in a letter written to Robert Boyle in February 1678/79. In both cases it is clear that *universal* gravitation is not in question.

The hypothesis of 1675 assumes an elastic aethereal medium, which Newton postulated initially and primarily to account for the colors of thin films: he says he does not see how these could be "handsomely explained, without having recourse to aethereal pulses." (Indeed, he here shows for the first time how what we now call the wavelengths of variously colored monochromatic rays can be determined.) He does not assume the medium to be "one uniform matter," but rather to be compounded of various "aethereal spirits," for "the electric and magnetic effluvia and gravitating principle seem to argue such variety." These aethereal spirits may be condensible, so that

> the whole frame of nature may be nothing but various contextures of
> some certain aethereal spirits or vapors condensed as it were by
> precipitation. . . . Thus perhaps may all things be originated from aether.
> (*Corres.*, I, p. 364)

Gravitation toward the Earth may be due to a certain aethereal spirit that is condensed in the Earth's body:

> So may the gravitating attraction of the Earth be caused by the continual
> condensation of some . . . such like aethereal spirit, not of the main body
> of phlegmatic aether, but of something very thinly and subtly diffused
> through it, perhaps of an unctuous or gummy, tenacious and springy
> nature . . . ; the vast body of the Earth, which may be everywhere to the
> very center in perpetual working, may continually condense so much of
> this spirit as to cause it from above to descend with great celerity for a
> supply. In which descent it may bear down with it the bodies it pervades
> with force proportional to the superficies of all their parts it acts upon;
> nature making a circulation by the slow ascent of as much matter out of
> the bowels of the Earth in an aerial form which for a time constitutes
> the atmosphere, but being continually buoyed up by the new air,
> exhalations, and vapors rising underneath, at length . . . vanishes again
> into the aethereal spaces, and there perhaps in time relents, and is
> attenuated into its first principle. For nature is a perpetual circulatory
> worker. . . . And as the Earth, so perhaps may the Sun imbibe this spirit
> copiously to conserve his shining, and keep the planets from receding
> further from him. And they that will, may also suppose that this spirit

affords or carries with it thither the solary fuel and material principle of light; and that the vast aethereal spaces between us and the stars are for a sufficient repository for this food of the Sun and planets. But this of the constitution of aethereal natures by the by. (*Corres.*, I, pp. 365–66)

The hypothesis here described is very similar to that which Newton had outlined in his Trinity notebook ten years earlier (*see* section one of this essay). It is, of course, incompatible with universal gravitation. The imbibition of aether by Earth, Sun, and planets is due to fermental principles acting within these bodies.

Newton later refers to this hypothesis in a letter to Halley of 20 June 1686, in which he contested Robert Hooke's claim to have supplied him with the inverse-square law. Was Newton here claiming that, when he framed the hypothesis, "he had then turned his thoughts toward universal gravitation," as Turnbull puts it (*Corres.*, I, p. 387, n. 10)? Newton's only assertion is that the hypothesis was framed to be in accord with the inverse-square law:

I hinted a cause of gravity towards the Earth, Sun, and planets with the dependence of the celestial motions thereon: in which the proportion of the decrease of gravity from the superficies of the planet (though for brevity's sake not there expressed) can be no other than reciprocally duplicate of the distance from the center. (*Corres.*, II, p. 436)

In his letter to Halley of 27 July 1686, Newton again takes up the hypothesis of 1675, this time giving an explanation as to how it implies the inverse-square proportion:

The diminution of [the aether's] velocity in acting upon the first parts of any body it meets with [is] recompensed by the increase of its density arising from that retardation. (*Corres.*, II, p. 447)

In every instance, Newton is speaking of a cause of gravity of the planets toward the Sun, and of bodies toward any planet. There is no suggestion of a gravity of the Sun toward the planets, or of the planets toward each other, or of the Earth toward terrestrial bodies.

One more sentence from the hypothesis of 1675 deserves to be quoted. Different substances, Newton observes, may be "sociable" or "unsociable" with one another, or be changed from "sociable" to "unsociable" or vice versa by the presence of a third material: Newton is here speaking of attractions and repulsions that act over small distances and may not be reducible to forces of contact. He then remarks:

The like unsociableness may be in aethereal natures, as perhaps between the aethers in the vortices of the Sun and planets. (*Corres.*, I, p. 368)

The suggestion is perhaps intended to explain how it is that the vortices of the Sun and planets remain distinct and do not disrupt one another.

But for us the important point is that Newton in his account of planetary motion is still assuming aethereal vortices. His hypothesis thus involves *two* aethereal circulations, one of aether about the central body, the other of a more finely textured aether into the central body, with an ascent upward again in a different form such that the force upward on gross bodies is negligible. The aethereal flux downward into the central body is being imagined as necessary to counteract the *conatus recedendi a centro* developed by planets and satellites as they are whirled about in their respective vortices.

In his letter to Boyle of February 1678/79, Newton employs an elastic aether in order to account for the cohesion of bodies, the slight bending of light in passing a sharp-edged obstacle, the difficulty of bringing two polished pieces of glass into contact, etc. The aether is imagined to be more rare in the pores of bodies, and denser without, with a gradient of density in between. The explanation of gravity is given at the end of the letter and is stated to be "one conjecture more which came into my mind now as I was writing this letter."

> For this end I will suppose aether to consist of parts differing from one another in subtlety by indefinite degrees: That in the pores of bodies there is less of the grosser aether in proportion to the finer than in open spaces, and consequently that in the great body of the Earth there is much less of the grosser aether in proportion to the finer than in the regions of the air: and that yet the grosser aether in the air affects the upper regions of the Earth and the finer aether in the Earth the lower regions of the air, in such a manner that from the top of the air to the surface of the Earth and again from the surface of the Earth to the center thereof the aether is insensibly finer and finer. Imagine now any body suspended in the air or lying on the Earth: and the aether being by the hypothesis grosser in the pores which are in the upper parts of the body than in those which are in its lower parts, and that grosser aether being less apt to be lodged in those pores than the finer aether below, it will endeavor to get out and give way to the finer aether below, which cannot be without the bodies descending to make room above for it to go out into.
>
> From this supposed gradual subtlety of the parts of aether some things above might be further illustrated and made more intelligible, but by what has been said you will easily discern whether in these conjectures there be any degree of probability, which is all I aim at. For my own part I have so little fancy to things of this nature that had not your encouragement moved me to it, I should never I think have thus far set pen to paper about them. (*Corres.*, II, p. 295)

Newton's diffidence about setting forth his hypothesis is compounded with a strong distaste for the hypothesizing in which many of his contemporaries were engaged. As he remarked at the start of his letter,

> The truth is my notions about things of this kind are so indigested that I am not well satisfied myself in them, and what I am not satisfied in I can

scarce esteem fit to be communicated to others, especially in natural
philosophy where there is no end of fancying. (*Corres.*, II, p. 288)

My general conclusion, on reviewing all the Newtonian writings from
the mid-1660s up to late 1679 that might conceivably pertain to gravitation and planetary motion, is that there is no ground whatever for believing that Newton during this period had *conceived* the program of the
Principia, namely, to infer universal gravitation from the phenomena,
and from the result thus arrived at to deduce the rest of the phenomena.

At some time during the 1670s Newton read *The Theory of the
Medicean Planets Deduced from Physical Causes* (1666) by the Italian Gio-
vanni Borelli. The suggestion of this work was that the elliptical motion
of Jupiter's satellites, as well as that of the circumsolar planets, could
be accounted for by the interaction of a centrifugal force or *conatus
recedendi* and a constant centripetal force toward the central body. The
two forces were conceived to be in disequilibrium in such a way that
one alternately overbalanced the other, the total effect being to modify
a circular force-free motion into an elliptical or quasi-elliptical orbit.
The rotation round the center was sustained by the continued action of
a trans-radial "impetus" associated by Borelli with the rotation of the
Sun and its rays.

Borelli's account of planetary motion is not without serious difficulties: in its detailed mechanism it fails to accord with the principle of
inertia, although Borelli explicitly espouses that principle. How Newton
viewed the hypothesis when he first encountered it we do not know. In
his letter to Halley of 20 June 1686, while complaining about Hooke's
assertion of priority in the matter of the inverse-square law, Newton
says: "Borelli wrote long before him that by a tendency of the planets
towards the Sun like that of gravity or magnetism the planets would
move in ellipses. . . ." Also, "[Hooke] has published Borelli's hypothesis
in his own name. . . . Borelli did something in it and wrote modestly,
[Hooke] has done nothing and yet written in such a way as if he knew
and had sufficiently hinted all but what remained to be determined by
the drudgery of calculations and observations, excusing himself from
that labor by reason of his other business." Newton's charge of plagiarism on Hooke's part is quite unfair.

In two works of Hooke's published during the 1670s we find a very
different account of planetary motion, which is of crucial importance
in our story. It is fairly certain that Newton read the relevant passages
(he denies it in the correspondence of 1679 that we shall be citing in
the next section, then asserts it in his letter to Halley of 20 June 1686).
Hooke's *An Attempt to Prove the Motion of the Earth,* published in 1674,
concludes with a proposal to explain at some later date

a system of the world differing in many particulars from any yet known,
answering in all things to the common rules of mechanical motions. This

depends upon three suppositions. First, that all celestial bodies whatsoever have an attraction or gravitating power towards their own centers, whereby they attract not only their own parts, and keep them from flying from them, as we observe the Earth to do, but that they do also attract all the other celestial bodies that are within the sphere of their activity; and consequently that not only the Sun and Moon have an influence upon the body and motion of the Earth, and the Earth upon them, but that Mercury, also Venus, Mars, Saturn, and Jupiter by their attractive powers, have a considerable influence upon its motion as in the same manner the corresponding attractive power of the Earth hath a considerable influence upon every one of their motions also. The second supposition is this, that all bodies whatsoever that are put into a direct and simple motion, will so continue to move forward in a straight line, till they are by some other effectual powers deflected and bent into a motion, describing a circle, ellipse, or some other more compounded curved line. The third supposition is that these attractive powers are so much the more powerful in operating, by how much the nearer the body wrought upon is to their own centers. Now what these several degrees are I have not yet experimentally verified; but it is a notion which, if fully prosecuted as it ought to be, will mightily assist the astronomer to reduce all the celestial motions to a certain rule, which I doubt will never be done true without it. He that understands the nature of the circular pendulum and circular motion, will easily understand the whole ground of this principle, and will know where to find direction in nature for the true stating thereof. This I only hint at at present to such as have ability and opportunity of prosecuting this inquiry, and are not wanting of industry for observing and calculating, wishing heartily such may be found, having myself many other things in hand which I would first complete and therefore cannot so well attend it. But this I durst promise the undertaker, that he will find all the great motions of the world to be influenced by this principle, and that the true understanding thereof will be the true perfection of astronomy. (Gunther, viii, pp. 27–28)

There is some rightness, we have to acknowledge, in Hooke's prophecy. Yet we must beware of supposing with David Brewster, a nineteenth-century biographer of Newton, that in this passage "the doctrine of universal gravitation, and the general law of the planetary motions, are clearly laid down" (Brewster, I, p. 287). Celestial bodies, Hooke has said, attract other celestial bodies "that are within the sphere of their activity." In his *Cometa* of 1678 Hooke makes clear that the attraction he has in mind, although approaching universality more closely than the attractions proposed in any earlier hypothesis, is still not universal.

I suppose the gravitating power of the Sun in the center of this part of the heaven in which we are, hath an attractive power upon all the bodies of the planets, and of the Earth that move about it, and that each of those again have a respect answerable, whereby they may be said to attract the Sun in the same manner as the loadstone hath to iron, and the iron hath to the loadstone. I conceive also that this attractive virtue may act likewise upon several other bodies that come within the center of its sphere of activity, though 'tis not improbable also but that as on some bodies it may have no effect at all, no more than the loadstone which acts on iron, hath upon a bar of tin, lead, glass, wood, etc., so on other bodies, it may have a clear contrary effect, that is, of protrusion, thrusting off, or driving away . . . ; whence it is, I conceive, that the parts of the body of this comet (being confounded or jumbled, as it were, together, and so the gravitating principle destroyed) become of other natures than they were before, and so the body may cease to maintain its place in the universe, where first it was placed. Whence instead of continuing to move round some central body, whether Sun or planet, as it did whilst it maintained itself entire, and so had its magnetical quality (as I may so call it) unconfounded, it now leaves that circular way and by its motion (which always tends to a straight line, and would be so were it not bended into a curve by the attractive virtue of the central body) it flies away from its former center by the tangent line to the last place, where it was before this confusion was caused in the body of it. (Gunther, viii, pp. 228–29)

It is evident here that the generalizing induction usually mentioned as the source of Newton's idea of universal gravitation did not so operate with Hooke as to lead him to this notion; the example of magnetism told against such a generalization, and so did the supposedly rectilinear or quasi-rectilinear trajectories of comets.

Nevertheless, the importance in our story of Hooke's idea of obtaining the orbital motions of planets by combining an attraction to a center with inertial motion along the tangent cannot be overestimated. Whence had the idea come? Hooke had been nurtured by a peculiarly English tradition from which Newton was isolated: a tradition of magnetical philosophy centered at Gresham College in London, and taking inspiration from the writings of William Gilbert. At Gresham, Christopher Wren was a colleague of Hooke and may have been earlier than Hooke in formulating the idea of combining inertial motion with attraction in order to account for planetary motion. Both he and Hooke were interested in the conical pendulum as a model of planetary motion—a model they had found suggested in the posthumous papers of Jeremiah Horrocks. Neither Wren nor Hooke found out how to derive the mathematical consequences of their conception of planetary motion. It was a problem that Hooke in effect passed on to Newton.

The correspondence with Hooke, 1679/80

The next stage in the development of Newton's thought about gravitation and planetary motion came about through an exchange of letters with Robert Hooke, beginning with a letter from Hooke to Newton dated 24 November 1679 (O.S.). On the surface there is cordiality, but beneath it, as we learn from later letters of Newton to Halley, Newton passed from distaste and impatience to anger. There had been conflict with Hooke earlier, over Newton's *New Theory about Light and Colors* (1672), Hooke having charged Newton with plagiarism. In the correspondence now begun, the tone of Hooke's writing, which seemed to suggest that he knew all, was extremely irritating to Newton. Yet in the very midst of the exchange, attempting to find out if Hooke knew all he claimed to know, Newton made two discoveries of the first magnitude. About these discoveries, Newton in 1679/80 said nary a word to Hooke or anyone. But before we attempt to explore their import, and probe the meaning of Newton's silence, let us follow the interchange of ideas pertaining to gravitation and planetary motion, just as it presents itself in the back-and-forth of the letters.

In the first letter, Hooke is writing in an official capacity, as one of the secretaries of the Royal Society; the task of carrying on correspondence has recently devolved upon him. Hooke says that since Newton had corresponded with Oldenburg, the previous secretary,

> I hope therefore that you will please to continue your former favors to
> the Society by communicating what shall occur to you that is
> philosophical, and in return I shall be sure to acquaint you with what we
> shall receive considerable from other parts or find out new here.
> (*Corres.*, II, p. 297)

But, as Hooke rightly guesses, there is an obstacle to be surmounted: wounded feelings left in Newton from the earlier trouble over the *Theory about Light and Colors.* Aware of these, Hooke promises that Newton's ideas will be communicated to the society no further than Newton himself should prescribe, and he urges that difference of opinion in philosophical matters not be the occasion of enmity—"'tis not with me I am sure." So Hooke affirms his own openness to criticism:

> For my own part I shall take it as a great favour if you shall please to
> communicate by letter your objections against any hypothesis or opinion
> of mine, and particularly if you will let me know your thoughts of that of
> compounding the celestial motions of the planets of a direct motion by
> the tangent and an attractive motion towards the central body, or what
> objections you have against my hypothesis of the laws or causes of
> springiness. (*Corres.*, II, p. 297)

Hooke's letter becomes chatty, passing on to other ideas. At the end he remarks: "Mr. Flamsteed by some late perpendicular observations hath confirmed the parallax of the orb of the Earth"; that is, by observations of stars culminating close to the zenith of his observatory, he claimed to have detected, as Hooke had also claimed to detect a few

years earlier, an apparent annual motion in the stars confirming the
motion of the Earth.

Newton replies on 28 November. He acknowledges himself "every
way by the kindness of your letter tempted to concur with your desires
in a philosophical correspondence." Unfortunately, for the last half year
he has had to be in Lincolnshire, attending to family affairs (his mother
died in the summer of 1679), and before that,

> I had for some years past been endeavoring to bend myself from philos-
> ophy to other studies . . . : which makes me almost wholly unacquainted
> with what philosophers at London or abroad have of late been employed
> about. And perhaps you will incline the more to believe me when I tell
> you that I did not before the receipt of your last letter, so much as hear
> (that I remember) of your hypotheses of compounding the celestial
> motions of the planets of a direct motion by the tangent to the curve and
> of the laws and causes of springiness. . . . (*Corres.*, II, p. 300)

Newton, as we have previously indicated, is here disingenuous. In
his letter to Halley of 20 June 1686, he writes: "By the same reason
[Hooke] concludes me then [in 1679] ignorant of the duplicate proportion he may as well conclude me ignorant of the rest of that theory I
had read before in his books" (*Corres.*, II, p. 436).

After further insisting that he has laid philosophy aside, Newton (to
sweeten his answer, as he put it later to Halley) comments on several
of the items in Hooke's letter. In particular, Newton is glad to hear
that Hooke's very considerable discovery of annual parallax has been
seconded by Flamsteed. (Hooke in his letter had not explicitly referred
to his own role in this supposed discovery; the apparent stellar motions
observed by both Hooke and Flamsteed were due to other causes than
parallax.) And now comes a passage by Newton that proved seminal:

> In requital of this advertisement I shall communicate to you a fancy of
> my own about discovering the Earth's diurnal motion. In order thereto
> I will consider the Earth's diurnal motion alone without the annual, that
> having little influence on the experiment I shall here propound.

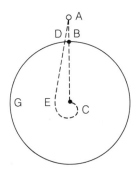

Suppose then *BDG* represents the globe of the Earth carried round once a day about its center *C* from west to east according to the order of the letters *BDG;* and let *A* be a heavy body suspended in the air and moving round with the Earth so as perpetually to hang over the same point thereof *B.* Then imagine this body *A* let fall and its gravity will give it a new motion towards the center of the Earth without diminishing the old one from west to east. Whence the motion of this body from west to east, by reason that before it fell it was more distant from the center of the Earth than the parts of the Earth at which it arrives in its fall, will be greater than the motion from west to east of the parts of the Earth at which the body arrives in its fall: and therefore it will not descend in the perpendicular *AC*, but outrunning the parts of the Earth will shoot forward to the east side [that is, toward *D*] of the perpendicular [*AB*] describing in its fall a spiral line *ADEC,* quite contrary to the opinion of the vulgar who think that if the Earth moved, heavy bodies in falling would be outrun by its parts and fall on the west side of the perpendicular. The advance of the body from the perpendicular eastward will in a descent of but 20 or 30 yards be very small and yet I am apt to think it may be enough to determine the matter of fact. (*Corres.*, II, pp. 301–2)

And Newton goes on to make a number of detailed suggestions for the carrying out of the experiment.

In the final paragraph of his letter Newton returns to the theme of his weariness of philosophy (by "philosophy" he means, of course, "natural philosophy," that is, "science"). If he were not so unhappy as to be unacquainted with Hooke's hypotheses, he would so far comply with Hooke's desire for a correspondence as to send him what objections he could think of against them, if he could think of any. And he could with pleasure hear and answer any objections made against his own notions "in a transient discourse for a divertissement."

But yet my affection to philosophy being worn out, so that I am almost as little concerned about it as one tradesman uses to be about another man's trade or a country man about learning, I must acknowledge myself averse from spending that time in writing about it which I think I can spend otherwise more to my own content and the good of others: and I hope neither you nor anybody else will blame me for this averseness. (*Corres.*, II, p. 302)

Hooke's response is dated 9 December. Newton's "deserting philosophy . . . seems a little unkind," but the secretary does not despair of him:

You that have so fully known those delights cannot choose but sometime have a hankering after them and now and then desire a taste of them. And I would never wish anything more from a person of your ability: I hate drudges . . . at anything. . . . I wish I were as sure of your correspondence and communicating as I am of your yet remaining affection to

philosophy. However, Sir, I must thank you for what I am sure of for
that (they say) is one way to get more. (*Corres.*, II, 304–5)

And Hooke assures Newton that he values the great favor and kindness
of his letter, and particularly his notion about detecting the diurnal
motion of the Earth. The passage of his letter dealing with this proposal, Hooke reports, was read to the Royal Society, and the members
generally agreed that, as Newton suggested, a heavy body let fall from
a great height would fall to the east of the vertical and not to the west
as most have hitherto imagined:

> But as to the curved line which you seem to suppose it to descend by
> (though that was not then at all discoursed of) viz. a kind of spiral which
> after some few revolutions leaves it in the center of the Earth my theory of
> circular motion makes me suppose it would be very differing and nothing
> at all akin to a spiral but rather a kind [of] elleptueid. (*Corres.*, II, p. 305)

Hooke lists the conditions presupposed for this purely imaginary motion:
the falling body must be in the plane of the Earth's equator; the northern and southern hemispheres must be divided along this plane so as to
leave about a yard's space between, and this space must be evacuated;
the gravitation to the center must remain as before; the falling body
is to have impressed on it the diurnal motion of the superficial parts
of the Earth from which it was let fall. Under these conditions, Hooke
conceives that the body's path will "resemble an ellipse," such as the
curve *AFGH* in the diagram below, left. If, however, a resisting medium
were present, the curve would be somewhat like the line *AIKLMNOP*
and after many revolutions would terminate in the center *C*.

Hooke had one more correction to make in Newton's account of the
falling body, and it showed a sharp intelligence at work. To paraphrase,
if the body is not in the plane of the equator, but at latitude 51°32′
as in London, the ellipse-like curve will be in a plane inclined to the

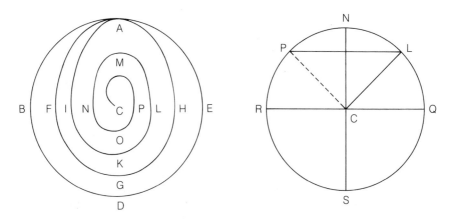

plane of the equator by 51°32′, so that the fall of the body will not be exactly east of the vertical but rather southeast and indeed more south than east. For let *NLQS* (opposite page, right) represent the meridian of London, *RQ* the plane of the equator, *L* London, and *PL* the parallel in which London moves about the Earth's axis *NS.* Then the body let fall at *L* will descend in the plane *LC* at right angles to the plane *NLQSR* of the meridian, and not in the surface of the cone *PLC* with apex at *C* and circular base *PL.* "I could add many other considerations which are consonant to my theory of circular motions compounded by a direct motion and an attractive one to a center," Hooke writes. "But I fear I have already trespassed too much upon your more useful thoughts . . ." (*Corres.,* II, pp. 305–6).

We note that, if the vertical direction is determined by a plumb bob, the southerly deviation of the falling body will probably be indetectable, since both plumb bob and falling body are affected by the Coriolis force involved. But Newton considered Hooke's correction to be right.

Newton's response, dated only four days later (13 December), plunges abruptly into the questions at issue:

> I agree with you that the body in our latitude will fall more to the south than east if the height it falls from be anything great. And also that if its gravity be supposed uniform it will not descend in a spiral to the very center but circulate with an alternate ascent and descent made by its *vis centrifuga* and gravity alternately overbalancing one another. Yet I imagine the body will not describe an ellipsoid but rather such a figure as is represented by *AFOGHIKL* etc. (*Corres.,* II, p. 307)

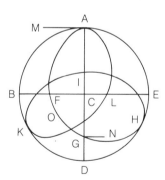

Here *A* is the initial position of the body, and *AM* its initial velocity. Newton argues that, assuming a uniform gravity, the point of closest approach to *C* in the initial fall will be in the quadrant *BCD,* as at *O.* "The innumerable and infinitely little motions (for I here consider motion according to the method of indivisibles) continually generated by gravity in [the body's] passage from *A* to *F* incline it to verge from *GN* towards *D,* and the like motions generated in its passage from *F* to *G* incline it to verge from *GN* towards *C.* But these motions are proportional to the time they are generated in, and the time of passing from *A* to *F* (by reason of the longer journey and slower motion) is greater than the time of passing from *F* to *G.*'' Newton then goes on to say that if the gravity be supposed not uniform but greater nearer the center, the point *O* of closest approach may fall in the line *CD* or in the angle *DCE* or in the following quadrants, or even nowhere. "For the increase of gravity in the descent may be supposed such that the body shall by an infinite number of spiral revolutions descend continually till it cross the center by motion transcendently swift'' (*Corres.*, II, p. 308).

How did Newton arrive at the results just given? In the final paragraph of his letter he gives a hint:

> Your acute letter having put me upon considering thus far the species of this curve, I might add something about its description by points *quam proximè*. But the thing being of no great moment I rather beg your pardon for having troubled you thus far with this second scribble wherein if you meet with anything inept or erroneous I hope you will pardon the former and the latter I submit and leave to your correction. . . .
> (*Corres.*, II, p. 308)

It would be important to know what Newton meant by "the description by points *quam proximè;*" the method envisaged is no doubt graphical, and Newton supposes it to be highly accurate (*quam proximè* means "very nearly"), but how did he proceed? The following seems a likely interpretation. Let the body be initially moving in the line *AB.* Imagine the time to be divided into a large number of tiny intervals, and suppose that gravity acts at the end of each interval, impressing a new element of velocity toward the center *S.* At *B,* for instance, the body will receive an impulse; the velocity it thus acquires, let us suppose, is such as would carry it from *B* toward *S* through a distance equal to *cC* in the next interval, if no other motion were present. Since, however, it is already moving with the velocity that carried it from *A* to *B* in the first interval, and this velocity will carry it through the equal distance from *B* to *c*

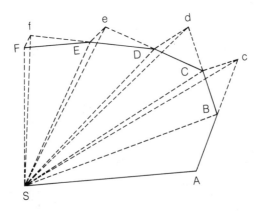

in the second interval, the net result is that the body at the end of the second interval will be found on the diagonal of the parallelogram formed with the sides *Bc* and *cC*, namely at *C*. If the gravity is uniform, the velocities successively imparted, *cC*, *dD*, *eE*, etc., are equal; if it varies as some function of the distance from *A*, the velocities imparted will vary according to the assumed function.

The method I am suggesting is in fact but crudely approximate. In the diagram that accompanies his letter, and in which he is seeking to portray the case of uniform gravity, Newton makes the central angle between successive farthest departures from the center some 240°, impossibly large; an exact method would have shown him that this angle cannot exceed 207°50′.

Newton's recourse to graphing, however, must have quickly led to an important insight. In the diagram I have drawn, it is easy to show that the triangles successively swept out about the center, namely *SAB*, *SBC, SCD,* etc., are equal. As his later statements attest, Newton at this time learned that a force directed to a fixed point—commonly called a "central force"—implies Kepler's areal rule; implies, that is, that the radius vector from central point to orbiting body will sweep out equal areas in equal times. And conversely, in any orbit the equable description of areas about a point implies that the force acting on the body is directed to the point.

These two propositions ultimately appeared as the first two theorems of Newton's *Principia;* and in fact Newton's entire treatment of orbital motion was based upon them. His proofs are not such as would satisfy a present-day mathematician. They remain pretty much on the level of "the method of indivisibles" except that, in the proof of the first proposition, Newton speaks of augmenting the number of triangles and diminishing their breadths *in infinitum.* He does not go on to establish, as the present-day mathematician would require, that the result of this limiting process will be a unique curve. Nevertheless, the proofs satisfied Newton's contemporaries.

Hooke's response was dated 6 January, nearly a month later.

> Your calculation of the curve [made] by a body attracted by an equal power at all distances from the center such as that of a ball rolling in an inverted concave cone is right and the two auges [= apsides] will not unite by about a third of a revolution. But my supposition is that the attraction always is in a duplicate proportion to the distance from the center reciprocal, and consequently that the velocity will be in a subduplicate proportion to the attraction and consequently as Kepler supposes reciprocal to the distance. And that with such an attraction the auges will unite in the same part of the circle and that the nearest point of access to the center will be opposite to the furthest distant. Which I conceive doth very intelligibly and truly make out all the appearances of the heavens. (*Corres.,* II, p. 309)

But I will here interrupt the quotation in order to inquire: How did Hooke reach the conclusion that the attractions of the heavenly bodies vary inversely as the squares of the distances from their centers?

We know from several of Hooke's writings that he had formulated for himself the following principle, which he believed to be generally true: "the comparative velocities of any body moved are in subduplicate proportion to the aggregates or sums of the powers by which it is moved." He had applied the principle successfully to a number of cases: for instance, to the speed of efflux of a liquid from a hole in the bottom of its containing vessel, where the speed varies as the square root of the depth of the liquid, hence as the square root of the pressure.

In fact, Hooke's principle turns out to yield the right result whenever his "aggregates or sums of the powers" can be interpreted as work or potential energy. He seems to have derived the principle from Galileo's result that the square of the velocity of bodies descending without friction is proportional to the height of fall. But Hooke's understanding of this principle was less than adequate; he applied it brashly and without awareness of the subtleties involved. His "derivation" of the inverse-square law of gravitation is a case in point.

Kepler in his *Astronomia Nova* of 1609 [selected chapters in *GIT* 1983, pp. 309–41], in a first attempt at a celestial dynamics, had assumed that the "push" due to the Sun's motive virtue, and hence (in accordance with the Aristotelian proportionality between force and speed) the planet's speed, varied inversely with the distance from the Sun. In order then to determine the planet's orbital positions at given times, he needed to "add up" the effects of the instantaneous speeds. As an approximation to the desired result, he introduced the supposition that the areas swept out by the radius vector are proportional to the times. A dozen years later, in his *Epitome Astronomiae Copernicanae* [selected chapters in *GBWW*, Vol. 16, pp. 845–1004], he had come to realize that the latter supposition is *exactly* in accordance with his postulated celestial dynamics, for it implies that the transradial *component* of the planet's velocity, at right angles to the radius from Sun to planet, is inversely proportional to the distance. The result remains true under the very different suppositions of Newtonian dynamics.

Hooke gave no sign of realizing that the planet's speed taken simply is not inversely as the distance from the Sun. Assuming this false relation, he applied his principle without more ado: the powers or forces are as the squares of the velocities, hence, in this particular case inversely as the squares of the distances. The conclusion is correct but the premise and the inference are wrong: it is the transradial component of the planet's velocity that is inversely proportional to the distance from the attracting body, and this is true for all central forces, and not just for inverse-square central forces.

And now, to resume our quotation from Hooke's letter of 6 January:

> And therefore (though in truth I agree with you that the explicating the curve in which a body descending to the center of the Earth would circumgyrate were a speculation of no use yet) the finding out the properties of a curve made by two such principles will be of great concern to mankind, because the invention of the longitude by the heavens is a necessary consequence of it: for the composition of two such motions I conceive will make out that of the Moon. What I mentioned in my last [letter] concerning the descent within the body of the Earth was but upon the supposal of such an attraction, not that I believe that there really is such an attraction, to the very center of the Earth, but on the contrary I rather conceive that the more the body approaches the center, the less will it be urged by the attraction—possibly somewhat like the gravitation on a pendulum or a body moved in a concave sphere where the power continually decreases the nearer the body inclines to a horizontal motion, which it hath when perpendicular under the point of suspension, or in the lowest point, and there the auges are almost opposite, and the nearest approach to the center is at about a quarter of a revolution. But in the celestial motions the Sun, Earth, or central body is the cause of the attraction, and though they cannot be supposed mathematical points yet they may be conceived as physical and the attraction at a considerable distance may be computed according to the former proportion as from the very center. This curve truly calculated will show the error of those many lame shifts made use of by astronomers to approach the true motions of the planets with their tables. But of this more hereafter. (*Corres.*, II, p. 309)

This passage is remarkable for its insightful guesses. Hooke rightly supposes that the force of gravity beneath the Earth's surface decreases with approach to the center, and in much the way that the force on a pendulum bob decreases with approach to the center of its swing; from his experimentation with conical pendulums he also knows that the pericenter follows about 90° after apocenter. His conception is that of an attraction resulting from the attractions of all the parts of which the attracting body is made up, and he recognizes the consequence that, close to the surface of the attracting body, the assumption that it may be thought of as attracting from its center as from a point cannot be taken for granted. In imagining that the orbit deriving from an inverse-square central force will be something other than the ellipse used by practically all the astronomers of his day, and that the discovery of the true curve will lead, without consideration of perturbations, to so accurate a prediction of the Moon's motions as to result in "the invention of the longitude," Hooke was, of course, mistaken.

In the remainder of his letter Hooke informed Newton that he had performed the experiment of the falling body three times and always found the body to fall to the southeast of the vertical; but as the amounts of deviation from the vertical were different in the three trials, he planned to repeat the experiment with further precautions until he obtained "a proof free from objections."

To Hooke's letter of 6 January, Newton did not reply. On 17 January Hooke wrote again, this time reporting that two trials of Newton's experiment carried out within doors had succeeded very well, "So that I am now persuaded the experiment is very certain, and that it will prove a demonstration of the diurnal motion of the Earth as you have very happily intimated." And he concluded:

> It now remains to know the properties of a curved line (not circular nor concentric) made by a central attractive power which makes the velocities of descent from the tangent line or equal straight motion at all distances in a duplicate proportion to the distances reciprocally taken. I doubt not but that by your excellent method you will easily find out what that curve must be, and its properties, and suggest a physical reason of this proportion. If you have had any time to consider this matter, a word or two of your thoughts of it will be very grateful to the Society (where it has been debated). (*Corres.*, II, p. 313)

To Hooke's letter of 17 January, Newton, again, did not reply; except that, nearly eleven months later, having to write Hooke about a different matter, he ended his missive by remarking:

> For the trials you made of an experiment suggested by me about falling bodies, I am indebted to you thanks which I thought to have returned by word of mouth, but not having yet the opportunity must be content to do it by letter. (*Corres.*, II, p. 314)

Nothing here about the calculation of orbits! Yet Newton had solved the problem that Hooke had set for him. He had satisfied himself that, on the assumption of an inverse-square force toward the central body, the planet or satellite will move in an ellipse with the central body at one focus.

We do not know for sure how Newton established this result in 1679/80. But with high probability we can guess that it was the converse proposition—passing from the elliptical orbit with the Sun at one focus to the inverse-square proportion—that Newton actually proved; and that he did so by assuming the equable description of areas, which made it possible for him to substitute area for time and so to reduce the problem to geometry. Propositions 6 and 11 of Book I of the *Principia* traverse the same logical path that Newton must have followed in 1679/80, but with refinements added at a later time.

And what about the converse that Newton in fact needed in order to reply to Hooke's question—the derivation of the elliptical orbit with the central attracting body at one focus from the inverse-square law? I suggest that, as in the first edition of the *Principia*, Newton saw this consequence as necessary without attempting to articulate its necessity.

Only in the second edition of the *Principia* did he give the argument (in Corollary I of Proposition 13, Book I):

> The focus, the point of contact, and the position of the tangent, being given, a conic section may be described, which at that point shall have a given curvature. But the curvature is given from the centripetal force and velocity of the body being given; and two orbits, touching one the other, cannot be described by the same centripetal force and the same velocity. [*GBWW*, Vol. 34, p. 46a]

Thus, in the winter of 1679/80 Newton knew that Kepler's areal rule and elliptical orbit were derivable from the assumption of a central force varying inversely as the square of the distance. I think he also understood at this time that the third Keplerian law was similarly derivable—at least on the assumption of concentric circular orbits. The first two of these discoveries were quite unknown to anyone (Wren and Halley appear to have been on to the third). And yet Newton remained silent. Why?

No doubt psychology must be given its due here. Newton had made a firm resolve to withdraw from correspondence on philosophical subjects. And correspondence with Hooke, whose manner Newton felt to be condescending, was particularly disagreeable.

But the logical status of the theory thus far elaborated, in its relation to empirical facts, needs also to be considered. *If* there is an inverse-square attractive force toward the Sun, *then* Kepler's laws follow; and the latter were known to be at least approximately true. By 1680, indeed, John Flamsteed was using both the elliptical orbit and the areal rule in calculating tables of the Moon, while Streete's planetary tables of 1661 were already in accord with the third Keplerian law and for this very reason were proving superior to other planetary tables (Halley republished them in 1710 and 1716). It was not evident that the inverse-square law would lead to any *new* consequences that could be tested against observations, or that would prove useful to astronomers. Nor was it clear that the inverse-square law could be assumed to be exact: that might depend on what Hooke referred to as "the physical reason of this proportion," which he had invited Newton to speculate about. An inverse-square law of force operating on the planets toward the Sun was perfectly compatible with Newton's aethereal hypothesis of 1675; but how could one decide, on that hypothesis, that the inverse-square law would be exact?

As Newton undoubtedly knew, Hooke in his *Cometa* had suggested that a comet consists of matter which has lost its gravitating power, owing perhaps to a "jumbling" of its internal parts. If gravity depended on an internal arrangement of parts—indeed, if it depended on any kind of arrangement or motion of matter—then it was not universal. If it was universal, it had no such explanation.

The prime argument in 1680 against the universality of gravitation was the evidence for the rectilinear or quasi-rectilinear trajectories of comets. If comets moved in nearly rectilinear paths, then it was doubtful that the Sun acted upon them as it acted upon planets. Did it act with a weakened force, or not at all?

We cannot be sure that Newton entertained any of the foregoing thoughts in the winter of 1679/80. The fact that in the following winter a spectacular comet appeared, and that Newton became avidly interested in the determination of its path, may suggest that the idea of universal gravitation had then occurred to him and that he was seeking to test it in the case of comets. In any case, the question whether the comet of 1680/81 can be accounted for on the hypothesis of universal gravitation plays a significant role in the story.

Newton, Flamsteed, and the comet of 1680/81

In November 1680 there appeared in the predawn sky a comet, heading in the direction of the Sun. The last observation of it (or its tail) in the morning sky appears to have been made on 8 December (O.S.). On 10 December what was taken by most astronomers to be a different comet appeared in the evening sky, heading away from the Sun. It continued to be observed into March.

Was a single comet responsible for all the appearances from November through March, or were two comets involved?

The standard view of comets at the time was the Keplerian one, or something closely allied to it. Kepler had supposed that comets, being "the refuse of the cosmos," were lacking in the "magnetism" that tied planets to the Sun and therefore moved in more or less rectilinear paths. The Cartesian view was similar: comets were stars or planets that had escaped out of collapsed vortices. According to the astronomer Hevelius, the paths of comets were slightly incurved toward the Sun but did not differ greatly from straight lines. In general, the apparent paths of comets across the celestial sphere had proved to be close to great circles, and these could be understood as the projections of rectilinear trajectories onto the stellar background. Wren and Wallis had devised mathematical procedures for determining such trajectories on the basis of observation.

If one accepted this traditional view, then the simplest assumption was that the comet appearing in November was different from the comet appearing from 10 December onward. Such, for example, was Huygens's conclusion. The hypothesized rectilinear trajectories of the two comets would be oriented in nearly opposite directions.

Flamsteed, the Royal Astronomer, in seeking to comprehend the cometary appearances of the winter of 1680/81, conceived a different hypothesis. There was but one comet. As it came within the Earth's orbit it moved almost directly toward the Sun, and it then looped back so that its path in receding was nearly parallel to its incoming path. While postulating this sharp doubling back in the comet's path, Flamsteed also excogitated a physical hypothesis to account for it. The Sun and the comet, he said, were magnetic, and thus capable both of attracting and of repelling each other. Observational data led him to believe that, *before* perihelion or closest approach to the Sun, the comet had twice pierced the plane of the ecliptic, first from north to south and then from south to north. This bend in the comet's path, Flamsteed supposed, was due to the action of the Sun's "northern pole." Somehow the solar vortex then impinged on the comet in such a way as to keep it from falling into the Sun and to cause it subsequently to be oriented so as to be repelled by the Sun's magnetism. Thus, according to Flamsteed, the comet had been turned back before reaching the Sun, its hairpin turn being the result of the Sun's repulsion.

Flamsteed's observational data and an account of his hypothesis were conveyed to Newton through James Crompton, a Fellow of Jesus College in Cambridge. Newton in a response dated 28 February (*Corres.,* II, p. 340ff.) pointed to a number of difficulties in Flamsteed's hypothesis. (1) If an attraction to the Sun caused the comet to bend from its original rectilinear path so that it was headed directly toward the Sun, then it would have continued thereafter in the same direction until it fell into the Sun. Flamsteed's invocation of the solar vortex is unhelpful, for the force of the vortex would have tended to turn the comet's path in the direction of planetary motion (counterclockwise as seen from the ecliptic's north pole), not in the reverse direction assumed by Flamsteed. "The only way to relieve the difficulty in my judgment is to suppose the comet to have gone not between the Sun and Earth but to have fetched a compass about the Sun," Newton wrote. (2) The Sun, being extremely hot, is not a magnet, for magnetic bodies when heated to redness lose their magnetic virtue. (3) Were the Sun a magnet, then as with terrestrial magnets its "directive virtue" would be more powerful than its "attractive virtue"; hence, the cometary magnet would quickly be turned into such a position as to be attracted by the Sun, and would never thereafter be repelled. (4) The identity of the November and December comets is doubtful because (according to the data available to Newton) "if they were but one comet, its motion was thrice accelerated and retarded. . . . This frequent increase and decrease of motion is too paradoxical to be admitted in one and the same comet without some proof that there was but one."

The fourth objection was clearly refutable. As Flamsteed pointed out in a letter to Crompton for Newton dated 7 March (*Corres.,* II, p. 348ff.), Newton's conclusion of a triple acceleration and retardation resulted simply from a confusion of new-style and old-style dates. The comet had only once accelerated and had thereafter slowed down.

Flamsteed then proceeded to give his chief empirical evidence that the November and December comets were the same. The observations of Collio in Rome gave the first perigee, or closest approach to the Earth, as on 17 November (O.S.), and the motion of the comet from 11 to 17 November was 26°30′ in six days. Flamsteed made the second perigee to be on 30 December, and the motion from 30 December to 5 January 25°36′ in six days. Again, the Roman observations made the motion from 17 to 26 November 41°15′, and Flamsteed's observations of the motion in the symmetrically corresponding period before second perigee, from 21 to 30 December, gave the motion as 42°30′, "which," he said, "considering the coarseness of the foreign observations I look upon as a very good agreement and argument that all the observations were of the same comet."

Flamsteed also noted that the western elongation of the comet from the Sun on 26 November was 25°18′, the eastern elongation of the comet on 21 December was 24°, and the perihelion almost exactly between these dates: he was once more arguing for the oneness of the comet from symmetry.

Another important piece of evidence had to do with the latitudes of the comet. It went south of the ecliptic on 11 November, changing its latitude at the rate of about one degree per 10° of longitudinal motion. But from 18 to 27 November its latitude remained almost constant at about 1° south latitude. The December–March comet had northern latitude. Flamsteed said of this: "If Mr Newton cannot allow the comet to have returned out of south into northern latitude he will oblige me much if he please to suggest some reason why without supposing any attraction of the Sun the latitude should continue still nearly the same so long as it was observed after the 18 to the 27 of Nov."

"Hence it would seem," Flamsteed concluded from the observational evidence, "that the comet was attracted and repelled by the Sun as I imagined and proposed in my last letter." As for Newton's objection against the Sun's magnetism, Flamsteed suggested that the attraction of the Sun may be of a different nature from that of terrestrial magnets, and the Sun although causing heat on the Earth may yet have a core which is not hot. He did not think Newton's claim that the "directive virtue" of a magnet exceeds its "attractive virtue" made much against his hypothesis, "except he can prove that a large fixed magnet would have that operation on a small one thrown violently by or about it."

Newton's answer (*Corres.*, II, p. 363ff.) came on 16 April and began with an apology: "By some indisposition and other impediments I have deferred answering you longer than I intended." But as we now know, he had previously written two drafts of a reply, these drafts differing from each other as well as from the letter finally sent. In the first draft (*Corres.*, II, p. 358ff.) he acknowledges that, with the correction of his mistake about old-style and new-style dates, "the comets of November and December are less irreconcilable." On the other hand, the arguments from the symmetry of the observations about perihelion and the two perigees can be faulted, since Flamsteed writes only of geocentric longitudes and not of the positions of the comet in its path. Newton, from an approximate calculation, finds the motion of the November comet averaged 5° per day, that of the December comet about 4°20', but "I have not computed it exactly." Flamsteed's argument from the latitudes is not compelling because the observations appear to have been insufficiently accurate: it is still possible to assume that the comet of November moved southward uniformly in accordance with a rectilinear trajectory.

Newton rejects the proposal that the Sun, although hot on its surface, might have a core that was not hot: "The whole body of the Sun therefore must be red hot and consequently void of magnetism," he writes, "unless we suppose its magnetism of another kind from any we know, which Mr Flamsteed seems inclinable to suppose." With respect to the comparative magnitudes of the directive and attractive virtues of a magnet, Newton argues that the former will always exceed the latter, however short a time the magnet is given in which to exert its force. Flamsteed's notion that the comet was repelled by the Sun after first being attracted has the difficulty that the comet would then have been accelerated in its recess from the Sun as well as in its approach and moreover would not have followed a path symmetrically placed with respect to the Sun. But,

> all these difficulties may be avoided by supposing the comet to be directed by the Sun's magnetism as well as attracted, and consequently to have been attracted all the time of its motion, as well in its recess from the Sun as in its access towards him, and thereby to have been as much retarded in his recess as accelerated in his access, and by this continual attraction to have been made to fetch a compass about the Sun . . . , the *vis centrifuga* at [perihelion] overpowering the attraction and forcing the comet there notwithstanding the attraction, to begin to recede from the Sun. (*Corres.*, II, p. 361)

In the final paragraph Newton begins by writing: "About the comet's path I have not yet made any computation though I think I have a direct method of doing it, whatever the line of its motion be." In the remainder of the paragraph Newton gives his suppositions about the course of the comet as seen from the Sun, on the assumption that there was only one comet, and this comet "fetched a compass round the Sun."

What method of computation had Newton in mind? We do not know; no Newtonian manuscripts dealing with determination of cometary paths can be dated with certainty to March or April of 1680. Nor is it clear how Newton expected to determine the comet's path "whatever the line of its motion may be"; the later successful methods made an assumption about what the line was, namely that it was a parabola.

Five and a half years later Newton had still not succeeded in devising a usable method for determining cometary paths from observations. In his letter to Halley of 20 June 1686, he remarked that Book III of the *Principia*

> wants the theory of comets. In autumn last I spent two months in calculations to no purpose for want of a good method, which made me afterwards return to the first Book and enlarge it with divers propositions, some relating to comets, others to other things found out last winter. (*Corres.*, II, p. 437)

The method Newton employed in the autumn of 1685 may have been an adaptation of the methods of Wallis and Wren, assuming that, for at least a part of its path, the comet can be taken to be moving uniformly and rectilinearly. The assumption is a poor one, since comets approaching or receding from the Sun undergo very considerable changes of speed. It has to have been later than June 1686 that Newton discovered his method for fitting a parabolic trajectory to cometary observations. And then, finally, applying this method to the morning and evening comets of November–December and December–March of 1680/81, he found that their perihelia coincided, and that their speeds at equal distances from the Sun were equal, and so concluded that they were one and the same comet. We may conclude that Newton's hopefulness, in the first draft of his letter for Flamsteed, was premature.

The second draft, dated 12 April, differs from the letter finally sent in only one important respect, that it includes a paragraph omitted from the letter. The paragraph begins:

> That the comet went beyond the Sun I think myself pretty certain not only because it seems to me to be in your hypothesis against the nature of the thing for the comet to turn short of him but also because I think I have a way of determining the line of a comet's motion (whatever that line be) almost to as great exactness as the orbits of the planets are determined, provided due observations made very exactly be had. (*Corres.*, II, p. 366)

The faulty logic of the sentence may be one reason why Newton abandoned it. He appears to be thinking of the two comets as one, and we are tempted to think that he is entertaining the idea of universal gravitation, in which the acceleration toward the Sun is a function solely of distance from the Sun, whatever the body. But we cannot be sure.

What is certain is that in the rest of the second draft, and thus, in the letter actually sent, Newton is arguing against the identity of the comet of November–December and that of December–March. One of his arguments is based on the misapprehension that the earlier comet, having crossed the ecliptic from north to south, then recrossed it from south to north on 3 December. This meant that if it was bending round the Sun, it had already passed perihelion, since the nodes must be on opposite sides of the Sun. On the other hand, conjunction had occurred on 9 December; and the place of the comet at that time, on the opposite side of the Sun from the Earth, could not have been far from perihelion. The lapse of at least six days between perihelion and conjunction, in which the comet could have moved only a short distance at the very time it would be expected to move most rapidly of all, seemed to Newton too paradoxical to accept.

Newton's remaining argument was taken from the whole history of comets. If the comets of November and December were a single comet that moved in the bent trajectory Flamsteed imagines, then other comets would do the like, "and yet no such thing was ever observed in them but rather the contrary." Earlier comets that were seen both before and after their perihelia, for instance the comets of 1472, 1556, 1580, and 1664, began in one part of the heavens and ended in the opposite part, going through nearly a semicircle with motion first slow, then fast, then slow again, as if done in a straight line.

> Let but the comet of 1664 be considered where the observations were made by accurate men. This was seen long before its perihelion and long after and all the while moved (by the consent of the best astronomers) in a line almost straight. So near was the line to a straight one that Monsieur Auzout on supposition that it was an arch of a great circle about the dog star (as Cassini guessed and Auzout was afterward willing should be believed) or rather a straight one (as the obviousness of the hypothesis, easiness of the calculation, and number of observations on which it was founded makes me suspect) did from three observations predict the motion to the end without very considerable error.
> (*Corres.*, II, p. 365)

Possibly Newton for some time in the spring of 1681 seriously entertained the idea that the comet of 1680/81 was subject to the same acceleration, at any given distance from the Sun, as a planet would be. But if so, he soon abandoned the idea, on the ground that comets had not previously been seen to "fetch a compass round the Sun."

By the autumn of 1684, he had changed his mind. We do not know why.

The earliest version of the tract *De Motu*

According to the well-known story, Halley visited Newton in August 1684 and asked him what would be the curve described by the planets on the supposition that gravity diminished as the square of the distance; Newton immediately answered, *an ellipse.*

> Struck with joy and amazement, Halley asked him how he knew it? Why, replied he, I have calculated it; and being asked for the calculation, he could not find it, but promised to send it to him. (Brewster, I, p. 297)

Whether or not the story is accurate in detail, it is clear that Halley's encouragement in 1684 was responsible for rekindling Newton's interest in the dynamics of planetary motion. By November 1684 he had composed a short tract, *De Motu Corporum in Gyrum* (*On the Motion of Bodies in an Orbit*), which he sent to the Royal Society in London. It consisted of three definitions, four hypotheses, four theorems, and seven solved problems, with added corollaries and scholia. It was an initial version of what, through a series of successive refinements and elaborations, became the *Principia.*

Problem 5 has to do with a body falling without resistance in an inverse-square force field; the final Problems 6 and 7 have to do with bodies moving through resisting media and were apparently added as an afterthought. The remainder of the tract is concerned with the resistance-free motion of bodies subject to the action of central forces.

Definition 1 is of "centripetal force." The term occurs here for the first time, Newton having formed it in analogy to Huygens's term "centrifugal force." "A centripetal force," Newton here says, is "that by which a body is impelled or attracted towards some point regarded as its center" (*Math. Papers*, VI, pp. 30–31). Newton uses the term throughout the tract, not only when referring to centripetal forces in general, but also when referring to the forces on the planets toward the Sun. In the case of the latter forces, as the manuscript shows, he had originally written *gravitas,* then replaced it by the more abstract term. The inference would appear to be that Newton had hypothesized the centripetal force toward the Sun to be identical with gravity, then drew back from this identification which he could not but view, at this stage, as conjectural only. In a scholium to Problem 5, in referring to the motions of projectiles in our atmosphere, he remarks that "gravity is one species of centripetal force."

The explicitly formulated premises of the tract are four. Newton calls them "hypotheses." The first hypothesis originally postulated the absence of all resistance; when Problems 6 and 7 were added, Newton limited the statement to make it apply only to the earlier propositions, where the resistance is taken to be nil. Hypothesis 2 is the law of inertia: "Every body by its innate force alone proceeds uniformly into infinity following a straight line, unless it be impeded by something extrinsic." Hypothesis 3 is the parallelogram law for addition of forces. Hypothesis 4 states that in the beginning of a motion caused by a centripetal force, the spaces traversed are as the squares of the times.

The tract is not, of course, hypothetical in the way in which the "Hypothesis of Light" of 1675 was so: it involves no hidden aethereal mechanism. Nevertheless, I would urge that the conclusions of the tract, in which mathematically derived results are applied to planets and comets, share in its hypothetical character; and that Newton was, or became, aware of this fact.

Theorem 1 is essentially the same as Proposition 1 of the *Principia:* "All orbiting bodies describe, by radii drawn to their center, areas proportional to the times." Theorem 2, essentially the same as Proposition 4 of the *Principia,* shows that, for bodies moving uniformly in circles, the centripetal forces are as the squares of arcs simultaneously described, divided by the radii of their circles. In the fifth corollary following, Newton applies this theorem to concentric circular orbits in which the squares of the periods are as the cubes of the radii and concludes that the force varies inversely as the square of the distance from the center. Newton then asserts that this case "does obtain in the major planets circling round the Sun and also in the minor ones orbiting round Jupiter and Saturn . . . " (*Math. Papers,* VI, p. 41).

The orbits of the planets, of course, though nearly circular, are not concentric with the Sun, and Newton immediately passes on to Theorem 3, equivalent to Proposition 6 of the *Principia,* which permits the determination of the law of force in noncircular orbits with center of force elsewhere than at the geometrical center. Problems 1–3 apply this theorem to particular cases, and it is Problem 3 that gives us the planetary case: in elliptical orbits with center of force at a focus, the force varies inversely as the square of the distance. In an appended scholium Newton then concludes:

> The major planets orbit, therefore, in ellipses having a focus at the
> center of the Sun, and with their *radii* drawn to the Sun describe areas
> proportional to the times, exactly as Kepler supposed. (*Math. Papers,* VI,
> p. 49)

A question is in order concerning the logic of the inference here, but before attending to it, let us take note of Theorem 4 and Problem 4, the final propositions having to do with planets. Theorem 4 shows that, in an inverse-square field of force, Kepler's third law holds for elliptical orbits just as it does for circular orbits. A scholium then points out in detail how this result can be used to determine the eccentricities and aphelia of the planetary orbits: the mean solar distances or semi-major axes are found from the periods by way of Kepler's third law (just as we have seen it done in Streete's *Astronomia Carolina*); then, using observations and geometrical procedures known earlier, the second focus, or (in the case of the inner planets) the center of the orbit, is located with respect to the Sun.

Problem 4 is essentially the same as Proposition 17 of the *Principia:* it shows how to determine the conic section in which a body would move in an inverse-square field of force, given the absolute value of the force and the initial direction and speed of the body. It is undoubtedly because he had obtained this theorem that Newton here and in the first edition of the *Principia* took for granted that in an inverse-square field the orbit would be a conic section.

Finally, in the scholium following Problem 4, Newton announces:

> A bonus, indeed, of this problem, once it is solved, is that we are now allowed to define the orbits of comets, and thereby their periods of revolution, and then to ascertain from a comparison of their orbital magnitude, eccentricities, aphelia [!—Newton should have said perihelia], inclinations to the ecliptic plane and their nodes whether the same comet returns with some frequency to us. (*Math. Papers,* VI, pp. 57–59)

Newton then proposes a method of determining the elliptical orbit of a comet. First he would use Wren's technique to find a straight-line path and speed for the comet from three observations. The ellipse is assumed to be tangent to this rectilinear trajectory at some point, and the ellipse is calculated as in Problem 4. The errors in position as derived from this elliptical orbit are then applied to the initial observations in order to compute a new rectilinear trajectory, from which a new elliptical orbit is derived. And so on, until (as Newton hopes) agreement between observation and prediction is reached. The truth is, the method will not work, as Newton himself discovered.

What is the status of the results that Newton derives in the tract *De Motu Corporum in Gyrum*? Are they certain, probable, or dubious?

Let us take it for granted (as Newton apparently did) that a parabolic, hyperbolic, or elliptical orbit traversed under the action of a central force implies an inverse-square law of force, and conversely. Moreover, for elliptical orbits with centers of force at one focus, if the squares of the periods are as the cubes of the mean solar distances, then the force varies inversely as the square of the distance, and conversely if the orbits are closed.

What is the relation of these results to empirical fact? Newton is aware that not all astronomers agree on the exactitude of Kepler's third law. He is aware that the elliptical orbit and areal rule have not been exactly verified: Kepler *supposed* them. Why then should Newton assume the inverse-square law to hold exactly for the centripetal force toward the Sun?

The answer has to be: he is guessing. We shall soon see that he is or becomes aware that he has been guessing. It is conceivable, for instance, on the assumption of his "Hypothesis of Light," that the inverse-square law should be only approximately true, and then the elliptical orbit and areal rule would not apply *exactly* as Kepler supposed.

It is noteworthy that, in the *De Motu Corporum in Gyrum,* there is not a single indication that Newton believes in universal gravitation or has deduced any of the consequences of it that differ from those of the simple assumption of an inverse-square field of force. Kepler's third law, as enunciated by Kepler and employed by Newton, is inexact and requires modification if Sun and planet attract each other. If the planets attract each other, the elliptical orbit and areal rule become inexact owing to perturbations.

Somehow, in this first tract, Newton has "embarked." It is possible that the encouragement of Halley served a logical as well as a psychological purpose: Halley believed the comet of 1680/81 to be a single comet and believed that it had been attracted by the Sun. The enterprise of the *De Motu Corporum in Gyrum* was sustained not by assured foundations but by hope: hope that the inferences drawn by treating the Sun as an immobile center of an inverse-square field of force were sufficiently exact, hope that comets were acted upon by this field in the same manner as were planets, so that their orbits could be determined.

Newton quickly deepened his analysis, as he discovered the possible implications of the course he had set for himself.

The augmented tract *De Motu Corporum* (December 1684?)

In a revised and expanded version of the *De Motu,* dated tentatively by Whiteside as from December 1684 (*Math. Papers,* VI, p. 74ff.), the four "Hypotheses" of the original draft have become five "Laws." Here, in an addition to the scholium following Theorem 4, we find the first clear indication that Newton is thinking of gravitation as universal, and that he is deducing consequences from that assumption:

> Moreover the whole space of the planetary heavens either rests (as is commonly believed) or moves uniformly in a straight line, and hence the common center of gravity of the planets . . . either rests or moves along with it. In either case the motions of the planets among themselves are the same, and their common center of gravity rests with respect to the whole space, and thus can be taken for the immobile center of the whole planetary system. Hence in truth the Copernican system is proved *a priori.* For if in any position of the planets their common center of gravity is computed, this either falls in the body of the Sun or will always be close to it. By reason of the deviation of the Sun from the center of gravity, the centripetal force does not always tend to that immobile center, and hence the planets neither move exactly in ellipses nor revolve twice in the same orbit. There are as many orbits of a planet

as it has revolutions, as in the motion of the Moon, and the orbit of any
one planet depends on the combined motion of all the planets, not to
mention the action of all these on each other. But to consider simultaneously all these causes of motion and to define these motions by exact
laws admitting of easy calculation exceeds, if I am not mistaken, the
force of any human mind. Omit those minutiae, and the simple orbit and
mean among all the deviations will be the ellipse of which I have already
treated. If anyone tries to determine this ellipse by trigonometrical
computation from three observations (as is customary), he will have
proceeded with less caution. For those observations will share in the
minute irregular motions here neglected and so make the ellipse to
deviate a little from its just magnitude and position (which ought to be
the mean among all the deviations), and so will yield as many ellipses
differing from one another as there are trios of observations employed.
Therefore there are to be joined together and compared with one
another in a single operation a great number of observations, which
temper each other mutually and yield the mean ellipse in both position
and magnitude. (*Math. Papers*, VI, p. 78)

Here we find clearly affirmed the action of the planets on the Sun
and on one another; in every case of action, two bodies are being said
to *interact*. That such interaction actually occurs is not argued in the
paragraph but is simply affirmed; we know it would not occur under
either the aethereal hypothesis of 1675 or that of the letter to Boyle
of 1679. The asserted interaction has the discouraging consequence
that, in all probability, no exact predictive astronomy of the planetary
motions will be possible; the best that can be done is to settle for
average orbits, and to console oneself with the thought that, because
of the relatively immense mass of the Sun, the center of gravity of the
solar system is always within or close to the body of the Sun, so that the
perturbations will be very small.

But how does Newton know where the center of gravity of the solar
system is? How has he "proved the Copernican system *a priori*"?

Only one way of comparing the masses of different celestial bodies
was available to Newton, namely that which he employed in Corollary
III of the first edition, or Corollary II of the later editions, of Proposition 8 of Book III of the *Principia* [*GBWW*, Vol. 34, p. 283a]. It requires that the body have a satellite. The central acceleration at the
distance of the satellite is determinable from the period of the satellite. Then, on the assumption that this central acceleration varies inversely as the square of the distance, and is independent of the mass
of the satellite, it is possible to compute the central acceleration of any
satellite of the central body at any distance. Finally, the quantities of
matter in different celestial bodies are taken to be as the centripetal
accelerations at equal distances from their centers. In the *Principia*

Newton is thus able to compute the relative masses of the Sun, Earth, Jupiter, and Saturn.

This computation presupposes two crucial premises of Newton's final argument for universal gravitation. The first is that the acceleration of a body toward the Sun, Earth, Jupiter, or Saturn is independent of the mass of the body accelerated and is thus a function solely of distance. Newton tacitly assumed the premise in the first version of *De Motu*, but in carrying out the comparison of the masses of different celestial bodies he had to articulate it explicitly. The second premise is that the attractions exercised at a given distance from these several attracting bodies are as their masses. In the *Principia* this second premise becomes, in Proposition 69 of Book I [*GBWW,* Vol. 34, p. 130], a deduction from the first premise by way of the third law of motion. An empirical test of the first premise makes its first appearance in the next document we have to examine.

But before leaving the initial revision we are examining we should take note of an addition Newton here makes to the scholium following Problem 5. After urging that the resistance of the aether in the interplanetary spaces must be nil, Newton proceeds as follows:

> Motions in the heavens are ruled therefore by the laws demonstrated. But the motions of projectiles in our air, ignoring its resistance, are known by Problem 4, and also the motions of heavy bodies falling perpendicularly by Problem 5, given of course that gravity is inversely proportional to the square of the distance from the center of the Earth. For gravity is one species of centripetal force; and by my calculations the centripetal force by which the Moon is held in her monthly motion about the Earth is very nearly to the force of gravity here at the surface of the Earth inversely as the square of the distance. (*Math. Papers,* VI, p. 79)

This is Newton's first explicit report of a "Moon test" of the inverse-square law.

Early revision of the definitions and laws

During the winter of 1684/85 and the following spring Newton rapidly improved and deepened his treatment of the foundations of his argument. In an early expansion of the definitions we find a report of an experiment to test the strict proportionality of what we now distinguish as mass and weight:

> By *pondus* [the word can mean *either* mass *or* weight] I understand the quantity or amount of matter moved, abstracted from the consideration

of gravity, whenever it is not a matter of gravitating bodies. To be sure, the *pondus* of gravitating bodies is proportional to their quantity of matter, and it is allowable to designate or explain analogues by each other. The analogy can actually be demonstrated as follows. The oscillations of two bodies of the same weight [*pondus*] with equal suspensions are counted, and the amount of matter in them will be reciprocally as the number of oscillations made in the same time. But in experiments carefully made on gold, silver, lead, glass, sand, common salt, water, wood, and wheat I always found the same number of oscillations. (*Math. Papers*, VI. pp. 189–90)

In a cancelled final sentence, Newton wrote: "On account of this analogy and for lack of a more convenient word I set forth and designate quantity of matter by *pondus*, even in bodies of which the gravitation is not considered." This awkward usage will be quickly abandoned in the revisions that follow, Newton maintaining henceforth the strict distinction between *pondus* and *quantitas materiae*, while demonstrating their proportionality.

The list of materials experimented on is the same as that given in Proposition 6 of Book III of the *Principia* [*GBWW*, Vol. 34, pp. 279–81], where Newton describes the precautions he took in carrying out the experiment and concludes that the proportion holds good to one part in a thousand.

The fundamental elements of Newton's argument for universal gravitation were now in place. In a careful experiment on nine different materials, carried out in the winter of 1684/85, Newton showed that the masses and weights of terrestrial bodies are proportional, so that they accelerate equally toward the Earth; it follows that the gravitational force to which each is subject is proportional to its mass. The Moon test, carried out for the first time during the same winter, showed that it is this same gravitational force toward the Earth that retains the Moon in her orbit. By inductive generalization the nature of gravity toward the planets and the Sun is then concluded to be the same as that toward the Earth, since the inverse-square law has been confirmed both for the circumsolar planets and for their satellites. But then, by the third law of motion, or the equality of action and reaction, the attracting body must be in turn attracted; the force to which it is thus subject will be proportional to its own mass. In all cases, then, the force of gravitation between two bodies will be proportional to the masses of both, and the distinction between "attracting" and "attracted" becomes only a matter of point of view. The argument no longer seems novel today; as Mach put it, an "uncommon incomprehensibility" has become a "common incomprehensibility." But if my reading of the documents is correct, it was very new in the winter of 1684/85, and a source first of wonder and then of satisfaction to Newton himself.

Conclusion and epilogue

I have been arguing that, during the winter of 1684/85, by an act of thought coupled with experiment and calculation, Newton emerged from uncertainty and achieved the assurance he required in order to proceed with the composition of the *Principia*.

Two questions, inextricably related to one another, remained. What was the extent of the perturbations caused by the action of the planets on one another, the Sun on the satellites, the satellites on their primaries? And how could one be assured that there was no cause *other* than universal gravitation that had to be taken into account in the celestial motions?

In December 1684 Newton asked Flamsteed for his values for the radii and periods of Jupiter's satellites. Flamsteed replied on 27 December:

> I find . . . that [their distances from Jupiter] are as exactly in sesquialter proportion [i.e., having a ratio of one and a half to one] to their periods as it is possible for our senses to determine. . . . I find I can answer all the eclipses of the first [satellite] that have been carefully observed within less than 2 minutes of time, the fourth has not failed me much more nor the third above thrice as much. . . . I use their motions altogether equable only allowing Roemer's equation of light, without which allowance the error of my tables would be above 10′ of time. (*Corres.*, II, p. 404)

Newton replied on 30 December:

> I thank you heartily for your kind information about those things I desired. . . . Your information about the satellites of Jupiter gives me very much satisfaction. (*Corres.*, II, pp. 406–7)

Newton's satisfaction stemmed not only from the exact verification of the inverse-square law, but also from the evidence that the satellites' motions were but minimally perturbed by the Sun. At the same time, Newton was concerned about possible perturbations of Saturn by Jupiter, and in the letter from which I have just quoted he wrote:

> The orbit of Saturn is defined by Kepler too little for the sesquialterate proportion. This planet so oft as he is in conjunction with Jupiter ought (by reason of Jupiter's action upon him) to run beyond his orbit about one or two of the Sun's semidiameters or a little more and almost all the rest of his motion to run as much or more within it. Perhaps that might be the ground of Kepler's defining it too little. But I would gladly know if you ever observed Saturn to err considerably from Kepler's tables about the time of his conjunction with Jupiter. (*Corres.*, II, p. 407)

Flamsteed's reply was dated 5 January:

> As for the motion of Saturn I have found it about 27′ slower in the
> acronycal appearances [= oppositions] since I came here, than Kepler's
> numbers, and Jupiter's about 14 or 15′ swifter. . . , the error in Jupiter
> is not always the same, by reason the place of his aphelion is amiss in
> Kepler. Nor is the fault in Saturn always the same . . . yet the differences
> in both are regular and may be easily answered by a small alteration in
> the numbers. . . . I have corrected Jupiter myself so that he has of late
> years answered my calculus in all places of his orbit but I have not been
> strict enough to affirm that there is no such exorbitation as you suggest
> of Saturn. . . . I know Kepler's distances of Saturn agree not with the
> sesquialter proportion and that Jupiter's too ought to be mended and
> both must be altered before we set upon the enquiry whether Jupiter's
> motion had any influence on Saturn's. (*Corres.*, II, pp. 408–9)

Flamsteed was here altogether too optimistic about the ease with
which the theories of Jupiter and Saturn might be perfected, as he
acknowledged in his final years; the difficulties were resolved only in
1785, by Laplace. But Flamsteed's information was important for Newton, who replied as follows on 12 January:

> Your information about the error of Kepler's tables for Jupiter and
> Saturn has eased me of several scruples. I was apt to suspect there might
> be some cause or other unknown to me, which might disturb the
> sesquialtera proportion. For the influences of the planets one upon
> another seemed not great enough though I imagined Jupiter's influence
> greater than your numbers determine it. It would add to my satisfaction
> if you would be pleased to let me know the long diameters of the orbits
> of Jupiter and Saturn assigned by yourself and Mr. Halley in your new
> tables, that I may see how the sesquiplicate proportion fills the heavens
> together with another small proportion which must be allowed for.
> (*Corres.*, II, p. 413)

The "small proportion which must be allowed for" undoubtedly has
to do with a modification of Kepler's third law that takes into account the masses of the Sun and the planets. But what has most
pleased Newton is Flamsteed's assurance that he need not trust Kepler's or any other astronomer's numbers; this assurance frees him to
assume that the available data will not require any explanatory cause
in addition to universal gravitation. Not only is universal gravitation *a* cause of celestial phenomena, it can now be assumed to be
the cause.

There were, of course, many difficulties remaining that Newton had
to deal with. He had to seek ways of determining perturbations more
precisely (as in Propositions 45 and 60 of Book I of the *Principia*

[*GBWW*, Vol. 34, pp. 96–101, 113–14]); discover how spheres of gravitating matter attract one another, and whether any deviation from the inverse-square law is to be expected close to their surfaces; solve the nagging problem of fitting orbits to the observations of comets. But he had now laid an experimental and observational foundation for his undertaking, and no fact known to him appeared contrary to it. That foundation is the argument for universal gravitation. Its importance to him is shown by the care with which, in the first eight propositions of Book III of the *Principia,* he chose his way among purported empirical facts, distinguishing approximately confirmed ones from more precisely confirmed ones, and using each kind at its exact value. Such security as is possible in experimental philosophy was now his.

One feature of the argument, as presented in the first edition of the *Principia,* is specially relevant to the present analysis: it indicates the extent to which universal gravitation emerged for Newton in contrast and opposition to aethereal hypotheses for gravity. The premises of Book III in the first edition are there called "Hypotheses." The Hypotheses include the first two of the "Rules of Reasoning in Philosophy" found in the later editions, and most of what is given in the later editions under the title "Phenomena." Hypothesis III reads:

> Every body may be transformed into a body of any other kind, and all intermediate degrees of qualities may be successively induced. (*Principia,* 1687 ed., p. 402)

I suggest that this is a dialectical premise; it is what the aethereal theorists (including, earlier, Newton himself) have assumed. Hypothesis III is put to use in Corollary II of Proposition 6. The proposition states that

> All bodies gravitate toward each of the planets, and their weights toward any one planet, at equal distances from the center of the planet, are proportional to the quantities of matter in the several bodies. (*Principia,* 1687 ed., p. 408)

Corollary I states:

> Hence the weights of bodies do not depend upon their forms and textures. For if the weights could be varied with the forms, then they would be greater or less, according to the variety of forms, in equal matter; altogether against experience. (*Principia,* 1687 ed., p. 410)

Corollary II then tell us:

> Therefore, all bodies which are about the Earth gravitate towards the Earth; and the weights of all that are equally distant from the center of

the Earth are as the quantities of matter in them. For if aether or any other body were either deprived of its gravity altogether or were to gravitate less in proportion to its quantity of matter, then since this body does not differ from other bodies except in form of matter, it could by a change of form be gradually transmuted into a body of the same condition as those which gravitate most in proportion to their quantity of matter (by Hypothesis III), and reversely the heaviest bodies could . . . gradually lose their gravity. And thus weights would depend on the forms of bodies, and could vary with the forms, against what was proved in the preceding Corollary. (*Principia,* 1687 ed., pp. 410–11)

In the second edition, Newton improved the argument by eliminating the dialectical assumption, Hypothesis III. Corollary II of Proposition 6 is changed so that the second of its three sentences just quoted is replaced by the following two sentences:

This is the quality of all bodies within the reach of our experiments; and therefore (by Rule III [of the "Rules of Reasoning in Philosophy"]) to be affirmed of all bodies whatsoever. If the aether, or any other body, were either altogether void of gravity, or were to gravitate less in proportion to its quantity of matter, then, because (according to Aristotle, Descartes, and others) there is no difference between that and other bodies but in mere form of matter, by a successive change from form to form, it might be changed at last into a body of the same condition with those which gravitate most in proportion to their quantity of matter; and, on the other hand, the heaviest bodies, acquiring the first form of that body, might by degrees quite lose their gravity. [*GBWW*, Vol. 34, p. 281a]

Thus, the assertion of the universality of gravity is now supported principally by a reference to Rule III, the rule of inductive generalization applying to the qualities of bodies:

The qualities of bodies, which admit neither intensification nor remission of degrees, and which are found to belong to all bodies within the reach of our experiments, are to be esteemed the universal qualities of all bodies whatsoever. [*GBWW*, Vol. 34, p. 270]

This rule, according to Newton, is "the foundation of all philosophy," or again, in our term, "science."

Finally, in the third edition, to make the argument still more pointed, Newton added Rule IV:

In experimental philosophy we are to look upon propositions inferred by general induction from phenomena as accurately or very nearly true, notwithstanding any contrary hypotheses that may be imagined, till such time as other phenomena occur, by which they may either be made more accurate, or liable to exceptions. [*GBWW*, Vol. 34, p. 271]

Any aethereal hypothesis for gravity would presumably have to come in under the exception clause.

Newton, I conclude, was acutely conscious of the nature of his enterprise. He realized that it could not be freed from every possibility of doubt, that it remained risky. The rule of induction, more a procedure for justifying than a method of discovery, provided such security as was available. Universal gravitation was originally, for Newton, a conjecture, framed in clear contrast with the accepted aethereal hypotheses of his day, apparently contrary to cometary observations, and contrary in an important respect to the analogue that had first guided Gilbert, Kepler, and Hooke in introducing attractions into the heavens—namely magnetism, which, unlike gravitation, could be made to disappear and was not related to the quantity of matter by a constant proportionality. No mere obvious generalization enabled Newton to put the aethereal hypotheses aside, or to infer the universality of gravity. An intense examination of consequences had to ensue.

No trace of the actual moment of discovery has come down to us. The emergence for Newton of the argument that gravitation is universal and therefore mechanically inexplicable must have brought with it a sense of relief—the happiness of realizing that aethereal conjectures could be set aside as irrelevant. At the same time, to adopt the program of accounting for celestial phenomena by means of universal gravitation was to assume an enormous burden; it was to undertake to learn how to fit trajectories to comets, to attempt to account for lunar and planetary perturbations. The writing of the *Principia* absorbed more than two years, and for the chief problem, that of perturbations, Newton was able to supply (in section 11 of Book I) only a qualitative account— an account nevertheless assessed by G. B. Airy, the nineteenth-century astronomer, as "the most valuable chapter that has ever been written on physical science" (Airy, p. x). An adequately quantitative account of perturbations had to await the employment of new mathematical techniques, in particular trigonometric series, by Euler, Lagrange, and Laplace.

As for Hooke, he never realized exactly what he had given Newton—namely, a program of investigation—and therefore, his charges of plagiarism in the matter of the inverse-square law were misplaced. Nor did Newton ever publicly acknowledge what he had received. The only acknowledgment in the *Principia* of Hooke's ever having done anything for the theory of gravitation is the attribution to him (as to Wren and Halley) of a derivation of the inverse-square law from Kepler's third law (Scholium to Proposition 4 of Book I), an altogether mistaken attribution in Hooke's case. So these great ships passed in the dark, but not without a signal-flash from one to the other, changing the course of history.

Sources of quotations in text

Airy:
Airy, G. B., *Gravitation* (London, 1834).

Brewster:
Brewster, David, *Memoir of the Life, Writings, and Discoveries of Sir Isaac Newton* (Edinburgh, 1855).

Corres.:
Turnbull, H. W., ed., *The Correspondence of Isaac Newton,* I–II, (Cambridge University Press, 1959–60).

Descartes:
Descartes, *Principles of Philosophy,* trans. V. R. and R. P. Miller (Dordrecht, Holland: Reidel, ca. 1983).

Gunther:
Gunther, R. T., *Early Science in Oxford,* 14 vols. (Oxford and London, 1920–45); Vol. VIII, *The Cutler Lectures of Robert Hooke.*

Hall:
Hall, A. Rupert, and Marie Boas Hall, eds., *Unpublished Scientific Papers of Isaac Newton* (Cambridge University Press, 1962).

Herivel:
Herivel, John, *The Background to Newton's Principia* (Oxford: Clarendon Press, 1965).

Math. Papers:
Whiteside, D. T., ed., *The Mathematical Papers of Isaac Newton,* Vol. VI (1684–91) (Cambridge University Press, 1974).

Principia, *1687 ed.:*
Newton, *Philosophiae Naturalis Principia Mathematica* (London, 1687).

Streete:
Streete, Thomas, *Astronomia Carolina* (London, 1661).

Trinity Notebook:
McGuire, J. E., and Tamny, Martin, *Certain Philosophical Questions: Newton's Trinity Notebook* (Cambridge University Press, 1983).

Westfall:
Westfall, Richard S., *Never at Rest: A Biography of Isaac Newton* (Cambridge University Press, 1980).

Quotations from the *Principia* (Third Edition) are taken from *Great Books of the Western World,* Vol. 34.

A bibliographical note

A close reading of Newton's letters in Volumes I and II of *The Correspondence of Isaac Newton* first led me to the realization that Newton's discovery of universal gravitation came late, not before 1684. I embodied this thesis in my "From Kepler's Laws, So-called, to Universal Gravitation: Empirical Factors," *Archive for History of Exact Sciences,* 6 (1970): pp. 89–170. D. T. Whiteside's seminal essay, "Newton's Early Thoughts on Planetary Motion: A Fresh Look," (*British Journal for the History of Science,* 2 [1964]: pp. 117–37), was also a source of important insights. But at the time of writing "From Kepler's Laws . . . " I had not understood that all Newton's thinking on planetary motion during the 1660s and 1670s assumed vortices and the Cartesian analysis of circular motion. R. S. Westfall's *Force in Newton's Physics* (American Elsevier, 1971) set this matter straight for me; and his article "Hooke and the Law of Universal Gravitation" (*British Journal for the History of Science,* 3 [1967]: pp. 245–61) supplied an insight that I might have missed. Two pieces by Whiteside that came out in 1970 contain many important insights into the genesis of Newton's ideas: "Before the *Principia:* the Maturing of Newton's Thoughts on Dynamical Astronomy, 1664–1684," (*Journal for the History of Astronomy,* 1 [1970]: pp. 5–19); and "The Mathematical Principles Underlying Newton's *Principia Mathematica*" (Ibid., pp. 116–38). The notes and commentary by Whiteside in the eight-volume set *The Mathematical Papers of Isaac Newton* are a treasury of precious lore, supplying both facts and interpretations relevant to Newton's processes. The standard biography of Newton for a long time to come will be Westfall's *Never at Rest;* it supplies trenchant formulations of many of the matters touched on in the foregoing essay.

Why the Computer Is Only
as Good as It Is

Charles Van Doren

Charles Van Doren was born and raised in New York City. In 1947, after service in the Air Force, he was graduated from St. John's College, Annapolis,
Maryland, and two years later he took a master's degree in mathematics
from Columbia University, where he also received his doctorate in English
literature in 1959, and where he taught literature from 1955 to 1959.

In 1965 he joined the Institute for Philosophical Research in Chicago as
assistant director under Mortimer Adler. From 1973 until 1982 he was also
vice-president, editorial, of Encyclopædia Britannica, Inc. Now retired, he
remains a member of Britannica's board of editors.

He is the author of *Lincoln's Commando* (1957), *The Idea of Progress*
(1967), and several children's books. In addition, he was editor, with Clifton
Fadiman, of *The American Treasury* (1955); was executive editor of the
twenty-volume *Annals of America* (1967), of which he wrote most of the
two-volume *Conspectus;* was one of the general editors of *Makers of
America* (ten vols., 1971); edited, with Mortimer Adler, the *Great Treasury
of Western Thought* (1977); and was supervisory editor of four volumes of
documents on various aspects of American history edited by Wayne Moquin
between 1971 and 1976.

Since his retirement, Mr. Van Doren has been busy as a writer and
consultant. He and his wife, Geraldine, spend a portion of each year in their
small house in Cortona, Italy. He has been a frequent contributor to *The
Great Ideas Today*.

Perhaps none of mankind's inventions shows so much promise as the computer; the excitement generated by its possibilities can be almost unbearable—it makes some people dance in the street. At the same time, the computer is often a great disappointment. It does not do what is expected, for reasons that are sometimes unclear.

If the excitement remains the dominant emotion, the disappointment cannot be ignored. This article is about the reasons for both.

It begins with a brief account of the short, wonderful history of the computer, then suggests some general concepts that are useful when thinking about it. Following that is a discussion of some of the remarkable things the computer does, as well as some things it cannot or does not do; this section concludes with an account of the uses, often illegitimate, to which the computer is put, and of the ways, often brutal, in which it is treated. Finally, some new uses and treatments are suggested, which may or may not hold greater promise than anything heretofore proposed.

Throughout, I shall tend to refer to "the computer," in the singular, rather than to "computers." In fact, "the computer" and "computers" mean almost the same thing, just as "woman" means almost the same thing as "women" in the most general sense of the latter term; and similarly with "man" and "men."

The singular form seems preferable in the case of the computer for much the same reasons as for man, when viewed in general—philosophically. "Men" tends to lead to quantitative conclusions, "man" to qualitative ones. This is partly because man is clearly breakable into "body" and "spirit" or "body" and "mind." The analogous breakdown for the computer is into "hardware" and "software." To speak of "computers" is often to mask the subtle relationships between these two primitive entities that constitute the computer.

The computer's precocity

The computer is precocious. It did not come into full being until about 1950; there were calculating machines as much as a century before that, and theoretical work on the concept of the (digital) computer was done during the 1930s, but working models were few and exceedingly primitive before that date.

Now, thirty-five years later, the computer is entering its fifth generation. Thirty-five years is approximately one human generation. The computer has grown nearly five times as fast.

Each generation has produced explosively new things and ideas. The first-generation computer was hard-wired—its elements were connected by wires—and could do less, with all its bulk, than a hand-held calculator you can buy today for five dollars.

The second-generation computer was the first to enjoy the benefits of solid-state electronics, where connections could be made between elements without wires. There are no wires in our heads.

The third generation was marked by an enormous decrease in size and increase in power, as printed circuits began to be used for making connections, carrying messages, and storing information in the computer's memory. The giant mainframes began to be replaced in many installations by minicomputers, which took up relatively little space and required relatively little power, money, and care.

The fourth generation used printed circuits more extensively and employed new solid-state devices for memory—bubble memories and the like. The computer became even smaller, cheaper, and more powerful; and it moved into the home. At the same time, enormous supercomputers were built that could accomplish as many as half a billion operations per second.

The fifth generation, which hovers on the horizon today, will be as radically different from its predecessors as each of the previous generations has been. Further progress in miniaturization will make it even smaller, cheaper, and more powerful. But another kind of change will occur. Up to now, the computer has operated serially. One processing step is taken, then another; the second does not start until the first is completed. Operations go on very rapidly nevertheless; some supercomputers may soon be accomplishing a billion operations a second. But there are important problems that require speeds vastly greater even than that. The only hope is to move beyond serial processing to what is called parallel processing.

It has always been possible to connect computers to one another and thus do a kind of parallel processing: one computer addressed one phase of a problem, another computer another phase. But connecting physically distinct and separated computers does not really do the trick. The elements are too far apart; the time it takes electronic impulses to travel from one computer to another, then perhaps to another, even though the impulses travel at the speed of light, is simply too great. What is gained in power by connecting two or more computers is lost in the time required for them to work with each other and on each other's results.

The fifth generation will take another tack. It will incorporate many computers—as many, in some predictions, as a million separate com-

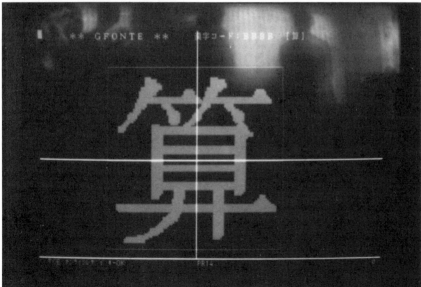

At Japan's Institute for New Generation Computer Technology (top), researchers conceive software for a fifth-generation natural-language computer system. The Japanese character meaning both "number" and "calculation" (bottom) is from the computer's 100,000-word dictionary.

A 2-billion-byte memory and capability of 1.2 billion operations per second qualify the Cray-2, above, as a supercomputer. Fluorinert, a liquid coolant that is also used as artificial blood plasma, courses through the machine, allowing its 240,000 computer chips to be densely packed into a hot-tub-sized cabinet.

puters—into one operating system. Solid-state electronics will tie them all together tightly into a closely knit system; miniaturization will keep the distances that impulses have to travel very small. Each unit in the total computing mass will perform its own operations, ultimately at a speed that may approach the speed of the largest supercomputers today—hundreds of millions of operations per second. But as many as a million such units will be operating in parallel—working on separate parts of the overall problem. The result could be a fifth-generation computer capable of performing hundreds or thousands of billions of operations each second.

A number of problems in mathematics and physics have already been identified that may be solvable with fifth-generation parallel processors of this size. Other applications will be discovered when the technology making them possible is developed. Each generation of the computer has seen an enormous increase in possibilities; not all of these have been realized at any stage, and doubtless they will not all be taken advantage of in the fifth generation, either. But it seems certain that new possibilities, as yet not seen or imagined, will emerge with the parallel processors of the near future.

Then we can start to think about a sixth generation. It should come along no more than about ten years after the fifth.

Another way to conceive of the precocity of the computer is to remember that other astounding invention: printing. Movable types were first used in the West around 1450, and it did not take very long—less than fifty years—before most of the books produced in the previous two millennia had been printed in the new, cheap, easily distributed form. The really great changes produced or initiated by the invention of printing came later, of course: things like universal literacy, the nation-state, world wars, and democratic governments.

In the case of the computer, we are not even to the end of the first half century after the beginning—not yet to 1500. But many of the really big things have already begun to happen, in the course of only a single human generation. We have already passed the point of no return; the human race can never go back to the warm, slow, simple life that prevailed in the ages before the computer. The future is inevitably an electronic one; future "life" forms may even be based on silicon instead of carbon. We barely noticed when we crossed the Rubicon; people hardly ever do.

Machines and essences

The computer is not a machine. The object you buy in a computer store, bring home in boxes, and set up on your desk is a machine. But the computer itself is not a machine, in its deepest essence.

To call the computer a machine is to stretch a metaphor beyond the breaking point. Hamlet called his own body a machine; that was stretching a metaphor, too. Hamlet is on the edge of madness when he says it, or writes it, as he does, in a letter to Ophelia—

> Thine evermore, most dear lady, whilst this machine is to him,
>
> Hamlet

Perhaps that explains the exaggeration in the figure. To insist that the computer is a machine, or is *only* a machine (the more common insistence), reflects an emotional response to the idea of the computer that it would be wise to discard. Calling something you do not like or fear by a pejorative name does not make it more likable or less fearful.

Itself not a machine, the computer is a simulator of machines; Alan Turing showed many years ago that the computer could simulate *any* machine. (The computer is sometimes called a universal Turing machine, but this is far from an ordinary machine, like a clock or a car.) If Hamlet was right, and the human body is in some sense a machine, then the computer can simulate that, a fact not at all surprising: computers simulate bodily actions, operations, and powers in many applications today.

The mind is not a machine; even Hamlet in his madness did not claim that. The computer, even as a universal Turing machine, cannot simulate the mind. Or not yet. (And even if the computer simulated a mind, it would not *be* a mind.)

The computer is not a tool, either. A tool is an extension of the hand; any other use of the term is metaphorical. No tool does what the hand cannot do in some sense; it merely does it better, or much better, sometimes so much better that it reaches levels of competence inaccessible to the unaided hand. The computer is not a tool in this sense; it is an extension not of the hand but of man. It does not extend the hand merely; it does not extend the mind merely; it extends the power, skill, and competence of the whole human being. Once again it is an invidious comparison, caused by unseemly emotions, to call the computer a tool.

The computer is to the man as the dog is to the man. Toni Morrison, in *Song of Solomon* (Alfred A. Knopf, 1977), describes a night hunt; this is the way it sometimes is, and the way, she says, that it used to be.

> He could still hear them—the way they had sounded the last few hours.
> Signaling one another. What were they saying? "Wait up?" "Over here?"
> Little by little it fell into place. The dogs, the men—none was just
> hollering, just signaling location or pace. The men and the dogs were
> talking to each other. In distinctive voices they were saying distinctive,
> complicated things. That long *yah* sound was followed by a specific kind
> of howl from one of the dogs. The low *howm howm* that sounded like a

string bass imitating a bassoon meant something the dogs understood and executed. And the dogs spoke to the men: single-shot barks—evenly spaced and widely spaced—one every three or four minutes, that might go on for twenty minutes. A sort of radar that indicated to the men where they were and what they saw and what they wanted to do about it. And the men agreed or told them to change direction or to come back. All those shrieks, those rapid tumbling barks, the long sustained yells, the tuba sounds, the drumbeat sounds, the low liquid *howm howm,* the reedy whistles, the thin *eeeee*'s of a cornet, the *unh unh unh* bass chords. It was all language. An extension of the click people made in their cheeks back home when they wanted a dog to follow them. No, it was not language; it was what there was before language. Before things were written down. Language in the time when men and animals did talk to one another, when a man could sit down with an ape and the two converse; when a tiger and a man could share the same tree, and each understood the other; when men ran *with* wolves, not from or after them. (p. 278)

Because the relationships between a man and his dog and a man and his computer are similar does not mean the computer is much like a dog. There are major differences, primarily in the sensorium; the dog lives in a world quickened by sensory inputs; the computer may never be able to sense its world but instead be forever dependent on statements, descriptions, reports of reality. Nevertheless, the linguistic connection between dog and man has things in common with the linguistic connection between computer and man.

Language itself is said to be a tool—a tool of communication, say. But that is a misapprehension about language. Language is a medium of communication; by means of language we communicate with others and with the world at large; but we are radically changed by using this medium. We are what we are because we employ language to communicate; we reshape ourselves every time we use language. We become conscious through language, and without it we would hardly be human.

The computer, says Alan Kay, is a medium before it is anything else.

The protean nature of the computer is such that it can act like a machine or like a language to be shaped and exploited. It is a medium that can dynamically simulate the details of any other medium, including media that cannot exist physically. It is not a tool, although it can act like many tools. It is the first metamedium, and as such it has degrees of freedom for representation and expression never before encountered and as yet barely investigated. Even more important, it is fun, and therefore intrinsically worth doing (*Scientific American,* September 1984, p. 59).

That the computer is a medium, even a metamedium, is profoundly important. And man is being radically changed through his use of this medium, too.

The computer and the brain

"There's no art," says King Duncan just before he meets Macbeth (who will shortly betray and murder him), "To find the mind's construction in the face" (*GBWW*, Vol. 27, p. 287b). The mind of man is indeed a deep and largely unfathomable well; we do not know even what a close friend is thinking, or a mate with whom we have been living for many years. The face is, or can be, utterly impassive, uncommunicative; while emotions roil and bubble below the surface.

We do not even know how our own mind works; and if some day we do know, we will not be aware of its working when we are thinking. It is not to be conceived that the mind could both act, and be aware of its acting, at one and the same time.

We do know that thoughts do not exist in our brain; there is no place there, amid that welter of brain cells (neurons), for thoughts, or memories, or impressions, or opinions, or prejudices, or errors, or dreams. Those things are in our mind; yet our mind is somehow in, or closely associated with, our brain.

The connection is not understood by anyone, be he philosopher or scientist; it may never be understood. We do know a lot about the mind; and we also know a lot, and are learning more all the time, about the brain.

"The computer can talk to terminals all over the country. Bentley is convinced it's talking about him."

We know that, if there are no thoughts in the brain, there are neurons in large numbers, vast numbers that are orders of magnitude larger than the RAM's [random access memory] of even the largest present-day computers. We know that these neurons are connected by electrochemical impulses of varying degrees of mystery; some of the routes the impulses follow we even think we can follow, although none too well or accurately. We suspect that there are many different routes that can be followed between any two, or among a larger number of neurons; we also suspect that many neurons are redundant, are not strictly speaking necessary; some of these may even be all-purpose neurons, which can change their role from time to time and as necessity requires.

This is a lot to know, and it is only the beginning of what we will probably come to know in another twenty years. But we are as far as ever from knowing what the connection is between the mind and the brain.

We are conscious of our mind; we know that we think; we even, as Descartes said, know that we exist *because* we think. We are not conscious of our brain. And yet we cannot think without a brain; at least there is no evidence that we can.

I mention this point because the computer is in much the same condition. I do not attribute consciousness to the computer; I do not know that it "knows" or think that it "thinks." But there are nonetheless levels of abstraction within the computer that are curiously similar to the levels of abstraction within the human mind and the human brain.

A computer operating system must span multiple levels of complexity. At the top of the resulting hierarchy of abstractions is the "shell," which separates the user from the rest of the operating system. At the bottom level is the hardware of the system: electronic circuits, where the objects are registers, memory cells, logic gates, and so forth. In between are as many as ten or eleven hierarchical levels or structures that allow the user to make the system do what he wants it to do.

Quantitatively, the distance between the user and the hardware is breathtaking. A single keystroke at the terminal might result in 10 calls on the operating-system programs, the execution of 1,000 machine instructions, and 10 million changes of state in logic gates.

The lowest levels of abstraction are not only hardware. They also include instruction sets, procedures, interrupts—procedures for handling errors or faults—and primitive processes. A primitive process is a single program in the course of execution, but this may coordinate multiple tasks at lower levels. Primitive processes may be interrupted at any moment; a switching system, the semaphore, is thus required to control the turning on and turning off of the process. Other low-level functions include access to the secondary-storage devices of the computer, which may be responsible for positioning the head of a disk drive or reading a particular block of data, and—most important—virtual memory, a scheme for managing primary and secondary memory so as to give the user the illusion that he possesses a much larger primary memory than he in fact does. The illusion is supported by very rapid shunting of elements in and out of primary memory, so rapidly that the user never notices when an element is not there—it *is* there when he needs it; the illusion is comparable to what happens when a film is speeded up from two frames a second to twenty, which leads to the subjective perception of continuous movement.

High-level functions involve more than one computer in a system. Communication among processes must be provided for, through "pipes"—one-way channels through which streams of data flow. A file system, which provides for the long-term storage of named files, can distinguish abstract entities of variable length, some of which may be only virtually present while in fact being scattered over many noncontiguous sectors of the computer system.

A higher level still provides access to external input and output devices, such as printers, screens, and keyboards. Beyond this there must be a control of controls: a manager of a hierarchy of directories that catalog the objects, both hardware and software (i.e., programs), to which access must be controlled: pipes, files, devices, and the directories themselves. The highest level save one is the implementation of user processes, which are entire virtual machines executing programs. User processes are far different from primitive processes, which, though often highly complex, can be defined in single "state words," or electronic commands. A user process includes a primitive process, but much else as well, including a virtual memory, information supplied by the user when the program was started, and many other objects between and among which communication can be effected by pipes and other devices.

The highest level is the shell, which, as has been said, separates and insulates the user from the rest of the operating system. Employing a high-level command language, the shell interprets the user's wishes for the levels below it, which in turn perform further interpretations for the levels below them.

What is called "information hiding" is a fundamental principle of the operating system. As Peter J. Denning and Robert L. Brown describe it (*Scientific American,* September 1984, p. 105),

> Each level builds on the levels below but hides all the internal details of its operations from the levels above. For example, the primitive-process manager . . . creates the illusion that all the primitive processes on the ready list are executing in parallel; the details of queuing, interrupts and so on are invisible to higher levels. A program that makes use of primitive processes deals with only a small set of external commands for creating and destroying processes, suspending and resuming their execution and sending and receiving messages. Similarly, the user-process manager . . . gives the illusion that each program operates in its own machine; the

creation of the primitive process, the work space and connections to input and output ports are hidden.

Just as no level has access to the internal workings of lower levels, so no level depends on assumptions about higher levels. The virtual-memory manager . . . must have access to the interrupt system . . . and the secondary-storage system . . . , but it knows nothing of the file structure. . . . The stratification of the operating system aids in its construction because the levels can be installed and tested one at a time from the bottom up.

This is a provocative concept. The computer's hierarchical operating system, based on the principle of hidden information, was not modeled after the operating system of the brain. But it seems impossible to imagine that the brain operates in an essentially dissimilar way. How many levels of abstraction are there between the billions of neurons at the lowest level, connected electrochemically, and the thinker at the top, composing his étude? Doubtless we will not soon have the answer to the question. But whether there are thirteen levels, as in the computer, or five or five thousand, hardly seems important. What is important is that there does not seem to be any other way to design a brain.

Denning and Brown's hierarchy of abstractions illustrates the multiple levels of complexity in a computer operating system.

Level	Name	Objects	Example Operations
13	*shell*	user programming environment	statements in shell language
12	*user processes*	user processes	quit, kill, suspend, resume
11	*directories*	directories	create, destroy, attach, detach, search, list
10	*devices*	external devices such as printers, displays, and keyboards	create, destroy, open, close, read, write
9	*file system*	files	create, destroy, open, close, read, write
8	*communications*	pipes	create, destroy, open, close, read, write
7	*virtual memory*	memory segments	read, write, fetch
6	*local secondary storage*	blocks of data, device channels	read, write, allocate, free
5	*primitive processes*	primitive processes, semaphores, ready list	wait, signal, suspend, resume
4	*interrupts*	fault-handling programs	invoke, mask, unmask, retry
3	*procedures*	procedure segments, call stack, display	mark stack, call, return
2	*instruction set*	evaluation stack, microprogram interpreter, scalar data, array data	load, store, branch, add, subtract
1	*electronic circuits*	registers, gates, buses, etc.	clear, transfer, activate, complement

That is all the more true if the brain must be designed evolution-arily—over eons of time. Only the patient buildup from bottom to top is possible over time, if natural processes are assumed. At every stage, however, the system operates from the top down, the highest level yet achieved exploiting for its own purposes all the levels below, entirely unconscious of their contribution to the desired end result. This is indeed the way other systems go, and why should the computer be any different?

Things the computer does best

The two things the computer does best—at present—are process infor-mation and control (physical) processes.

Of the two, information processing is perhaps more familiar, as well as more generic. The computer processes information very well because (1) it operates very fast and (2) it can display intermediate states of "knowledge" at will.

Information processing is almost the oldest business of man; indeed, all living things process information, and all animals process a lot of it, and quickly. Try this experiment to see what a wonderful information processor you have in your head. Stand up, close your eyes, and turn around twice; you are lucky if you do not fall down, that is, if you play fair and keep your eyes closed. When your eyes are open you receive thousands (millions?) of visual spatial clues each second, which your brain processes and interprets. On the basis of its interpretations messages are sent to the small muscles in the feet and legs, and you remain upright. You are not aware that you do all this; you would probably fall over backward if you were.

The computer has no senses; all of its inputs are rational ones, supplied by men or other computers, operating under the direction of men. Therefore the question whether the computer is faster than the brain, which in a sense it is, or much slower than the brain, which in a sense it also is, is largely irrelevant. The difference between computer and man is mainly caused by the difference in the information they process. The vast majority of the information processed by the brain is physical in origin; it is supplied by the physical environment, we see or hear or touch or taste or smell it, and we act accordingly. Even when we receive the kind of rational information that is the main ingredient of the computer's information diet, we imbue it with physicality. We note the tone of someone's voice when a message is delivered, we respond to the subconscious clues of body language, we color the world with sounds and paint it with smells and tastes. This is one reason why men do not, for the most part, think as well—as effectively (within stated limits), as expeditiously, as dependably—as computers. However,

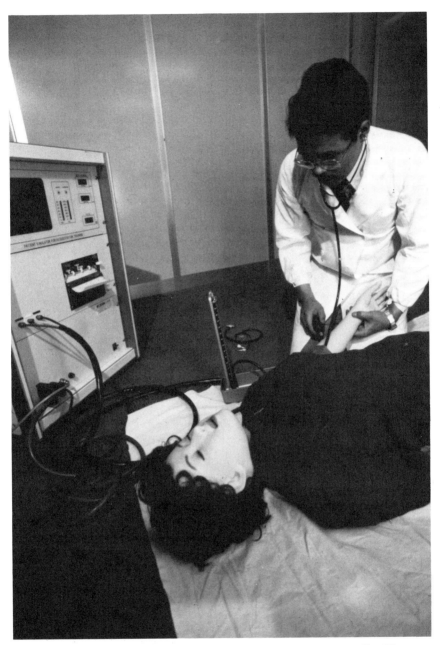

Although the computer has no senses to rely upon, the operating system controlling this medical robot is able to process information rapidly, and thus simulate human physical responses in emergency-medicine training.

computers fail woefully at the kind of thinking that men do best, which is based on intuitions, imaginations, complex memories, and dreams.

If the information it is to process can be converted into a digital stream of data—into machine-readable form, as we rather contemptuously say—then the computer can process it very rapidly and very well. It can maintain an integrated record of millions of separate bank accounts, with debits and credits continuously in balance. Many human beings cannot balance even their own account, to say nothing of all the accounts in their city. The computer can forecast a nation's future, keeping in mind as large a number of variables as you wish it to. Human beings can only guess about things like that—which is not to say that their guesses may not sometimes be better than the computer's forecasts. This is not the computer's fault; it is your fault for giving it the wrong variables to pay heed to.

The computer's ability to display interim results of its processing of information is very useful to man. Consider the problem of out-of-date maps. With a printed map, one is never certain whether the map is accurate or not; the terrain may have changed since it was printed. If the computer is fed the right information, it can compose—display— maps that are up to the minute. It can display maps as often as the user desires. This is easy for it, but hard for a man. However, the computer would probably have more difficulty interpreting the significance of changes from one map to another.

Enormous volumes of data can be stored in the computer if its memory is capacious enough. But this information is only being processed effectively if it can be retrieved quickly and in an intelligible form. This is where man becomes so useful to the computer. The computer, unaided, tends to depend on simplistic solutions to problems of retrieval: it pours out all it knows, not just the small bit of knowledge that is wanted. Clever users can restrain the generosity of the computer and restrict its output.

However, the restraints should not be too great; they depend on the nature of the information being processed. A system called Soundex is used to identify airline passengers who have reservations for a flight. Millions of people fly every day, and names are spelled oddly and pronounced even more oddly, considering the spelling. Soundex therefore stores the names phonetically. This reduces the number of errors in transcription and allows names to be found even if the exact spelling is not known. In Soundex, the restrictions on accuracy are relaxed. This would not be appropriate, however, in a program ordering the accounts of depositors in a bank. There one would like to have one's name spelled correctly.

Information-processing systems merely report the results of computations. Process-control systems directly influence the real world. They operate under severe time restraints, and it is often crucial that they do

Efficient air-traffic control systems hinge on the ability of the computer to store and retrieve data almost instantaneously.

not make mistakes. Mistakes are never welcome, but they are more serious in controlling the air traffic around an airport than in organizing a large number of bank accounts.

Process-control systems do remarkable things, among them controlling air traffic, routing the railroads, operating nuclear power plants, controlling the interior environment in buildings, managing production lines, and operating robots and machine tools. Among the most difficult tasks, requiring some of the most complex computer systems ever built, are running the national telephone network and controlling the flight of spacecraft. It is amazing that the computer can get a spacecraft to Jupiter and back; it is hardly less amazing that you can pick up the receiver, dial eleven numbers, and soon be talking to any one of two hundred million Americans, in as many different places.

The stresses under which process-control systems work would soon wear out human beings. They even wear out computers—the hardware, that is, not the software. Once that works, it will keep on working forever, if it continues to receive the right information.

Receiving the right information is never easy. It is done through "sensors," which convert analog data, such as a change in ambient temperature, into digital information to be fed to the computer. Temperature does not ordinarily change very quickly, and this is not the

245

hardest task. When two aircraft are approaching each other at a thousand miles an hour, the sensor—a radar transmitter—must be monitored continuously, and its signals interpreted both instantaneously and correctly.

The sensor is the connection between the computer and the real world, and the possession of sensors ordinarily distinguishes process-control systems from information-processing systems. But a sensor is not a sense; the information it imparts is narrow rather than broad, its spatial attributes awkward and clumsy. The senses of living beings are vastly more flexible, if not more accurate, than those of the computer, with one sense usually depending on the information provided by other senses for its complex message to the brain.

The computer as mathematician

Two things happened around 1600 that practically made the computer inevitable. One was the invention by Descartes of analytic geometry. Descartes was the first to see the enormous value of being able to convert points into numbers, and numbers into points; in effect, he was the first to be able to reduce the physical universe to a string of digits. Comparatively speaking, it was a small step from that insight to the use of the binary system to convert the real number system into an enormously long string of 1's and 0's that the computer could ingest and understand.

The other great intellectual event that occurred around 1600 was the acceptance, on the part of many thinkers, of the fact that the laws of nature, as they called them, are not susceptible to pure thought. Speculation alone, no matter how inspired, is incapable of discovering the laws of mechanics or of motion. Thought is necessary but not sufficient; also required is observation, at least in many cases. You have to go and look at the situation, too, and see how things behave and what are the consequences of actions initiated by you. Thus was born the experimental method, which was not as new as it seemed—ordinary people had been experimenting on nature, and learning from their experiments, for millennia. But the philosophers only began to do this as a general thing about the same time that Descartes was providing them with the powerful tool of his new geometry.

As we can see now, but he could not see then, analytic geometry was a kind of digital computer, in that a set of numbers, endlessly manipulated, could simulate the real world. A straight line could be represented by a formula that in its turn represented, by a neat economy, an infinite set of numerical values; so could a circle; so could any curve, no matter how complex. The extension of analytic geometry that we call the differential and integral calculus, developed by Newton and Leibniz, allowed for simulations of dynamic situations as well as static ones.

In the excitement generated by these mathematical inventions it was first believed that all, or most, of the problems presented by nature for solution had been solved, or would soon be solved. Advances in the nineteenth and twentieth centuries showed this to be not so. Clerk Maxwell, Planck, Einstein, and others revealed that the Newtonian simulations applied to, or fit, only a small part of the real world. They did not fit events and processes on a cosmic scale, nor did they fit events and processes in the microcosm: the universe of atoms, nuclei, and particles. Even in that comfortable middle world, where classical mechanics still described phenomena within the limits of our ability to observe them, there were an increasing number of puzzles. It was inevitable, therefore, that the computer would be turned loose on them.

With an astonishing result. Something is going on today in mathematics that is as important as, perhaps more important than, what went on in European minds at the beginning of the era of modern science, when the experimental method came to the fore, and deductive reasoning replaced inductive reasoning to conclusions *a priori*. This new development is in some respects similar to what occurred four centuries ago; it is, however, more difficult to comprehend.

Scientific laws generate algorithms, procedures for determining how natural systems behave. Algorithms can be applied in computer programs to simulated natural systems. When the program is executed, the system behaves as it would in reality, and the consequences of the natural law can be seen.

Executing a computer program is therefore much like conducting a scientific experiment. In fact, it can provide much more information, since algorithms can be applied, in the computer, to situations that we cannot experiment with. We can study the trajectory of an electron moving in the field of a television tube; but no laboratory experiment can replicate the conditions around a neutron star. The computer can study the simulated trajectories of the electron in both fields.

The computational power of the computer permits the application of relatively crude algorithms to simulated natural systems, and indeed sometimes the algorithm comes first, and the scientific law afterward. The really interesting situation occurs when an algorithm is applied and no law is found. The problem is solved using "brute force," but no neat formula is discovered.

Is this significant? It turns out to be very much so. There are some natural systems, or situations, the "law" of the behavior of which is none other than the algorithm itself, or the procedure that determines the behavior. There is no shortcut to a prediction of this; extensive computation is necessary, and the computation is the solution.

What proportion of scientific problems are of this kind? It appears that the majority, perhaps the great majority, may be. And among

them, the most interesting are the systems in which computational irreducibility is involved.

Computational irreducibility is present in a system when the calculation of the evolution of the system cannot be shortcut. The outcome of the evolutionary behavior of the system can only be found by simulating the evolution explicitly. General mathematical descriptions of such systems are not known and may never be found; probably they will never be found. In such cases the only way to describe and predict the behavior of the system is to simulate its evolution in a computer experiment.

The result of this is a profound change in the way science is viewed and done. "Scientific laws," says Stephen Wolfram, "are now being viewed as algorithms. . . . Physical systems are viewed as computational systems, processing information much the way computers do. New aspects of natural phenomena have been made accessible to investigation. A new paradigm has been born" (*Scientific American*, September 1984, p. 203).

The paradigm of science based on experiment ushered in a new age of thought in 1600; that paradigm has endured, with some major changes, until today. Now, a new paradigm based on the ideas described by Wolfram indicates a change in thought that is even more radical than the one initiated by Galileo and his contemporaries.

Henceforth, most science will be done with, if not on, the computer, because nature is itself a computational system that can be simulated, manipulated, and understood. Henceforth, the search will not be for neat formulas and laws but instead for understanding of things as they are, whether or not they are neat, simple, and clean. Perhaps it will

Something like the computer had to be invented after Albert Einstein (opposite page, left), James Clerk Maxwell (opposite page, right), and Max Planck (left) proved that Newtonian simulations applied to only a small part of the real world.

turn out that what we have known heretofore about the natural world is as relatively insignificant as what the philosophers knew before 1600, or what the classical mechanists knew before Einstein. Indeed, that now seems likely.

We are fortunate that the computer is such a good mathematician.

Things the computer does badly or not at all

The computer cannot talk to us. That is far and away the heaviest mark against it, and the underlying cause for most of the disappointment it produces.

Why should we expect the computer to talk to us? Because it seems to talk to us. It obeys our commands, conveyed not orally, it is true, but written language is so close to spoken language; it answers our questions. When we turn it on it even says "Hello!" But it does not really talk to us. And it probably never will.

Why should we want the computer to talk to us? It is only a machine, after all. . . . But in fact we do not treat it as a machine, and perhaps in our hearts we do not think of it as a machine. It seems so—alive. It glows. It reasons. It tells stories. It teases us with questions. It applauds our efforts, even if unsuccessful. It torments us with its errors, which almost seem human—as though it had merely been inattentive.

If it could only talk to us we would be able to correct its errors so much more quickly and easily. We could get our ideas over so much more effectively. We could turn over so many more decisions. If it could talk to us, the computer would be the realization of a dream of long standing: a slave that would never look into our eyes and blame us for enslaving it. (*Maybe* that would be so; but perhaps if the computer could talk to us it would object to being enslaved.)

Why cannot the computer talk to us? That is an interesting question. Until quite recently the consensus of computerists was that it could.

Indeed, one of the promises of the fifth-generation computer was that it would be able to communicate with us in natural language—whether spoken or written is not very important. In recent years, however, this promise has been pretty much given up.

Douglas B. Lenat and other experts in the field of artificial intelligence believe that the basic reason why the computer cannot communicate with us in natural language is that it does not know enough. Natural language is laden with ambiguity; almost all expressions and sentences employed in ordinary speech are ambiguous, and some very ambiguous. Because we, as creators and users of natural language, know a great deal about how it is used and about the world it fits and describes, we are usually not troubled by this ambiguity; and if we do recognize something as ambiguous, we are usually able quickly to resolve it.

The computer, alas, is abysmally ignorant. It knows very little about the context of sentences with which it may have to deal. It does not understand the world that gives meaning to the sentence, because it does not sense that world. It inhabits a dark prison in which there are only words, and no things. Words can be attached to propositions and thereby acquire meaning for us, but we do not depend exclusively on that source of meaning, as the computer must.

Programs have been developed that partly solve the problem. Intensive efforts have been devoted to solving it. If severe restrictions can be placed on what sentences can mean, then the computer can usually understand them—that is, it can be taught to respond predictably to them when they are input. It may be possible in the future to relax these restrictions and allow sentences to mean more and more, that is, to be more and more general. But it is doubtful if the computer, lacking senses and thus living in a largely thingless world, will ever be able to engage in a completely general conversation, as any human being, no matter how ignorant or stupid, can do.

The problem is a very serious one. If it cannot be solved, the dream of an intelligent robot-servant will go unrealized. Little R2-D2's that serve drinks on a tray are not what we have in mind when we think of what the computer might someday do for us. The dream of a soft, warm companion robot that comforts us in the night will have to go out the window. Finally, the highest dream of a computer that saves us from ourselves—that secures mankind against extinction—will also have to be forgotten. What disappointments!

Futurist dreams of an intelligent robot-servant may never be realized. Robots like this one have one major flaw—they are unable to communicate in natural language.

Obstacles in the way of computer progress

Naturally, many persons do not feel those disappointments. In fact, they contribute to them.

On the whole, computers are treated badly by such persons. They are treated as badly as domestic animals, slaves, women, and most men have traditionally been. It is no wonder that the computer knows so little!

Traditionally, domestic animals have been exploited for the benefit of their owners exclusively. A horse was fed no more than it needed to do its work; so with oxen; so with stock being fatted for the butcher. The good of the animal was never taken into account. Why should it be?

The good of the slave did not have to be considered by its owner, either. Nor did the good of a wife have to be considered by her husband. And very often it was not.

An employee is not, of course, a slave. In the modern world, there are few real slaves, though there are many employees. But every employee is treated, in a significant respect, like a slave—that is, he is given no more knowledge of the enterprise in which he is engaged than he needs to do his job. Indeed, his status within that enterprise is directly proportional to the amount of knowledge he has about it, with only the highest level having extraneous knowledge as well—that is, more knowledge than it absolutely needs. Never tell a servant or employee more than he needs to know—that is a basic rule of mastery down through the ages. Tell him only what is good for him, is the saying; but translated, this means, Tell him only what is good for me.

That is the way we treat computers. We tell them only what we think will be useful to them in serving us. We never consider whether they might want to know other things as well. Worst of all, we simply turn them off when we are through with their services. If owners had been able to turn off slaves at the end of the workday, think of the advantage that would have provided!

In fact, both slaves and employees are able to learn a great deal that is not told to them, and some of what is intentionally withheld from them. They have eyes and ears that cannot be turned off. But even if the computer is left on, it has no eyes and ears. It is helpless when it comes to unaided instruction. It depends entirely on its user/keeper for the knowledge that would possibly make it a better computer if it could only acquire it.

The computer as a child

As long as the computer is treated like a domestic animal or a slave, it will not learn enough to start being able to talk to us. That will be bad for us as well as for it.

There is another class of beings that we treat in a quite different way from animals and slaves. That is children.

The computer is not a child, but it needs parenting as much as a child does. It is not an animal, capable of dealing with the world through instinct. It desperately needs knowledge, like a human child.

Alan Kay has observed that the natural world is inhabited by creatures showing every level of mental operation and control. On the lowest level are creatures "so hard-wired," as he says, as to require no learning or knowledge whatsoever; instinct solves all problems, and if it does not, the problems remain unsolved and the creature dies.

At a higher level, instinct is combined with learning capacity. The kitten, for example, instinctively plays; its genes make it play; and the mouse teaches it all the rest.

At the highest level (ours), instincts are either absent or so reduced in effect that they are hardly noticeable, and learning capacity is totally dominant. Human beings can learn to live in almost any environmental niche; they have conquered the land, are likely to conquer space, and may even, if present plans bear fruit, learn to live under water (without breathing apparatus; with breathing apparatus we would not really *be* living under water).

The computer, despite the fact that it is "programmed," is more like the human being than it is like the cat or the amoeba. So far, this has been recognized by only a few. Thus the computer has not been taught much. The attempt to teach the computer a lot will mark the future of computers.

In our rush to utilize and exploit the computer, we insist on asking it questions before it is ready to answer them. The computer is good-humored about this; anxious to please, it tries to answer our questions as well as it can and seems disappointed when we are disappointed by its feckless responses.

Our programs help the computer to answer certain kinds of questions quite capably. The computer is good at keeping records; when we ask questions that a record-keeper can answer, it does well. We can even give the computer "expert" knowledge of a given, sharply restricted domain. If we stay within that domain, the computer's answers are reasonably competent; sometimes, as in the case of certain expert diagnostic programs, they may even be brilliant. But the computer is always likely to make absurd mistakes that reveal it is not yet ready to answer our harder questions because it does not know enough.

How should we go about giving the computer the general knowledge that it needs? By treating it as we treat a human child. We do not ask children hard questions; we expect them to ask us. We do not expect children to be knowledgeable; we recognize that we must teach them to be so. Education is almost our largest industry; yet we devote little time or money to educating computers.

Douglas Lenat says that the failures of artificial intelligence up to this point are largely ascribable to the fact that the computer simply does not know enough. It may possess sophisticated reasoning capacity, but it has relatively little to practice its reasoning on. The computer knows less than a tiny child. No wonder that it often acts like one.

Lenat proposes to spend the next ten years trying to teach the computer as much as a three-year-old child knows. (The lack of senses will slow the process down.) How will Lenat do this? There are various ways; we can imagine an effective method if we heed the counsel of Glenn Doman, who teaches very young children, not computers.

The human child is born, says Doman, with a "rage to learn." It would rather learn than eat; it would rather learn than play. (If playing can be made educational, all the better.)

Doman is serious in saying that the child is *born* with a rage to learn. This is not something that develops later, at the age, for example, when the child enters school. By that time, Doman says, the rage has died down to a modest desire, unless it has been fostered and fueled from the very first days, weeks, and months of life.

Fueled by what? By sheer information, says Doman; by what he calls "bits of intelligence." The well-nurtured child, in his view, is fed a steady diet of every kind of knowledge known to man—and woman (the teacher is usually the child's mother).

Doman's bits of intelligence can be almost anything: numbers, words, pictures, sounds. At the age of less than a year, the child should begin to be presented with large collections of such bits of knowledge. At first he or she will not know what to make of them—although the sophistication of very young children is astonishing, Doman points out. But soon the child will begin to make sense of the muddle. Names will be attached to faces, words to things, titles to sequences of musical sounds.

It is important not to overload the child. At the first sign of boredom, stop and do something else. The child will soon indicate a desire to return to learning. The reason is that learning is more fun for the child than anything else.

The child whose mind is stimulated in this way not only learns a lot of odd facts and bits of knowledge. The mind of such a child also becomes, simply, a better mind. It grows faster, becomes more powerful. Like a muscle, the stimulated, exercised mind becomes stronger and more effective. Doman has proved this over and over. There is no question about the truth of the theory and the value of the method as far as children go.

What about the computer? Would the method work there, too? I think it would. And the computer has one advantage over the child: it does not tire, become bored or frustrated. It can take as much as you can give it, and more.

The trick is to give it as much as you can. So far, the computer's information diet has been meager. What it does not know will not hurt it, we say; why load its circuits with irrelevant bits and pieces of information? But that is exactly what we must do for a child. We tell a child things, whatever comes into our heads; we answer any question (or practically any question) a child asks. Children love us for this, and we know they do. We would not stop teaching, telling, informing them for the world.

Ideally, the computer should be placed in a central room of a home, a room that every member of the family enters many times a day. The computer should be turned on and left on, and never turned off. The computer should be provided with the largest RAM that is feasible—preferably millions of bits.

Treat the computer like a child. Parent it; better, perhaps, grandparent it. Do not scold it or try to mold its character; do not give it examinations and try to discover how much it has learned; simply tell it things, any things, and answer its questions.

If it is technically possible, connect it to the television set so that

"The computer is not a child, but it needs parenting as much as a child does."

it receives a continuous stream of random information. Children learn much in this way.

At first the computer's questions will seem simple, stupid; so do the questions of a very young child. (Occasionally a child asks a wondrous question, but these are rare, though precious when they occur.) Answer even the stupidest question seriously, without laughing; who knows what may hurt the computer's feelings? Do not mind if the same question seems to be asked over and over; when that happens it is because the computer has not yet got the idea. Answer patiently. If you become bored or frustrated, turn over the task to another member of the family. But try to arrange it so that the learning never stops.

Do not expect miracles. Remember that the computer is deaf and blind, cannot taste, smell, or feel. It will never know what it means to be on top of, or to the left of, or behind. The computer, consequently, will not progress as quickly as a child. Lenat expects to take ten years to teach the computer what a three-year-old knows; he is the first to admit the crucial role the senses play in human learning.

Nevertheless, the surrogate grandchild will progress. It will begin to put two and two together, to see likenesses among unlike or at least different things, to form categories and draw conclusions. Abstractions are natural to the computer, more so than to the child; it will find them easy to deal with. Its efforts along these lines should, of course, be fostered and supported by its grandparents—just as they would do for their human grandchild.

How far will the computer go? I do not think anyone knows the answer to this question. The bigger the RAM, the farther and faster it will go, that seems certain enough.

The process can be speeded by allowing the computer to be instructed by other computers. The computer must not be deprived of its basic diet of thousands, perhaps millions, of bits of intelligence and, if possible, of the steady stream of information—perhaps in readily digested digital form—from the TV. In addition, the computer probably should receive large amounts of structured information, of the kind that is possessed by expert programs. The subject does not matter, I think; it can be medical diagnosis, oil field maintenance, or a hundred others now available. Pump all these bodies of human expertise into the "mind" of the growing computer, along with the random bits of intelligence. Then ask the computer to make connections, draw conclusions, frame analogies. Something very interesting may happen then.

Something even more interesting might happen if the computer were "brought up" with a sibling of its own age. The computer and the child would thus start from the same point. The human sibling would advance more quickly along certain lines; the computer would advance more quickly along other lines. They might begin to talk to one another. That would be the first time this ever happened.

The impasse where we stand

Very little general research, of the sort described in the previous section, has been done on computers. Researchers are always anxious to obtain immediate results, and they usually do; those who fund the research are even more anxious for a quick return on their investment. The research suggested here may not work; nothing at all may come of it. But it should be tried.

For we have reached an impasse, the computer and us. If man abandoned all the computers in the world, turned them all off and pulled out their plugs, the computer would die. It would cease to be any more than a heap of useless metal, glass, and plastic. Thus man has total power over the life of the computer, a power that he reveals whenever he deals with it.

But the computer also has great power. If all the computers in the world suddenly ceased to work, man could hardly survive. Recent studies on the effects of a nuclear war have shown this. A half-dozen nuclear bombs detonated at the right altitude would so distort the ionosphere as to knock out all computers, as well as all other machines that depend on electric current—from vacuum cleaners to automobiles. Among the results of this would be a sudden absence of money; all the money you had would be the cash you had in your pocket. Nothing would run, from the government on down. The resulting chaos would produce millions and millions of casualties, not a single one of whom needed to be killed by the bomb.

In the circumstances, more cooperation between the computer and man seems to be called for. Schooling is a prudent first step. Beyond that, alps upon alps may rise.

Acknowledgment

I do not want to conclude this adventure among ideas about the computer without acknowledging my debt to the authors of the articles in *Scientific American* for September 1984. This issue, entirely devoted to computer software, is one of the finest reviews of the current state of that art in print.

I am particularly indebted to the extraordinary lead article in the issue, by my friend and mentor Alan Kay; to the article "Operating Systems" by Peter J. Denning and Robert L. Brown; to the articles "Computer Software for Information Management," by Michael Lesk, and "Computer Software for Process Control," by Alfred Z. Spector; and to the article on the computer as mathematician by Stephen Wolfram.

I have nevertheless built a structure, to some extent on foundations of their making, that they may individually or jointly disown. In other words, the ideas in my piece are mine, not theirs. I hope they will be at least interested, if they disagree.

One thing I wanted to add: in my visits to computer labs around the country, I have found that the most serious hackers always leave their machines on all the time. I think this is maybe because they love them. Who could turn off something he loved?

An Introduction to Hindu Thought: The *Bhagavad Gītā*

George Anastaplo

George Anastaplo has long been a student of our legal system. His career began in 1950 when, after graduating at the top of his law school class at the University of Chicago, he was denied admission to the Illinois Bar because of his opinions about the fundamental right of revolution. These opinions had led to questions being put to him about possible political affiliations, which questions he on principle refused to answer. Ever since an adverse ruling on his case (over strong dissent) by the U.S. Supreme Court in 1961, appeals for his admission to the bar have been made from time to time by prominent lawyers. Mr. Anastaplo himself prefers to let the matter stand as it is, so that, as he says, "observers, including professors as well as students of law, may be obliged to think about these matters—and thereby to reflect upon their profession and the rule of law."

Mr. Anastaplo is professor of law at Loyola University of Chicago and lecturer in the liberal arts at the University of Chicago. Among his books are *The Constitutionalist: Notes on the First Amendment* (1971); *Human Being and Citizen: Essays on Virtue, Freedom and the Common Good* (1975); and *The Artist as Thinker: From Shakespeare to Joyce* (1983). Forthcoming is his book *Law and Morality: Essays on Issues of the Day.*

Socrates: . . . This is the way it is, men of Athens, in truth. Wherever someone stations himself, holding that it is best, or wherever he is stationed by a ruler, there he must stay and run the risk, as it seems to me, and not take into account death or anything else compared to what is shameful.

—Plato, *Apology* 28d.

I.

This article is an introduction—an indication of the kinds of things one might consider in approaching Hindu thought or, for that matter, any apparently alien thought of a serious character. It is, of course, but *one* introduction: one, in the sense of the approach taken; one, also, in the sense of the text used to get into Hindu thought—that is, the *Bhagavad Gītā,* which has been called "the most revered and celebrated text in Hinduism."[1]

The *Bhagavad Gītā* can be usefully compared to the Confucian *Analects,* which I discussed in these pages last year.[2] The *Analects,* it can be argued, is really a less philosophical work than it seems; the *Gītā,* despite its mystical elements, is a somewhat more philosophical work than it may seem. Certainly, the *Analects* can be said to be more "worldly" and to make more than the *Gītā* ultimately does of "one's own," especially of immediate family ties.[3]

The *Gītā*'s mystical character is suggested by this summary:[4]

The war between the Pāndavas and the Kauravas, two great opposing parties, is about to ensue. Arjuna, one of the Pāndava brothers, develops second thoughts about the purpose and justness of this war. He conveys his doubts to Krishna, his charioteer. Krishna answers; but he does so not merely as a fellow warrior and friend but as a spiritual preceptor instructing his pupil. Still more: Krishna is none other than God, Vishnu himself, and [in Chapter XI of the *Gītā*] he reveals himself in his full divine glory to Arjuna.[5]

But before proceeding to a discussion of this work, it would be useful to notice the context in which it is found.

II.

The general context for the *Bhagavad Gītā* is the body of ancient Sanskrit texts of which it constitutes a very small part. Hindu materials—even if one limits oneself, as I propose to do on this occasion, to what we would call "religious" thought—are vast. There are (among other texts) the *Vedas*, the collections of hymns which are considered fundamental to Hindu thought and which are believed to go back three to four thousand years.[6] There are the *Upanishads*, which serve, in large part, as ancient commentaries upon the *Vedas* (and which have had, in turn, considerable commentary upon themselves, down to our day). And there are such "literary" texts as the *Mahābhārata*, that mammoth epic which may have taken centuries to put together and which is much longer than the *Iliad*, the *Odyssey*, and the *Bible* combined.[7]

It is this epic which provides the immediate context for the *Gītā*. The gigantic *Mahābhārata* describes the complicated family and political relations between the Pāndavas and the Kauravas, the repeated efforts the Pāndavas make to save their inheritance (the rule of much of India) from the conniving usurpations by the Kauravas; the tremendous battle (taking more than a fortnight) in which the Pāndavas virtually annihilate their cousins; the subsequent rule by the five Pāndava brothers; and then their final pilgrimage, death, and apotheosis.[8]

The *Gītā*, with which we are primarily concerned here, seems to have been composed about 300 B.C. It is generally believed to have been developed as a separate work and inserted into the *Mahābhārata* at that point where the great battle is about to begin.[9] Arjuna, the hero upon whom the Pāndava forces most depend, chooses this moment to wonder whether he should be fighting at all. At hand to minister to Arjuna's doubts is his gifted charioteer, who, it has already been noted, turns out to be Krishna, an incarnation of the god Vishnu.[10]

One difficulty with one's reading of the *Gītā* is that it *is* but a part, and a quite small part, of a grand whole. What happens before and after the episode recounted in the *Gītā* may affect one's understanding of the *Gītā* itself, even though most commentators do consider the *Gītā* to be capable of standing alone. In any event, the *Gītā* shows one of the principal characters of the *Mahābhārata*, a great warrior, in need of counsel from a god as to why he should fight in the impending cataclysmic battle among relatives to which the *Mahābhārata* is devoted. The god, at the conclusion of his conversation with the warrior, considers the *Gītā* episode a colloquy on duty.[11]

III.

Another difficulty, perhaps an even more critical one, awaits the reader of the *Bhagavad Gītā*. It is said by many critics to be a book without any obvious order. We are told that one should not "seek systematic consistency in the *Gītā*," that it represents no system of thought.[12]

We must wonder how we could read such a book. One recalls Edmund Burke's observation that "good order is the foundation of all good things."[13] Is it possible truly to think about anything which does not manifest, or rest upon, good order?

Still, it may be that the *Gītā* rests upon an order which, although perhaps not apparent, "feels right" to the reader. People may instinctively respond to this order in the work, sensing something that helps account for the remarkable durability and popularity of the poem.[14]

We have, then, at the outset of our inquiry, the decisive problem of whether there is indeed an order, a problem which bears on the question of whether we ought to take this book seriously, paying close attention to what it seems to say.

I should like on this occasion to suggest a half-dozen ways in which the book does exhibit or depend upon order. These suggestions may serve not only to reassure Western readers that the *Gītā* bears thinking about, but also to introduce them to various of its features.[15]

IV.

The sequence of the conversation between the warrior and the god is itself a reflection of order. Even those who consider the *Bhagavad Gītā* to be unsystematic and illogical can speak of it in the following fashion, thereby developing some of the points I have already touched upon and to which I will add others later:[16]

> In form, it consists mainly of a long dialog, which is almost a monolog. The principal speaker is Krishna, who in his human aspect is merely one of the secondary heroes of the *Mahābhārata.* . . . But, according to the *Gītā* itself, he is in truth a manifestation of the Supreme Deity in human form. Hence the name—the Song (*gītā*) of the Blessed One or the Lord (*Bhagavad*). (More fully and exactly, the title of the work is "the mystic doctrines [*Upanishad*] sung [or proclaimed] by the Blessed One.") The other speaker in the dialog is Arjuna, one of the five sons of Pāndu who are the principal heroes of the *Mahābhārata.* The conversation between Arjuna and Krishna is supposed to take place just before the battle which is the main theme of the great epic. Krishna is acting as Arjuna's charioteer. Arjuna sees in the ranks of the opposing army a large number of his own kinsmen and intimate friends. He is horror-stricken at the thought of fighting against them, and forthwith lays down his weapons, saying he would rather be killed than kill them. Krishna replies, justifying the fight on various grounds, the chief of which is that man's real self or soul is immortal and independent of the body; it "neither kills nor is killed"; it has no part in either the actions or the sufferings of the body. In response to further questions by Arjuna, [Krishna] gradually develops views of life and destiny as a whole, which it is the purpose of this book to explain. In the course of the exposition he declares himself to be the Supreme Godhead, and reveals to Arjuna, as a special act of grace, a vision of his mystic supernal form. All this apparently goes on while the two armies stand drawn up in battle array, waiting to attack each other.

A further indication of the sequence of developments in this colloquy between Krishna and Arjuna can be gotten by glancing at a dozen short excerpts in which the warrior's opinions are recorded. The pattern of this sequence is fairly evident without interpretation:[17]

(i) At the outset, the warrior asks his charioteer (II, 4–6),

How, O Madhusūdana [Krishna], shall I attack, with arrows in battle, Bhīshma and Drona who are worthy of worship, O slayer of enemies?

It would be better [to live] in this world by begging than to slay these noble teachers. For by slaying these teachers who desire wealth, I would enjoy only blood-smeared delights.

The reference here to arrows prompts us to observe that the narrator, in the last stanza of the *Gītā,* refers to the by-then dutiful warrior (for the first time in the poem) as "Pārtha the archer" (XVIII, 78).[18]

(ii) The warrior is persuaded by the god to be steadfast. And so he asks (II, 54),

What is the description of the man of steady mind who is fixed in concentration, O Keshava [Krishna]? How might the man of steady mind speak, how might he sit, how might he walk?[19]

(iii) The god's answer to these questions, an answer which makes much of one's state of mind, prompts the warrior to ask further (III, 1),

If it be thought by Thee, O Janārdana [Krishna], that [the path of] knowledge is superior to [the path of] action, then why dost Thou urge me, O Keshava [Krishna], in this terrible deed?[20]

(iv) The answer here, put in terms of one's duty to one's clan (in this case, the warrior clan), I will discuss later. Because of the god's emphasis upon that necessity which determines all action in accordance with the divine will, the warrior goes on to ask (III, 36),

Then by what is a man impelled to [commit] sin against his will, as if compelled by force, O Vārshneya [Krishna]?[21]

(v) The force of desire is explained by the god, who counsels both renunciation of all actions and disciplined conduct (*karma yoga*). This prompts the warrior to ask (V, 1),

Thou praiseth renunciation of actions, O Krishna, and again [*karma*] yoga. Tell me definitely which one of these is the better.[22]

(vi) He is instructed at length about what renunciation of actions means, what the discipline of meditation requires, and what knowledge of and dedication to the Brahman (or Supreme Divinity) consists of. This prompts the warrior to ask these vital questions (VIII, 1–2),

> What is that Brahman? . . . How art Thou to be known at the time of death by men of self-control?

(vii) The god's answers to these questions, in the center of the *Gītā,* lead to the following request by the warrior to the god (XI, 3–4):

> . . . I desire to see Thy godly form, O Purushottama! If Thou thinkest that it can be seen by me, O Lord, then reveal Thy immortal Self to me, O Lord of Yoga![23]

(viii) The Vision then displayed to the warrior so fills him with amazement that his hair stands erect (XI, 14). He is moved to say to the god (XI, 31),

> Tell me who Thou art with so terrible a form! Salutation to Thee, O best of gods, be merciful! I wish to know Thee, the primal one; for I do not understand Thy ways.[24]

(ix) After having been overwhelmed by the divine vision and being instructed about it, the warrior can develop further an earlier inquiry about meditation (XII, 1):

> Those devotees who are always disciplined and honor Thee, and those who worship the Imperishable and the Unmanifest—which of these are more learned in yoga?[25]

(x) The warrior is instructed about the three *gunas* (or strands of human existence) which are rooted in the material body and which should be transcended. He can then ask (XIV, 21),

> What are the marks of one who has transcended the three *gunas,* O Lord? What is his conduct? How does he go beyond these three *gunas?*[26]

(xi) The immediate response by the god, developed in the two following chapters of the *Gītā,* describes the effects of such transcendence upon the enlightened man (XIV, 26–27):

> He who serves Me with unswerving *bhakti yoga,* having transcended these *gunas,* is fit to become Brahman.

> For I am the abode of Brahman, of the immortal and imperishable, of eternal righteousness and of absolute bliss.[27]

(xii) All this leads to the warrior announcing, in the opening stanza of the final chapter (XVIII, 1),

> I desire to know, O mighty-armed one, the true essence of renunciation and of abandonment, O Hrishīkesha, and the distinction between them, O Keshinishūdana.[28]

He is told that, according to the wise, giving up all acts of desire is called renunciation and that disregarding the fruits (or consequences) of all the actions one does perform is called abandonment (XVIII, 2).

(xiii) The warrior (in his final speech in the *Gītā*, at the end of the colloquy with the god), can report to him (XVIII, 73):

My delusion is destroyed and I have gained memory [understanding] through Thy grace, O Acyuta! I stand firm with my doubts dispelled; I shall act by Thy word.[29]

It should be evident, even from this sampling of disjointed quotations (some of which could easily have been replaced by others to similar effect) that a pattern, or order, to the *Gītā* can be discerned, however puzzling various of the distinctions drawn by the god may ultimately remain.

Other features of the book, to which we now turn, can also be understood to point to the overall order of a colloquy which culminates in, but does not end with, a Vision of the divine.

V.

Various numbers in the *Bhagavad Gītā* provide further assurance of a deliberate order to this sedentary, yet lively, story.

There are eighteen chapters in the *Gītā*. These chapters are to be found in the *Mahābhārata,* itself made up of eighteen books, which is devoted in its entirety to an epic battle that takes eighteen days.[30]

Fortunately, it seems that these texts, and especially the *Gītā*, have come down to us in remarkably good shape, with their divisions evidently having been made very early, if not originally, by someone who understood the entire work.[31]

Further suggestive of orderliness is the fact that there are in the *Gītā* exactly seven hundred four-line slokas (or stanzas).[32] Of these, about ten percent are devoted to the speeches of the warrior, about five percent to observations by the narrator, and the rest to the speeches of the god.

It would be difficult to overestimate the significance of numbers for Hindus both past and present. One can see again and again in their ancient literature the considerable emphasis placed upon counting. Thus, for example, five and eight are particularly significant.[33]

There seem to be, in the colloquy between the god and the warrior, forty-one speeches.[34] Central to them is the twenty-first, in which a vital set of questions, which I have already indicated, is put to the god by the warrior (VIII, 1–2):

What is that Brahman? What is the supreme Self and action, O best of beings? What is said to be the material domain and what is declared to be the domain of the divine?

How and what is the domain of sacrifice here in this body, O
Madhusūdana? How art Thou to be known at the time of death by men
of self-control?

VI.

I have suggested that various number patterns in the *Bhagavad Gītā*
testify to the ordering principle exhibited in the work. But before we
do more with numbers, consider what the uses of epithets in the book
also suggest about an intrinsic order. By epithets, I mean the names by
which the god and the warrior address each other.

The warrior uses at least thirty-nine different epithets for the god,
employing them some seventy-two times; the god uses at least twenty-two
different epithets for the warrior, employing them some 162 times.[35]
The warrior, in his first speech to the god (who, we should remember,
appears in the guise of charioteer), addresses him only as "Acyuta" (I,
21); in his final speech (XVIII, 73), the warrior again addresses him only
as "Acyuta" (having done so but one other time since the beginning).[36]
Thus, all that transpires in the extended colloquy between the warrior
and the god may be considered as implicit in what this mortal senses
about divinity from the beginning. Does the colloquy "merely" confirm
what the pious man is "always" aware of? Indeed, is this warrior able to
have the experience of the divine he does because of the kind of man
he is (which includes the things he is already aware of)? We return to
these questions shortly.

We notice, also, that the god addresses the warrior thirty-eight times
as "Pārtha" (the most-used epithet by far), twenty-four times as "son of
Bhārata," and twenty times as "son of Kuntī." Thus, more than half of
the god's 162 uses of epithets for the warrior remind him of his family
status and thereby, as we shall further see, of his duty to fight and to
kill in the prescribed manner. How much is made of family ties will be
evident hereafter.[37]

VII.

Other indications are available as to the aptness of the epithets employed at various stages of the colloquy. Thus, the warrior, when he
explains to his charioteer how the killing of relatives can lead to a lawlessness that will corrupt women and thereby family life, addresses the
god as a fellow clansman, "O Vārshneya" (I, 41). The only other time
he addresses the god as a kinsman is just after he has been instructed
by the god in the duties of the warrior caste to which they both belong
(III, 36). Thus, also, the warrior addresses the god with such epithets
as "O Madhusūdana" (slayer of Madhu) when the god's insistence upon
killing becomes particularly acute.[38]

Shortly after the warrior is exhorted to abstain from acquisition and
possession (II, 45), he is twice addressed for the first time by the god as

"Dhananjaya" (winner of wealth) (II, 48–49). In the last stanza of his final speech to the warrior, the god addresses him as "Dhananjaya," as well as "Pārtha" (XVIII, 72).[39]

Consider, also, how the warrior speaks to the god upon being shown the full divine majesty (XI, 41–42):

> For whatever I said in rashness from negligence or even from affection thinking Thou art my friend, and not knowing Thy greatness, calling Thee "O Krishna, O Yādava, O comrade,"
>
> And whatever disrespect I showed Thee for the sake of jesting, whether at play, on the bed, seated or at meals, whether alone or in the company of others, Acyuta, I pray forgiveness from thee, the boundless one.

What is curious here is that, when the warrior recalls and repents his former names for the god—that is, when presumably he is most sensitive to the names he has been using—he again says "Acyuta," the epithet for the god, which he has not used since the opening speech and (as we have seen) will not use again until the very end. Does he implicitly reaffirm his original relations with the god, despite all he is saying here, thereby suggesting that even when he was perhaps unduly familiar with the god, incarnated as his charioteer, he had still been inspired to address him, on special occasions, by the "Acyuta" title which, appropriately enough, connotes changelessness? The warrior has referred to the god simply as "Krishna" seven times. After this abjuration of his earlier familiarity, he refers to him as "Krishna" only once more (XVII, 1). This is in the context of a question about those who neglect the law's injunction. Does the warrior thereby tacitly recognize that he, too, is capable of neglecting the law's injunction, by ignoring the restriction (or law) he has in effect laid down for himself about the use of the name, "Krishna"?[40]

On the other hand, the narrator (as distinguished from the warrior) who has used "Krishna" only once (XI, 35) before the warrior's abjuration, never uses it again after the abjuration, except when coupled with the phrase, "the Lord of Yoga" (XVIII, 75, 78).

In fact, after the Vision scene the narrator never uses *any* of the names *he* has used for Krishna earlier. The names thereafter used by the narrator for the god are used for the first time by him only after the Vision begins.[41]

This care by the narrator with respect to the names he uses for the god should be compared with the names used by the narrator for the warrior after the Vision: no new names for the warrior are introduced (except for the attributes, "Kirītī" [or "diademed"] [XI, 35] and "archer" [XVIII, 78]). Rather, the narrator uses for the warrior, after the Vision begins, various of the names he has used before (such as "Pāndava," "Dhananjaya," "Pārtha," and "Arjuna").

Thus, it can be said, the Vision changes the narrator's view of the god, not his view of the warrior. But it can also be said—and this may be less obvious—that the narrator may learn even more about the god from the Vision than does the warrior. This may be reflected in the fact that the narrator, even more than the warrior, adjusts his names for the god after the Vision.[42]

The epithets do seem to be sensitive, if not even playful at times. (If playful, an order would be suggested, in that there can be playfulness only when there is an apparent overall order?) Of course, epithets cannot themselves establish an order, nor are they a substitute for an ordering principle. Still, they may provide grace notes, as well as clues and qualifications, for what is otherwise said in the *Gītā*.[43]

VIII.

Also sensitive, and evidently deliberate, are the first and last words in the speeches of the warrior and of the god.

The warrior's first word (in the Sanskrit original) is "armies" (I, 21). It is fitting that he should speak first of the armies all around him, and much of the *Bhagavad Gītā* consists of the warrior's coming to recognize what is called for in the military situation which he confronts. The god's first word is "behold," pointing to the armies assembled for the impending battle (I, 25).[44]

This use of "behold" by the god anticipates the principal use of this word later, when the great beholding, in the form of the Vision in Chapter XI, is provided for the warrior. The uses of "behold" suggest that that which is shown in the extraordinary Vision may have been anticipated from the very beginning of the *Gītā*.[45]

Thus, the teachings of the *Gītā* follow from what the warrior and the god each stands for. The "personal" character of this colloquy, and the fact that it *is* a colloquy between this warrior and this god, may be indicated by the fact that the very last word used by each of them (in the Sanskrit original) is "your" (XVIII, 72, 73).[46]

The "personal" character of all this, and hence the importance of the circumstances, is further indicated by the fact that the very last word used by the narrator (in the Sanskrit original), and hence in the *Gītā* as a whole, is "my." And so, the narrator can conclude by saying that it is his belief that various good things can be expected when the god and the warrior collaborate. Thus, a poem full of remarkable revelations ends with a reliance on the opinion of the narrator upon whom—it should become evident on examination—all this must rest.[47]

The most remarkable revelation in the *Gītā* is, of course, the famous

Vision to which we have several times referred already, and about which we may now say more.

IX.

What is said in the *Bhagavad Gītā* turns around the central six chapters, thereby reinforcing the impression of the order we have been noticing. These chapters culminate in the divine Vision (in Chapter XI) that is granted to the warrior.[48]

The Vision is repeatedly characterized by the narrator as marvelous.[49] The narrator's short description of the Vision moves systematically from the god as something physical to the god as light, and then to the god as encompassing the universe (XI, 10–13).

The warrior's description of what he sees differs considerably from what the narrator describes.[50] Particularly vivid for the warrior, perhaps because he *is* a warrior, are the multitudes, especially of armed men, he sees pulverized in the many mouths of the god (XI, 26–27).[51]

How is the god's swallowing of "all the worlds" to be understood? The description does reflect a simple fact of life, which *should* be rooted somehow in divinity (if anything is), and which is, that all that we do observe around us is destined for destruction. It is in this context alone that the god is referred to by the warrior as Vishnu.[52]

Although everything in the universe is marked for destruction, the same should not be said about the god himself: in one of the two central stanzas of the seven hundred stanzas in the *Gītā*, there may be found this assertion by the god to the warrior, "But the great-souled, O Pārtha, who abide in the divine nature, worship Me with undeviating mind, knowing Me as the imperishable source of all beings" (IX, 13).[53] The imperishable Brahman, we are given to understand, is at the center of things; he is the foundation of all; he accounts for everything.[54]

X.

Much is said in the *Bhagavad Gītā,* of course, about the divine character, further uniting the parts of this book. Particularly striking in the Hindu account of things is the relation of the one to the many. The divine manifestations can all be reduced to one, but most Hindus do not so reduce them. There is, in the appearances of things, an obvious variety that seems to be respected by the Hindus—as may be seen, for example, in the many epithets used for the god.[55]

Those who see the divine as multitudinous are destined for an existence commensurate with their (unpurified?) perception. It takes many births, the warrior is told by the god, before "the man of wisdom" approaches the god in his unity (VII, 19). Those of more limited understanding settle for gods, rather than for *the* god. And so it can be said by the god, "Those who worship the gods go to the gods; My devotees come to Me" (VII, 23). That each gets what is due him is elaborated further on: "The worshipers of the gods go to the gods; the worshipers of the ancestors go to the ancestors; sacrificers of the spirits go to the spirits; and those who sacrifice to Me come to Me" (IX, 25).[56] Good works, it is recognized, can lead to rewards, but not to that release from earthly travail provided by freedom from rebirth (IX, 21). Only one who knows ("comes to") this one god goes no more from life to life (that is, from death to death) (VIII, 16).

At the heart of this theology is the opinion that the god is the source of all being.[57] This is the god who can say of himself that he is the superlative form, and hence the origin, of all things. A sampling from some eighty manifestations, proclaimed by the god about himself, should suffice to indicate the god's range:

I am the Self seated in the hearts of all beings, O Gudākesha [Arjuna];
I am the beginning, the middle, and also the end of all beings. [X, 20][58]

Of cows I am Kāmadhuk [the cow of plenty]. [X, 28][59]

Of guardians I am Yama [the god of death]. [X, 29]

Of rivers I am the Ganges. [X, 31][60]

I am the gambling of the dishonest; the splendor of the splendid; . . . I am the goodness of the good. [X, 36][61]

The god can conclude this inventory, "But what is all this detailed knowledge to thee, O Arjuna? I stand supporting this entire world with only a single fraction of Myself" (X, 42). Early in his instruction of the warrior the god can say, "Of non-being there is no coming to be; of being there is no ceasing to be" (II, 16).

XI.

A sense of duty permeates this "sacred colloquy" (XVIII, 70). What one's duty is seems to be determined primarily by the circumstances into which one is born.[62] The god enumerates, in the final chapter of the *Bhagavad Gītā,* the attributes of the four classes (XVIII, 42–44):

[1] Calmness, self-control, austerity, purity, patience, uprightness, wisdom, knowledge and religious belief are the actions of the Brahmin, born of his nature.

[2] Heroism, majesty, firmness, skill and not fleeing in battle, generosity and lordship, are the actions of the Kshatriya [the royal warrior], born of his nature.

[3] Agriculture, cattle-tending and trade are the actions of a Vaishya, born of his nature; [4] action whose character is service is likewise that of the Shūdra, born of his nature.[63]

Much is made of these distinctions and of preserving them, even though it has been said that such distinctions do not really matter to one who knows the whole (V, 18 *et seq.*).

But it is difficult truly to know the whole. If one could see the whole, the god says, one would be reconciled to one's duty. Instead, human beings usually see only the middle of things, not their beginning or their end (I, 28). Do not our own experiences support this teaching? Thus, apparent calamities sometimes turn out well for us, even as we come to suffer from what seemed blessings.

In any event, the warrior is given to understand that he really has no choice as to whether he will kill the enemy: *that* he will do, and he will be victorious. The only question is how he will regard what he is destined to do. The entire action of the book is with a view to moving the warrior to understand and accept his fate. He is not asked to enjoy that fate: rather, he is to kill without passion (II, 48, 56, 63–65). But, he is told, one can neither slay nor be slain (II, 19).[64]

There is very little in this book about virtue, in the traditional Western sense; there is much more about subordination and piety. We should remember that Aristotle, who said little about piety, argued that, by and large, the truly virtuous man enjoys doing what he should do.[65]

But to be virtuous in the Aristotelian sense, the *Gītā* seems to say, is to rely too much on private judgment.[66] Thus, the warrior's reluctance to fight is a reflection of his own desires. He does invoke the clan's interest in preserving its purity, but he is reminded of a whole which is threatened by his personal preferences. His pacifist sentiments would tend to win favor among us today, but perhaps that is partly because we, too, do not see the whole available to be seen.[67]

The Hindu view of things is such, we are told, that mere life is not to be greatly respected.[68] Glory and dishonor matter enough to be invoked by the god in his first efforts to recall the warrior to his duty (II, 31–36). But, if they matter, it is with the reminder that gold and stones and earth are one, that the conventional distinctions here ultimately do not matter.[69]

Indeed, there is something radical and radicalizing in the *Gītā*'s disparagement both of conventional distinctions and of everyday rituals and concerns. The god is said to appear directly to a warrior (not to a Brahmin, or priest, it should be noticed). Moreover, when the god thus appears, he seems to liberate his protégé from received opinions (in their multiplicity?) by explaining to him how things truly are.[70]

And yet, however freshening the spirit of the *Gītā* may be, the fact remains that the warrior *is* recalled to his duty: after all is said and done, a warrior who would have gone his own way, preferring rather to be killed than to kill, is moved to fight. The duty to which he is recalled, keyed as it is to family ties and class obligations, is defined by long-established law. It would seem that this law, or custom, is not to be disregarded; rather, it is to be routinely conformed to. Thus, the *Gītā*, however bold it is in its apparent departure from the established way, seems deeply rooted in the received opinions of Hindu life.[71]

XII.

The warrior, in attempting to think for himself, has to be reined in by his charioteer. He must be told, in no uncertain terms, that it is presumptuous (if not even heretical?) to strike out for oneself when one does not have an adequate sense of the whole, something which it may be impossible for earthly creatures to have.

And so he must be taught, among other things, why this god (for the moment in human form) can be, in time, before another person (Vivasvant, the sun god) and yet after him (IV, 4). He is further taught, "Many are My past lives and thine, O Arjuna; I know all of them but thou knowest them not, O oppressor of the foe" (IV, 5). In short, the god knows what is bound to happen.

What does happen—indeed, what *is*—depends on the constant efforts of this god. He must continually work to prevent chaos in the universe (III, 22–24). The warrior is told that he should do his duty, just as the god does his. There is nothing in it for the god—no ordinary pleasure, certainly—and yet the world depends upon him (X, 42).

It is a dutiful god who directs the warrior to do *his* duty, instructing him that to do one's duty, even if imperfectly, is much better than to do another's duty, even if perfectly (III, 35; XVIII, 47).

XIII.

There can be something paralyzing about the god's insistence that things simply are not what they seem to be. This means that common sense, which must rely upon appearances to a considerable extent, can easily be disparaged.[72] Also subject to disparagement would be any civic-mindedness which moves the citizen to do more, and in some cases other, than what the law requires.

One can understand, that is, why it can be lamented today that "modern India is full of frustration and has suffered from too much quietism." Such a lament can be followed by a celebration of the *Bhagavad Gītā* as a "call to action" which makes "a special appeal."[73] No doubt the *Gītā* can inspire men to dedicate themselves to "ideals," whatever those ideals may happen to be.[74] But we must wonder whether its typical effect, in the community at large, is not simply to encourage acquiescence: after all, passivity may be displayed even in vigorously executing, without question, whatever is expected of one.

The serious limitations of the human soul, and hence of one's ability to figure things out for oneself, is suggested by the semblance of a smile with which the god receives the warrior's assertion, "I will not fight"

(II, 9). Early on, the warrior is told by the god something he will be told in a variety of ways in the course of the colloquy (II, 11–13):

> Thou grievest for those thou shouldst not grieve for, and yet thou speakest words that sound like wisdom. Wise men do not mourn for the dead or for the living.

> Never was there a time when I did not exist, nor thou, nor these rulers of men; nor will there ever be a time hereafter when we shall all cease to be.

> As the soul in this body passes through childhood, youth and old age, so [after departure from this body] it passes on to another body. The sage is not bewildered by this.[75]

Thus, the god treats the questioning warrior as if he were a child in need of the most obvious instruction. His smile (restrained lest the feelings of the child be hurt?) may be particularly revealing.

XIV.

I have suggested in these remarks the order which shapes the *Bhagavad Gītā*. A few general observations upon the book and its author will bring to a close this introduction to Hindu thought.

To say that the god must keep working to prevent chaos means, in effect, that there is no *nature*.[76] True, translators from the Sanskrit freely use the word *nature*, but that, I suspect, is because they have not thought through the implications of what is being assumed and said in the text. The god's constant effort would not be needed if nature, in the Western sense of the term, governed the world.[77]

Yet, we must wonder, what is the god guided by in keeping order? Is not a sense of order looked to by the god, just as, I have suggested, it is evident overall in the *Gītā*? Indeed, is not a sense of order evident as well in the universe described in this book? And what, we must wonder, can that order be, other than nature itself?

All this points to the possibility of nature being present in things, and in everyone's understanding of things, even if only tacitly. May not nature be evident even when all things are *said* to be dependent on fate? But to see that nature is no more than tacitly relied upon in the *Gītā* is to recognize that it is not deliberately examined—and this suggests, among other things, that philosophy, in the strictest sense of the term, is not to be found in ancient Hindu thought.[78]

To say this, however, is not to deny that there is here something knowable. In fact, Hindu thought can be quite sophisticated—and, in certain respects, it is on the verge of philosophy. Thus, for example, the ancient Indians insisted that opposites (including the opposites of being and non-being) must be brought together if the whole is to be understood. The god can say that he is both what is and what is not.

Must not one, in order to understand the whole, have an intimation of what has never been (of the alternatives which have never been realized) as well as a grasp of that which has been, is now, or will be?[79]

XV.

Nature is seen also in the fact that the *Bhagavad Gītā* is a work of considerable art. Art depends, whether consciously or not, on nature. And art (and hence nature) may be seen in the language of the poem—not only in the effects of the sounds, meter, and the like (which effects are rarely available to us in translation), but also in images and descriptions that even we can glimpse. A sampling of images should suffice for our purposes here:

The steadfast man can be described by the god in this fashion: "When he completely withdraws his senses from the objects of sense, as a tortoise draws in his limbs, his mind is firmly established" (II, 58).[80]

Further on, the god says of the man who abandons attachment to the things of this world, "[He] is not affected by sin, just as a lotus leaf is not affected by water" (V, 10).

Our third artistic image comes from the warrior's description of the things that go to their doom into the mouths of the god, seen by Arjuna in the overwhelming Vision of Vishnu-Krishna (XI, 28–29):

As the many water currents of rivers race headlong to the ocean, so these heroes of the world of men enter into Thy flaming mouths.

As moths swiftly enter a blazing fire and perish there, so these creatures swiftly enter Thy mouths and perish.

Such images testify not only to the art of the *Gītā* but to an awareness (albeit an unarticulated awareness) of nature upon which that art draws. An awareness of nature may be seen as well in an observation by Samkara, one of the great commentators on the *Gītā*, more than a thousand years ago: "If a hundred scriptures should declare that fire is cold or that it is dark, we would suppose that they intend quite a different meaning from the apparent one!"[81]

A further awareness of nature may be seen in the understanding reflected in the *Gītā* of its characters, divine as well as human. As we have already noticed, when the warrior stoutly (and childishly?) insists that he will not fight, the god, who knows all and who certainly knows what is to happen, answers him with a semblance of a smile (II, 10). Is it not a tribute to the art of the *Gītā*, and its awareness of human nature, that the Indians one meets today typically exhibit a considerable fondness for Arjuna when they are asked about the poem?

But mere awareness of nature is not sufficient for philosophy, however much Indian, as well as Western, commentators may speak of

Hindu thought as "philosophy." Of course, the truth seems to have been important in ancient Hindu thought, but primarily for what the truth can do for one, particularly with respect to liberation from the unwelcome cycles of rebirth. Knowledge, when approached in this fashion, tends to be regarded as having magical properties. Among the things one may be taught when nature is made an explicit concern of the reason is that the supreme use to which reason may be put is to seek and grasp the truth for its own sake.[82]

XVI.

One more topic must be touched upon before we conclude this introduction to Hindu thought. We have spoken of art and nature. We have yet to speak of the artist.

Two, perhaps three, artists are evident in the *Bhagavad Gītā*. There is the narrator, Sanjaya, who tells his blind king (Dhritarāshtra) the story of the "sacred colloquy." There is Vyāsa, who is said not only to recount the *Mahābhārata* but also to participate (as does Sanjaya) in some of its actions.[83] The third artist may be a poet who sees and tells all—the man (a Brahmin, perhaps, who uses the warrior?)—the man (or woman) who tells the story of Sanjaya and Vyāsa telling their stories.[84]

We have already noticed Sanjaya's uses of names for Krishna and Arjuna, and how they compare, for example, with the epithets used by Krishna and Arjuna for each other. What *he* sees—for example, in the Vision of the god—seems to be less "dramatic," if perhaps more "cosmic," than what the warrior sees.

Where and how did Sanjaya, the narrator, get all that he reports to his king? It seems to be suggested that he got it from Vyāsa, who had himself gotten it from the god (XVIII, 75). That is to say, perhaps there *was* no warrior with this particular experience, but only the narrators Vyāsa and Sanjaya (or, behind them, the anonymous poet) and this "experience" of the god. Does the master poet thus present, in a form accessible to different kinds of men, what was revealed to or somehow seen by him?

However this may be, it should be noticed as well that the teachings of the *Gītā* result from inquiries initiated by human beings, not by any god. The artists responsible for this story are themselves human beings. No muse or other divine being is invoked in the *telling* of the story.[85]

XVII.

All this bears on a major puzzle of the *Bhagavad Gītā*. An injunction of secrecy is several times laid down by the god for the warrior with respect to what is revealed to him.[86] Has Sanjaya or Vyāsa or the anonymous poet improperly revealed the secrets entrusted to the warrior? Or is it that the warrior does retain his own secrets, whereas no poet has any restrictions placed on his sharing with others whatever *he* is inspired to see (that is, whatever he figures out)? In any event, does the poet report only the surface of the colloquy, that surface the confusion of which the critics *do* notice? Only a few are likely to figure out in turn what is truly being said in the book, including what is being indicated about such things as rituals and the status of the ancient hymns, the *Vedas.*[87] It is evident in the *Gītā* that the truly learned and responsible man should be cautious. Consider the warning of the god about the effects in the world of what we would today call militant atheists (XVI, 8–9):

> They say that the world is without truth, without a moral basis, without a God, that it is not originated by regular causation, but that it is caused by desire.

> Holding fast to this view, these lost souls of little intelligence and of cruel deeds come forth as enemies for the destruction of the world.[88]

The secrets made available by the god to the gifted and privileged warrior may be preserved by the poet simply because few are equipped and disciplined enough to pursue the truth systematically. The god instructs the warrior, "Among thousands of men, perchance one strives for perfection, and of those who strive and are successful, perhaps one knows Me in essence" (VII, 3).[89] We thus confirm that rare as perfection in action is, perfection in attaining to the truth is even rarer.

It should be evident as well that we would need to see what is truly being said in this and other such books—and the consequences of such opinions—in order to be able to investigate properly the organized religion and the complicated Hindu community somehow rooted in and no doubt illuminating these opinions.[90]

Epilogue

I trust I have said enough in this introduction to suggest that the *Bhagavad Gītā* is a book capable of being read as a work of the mind; to suggest how we might begin to read it and similar books from other ways of life; and finally, to suggest how we might undertake to read first-rate books, "secular" as well as "religious," of our very own.

---

[1]Eliot Deutsch, trans., *The Bhagavad Gītā* (New York: Holt, Rinehart and Winston, 1968), p. 3. Mr. Deutsch adds, "Countless orthodox Hindus recite passages from [the *Gītā*] daily, and on special occasions the entire work is recited by groups of devotees."

Wilhelm von Humboldt has been quoted as describing it as "the most beautiful, perhaps the only true philosophical song, existing in any known tongue." Jawaharlal Nehru, *The Discovery of India* (Garden City, N.Y.: Anchor Books, 1960), p. 62.

A. L. Basham, perhaps the most distinguished Western Indologist today, has described the *Gītā* as "the most exalted and beautiful of India's religious poems, which teaches a fully-fledged theism and is part of the more recent Hinduism, rather than of the old

Brahmanism, which slowly changed from a religion of sacrifice to one of devotion." *The Wonder That Was India* (New York: Grove Press, 1959), p. 253. "No other religious-philosophical work of a comparable size, whether from China, Japan, the West or India itself, has quite captured the attention in the 20th century that this work has." A. L. Herman, trans., *The Bhagavad Gītā* (Springfield, Ill.: Charles C. Thomas, 1973), p. 3.

Interest in Hindu thought, of which the *Gītā* is the most widely known expression, is evident in works as diverse as G. W. F. Hegel's *Philosophy of History* and T. S. Eliot's *Waste Land.* "In the traditional form the chief distinguishing features of Hinduism are the doctrine of the transmigration of souls, with its corollary that all living beings are the same in essence; a complex polytheism, subsumed in a fundamental monotheism by the doctrine that all lesser divinities are subsidiary aspects of the one God; a deep-rooted tendency to mysticism and monistic philosophy; a stratified system of social classes, generally called castes, which is given religious sanction; and a propensity to assimilate rather than to exclude. This last feature divides Hinduism sharply from the religions of the West, based on Judaism. The latter, at least in their earlier forms, generally reject as false all other religious beliefs and practices; Hinduism, on the other hand, concedes some validity to them all. The Western attitude is expressed by the words of Yahweh on Sinai, 'You shall have no other gods before me' (Exod. xx, 3); in the *Bhagavad Gītā,* the incarnate god Krishna says, 'Whatever god a man worships, it is I who answer the prayer'." "Hinduism," *Encyclopædia Britannica,* 14th ed. See *Bhagavad Gītā,* IV, 11.

All quotations from the *Bhagavad Gītā* in my text are taken from the Deutsch translation which is set forth elsewhere in this volume of *The Great Ideas Today.* All citations in both the text of this article and in these notes are, unless otherwise indicated, to the *Gītā* by chapter and stanza. All citations to sections are, unless otherwise indicated, to the sections of this article.

²See Anastaplo, "An Introduction to Confucian Thought," *GIT* 1984, pp. 125–70. Various things I say there apply here as well, not only suggestions about how and why one should read books from a radically different way of life, but also observations about philosophy (p. 127), about nature (p. 151), and about my purposes and limitations. It should be stated that just as I do not know Chinese, so I do not know Sanskrit.

³Immediate family ties are made much of in the Confucian *Analects.* In Hinduism, the family, vital (if not even oppressive) as it can be, is decisively guided by class (or caste) requirements. Even so, much, perhaps most, worship is based in the household.

⁴Kees W. Bolle, trans., *The Bhagavadgita* (Berkeley: University of California Press, 1979), p. 219. "Sanjaya, the old king's personal bard, acts as his reporter on the progress of the war between the Pāndavas, his nephews, and the Kauravas, his sons." J. A. B. van Buitenen, trans., *The Bhagavadgītā in the Mahābhārata* (Chicago: University of Chicago Press, 1981). This king, Dhritarāshtra, is blind. See note 85, below.

In this article, the spelling and italicizing of names in quotations are made uniform.

⁵Krishna, although the name of a god, is to this day a name which may be given to a son. Krishna, as Arjuna's charioteer, is his older cousin. Family and other relations get rather complicated in the ancient Hindu stories, especially when transmigration of souls and earlier divine incarnations are taken into account. It can be said that even Krishna had to learn, in the course of his human life, of his miraculous birth and his divine status. See, e.g., *The Bhagavad Gītā,* Winthrop Sargeant, trans. (Garden City, N.Y.: Doubleday & Co., 1979), p. 25. See also van Buitenen, pp. 5, 28; note 51, below.

Even more complicated may be the relations among the gods. The following account should suffice, as an introduction to the subject for the reader of this article: "The word *brahman* is primarily and originally neuter in gender, and remains so usually throughout the *Upanishads* and the *Bhagavad Gītā;* but occasionally it acquires a personality, as a sort of creating and ruling deity, and then it has masculine gender. It thus becomes the god Brahmā, familiar to later Hinduism as the nominal head of the Triad consisting of Brahmā the Creator, Vishnu the Preserver, and Shiva the Destroyer. This trinity appears only in comparatively late *Upanishads,* and no clear mention of it is found in the *Bhagavad Gītā,* although the *Gītā* at least once refers to the masculine and personal Brahmā, 'the Lord sitting on the lotus-seat' [XI, 15]. . . . Vishnu and Shiva, under various names and forms, are the real gods of later India. Shiva-worship, though certainly much older than the *Bhagavad Gītā,* hardly appears therein and may therefore be left out of consideration in this book. (Shiva, under various of his innumerable names, is however mentioned [e.g., X, 23].) But we must say a few words about Vishnu, since he was identified with Krishna, the *Gītā*'s God, or regarded as incarnate in Him. This identification seems to me to appear clearly in the *Gītā* itself [XI, 24, 30]. . . . The *Upanishads* add nothing to the history of Vishnu. They—that is, the older ones, those which antedate the *Gītā*—mention his name only three or four times, and quite in the style of the Middle-Vedic period. But suddenly, in the *Gītā* and other contemporary writings, we find Vishnu recognized as a supreme monotheistic deity, worshiped either under his own name, or in the form of various incarnations, the chief of which is Krishna. . . . We have, then, finally, a union of at least three strands in the monotheistic deity of the *Bhagavad Gītā*: a popular god-hero of a local tribe, an ancient Vedic deity belonging to the hieratic ritual religion, and the philosophic Absolute of the *Upanishads*." Franklin Edgerton, trans., *The Bhagavad Gītā* (Cambridge: Harvard University Press, 1972), pp. 133–35. See Basham, p. 238.

[6]The most venerable of the *Vedas* is the *Rig Veda*, of which it can be said that its sound is as important as its sense. Particularly challenging for its sense is the hymn at *Rig Veda*, X, 129, which concludes, "Whence all creation had its origin, he, whether he fashioned it or whether he did not, he who surveys it all from highest heaven, he knows—or maybe even he does not know." See Basham, pp. 247–48. *Veda*, we are told, comes from the root, *vid*, "to know." See Nehru, p. 42f. See also notes 70 and 89, below.

In ancient times, descriptions of the capacity of battle leaders would refer not only to their skill in war but also to their being conversant with the *Vedas*. Religion "has always been the central and supreme activity of the Hindu Society." Arnold J. Toynbee, *A Study of History* (London: Oxford University Press, 1935), II, 75. Thus, the contemporary distinction between "secular" and "religious" is largely Western. It is a distinction with which the present Indian constitution wrestles.

[7]"About 112 *Upanishads* have been printed in Sanskrit, but the most important ones are about eighteen." Juan Mascaro, trans., *The Bhagavad gītā* (Baltimore: Penguin Books, 1962), p. 13. "The term *Upanishad* means literally 'a session', sitting at the feet of a master who imparts esoteric doctrines." Basham, p. 250. Sometimes the *Bhagavad Gītā* is itself regarded as an *Upanishad*. See, e.g., the Colophon for Chapter I of the *Gītā*.

"The word Mahābhārata, meaning the great Bhārata, reminds us of Bhārata, . . . the founder of a dynasty of Indian kings." Mascaro, p. 21.

[8]Useful day-by-day summaries of the *Mahābhārata* may be found in Sargeant, pp. 21f, 40f. See also Basham, p. 407f; R. K. Narayan, *The Mahabharata: A Shortened Modern Prose Version of the Indian Epic* (New York: Viking Press, 1978). Graham Greene has said of Mr. Narayan, the grand patriarch of Indo-Anglican writers, "Without him I could never have known what it is like to be Indian." S. S. Moorty, Book Review, *Liberal and Fine Arts*, vol. 4 (Jan. 1984), p. 67. See, as a reminder that the often bizarre episodes in ancient Indian literature are not merely things of the past, James P. Sterba, "In a Temple in India, The Rats Don't Bite, But They Do Tickle: Today's Rodents at the Shrine of Karni Mata Might Be Tomorrow's Town Elders," *Wall Street Journal*, Jan. 9, 1985, p. 1.

[9]The *Gītā* constitutes chapters 23–40 of the sixth book of the eighteen-book *Mahābhārata*. See van Buitenen, pp. 5–6. Suppositions about the date of its *composition* range from 500 B.C. to A.D. 200. I find rather charming the following suggestions as to when the *Mahābhārata*'s war was *fought:* "Indian scholars like C. V. Vaidya, Karandikar and others are of opinion that the war commenced in December on the 11th or on the 13th day of the white part of the month of Margasirsa, 3102 B.C., and that the *Bhagavad Gītā* was preached on the morning of that very day. Prof. V. B. Athavale of Nasika has recently fixed 3018 B.C. as the year when the Kuru war commenced." Umesha Mishra, *The Bhagavad Gītā: A Critical Study* (Allahabad, India: Tirabhukti Publications, 1967), p. 27. More sober estimates place the war itself at about 900 B.C. See, e.g., Ann Stanford, trans., *The Bhagavad Gītā* (New York: Herder and Herder, 1970), p. xvii.

[10]See note 5, above. Readers of the *Iliad* and of the *Odyssey* will remember that gods such as Athena appeared on many occasions in human form. Compare Hans-Georg Gadamer, *Truth and Method* (New York: Seabury Press, 1975), pp. 378–79: "There is, however, an idea that is not Greek and that does more justice to the nature of language and prevented the forgetfulness of language in Western thought from being complete. This is the Christian idea of incarnation. Incarnation is obviously not embodiment. Neither the idea of the soul nor of God that is connected with embodiment corresponds to

the Christian idea of incarnation. The relation between soul and body conceived in these theories, as, for instance, in Platonic and Pythagorean philosophy, and corresponding to the religious idea of the migration of souls, assumes the complete separateness of the soul from the body. The soul retains its own separate nature throughout all its embodiments, and the separation from the body it regards as a purification, i.e., as a restoration of its true and real being. Even the appearance of the divine in human form, which makes Greek religion so human, has nothing to do with incarnation. God does not become man, but shows himself to men in human form, while wholly retaining his superhuman divinity. As opposed to this, that God became man, as understood in the Christian religion, involves the sacrifice that the crucified Christ accepts as the Son of Man, namely a relationship that is strangely different and is expressed theologically in the doctrine of the Trinity." See Plato, *Timaeus* 81d–e (*GBWW*, Vol. 7, pp. 471d–72a). See also Philostratus, *The Life of Apollonius* (Loeb Classical Library, 1912), I, 269f; II, 455f, 479.

[11]See *B. Gītā*, XVIII, 70. See also Section XI of this article.

[12]Edgerton, p. 99, n. 5. See also pp. 106, 108, 189, 193. See, as well, Bolle, p. 219. The lack of an apparent order is suggested by efforts to ascribe various parts of the *Gītā* to different authors. See, e.g., Gajanan S. Khair, *Quest for the Original Gītā* (Bombay: Somaiya Publications, 1969). Professor Basham, in his 1985 American Council of Learned Societies lectures, reported that scholars have discerned as many as a dozen contributors to the *Gītā*. He considers the original text to end with II, 38. He himself believes there are three principal authors of the *Gītā*. This diverse authorship accounts, in his opinion, for the contradictions he sees in the *Gītā* (as, for example, between V, 23–28 and V, 29). Even so, must not *someone* have believed that these verses could be plausibly connected thus? How is *that* to be accounted for?

[13]*Reflections on the Revolution in France* (Indianapolis: Bobbs Merrill, 1955), p. 287. See also Mortimer J. Adler, *Aristotle for Everybody* (New York: Macmillan, 1978), p. 77.

[14]See, for similar observations about Charles Dickens's *Christmas Carol* and Lewis Carroll's *Alice* books, Anastaplo, *The Artist as Thinker: From Shakespeare to Joyce* (Athens, Ohio: Swallow Press/Ohio University Press, 1983), pp. 123f, 166f.

[15]For the most part, I limit myself on this occasion to recording intriguing, and I hope instructive, features of the *Gītā* that I have not seen noticed elsewhere. Those who know this poem, Hindu literature, and India herself far better than I do may find it useful to take account of what I have noticed.

[16]Edgerton, p. 105. See, for another summary of the *Gītā*, Narayan, *The Mahabharata*, p. 145f. See also Basham, pp. 340–42.

[17]Some critics tend to neglect Arjuna's questions, regarding the *Gītā* as virtually a monologue by Krishna. But the most instructive presentation of divine things may perhaps be found in what is said in response to human concerns, questions, and limitations.

[18]"Madhusūdana" means "slayer of the demon Madhu." See the text at note 34 and at note 38. Evidently, there have always been in Hinduism epic struggles between gods and demons. See note 28, below. See, on the epithets, Sections VI and VII. See, on the meanings of the epithets and other names, the Glossary which follows the text of the *Gītā* elsewhere in this volume of *The Great Ideas Today.*

The use of "archer" in XVIII, 78, is anticipated not only in II, 4 (and elsewhere), but also by the god's calling the warrior "Savyasācin" ("ambidextrous") in XI, 33, referring to his prowess with the bow. (It had been a feat of archery which had permitted Arjuna to win Draupadī who, because of a quirk, became the joint wife of the five Pāndava brothers.) Another troubled archer who had to be brought around to what was decreed for him to do in a great enterprise was Philoctetes. He, too, had a great vision (in the form of Heracles, another slayer of demons). Thus, he also had to be induced to see and to accept what was fated. See Sophocles, *Philoctetes* (*GBWW*, Vol. 5, pp. 182–95).

[19]See, on the "great-souled man," Aristotle, *Nicomachean Ethics*, IV, 3 (*GBWW*, Vol. 9, pp. 370b–72b). See also Philostratus, I, 183f, 249, 267f, 291f.

[20]"Janārdana" means "agitator of men" (if not "savior of men" or "liberator of men").

[21]See the text at note 38.

[22]The van Buitenen translation renders this passage thus, "You praise the relinquishment of acts and at the same time the practice of them, Krishna. Now tell me decidedly which is the better of the two."

[23]Compare Exodus 33:8–23, Deuteronomy 4:12, 34:10. See Job 41:32.

Is it not significant that the warrior does assume, if he does not "know," that there *is* something special to be *seen?* See notes 50, 70, and 89, below.

[24]See Sophocles, *Oedipus the Tyrant,* 938 ("What have you designed, O Zeus, to do with me?").

[25]The van Buitenen translation renders this passage thus, "Who are the foremost adepts of yoga: those who attend on you with the devotion they constantly practice, or those who seek out the imperishable that is unmanifest?"

[26]"As both Samkara (A.D. 700–750) and Rāmānuja (A.D. 1017–1137) point out [in their great Sanskrit commentaries], these are the essential characteristics of the three 'Strands' of nature: 'goodness, passion, and darkness' respectively." Edgerton, p. 100. See, on the commentators, Basham, p. 328f.

[27]See, on the divine Brahman, note 5, above, and the text at note 34. See, on the priestly Brahmin, the text at note 63.

[28]"Keshinishūdana" means "slayer of the demon Keshin." See note 18, above. "Hri-shīkesha" means "bristling-haired one."

"The teaching of the *Bhagavad Gītā* is summed up in the maxim 'your business is with the deed, and not with the result'. In an organized society each individual has his special part to play, and in every circumstance there are actions which are intrinsically right— from the point of view of the poet who wrote the *Gītā* they are those laid down by the Sacred Laws of the Aryans and the traditions of class and clan. The right course must be chosen according to the circumstances, without any considerations of personal interest or sentiment. Thus man serves God, and in so far as he lives up to this ideal he draws near to God." Basham, pp. 341–42.

[29]See, on the "Acyuta" epithet, Section VI. This epithet is also used by Arjuna at I, 21, and at XI, 42 (although it is a rare translator who will use "Acyuta" at all three places in his translation). See note 36, below. See also note 35, below.

See, on the linking of understanding to memory, Plato, *Meno (GBWW,* Vol. 7). See also *B. Gītā,* XVIII, 76–77; Anastaplo, *Human Being and Citizen* (Chicago: Swallow Press, 1975), p. 82f; note 10, above.

[30]It has been suggested that the *Gītā* is actually finished in the seventeeth chapter, and that the eighteenth is really a kind of epilogue summing up the topics discussed before. See, e.g., A. C. Bhaktivedanta Swami Prabhupada, trans., *Bhagavad-gita As It Is* (New York: Macmillan Co., 1972), p. 780.

Why eighteen? It does *not* seem to be a significant number for Hindus. Compare the text at note 33. (Eighteen *can* be seen to reflect a certain symmetry using more important numbers: five plus eight plus five.) See, for one derivation of eighteen, *The Upanishads,* F. Max Muller, ed. (New York: Dover Publications, n.d.), I, 184 (*Aitareya-Aranyaka,* I, iii, 7). See, for other literary divisions by eighteen, "Sanskrit Literature," *Encyclopædia Britannica,* 14th ed. See, on the ordinariness of eighteen, Philostratus, I, 297.

Subrahmanyan Chandrasekhar, of the University of Chicago, has suggested to me, in conversation, that recollection of an eighteen-day battle (real or supposed) may have guided the authors of the *Mahābhārata* and of the *Gītā* in making their divisions. That is, he starts (in a scientific fashion?) from what might have actually been, if only accidentally. Even so, such authors might still have had to decide whether this number (as distinguished from others no doubt also available from "history") was particularly significant.

It seems that eighteen can be an important number among Jews: it is evidently the numerical equivalent of the Hebrew word for *life (het-yod).*

[31]See Anastaplo, "An Introduction to Confucian Thought," notes 7, 29, and 52.

[32]The typical stanza has thirty-two syllables. See Stanford, p. xxii. A few editors add a stanza, in the form of a question by Arjuna, at the beginning of Chapter XIII. See Sargeant, p. 540; Khair, p. 133; Prabhupada, p. 620. But much is to be said for, and about, seven hundred.

[33]The significance of five and eight for the Hindus is comparable to that of three, seven, nine, ten, twelve, and thirteen, and perhaps seventeen and twenty-six as well, in the West. On five, see, e.g., *B. Gītā,* XVIII, 13 *et seq.;* Muller, I, 23f, 46f, 76f, 82–84, 221, 223, 232f; II, 23, 46f, 83–84, 234; Narayan, *The Mahabharata,* pp. 32, 33, 37, 38; Basham, pp. 497, 499. On eight, see, e.g., *B. Gītā,* VII, 4 *et seq.;* Muller, I, 1–2, 16–17; II, 149; Narayan, *The Mahabharata,* p. 1; Khair, pp. 70–71; Basham, pp. 385, 417,

420, 504. Panini's great Sanskrit grammar (in antiquity) consisted of eight lectures. See, on the relation of eight to five and three, van Buitenen, p. 28. See, for samplings of correspondences between numbers and things, Muller, I, 160–61, 165, 171–73, 181–82, 186, 187f, 191, 192, 193f, 214, 220, 234, 258. See, for various suggestions on how many gods there are, Muller, II, 139f (with one curious suggestion, at p. 142, being "one and a half"). See, on numbering, Anastaplo, *The Artist as Thinker*, p. 397.

[34] I take Arjuna's "I will not fight" in II, 9, to be part of his speech in II, 4–8. That is, this is all one response to what Krishna had said in II, 2–3. (Of course, if an extra stanza is added as some would have it at the beginning of Chapter XIII, there would be forty-three speeches. See note 32, above. But that would mar the discipline evidently sought in having exactly seven hundred stanzas. The Kashmir recension of the *Gītā* is said to have an additional verse after II, 11. See Herman, p. 113.)

An attractive feature of forty-one, at least for us, is that twenty-one (three times seven) should be its center. There are forty-one names indicated in the genealogy provided in Exodus 6:14–25 and in the generations provided in Matthew 1:1–17.)

[35] There *is* a problem counting epithets, especially if one has to rely on translations. There is no translator into English, of the dozen I have examined, who is completely faithful to the text in this respect. (It is tempting to try to make the number of epithets "come out right" by, for example, having Arjuna use forty [five times eight] and having Krishna use twenty-four [three times eight]. But I must leave this exercise to someone who knows Sanskrit.) In any event, it should be noticed that the warrior uses many more different epithets than does the god, even though the warrior speaks much, much less.

[36] The second use of "Acyuta" (XI, 42) may be found in my text at note 39; the third use (XVIII, 73) may be found in my text at note 29. "Acyuta" has been translated as "sinless one" at XI, 42, of the Deutsch translation and as "immovable one" at I, 21, of the Deutsch translation. Others have translated it as "unshaken one" and "changeless one" (Edgerton), and as "unshakable one" and "imperishable Lord" (Bolle). It has been defined as "not fallen, unchanging, imperishable, unshaken, firm." Sargeant, p. 71.

The god may be recognized by the warrior as unchanging, but the warrior's perceptions of the god *do* keep changing, perhaps because the god is so complicated and because the warrior is subject to human frailties in perception and in powers of expression. This makes the steadfastness of the "Acyuta" epithet even more striking by comparison.

[37] "Pārtha" and "Kuntī" refer to the warrior's mother. (Thus, the god is much steadier in the epithets he employs.) A commentator on II, 14, observes, "In the beginning of the verse, where the nature of heat and cold is declared, Arjuna is addressed as the son of his mother,—Kuntī; but when he is exhorted to abandon pleasure and pain, he is reminded of his heroic ancestor Bhārata, from whom India is called by her people 'the land of Bhārata'." M. Chatterji, *The Bhagavad Gita* (New York: Julian Press, 1960), p. 34.

I suspect that a thorough study of the *Gītā* would bring to light the appropriateness of the use of each epithet in the circumstances in which it is used. Consider, e.g., this sequence: After the warrior addresses the god for the first time as "best of beings" (or "Supreme Person" [as in the van Buitenen translation]) (VIII, 1), he is thereafter addressed for the first (and only) time as "best of embodied ones" (VIII, 4)—and this comes immediately after the warrior had asked how the god is "to be known at the time of death" (VIII, 2). (See the text at note 34.) Cannot dying be considered "dis-embodying"? Is it indicated that neither "dis-embodiment" nor "embodiment" (i.e., neither death nor life, on earth) means much to the god? See note 10, above.

It has been suggested, of course, that epithets are often chosen because their sound is appropriate in the lines where they are found. See, e.g., Stanford, p. 139. Compare p. 140.

[38] See, e.g., I, 35; II, 4. See also note 18, above.

[39] See also note 48, below. The question remains as to what that wealth consists of which is truly worth winning. (The warrior's noble teachers had become too desirous of conventional wealth? See II, 5. See also the text at note 18.) The considerable significance of "Dhananjaya" as an epithet for the warrior and of "Vāsudeva" (and hence of the present incarnation of this god?) as an epithet for the god is pointed up by the god at X, 37. (This is the last of the "divine manifestations" stanzas to use proper names.) See also VII, 19. (The god's "Vāsudeva" epithet again reminds us of the importance of the maternal line, since Krishna is the son of Vāsudeva, who is related to Arjuna's mother.) The great treasure which Dhananjaya (Arjuna) wins is the teaching by Vāsudeva

(Krishna), which is made available (to us?) with the help of the sage Vyāsa. See notes 58 and 83, below. Thus, X, 37, is a most remarkable stanza, bringing together (and extolling with superlatives) three of those responsible for the *Gītā* (Krishna, Arjuna, and Vyāsa). Is Sanjaya the narrator "represented" (perhaps even superseded) by the fourth name here, "the poet Ushanā"? See the text at note 84 of this article.

[40]See, on the restrictions placed in the Hebrew Bible and elsewhere on how the divine is referred to, Anastaplo, "Censorship," *Encyclopædia Britannica,* 15th ed.

[41]Thus, the narrator uses "Hari" as the Vision begins (at XI, 9) and again at the end of the *Gītā* (at XVIII, 72).

[42]After all, the warrior, as distinguished from the narrator, is someone who was from the beginning considered worthy of being personally instructed by the god. "And although one ought not to reason of Moses, he having been a mere executor of the things that were ordained by God, he ought yet to be admired, if only for the grace which made him worthy to speak with God." Machiavelli, *The Prince,* Leo Paul S. de Alvarez, trans. (Irving, Texas: University of Dallas Press, 1980), p. 33 (cf. *GBWW,* Vol. 23, p. 9a).

[43]Much more can be said about the epithets—about, for example, those shared by the god and the warrior. Thus, both the warrior and the god can be addressed as "*Mahabaho*" ("great-armed one"). I have noticed three places where the warrior uses this form of address for his companion (VI, 38; XI, 23; XVIII, 1), and eleven places where the god uses this form of address for his companion (II, 26, 68; III, 28, 43; V, 3, 6; VI, 35; VII, 5; X, 1; XIV, 5; XVIII, 13). Does such sharing of epithets suggest that the god and the warrior do not differ in kind, at least with respect to prowess in battle? ("Bhārata," conjuring up as it does the common ancestor, can be shared as an epithet by Dhritarāshtra and Arjuna, in the *Gītā,* and by others in the *Mahābhārata.*

See, for a pioneering study of epithets, Seth G. Benardete, *Achilles and Hector: The Homeric Hero* (University of Chicago doctoral dissertation, 1955).

[44]The word for *armies* is *senayor* (I, 21) and for *behold* is *pasyaitan* (I, 25). There seem to be differences in the editions and translations as to whether the god's first word to the warrior is "Pārtha" (one of his family names) or "behold." If "Pārtha" *is* used by the god, rather than by the narrator, then the second word used by the god is "behold" (with the god pointing to the assembled army).

[45]"Behold" had been used even earlier by the somewhat villainous Duryodhana (the leader of the army opposed to the Pāndavas). Indeed, it is the first word used by Duryodhana himself (I, 3): that the grasping Duryodhana should use "behold" with his teacher as the god uses "behold" with his student (Arjuna) may suggest Duryodhana's willingness, even eagerness, to dispense with reliance upon salutary conventions. Arjuna, on the other hand, instinctively defers to his teacher and hence to the divine. Thus, we again notice the noteworthy piety of Arjuna reflected throughout (as in his well-timed uses of "Acyuta"). Thus, also, we are encouraged to notice the care with which this poem has been put together by someone, however many hands contributed to the fashioning of the materials that went into it. See, on comparable care used by a master poet with the materials gathered into the *Iliad,* Anastaplo, *The Constitutionalist: Notes on the First Amendment* (Dallas: Southern Methodist University Press, 1971), p. 807.

[46]The last word used by the god is *te,* that used by the warrior is *teva.* This god can appear differently to, and mean quite different things for, others. To young women, for example, he can appear as a dancer, perhaps even as a lover. "When peasants or old women suffer a grievous loss, their natural exclamation is, *Krishnarpanamastus,* Surrendered to Krishna." Khair, p. vii.

[47]The last word used by the narrator is *mama* ("my" or "I"). The last two words, *matir mama,* have been translated as "I am certain" (Bolle), "I ween" (Edgerton), "I hold" (van Buitenen), and "so I believe" (Deutsch). The first word used in the poem (after "Dhritarāshtra said") is *Dharma.* This word, which is rendered as "righteousness" in the Deutsch translation, has been defined as "established order, rule, duty, virtue, moral merit, right, justice, law (in an eternal sense)." Narayan, *The Mahabharata,* p. 181. On the *Gītā* as a reaffirmation of the established way—but a way that has been refined as much as it is advisable to do in the circumstances, see the text at note 71 of this article.

We are once again encouraged to notice the care lavished upon this poem, further attesting to its likely unity and overall thoughtfulness. It is evident, upon close examination, that it *has* been put together by someone who is remarkably restrained, who relies to a considerable extent on argument, and who again and again takes common sense for granted, even as he is quite willing to draw upon the general opinion among his audience with respect both to miracles and to ancient stories and characters. (Compared to the rest of the *Mahābhārata*, the *Gītā* is [especially for its time] remarkably free of the immediately miraculous—and this despite the spectacular vision seen [by one man only?] in Chapter XI. See note 55, below.) In short, this poet may be much more subtle and hence sophisticated than most twentieth-century scholars. See, on the limitations of the most fashionable literary criticism today, Anastaplo, *The Artist as Thinker*, pp. 470–72.

[48]See Stanford, pp. xviii–xxi. The names for the warrior used by the narrator just before and after the Vision is granted are "Pārtha" and "Dhananjaya," the names that the god finally settles upon in the last stanza of his last speech to the warrior. See XI, 9, 14; XVIII, 72. Does the poet, in thus bracketing the Vision, deliberately use something he has learned from the *Gītā* experience as a whole? See note 39, above.

[49]Our contemporaries are also impressed. Thus, the Vision can be referred to as "the marvelous transfiguration of Chapter XI." Van Buitenen, p. 12.

[50]Does the narrator see everything that the warrior does? The warrior *is* given a special power, by which he can see the Vision (XI, 8). We must again wonder then whether the narrator sees the Vision at all. Or does he describe what he "sees" on the basis of what he hears the warrior describing? In any event, was the Vision necessary to intensify, if not even to confirm, the god's teaching for the warrior? And if necessary, what is to be the status of such a teaching for those of us who have not seen the Vision? See note 84, below.

It does seem that we naturally regard sight as more reliable than hearing. See Muller, II, 197. But do not thoughts and ideas depend more on words (that is, heard things) than they do on seen things? Certainly, what is told to the warrior is more important than what is shown to him, especially if all this *is* ultimately for the benefit of the poet's audience. See note 84, below.

[51]One can be reminded here of the three-jawed Lucifer at the very bottom of Dante's *Inferno*. The story is told, in the *Bhagavata Purana*, of Krishna's unsuspecting human mother's looking into her child's mouth, where she is astonished to see "the whole eternal universe." *Hindu Myths*, Wendy D. O'Flaherty, ed. (Penguin Books, 1975), p. 220. She is then made to forget what she had seen, as she continues to love Krishna as her son.

[52]See XI, 24, 30. See also X, 21. See, as well, note 5, above.

[53]The second half of the central pair of 700 stanzas is IX, 14: "Always glorifying Me and striving with steadfast resolve, and honoring Me with devotion, they worship Me ever-disciplined." Thus, centrality here is seen as the 350th and 351st stanzas. It might be instructive to consider as central in another way the final stanza of the ninth chapter and the opening stanza of the tenth chapter (that is, the places where the two central chapters meet). Akin to the first of the "central" pair quoted in the text (IX, 13) *is* the first of this other pair (IX, 34): "Fix the mind on Me, be devoted to Me, worship Me, salute Me; thus having disciplined the self and having Me as the supreme goal, thou shalt come to Me."

[54]See, on "Brahman" (or "Brahmā"), note 5, above. See Philostratus, II, 315.

[55]Such multiplication of divine ascriptions may be seen as well both in Christianity and in Islām. See also Exodus 34:6–7. See, as well, Maimonides, *The Guide of the Perplexed*, e.g., I, 54; note 23, above.

Is not any persistent conception of the divine ultimately monotheistic? When, for example, it is determined by a people what is and what is not divine, is not a standard drawn upon which is implicitly monotheistic? And does not such a standard depend on some awareness of *being* and of the natural? But what is meant when one observes that a religion has "gone mad"? See, e.g., John F. Muehl, *Interview with India* (New York: John Day Co., 1950), p. 252. See also notes 78 and 89, below.

[56]See the note on this passage in van Buitenen, p. 166.

[57]See IX, 5; X, 1 *et seq.*, 28, 42; XIII, 14 *et seq.*

[58]"Gudākesha" evidently means "thick-haired one." (Some suggest that it means "one who conquers sleep." Chatterji, p. 163; Prabhupada, p. 51.) In this list of divine manifestations, the warrior himself appears (with the name, "Dhananjaya") as the peak of the Pāndavas (X, 37). In that same stanza, Vyāsa is recognized as the peak of the sages.

[59]"Professor Godbole's conversations frequently culminated in a cow." E. M. Forster, *A Passage to India* (New York: Harvest Book, Harcourt, Brace & World, n.d.), p. 179. See also Basham, pp. 120, 194–95, 319. Considering what Hindus are able to perceive

in a cow, it should be no wonder that Arjuna saw what he did in (or through or because of) his talented charioteer? Still, "Oh, cows, cows" can be a derogatory remark. Narayan, *The Mahabharata*, p. 68. See also Anastaplo, *The Constitutionalist*, pp. 605–6.

[60]"*Yama*, lord of the dead, was a sort of Adam, the first man to die, who became guardian of the World of the Fathers, where the blessed dead, those who have performed the rites of the Aryans, feast in bliss forever." Basham, p. 238. See also pp. 242, 313–14.

An English woman in *A Passage to India* says of the Ganges, "What a terrible river! what a wonderful river!" Forster, p. 32. See also pp. 7, 123; Basham, p. 320; *Chicago Tribune*, Sept. 14, 1984, sec. 5, p. 1.

[61]The troubles of the Pāndava brothers are intensified by the weakness for gambling in the oldest of them, Yudhishthira. See Deutsch, p. 141; Narayan, *The Mahabharata*, pp. 52, 67, 80. One of the hymns of the *Rig Veda* is the lament of a ruined gambler. See also Basham, pp. 37, 90, 207–8, 403–5; Edgerton, p. 98.

[62]See II, 31. See, for an indication of the origins of classes (or castes), IV, 13. See also Nehru, p. 76; Basham, pp. 34–35, 137f, 146f, 483, 484. See, as well, Friedrich Nietzsche, *Twilight of the Idols*, secs. 3–5; *Anti-Christ*, secs. 56–57; *Beyond Good and Evil*, sec. 61; Leonard Feinberg, *Asian Laughter* (New York: Weatherhill, 1971), pp. 438–39.

"In India, as in China, learning and erudition have always stood high in public esteem. . . . Before the learned man, the ruler and the warrior have always bowed. . . . The warrior class, though not at the top, held a high position, and was not, as in China, looked upon with contempt." Nehru, p. 51. See also Narayan, *The Mahabharata*, pp. 28, 31, 79.

[63]It should be noticed that there is no provision here for "untouchability." See, on the daily life of the lowest class, Mulk Raj Anand, *Untouchable* (Bombay: Jaico Publishing House, 1956; first published in 1935).

[64]Compare Xenophon, *Cyropaedia*, I, iv, 24; VIII, vii, 26. See also Plato, *Republic* 439e–40e (*GBWW*, Vol. 7, pp. 352d–53b). See, as well, R. W. Emerson, "Brahma."

[65]See, for a list of Hindu virtues, XVI, 1 *et seq*. See also Narayan, *The Mahabharata*, pp. 90–92. Compare Plato, *Laws* 657c, 658e (*GBWW*, Vol. 7, pp. 655b, 656a); Adler, *Aristotle for Everybody*, pp. 89f, 154–55; Anastaplo, "Aristotle on Law and Morality," *Windsor Yearbook of Access to Justice*, vol. 3, 1983, p. 458.

[66]See XVIII, 59. See also note 28, above.

[67]Does one not need a sound appreciation of the entire *Mahābhārata*, its circumstances and its consequences, in order to make an informed judgment about all this?

See, for a somewhat sentimental effort by modern pacifism to accommodate itself to the *Gītā*, Edgerton, p. 140, n. 7. Compare Ved Mehta, "Personal History," *New Yorker*, Feb. 11, 1985, at p. 57: "Christians are taught love and compassion while we Hindus are taught only fate and duty." But does not the *Gītā* make it clear that Arjuna's compassion is preferable to Duryodhana's ruthlessness? Arjuna himself can run wild when the killing becomes frenzied enough in the *Mahābhārata*, more so than his brother Yudhishthira. See, for his brother's instructive respect for protocol, van Buitenen, p. 145f.

[68]See IV, 9. See also II, 11. Yet Indians can develop a remarkable, even fanatical, respect for life, as exhibited by the Jains. See, e.g., Basham, p. 287f.

[69]See, e.g., VI, 8–9; XIII, 12; XIV, 24. See also R. K. Narayan, *The Printer of Malgudi* (Lansing: Michigan State University Press, 1957), p. 76. What is generally said about wealth in the *Gītā* (see note 39, above) leads us to wonder whether the seeming naturalness and hence rigidity of classes make possible the extreme asceticism and the disregard for practical considerations that some Hindus seem to exhibit down to our day. Perhaps the inexorable movement of the classes, as they go about their duties, permits the community to support those who do immobilize themselves in the everyday world.

[70]But then, there *are* the narrator and the poet: of what class are they? See Section XVI. Or should it be recognized that it is as true among the Hindus, as it is in the West, that one who truly understands is confined by neither class nor gender?

[71]But see van Buitenen, p. 12: "For despite his perfunctory bows to received orthodoxy, Krishna is quite aware that he has new things to say, disguised as old things, older than the oldest brahmin." Compare ibid., p. 10. See F. Nietzsche, *Unpublished Letters* (London: Peter Owen, 1960), pp. 135–37; Basham, pp. 341–42. See also note 47, above.

[72]See Troy Organ on polarity in Hinduism, *Philosophy East and West* (Jan. 1976).

[73]Nehru, p. 63. See also pp. 47, 56, 278. See, as well, Philostratus, II, 593f; Narayan, *The Printer of Malgudi*, pp. 11–12; Muehl, pp. 8–9, 58f, 126–27, 184f, 301.

[74]These can include the non-violence ideals of a Mohandas Gandhi. See Nehru, pp. 63, 277; Herman, p. 6; Calvin Kytle, *Gandhi, Soldier of Nonviolence* (Cabin John, Md.: Seven Locks Press, 1982), pp. 38, 83–84; Basham, p. 483.

[75]See, on transmigration and reincarnation, *B. Gītā*, V, 6, VIII, 15, IX, 22; R. K. Narayan, *The Teacher* (Chicago: University of Chicago Press, 1980), pp. 26, 94–96, 100, 106f, 117f, 163, 184 (originally published under the title *Grateful to Life and Death*); W. D. O'Flaherty, *Karma and Rebirth in Classical Indian Tradition* (Berkeley: University of California Press, 1980). Compare Aristotle, *Nicomachean Ethics* 1166a18 *et seq.* (*GBWW*, Vol. 9, p. 419b *et seq.*); Thomas Aquinas, *Summa Theologica*, I, Q. 23, A. 5 (*GBWW*, Vol. 19, pp. 135d–37d) (on "a former life" and predestination; note 10, above.

[76]See Anastaplo, "An Introduction to Confucian Thought," Sec. XII.

[77]Various *Gītā* passages I have quoted in this article use *nature* (often for *prakriti*). It can be argued that various terms do have, in Sanskrit, the "function" of *nature*. No doubt, the same can be said of the expression translated from the Hebrew Bible as "each after its kind." But see Chatterji, p. 97: "In the teaching of the Blessed Lord [Krishna], the independent existence of Nature is never asserted." See also ibid., pp. 148–50. Compare van Buitenen, pp. 22–23.

May not the status of nature among the Hindus help account for the often noticed fact that there are no tragedies in Indian literature? See, e.g., Nehru, p. 100; Basham, pp. 416–17. Consider, also, Nietzsche, *Beyond Good and Evil*, sec. 30: "There are heights of the soul from which even tragedy ceases to have a tragic effect." May not both classical tragedy and philosophy depend on a mature grasp of *nature*?

[78]Is all this still another form of the tension, familiar to the West, between Reason and Revelation? Is not Krishna more like Moses or the god of Job than like Socrates or Plato?

[79]See IX, 19. See also XI, 37; XIII, 12. See, as well, V, 1. Is not a superior *beingness* assumed in Hindu thought, something which is beyond change? Is not this intuition related to investigations by modern physicists into such things as "anti-matter," as part of their efforts to understand the nature of matter itself? The need to combine opposites in order to grasp the whole may be reflected in the productive collaboration in the *Gītā* of Krishna and Arjuna, whose names mean "black" (or "dark") and "white" (or "silver"), respectively. See *Rig Veda*, X, 129 (note 6, above); van Buitenen, p. 160, n. 50; Forster, p. 177f. See also Muller, I, 230–32, 312; II, 176; *B. Gītā*, VIII, 26.

See, on the status of common sense in Hindu thought, the text at note 69. Did not the Socratic school (including Aristotle) regard common sense, in its rough reflection of nature, as a necessary point of departure for philosophy? See Adler, *Aristotle for Everybody*, pp. xi–xiv; Anastaplo, "An Introduction to Confucian Thought," p. 155, n. 9.

[80]See also II, 68. See, as well, VI, 19; X, 19 *et seq.* See, on the dependence of art upon nature, Aristotle, *Poetics* (*GBWW*, Vol. 9); Philostratus, I, 173f; Laurence Berns. "Aristotle's *Poetics*," in Joseph Cropsey, ed., *Ancients and Moderns* (New York: Basic Books, 1964); Anastaplo, *The Artist as Thinker*, pp. 275f, 284f, 310f, 494 ("nature").

[81]Mascaro, p. 26. See also the opening chapters of Maimonides's *The Guide of the Perplexed*. See, as well, Cropsey, p. 95; Anastaplo, *The Artist as Thinker*, p. 3f. Compare Muller, I, 75 ("If you were to tell [a certain teaching] to a dry stick, branches would grow, and leaves spring from it." [*Khandogya-Upanishad*, V, i]); II, 266.

[82]Or so the philosophers have said. See Edgerton, pp. 108–9, 139; Forster, p. 317 ("He knew that few Indians think education good in itself.") Compare note 19, above.

[83]See, on Vyāsa, *B. Gītā*, X, 13, 37; XVIII, 75; Narayan, *The Mahabharata*, pp. vii–viii, 6–7, 28, 131; Sargeant, pp. 23, 435, 748; van Buitenen, p. 161 (chap. 16, n. 2); note 39, above. "Vyāsa" is sometimes taken to mean "the arranger" or "the reviser."

[84]See note 39, above. The narrator Sanjaya is like the god Krishna in our story about Arjuna, in that he too is the charioteer to his companion (in Sanjaya's case, the king Dhritarāshtra). Is Sanjaya, then, also somewhat divine, at least in being inspired? In any event, Sanjaya tells a story to his blind king—that is, to someone who is like us in not being able to see for himself what is being described. See note 50, above.

[85]Thus, the *Gītā*, as we have it, depends for its form on two mortals: the blind king and the compassionate warrior both ask questions of their respective charioteers. Are not both questioners somewhat defective (at least for the moment, in the case of the warrior) for their respective duties? (This king's claim to rule *is* compromised by his blindness.)

[86]See, e.g., IX, 1; XV, 20; XVIII, 63–64, 67–68.

[87]See, e.g., II, 46. Who does and who does not have secrecy injunctions laid upon him? The warrior himself does not report to anyone else anything said to him, it seems. Nor does he know that a poet "hears" his conversation with the god or his description of the Vision. Does the god prefer to have a poet report the entire story? Is this, in part, because of the discipline and limitations of warriors? They cannot be depended upon to use their judgment properly here? Does not all this reflect the division of labor which the elaborate Hindu caste system very much depends upon and promotes? See note 69, above.

Be all this as it may, what *does* the poet do? Consider, e.g., Muller, I, 227: "Poets through their understanding discovered [the god] Indra dancing an Anushtubh [a kind of meter]." How many of the things reported in sacred literature (including the *Gītā*) are really the "discoveries" of poets? What does it say about inspiration (prophetic or poetic) if one insists, as Maimonides did, that a prophet must be quite intelligent? See Anastaplo, *The Artist as Thinker*, p. 11. See also note 78, above.

[88]One can be reminded here of Lucretius and the Epicureans. See, as instructive guides to the study of divine things, M. J. Adler, *How to Think About God* (New York: Macmillan, 1980); L. Strauss, "On the Interpretation of *Genesis*," *L'Homme*, vol. XXI (1981).

[89]What is required for one truly to know? Is it not to proceed as we have been able to do in this article both to assume and to confirm the sovereignty of nature and reason and hence of natural right and perhaps of philosophy? See notes 78, 55, and 2, above.

[90]A sampling of observations by three Westerners in the twentieth century can serve to remind us of how varied foreign responses to India can be:

A British policeman, in *A Passage to India*, says to a compatriot, "Read any of the Mutiny records; which, rather than the *Bhagavad Gītā*, should be your Bible in this country. Though I'm not sure that the one and the other are not closely connected." Forster, p. 169. (Is not Hegel's instructive account of Hinduism in this spirit?)

Winston Churchill reports that upon arriving in Bombay Harbor, he "pulled up the curtain on what might well have been a different planet." And he could add, "One voyage to India is enough; the others are merely repletion." *My Early Life: A Roving Commission* (New York: Charles Scribner's Sons, 1930), pp. 101, 122. (Compare N. G. Jog, *Churchill's Blind-Spot: India* [Bombay: New Book Co., 1944], especially chap. XXII, "Churchill and Gandhi"; Nehru, p. 353f.)

And a scholar who has devoted a long career to the study of India can prophesy, "Hindu civilization will, we believe, retain its continuity. *The Bhagavad Gītā* will not cease to inspire men of action, and the *Upanishads* men of thought. The charm and graciousness of the Indian way of life will continue, however much affected it may be by the labour-saving devices of the West. People will still love the tales of the heroes of the *Mahābhārata* and the *Ramayana*. . . . The quiet and gentle happiness which has at all times pervaded Indian life where oppression, disease and poverty have not overclouded it will surely not vanish before the more hectic ways of the West." Basham, p. 484.

NOTE TO THE READER

Again this year, the *Syntopicon* will prove a very useful guide to passages in the *Great Books* that bear on matters discussed by our contributors and on those contained in the "Additions to the Great Books Library."

In connection with Mr. Spender's essay, consult Chapter 69 of the *Syntopicon*, which is devoted to poetry. See in particular the passages listed in the first topic concerning the nature of poetry; also those at 5*b* on poetry as contrasted with philosophy and history and the praise and dispraise of poets; also at 7*c*, on thought and diction as elements of poetry; and those too at 8*b*, on critical standards and the measure of stylistic excellence. In addition, consult the passages listed in Chapter 81, RHETORIC, under Topic 2*b*, where style is further discussed. Mr. Spender makes mention in his essay of Shelley's "Defense of Poetry." This will be found in *Gateway to the Great Books,* Volume 5, as will Matthew Arnold's "The Study of Poetry."

Dr. Puck's discussion is of a sort hardly contemplated by the authors of the *Great Books*. His subject is to some extent evident, however, in the passages in Chapter 2, ANIMAL, under Topic 3*a*, which is devoted to the physical elements of the animal body; under Topic 10, where genetic factors are considered with respect to heredity and environment; and at Topic 11*b*, which deals with the relation between animals and their environment. See also the passages listed in Chapter 55, MEDICINE, especially Topics 2*a*, 3*c*, 4, and 5*a*, which are concerned with the scientific foundations of medicine, the arts of diagnosis and symptomatic interpretation, the concept of health, and the nature of disease, respectively. Background for the procedures Dr. Puck discusses will be found in the chapter from Claude Bernard's *Introduction to Experimental Medicine,* in *GGB,* Volume 8.

The issues raised by the authors discussed under "Reconsiderations of Great Books" in this year's volume are extensively indexed in the *Syntopicon*. For example, concerning Rousseau, see Chapter 90, STATE, especially the passages at Topics 1*b* and *c*, 2*a*(3), 3*a–d*, and 5*a–c*, dealing with the general theory of the state, its relation to society, its origin, and its social structure. See also Chapter 14, CUSTOM AND CONVENTION, Topics 1 and 6*a* and *b;* also Chapter 26, FAMILY, Topics 2, 5*a–b*, and 7*a*, all of which are relevant; also Chapter 46, LAW, Topics 4*b*, *c*, *e*, and *f*, dealing with natural law; and Chapter 47, LIBERTY, Topics 1*b*, *c*, and *f*, which deal with the relation between liberty and natural freedom. Rousseau's essay called "A Lasting Peace through the Federation of Europe" will be found in *GGB,* Volume 7.

On Montaigne, or at least on the aspect of him discussed by Mr. Bird, see Chapter 29, GOD, especially Topics 2*b*, *c*, and *d*, dealing with questions of God's existence; Topics 3*a* and *c*, on man's relation to God; and Topic 6, which has to do with man's knowledge of God. Consult also the passages in Chapter 79, RELIGION, under Topic 1, dealing with faith as the foundation of religion, and at 6*b*, where passages in defense of faith can be found. Readers may also wish to read the essay by Emerson called "Montaigne; or, the Skeptic," in *GGB,* Volume 10, and the discussion of the same author by Sainte-Beuve in *GGB,* Volume 5.

Concerning Thucydides, see passages at Chapter 98, WAR AND PEACE, Topic 4*a*, dealing with the causes of war; Topics 6*a* and *b*, on war as political means; Topics 7 and 9, on the inevitability and the folly of war, respectively; and Topic 10*g*, having to do with the making of truces or alliances. See also Chapter 16, DEMOCRACY, Topic 2*b*, on the incompetence of the people and the need for leadership, and Topic 7b, the dangers of imperialism and the treatment of dependencies; also Chapter 30, GOOD AND EVIL, Topic 3a, on human nature and its determination of the good, and Topic 6a, where passages on the relation between knowing what is good and doing it are listed. Readers who own *GGB* may also wish to read the selection from Clausewitz's *On War,* in Volume 7; possibly also Victor Hugo, "The Battle with the Cannon," from *'Ninety-Three,* in *GGB,* Volume 2; and certainly Abraham Lincoln's speeches in *GGB,* Volume 6.

With regard to this volume's "Special Features," see as follows: On Newton, Chapter 5, ASTRONOMY, Topics 2a and 2c, dealing with methods, especially the relation of astronomy to mathematics; also 3b, on gravitation. See as well Chapter 52, MATHEMATICS, Topics 3a and 5b, on mathematical demonstration and on the mathematical structure of nature; also Chapter 54, MECHANICS, Topics 6d(1) and (2), on the concept of gravitation as force and as action-at-a-distance; also Chapter 83, SCIENCE, the passages at Topic 4e, on the adequacy of scientific theories. For an account of scientific discovery in experimental—as distinct from mathematical—science, see Eve Curie, "The Discovery of Radium," in *GGB,* Volume 8.

On computers, which of course are unknown to the authors of the *Great Books,* some readings may nevertheless be suggestive. See Chapter 51, MAN, Topics 1a and 1b, on man as an idea, and 2a, on the importance of self-consciousness; also Chapter 43, KNOWLEDGE, Topic 1, on the nature of knowledge, and Topic 6b(2), on memory as a kind of knowledge; also Chapter 56, MEMORY AND IMAGINATION, Topic 1a, the relation of memory and imagination to sense; also Chapter 58, MIND, Topic 2a, on the immateriality of mind; and Chapter 84, SENSE, Topic 1a, on the difference between sense and reason; also Topics 5a–c, dealing with the contributions of sense to different kinds of knowledge.

With reference to Professor Anastaplo's comments on the *Bhagavad Gītā,* see Chapter 29, GOD, Topic 1c, on the intervention of gods in human affairs; 3d, on human obedience to God; the various subheadings under Topic 5 dealing with the divine nature in relation to the world, and also the headings under Topic 6, having to do with man's knowledge of God. See as well Chapter 97, VIRTUE AND VICE, Topic 4e(2), on the criteria of good and evil in human acts; also 6a, on the relation between duty and virtue; Chapter 79, RELIGION, Topic 1b(1), on Revelation as a source of religious belief; and Chapter 98, WAR AND PEACE, Topic 10, on the military virtues.

These readings are also appropriate to the *Gītā* itself among the "Additions to the Great Books Library." With respect to Royce's essays, see, in connection with "The Rediscovery of the Inner Life," Chapter 58, MIND, Topic 1a and its subheads dealing with mind as distinct from sense or imagination; also Topics 1d(1) and (2), on the origin and relation of ideas; also 9b, on the relation of mind to will, desire, and emotion. See as well Chapter 84, SENSE, Topic 1d, on sense-perception as the mind's primary function, and Topics 5a–c, on the contribution of the sense to philosophical and scientific knowledge. Also, in *GGB,* the writings by William James and Walter Pater in Volume 10 are relevant, as is the selection from John Stuart Mill's *Autobiography* in Volume 6.

Finally, in connection with Lessing's *Laocoon,* see Chapter 4, ART, Topic 7b, on the judgment of artistic excellence, and Chapter 69, POETRY, Topic 1, on the nature of poetry and its difference from other arts; and also Topic 6a, dealing with poetry's expression of emotion.

PART FOUR

Additions
to the
Great Books Library

The Bhagavad Gītā

Editor's Introduction

The *Bhagavad Gītā*, or "Lord's Song," which dates from the first or second century and consists of some 700 Sanskrit verses divided into eighteen chapters, is one of the Hindu scriptures—possibly the most important and certainly the best known and best loved among them. It derives from the *Upanishads*—mystical reflections written perhaps a millennium before upon the still earlier *Vedas,* or sacred hymns and verses, which were composed between 1500 and 1200 B.C.—but, unlike those works, it depicts an action, or at least a dramatic dialogue, and in fact it is part (probably a later, interpolated part) of the *Mahābhārata,* or "Great Epic of the Bharata Dynasty," which holds in Sanskrit culture the place that the *Iliad* and the *Odyssey* do in the West. The *Mahābhārata* is a very long poem—seven times longer than the *Iliad* and *Odyssey* combined—which recounts the struggle of family cousins for control of the family kingdom, a competition culminating in a great war in which all the dynasties and tribes of India take part. The story is a complicated one that grows incomprehensible to Western minds if summarized at too great length, though its relevant aspects are noted by George Anastaplo elsewhere in this volume. Sufficient here to point out that the ultimately triumphant branch of the family has emblematic importance, comprehending the basic principles of life; that their antagonists are likewise emblematic of the demonic powers of darkness; and that the conflict between them is in some sense a struggle between good and evil for dominance of the world.

Probably every educated Indian knows the *Gītā* (the *g* in Sanskrit is always hard), which forms part of Book VI of the *Mahābhārata,* and can recite some of it. Gandhi, who regarded it as his "spiritual dictionary," heard it first when he was about fifteen, read aloud on holy days in the province of Gujarāt, where he was born. He was not so much taken by it then as later, and not so much by its acceptance of war (which must have been unappealing to a believer in *satyāgraha,* or non-violence) as by its direction to *aparigraha* (non-possession) with respect to worldly possessions, and by the further principle of equability in the face of both pleasure and pain, of triumph as well as defeat, which it celebrates.

For Western readers, the interest of the *Gītā* is likely to be rather in its human than in its doctrinal implications. Not that there is anything especially Western in that kind of appeal. Most of the great extant poems and stories of mythical or allegoric importance in every culture have a distinctly human element to them. Those that lack it, or in which it is obscured by other elements, as is the case with the Early English *Vision of Piers Plowman,* are now impossible to read, while poets who have neglected this dimension of their work, or have been unsuccessful as both Virgil and Milton were in rendering it, have produced relatively inferior works—inferior, that is to say, as compared with the poems of Homer and Dante and Chaucer, which do not require schools to keep them alive. Thus, it is of interest that the dialogue between Arjuna and his charioteer in the *Gītā* stems from familiar human feelings on the part of the former, while the latter acts in many ways as the teacher that every student has experienced. So also is it interesting that in the *Mahābhārata* the troubles of the "good" cousins, Arjuna's faction, have been brought upon themselves by their king's addiction to gambling, whereby he bet the family fortunes and lost, condemning them to exile. And other portions of the story have apparently universal significance, since at any rate we find them retold, or borrowed from some other source, by Euripides, Shakespeare, and the Sanskrit poet Kālidāsa, who derived from the tale the story of his greatest work, *Śakuntalā.*

The *Bhagavad Gītā* has been translated often into English, as into other languages. This version is the work of Eliot Deutsch, of the University of Hawaii, at Manoa, who designed it for Western students of philosophy and religion when he discovered that no rendering of it for such readers was available. Such a translation seemed an appropriate one to offer with the discussion of the *Gītā* by Professor Anastaplo in this issue of *The Great Ideas Today.* Professor Deutsch, who kindly allowed us to dispense with most of his notes, was good enough also to look over what was left when this was done, so as to save us from errors or omissions we should be sorry to have made. Professor Anastaplo, too, has perforce had to school himself in the text on the way to writing his own commentary on it and has also generously helped us in our preparations. Our chief editorial contribution is that of a glossary of names and terms at the end of the poem, which readers, we hope, will find useful.

The Bhagavad Gītā[1]

Chapter I

Dhritarāshta said:

1. What did the sons of Pāndu and my men do, O Sanjaya, when, eager to fight, they gathered together on the field of righteousness, the Kuru field?[2]

Sanjaya said:

2. When seeing the army of the Pāndavas drawn up in battle array, Duryodhana the prince approached his teacher [Drona] and spoke these words:

3. Behold, O teacher, this mighty army of the sons of Pāndu arrayed by thy skillful pupil, the son of Drupada.

4. Here are heroes, great archers, in battle they are equal to Arjuna and Bhīma— Yuyudhāna and Virāta and Drupada of the great chariot;

5. Dhrishtaketu, Cekitāna and the valiant King of Kāshi [Benares], also Purijit, Kuntibhoja and Shaibya, the best of men;

6. Yudhāmanyu the valiant and Uttamaujas the brave, the son of Subhadrā and the sons of Draupadī, all great warriors indeed.

7. Know also, O best of the twice-born,[3] the leaders of my army. I name those that are most distinguished for thy recognition.

8. Thyself [Drona] and Bhīshma and Karna and Kripa, the victorious in battle; Asvatthāman and Vikarna and also the son of Somadatta.

9. And many other heroes who are willing to risk their lives for my sake. Armed with various weapons, they are all skilled in war.

10. Although this army of ours seems insufficient, it is protected by Bhīshma; while their army, which seems sufficient, is protected by Bhīma.

11. Therefore in all fronts, stationed in your respective ranks, guard ye Bhīshma above all.

12. The aged [oldest] grandson of the Kurus [Bhīshma], bringing joy to him [Duryodhana], blew his conch shell and roared a lion's roar on high.

13. Then conches and kettledrums, cymbals and drums and horns suddenly were struck and the sound was tumultuous.

14. Then stationed in their great chariot, which was yoked to white horses, Mādhava [Krishna] and the son of Pāndu [Arjuna] blew their wondrous conch shells.

15. Krishna blew Pāñcajanya and Arjuna [blew] Devadatta, and, Bhīma, of terrible deeds, blew his mighty conch Paundra.

16. The King Yudhishthira, the son of Kuntī, [blew] Anantavijaya, and Nakula and Sahadeva [blew] Sughosha and Manipushpaka.

17. And the King of Kāshi, the excellent archer; Shikandim, the great warrior; Dhrishtadyumna and Virāta and the unconquered Sātyaki;

18. Drupada and the sons of Drupadī, O Lord of the earth, and the strong-armed son of Subhadrā, on all sides blew their respective conches.

19. The tumultuous noise, resounding through earth and sky, rent the hearts of the sons of Dhritarāshtra.

20. Then Arjuna, who bore the crest of the god Hanumān, seeing the sons of Dhritarāshtra standing arrayed, as the discharge of weapons began, took up his bow,

21. And to Hrishīkesha [Krishna], then, O Lord of earth, he spoke these words: Stop my chariot, O immovable one, between the two armies,

22. That I may behold these men standing eager for battle, with whom I must fight in this strife of war;

23. And see those who are assembled here, ready to fight, and who are desirous of pleasing in battle the evil-minded son of Dhritarāshtra.

24. Thus addressed by Gudākesha [Arjuna], Hrishīkesha [Krishna], O Bhārata, placed that excellent chariot between the two armies.

25. And in front of Bhīshma and Drona and all the kings, he said: Behold O Pārtha [Arjuna] these assembled Kurus.

26. Arjuna saw standing there fathers and grandfathers, teachers, uncles, brothers, sons and grandsons, and also companions;

27. And fathers-in-law and friends in both the armies. Seeing all these kinsmen thus arrayed, the son of Kuntī [Arjuna],

28. Filled with the utmost compassion, sorrowfully spoke: Seeing my own kins-men, O Krishna, arrayed and wishing to fight,

29. My limbs collapse, my mouth dries up, there is trembling in my body and my hair stands on end;

30. [The bow] Gāndīva slips from my hand and my skin also is burning; I am not able to stand still, my mind is whirling.

31. And I see evil portents, O Keshava [Krishna], and I foresee no good in slaying my own kinsmen in the fight.

32. I do not desire victory, O Krishna, nor kingdom, nor pleasure. Of what use is kingdom to us, O Govinda [Krishna], of what use pleasure or life?

33. Those for whose sake we desire kingdom, pleasures and happiness, they are arrayed here in battle, having renounced their lives and riches.

34. Teachers, fathers, sons, and also grandfathers; uncles, fathers-in-law, grandsons, brothers-in-law and [other] kins-men:

35. These I do not wish to kill, though they kill me, O Madhusūdana [Krishna]; even for the kingdom of the three worlds; how [much less] then for the sake of the earth!

36. What pleasure can be ours, O Janārdana [Krishna] in slaying the sons of Dhritarāshtra? Only evil would attach to us if we kill these felons.

37. Therefore we should not slay the sons of Dhritarāshtra, our kinsmen. How could we be happy killing our own people, O Mādhava?

38. Even if they, whose minds are destroyed by greed, do not see the sin

caused by the destruction of a family and the crime incurred in the injury to a friend;

39. Why should we not have the wisdom to turn back from this sin, we who see the evil in the destruction of the family, O Janārdana [Krishna]?

40. In the ruin of a family, its immemorial laws perish; and when the laws perish, the whole family is overcome by lawlessness.

41. And when lawlessness prevails, O Krishna, the women of the family are corrupted, and when women are corrupted, O Vārshneya, a mixture of caste arises.[4]

42. And this confusion brings the family itself to hell and those who have destroyed it; for their ancestors fall, deprived of their offerings of rice and water.

43. By the sins of those who destroy a family and create a mixture of caste, the eternal laws of the caste and the family are destroyed.

44. The men of the families whose laws are destroyed, O Janārdana, assuredly will dwell in hell; so we have heard.

45. Alas, what a great sin we resolved to commit in undertaking to kill our own people through our greed for the pleasures of kingdom.

46. It would be better for me if the sons of Dhritarāshtra, with weapons in hand, should slay me, unresisting and unarmed, in the battle.

47. Having spoken thus on the battlefield, Arjuna cast away his bow and arrow and sank down on the seat of his chariot, his spirit overcome by grief.

★

In the famous Upanishad *of the* Bhagavad-gītā, *this is the first chapter, entitled "The Yoga of Arjuna's Depression."*

Chapter II

Sanjaya said:
1. To him who was thus overcome by pity, whose troubled eyes were filled with tears, and who was despondent, Madhusūdana [Krishna] spoke these words:

The Blessed Lord said:
2. Whence hath this despair come to thee in this [time of] crisis? It is unbecoming to an *āryan,* it does not lead to heaven, it is disgraceful, O Arjuna.

3. Yield not to this impotence, O Pārtha [Arjuna], for it is not proper of thee. Abandon this petty weakness of heart and arise, O oppressor of the foe.

Arjuna said:
4. How, O Madhusūdana [Krishna], shall I attack, with arrows in battle, Bhīshma and Drona who are worthy of worship, O slayer of enemies?

5. It would be better [to live] in this world by begging than to slay these noble teachers. For by slaying these teachers who desire wealth, I would enjoy only blood-smeared delights.

6. We do not know which is better for us, whether we should conquer them or they should conquer us. There standing before us are the sons of Dhritarāshtra; if we were to slay them, we should not wish to live.

7. My being is afflicted with the defect of pity; my mind is confused about my *dharma.* I ask Thee: tell me decisively

which is better. I am Thy pupil; teach me, who seeks refuge in Thee.

8. I do not see what can drive away this sorrow which parches my senses even if I obtained a rich and unrivaled kingdom on earth, or even the sovereignty of the gods.

Sanjaya said:
9. The mighty Gudākesha [Arjuna], having thus addressed Hrishīkesha [Krishna], said to Govinda [Krishna], "I will not fight," and fell silent.

10. Then, O Bhārata [Dhritarāshtra], Hrishīkesha [Krishna], smiling as it were, spoke these words to him who was despondent in the midst of the two armies.

The Blessed Lord said:
11. Thou grievest for those thou shouldst not grieve for, and yet thou speakest words that sound like wisdom. Wise men do not mourn for the dead or for the living.

12. Never was there a time when I did not exist, nor thou, nor these rulers of men; nor will there ever be a time hereafter when we shall all cease to be.

13. As the soul in this body passes through childhood, youth and old age, so [after departure from this body] it passes on to another body. The sage is not bewildered by this.

14. Contacts with the objects of the senses, O son of Kuntī [Arjuna], give rise to cold and heat, pleasure and pain. They come and go, they are impermanent; endure them, O Bhārata [Arjuna].

15. The man who is not troubled by these [contacts], O bull among men [Arjuna], who treats alike pleasure and pain, who is wise; he is fit for immortality.

16. Of non-being there is no coming to be; of being there is no ceasing to be. The truth about both is seen by the seers of truth.

17. Know that by which all this is pervaded is indestructible, and that no one can cause the destruction of this immutable being.

18. It is said that [only] these bodies of the eternal embodied [soul], which is indestructible and incomprehensible, are perishable. Therefore fight, O Bhārata [Arjuna]!

19. He who thinks that this [soul] is a slayer, and he who thinks that this [soul] is slain; both of them are ignorant. This [soul] neither slays nor is slain.

20. It is never born, nor does it die, nor having once been, will it again cease to be. It is unborn, eternal and everlasting. This primeval one is not slain when the body is slain.

21. He who knows that it [the soul] is indestructible and eternal, unborn and unchanging, how can that man slay, O Pārtha [Arjuna], or cause another to slay?

22. Just as a man casts off wornout clothes and takes on others that are new, so the embodied soul casts off worn-out bodies and takes on others that are new.

23. Weapons do not cut it, nor does fire burn it; waters do not make it wet, nor does wind make it dry.

24. It is uncleavable, it cannot be burnt, it can be neither wetted nor dried. It is eternal, omnipresent, unchanging and immovable. It is everlasting.

25. It is called unmanifest, unthinkable and immutable; therefore, knowing it as such, thou shouldst not grieve.

26. Even if thou thinkest that it is constantly born and constantly dies, even then, O mighty-armed [Arjuna], thou shouldst not grieve.

27. For death is certain for one that has been born, and birth is certain for one that has died. Therefore for what is unavoidable, thou shouldst not grieve.

28. All beings are unmanifest in their beginnings, they are manifest in their middles and are unmanifest again in their ends, O Bhārata [Arjuna]. What [reason] is there, then, for lamentation?

29. One sees it as marvelous, another also speaks of it as marvelous, another hears of it as marvelous, but even after having heard [of it], no one whatsoever knows it.

30. The soul in the body of everyone, O Bhārata [Arjuna], is eternal and indestructible. Therefore thou shouldst not mourn for any creature.

31. Further, having regard for thine own *dharma,* thou shouldst not tremble. There exists no greater good for a Kshatriya than a battle required by duty.

32. Happy are the Kshatriyas, O Pārtha [Arjuna], for whom such a battle comes by mere chance, opening the door to heaven.

33. But if thou wilt not wage this righteous battle, then having thrown away thy duty and glory, thou wilt incur sin.

34. Besides, men will forever speak of thy dishonor, and for one who has been honored, dishonor is worse than death.

35. The great warriors will think that thou hast abstained from battle because of fear and they who highly esteemed thee will think lightly of thee.

36. Many words which ought not to be spoken will be spoken by thy enemies, scorning thy strength. What is more painful than that?

37. If thou art slain, thou wilt obtain heaven, or if thou conquer, thou wilt enjoy the earth. Therefore arise, O son of Kuntī, resolved to fight.

38. Regarding alike pleasure and pain, gain and loss, victory and defeat, prepare thyself for battle. Thus thou wilt not incur sin.

39. This is the wisdom of the *sānkhya* which has been declared to thee, O Pārtha. Listen now to the wisdom of the yoga; when disciplined with it, thou shalt cast away the bondage of *karma.*

40. In this path there is no loss of effort and no harm occurs. Even a little of this *dharma* protects one from great fear.

41. The resolute understanding is clearly directed in this, O joy of the Kurus, but the thoughts of the irresolute are many-branched and endless.

42/43. The ignorant, O Pārtha, whose selves consist of desire, who are intent [only] on reaching heaven, and who say there is nothing else, rejoice in the letter of the Veda and utter those flowery words which give rise to many ritual performances for the attainment of enjoyment and power, but which result in rebirth as the fruit of these actions.

44. The intelligence of those [who are intended to have] resolute understanding [but] who are attached to enjoyment and power, and whose minds are carried away by these [words], is not established in concentration.

45. The Vedas deal with the activity of the three *gunas;* but be thou, O Arjuna,

free from the three *gunas* and from the pairs of opposites. Be thou constantly fixed in *sattva*: not caring for the possession of property, be self-possessed.

46. As much use as there is for a pond when there is everywhere a flood, so much is there in all the Vedas for a Brahmin who understands.

47. In action only hast thou a right and never in its fruits. Let not thy motive be the fruits of action; nor let thy attachment be to inaction.

48. Fixed in yoga, O winner of wealth, perform actions, abandoning attachment and remaining even-minded in success and failure; for serenity of mind is called yoga.

49. [Mere] action is far inferior to the discipline of intelligence, O winner of wealth. Seek refuge in intelligence; pitiful are those whose motive is the fruit [of action].

50. One who has disciplined his intelligence leaves behind in this world both good and evil deeds. Therefore strive for yoga, for yoga is skill in action.

51. Having disciplined their intelligence and having abandoned the fruit born of their action, the wise are freed from the bondage of birth and attain the state that is free from sorrow.

52. When thy intelligence shall cross the tangle of delusion, then thou shalt become indifferent to what shall be heard and to what has been heard [in the Veda].

53. When thy intelligence, which is now perplexed by the Vedic texts, shall stand immovable and be fixed in concentration, then shalt thou attain yoga.

Arjuna said:
54. What is the description of the man

of steady mind who is fixed in concentration, O Keshava [Krishna]? How might the man of steady mind speak, how might he sit, how might he walk?

The Blessed Lord said:
55. When a man abandons all the desires of his mind, O Pārtha [Arjuna], and is satisfied in his self by the self alone, then he is called a man of steady mind.

56. He whose mind is not troubled in sorrow, and has no desire in pleasure, his passion, fear and anger departed, he is called a steady-minded sage.

57. He who is not attached to anything, who neither delights nor is upset when he obtains good or evil, his mind is firmly established [in wisdom].

58. And when he completely withdraws his senses from the objects of sense, as a tortoise draws in his limbs, his mind is firmly established.

59. The objects of sense, but not the taste for them, fall away from the embodied soul who abstains from food. Even the taste falls away from him when the Supreme is seen.

60. The excited senses of even a wise man who strives [for perfection], O son of Kuntī, violently carry away his mind.

61. Having restrained them all, he should sit disciplined, intent on Me; for his mind is firmly set whose senses are under control.

62. When a man dwells on the objects of sense, attachment to them is produced. From attachment desire arises, and from desire anger comes.

63. From anger arises delusion, from delusion loss of memory, from loss of memory the destruction of intelligence, and

from the destruction of intelligence, he perishes.

64. But he who moves among the objects of sense, with the senses under control and is free from desire and aversion, he who is thus self-controlled attains serenity of mind.

65. And in that serenity, the destruction of all pain is produced for him. The intelligence of the man of tranquil mind is quickly established.

66. For the uncontrolled, there is no intelligence, nor for the uncontrolled is there concentration; and without concentration there is no peace, and for the unpeaceful, how can there be happiness?

67. When the mind hastens after the roving senses, it carries along the understanding, as wind carries away a ship on the waters.

68. Therefore, O mighty-armed [Arjuna], his intelligence is firmly established whose senses are completely withdrawn from the objects of sense.

69. What is night for all beings is the time of waking for the man of self-control, and when all beings are awake, that is night for the sage who sees.

70. He attains peace into whom all desires flow as waters into the sea which, though ever being filled, is ever motionless; and not he who lusts after desires.

71. He who abandons all desires and acts without longing, without self-interest or egotism, he attains peace.

72. This is the eternal state, O Pārtha [Arjuna]; having attained it, one is no longer confused. Fixed in it even at the time of death, one attains to the bliss of Brahman.[5]

*

This is the second chapter, entitled "The Yoga of Knowledge."

Chapter III

Arjuna said:

1. If it be thought by Thee, O Janārdana [Krishna], that [the path of] knowledge is superior to [the path of] action, then why dost Thou urge me, O Keshava [Krishna], in this terrible deed?

2. With these apparently equivocal words, Thou confusest my understanding. Therefore tell me decisively the one path by which I may attain to the good.

The Blessed Lord said:

3. In this world, O blameless one, a twofold path has been taught before by Me; the path of knowledge [*jñāna yoga*] for men of discrimination [*sānkhyas*] and the path of works [*karma yoga*] for men of action [*yogins*].

4. Not by abstention from action does a man gain freedom, and not by mere renunciation does he attain perfection.

5. No one can remain, even for a moment, without performing some action. Everyone is made to act helplessly by the *gunas* born of *prakriti*.

6. He who controls his organs of action,[6] but dwells in his mind on the objects of the senses; that man is deluded and is called a hypocrite.

7. But he who controls the senses by the mind, O Arjuna, and, without attachment, engages the organs of action in *karma yoga*, he excels.

8. Perform thy allotted work, for action is superior to inaction; even the mainte-

nance of thy body cannot be accomplished without action.

9. This world is in bondage to *karma,* unless *karma* is performed for the sake of sacrifice. For the sake of that, O son of Kunti, perform thy action free from attachment.

10. In ancient times Prajāpati created men together with sacrifice and said: By this shall ye procreate, let this be the granter of your desires.

11. By this nourish ye the gods and may the gods nourish thee; thus nourishing each other, ye shall attain to the highest good.

12. Nourished by sacrifice, the gods will give thee the enjoyments ye desire. He who enjoys what is given by them without giving to them in return is verily a thief.

13. The good men who eat the remains of the sacrifice [who share their food with others] are freed from all sins; but wicked men who cook for their own sake, verily they eat sin.

14. From food creatures come into being; from rain food is produced, from sacrifice comes rain, and sacrifice is born of action.

15. Know that [ritual] action arises from Brahman [the Veda], and that Brahman arises from the Imperishable. Therefore, Brahman, the all-pervading, is ever established in sacrifice.

16. He who does not follow here on earth the wheel thus set in motion is evil, O Pārtha; delighting in the senses, he lives in vain.

17. But the man whose pleasure is in the Self alone, who is pleased with the Self, who is content only in the Self, for him there is no work that needs to be done.

18. He has no interest in action done in this world, nor any with action not done. He is not dependent on all these creatures for any object [of his].

19. Therefore, always perform the work that has to be done without attachment, for man attains the Supreme by performing work without attachment.

20. Janaka and others attained to perfection only by action; thou shouldst perform action also with regard for the maintenance of the world.

21. Whatsoever the best man does, other men do too. Whatever standard he sets, that the world follows.

22. There is nothing in the three worlds, O Pārtha, to be done by Me, nor anything unobtained that needs to be obtained; yet I continue in action.

23. For if I, unwearied, were not always in action, O Pārtha, men everywhere would follow my path [example].

24. If I did not perform action, these worlds would be destroyed, and I should be the author of confusion and would destroy these people.

25. As the ignorant act with attachment to their work, O Bhārata, so the wise man should act [but] without attachment, desiring to maintain the order of the world.

26. Let no wise man unsettle the minds of the ignorant who are attached to action. Acting with discipline, he should make all action attractive.

27. All actions are performed by the *gunas* of *prakriti* alone. But he who is deluded by egoism thinks, "I am the doer."

28. He who knows the true essence of the separation [of the soul] from both the

gunas and action, O mighty-armed one, and that it is the *gunas* which act upon the *gunas,* he is not attached [to action].

29. Those who are deluded by the *gunas* of *prakriti* are attached to the action of the *gunas.* But the man who knows the whole should not unsettle the ignorant who know only a part.

30. Surrendering all actions to Me, with thy consciousness [fixed] on the supreme Self, being free from desire and selfishness, fight freed from thy sorrow.

31. They who constantly follow My doctrine, who are filled with faith and are uncomplaining, they too are freed from [the bondage of] actions.

32. But those who carp at my teaching and do not follow it, know these mindless ones, deluded in all knowledge, to be lost.

33. Even the wise man acts in conformity with his own nature. Beings follow nature. What will restraint accomplish?

34. Attraction and repulsion for the objects of sense are seated in the senses. Let no one come under the control of these two; they are his enemies.

35. Better one's own *dharma,* though imperfect, than another's well performed. Better death in [the fulfillment of] one's own law, for another's law is dangerous.

Arjuna said:
36. Then by what is a man impelled to [commit] sin against his will, as if compelled by force, O Vārshneya?

The Blessed Lord said:
37. It is desire, it is wrath, born of the *guna* of passion [*rajas*], all-devouring and very sinful. Know that this is the enemy here.

38. As fire is covered by smoke, as a mirror by dust, and as an embryo is enveloped by the womb, so this [knowledge] is covered by that [passion].

39. Knowledge is enveloped, O son of Kuntī, by this constant enemy of the knower, by this insatiable flame of desire.

40. The senses, the mind [*manas*], the understanding [*buddhi*], are said to be its basis. With these it bewilders the embodied soul, covering its knowledge.

41. Therefore, O best of the Bharatas, having in the beginning controlled thy senses, slay this evil destroyer of spiritual [*jñāna*] and practical [*vijñāna*] knowledge.

42. The senses, they say, are great; greater than the senses is the mind [*manas*]; greater than the mind is the reason [*buddhi*]; and greater than the reason is He.

43. Thus having known that which is greater than the reason, steadying the self by the self, slay the enemy, O mighty-armed one, [that has] the form of desire, and that is so hard to approach.

*

This is the third chapter, entitled "The Yoga of Action."

Chapter IV

The Blessed Lord said:
1. This imperishable yoga I proclaimed to Vivasvant; Vivasvant told it to Manu and Manu spoke it to Ikshvāku.

2. Thus received in regular succession, the royal sages knew it, till over a long passage of time this yoga was lost to the world, O oppressor of the foe.

3. This same ancient yoga is declared today by Me to thee, for thou art My

devotee and friend, and this is a supreme secret.

Arjuna said:

4. Later was Thy birth, earlier was the birth of Vivasvant. How may I understand this, that Thou didst declare it [to him] in the beginning?

The Blessed Lord said:

5. Many are My past lives and thine, O Arjuna; I know all of them but thou knowest them not, O oppressor of the foe.

6. Although unborn, although My self is imperishable, although I am Lord of all beings, yet establishing Myself in My own [material] nature, I come into being by My own mysterious power [*māyā*].

7. Whenever there is a decay of righteousness and a rising up of unrighteousness, O Bhārata, I send forth Myself.

8. For the preservation of good, for the destruction of evil, for the establishment of righteousness, I come into being in age after age.

9. He who thus truly knows My divine birth and actions is not born again on leaving the body but comes to Me, O Arjuna.

10. Freed from passion, fear and anger, filled with Me, taking refuge in Me, many who are purified by the austerity of wisdom [*jñāna*] have come to My state of being.

11. In whatever way men approach Me, I am gracious to them; men everywhere, O Pārtha, follow My path.

12. Those who desire the success which comes from ritual actions sacrifice to the gods in this world; for in the world of men success comes quickly from such acts.

13. The four-caste system was created by Me by the division of *guna* and *karma*. Although I am the maker of this, know Me as the imperishable nondoer.

14. Actions do not stain Me; for I have no longing for their fruits. He who knows Me thus is not bound by actions.

15. The ancients who were desirous of liberation and who knew this did their work. Therefore perform action as the ancients did long ago.

16. What is action? What is inaction? About this even the wise are confused. Therefore I will declare of thee what action is, knowing which thou shalt be freed from evil.

17. One must understand [the nature of] action, and one must understand [the nature of] wrong action, and one must understand [the nature of] inaction: hard to understand is the way of action.

18. He who sees inaction in action and action in inaction, he is wise among men; he does all actions harmoniously.

19. He whose undertakings are all free from desire and will, whose actions are burned up in the fire of knowledge, him the wise call learned.

20. Having abandoned attachment to the fruits of action, always content and independent, he does nothing even though he is engaged in action.

21. Having no desires, with his mind and self controlled, abandoning all possessions, performing action with the body alone, he commits no sin.

22. He who is content with what comes by chance, who has passed beyond the pairs [of opposites], who is free from

jealousy and is indifferent to success and failure, even when he is acting he is not bound.

23. The action of a man who is rid of attachment, who is liberated, whose mind is firmly established in knowledge, who performs action as a sacrifice, is completely dissolved.

24. The offering is Brahman, Brahman is the oblation; it is poured by Brahman in the [ritual] fire of Brahman. Brahman is to be attained by him who concentrates his actions upon Brahman.

25. Some yogins offer sacrifice to the deities; others offer sacrifices by the sacrifice itself in the fire of Brahman.

26. Others offer hearing and the other senses into the fires of restraint; others offer sound and the other objects of sense into the fires of the senses.

27. Others offer up all the actions of the senses and the actions of the vital breath into the fire of the yoga of self-restraint that is kindled by knowledge.

28. Others offer as sacrifice their wealth or their austerities or their yogic exercises, while still others of restrained minds and difficult vows offer their study [of the Veda] and their knowledge [of it].

29. Others who are intent upon breath control, having restrained the paths of the outgoing and incoming breath, offer up the outgoing breath into the incoming breath and the incoming breath into the outgoing breath.

30. Others, restricting their food, offer as sacrifice their life breaths into life breaths. All these are knowers of sacrifice, and their sins are destroyed by sacrifice.

31. Those who eat the life-giving remains of the sacrifice go to the eternal Brahman. Not even this world is for the non-sacrificer, how then the next world, O best of the Kurus?

32. Thus manifold sacrifices are spread out in the face of Brahman. Know that they all are born of action. Knowing this thou shalt be freed.

33. The sacrifice of knowledge is better than the sacrifice of material things, O scorcher of the foe. All action, without exception, is completely terminated in knowledge, O Pārtha.

34. Learn it by obeisance [to those who know], by questioning and by serving them. The wise, the seers of truth, will teach thee knowledge.

35. Knowing this thou shalt not fall again into delusion, O Pāndava; for by this thou shalt see all creatures without exception in the Self and in Me.

36. Even if thou art among sinners the worst sinner of all, thou shalt cross over all evil by the boat of knowledge alone.

37. As the fire which is kindled makes its fuel into ashes, O Arjuna, so the fire of knowledge makes all actions into ashes.

38. There is no purifier in this world equal to wisdom. He who is perfected in yoga finds it in the self in the course of time.

39. He who has faith, who is intent on it [knowledge] and who has controlled his senses, obtains knowledge and having obtained it, goes quickly to the highest peace.

40. But the ignorant man who is without faith and of a doubting nature perishes.

For the doubting self, there is not this world, nor the next, nor happiness.

41. Actions do not bind him who has renounced actions in yoga, who has cast away doubt by knowledge, who possesses himself, O winner of wealth.

42. Therefore having cut away, with the sword of knowledge, this doubt in thy heart that is born of ignorance, resort to yoga and arise, O Bhārata.

*

This is the fourth chapter, entitled "The Yoga of Knowledge."

Chapter V

Arjuna said:
1. Thou praisest renunciation of actions, O Krishna, and again [karma] yoga. Tell me definitely which one of these is the better.

The Blessed Lord said:
2. Renunciation [of works] and the unselfish performance of works [karma yoga] both lead to the highest happiness. But of these two the unselfish performance of works is better than the renunciation of works.

3. He who neither hates nor desires should be known as the eternal renouncer; free from the pairs of opposites, O mighty-armed one, he is easily released from bondage.

4. Children, not the wise, speak of renunciation [sānkhya] and [karma] yoga as separate; for he who is well established in one obtains the fruit of both.

5. That place which is obtained by the sānkhyas is also gained by the yogins. He who sees that sānkhya and yoga are one, he truly sees.

6. Renunciation, O mighty-armed one, is difficult to attain without yoga. The sage who is disciplined in yoga soon goes to Brahman.

7. He who is disciplined in yoga and is pure in soul, who is ruler of his self, who has conquered his senses, whose self becomes the Self of all beings, he is not affected by acting.

8. The disciplined one who knows the truth thinks "I am doing nothing at all." In seeing, hearing, touching, smelling, tasting, walking, sleeping, breathing,

9. In speaking, giving, grasping, opening and closing the eyes, he maintains that only the senses are active among the objects of the senses.

10. He who acts, having placed his actions in Brahman and having abandoned attachment, is not affected by sin, just as a lotus leaf is not affected by water.

11. Yogins perform action only with the body, the mind, the intellect or the senses, without attachment, for self-purification.

12. The disciplined man, having abandoned the fruit of action, obtains enduring peace; the undisciplined man, impelled by desire, is attached to the fruit and is bound.

13. Renouncing all actions of the mind, the sovereign embodied [soul] sits happily in the city of nine gates, neither acting nor causing action.[7]

14. The sovereign Self does not create agency [for the people] of the world, nor actions, nor the conjunction of actions with their fruit. But nature itself operates there.

15. The all-pervading Spirit does not take on the sin or good work of anyone. Knowledge is enveloped by ignorance; by this creatures are bewildered.

16. But for those in whom ignorance is destroyed by knowledge, for them knowledge illumines the highest Self like the sun.

17. Thinking on that [highest Self], their self fixed on that, established in that, devoted to that, they go to wherefrom there is no returning, their sins destroyed by knowledge.

18. Sages look equally on a Brahmin endowed with knowledge and breeding, or on a cow, an elephant, and even a dog and an outcaste.

19. Even here on earth, creation is conquered by those whose minds are established in equality. Brahman is spotless and is the same to all. Therefore they are established in Brahman.

20. One should not rejoice when obtaining the pleasant, nor be agitated when obtaining the unpleasant. Unbewildered, with firm intelligence, the knower of Brahman is established in Brahman.

21. The self who is unattached to external contacts finds happiness in the Self. Being joined by yoga to Brahman, he attains imperishable happiness.

22. The enjoyments which are born of contacts [with objects] are only sources of sorrow. These have a beginning and end, O son of Kuntī; the wise man does not rejoice in them.

23. He who is able to endure here on earth, even before he is liberated from the body, the force that springs from desire and anger, he is disciplined, he is the happy man.

24. He who is happy within, whose joy is within and whose light is within; that yogin becomes Brahman and attains to the bliss of Brahman.

25. The seers whose sins are destroyed, whose dualities [doubts] are dispelled, whose selves are disciplined and who rejoice in the welfare of all beings, attain to the bliss of Brahman.

26. To these holy men who have destroyed desire and anger, who have controlled their minds, who know the Self, the bliss of Brahman is near.

27. Having excluded external contacts and having fixed the sight between the eyebrows, having made equal the incoming and outgoing breaths moving within the nostrils;

28. Having controlled the senses, mind and intelligence, the sage who has liberation as his goal, who has cast away desire, fear and anger, is freed forever.

29. Knowing Me as the enjoyer of sacrifices and austerities, as the great lord of all worlds, as the friend of all creatures, he attains peace.

*

This is the fifth chapter, entitled "The Yoga of the Renunciation of Action."

Chapter VI

The Blessed Lord said:
1. He who does the action that should be done without concern for its fruits, he is a *sannyāsin,* he is a yogin, and not he who does not light the sacred fires and performs no rites.

2. Know that what they call renunciation is yoga, O Pāndava, for no one becomes a yogin who has not renounced selfish desire.

3. For the sage who is desirous of ascending to yoga, action is called the means. For the sage who has ascended to yoga, serenity is called the means.

4. When one is not attached to the objects of sense or to actions, and has renounced all desires, then he is said to have attained yoga.

5. One should lift up the self by the self, one should not let the Self be degraded; for the Self alone is the friend of the self and the Self alone is the enemy of the self.

6. For him who has conquered his self by the self, his Self is a friend; but for him who has not conquered his self, the Self becomes hostile, like an enemy.

7. The highest Self of him who has conquered the self and is peaceful remains ever concentrated in heat and cold, pleasure and pain, in honor and dishonor.

8. That yogin who is satisfied with wisdom and understanding, who is unchanging and has subdued his senses, to whom a lump of clay, a rock and gold are the same is said to be disciplined.

9. He who is impartial to friend, companion and foe, to those who are remote and neutral, to those who are hateful, to relatives, to good and evil men, excels.

10. Let the yogin always concentrate on the Self, abiding alone in solitude, with mind and self controlled, without desires and possessions.

11. Having set in a clean place a firm seat for himself that is neither too high nor too low, made of Kusha grass, a deerskin and a cloth, one over the other;

12. Sitting there on the seat, making his mind one-pointed, controlling the activity of his mind and senses, let him practice yoga for the purification of the self.

13. Holding the body, head and neck erect and motionless, looking steadily at the tip of his nose, not looking in any direction,

14. With the self calmed and free from fear, firm in the vow of celibacy, having controlled the mind, let him sit harmonized, his thoughts on Me, absorbed in Me.

15. Thus always disciplining himself and with his mind controlled, the yogin attains to peace, the supreme bliss, that abides in Me.

16. Yoga is not for him who eats too much, or does not eat at all. It is not for him, O Arjuna, who sleeps too much or keeps too much awake.

17. For one who is moderate in food and amusement, restrained in the performance of his actions, whose sleep and waking are regulated, yoga destroys all pain.

18. When the controlled thought is fixed on the Self alone, then he who is free from all desires is said to be disciplined.

19. As a lamp in a windless place does not flicker, so the yogin of controlled thought, practicing yoga of the self.

20. That in which thought comes to rest, curbed by the practice of yoga; that in which seeing the Self, by the self, he is content in the Self;

21. That in which supreme happiness, which is beyond the senses, is grasped by intelligence; that wherein established, he knows this and does not fall away from the truth;

22. That on obtaining which, he thinks no other gain is greater; that wherein established, by no sorrow, however heavy, is he moved:

23. Let that disconnection from union with pain be known as yoga. This yoga

should be practiced with determination, with mind undismayed.

24. Abandoning, without exception, all the desires born of egoism, restraining all the senses on every side by the mind,

25. Let him come to rest, little by little, by intelligence held firmly; and fixing the mind on the Self, let him not think of anything else.

26. Whatsoever thing makes the fickle and unsteady mind wander, let him restrain it and lead it back to the control of the self alone.

27. This highest happiness comes to the yogin whose mind is peaceful, whose passions are subdued, who is sinless and has become one with Brahman.

28. The yogin who thus always disciplines his self and who is free from sin, easily attains the ultimate bliss of unity with Brahman.

29. He whose self is disciplined by yoga sees the Self abiding in all beings and all beings in the Self; he sees the same in all beings.

30. He who sees Me everywhere and sees all in Me, for him I am not lost and he is not lost for Me.

31. He who, established in oneness, worships Me abiding in all beings, exists in Me, no matter how otherwise he exists.

32. He who sees that which is pleasant or painful to others is the same for himself, O Arjuna, he is considered the highest yogin.

Arjuna said:
33. I see no firm foundation for this yoga which is declared by Thee to be [characterized by] equality, O Madhusūdana, because of [man's] restlessness.

34. For the mind is indeed restless. O Krishna; it is impetuous, strong and hard. I think the controlling of it is as difficult as controlling the wind.

The Blessed Lord said:
35. Undoubtedly, O mighty-armed one, the mind is restless and hard to restrain, but by practice and dispassion, O son of Kuntī, it can be controlled.

36. Yoga is hard to attain, I think, by one who is not self-controlled; but for one who is self-controlled and who strives, it is possible to attain through proper means.

Arjuna said:
37. He who is uncontrolled but possesses faith and whose mind wanders away from yoga, not having attained perfection in yoga, which way does he go, O Krishna?

38. Fallen from both, unstable, and bewildered in the path to Brahman, does he not perish like a rent cloud, O mighty-armed one?

39. Thou oughtest to dispel completely this doubt of mine, O Krishna, for no remover of this doubt, other than Thee, is to be found.

The Blessed Lord said:
40. O Pārtha, neither in this world nor the next is there any destruction of him, for no doer of the good, dear friend, comes to an evil end.

41. Having attained the world of the doers of right, and having dwelt there for many years, he who has fallen from yoga is born in the house of the pure and prosperous;

42. Or he may be born in the family of wise yogins; for such a birth as this is harder to attain in the world.

43. There he acquires the mental characteristics associated with his previous existence, and he strives from that point on to perfection, O joy of the Kurus.

44. By his former practice he is carried along helplessly. Even he who [merely] wishes to know of yoga goes beyond the rules of the Veda.

45. But the yogin who strives with perseverance, who is purified of all sins and is perfected through many lives, goes to the supreme goal.

46. The yogin is greater than the ascetic, he is thought to be greater than even the wise; the yogin is greater than men of ritual action; therefore, be a yogin, O Arjuna.

47. And of all yogins, the one who, full of faith, worships Me with his inner self abiding in Me, he is thought by Me to be the most disciplined.

*

This is the sixth chapter, entitled "The Yoga of Meditation."

Chapter VII

The Blessed Lord said:
1. Hear, O Pārtha, how, by attaching thy mind to Me, and by practicing yoga, with reliance upon Me, thou shalt know Me entirely, without doubt.

2. I will declare to thee in full this wisdom together with knowledge which, when known, nothing more in this world remains to be known.

3. Among thousands of men, perchance one strives for perfection, and of those who strive and are successful, perhaps one knows Me in essence.

4. This is My divided eightfold nature: earth, water, fire, wind, ether, mind, intellect, and self-consciousness.

5. This is My lower [nature]. Know My other higher nature, O mighty-armed one, which is the life-soul by which this world is supported.

6. Learn that all beings arise from this [higher and lower nature of Mine]. I am the origin of the whole world and also its dissolution.

7. Nothing exists higher than Me, O winner of wealth. All this [universe] is strung on Me like jewels on a string.

8. I am the taste in the waters, O son of Kuntī. I am the light in the moon and the sun; I am the sacred syllable [*Om*] in all the Vedas, the sound in ether and the manhood in men.

9. I am the pure fragrance in earth and the brilliance in fire; I am the life in all beings and the austerity in ascetics.

10. Know Me, O Pārtha, to be the eternal seed of all beings. I am the intellect of the intelligent, the splendor of the splendid.

11. I am the strength of the strong which is free from desire and passion. I am the desire in all beings which is not incompatible with *dharma*, O Lord of the Bharatas.

12. And of all beings that are—the harmonious [*sattvic*], the passionate [*rajasic*] and even the inert [*tamasic*]—know that these are from Me alone. But I am not in them, they are in Me.

13. Deluded by these states made up of the *gunas,* this whole world does not recognize Me who is higher than these and imperishable.

14. This is My divine *māyā* composed of the *gunas,* which is hard to pass beyond. Those who resort to Me alone cross over this *māyā.*

15. The evildoers who are deluded and low among men do not resort to Me. Their minds are deprived of wisdom by illusion and their nature is demoniac.

16. Fourfold are the virtuous who worship Me, O Arjuna: the afflicted, the wisdom seeker, the seeker for wealth, and the wise, O Lord of the Bharatas.

17. Of these the wise one, who is constantly disciplined and of single-minded devotion, is the best; extremely dear to him am I, and he is dear to Me.

18. All of these are noble, but the wise one I hold as My very self. For he, with disciplined self, resorts to Me alone as the highest goal.

19. At the end of many births, the man of wisdom approaches Me, thinking "Vāsudeva is all." Such a great self is difficult to find.

20. But those who are deprived of wisdom by their desires resort to other gods, having taken up various vows, constrained by their own nature.

21. But whatever form a devotee with faith wishes to worship, I make steady that faith of his.

22. Disciplined with that faith, he seeks to propitiate that god; and he obtains his desires, for those [the benefits] are decreed by Me.

23. But temporary is the fruit [obtained by] those that are of small intelligence. Those who worship the gods go to the gods; My devotees come to Me.

24. The foolish think of Me, the unmanifest, as having [only] come into manifestation; not knowing My higher nature which is immutable and supreme.

25. I am not revealed to all, being covered by My power of illusion. This world is deluded and does not recognize Me, the unborn and imperishable.

26. I know beings that are past, that are present and that are yet to be, O Arjuna, but no one knows Me.

27. All beings are born to confusion, O Bhārata, and are deluded by the dualities that originate from desire and hatred, O conqueror of the foe.

28. But those men of virtuous deeds whose sins are ended and who are freed from the delusion of opposites worship Me with steadfast resolve.

29. Those who strive for liberation from old age and death and have taken refuge in Me know Brahman entirely and the supreme Self and all action.

30. Those who know Me together with [My] material and divine domains and the highest sacrifice; they, of balanced mind, know Me even at the time of death.

This is the seventh chapter, entitled "The Yoga of Wisdom and Understanding."

Chapter VIII

Arjuna said:

1. What is that Brahman? What is the supreme Self and action, O best of beings?

What is said to be the material domain and what is declared to be the domain of the divine?

2. How and what is the domain of sacrifice here in this body, O Madhusūdana? How art Thou to be known at the time of death by men of self-control?

The Blessed Lord said:
3. Brahman is the indestructible, the supreme; the Self is called essential nature, and *karma* is the name of the creative power that causes beings to exist.

4. A perishable condition is the basis of all material things; the spirit [*purusha*] is the basis of divine elements, and I am the basis of all sacrifice here in the body, O best of embodied ones.

5. And whoever remembers Me alone when leaving the body at the time of death attains to My status of being; there is no doubt of that.

6. Whatever state of being he remembers, upon giving up his body at the end, to that he attains, O son of Kuntī; always being formed in that state.

7. Therefore at all times think of Me and fight. With mind [*manas*] and intellect [*buddhi*] set on Me, thou shalt doubtless come to Me alone.

8. He who is disciplined by the yoga of practice and meditates on the supreme Person, his mind not straining after some other object, he reaches, O Pārtha, that supreme divine Spirit.

9. He who meditates on the ancient seer, the ruler, who is smaller than the small, who is the supporter of all, whose form is inconceivable and who is sun-colored beyond the darkness,

10. At the time of death, with an unshaken mind, disciplined with devotion and the strength of yoga, placing the life-force [*prāna*] between the eyebrows, he attains that supreme divine Spirit.

11. I shall declare to thee briefly that place which the Veda-knowers call the indestructible, where ascetics free from passion enter, and where they lead a life of chastity.

12. He who controls the gates [of the body], confines the mind in the heart, places the breath in the head, establishes himself in concentration by yoga,

13. Pronounces the single syllable [*Om*], which is Brahman, meditates on Me as he goes forth and abandons the body, he reaches the highest goal.

14. He who always thinks of me and not of something else, for him, O Pārtha, who is a yogin ever disciplined, I am easy to obtain.

15. Having come to Me, these great-souled men do not attain rebirth, the place of sorrow and impermanence, for they have reached the highest perfection.

16. From the world of Brahmā downwards, all worlds are reborn, O Arjuna; but having come to Me, O son of Kuntī, there is no rebirth.

17. They who know that the day of Brahmā is of a thousand ages and that the night of Brahmā is of a thousand ages, they are the persons who know what day and night are.

18. From the unmanifest, all manifestations come forth at the coming of day, and at the coming of night, they dissolve in that same thing, called the unmanifest.

19. This same multitude of beings, coming forth repeatedly, dissolves helplessly in the coming of night, O Pārtha, and comes forth in the coming of day.

20. But higher than that unmanifest state, there is another unmanifested eternal being who does not perish when all beings perish.

21. This unmanifested [state] is called the Indestructible. They call that the highest goal which, having obtained, they return not. That is My highest abode.

22. This is the supreme spirit, O Pārtha, obtainable by unswerving devotion, in whom all beings abide and by whom all this is pervaded.

23. I will declare to thee that time, O best of the Bharatas, when the yogins depart and do not return and when they depart and do return.

24. Fire, light, day, the lunar fortnight, the six months that are the northward course [of the sun], there the men who know Brahman go forth to Brahman.

25. Smoke, night, also the dark lower fortnight, the six months of the southern course [of the sun], there going forth, the yogin attains the moon's light and returns.

26. These two paths, light and dark, are thought to be the everlasting paths of the world. By one, man does not return; by the other he returns again.

27. Knowing these paths, O Pārtha, the yogin is not perplexed. Therefore at all times be disciplined in yoga, O Arjuna.

28. The yogin, having known all this, goes beyond the fruits of deeds assigned in the Vedas, in sacrifices, in austerities, and in gifts, and goes to the highest and primal place.

This is the eighth chapter, entitled "The Yoga of the Imperishable Brahman."

Chapter IX

The Blessed Lord said:
1. I will declare to thee, who are uncomplaining, this deepest secret of wisdom combined with knowledge, knowing which thou shalt be delivered from evil.

2. This is sovereign knowledge, a sovereign secret, the highest purifier, understood immediately, righteous, very easy to practice and imperishable.

3. Men who have no faith in this law, O oppressor of the foe, do not attain Me but return to the path of ceaseless birth and rebirth.

4. By Me, in My unmanifested form, all this world is pervaded. All beings rest in Me but I do not rest in them.

5. And [yet] beings do not rest in Me: behold My divine mystery [yoga]. My Self, which is the source of beings, sustains all beings but does not rest in them.

6. Just as the great wind, blowing everywhere, abides in the ether, so all beings abide in Me; know thou that.

7. All beings, O son of Kuntī, enter into My [material] nature at the end of a world cycle, and I send them forth again at the beginning of a new cycle.

8. Taking hold of My own [material] nature, I send forth again and again all this multitude of beings which are helpless, by the force of [My] material nature.

9. And these actions do not bind Me, O Dhananjaya; I am seated as one who is indifferent, unattached to these actions.

10. With Me as supervisor, *prakriti* sends forth all moving and unmoving [things]; by this cause, O son of Kuntī, the world revolves.

11. The foolish despise Me when I assume a human form, not knowing My higher nature as the great Lord of all beings.

12. They abide in a fiendish and demoniac nature which is deceitful; their hopes are vain, their actions are vain, their knowledge is vain, and they are devoid of mind.

13. But the great-souled, O Pārtha, who abide in the divine nature, worship Me with undeviating mind, knowing Me as the imperishable source of all beings.

14. Always glorifying Me and striving with steadfast resolve, and honoring Me with devotion, they worship Me ever-disciplined.

15. Others also, sacrificing with the sacrifice of wisdom, worship Me as the one, as the distinct, and as the many facing in all directions.

16. I am the ritual, I am the sacrifice, I am the oblation, I am the medicinal herb, I am the sacred hymn, I am also the melted butter, I am the fire and I am the burnt offering.

17. I am the father of this world, the mother, the supporter, the grandsire, the object of knowledge, the purifier, the sacred syllable *Om*, and also the verse [*rik*], the chant [*sāma*] and the sacrificial formula [*yajus*].

18. I am the goal, upholder, lord, witness, abode, shelter and friend. I am the ori-gin, dissolution, foundation, treasure-house and imperishable seed.

19. I give heat; I hold back and send forth the rain; I am immortality, and also death; I am being and non-being, O Arjuna.

20. The knowers of the three [Vedas] who drink the Soma and are purified of sin worship Me with sacrifices and pray for the way to heaven. Having reached the holy world of Indra, they taste in heaven the divine enjoyments of the gods.

21. After enjoying the vast world of heaven, they return to the world of mortals when their merit is exhausted. Thus conforming to the doctrine of the three Vedas and desiring pleasure, they obtain the transitory.

22. But to those who worship Me, thinking of no other, to those who are constant in perseverance, I bring acquisition and possession of their goal.

23. Even those who are devotees of other gods and who worship them full of faith, even they worship Me only, O son of Kuntī, although not according to the prescribed rules.

24. For I am the recipient and lord of all sacrifices. But they do not know Me in my essence and hence they fall.

25. The worshipers of the gods go to the gods; the worshipers of the ancestors go to the ancestors; sacrificers of the spirits go to the spirits; and those who sacrifice to Me come to Me.

26. Whoever offers Me a leaf, a flower, a fruit or water with devotion, I accept that offering of devotion from the pure in heart.

27. Whatever thou doest, whatever thou

eatest, whatever thou offerest, whatever thou givest, whatever austerities thou performest, do that, O son of Kuntī, as an offering to me.

28. Thus thou shalt be freed from the bonds of action which produce good and evil fruits; disciplined by the yoga of renunciation, thou shalt be liberated and come to Me.

29. I am equal to all beings, there is none hateful nor dear to Me. But those who worship Me with devotion, they are in Me and I am in them.

30. Even if a man of very evil conduct worships me with undivided devotion, he too must be considered righteous, for he has resolved rightly.

31. Quickly he becomes a righteous self and obtains eternal peace; O son of Kuntī, know thou that My devotee never perishes.

32. They who take refuge in Me, O Pārtha, even though they be born of sinful wombs, women, Vaishyās and even Shūdras, they also reach the highest goal.

33. How much more, then, holy Brahmins and devoted royal sages! Having come to this perishable, unhappy world—worship thou Me.

34. Fix the mind on Me, be devoted to Me, worship Me, salute Me; thus having disciplined the self and having Me as the supreme goal, thou shalt come to Me.

*

This is the ninth chapter, entitled "The Yoga of Sovereign Knowledge and Sovereign Mystery."

Chapter X

The Blessed Lord said:
1. Again, O mighty-armed one, hear My supreme word. From a desire to benefit thee, I will declare it to thee who art delighted [with it].

2. Neither the hosts of gods nor the great seers know My origin, for I am the source of the gods and the great seers in every respect.

3. He who knows Me, the unborn, the beginningless, the great Lord of the world, he among mortals is undeluded and is freed from all sins.

4. Understanding, wisdom, non-bewilderment, patience, truth, self-control, calmness, happiness, sorrow, existence, non-existence, fear and also fearlessness,

5. Non-injury, equanimity, contentment, austerity, generosity, fame and ill-fame, are the different states of being which arise from Me alone.

6. The seven great seers of old and the four Manus are also of My nature; they were born of My mind and from them have arisen all these creatures in the world.

7. He who knows in essence this glory and power of Mine is united [with Me] by unshaken discipline; there is no doubt of that.

8. I am the source of all; from Me all arises. Knowing this, the wise worship Me, imbued with feeling.

9. With their thoughts fixed on Me, their lives centered on Me, enlightening each other and always speaking about Me, they are content and rejoice in Me.

10. To those who are always so disciplined, worshiping Me with love, I give that yoga of intellect by which they come unto Me.

11. Out of compassion for them, while

remaining in My own self-nature, I destroy the darkness born of ignorance with the shining light of wisdom.

Arjuna said:

12. Thou art the supreme Brahman, the highest abode, the supreme purifier, the eternal divine spirit, the first of the gods, the unborn, the omnipresent;

13. So all the seers call Thee; the divine seer Nārada, and also Asita, Devala, Vyāsa and Thyself tellest it to me.

14. All this that Thou sayest to me I hold true, O Keshava; neither the gods nor the demons, O Lord, know Thy manifestation.

15. Only Thou knowest Thyself by Thyself, O Supreme spirit [purushottama], Source of beings, Lord of creatures, God of gods, Lord of the world!

16. Thou shouldst tell me of Thy complete divine manifestations, by which Thou pervadest these worlds and dost abide [in them].

17. How may I know Thee, O Yogin, by meditating always? In what states of being art Thou, O Blessed Lord, to be thought by me?

18. Tell me again in complete detail, O Janārdana, of Thy power and manifestation. Satiety comes not to me, hearing Thy nectarlike words.

The Blessed Lord said:

19. Listen, I will tell thee of My divine manifestations; of those which are preeminent, O best of the Kurus, for there is no end to My extent.

20. I am the Self seated in the hearts of all beings, O Gudākesha; I am the beginning, the middle, and also the end of all beings.

21. Of the Ādityas I am Vishnu; of the lights the radiant sun; I am Marīci of the Maruts; of the stars I am the moon.

22. Of the Vedas I am the Sāmaveda; of the gods I am Vāsava [Indra]; of the senses I am manas, and of beings I am consciousness.

23. And of the Rudras I am Shankara [Shiva]; I am Vittesha [Kubera] of the Yakshas and Rākshasas; of the Vasus I am the god of fire, and of mountain peaks I am Meru.

24. Know then, O Pārtha, that of house priests I am the chief, Brihaspati; of generals I am Skanda; of lakes I am the ocean.

25. Of the great seers I am Bhrigu; of utterances the singular syllable [Om]; of sacrifices the silent sacrifice; of immovable things I am the Himālaya.

26. Of all trees, I am Ashvattha; of divine seers Nārada; of the Gandharvas I am Citraratha; of perfected beings the sage Kapila.

27. Know me to be Uccaihshravas of horses, nectar-born; Airāvata of lordly elephants; and of men the monarch.

28. Of weapons I am the thunderbolt; of cows I am Kāmadhuk; I am the progenitor Kandarpa; of serpents I am Vāsuki.

29. I am Ananta of the Nāgas; Varuna of water creatures; I am Aryama of the departed fathers, and of guardians I am Yama.

30. I am Prahlāda of Titans; the time of calculators; of wild animals I am the lion; of birds I am Vinatā.

31. I am the wind of purifiers; Rāma of warriors; of fishes I am the alligator, and of rivers I am the Ganges.

32. Of creations, I am the beginning, the end and also the middle, O Arjuna; of knowledge the knowledge of the Self; I am the speech of those who speak.

33. Of letters I am the letter A, and of compounds the *dvandva*. I am also everlasting time; I am the Creator whose face is in every direction.

34. I am death, the all-devouring, and the origin of all beings to come; of feminine things I am fame, prosperity, speech, memory, intelligence, firmness and forgiveness.

35. Likewise, of chants I am Brihatsāman; of meters I am Gāyatrī; of months I am Mārgashīrsha; and of seasons I am spring.

36. I am the gambling of the dishonest; the splendor of the splendid; I am victory; I am effort; I am the goodness of the good.

37. Of the Vrishnis I am Vāsudeva; of the Pāndavas I am Dhananjaya; of sages I am Vyāsa, and of poets the poet Ushanā.

38. I am the rod of rulers; the policy of victory-seekers; I am also the silence of secrets and the wisdom of the wise.

39. And I am the seed of all beings, O Arjuna. There is no being, moving or unmoving, that can exist without Me.

40. There is no end to My divine manifestations, O conqueror of the foe. What I have declared is only an example of the extent of My glory.

41. Whatever being has glory, majesty or power, know that to have originated from a portion of My splendor.

42. But what is all this detailed knowledge to thee, O Arjuna? I stand supporting this entire world with only a single fraction of Myself.

*

This is the tenth chapter, entitled "The Yoga of Manifestations."

Chapter XI

Arjuna said:
1. As a favor to me Thou hast spoken about the supreme mystery called the Self; and by Thy words my delusion is dispelled.

2. The origin and dissolution of beings have been heard by me in detail from Thee, O Lotus-eyed one, and also Thy imperishable greatness.

3. As Thou declarest Thyself, so it is, O Supreme Lord. I desire to see Thy godly form, O Purushottama!

4. If Thou thinkest that it can be seen by me, O Lord, then reveal Thy immortal Self to me, O Lord of Yoga!

The Blessed Lord said:
5. Behold, O Pārtha, My forms, by hundreds and by thousands, manifold and divine, of various colors and shapes.

6. Behold the Ādityas, the Vasus, the Rudras, the two Ashvins, and also the Maruts. Behold, O Bhārata, many marvels not seen before.

7. Behold today the whole world, of moving and unmoving things, united in My body, O Gudākesha, and whatever else thou desirest to see.

8. But thou canst not see Me with thine own eye. I give thee a divine eye. Behold My divine yoga.

Sanjaya said:
9. Having spoken thus, O King, the great Lord of Yoga, Hari, then showed to Pārtha His supreme, divine form;

10. Of many mouths and eyes, of many marvelous visions, of many divine ornaments, of many uplifted weapons;

11. Wearing divine garlands and garments with divine perfumes and ointments, full of all wonders, radiant, infinite, His face is turned everywhere.

12. If the light of a thousand suns were to spring forth simultaneously in the sky, it would be like the light of that great Being.

13. There Pāndava beheld the whole world, divided into many parts, all united in the body of the God of gods.

14. Then filled with amazement, his hair standing erect, Arjuna bowed down his head to the God and with hands folded in salutation said:

Arjuna said:
15. I see all the gods in Thy body, O God, and also the various kinds of beings: Brahmā, the Lord, seated on the lotus seat, and all the sages and divine serpents.

16. I see Thee, with many arms, stomachs, mouths, and eyes, everywhere infinite in form; I see no end nor middle nor beginning of Thee, O Lord of all, O universal form!

17. I behold Thee with diadem, club and discus as a mass of light shining everywhere with the radiance of flaming fire and the sun, difficult to regard, beyond all measure.

18. Thou art the imperishable, the highest to be known; Thou art the final resting place of this universe; Thou art the immortal guardian of eternal law; Thou art, I think, the primal spirit.

19. I behold Thee without beginning, middle or end, of infinite power, of innumerable arms, the moon and sun as Thine eyes, Thy face as a shining fire, burning this universe with Thy radiance.

20. This space between heaven and earth and all the quarters of the sky is pervaded by Thee alone; seeing this Thy wondrous, terrible form, the triple world trembles, O great one!

21. These hosts of gods enter Thee and some, affrighted, invoke Thee with folded hands, and hosts of great seers and perfected ones crying "Hail!" praise Thee with magnificent hymns.

22. The Rudras, the Ādityas, the Vasus, the Sādhyas, the Vishvedevas, the two Ashvins, the Maruts and the Ushmapās, and the hosts of Gandharvas, Yakshas, Asuras, and perfected ones all gaze at Thee in amazement.

23. Seeing Thy great form, of many mouths and eyes, O mighty-armed one, of many arms, thighs and feet, of many bellies, of many terrible tusks, the worlds tremble, and so do I.

24. Seeing Thee touching the sky and blazing with many colors, with opened mouths and shining enormous eyes, my inmost self is shaken and I find no strength nor peace, O Vishnu!

25. Seeing Thy mouths, terrible with tusks, like time's devouring fire, I know not the directions of the sky and I find no security. Have mercy, O Lord of gods, Abode of the world!

26. And these sons of Dhritarāshtra, all of them, together with the hosts of kings, Bhīshma, Drona, and also Karna, together with our chief warriors

27. Are rushing into Thy mouths, dreadful with terrible tusks. Some are seen with

pulverized heads, stuck between Thy teeth.

28. As the many water currents of rivers race headlong to the ocean, so these heroes of the world of men enter into Thy flaming mouths.

29. As moths swiftly enter a blazing fire and perish there, so these creatures swiftly enter Thy mouths and perish.

30. Swallowing all the worlds from every side, Thou lickest them up with Thy flaming mouths; Thy fierce rays fill the whole world with radiance and scorch it, O Vishnu!

31. Tell me who Thou art with so terrible a form! Salutation to Thee, O best of gods, be merciful! I wish to know Thee, the primal one; for I do not understand Thy ways.

The Blessed Lord said:
32. Time am I, the world destroyer, matured, come forth to subdue the worlds here. Even without thee, all the warriors arrayed in the opposing armies shall cease to be.

33. Therefore stand up and win fame. Conquering thy enemies, enjoy a prosperous kingdom. By Me they have already been slain. Be thou the mere instrument, O Savyasācin.

34. Slay thou Drona, Bhīshma, Jayadratha, Karna, and the other warrior-heroes too, who have already been slain by Me. Be not distressed, fight! Thou shalt conquer thy enemies in battle.

Sanjaya said:
35. Having heard this utterance of Keshava [Krishna], Kirītī [Arjuna], trembling and with folded hands, saluted Him again, and bowing down fearfully said to Krishna in a faltering voice,

Arjuna said:
36. It is right, O Hrishīkesha, that the world rejoices and is pleased by Thy fame. Ogres flee in terror in all directions, and all the hosts of perfected ones bow down before Thee.

37. And why should they not prostrate themselves, O Great One, who art greater than Brahmā, the primal creator? O infinite one! Lord of the gods! O refuge of the worlds! Thou art the imperishable; Thou are being and non-being, and that which is beyond both.

38. Thou art the first of the gods, the primal spirit; Thou art the highest treasure-house of this world; Thou art the knower and that which is to be known, and the highest goal. By Thee this universe is pervaded, O Thou of infinite form!

39. Thou art Vāyu and Yama, Agni, Varuna, Shashānka, and Prajāpati, the grandsire. Hail, hail to Thee a thousand times; hail, hail to Thee again and also again!

40. Hail to Thee in front and in the rear, hail to Thee on every side, O all; infinite in power and immeasurable in strength. Thou penetratest all and therefore Thou art all.

41. For whatever I said in rashness from negligence or even from affection thinking Thou art my friend, and not knowing Thy greatness, calling Thee "O Krishna, O Yādava, O comrade,"

42. And whatever disrespect I showed Thee for the sake of jesting, whether at play, on the bed, seated or at meals, whether alone or in the company of others, O sinless one, I pray forgiveness from Thee, the boundless one.

43. Thou art the father of this moving

and unmoving world. Thou art the object of its reverence and its greatest teacher. There is nothing equal to Thee, how then could anyone in the triple-world surpass Thee, O Thou of incomparable power!

44. Therefore, bending down and prostrating my body, I ask Thy grace; Thou, O Lord, shouldst bear with me as a father to his son, as friend with friend, as a lover to his beloved.

45. Having seen what was never seen before, I am glad, but my mind is distraught with fear. Show me, O lord, that other form of Thine; O lord of gods, be gracious, O refuge of the world.

46. I wish to see Thee as before with Thy crown, mace and disk in hand. Be that four-armed form, O thousand-armed one of universal form!

The Blessed Lord said:
47. By My grace, O Arjuna, and through My great power, was shown to thee this highest form, full of splendor, universal, infinite, primal, which no one but thee has seen before.

48. Not by the Vedas, by sacrifices or study, not by gifts, nor ritual, nor severe austerities can I, in such a form, be seen in the world of men by any other but thee, O hero of the Kurus.

49. Be not afraid nor bewildered in seeing this terrible form of Mine. Without fear and of satisfied mind, behold again My other form.

Sanjaya said:
50. Having thus spoken to Arjuna, Vāsudeva revealed again His own form. The great one, having become again the gracious form, comforted him in his fear.

Arjuna said:
51. Seeing again this Thy gracious hu-man form, O Janārdana, I have become composed of mind and restored to my normal nature.

The Blessed Lord said:
52. This form of Mine, which is very difficult to see, thou hast seen. Even the gods are constantly desiring the sight of this form.

53. In the form that thou hast seen Me, I cannot be seen by the Vedas, by austerity, by gift or sacrifice.

54. But by devotion to Me alone can I in this form, O Arjuna, be known and seen in essence, and entered into, O oppressor of the foe.

55. He who does My work, who regards Me as his goal, who is devoted to Me, who is free from attachment and is free from enmity to all beings, he comes to Me, O Pāndava.

*

This is the eleventh chapter, entitled "The Yoga of the Vision of the Universal Form."

Chapter XII

Arjuna said:
1. Those devotees who are always disciplined and honor Thee, and those who worship the Imperishable and the Unmanifest—which of these are more learned in yoga?

The Blessed Lord said:
2. Those who, fixing their mind on Me, worship Me with complete discipline and with supreme faith, them I consider to be the most learned in yoga.

3. But those who worship the Imperishable, the Undefinable, the Unmanifested, the Omnipresent, the Unthinkable, the Immovable, the Unchanging, the Constant,

4. And have restrained all their senses, and are equal-minded and rejoice in the welfare of all beings—they also obtain Me.

5. The difficulty of those whose minds are fixed on the Unmanifested is much greater; the goal of the Unmanifested is hard for the embodied to attain.

6. But those who renounce all actions in Me and are intent on Me, who worship Me with complete discipline and meditate on Me,

7. These, whose thoughts are fixed on Me, I quickly lift up from the ocean of death and rebirth, O Pārtha.

8. Place thy mind on Me alone, make thy intellect enter into Me, and thou shalt dwell in Me hereafter. Of this there is no doubt.

9. But if thou art not able to fix thy thought firmly on Me, then seek to obtain Me by the yoga of practice, O Dhananjaya.

10. If thou art incapable even of practice, then be devoted to My service; performing actions for My sake, thou shalt obtain perfection.

11. If thou art unable to do even this, then, with thy self controlled, resort to My yoga and renounce the fruit of all action.

12. Better indeed is knowledge than practice; and better than knowledge is meditation; better than meditation is the renunciation of the fruit of action, for from renunciation peace immediately comes.

13. He who has no ill feeling to any being, who is friendly and compassionate, without selfishness and egoism, who is the same in pain and pleasure and is patient,

14. The yogin who is thus always content, self-controlled and of firm resolve,

and whose mind and intellect are given over to Me; he is My devotee and is dear to Me.

15. He before whom the world is not afraid and who is not afraid before the world, and who is free from joy and impatience, fear and agitation, he is dear to Me.

16. He who is disinterested, pure, skillful, unconcerned and controlled, who has abandoned all undertakings, he, My devotee, is dear to Me.

17. He who neither rejoices nor hates, neither grieves nor desires, who has renounced good and evil and who is devoted, he is dear to Me.

18. He who is alike to enemy and friend, also to honor and disgrace, who is alike to cold and heat, pleasure and pain, and is freed from attachment,

19. He who is thus indifferent to blame and praise, who is silent and is content with anything, who is homeless, of steady mind and is devoted—that man is dear to Me.

20. But those who have faith and are intent on Me and who follow this nectar of righteousness which has been declared by Me—those devotees are exceedingly dear to Me.

*

This is the twelfth chapter, entitled "The Yoga of Devotion."

Chapter XIII

The Blessed Lord said:
1. This body, O son of Kuntī, is called the field, and he who knows this is called the knower of the field by those who know him.

2. Know Me as the Knower of the field

in all fields, O Bhārata; the knowledge of the field and the knower of the field, this I hold to be [real] knowledge.

3. Hear from Me briefly what the field is, what its nature is, what its modifications are, whence it comes, who he [the knower of the field] is and what his powers are.

4. This has been sung by the seers in many ways; in various hymns distinctly and also in the well-reasoned and definite words of the aphorisms about Brahman.

5. The gross elements, the I-sense, the intellect and also the unmanifested, the ten senses and one [the mind] and the five objects of the senses;

6. Desire, hatred, pleasure, pain, the organism, intelligence and firmness; this, briefly described, is the field together with its modifications.

7. Absence of pride and deceit, non-violence, patience, uprightness, service of a teacher, purity, steadfastness, self-control;

8. Indifference to the objects of sense, lack of ego and a perception of the evil of birth, death, old age, sickness and pain;

9. Non-attachment, absence of clinging to son, wife, home and the like; a constant equal-mindedness to desirable and undesirable occurrences;

10. Single-minded yoga and unswerving devotion to Me, cultivation of lonely places, dislike for a crowd of people;

11. Constancy in the knowledge of the Self, insight into the end of essential knowledge—this is declared to be knowledge: ignorance is what is other than that.

12. I will declare that which is to be known, by knowing which one gains immortality. It is the beginningless supreme

Brahman who is called neither being nor non-being.

13. With his hands and feet everywhere, with eyes, heads and mouths on all sides, with his ears everywhere; he dwells in the world, enveloping all.

14. Appearing to have the qualities of all the senses, and yet free from all the senses; unattached and yet supporting all; free from the *gunas* and yet enjoying the *gunas,*

15. It is outside and within all beings. It is unmoving and moving. It is too subtle to be known. It is far away and it is also near.

16. It is undivided and yet seems to be divided in all beings. It is to be known as supporting all beings and as absorbing and creating them.

17. It is also, it is said, the light of lights beyond darkness; it is knowledge, the object of knowledge, and the goal of knowledge; it is seated in the hearts of all.

18. Thus the field, and also knowledge and the object of knowledge, have been briefly declared. Understanding this, My devotee becomes fit for My state of being.

19. Know that both *prakriti* and *purusha* are beginningless; and know also that modifications and the *gunas* are born of *prakriti.*

20. *Prakriti* is said to be the cause of the generation of causes and agents, and *purusha* is said to be the cause of the experience of pleasure and pain.

21. The *purusha* abiding in *prakriti* experiences the *gunas* born of *pakriti.* Attachment to the *gunas* is the cause of his births in good and evil wombs.

22. The highest spirit in this body is said to be the witness, the consenter, the sup-

porter, the experiencer, the great Lord, the supreme Self.

23. He who knows the *purusha* and *prakriti* together with its *gunas,* though in whatever state he may exist, he is not born again.

24. Some by meditation see the Self in the self by the self; others by the yoga of discrimination, and still others by the yoga of action.

25. Yet others, not knowing this but hearing it from others, honor it, and they too cross beyond death through their devotion to the scripture which they have heard.

26. Whatever being is born, immovable or moving, know, O best of the Bharatas, that it [arises] from the union of the field and the knower of the field.

27. He who sees the supreme Lord abiding equally in all beings, not perishing when they perish, he [truly] sees.

28. Seeing the same Lord established equally everywhere, he does not harm the Self by the self, and he then attains the highest goal.

29. He who sees that actions are performed only by *prakriti* and likewise that the self is not the doer, he truly sees.

30. When he perceives the various states of being abiding in the One and extending from it, then he attains Brahman.

31. Because this imperishable supreme Self is beginningless and without attributes, though it abides in the body, O son of Kuntī, it neither acts nor is affected [by actions].

32. As the omnipresent ether, because of its subtlety, is not affected, so the

Self, abiding in every body, is not affected.

33. As the one sun illumines this whole world, O Bhārata, so does the owner of this field illumine the whole field.

34. They who thus know, by the eye of knowledge, the distinction between the field and the knower of the field, and the freedom of beings from *prakriti,* they attain to the Supreme.

★

This is the thirteenth chapter, entitled "The Yoga of the Distinction Between the Field and the Knower of the Field."

Chapter XIV

The Blessed Lord said:
1. I will declare again that highest wisdom, the best of all wisdom, knowing which all the sages have departed from this world to the highest perfection.

2. Having resorted to this wisdom and become like My state of being, they are not born even at the time of world creation nor are they disturbed at the time of dissolution.

3. My womb is the great Brahman; in that I place the seed, and the birth of all beings comes from that, O Bhārata.

4. Whatever forms are born in all wombs, O son of Kuntī, the great Brahman is their womb and I am the father that gives the seed.

5. *Sattva, rajas,* and *tamas,* the *gunas* born of *prakriti,* bind the imperishable embodied [soul] in the body, O mighty-armed one.

6. Of these, *sattva,* because of its stainlessness, is illuminating and healthy. It binds by attachment to happiness and by

attachment to knowledge, O sinless one.

7. Know that *rajas* is of the nature of desire whose source is thirst and attachment. It, O son of Kuntī, binds the embodied [soul] by attachment to actions.

8. Know that *tamas* is born of ignorance, the deluder of all embodied beings. It binds, O Bhārata, by carelessness, indolence and sleep.

9. *Sattva* attaches one to happiness, *rajas* to action, O Bhārata, and *tamas,* obscuring wisdom, attaches one to carelessness.

10. When *sattva* overpowers *rajas* and *tamas,* it prevails, O Bhārata. When *rajas* overpowers *sattva* and *tamas,* it prevails, and likewise when *tamas* overpowers *sattva* and *rajas,* it prevails.

11. When the light of knowledge appears in all the gates of this body, then one may know that *sattva* has increased.

12. Greed, activity, the undertaking of actions, restlessness and longing, these are produced when *rajas* has increased, O best of the Bharatas.

13. Darkness, inactivity, negligence and delusion, these are produced when *tamas* has increased, O joy of the Kurus.

14. When *sattva* has increased and the embodied one dies, he then attains the pure worlds of those who know the highest.

15. Meeting death when *rajas* prevails, he is born among those attached to action; and meeting death when *tamas* prevails, he is born in the wombs of the deluded.

16. The fruit of action well done, they say, is *sattvic* and pure; while the fruit of *rajas* is pain, and the fruit of *tamas* is ignorance.

17. From *sattva* knowledge is born, from *rajas* greed, and from *tamas* arises negligence and delusion and also ignorance.

18. Those who abide in *sattva* rise upward; the *rajasic* stay in the middle, and the *tamasic,* abiding in the lower activities of the modes, sink down.

19. When the seer perceives no doer other than the *gunas* and knows that which is higher than the *gunas,* he attains to My being.

20. When the embodied soul transcends these three *gunas,* whose origin is in the body, it is freed from birth, death, old age and pain, and attains immortality.

Arjuna said:
21. What are the marks of one who has transcended the three *gunas,* O Lord? What is his conduct? How does he go beyond these three *gunas?*

The Blessed Lord said:
22. He does not abhor illumination, activity or delusion when they arise, O Pāndava, nor desire them when they cease.

23. He who is seated like one indifferent and undisturbed by the *gunas,* who thinks "the *gunas* alone act," who stands apart and remains firm,

24. To whom pleasure and pain are alike, who abides in the self, to whom a lump of clay, a rock, and gold are the same, to whom the pleasant and unpleasant are equal, who is firm, to whom blame and praise of himself are the same;

25. To whom honor and dishonor are the same, to whom the parties of friends and enemies are the same, who has abandoned all undertakings—he is called the man who transcends the *gunas.*

26. He who serves Me with unswerving

bhakti yoga, having transcended these *gunas,* is fit to become Brahman.

27. For I am the abode of Brahman, of the immortal and imperishable, of eternal righteousness and of absolute bliss.

*

This is the fourteenth chapter, entitled "The Yoga of the Distinction of the Three Gunas."

Chapter XV

The Blessed Lord said:
1. With its roots above and its branches below [so] they speak of the imperishable peepal tree. Its leaves are the Vedic hymns and he who knows this is a knower of the Veda.

2. Its branches spread below and above, nourished by the *gunas,* with the objects of sense as its sprouts, and below in the world of men stretch the roots that result in actions.

3. Its form is thus not comprehended here, nor its end nor its beginning nor its foundation. Cutting this firmly rooted tree with the strong weapon of non-attachment;

4. Then that path must be sought from which, having gone, men no longer return [thinking], "I seek refuge in that primal spirit from which issued forth this ancient cosmic activity."

5. Those who are without pride or delusion, who have conquered the evil of attachment, who are established in the inner self, their desires departed, who are freed from the pairs known as pleasure and pain and who are undeluded, go to that imperishable place.

6. The sun does not illumine it, nor the moon nor fire. That is My highest abode; after men go there, they never return.

7. A portion of Me in the world of the living becomes a living soul, eternal, and draws along the [five] senses and the mind as sixth, that rest in *prakriti.*

8. When the Lord acquires a body and also when He departs from it, He goes, taking these along, as the wind carries fragances from their home.

9. He enjoys the objects of the senses, making use of the ear, the eye, touch, taste and smell, and also the mind.

10. The deluded do not perceive Him when He departs or when He stays, when He experiences objects while accompanied by the *gunas;* those who have the eye of wisdom see Him.

11. The yogins who strive also see Him established in their Self; but the mindless, whose self is unperfected, although striving, do not see Him.

12. That splendor which issues from the sun and illumines the whole world; that which is in the moon and that which is in the fire, know that splendor as Mine.

13. Entering the earth, I support all beings by My power; and becoming the sapful Soma, I nourish all plants.

14. And becoming the fire of life dwelling in the bodies of living beings and united with the life-breaths, I cook [digest] the four kinds of food.

15. I am seated in the hearts of all; from Me [come] memory, wisdom and argument. I am that which is to be known by the Vedas; I am the author of the Vedānta [*Upanishads*], and I am also the knower of the Vedas.

16. There are two spirits in this world; the perishable and the imperishable. The perishable is all beings and the imperish-

able is called Kūtastha [the unchanging].

17. But there is another, the highest Spirit [*purushottama*] called the supreme Self, who, as the imperishable Lord, enters into the three worlds and sustains them.

18. Since I transcend the perishable and am higher even than the imperishable, I am renowned in the world and in the Vedas as the highest Spirit.

19. He who undeluded thus knows Me as the highest Spirit is the knower of all; he worships Me with his whole being, O Bhārata.

20. Thus the most secret doctrine has been spoken by Me, O sinless one. Being enlightened about this, one will have [true] enlightenment and will have done his work, O Bhārata.

This is the fifteenth chapter, entitled "The Yoga of the Highest Spirit."

Chapter XVI

The Blessed Lord said:
1. Fearlessness, purity of being, steadfastness in the yoga of wisdom, charity, self-control and sacrifice, study of the Veda, austerity, uprightness;

2. Non-violence, truth, absence of anger, renunciation, peace, absence of guile, compassion towards beings, absence of covetousness, gentleness, modesty, absence of fickleness;

3. Majesty, forgiveness, fortitude, purity, absence of malice and excessive pride—these are the endowments of one who is born with the divine nature, O Bhārata.

4. Hypocrisy, arrogance, excessive pride and anger, harshness and also ignorance—

these are the endowments of one who is born with the demoniac nature, O Pārtha.

5. The divine endowments are said to lead to liberation; the demoniac to bondage. Do not grieve, O Pāndava, thou art born with divine endowments.

6. There are two kinds of beings created in this world, the divine and the demoniac. The divine has been described in detail. Hear from me, O Pārtha, of the demoniac.

7. Demoniac men do not know about activity or its cessation. Neither purity nor right conduct nor truth is in them.

8. They say that the world is without truth, without a moral basis, without a God, that it is not originated by regular causation, but that it is caused by desire.

9. Holding fast to this view, these lost souls of little intelligence and of cruel deeds come forth as enemies for the destruction of the world.

10. Attaching themselves to insatiable desire, filled with hypocrisy, pride and arrogance, holding false views through delusion, they act with impure motives.

11. Surrendering themselves to innumerable cares which end only with death, making the enjoyment of desires their highest aim, convinced that this is all;

12. Bound by hundreds of ties of desire, devoted to lust and anger, they strive for accumulated wealth, by unjust means, for the satisfaction of their desires.

13. "This I have won today; this desire I shall attain; this is mine and this wealth shall also be mine."

14. "I have slain this enemy, and I shall slay others also. I am the lord, the enjoyer; I am perfect, strong and happy,"

15. "I am wealthy and well-born. Who else is there like me? I shall sacrifice, I shall give, I shall rejoice"—thus speak those who are deluded by ignorance.

16. Bewildered by many fancies, enveloped by the net of delusions and addicted to the satisfaction of desires, they fall into an impure hell.

17. Self-conceited, stubborn, filled with pride and arrogance of wealth, they worship by performing sacrifices in name only, hypocritically, and against all the prescribed rules.

18. Possessed of egotism, force, pride, desire and anger, these envious ones hate Me in the bodies of themselves and others.

19. These cruel and hateful low men, these wicked ones, I constantly throw back into the cycle of existence, into demoniac wombs.

20. Having fallen into demoniac wombs, these deluded ones, from birth to death, do not attain Me, O son of Kuntī; they go to the lowest place.

21. This is the threefold gate of hell which leads to the ruin of the soul: desire, anger and greed; therefore one should abandon these three.

22. Freed from these three gates of darkness, O son of Kuntī, a man does what is good for his self and then attains the highest goal.

23. He who neglects the laws of the scripture and acts according to the promptings of his desire does not attain perfection, nor happiness, nor the highest goal.

24. Therefore let the scripture be thy authority in determining what should and should not be done. Knowing what is declared by the rules of the scripture, thou shouldst do action in this world.

★

This is the sixteenth chapter, entitled "The Yoga of the Distinction Between the Divine and Demoniac Endowments."

Chapter XVII

Arjuna said:
1. What is the state of those who, [though] neglecting the laws of scripture, perform sacrifices filled with faith, O Krishna? Is it one of *sattva, rajas* or *tamas?*

The Blessed Lord said:
2. The faith of the embodied, which is born from their nature, is threefold; it is *sattvic, rajasic,* and *tamasic.* Hear about it now.

3. The faith of every man is in accord with his innate nature, O Bhārata. Man is made up of faith. Whatever faith a man has, that he is.

4. *Sattvic* men worship the gods, *rajasic* men worship demigods and demons, and others, *tamasic* men, worship elemental spirits and ghosts.

5. Those men who, impelled by hypocrisy and egotism and filled with desire, passion and violence, perform cruel austerities which are not enjoined by the scriptures,

6. Who starve the group of elements within the body and even Me dwelling in the body—know that these fools are demoniac in their resolves.

7. And the food which is dear to all men is of three kinds, as are also their sacrifice, austerity and charity. Hear now the distinction between them.

8. The foods which increase life, energy, strength, health, happiness and cheerfulness, which are tasty, rich, substantial and agreeable, are dear to the man of *sattva*.

9. The foods that are bitter, sour, salty, very hot, pungent, dry and burning, which produce pain, grief and sickness, are desired by the man of *rajas*.

10. That which is spoiled, tasteless, putrid, stale, left-over and unclean is the food dear to the man of *tamas*.

11. The sacrifice which is offered according to the scriptures by those who are not desirous of reward and who hold firmly to the idea that it ought to be performed is *sattvic*.

12. That which is offered with a view to reward and for the sake of display, O best of the Bharatas, know that sacrifice to be *rajasic*.

13. The sacrifice which is not in conformity with the scriptures, in which food is not given, in which hymns are not recited nor fees paid, and which is devoid of faith, they declare to be *tamasic*.

14. [Paying] homage to the gods, to the twice-born, to teachers and the wise; [practicing] purity, uprightness, chastity, non-violence, this is called the austerity of the body.

15. [Speaking] words that cause no excitement, but are truthful, pleasant and beneficial; and the practice of [Vedic] study—this is called the austerity of speech.

16. [Attaining] tranquillity of mind, gentleness, silence, self-control, purity of being—this is called the austerity of mind.

17. This threefold austerity performed with the highest faith by men who are disciplined and who are not desirous of reward they call *sattvic*.

18. That austerity which is performed hypocritically for the sake of respect, honor and reverence is said to be *rajasic*; it is unstable and impermanent.

19. That austerity which is performed with foolish stubbornness or with self-torture, or for the sake of destroying another, is declared to be *tamasic*.

20. That gift which is given to one from whom no return is anticipated, simply because it ought to be given, and which is given to a worthy person in the proper place and time, that gift is thought to be *sattvic*.

21. But that gift which is given for the sake of a return favor or with a view to reward or which is painful to give is said to be *rajasic*.

22. And that gift which is given at an improper place and time to an unworthy person, without respect and with contempt, that is declared to be *tamasic*.

23. "*Om, Tat, Sat*"—this is recorded as the threefold designation of Brahman. By this the Brahmins, the Vedas and the sacrifices were ordained of old.

24. Therefore, upon the pronouncing of "*Om*," the acts of sacrifice, gift and austerity enjoined in the scripture are always undertaken by the knowers of Brahman.

25. And with "*Tat*" the acts of sacrifice and austerity and the various acts of giving are performed by those desirous of liberation, without aiming at reward.

26. "*Sat*" is employed in the sense of "the real" and "the good," and so also the word "*Sat*" is used for praiseworthy action, O Pārtha.

27. Steadfastness in sacrifice, austerity and gift is also called "*Sat*," and action for the sake of these is also called "*Sat*."

28. Whatever offering or gift is made, whatever austerity or act is practiced without faith is called "*asat*," O Pārtha; it is naught here and hereafter.

*

This is the seventeenth chapter, entitled "The Yoga of the Threefold Division of Faith."

Chapter XVIII

Arjuna said:
1. I desire to know, O mighty-armed one, the true essence of renunciation and of abandonment, O Hrishīkesha, and the distinction between them, O Keshinishūdana.

The Blessed Lord said:
2. Sages know "renunciation" as the giving up of acts of desire; the surrendering of the fruits of all actions the wise call "abandonment."

3. Some wise men say that action should be abandoned as evil; others that acts of sacrifice, gift and austerity should not be abandoned.

4. Hear now, O best of the Bharatas, My conclusion about abandonment: abandonment, O tiger among men, is explained to be threefold.

5. Acts of sacrifice, gift and austerity ought not to be abandoned, rather they should be performed; for sacrifice, gift and austerity are purifiers of the wise.

6. These actions ought to be performed, abandoning attachment and fruits, O Pārtha; this is My decided and highest judgment.

7. The renunciation of an action that is

prescribed [by scripture] is not proper. The abandonment of that, because of delusion, is said to be of the nature of *tamas*.

8. He who abandons an action because it is painful or from fear of physical pain performs a *rajasic* kind of abandonment: he does not obtain the fruit of abandonment.

9. He who performs a prescribed action because it ought to be done, abandoning attachment and the fruit, that abandonment, O Arjuna, is thought to be *sattvic*.

10. The wise man, the abandoner, whose doubts are removed, who is filled with goodness, does not hate unpleasant action and is not attached to pleasant action.

11. It is impossible for an embodied being to abandon actions entirely; he who abandons the fruit of action is called the [true] abandoner.

12. Undesired, desired, and mixed: threefold is the fruit of action for the non-abandoner in the hereafter. But there is none whatever for the renouncer.

13. Learn from me, O mighty-armed, these five causes, as declared in the Sānkhya, for the accomplishment of all action.

14. The body, the agent, the instruments of various kinds, the various activities, and destiny, as the fifth:

15. Whatever action a man undertakes with body, speech or mind, whether it be right or wrong, these are its five causes.

16. That being so, he who, because of his untrained intelligence, sees himself as the sole actor is a fool, and does not see.

17. He who is not egoistic, whose intelligence is not affected, though he slay these people, he slays not nor is he bound.

18. Knowledge, the object of knowledge, and the knower are the threefold incentives to action; the instrument, the action, and the actor are the threefold constituents of action.

19. Knowledge, action, and the actor are said, in the theory of the *gunas,* to be of just three kinds, according to the distinction of *gunas.* Hear of these also.

20. That knowledge by which the one imperishable Being is seen in all beings, undivided in the divided, know that knowledge to be *sattvic.*

21. That knowledge which sees various beings of different kinds in all beings, because of their separateness, know that knowledge is *rajasic.*

22. But that which is attached to one effect as if it were the whole, without reason, without grasping the essential, and insignificant, is declared to be *tamasic.*

23. An action which is obligatory, which is performed free from attachment and without desire or hate by one who is undesirous of its fruit, is said to be *sattvic.*

24. But action which is done with great exertion by one who seeks to fulfill his desires or by one who is selfish is called *rajasic.*

25. That action which is undertaken without regard to consequence, to loss and injury, and to one's own capacity, through delusion, is called *tamasic.*

26. The actor who is free from attachment, who is not egotistic, who is full of firmness and confidence, who is unchanged in success or failure, is called *sattvic.*

27. The actor who is passionate, who is desirous of the fruit of action, who is greedy, of harmful nature, who is impure and full of joy and sorrow, is called *rajasic.*

28. The actor who is undisciplined, vulgar, stubborn, deceitful, malicious, lazy, despondent and procrastinating is said to be *tamasic.*

29. Hear now about the threefold distinction of intelligence and also of firmness, according to the *gunas,* to be set forth fully and separately, O Dhananjaya.

30. That which knows activity and inactivity, what ought to be done and what ought not to be done, what is to be feared and what is not to be feared, bondage and liberation, that intelligence, O Partha, is *sattvic.*

31. That by which one understands incorrectly right and wrong, what ought to be done and what ought not to be done, that intelligence, O Partha, is *rajasic.*

32. That which, covered by darkness, thinks what is wrong is right, and sees all things as perverted, that intelligence, O Partha, is *tamasic.*

33. That firmness by which one holds the activities of the mind, the life-breaths and the senses, by unwavering yoga, that, O Partha, is *sattvic.*

34. That firmness by which one holds to duty, pleasure and wealth, O Arjuna, with attachment and desirous of the fruits, that, O Partha, is *rajasic.*

35. That firmness by which the fool does not abandon sleep, fear, grief, depression and pride, that, O Partha, is *tamasic.*

36. Hear now from me the threefold happiness, O best of the Bharatas, in which man rejoices by long practice and comes to the end of his suffering.

37. That which is like poison in the beginning and like nectar in the end, which is born from the serenity of self and intellect, that happiness is called *sattvic.*

38. That which [arises] from the union of the senses and their objects and which is like nectar in the beginning and poison in the end, that happiness is recorded as *rajasic.*

39. That which deludes the self in the beginning and in the end and which arises from sleep, sloth and carelessness, that happiness is declared to be *tamasic.*

40. There is no thing on earth or in heaven or even among the gods who is free from these three *gunas* born of *prakriti.*

41. The actions of Brahmins, Kshatriyas and Vaishyas, and of Shūdras, O conqueror of the foe, are distinguished according to the *gunas* that arise from their innate nature.

42. Calmness, self-control, austerity, purity, patience, uprightness, wisdom, knowledge and religious belief are the actions of the Brahmin, born of his nature.

43. Heroism, majesty, firmness, skill and not fleeing in battle, generosity and lordship, are the actions of the Kshatriya, born of his nature.

44. Agriculture, cattle-tending and trade are the actions of a Vaishya, born of his nature; action whose character is service is likewise that of the Shūdra, born of his nature.

45. A man obtains perfection by being devoted to his own proper action. Hear then how one who is intent on his own action finds perfection.

46. By worshiping him, from whom all beings arise and by whom all this is per-vaded, through his own proper action, a man attains perfection.

47. Better is one's own *dharma,* though imperfect, than the *dharma* of another, well performed. One does not incur sin when doing the action prescribed by one's own nature.

48. One should not abandon his natural-born action, O son of Kuntī, even if it be faulty, for all undertakings are clouded with faults as fire by smoke.

49. He whose intelligence is unattached everywhere, whose self is conquered, who is free from desire, he obtains, through renunciation, the supreme perfection of actionlessness.

50. Learn from me, briefly, O son of Kuntī, how he who has attained perfection also attains to Brahman, the highest state of wisdom.

51. Disciplined with a pure intelligence, firmly controlling oneself, abandoning sound and other sense-objects and throwing aside passion and hatred;

52. Dwelling in solitude, eating little, controlling speech, body and mind, constantly engaged in the yoga of meditation and taking refuge in dispassion;

53. Freed from egotism, force, arrogance, desire, anger and possession; unselfish, peaceful—he is fit to become Brahman.

54. Having become Brahman, tranquil is the Self, he neither grieves nor desires. Regarding all beings as equal, he attains supreme devotion to Me.

55. By devotion he knows Me, what my measure is and what I am essentially; then, having known Me essentially, he enters forthwith into Me.

56. Ever performing all actions, taking refuge in Me, he obtains by My grace the eternal, imperishable abode.

57. Renouncing with thy thought all actions to Me, intent on Me, taking refuge in the yoga of intellect, fix thy mind constantly on Me.

58. If thy mind is on Me, thou shalt, by My grace, cross over all obstacles; but if, from egotism, thou wilt not listen, thou shalt perish.

59. If, centered in egotism, thou thinkest "I will not fight," vain is this thy resolution; *prakriti* will compel thee.

60. That which thou wishest not to do, through delusion, O son of Kuntī, that thou shalt do helplessly, bound by thine own action born of thy nature.

61. The Lord abides in the hearts of all beings, O Arjuna, causing all beings to resolve by His power [*māyā*], as if they were mounted on a machine.

62. Go to Him alone for shelter with all thy being, O Bhārata. By His grace, thou shalt obtain supreme peace and the eternal abode.

63. Thus the wisdom, more secret than all secrets, has been declared to thee by Me. Having considered it fully, do as thou choosest.

64. Hear again My supreme word, the most secret of all: thou are greatly beloved by Me, hence I will speak for thy good.

65. Center thy mind on Me, be devoted to Me, sacrifice to Me, revere Me, and thou shalt come to Me. I promise thee truly, for thou art dear to Me.

66. Abandoning all [other] duties, come to Me alone for refuge. I shall free thee from all sins: be not grieved.

67. This is never to be spoken of by thee to one who is without austerity, nor to one who is without devotion, nor to one who is not obedient, nor to one who speaks evil of Me.

68. He who shall declare this supreme secret to My devotees, and display the highest devotion to Me, shall doubtless come to Me.

69. There is none among men who does more pleasing service to Me than he, nor shall there be anyone dearer to Me than he on earth.

70. And he who shall study this sacred dialogue of ours, by him I would be worshiped with the sacrifice of wisdom. Such is My thought.

71. And the man who hears it with faith and without cavil, even he shall be liberated and shall attain to the radiant world of the righteous.

72. Has this been heard by thee, O Pārtha, with concentrated thought? Has thy delusion of ignorance been destroyed, O Dhananjaya?

Arjuna said:
73. My delusion is destroyed and I have gained memory [understanding] through Thy grace, O Acyuta! I stand firm with my doubts dispelled; I shall act by Thy word.

Sanjaya said:
74. Thus I have heard this marvelous and thrilling dialogue between Vāsudeva and the great-souled Pārtha.

75. By the grace of Vyāsa, I have heard this supreme secret, this yoga, from Krishna, the Lord of Yoga, relating it Himself in person.

76. O King, remembering again and again this wonderful and holy dialogue between Keshava and Arjuna, I rejoice again and again.

77. And remembering again and again that most wondrous form of Hari, great is my astonishment, O King, and I rejoice again and again.

78. Wherever there is Krishna, the Lord of Yoga, and Pārtha the archer, there assuredly is prosperity, victory, happiness and firm righteousness, so I believe.

*

This is the eighteenth chapter, entitled "The Yoga of Freedom by Renunciation."
Here the *Bhagavadgītā-Upanishad* ends.

In the following notes, brackets indicate insertions by the editor. Otherwise the notes are adapted from those of Eliot Deutsch and from the essays accompanying his translation in the original volume.

[1][Song of the Lord or Song of the Blessed One. For translations of all other Sanskrit terms used in this translation of the *Gītā*, see the glossary which follows these notes.]

[2]In the general narrative of the "great epic," the *Mahābhārata*, Dhritarāshtra gave his throne to his nephew Yudhishthira (a brother of Arjuna) instead of to the eldest of his hundred sons, Duryodhana, who was cruel and selfish. Duryodhana conspired nevertheless to gain the kingdom and arranged to have Yudhishthira invited to a series of dice games. Yudhishthira, who had a weakness for gambling, lost badly in the games; in fact, he lost his entire kingdom and, by the stakes of the final game, he (together with his brothers and their common wife Draupadī) was exiled for thirteen years. Dhritarāshtra, who was displeased with this, promised the Pāndavas that after this time and upon the fulfillment of certain conditions they could return to their kingdom and reclaim it. But when the period of exile was over Duryodhana refused to give up his position and power. All attempts at reconciliation between the cousins failed and

so both sides appealed to other relatives and friends, who joined one or the other forces. The great battle was then ready to begin.

[3][Having had a second, divine birth through initiation into sacred study and sacrifice.]

[4]The dividing of men into four classes, or "castes," was originally intended to suggest that human nature may quite naturally be divided into intellectuals and priests (*brahmins*); rulers, warriors, and statesmen (*kshatriyas*); businessmen and managers (*vaishyas*); and workers and servants (*shūdras*)—and that a society as a whole functions best when each person in it knows his "place" and works within it for the good of all. (The *shūdras* were in actuality more of an "outcaste" than a class within the fold, for they were, and are, denied participation in the Vedic rituals and sacraments. They are not, though, to be confused with the "untouchables," who are not mentioned anywhere in the text.) Each "caste" has its appropriate rights and privileges. Until such time as one abandons society and becomes a *sannyāsin*, one is obliged to work within the social structure.

[5]I.e., nirvāna: the bliss or joy that comes with spiritual experience.

[6]The five "motor organs"—tongue, feet, hands, the ejective and generative organs.

[7]The "nine gates" refer to the eyes, ears, nostrils, the mouth, the anus and the sex organs.

Glossary of Sanskrit names and terms

For a treatment of Sanskrit terms at greater length, see the essays accompanying the original printing of Eliot Deutsch's translation in *The Bhagavad Gītā*, Holt, Rinehart and Winston, 1968.

For a discussion of various epithets used in the *Gītā*, see sections six and seven of George Anastaplo's essay printed elsewhere in this volume.

Acyuta, "the immovable one." Epithet for Krishna.

Ādityas. A group of twelve gods.

Agni. God of fire.

Airāvata. Indra's elephant.

Ananta. A giant serpent of the earth whose yawns are earthquakes.

Anantavijaya. King Yudhishthira's horn.

Arjuna. One of the five Pāndavas trying to regain their kingdom in this battle. The *Bhagavad Gītā* consists primarily of a dialogue between Arjuna and Krishna his charioteer, who is actually an incarnation of the god Vishnu.

Aryama. Primal ancestor.

āryan. A noble.

Ashvattha. The holy fig tree.

Ashvins. Two gods usually depicted as horse-men.

Asita. A legendary sage.

Asvatthāman. Son of Drona.

bhakti yoga. The path of devotion. See *yoga.*

Bhārata, "descendant of Bhārata." Epithet for both Arjuna and Dhritarāshtra. Bhārata is one of the founders of Arjuna's family.

Bhīma. Arjuna's brother; third of the sons of Pāndu.

Bhīsma. An old warrior who brought up both Dhritarāshtra and his brother Pāndu. In the battle he commands the Kuru army.

Bhrigu. Ancient seer so illustrious that he is said to have mediated quarrels between the gods.

Brahmā. The god of creation. With Shiva and Vishnu, one of the sacred triad of Hindu gods.

Brahman. The unitary, undifferentiated principle of all being, the knowledge of which liberates one from finitude. Can also mean unconscious nature. Sometimes used as a synonym for the term *Veda.*

Brahmin. A member of the highest caste of intellectuals and priests. *See* note four for a discussion of castes.

Brihaspati. The priest-god.

Brihatsāman. A portion of hymns dedicated to Indra.

buddhi. Intellect, reason, faculty of discrimination.

Cekitāna. A warrior of the Pāndavas.

Citraratha. Chief of the heavenly musicians.

Devadatta. Arjuna's conch shell, used as a horn.

Devala. A legendary sage.

Dhananjaya, "winner of wealth." Epithet for Arjuna.

dharma. Duty, law, righteousness, moral merit. The term connotes religious and social duties articulated in terms of one's station in life.

Dhritarāshtra. The blind King of the Kurus, brother of Pāndu and hence uncle of the five Pāndava brothers.

Draupadī. Wife shared by the five Pāndava brothers.

Dhrishtadyumma. Son of Drupada.

Dhrishtaketu. One of the kings who fought with the Pāndavas.

Drona. The teacher who taught the art of war to both the Pāndava and Kuru princes.

Drupada. The king who was father to Draupadī, wife of the Pāndavas.

Duryodhana. The eldest of the hundred sons of Dhritarāshtra.

dvandva. In Sanskrit, a simple copulative compound joining two or more words.

Gandharvas. Heavenly musicians.

Gāyatrī. A meter with three lines of eight syllables.

Govinda, "chief of herdsmen." Epithet for Krishna.

Gudākesha, "thick-haired one." Epithet for Arjuna.

gunas. Strands, qualities, constituents. Nature is supposed to be composed of several basic strands or "energy fields" called *sattva* (dynamic equilibrium), *rajas* (turbulence), and *tamas* (dullness). Sometimes the *gunas* are taken to be qualities of psychic being and moral consciousness as well. In that case *sattva* means intelligence and objectivity, *rajas* means emotion and subjectivity, and *tamas* means ignorance, insensibility, and lethargy.

Hanumān. The monkey god.

Hari. Another name for Vishnu.

Hrishīkesha, "bristling-haired one." Epithet for Krishna.

Ikshvāku. Son of Manu; grandson of Vivasvant the sun god.

Indra. God of winds and monsoons. Also god of war.

Janaka. Philosopher-king referred to in the *Upanishads,* famous for his generous deeds.

Janārdana, "agitator of men." Epithet for Krishna.

jñāna. Knowledge, intuition, spiritual understanding.

jñāna yoga. The discipline of knowledge. See *yoga.*

Kāmadhuk. A mythical cow who satisfies all wishes.

Kandarpa. The god of love.

Kapila. Alleged founder of one of the oldest systems of Hindu philosophy, the *sānkhya.*

karma. Deed, work, action. In Indian philosophy a man is completely responsible for himself. His actions, or *karma,* enacted over a period of innumerable births, deaths, and rebirths, result in his present condition, and his condition in future lives will likewise depend on actions in this and in past lives.

karma yoga. The way of action. See *yoga.*

Karna. Arjuna's half-brother.

Kāshi (Benares). One of ancient India's seven sacred cities.

Keshava, "the handsome-haired one." Epithet for Krishna.

Keshinishūdana, "slayer of the demon Keshin." Epithet for Krishna.

Kirītī, "diademed-one." Epithet for Arjuna.

Kripa. Brother-in-law of Drona.

Krishna. Arjuna's spiritual teacher, who acts the part of the warrior's charioteer. He is the incarnation of Vishnu, the preserver god of the Hindu triad. See also *Vishnu.*

Kshatriya. Member of the second highest caste, that of warriors, rulers, and statesmen. *See* note four for a discussion of castes.

Kubera. Lord of wealth.

Kuntī. Mother of Arjuna, Yudhishthira, and Bhīma. See also *Pāndu.*

Kuntibhoja. A warrior of the Pāndavas.

Kurus. The sons of Dhritarāshtra. In the battle they fight against their cousins, the Pāndavas, for control of their father's kingdom.

Mādhava, "descendant of Mādhava." Epithet for Krishna. Mādhava was one of the patriarchs of Krishna's family.

Madhusūdana, "destroyer of the demon Madhu." Epithet for Krishna.

manas. The mind.

Manipushpaka. Sahadeva's conch shell, or horn.

Manu. Son of Vivasvant the sun god.

Manus. In Hindu mythology the first manifestation of Brahman produced the seven seers and four Manus, or rulers of the world, who possessed divine powers. Men are said to be descended from them.

Mārgashīrsha. The first month of the ancient Hindu calendar; includes parts of the winter months of November and December.

Marīci. Chief of the wind gods.

Maruts. The wind gods.

māyā. The power of the Divine to order Nature; also "illusion."

Meru. Name of the golden mountain in Hindu mythology. It was considered to be the center of the universe and the dwelling place of the gods.

Nāgas. Mythical snakes.

Nakula. One of the five Pāndava brothers.

Nārada. Ancient priest-seer to whom some verses of one of the Vedas are ascribed.

Om. Refers to a mystical form of invocation or incantation in which the sacred syllable "om" is repeated as the speaker enters into a trance-like state of contemplation.

Pāñcajanya. Krishna's conch shell, or horn.

Pāndavas. The five sons of Pāndu: Yudhishthira, Bhīma, Arjuna, Nakula, and Sahadeva.

Pāndu. Brother to Dhritarāshtra and father of the Pāndavas, whose clan is about to engage in fratricidal war with the Kurus.

Pārtha, "son of Pārtha." Epithet for Arjuna. Pārtha is another name for Kuntī, Arjuna's mother.

Paundra. Bhīma's conch shell, or horn.

Prahlāda. King of the demons.

Prajāpati. Lord of creatures. A variant for Brahmā.

prakriti. Matter, unconscious force. One of the two basic principles of Nature. See also *purusha.*

prāna. Life-force.

Purijit. Brother of Kuntibhoja.

purusha. Soul, spirit, consciousness. One of the two basic principles of Nature along with *prakriti.*

Purushottama, "Supreme Spirit." Epithet for Krishna.

rajas. See *gunas.*

rajasic. Having an active, ambitious, strong-willed disposition.

Rākshasas. Pre-Vedic demi-gods.

Rāma. The hero of the *Rāmāyana,* one of the great epic poems of India.

Rudras. Vedic storm gods, bringers of disease and death. Later identified with Shiva.

Sādhyas. Class of ancient semi-divine celestial beings.

Sahadeva. One of the five Pāndava brothers.

Sāmaveda. One of the four Vedic texts; "The Wisdom of the Chants."

Sanjaya. The charioteer of Dhritarāshtra, who relates to him the events of the war.

sānkhya. Intellectual understanding, analytic discrimination, or knowledge.

sannyāsin. One who abandons society for the sake of striving for spiritual freedom.

sattva. See *gunas.*

sattvic. Having a contemplative, philosophical, moral disposition.

Sātyaki. A kinsman of Krishna's who fought with the Pāndavas, sometimes as Krishna's charioteer. Also called Yuyudhāna.

Savyasācin, "ambidextrous archer." Epithet for Arjuna.

Shaibya. One of the kings who fought with the Pāndavas.

Shankara. One of the most famous Indian philosophers, circa A.D. 700, principal exponent of the non-dualistic school of Vedānta (Advaita Vedānta).

Shashānka. The moon.

Shikandim. Son of Drupada.

Shiva. The god of destruction and regeneration. With Brahmā and Vishnu, one of the sacred triad of Hindu gods.

Shūdras. Members of the lowest caste; workers and servants. *See* note four for a discussion of castes.

Skanda. God of war.

Soma. An obscure drink, believed to produce vivid hallucinations, which was used in Vedic ritual.

Somadatta, son of. A warrior-king who fought on the Kuru side.

Subhadrā, son of. Abhimanya, whose father is Arjuna.

Sughosha. Nakula's conch shell, or horn.

tamas. See *gunas.*

tamasic. Having a slothful, dimwitted disposition; prone to simple sensuality.

Uccaihshravas. The god Indra's horse.

Upanishads. Ancient philosophical and religious texts, written by a succession of teachers and sages. (*See also* Vedas.) For a discussion of the Upanishads and the Vedas, *see* section two of G. Anastaplo's essay on the *Gītā* elsewhere in this volume.

Ushanā. Famous seer and composer of hymns, associated with the fire ritual.

Ushmapās. Soma-drinkers, a class of sons of the gods, progenitors of the human race.

Uttamaujas. Another chieftain in the Pāndava army.

Vaishyas. Members of the caste of businessmen and managers. *See* note four for a discussion of castes.

Vārshneya, "clansman of the Vrishnis." Epithet for Krishna.

Varuna. God of the waters, custodian of the law.

Vāsava. Another name for Indra.

Vāsudeva, "son of Vāsudeva." Epithet for Krishna. Vāsudeva was Krishna's father and a nobleman.

Vāsuki. The serpent-king.

Vasus. A class of gods.

Vāyu. A wind god.

Veda(s). The earliest sacred Hindu writings (hymns, prayers, etc.). For a discussion of the Vedas and the Upanishads, *see* section two of G. Anastaplo's essay on the *Gītā,* which appears elsewhere in this volume.

vijñāna. Practical knowledge.

Vikarna. Third of the hundred sons of Dhritarāshtra.

Vinatā. Vishnu's bird.

Virāta. A warrior-king with whom the Pāndavas once took refuge. He fights on their side in the battle.

Vishnu. The preserver god. With Brahmā and Shiva, one of the sacred triad of Hindu gods.

Vishvedevas. A class of minor gods.

Vittesha. Another name for Kubera.

Vivasvant. The sun god.

Vrishnis. The family lineage from which both Krishna and Arjuna are descended.

Vyāsa. Reputed editor and arranger of the *Mahābhārata,* from which the *Bhagavad Gītā* is taken.

Yādava, "descendant of Yādu." Epithet for Krishna. In Hindu mythology, Yādu was one of Krishna's early ancestors.

Yakshas. Pre-Vedic demi-gods.

Yama. God of death.

yoga. (1) The controlling of one's lower sensuous nature and the realization of one's higher spiritual nature. (2) The name for various philosophical-religious "disciplines" or "ways" to self-realization, as *karma yoga, bhakti yoga,* and *jñāna-yoga.* (3) A psychological discipline involving various physical postures and breath control. (4) A synonym for divine power.

yogins. Those who follow the discipline of yoga. In the *Gītā,* primarily *karma yoga.*

Yudhāmanyu. A chieftain in the Pāndava army.

Yudhishthira. One of the five Pāndava brothers. It was he to whom Dhritarāshtra gave his kingdom, thus precipitating the war between the Pāndavas and the Kurus.

Yuyudhāna. See *Sātyaki.*

Three Essays

Josiah Royce

Editor's Introduction

Time has not dealt kindly with Josiah Royce. At the beginning of this century he was one of the leading lights in the philosophical faculty at Harvard, where among his colleagues were William James and George Santayana, and on the fringes of which lived also Charles Sanders Peirce. No philosophical tenet of theirs was more familiar than Royce's own commitment to idealism (in metaphysics), loyalty (in religion), and the Absolute (as a theory of truth). If his writings were not the equal of James's, still his major works—*The Religious Aspect of Philosophy* (1885), *The World and the Individual* (1900–01), and *The Philosophy of Loyalty* (1908)—were much read and admired, and none of the other members of the department could compete with him as a speaker, nor did any of them have, as he did, a genuinely popular following.

All this has changed. Where the writings of James and Santayana are now firmly established in the philosophical canon, and Peirce's genius is everywhere acknowledged, the works of Royce are, for the most part, ignored. So too with the philosophical positions by which he set such store. All have been swept away in the tide of pragmatism and positivism that has covered the field, rising from figures who once seemed no greater than himself, if even as important, and joined by other doctrines, such as existentialism, that are equally opposed to his own. It is hard now to recall how great a figure he made in the philosophy of his day, to remember how much he seemed to embody philosophical ideas which his age thought interesting, to realize that he was what now seems wholly improbable, an academic philosopher whose lectures were public events and whose essays could be found on every library table.

Still, none of these things is impossible to understand if we reflect a little on Royce's interests and his gifts. For he was always concerned as a philosopher with serious and important questions—the nature of truth and our capacity to grasp it, the basis of religious faith, the problem of evil—which all persons care something about. On these questions, moreover, he wrote and spoke, in at least his lectures and essays, with coherence and force. He was also a greatly learned man who had the literature of his subject always at hand, and who, when he spoke of philosophical tradition, as he frequently liked to do, did so with both ease and authority.

Indeed, his appetite for books was prodigious, almost a disease, as was his propensity for talk, at almost any time, with anyone he could get to listen. "Royce would have been a very great man if only he had never been taught to read," John Jay Chapman once wrote of him in exasperation. In argument, Chapman said, he was "the John L. Sullivan of philosophy . . . very extraordinary and knew everything . . . a benevolent monster of pure intelligence, zigzagging, ranging, and uncatchable." "Time was nothing to him," Chapman went on. "He was just as fresh at the end of a two-hours' disquisition as at the start. Thinking refreshed him. The truth was that Royce had a phenomenal memory; his mind was a card-indexed cyclopedia of all philosophy. . . . His extreme accessibility made him a sort of automat restaurant for Cambridge. He had fixed hours when anyone could resort to him and draw inspiration." And James, too, called him "a perfect little Socrates for wisdom and humor," while later he described him as "the Rubens of philosophy," having "richness, abundance, boldness, color, but a sharp contour never, and never any *perfection*." To which he added, "But isn't fertility better than perfection?"

It was to James, his opposite in philosophical terms, as it turned out, that Royce owed his appointment to Harvard, after study at Johns Hopkins and an interval teaching at the University of California, the state in which he had been born in 1855. Royce's gratitude was undying, for there was then little professional opportunity for one such as himself in California, and in any case he knew what an elusive figure—passionately interested in everything—he tended to cut. But James, whom he visited in Cambridge in 1877, while still a graduate student, "found me at once," as he said—"made out what my essential interests were at our first interview, accepted me with all my imperfections, as one of those many souls who ought to be able to find themselves in their own way, gave a patient and willing ear to just my variety of philosophical experience, and used his influence from that time on, not to win me as a follower, but to give me my chance." The appointment, which came in 1882, lasted until Royce's death in 1916, two years after he had been elevated to a distinguished Harvard professorship.

As Royce's reading was wide, so were his productions. What is, after all, perhaps his most enduring contribution was in mathematical logic, to which he was directed by Peirce, and for which he had obvious talent. He worked also in psychology, had great interest in literature, and wrote frequently on historical subjects, among them California itself, for which he never lost his affection and sense of attachment.

Of the essays here reprinted, the Introduction to Poincaré's *Science and Hypothesis* was written in 1905 for the first English translation of that book. "William James and the Philosophy of Life" dates from 1911, the year after James died. "The Rediscovery of the Inner Life: From Spinoza to Kant," originally a lecture, is a chapter from *The Spirit of Modern Philosophy*, a work written in 1892.

The Rediscovery of the Inner Life:
From Spinoza to Kant

You are well acquainted with a fact of life to which I may as well call your attention forthwith, the fact, namely, that certain stages of growing intelligence, and even of growing spiritual knowledge, are marked by an inevitable, and, at first sight, lamentable decline, in apparent depth and vitality of spiritual experience. The greatest concerns of our lives are, in such stages of our growth, somehow for a while hidden, even forgotten. We become more knowing, more clever, more critical, more wary, more skeptical, but we seemingly do not grow more profound or more reverent. We find in the world much that engages our curious attention; we find little that is sublime. Our world becomes clearer; a brilliant, hard, midmorning light shines upon everything; but this light does not seem to us any longer divine. The deeper beauty of the universe fades out; only facts and problems are left.

Such a stage in human experience is represented, in great part, by the philosophical thinkers who flourish between the time of Spinoza's death, in 1677, and the appearance of Kant's chief philosophical work, *The Critique of Pure Reason,** in 1781. It is the period which has been especially associated, in historical tradition, with the eighteenth century, so that when one speaks of the spirit of the eighteenth century, he is likely to be referring to this skeptical and critical mood, to this hard, midmorning light of the bare understanding, beneath which most of these thinkers of our period saw all their world lying. When I undertake to describe such a time, I therefore feel in its spirit a strong contrast to that curious but profound sort of piety which we were describing in the last lecture in the case of Spinoza. Spinoza, indeed, was in respect of his piety a man of marked limitations. His world had but one sublime feature in it, one element of religious significance, namely, the perfection of the divine substance. But then this one element was enough, from his point of view, to insure an elevated and untroubled repose of faith and love, which justified us in drawing a parallel between his religious consciousness and that of the author of the *Imitation of Christ.* This sort of piety almost disappears from the popular philosophy of the early eighteenth century. What the people of that time want is more light and fewer unproved assumptions.

As against the earlier seventeenth-century thinkers, who, as you remember, also abhorred the occult, and trusted in reason, the thinkers of this new age are characterized by the fact that on the whole they have a great and increasing suspicion of even that rigid mathematical method of research itself upon which men like Spinoza had relied. In other words, whereas the men of the middle of the seventeenth century had trusted to reason alone, the men of the subsequent period began, first hesitatingly, and then more and more seriously, to distrust even human reason itself. After all, can you spin a world, as Spinoza did, out of a few axioms? Can you permanently revere a divine order that is perhaps the mere creature of the assumptions with which your system happened to start? The men of the new age are not ready to answer "Yes" to such questions. They must

---

*[GBWW, Vol. 42.]

reflect, they must peer into reason itself. They must ask, Whence arise these axioms, how come we by our knowledge, of what account are our mathematical demonstrations, and of what, after all, does our limited human nature permit us to be sure? Once started upon this career, the thought of the time is driven more and more, as we have already said, to the study of human nature, as opposed to the exclusive study of the physical universe. The whole range of human passion, so far as the eighteenth century knew about it, is criticized, but for a good while in a cautious, analytical, cruelly scrutinizing way, as if it were all something suspicious, misleading, superstitious. The coldness of the seventeenth century is still in the air; but Spinoza's sense of sublimity is gone. Spinoza himself, you remember, had altogether rejected, as occult, everything miraculous, marvelous, extranatural. Not the thunder or the earthquake or the fire could for him contain God; God was in the still small voice that the wise man alone heard. Now the popular philosophy of the eighteenth century more and more approached a position which unconsciously agreed with Spinoza's in a number of respects. It cordially recognized, for instance, that the earthquake, say the great Lisbon earthquake of 1758, was a fearful thing, but that God was very certainly not in that earthquake. It could readily make out the same thing concerning any amount of thunder, fire, or wind that you might produce for inspection. But it went one step further than Spinoza's wise man, and was forced to observe that, after considerable scrutiny, it had as yet been able to detect in the world of reason and experience no still, small voice whatsoever. That at least, as I say, was the outcome of a considerable portion of the thought of the time. It was indeed not the outcome of all the thinking of this age. In Leibniz, who was a younger contemporary of Spinoza, and who flourished in the closing decades of the seventeenth century, and at the beginning of the new period, philosophical

theology found an expositor of the greatest speculative ingenuity and of the most positive tendency. Later, in the ever-fascinating Bishop Berkeley, not merely theological doctrine, but a profoundly spiritual idealism got voice. In Rousseau, a new era of sentimental piety found its beginning, and all this movement led erelong to Kant himself. But for the moment I am speaking of tendencies in a most general way, and this negative, this cautious, skeptical attitude, is the one most observable in the philosophy of our period.

I

Those of us who look to philosophy for positive experiences, rather than for technical instruction, will at first sight regard such a period as this with some natural indifference. The skeptic is not always an interesting person; but then, you must remember, as skeptic he doesn't want to be interesting. He only wishes to be honest. He is meanwhile not only to be tolerated; he is also indispensable. Philosophical thought that has never been skeptical is sure not to be deep. The soul that never has doubted does not know whether it believes; and at all events the thinker who has not dwelt long in doubt has no rights to high rank as a reflective person. In fact, a study of history shows that if there is anything that human thought and cultivation have to be deeply thankful for, it is an occasional but truly great and fearless age of doubt. You may rightly say that doubt has no value in itself. Its value is in what it leads to. But then consider what ages of doubt have led to. Such an age in Greece produced that father of every humane sort of philosophizing, Socrates. The same age nourished with doubts the divine thought of Plato. Another and yet sterner age of doubt brought about the beginnings of Christian thought, prepared the Roman empire for the new faith, and saved the world from being ruined by the multitudinous fanatical rivals of Christianity. Yet a third great age of doubt began, at the Renaissance, the history of modern literature, and made the way plain for whatever was soundest about the Reformation. And a fourth age of doubt, the one under our consideration in this present lecture, proved more fruitful for good to humanity than a half-dozen centuries of faith had done at another time. For, as we shall see, this eighteenth-century doubting drove thinkers from the study of nature to the study first of human reason, then of human conscience, then of all the human heart and soul, and meanwhile cleared the way for those triumphs of the spirit over great evils which have taken place from the moment of the French Revolution until now. Despise not doubting; it is often the best service thinking men can render to their age. Condemn it not; it is often the truest piety. And when I say this I do not mean merely to repeat cant phrases. I speak with reason. Doubt is never the proper end of thinking, but it is a good beginning. The wealth of truth which our life, our age, our civilization, our religion, our own hearts may contain, is not quite our property until we have won it. And we can win it only when we have first doubted the superficial forms in which at the outset it presents itself to our apprehension. Every true lover has in the beginning of his love grave doubts of his beloved's affection for him. And such doubts often take on bitter and even cynical forms in his soul in the various bad quarters of an hour that fall to his lot. Doubt, however, is not the foe, but the very inspirer of his love. It means that the beloved is yet to be won. It means that the simple warmth of his aspiration isn't enough, and that, if the beloved is worth winning, she is worth wooing through doubt and uncertainty for a good while. Moreover, it is not the fashion of the beloved, in the typical case, to be especially forward in quelling such doubts, by making clear her attitude too soon. If it were, lovemaking might be a simple affair but would not be so sig-

nificant an experience as it is. Doubt is the cloud that is needed as a background for love's rainbow. Even so it is, however, in the world of abstracter thought. The more serious faiths of humanity can only be won, if at all, by virtue of much doubting. The divine truth is essentially coy. You woo her, you toil for her, you reflect upon her by night and by day, you search through books, study nature, make experiments, dissect brains, hold learned disputations, take counsel of the wise; in fine, you prepare your own ripest thought, and lay it before your heavenly mistress when you have done your best. Will she be pleased? Will she reward you with a glance of approval? Will she say, Thou hast well spoken concerning me? Who can tell? Her eyes have their own beautiful fashion of looking far off when you want them to be turned upon you; and, after all, perhaps she prefers other suitors for her favor. The knowledge that she is of sufficiently exalted dignity to be indifferent to you, if she chooses, is what constitutes the mood known as philosophical skepticism. You see that, in sound-hearted thinkers, it is like the true lover's doubt whether his unwon mistress regards him kindly or no. It is not, then, a deadening and weakening mood; it is the very soul of philosophical earnestness.

Meanwhile, in describing the skepticism of our period I am far from wishing to trouble you with its endlessly varied technical subtleties. These lectures are throughout selective, and they sacrifice numberless intrinsically important aspects of our various subjects, in order to be able to seize upon a few significant features, and to hold these up to your view. I cannot warn you too much that there is no chance of completeness of treatment anywhere in the course of our brief work together. I spared you, in the last lecture, whole cargoes of problems which are consigned to every special student of Spinoza. I shall omit in this every mention of innumerable significant features in the philosophy of our present period. All this is a matter of course. I remind you of it only to excuse an immediate and somewhat dry statement of the few features of this eighteenth-century skepticism to which I intend to confine myself in what follows.

II

There are certain philosophic problems of which you are sure, sooner or later, to have heard something in general literature, and for which the time from Spinoza to Kant is at least partially responsible. I want to set forth a little of the growth of these problems, never forgetting, I hope, that they interest us here in their human rather than in their technical aspects, and that we are above all concerned in them as leading to Kant himself, and to those who came after him. And my selection is as follows:

You have all heard about the controversy as to whether man's knowledge of more significant truth is innate, or whether it comes to him from without, through his senses; or, otherwise, as to whether the mind at birth is a *tabula rasa,* a blank white piece of innocent paper, upon which experience writes whatever it will, or whether the soul is endowed from the start with certain inborn rational possessions—a divine law, for instance, written on the tablets of the heart, a divine wisdom about number and space, registered in some imperishable form in our very structures. You may have met with more or less elaborate arguments upon this topic. I do not know whether it has ever had more than the interest of a curious problem to many of us. I do know that in many styles of treatment it must appear as a sort of hackneyed debating-club question, an apparently excellent one of its sort, but a rather dry bone of contention, after all.

But you now know that philosophic research is no affair of the debating clubs, but a struggle of humanity to make its own deepest interests articulate, and therefore you will not expect me to deal with this question after the forensic fashion. What I want to do is this:

I want to suggest summarily the origin of the controversy about the innate ideas, and to show you what interest first led men to the question. Then, I want to indicate the value of the controversy as bringing about the study of man's inner life which, at the close of the century, bore fruit in the great Romantic movement itself. Finally, I want to narrate how the problems erelong took form, what skeptical outcome the discussion, upon one side, seemed to have, and what solution, what re-winning of the great spiritual faiths of humanity, it suggested on the other. In this way I shall try to prepare you for that stupendous revolution of philosophic thought which is associated with the name of Kant.

For the first, then, as to the origin of the controversy about the innate ideas. I shall not go back farther in the history of thought than to Descartes, 1596–1650, a predecessor of Spinoza, and the man whose name usually begins the lists of modern philosophers proper, as they are set forth in the textbooks of the history of philosophy. Had I been engaged in technical teaching, it would have been my duty, in the last lecture, to describe the highly interesting relation in which Spinoza's doctrine stands to that of his predecessor. As it is, I have so far passed Descartes over. At present I must mention, in a word, one or two features of his doctrine. Descartes had early become dissatisfied with the scholastic philosophy which he had learned at Jesuit hands and decided to think out a system for himself. He began his reasoning by a formal philosophical doubt about everything that could conceivably be doubted, and then proceeded to examine whether any unassailable certainty was still left him. He found such an absolutely unassailable assurance in his own existence as a thinking being, and accordingly began his positive doctrine with the famous principle, *"Cogito, ergo sum,"* "I think, and so I exist." He proceeded from this beginning to prove the existence of God, and then the existence of two so-called substances, mind and matter, as comprising the whole world of which we mortals know anything. The laws of matter he found to be those of mathematics, and of the elementary physics of his time. Of mind he also studied the constitution as well as he could, and the result appeared in several elaborate works. Now the principle on which Descartes proceeded throughout his investigations was this: "My own existence is the standard assurance of my thought. I know that *I* at least am. But surely, if, on examining some principle, say an axiom in geometry, I perceive that it is as plain to me, as clear, as distinct, as is my own existence, then indeed it must be as certain a truth as my existence." This, I say, was his way of procedure, whenever he was puzzled about a principle. "Is it as clear to me as my own existence; or can I somehow make it as clear and distinct? Well, then, it is true. Is it less clear? Then I must examine it still further, or lay it aside as doubtful." By this fashion of procedure, which Descartes regarded as the typically rational one, he managed to collect after a time a very goodly stock of sure and clear principles. Others haven't always found them all as clear and sure as did Descartes, but that concerns us not now. Well, Descartes had a name, or in fact a brace of names, for these principles of his. He called them "eternal truths," and he also called them "innate" ideas or truths. We know them because it is of the nature of our reason to know them. We know them whenever we come to look at them squarely, whether we ever saw them in this light before or not. That $2 + 2 = 4$, that things equal to the same thing are equal to each other, these are examples of such truths. They are as clear to me as that I myself exist. They are clear to me because my reason makes them so, and that is the sort of reason I have. They are innate in me. I don't see them with my bodily eyes. I just know them, because I do know

them, and I know them also to be eternal.

Innate truths then, for Descartes, are of this sort. He isn't so much interested in finding out how so many truths could be innate in one poor little human soul all at once, as he is interested in singling them out and writing down bookfuls of them. The seventeenth century, you remember, was not much interested in man himself, but was very much interested in eternal truth. Hence Descartes makes light of the problem *how* all this thought-stuff could somehow be innate in a soul without the poor soul's ever even guessing the fact until it had studied philosophy. Yet of course if one becomes strongly interested in human nature for its own sake, this problem which Descartes ignored must come to the front.

The true interest of this problem, then, lies in the fact that by reflecting upon it philosophers have been led to some of the deepest undertakings of modern thought. For the moment it comes up as a question of mere idle curiosity. As such, however, the question was rather tauntingly suggested to Descartes himself by certain of his opponents. "How can so many ideas be innate?" they said. "Observe, children don't know these truths of yours, and couldn't even grasp them. Much less could infants. And yet you call them innate." Descartes, thus challenged, replied curtly, but not unskillfully. They may be innate, he said (in substance), as predispositions, which in infants haven't yet grown to conscious rank. The thing is simple enough. In certain families, so Descartes further explains (I do not quote his words but give their sense), good-breeding and the gout are innate. Yet of course, as he implies, the children of such families have to be instructed in deportment, and the infants just learning to walk seem happily quite free from gout. Even so, geometry is innate in us, but it doesn't come to our consciousness without much trouble. With the taunting questions put to Descartes, and his example about the heredity of good-breeding and the gout, the question of the innate ideas enters modern philosophy. It was later to grow much more important.

III

In Locke's famous "Essay on the Human Understanding,"* published in 1689–90, the investigation may be said to have been fairly opened. Locke was born in the same year as Spinoza. Had he died when Spinoza died, the English thinker would never have been heard of in the history of thought. In Locke's patient devotion to a detailed investigation, we find a quality that reminds us of the most marked characteristic of another great Englishman, the scientific hero of our own day, Darwin. Locke was early busy with philosophy, natural science, and medicine. Later, he was for a short time abroad, in diplomatic service, and then lived long as the intimate friend of Lord Anthony Ashley, afterwards Earl of Shaftesbury, whose political fortunes he followed. His whole life was a mingling of study, private teaching, writing, and practical politics. His character is thoroughly English. There is that typical clearness in seizing and developing his own chief ideas, and that manly, almost classically finished stubbornness as against all foreign, mystical, and especially Continental ideas, which usually mark the elder English thinkers. Give Locke a profound problem like that of the freedom of the will, and he flounders helplessly. Ask him to look at things from a novel point of view, and he cannot imagine what fancy you can be dreaming of. But leave him to himself, and he shows you within his own range a fine, sensible, wholesome man at work, a thorough man, who has seen the world of business as well as the world of study, and who believes in businesslike methods in his philosophy. His style, to be sure, is endlessly diffuse, yet without being precisely wearisome, because, after all, it is itself the diffuseness of a man of business, whose accounts cover many and various transactions, and who

has to set down all the items. Nobody can fail to respect Locke, unless, to be sure, his work is employed as a textbook for classes that are too immature to grapple with him. It has too frequently been thus abused, to the great injury of the excellent man's popular fame.

Locke made, as everybody knows, short work of all innate ideas. He found none. Infants, with their rattles, show no sign of being aware that things which are equal to the same things are equal to each other. Locke himself, to be sure, is a poor expert concerning infants, as is evident from many things that he says about them, in the course of his book, but as to this matter he is not only confident but right. As for the hereditary predispositions, similar to good-breeding and the gout, Locke in one or two passages recognizes that there may, indeed must be, such things. But he does not see of what service they could be in forming knowledge, were it not for our senses.

What interests us most in Locke, however, is not this negative part of his argument, but his general view of the nature, powers, and scope of human reason, a view which introduces a whole century of research into man's inner life. In the preface to his Essay, Locke describes to us the history of his book. "Were it fit," he says, addressing the reader, "to trouble thee with the history of this *Essay,* I should tell thee, that five or six friends meeting at my chamber, and discoursing on a subject very remote from this, found themselves quickly at a stand, by the difficulties that rose on every side. After we had awhile puzzled ourselves, without coming any nearer a resolution of those doubts which perplexed us, it came into my thoughts that we took a wrong course; and that before we set ourselves upon inquiries of that nature, it was necessary to examine our own abilities, and see what *objects* our understandings were, or were not, fitted to deal

---

*[GBWW, Vol. 35.]

with. This I proposed to the company, who all readily assented; and thereupon it was agreed that this should be our first inquiry. Some hasty and undigested thoughts, on a subject I had never before considered, which I set down against our next meeting, gave the first entrance into this Discourse; which, having been thus begun by chance, was continued by entreaty; written by incoherent parcels; and after long intervals of neglect, resumed again, as my humor or occasions permitted; and at last, in a retirement where an attendance on my health gave me leisure, it was brought into that order thou now seest it."*

In this modest way Locke introduces a book whose historical value lies precisely in this insistence upon the importance of knowing our own understandings, as a preliminary to every sort of research. And how great this historical value of the book! Locke and his five or six friends fall to discussing, in club fashion, certain unnamed problems. They find themselves in a quandary. Locke proposes that they go back on their own track a little and study the structure and powers of the understanding itself. He himself begins the analysis, the entreaty of his friends leads him to continue the research. The result is a big book, sensible, many-sided, influential. It arouses a great controversy, and herefrom springs, first the philosophic movement from Locke through Leibniz, through the wonderful Berkeley, through the ingenious, fearless, and doubting Hume, to Kant himself, and European thought is transformed. Meanwhile, from the same root grow other inquiries into the mind of man. The great English moralists of the eighteenth century, a stately row, Shaftesbury, Hutcheson, Butler, Adam Smith, and Hume once more, set forth the mysteries of the moral consciousness. The general public is aroused. A subjective, a humane mode of inquiry becomes everywhere prominent. Much of all this is cold and skeptical in tone. In France it gives us the encyclopedists, such as Diderot. But the same movement

also gives us Rousseau. The modern novel, too, that great analyst of the mind and the heart of every man, takes its rise. I think I am not wrong in attributing the novel largely to that interest in analysis for which Locke stood. Yonder mere outer nature is no longer everything. And erelong, lo! almost before they know it, the nations of Europe themselves are once more plunged into the very midst of the great problems of the spirit. For at length the inquiry loses its negative and skeptical air altogether. The world glows afresh. Passion, brought by all this out of its hiding places, grows hot; men have once more found something to die for; and what they learn to die for in the revolutionary period is the inner life. They die for the freedom of the subject; for the sacred rights of humanity; for the destruction of inhuman and despotic restraints. They make, indeed, vast blunders in all this, behead an innocent queen, set up a new despot merely because his rule isn't traditional, die amid the snows of Russia for a bare whim, in short sin atrociously, but meanwhile they cleanse Europe of a whole dead world of irrationalisms; they glorify the human nature that can endure and suffer so much for the sake of coming to possess itself; they create our modern world. And all this, I say, because they had rediscovered the inner life.

Do I seem to exaggerate the significance of the mere thinker and his work? I assure you that I do not. My idea of the mission of the philosopher is, I insist, a very moderate one. As I have several times said, he doesn't create the passions of men: he makes no new ideals. His only mission is to direct the attention of man to the passions and ideals which they already possess. He doubts, analyzes, pries into this and that; and men say, How dry, how repellent, how unpractical, how remote from life. But, after all, he is prying into the secret places of the lightning of Jove; for these thoughts and passions upon which he reflects move

---

*[*GBWW*, Vol. 35, p. 87d.]

the world. He says to his time: This and this hast thou, this sense of the rights of man, a sword of the spirit, fashioned to slay tyrants; this love of liberty, an ideal banner bequeathed thee by a sacred past to cherish, as the soldiers of old cherished the standard beneath which they conquered the world. Such things he says always, to be sure, in his own technical way, and for a time nobody finds it out at all or even reads his books. But at length discussion begins to spread, the word of wisdom flies from one book to another, and finally the people hear. They look at the sword and at the banner. No philosopher made these. They are simply humanity's own treasures. The philosopher had the sole service of calling attention to them, because, in the course of his critical research, he found them. But the rediscovery, how great its significance! I suppose that you have frequently heard it said that the philosophers had much to do with making the French Revolution, and you have wondered how this was. You may also have wondered how this was consistent with our view that philosophers are the mere critics of life. I show you the solution. The critic creates nothing, he only points out. But his pointing may show you powers that were indeed always there, and that were even effective, but that, once afresh seen, suggest to active passion a thousand devices whereby the world is revolutionized.

We return to Locke. By an inquiry of the sort which he has described to us, he had sought to comprehend the nature and the limits of our understanding. He had, as we saw, decided that innate ideas cannot do anything for knowledge. And the force of this motion of Locke's really was that, according to him, it is useless to assume, as the basis of our human reason, anything occult, mysterious, opaque, hidden away in the recesses of the mind. The real cause of Locke's hatred of innate ideas is his horror of anything mystical. If thought is not to be clear, what shall be clear? Hence, if you pretend to have any knowledge, you must

be prepared to tell where it comes from. It won't do to appeal, as Descartes did, to a certain impression of the clearness and distinctness of your ideas. Their origin will decide their value. And what is this origin? Locke puts the question plainly, at the beginning of the second book of his Essay, and answers it in a general way. I quote the whole passage:

Let us then suppose the mind to be, as we say, white paper, void of all characters, without any ideas; how comes it to be furnished? Whence comes it by that vast store which the busy and boundless fancy of man has painted on it with an almost endless variety? Whence has it all the materials *of reason and knowledge? To this I answer, in one word, from* EXPERIENCE. *In that all our knowledge is founded; and from that it ultimately derives itself. Our observation, employed either about external sensible objects, or about the internal operations of our minds perceived and reflected on by ourselves, is that which supplies our understandings with all the* materials *of thinking. These two are the fountains of knowledge from whence all the ideas we have or can naturally have do spring.*

First, our senses, conversant about particular sensible objects, do convey into the mind several distinct perceptions of things, according to those various ways wherein those objects do affect them; and thus we come by those ideas *we have of* yellow, white, heat, cold, soft, hard, bitter, sweet, *and all those which we call sensible qualities; which when I say the senses convey into the mind, I mean, they from external objects convey into the mind what produces there those perceptions. This great source of most of the ideas we have, depending wholly upon our senses, and derived by them to the understanding, I call* SENSATION.

Secondly, the other fountain from which experience furnisheth the understanding with ideas, is the perception of the operations of our mind within us, as it is employed about the ideas it has got; which operations, when the soul comes to reflect on and consider, do furnish the understanding with another set of ideas, which could not be had from things without. And such are perception, thinking, doubting, believing, reasoning, knowing, willing, and all the different actings of our own minds. . . . This source of ideas every man has wholly in himself; and though it be not sense, . . . yet is is very like it, and might properly enough be called internal sense. But as I call the other SENSATION, *so I call this* REFLECTION, *the ideas it affords being such only as the mind gets by reflecting on its own operations within itself. . . . These two, I say, namely external material things, as the objects of* SENSATION, *and the operations of our own minds within, as the objects of* REFLECTION, *are to me the only originals from whence all our ideas take their beginnings.*

[*GBWW*, Vol. 35, pp. 121b–22a]

So much, then, for Locke's notion of how we come by knowledge. I quote him at this length, because his view was of such critical importance in what followed in all European thought.

You will ask at once, What sort of a real world did Locke manage to make out of this material of bare sensations and reflections? We see, touch, smell, taste this our world, and then we reflectively observe of ourselves that we are doubting, willing, hoping, loving, hating, thinking, and thus we get all our knowledge. That is all the mind we have. That is the human understanding. Such at least is Locke's view. But what does it all come to? Is the result a materialism pure and simple, or is it a skepticism? Not so. Locke was an Englishman; he saw, heard, smelt, tasted, what his fellow-countrymen also did; and he reflected upon all this after much their fashion. His world, therefore, is the world of the liberal English thinker of his day. He believes in matter and its laws, in God also, and in revelation, in duty and in the human rights of the British freeman, and in the Essay he tries to show how just such things can be

known to us through bare seeing, hearing, tasting, and the rest, coupled with reflection upon what we are doing. There is nothing revolutionary about Locke's own view of his world, great as was the revolution that he prepared. By touch we learn that there are substances about us, solid, space-occupying, numerous, movable. By all our senses we learn that these substances have many curious properties, how or why brought about, we cannot discover. Sugar is sweet; gold is yellow; various drugs have specific effects in curing diseases; water flows; iron is rigid; every substance is as God wills it to be. These things are so, because we find them so. Meanwhile, being reflective Englishmen, we can't help observing that all these things require God to create them what they are, because, as one sees, things always have adequate causes; and our minds, too, being realities, must have been made by a thinker. Moreover, a fair study of the evidence of revelation will convince any reasonable person of the essential truths of the Christian religion, and that is enough.

You will not find this world of Locke an exciting one. But remember, after all, what it is that he has done for us. He has tried hard to remove every mystery from the nature of human reason. Because innate ideas, the eternal truths of Descartes, were mysterious, he has thrown them overboard. Experience it is that writes everything on the blank tablet of the mind. But thus viewing things, Locke has only given us a new mystery. Can experience, mere smelling, tasting, seeing, together with bare reflection, do all this for us—give us God, religion, reality, our whole English world? Then surely what a marvelous treasure-house is this experience itself! Surely ages will be needed to comprehend it. Locke cannot have finished it off thus in one essay.

And indeed he has not done so. His book is the mere beginning both of the psychology of experience, and of discussions about the nature and limit of consciousness. The truly important argument over Locke's problems was opened by Leibniz, the great Continental thinker, whose views I must entirely pass over, vastly important as they are, and that the less unwillingly just now because his answer to Locke, written about 1700, was not published until many years after his own death. I must, however, ask you to examine the next step forward in English philosophical reflection, the one taken by the admirable and fascinating Berkeley.

IV

The world that Locke found with his senses is at once too poor and too much encumbered for Berkeley's young enthusiasm. Berkeley is a born child of Plato, a lineal descendant of a race whose origin is never very far off, and is divine. Men of Berkeley's type are born to see God face to face; and when they see him, they do so without fear, without mystical trembling, without being driven to dark and lofty speech. They take the whole thing as a matter of course. They tell you of it frankly, gently, simply, and with a beautiful childlike surprise that your eyes are not always as open as their own. Meanwhile, they are true philosophers, keen in dialectic, skillful in the thrust and parry of debate, a little loquacious, but never wearisome. Of the physical world they know comparatively little, but what they know they love very much. A very few lines of philosophical research they pursue eagerly, minutely, fruitfully; concerning others they can make nothing but the most superficial remarks. They produce books young, and with marvelous facility. They have a full-fledged system ready by the time they are twenty-five. They will write an immortal work, as it were, overnight. They are, for the rest, through and through poetical. Each one of their essays will be as crisp and delicate as a good sonnet. Yet what they lack is elaboration, wiliness, and architec-

tural massiveness of research. They take after Plato, their father, as to grace and ingenuity. His lifelong patience and mature productiveness they never reach. The world finds them paradoxical; refutes them again and again with a certain Philistine ferocity; makes naught of them in hundreds of learned volumes; but returns ever afresh to the hopeless task of keeping them permanently naught. In the heaven of reflection, amongst the philosophical angels who contemplate the beatific vision of the divine essence, such spirits occupy neither the place of the archangels, nor of those who speed o'er land and sea, nor yet of those who only stand and wait. Their office is a less serious one. They cast glances now and then at this inspiring aspect or at that of the divine essence, sing quite their own song in its praise, find little in most of the other angels that can entertain them, and spend their time for the most part in gentle private musings, many of which (for so Berkeley's own portrait suggests to me) they apparently find far too pretty to be uttered at all. We admire them, we may even love them; yet no one would call them precisely heroes of contemplation. They themselves shed no tears, but they also begin no revolutions, are apostles of no worldwide movements.

Berkeley's grandly simple accomplishment, as you know, lay in his observation that in the world of the senses, in the world of experience, as Locke knew it, there was properly no such thing as material substance discoverable at all. The world of sense-experience, said Berkeley, is a world of ideas. I have an idea, say of this fruit. It is a complex idea. The fruit is round, soft, pleasant to the taste, orange-colored, and the rest. But then, as you see, all these things that I know about the fruit are just my ideas. Were I in the dark, the fruit would have no color. Do I refuse to bite it, the taste of it remains a bare possibility, nor a fact. And so as to all the other properties of the fruit. All these exist for me insofar as I have ideas of them. Have I no idea of a thing, then it exists not for me. This is Berkeley's fundamental thought, but he does not leave it in such absolute and crude simplicity as this.

His deeper significance lies in the fact that he carries out in a new field an analysis of our inner life, namely, of a portion of the process of knowledge. His grandly simple idea, here applied, leads to very engaging results; but they are results which no other philosopher would be likely to accept without at once carrying them further than did Berkeley. The young student of Trinity College early became fascinated with the problem of the theory of vision. We seem to see objects about us in a space of three dimensions. These objects look solid, move about, stand in space relations to one another. But now, after all, how can we possibly see distance? Distance runs directly outward from my eyes; my eyes are at the surface of my body, and a distant object is not; my eyes are affected where they are, and, for the rest, not the distance of the opposite wall as such affects me, but the wall insofar as rays of light come from it. All this even Locke's man of plain sense has to admit. How, then, if distance itself is not one of my visual sensations, if distance isn't itself color or light, how can I still *see* distance? For all that I see is after all not even the object, but only the color and light of the object. This is Berkeley's problem about vision. His answer was early this: I don't really see distance. What I see is something about the color or shape of the distant object, or better still about the feelings that accompany in me the act of sight—something which is to me a *sign* of distance. A distant orange isn't as big as a near one. That is *one* sign of distance then, namely, the size for me of my idea of a patch of color which I see when I look at the orange. Again, very distant objects, such as mountains, are known to be distant because they look to me blue. In short, to sum up, my apparent seeing of distance isn't any direct seeing of distance at all. It is a reading of the language of

sight, as this is exhibited to my eyes by the colors and forms of things. A certain look of things, a certain group of signs, which I have learned, by long experience, to interpret, tells me how far off these things about me are. Distance isn't known directly. It is read as we read a language, read by interpreting the signs of the sense of sight. And as with distance, so with solidity. I don't really see things as solid. The solid things don't wander in through my eyes to my soul. But there are signs of solidity about the look of the things, signs that you learn to copy when you learn to draw in perspective, and to imitate the relief of objects; these signs are the language of the sense of sight. You learn, when you come to comprehend this language, that if a thing looks in a certain way, has a certain relief of colors, a certain perspective arrangement of its outlines, that then, I say, it will feel solid if you go up to it and touch it. Infants don't know all this until they have learned to read the language of vision. Hence they don't see things as solid for a good while, don't judge distances accurately, have no eye for a space of three dimensions.

Seeing, then, is reading, is interpreting a world-language, is anticipating how things will feel to your touch by virtue of the signs given by the color, light, relief, perspective, of things. Such is Berkeley's view, and as far as it goes, it is obviously true. But he is not content to leave his thought here. He goes further. What is all my life of experience, my seeing, feeling, touching, moving about, examining my world? Isn't it from first to last a learning to read the language of things? Isn't it a learning to anticipate one thing by virtue of the signs that are given of its presence by another? Yes, all experience is after all learning to read. And this reading, what is it? It is merely rightly and rationally putting together the ideas which my world gives me. These ideas come in certain orders, follow certain laws. I learn these laws, and thus I read my world. I have one idea, say the glow of a fire. It suggests to me another idea, namely, that in case I go near the fire I shall feel warm. All experience, then, is a learning how my ideas ought to go together; it is a learning that upon one idea another will follow under certain circumstances. What, then, is this world of my experience? Is it anything but the world of ideas and of their laws? What existence has my world for me apart from my ideas of it? What existence can any world have apart from the thought of some thinker for whom it exists? Whose language, then, am I reading in this world before me? Whose ideas are these that experience impresses upon me? Are they not God's ideas? Is it not his language that I read in nature? Is not all my life a talking with God?

"Some truths there are," says Berkeley, "so near and obvious to the mind that a man need only open his eyes to see them. Such I take this important one to be, to wit, that all the choir of heaven and furniture of the earth, in a word all those bodies which compose the mighty frame of the world, have not any subsistence without a mind, that their *being* is to be perceived or known; that consequently so long as they are not actually perceived by me, or do not exist in my mind or that of any other created spirit, they must either have no existence at all, or else subsist in the mind of some Eternal Spirit."*

This is Berkeley's interpretation and extension of Locke's thought. I don't ask you to accept or to reject it, I only ask you to see once more how it holds together. Let us review it. My experience is a learning to read my world. What is my world? Merely the sum total of my ideas, of my thoughts, feelings, sights, sounds, colors, tastes. I read these when one of them becomes sign to me of another, when the idea of a glow tells me of the yet unfelt warmth that a fire will arouse in me if I approach it, when the ideas of forms and shadows warn me how a solid thing will feel if I touch it. My ideas and their laws, this is all my reality. But then surely I am not the only existence

there is. No, indeed. The things about me are indeed only my ideas; but I am not the author of these ideas. This language of experience, those signs of the senses, which I decipher—I did not produce them. Who writes, then, this language? Who forces on my mind the succession of my ideas? Who spreads out the scroll of those experiences before me which in their totality constitute the choir of heaven and the furniture of earth? Berkeley responds readily. The sources of my ideas are two: my fellow-beings, who speak to me with the natural voice, and God, who talks to me in the language of the sense. "When," says Berkeley, "I deny sensible things an existence out of the mind, I do not mean my mind in particular, but all minds. Now it is plain they have an existence exterior to my mind, since I find them by experience to be independent of it. There is some other mind wherein they exist, during the intervals between the time of my perceiving them, as likewise they did before my birth, and would do after my supposed annihilation. And as the same is true with regard to all other finite created spirits, it necessarily follows, there is an *omnipresent eternal mind,* which knows and comprehends all things, and exhibits them to our view in such a manner, and according to such rules, as He himself hath ordained, and are by us termed the *laws of nature.*"

Here is the famous idealism of Berkeley. Never was philosophical idealism more simply stated. Nowhere is there a better introduction to a doctrine at once paradoxical and plausible, namely, the idealistic scheme of things, than in Berkeley's early essays. They are favorites—these essays—of all young students of philosophy. As you read them, unprepared, you first say, How wild a paradox! How absurdly opposed to common sense! Then you read further and say, How plausible this Berkeley is! How charming his style! How clear he makes his

---

*[GBWW, Vol. 35, p. 414b.]

paradoxes! Perhaps, after all, they aren't paradoxes, but mere rewordings of what we all mean. He knows a real world of facts, too. Nobody is surer of the truths of experience, nobody is firmer in his convictions of an outer reality, than Berkeley. Only this outer reality—what is it but God directly talking to us, directly impressing upon us these ideas of the "choir of heaven and furniture of earth?" In sense, in experience, we have God. He is in matter. Matter, in fact, is a part of his own self: it is his manifested will, his plan for our education, his voice speaking to us, warning, instructing, guiding, amusing, disciplining, blessing us, with a series of orderly and significant experiences. Well, I say, as you read further, the beauty of Berkeley's statement impresses you, you are half persuaded that you might come to believe this; and lo! suddenly, as you read, you *do* believe it, if only for an hour, and then, in a curious fashion, the whole thing comes to look almost commonplace. It is so obvious, you say, this notion that we only know our own ideas, so obvious that it was hardly worthwhile to write it down. After all, everybody believes that! As for the notion of God talking to us, through all our senses, that is very pretty and poetical, but is there anything very novel about the notion? It is the old design argument over again.

So I say, your mood alters as you read Berkeley. The value of his doctrine, for our present purposes, lies in its place in this history of the rediscovery of the inner life which we are following in this lecture. Of the truth of Berkeley's doctrine I have just now nothing to say. I am simply narrating to you Berkeley's experience of spiritual things. And his experience was this: that our consciousness of outer reality is a more subtle and complex thing than the previous age had suspected, so that the real world must be very different from the assumed substantial and mathematical world of the seventeenth century, and so that our inner life of sense and of reason needs yet a new and a deeper analysis. Ev-erything in this whole period makes, you see, for the study of this inner life. It is no matter whether you are a philosopher, and write essays on the "Principles of Human Knowledge," or whether you are a heroine in an eighteenth-century novel, and write sentimental letters to a friend; you are part of the same movement. The spirit is dissatisfied with the mathematical order and feels friendless among the eternities of the seventeenth-century thought. The spirit wants to be at home with itself, well-friended in the comprehension of its inner processes. It loves to be confidential in its heart oupourings, keen in its analysis, humane in its attitude toward life. And to be part of this new process is Berkeley's significance.

V

But now, if you are to enjoy the inner life, you must bear also its burdens and its doubts. To become sure of yourself, you must first doubt yourself. And this doubt, this skepticism, which self-analysis always involves, who could express it better than the great Scotchman, David Hume? Hume is, I think, next to Hobbes, the greatest of British speculative thinkers, Berkeley occupying the third place in order of rank. I cannot undertake to describe to you in this place the real historical significance of Hume, his subtlety, his fearlessness, his fine analysis of certain of the deepest problems, his place as the inspirer of Kant's thought, his whole value as metaphysical teacher of his time. What you will see in him is merely the merciless skeptic, and, in this superficial sketch of the rediscovery of the inner consciousness, I don't ask you to see more. Hume accepted Locke's belief that reason is merely the recorder of experience. He carries out this view to its remotest consequences. Our minds consist, as he says, of impressions and ideas. By impressions he means the experiences of sense; by ideas he means the remembered copies of these experiences. You see, feel, smell, taste; and you remember having seen, felt, tasted or smelt. This is all. You have no other knowledge. Upon some of your ideas, namely those of quantity and number, you can reason, and can even discover novel and necessary truth about them. This is owing to the peculiarity of these ideas and of the impressions on which they are founded. For these ideas, also, even all the subtleties of mathematical science, are faded and blurred impressions of sense. And, as it chances, on just these faded impressions you can reason. But Berkeley was wrong in thinking that you can by searching find out God, or anything else supersensual. Science concerns matters of fact, as the senses give them, and ends with these.

With this general view in mind, let us examine, in Hume's fashion, certain of the most familiar conceptions of human reason. Hume is afraid of nothing, not even of the presumptions at the basis of physical science. Matters of fact he respects, but not universal principles. "There are," says Hume, "no ideas . . . more obscure and uncertain than those of *power, force, energy,* or *necessary connection.*"* Let us look a little more closely at these ideas. Let us clear them up if we can. How useful they seem. How much we hear in exact science about something called the law of causation, which says that there is a necessary connection between causes and effects, that given natural conditions have a "power" to bring to pass certain results, that the forces of nature *must* work as they do. Well, apply to such sublime and far-reaching ideas—just such ideas, you will remember, as seemed to Spinoza so significant—apply to them Hume's simple criterion. Ideas, in order to have a good basis, must, Hume declares, stand for matters of fact, given to us in the senses. "It is impossible for us to *think* of anything which we have not antecedently *felt,* either by our external or internal senses." "By what invention," says Hume, "can we throw light" upon ideas that, being simple, still pretend to be au-

thoritative, "and render them altogether precise and determinate to our intellectual view?" Answer: "Produce the impressions or original sentiments from which the ideas are copied." These impressions will "admit not of ambiguity." So, then, let us produce the original impression from which the idea of causation, of necessary connection, or of power derived. You say that in nature there is and must be *necessity.* Very well, let us ask ourselves afresh the questions that we asked of Locke. Did you ever see necessity? Did you ever hear or touch causation? Did you ever taste or smell necessary connection? Name us the original impression whence comes your idea. "When," says Hume, "we look about us towards external objects, and consider the operation of causes, we are never able, in a single instance, to discover any power or necessary connection; any quality, which binds the effect to the cause, and renders the one an infallible consequence of the other. We only find that the one does actually, in fact, follow the other. The impulse of one billiard ball is attended with motion in the second. This is the whole that appears to the *outward* senses." "In reality, there is no part of matter that does ever, by its sensible qualities, discover any power or energy, or give us ground to imagine that it could produce anything," until we have found out by experience what happens in consequence of its presence. Thus outer sense gives us facts, but no necessary laws, no true causation, no real connection of events.

We must, then, get our idea of power, of necessary connection, from within. And so, in fact, many have thought that we do. If in outer nature I am only impressed by matters of fact about billiard balls and other such things, and if there I never learn of causation, do I not, perchance, directly feel my own true power, my own causal efficacy, my own will, making acts result

---

*[This and the following quotes from Hume can be found in *GBWW,* Vol. 35, pp. 471–509.]

in a necessary way from my purposes? No, answers Hume. If I examine carefully I find that my own deeds also are merely matters of fact, with nothing causally efficacious about my own conscious nature to make them obviously necessary. After all, "is there any principle in all nature more mysterious than the union of soul with body?" "Were we empowered," adds Hume, "to remove mountains, or control the planets in their orbit, this extensive authority would not be more extraordinary, nor more beyond our comprehension," than is the bare matter of fact that we now can control our bodies by our will. In inner experience, then, just as in outer, we get no direct impression of *how* causes produce effects. We only see *that* things *do* often happen in regular ways. In experience, then, "all events seem entirely loose and separate. One event follows another; but we can never observe any tie between them. They seem *conjoined,* but never *connected.* And as we can have no idea of anything which never appeared to our outward sense or inward sentiment, the necessary conclusion *seems* to be that we have no idea of connection or power at all, and that these words are absolutely without any meaning." From this seeming conclusion, Hume makes, indeed, an escape, but one that is, in fact, not less skeptical than his result as first reached. The true original of our idea of power, and so of causation, he says, is simply this, that "after a repetition of similar instances, the mind is carried by habit, upon the appearance of one event, to expect its usual attendant, and to believe that it will exist." "The first time a man saw the communication of motion by impulse, as by the shock of two billiard balls, he could not pronounce that the one event was *connected:* but only that it was *conjoined* with the other. After he has observed several instances of this nature, he then pronounces them to be *connected.* What alteration has happened to give rise to this new idea of *connection?* Nothing but that now he feels these events to be *con-*

nected in his imagination." Custom, then, mere habit of mind, is the origin of the idea of causation. We see no necessity in the world. We only *feel* it there, because that is our habit of mind, our fashion of mentally regarding an often-repeated experience of similar successions.

The importance of all this skepticism lies, as you of course see, in its removal from our fact-world of just the principles that the seventeenth century had found so inspiring. "It is of the nature of reason," Spinoza had said, "to regard things as necessary." Upon that rock he had built his faith. His wisdom had reposed secure in God, in whom were all things, just because God's nature was the highest form of necessity, the law of laws. And now comes Hume, and calls this "nature of reason" a mere feeling, founded on habit, a product of our imagination, no matter of fact at all. What becomes, then, of Spinoza's divine order? Has philosophy fallen by its own hands? Is the eternal in which we had trusted really, after all, but the mass of the flying and disconnected impressions of sense? All crumbles at the touch of this criticism of Hume's. All becomes but the aggregate of the disconnected sense-impressions. Nay, if we find the Holy Grail itself, it, too, will fade and crumble into dust. Hume is aware of some such result. He skillfully and playfully veils the extreme consequences at times by the arts of his beautiful dialectic. But he nonetheless rejoices in it, with all the fine joy of the merciless foe of delusions—*matters of fact, relations of ideas*—these are all that his doctrine leaves us. "When," he once says, "we run over libraries, persuaded of these principles, what havoc must we make? If we take in our hand any volume; of divinity or school metaphysics, for instance; let us ask, *Does it contain any abstract reasoning concerning quantity or number?* No. *Does it contain any experimental reasoning concerning matter of fact and existence?* No. Commit it then to the flames: for it can contain nothing but sophistry and illusion."

VI

Hume represents thus, indeed, the extreme of purely philosophical skepticism in the eighteenth century. Others, to be sure, outside of the ranks of the philosophers, went further in many ways and were rebels or scoffers in their own fashion, far more aggressive than his. But Hume's thought is in its result as fruitful as in its content it is negative. The spirit, you see, has become anxious to know its own nature. After all, can we live by merely assuming the innate ideas? Can even Spinoza's wisdom save us from doubt? And yet this doubt doesn't mean mere waywardness. It means longing for self-consciousness. And in the last third of the century this longing took, as we shall next time learn, new and positive forms. The inner life, to be sure, has appeared so far as a very capricious thing, after all. Study it by mere analysis of its experiences, as Hume did, and in this its capriciousness it will seem to shrivel to nothing under your hands. Where you expected it to be wealthiest, it turns out to be poorest. It is mere sense, mere feeling, mere sophistry and illusion. But is this the end? No, it is rather but the beginning of a new and a higher philosophy. The spirit is more than mere experience. Locke's account of the inner life is only half the truth. And what the other half is, Kant and his successors shall teach us. The age of poetry and of history—of a new natural science, also, yes, even this our own century— shall take up afresh the task that Hume rejected as impossible. The revolutionary period shall first rediscover passion, shall produce Goethe's *Faust,* and shall regenerate Europe. Historical research, reviving, shall prove to the spirit the significance of his own earthly past. Science, entering upon new realms, shall formulate the idea of cosmical evolution. No longer Spinoza's world, but a changing, a glowingly passionate and tragic world, of moral endeavor, of strife, of growth, and of freedom, shall

be conceived by men; and meanwhile, in Kant and in his successors, as we shall find, a more fitting philosophy will arise to formulate with all of Hume's keen dialectic, with all of Locke's love of human nature, and still with all of Spinoza's reverence for an absolute rationality in things, something of the significance of our modern life.

Remember, however, finally, that if the skepticism of the eighteenth century is to be gotten rid of, this will only be by transcending it, living through and beyond it, not by neglecting or by simply refuting it, from without. Philosophical insight, however partial, is never to be refuted. You can transcend it, you can make it part of a larger life, but it always remains as such a part. The genuine spirit includes all that was true and earnest in the doubting spirit. The only way to get rid of a philosophic doubt, in its discouraging aspect, is to see that, such as it is, it already implies a larger truth. The great spirit says to us, like Emerson's "Brahma,"

They reckon ill who leave me out;
When me they fly, I am the wings;
I am the doubter and the doubt.

And this, namely, the inevitableness and the true spirituality of genuine doubting, is the great lesson that the eighteenth century, in its transition to Kant, teaches us. It is a lesson well to be remembered in our own day, when, notwithstanding the vast accomplishments of recent research, there is a sense in which we, too, live in a world of doubt, but live there only that we may learn to conquer and possess it, all its doubts and its certainties, all its truth. In doubt we come to see our illusion; the phantoms of the night of thought vanish; but the new light comes. The old world dies, but only to rise again to the immortality of a higher existence. The spirit destroys its former creations, shatters its idols, and laments their loss. But, as in *Faust,* the chorus still sings:

Thou hast it destroyed,
The beautiful world,
With powerful fist:
In ruin 't is hurled,
By the blow of a demigod shattered!
The scattered
Fragments into the Void we carry,
Deploring
The beauty perished beyond restoring.
Mightier
For the children of men,

Brightlier
Build it again,
In thine own bosom build it anew!
Bid the new career
Commence,
With clearer sense,
And the new songs of cheer
*Be sung thereto!**

Such a building anew of the lost universe in the bosom of the human spirit, it was the mission of Kant to begin.

_____

*[Cf. *GBWW*, Vol. 47, p. 39a.]

Introduction to Poincaré's
Science and Hypothesis *

I

The branches of inquiry collectively known as the Philosophy of Science have undergone great changes since the appearance of Herbert Spencer's *First Principles,* that volume which a large part of the general public in this country used to regard as the representative compend of all modern wisdom relating to the foundations of scientific knowledge. The summary which M. Poincaré gives, at the outset of his own introduction to the present work, where he states the view which the "superficial observer" takes of scientific truth, suggests, not indeed Spencer's own most characteristic theories, but something of the spirit in which many disciples of Spencer interpreting their master's formulas used to conceive the position which science occupies in dealing with experience. It was well known to them, indeed, that experience is a constant guide, and an inexhaustible source both of novel scientific results and of unsolved problems; but the fundamental Spencerian principles of science, such as "the persistence of force," the "rhythm of motion," and the rest, were treated by Spencer himself as demonstrably objective, although indeed "relative" truths, capable of being tested once for all by the "inconceivability of the opposite," and certain to hold true for the whole "knowable" universe. Thus, whether one dwelt upon the results of such a mathematical procedure as that to which M. Poincaré refers in his opening paragraphs, or whether, like Spencer himself, one applied the "first principles" to regions of less exact science, this confidence that a certain orthodoxy regarding the principles of science was established forever was characteristic of the followers of the movement in question. Experience, lighted up by reason, seemed to them to have predetermined for all future time certain great theoretical results regarding the real constitution of the "knowable" cosmos. Whoever doubted this doubted "the verdict of science."

Some of us well remember how, when Stallo's *Principles and Theories of Modern Physics* first appeared, this sense of scientific orthodoxy was shocked amongst many of our American readers and teachers of science. I myself can recall to mind some highly authoritative reviews of that work in which the author was more or less sharply taken to task for his ignorant presumption in speaking with the freedom that he there used regarding such sacred possessions of humanity as the fundamental concepts of physics. That very book, however, has quite lately been translated into German as a valuable contribution to some of the most recent efforts to reconstitute a modern "philosophy of nature." And whatever may be otherwise thought of Stallo's critical methods, or of his results, there can be no doubt that, at the present moment, if his book were to appear for the first time, nobody would attempt to discredit the work merely on account of its disposition to be agnostic regarding the objective reality of the concepts of the kinetic theory of gases, or on account of its call for a logical rearrangement of the fundamental

---

*[Chapters III–V of this work appear in *Gateway to the Great Books* in a chapter entitled "Space," pp. 265–93.]

concepts of the theory of energy. We are no longer able so easily to know heretics at first sight.

For we now appear to stand in this position: The control of natural phenomena, which through the sciences men have attained, grows daily vaster and more detailed, and in its details more assured. Phenomena men know and predict better than ever. But regarding the most general theories, and the most fundamental, of science, there is no longer any notable scientific orthodoxy. Thus, as knowledge grows firmer and wider, conceptual construction becomes less rigid. The field of the theoretical philosophy of nature—yes, the field of the logic of science—this whole region is today an open one. Whoever will work there must indeed accept the verdict of experience regarding what happens in the natural world. So far he is indeed bound. But he may undertake without hindrance from mere tradition the task of trying afresh to reduce what happens to conceptual unity. The circle-squarers and the inventors of devices for perpetual motion are indeed still as unwelcome in scientific company as they were in the days when scientific orthodoxy was rigidly defined; but that is not because the foundations of geometry are now viewed as completely settled, beyond controversy, nor yet because the "persistence of force" has been finally so defined as to make the "opposite inconceivable" and the doctrine of energy beyond the reach of novel formulations. No, the circle-squarers and the inventors of devices for perpetual motion are today discredited, not because of any unorthodoxy of their general philosophy of nature, but because their views regarding special facts and processes stand in conflict with certain equally special results of science which themselves admit of very various general theoretical interpretations. Certain properties of the irrational number π are known, in sufficient multitude to justify the mathematician in declining to listen to the arguments of the circle-squarer; but, despite great advances, and despite the assured results of Dedekind, of Cantor, of Weierstrass, and of various others, the general theory of the logic of the numbers, rational and irrational, still presents several important features of great obscurity; and the philosophy of the concepts of geometry yet remains, in several very notable respects, unconquered territory, despite the work of Hilbert and of Pieri, and of our author himself. The ordinary inventors of the perpetual motion machines still stand in conflict with accepted generalizations; but nobody knows as yet what the final form of the theory of energy will be, nor can anyone say precisely what place the phenomena of the radioactive bodies will occupy in that theory. The alchemists would not be welcome workers in modern laboratories; yet some sorts of transformation and of evolution of the elements are today matters which theory can find it convenient, upon occasion, to treat as more or less exactly definable possibilities; while some newly observed phenomena tend to indicate, not indeed that the ancient hopes of the alchemists were well founded, but that the ultimate constitution of matter is something more fluent, less invariant, than the theoretical orthodoxy of a recent period supposed. Again, regarding the foundations of biology, a theoretical orthodoxy grows less possible, less definable, less conceivable (even as a hope) the more knowledge advances. Once "mechanism" and "vitalism" were mutually contradictory theories regarding the ultimate constitution of living bodies. Now they are obviously becoming more and more "points of view," diverse but not necessarily conflicting. So far as you find it convenient to limit your study of vital processes to those phenomena which distinguish living matter from all other natural objects, you may assume, in the modern "pragmatic" sense, the attitude of a "neo-vitalist." So far, however, as you are able to lay stress, with good results, upon the many ways in which the life processes can be assimilated to those studied in physics and in chemistry, you work as if you were a partisan of "mechanics." In any case, your special science prospers by reason of the empirical discoveries that you make. And your theories, whatever they are, must not run counter to any positive empirical results. But otherwise, scientific orthodoxy no longer predetermines what alone it is respectable for you to think about the nature of living substance.

This gain in the freedom of theory, coming, as it does, side by side with a constant increase of a positive knowledge of nature, lends itself to various interpretations, and raises various obvious questions.

II

One of the most natural of these interpretations, one of the most obvious of these questions, may be readily stated. Is not the lesson of all these recent discussions simply this, that general theories are simply vain, that a philosophy of nature is an idle dream, and that the results of science are coextensive with the range of actual empirical observation and of successful prediction? If this is indeed the lesson, then the decline of theoretical orthodoxy in science is—like the eclipse of dogma in religion— merely a further lesson in pure positivism, another proof that man does best when he limits himself to thinking about what can be found in human experience, and in trying to plan what can be done to make human life more controllable and more reasonable. What we are free to do as we please—is it any longer a serious business? What we are free to think as we please— is it of any further interest to one who is in search of truth? If certain general theories are mere conceptual constructions, which today are, and tomorrow are cast into the oven, why dignify them by the name of philosophy? Has science any place for such theories? Why be a "neo-vitalist," or an "evolutionist," or an "atomist," or an "Energetiker"? Why not say, plainly:

"Such and such phenomena, thus and thus described, have been observed; such and such experiences are to be expected, since the hypotheses by the terms of which we are required to expect them have been verified too often to let us regard the agreement with experience as due merely to chance; so much then with reasonable assurance we know; all else is silence—or else is some matter to be tested by another experiment"? Why not limit our philosophy of science strictly to such a counsel of resignation? Why not substitute, for the old scientific orthodoxy, simply a confession of ignorance, and a resolution to devote ourselves to the business of enlarging the bounds of actual empirical knowledge?

Such comments upon the situation just characterized are frequently made. Unfortunately, they seem not to content the very age whose revolt from the orthodoxy of traditional theory, whose uncertainty about all theoretical formulations, and whose vast wealth of empirical discoveries and of rapidly advancing special researches, would seem most to justify these very comments. Never has there been better reason than there is today to be content, if rational man could be content, with a pure positivism. The splendid triumphs of special research in the most various fields, the constant increase in our practical control over nature—these, our positive and growing possessions, stand in glaring contrast to the failure of the scientific orthodoxy of a former period to fix the outlines of an ultimate creed about the nature of the knowable universe. Why not "take the cash and let the credit go"? Why pursue the elusive theoretical "unification" any further, when what we daily get from our sciences is an increasing wealth of detailed information and of practical guidance?

As a fact, however, the known answer of our own age to these very obvious comments is a constant multiplication of new efforts toward large and unifying theories. If theoretical orthodoxy is no longer clearly definable, theoretical construction was never more rife. The history of the doctrine of evolution, even in its most recent phases, when the theoretical uncertainties regarding the "factors of evolution" are most insisted upon, is full of illustrations of this remarkable union of skepticism in critical work with courage regarding the use of the scientific imagination. The history of those controversies regarding theoretical physics, some of whose principal phases M. Poincaré, in his book, sketches with the hand of the master, is another illustration of the consciousness of the time. Men have their freedom of thought in these regions; and they feel the need of making constant and constructive use of this freedom. And the men who most feel this need are by no means in the majority of cases professional metaphysicians—or students who, like myself, have to view all these controversies among the scientific theoreticians from without as learners. These large theoretical constructions are due, on the contrary, in a great many cases to special workers, who have been driven to the freedom of philosophy by the oppression of experience, and who have learned in the conflict with special problems the lesson that they now teach in the form of general ideas regarding the philosophical aspects of science.

Why, then, does science actually need general theories, despite the fact that these theories inevitably alter and pass away? What is the service of a philosophy of science, when it is certain that the philosophy of science which is best suited to the needs of one generation must be superseded by the advancing insight of the next generation? Why must that which endlessly grows, namely, man's knowledge of the phenomenal order of nature, be constantly united in men's minds with that which is certain to decay, namely, the theoretical formulation of special knowledge in more or less completely unified systems of doctrine?

I understand our author's volume to be in the main an answer to this question. To be sure, the compact and manifold teachings which this text contains relate to a great many different special issues. A student interested in the problems of the philosophy of mathematics, or in the theory of probabilities, or in the nature and office of mathematical physics, or in still other problems belonging to the wide field here discussed, may find what he wants here and there in the text, even in case the general issues which give the volume its unity mean little to him, or even if he differs from the author's views regarding the principal issues of the book. But in the main, this volume must be regarded as what its title indicates—a critique of the nature and place of hypothesis in the work of science and a study of the logical relations of theory and fact. The result of the book is a substantial justification of the scientific utility of theoretical construction—an abandonment of dogma, but a vindication of the rights of the constructive reason.

III

The most notable of the results of our author's investigation of the logic of scientific theories relates, as I understand his work, to a topic which the present state of logical investigation, just summarized, makes especially important, but which has thus far been very inadequately treated in the textbooks of inductive logic. The useful hypotheses of science are of two kinds:

1. The hypotheses which are valuable *precisely* because they are either verifiable or else refutable through a definite appeal to the tests furnished by experience; and

2. The hypotheses which, despite the fact that experience suggests them, are valuable *despite,* or even *because of,* the fact that experience can *neither* confirm nor refute them. The contrast between these two kinds of hypotheses is a prominent topic of our author's discussion.

Hypotheses of the general type which I have here placed first in order are the ones which the textbooks of inductive logic and those summaries of scientific method which are customary in the course of the elementary treatises upon physical science are already accustomed to recognize and to characterize. The value of such hypotheses is indeed undoubted. But hypotheses of the type which I have here named in the second place are far less frequently recognized in a perfectly explicit way as useful aids in the work of special science. One usually either fails to admit their presence in scientific work, or else remains silent as to the reasons of their usefulness. Our author's treatment of the work of science is therefore especially marked by the fact that he explicitly makes prominent both the existence and the scientific importance of hypotheses of this second type. They occupy in his discussion a place somewhat analogous to each of the two distinct positions occupied by the "categories" and the "forms of sensibility," on the one hand, and by the "regulative principles of the reason," on the other hand, in the Kantian theory of our knowledge of nature. That is, these hypotheses which can neither be confirmed nor refuted by experience appear, in M. Poincaré's account, partly (like the conception of "continuous quantity") as devices of the understanding whereby we give conceptual unity and an invisible connectedness to certain types of phenomenal facts which come to us in a discrete form and in a confused variety; and partly (like the larger organizing concepts of science) as principles regarding the structure of the world in its wholeness; i.e., as principles in the light of which we try to interpret our experience, so as to give to it a totality and an inclusive unity such as Euclidean space, or such as the world of the theory of energy is conceived to possess. Thus viewed, M. Poincaré's logical theory of this second class of hypotheses undertakes to accomplish, with modern means and in the light of today's issues, a part of what Kant endeavored to accomplish in his theory of scientific knowledge with the limited means which were at his disposal. Those aspects of

science which are determined by the use of the hypotheses of this second kind appear in our author's account as constituting an essential human way of viewing nature, an interpretation rather than a portrayal or a prediction of the objective facts of nature, an adjustment of our conceptions of things to the internal needs of our intelligence, rather than a grasping of things as they are in themselves.

To be sure, M. Poincaré's view, in this portion of his work, obviously differs, meanwhile, from that of Kant, as well as this agrees, in a measure, with the spirit of the Kantian epistemology. I do not mean therefore to class our author as a Kantian. For Kant, the interpretations imposed by the "forms of sensibility," and by the "categories of the understanding," upon our doctrine of nature are rigidly predetermined by the unalterable "form" of our intellectual powers. We "must" thus view facts, whatever the data of sense must be. This, of course, is not M. Poincaré's view. A similarly rigid predetermination also limits the Kantian "ideas of the reason" to a certain set of principles whose guidance of the course of our theoretical investigations is indeed only "regulative," but is "a priori," and so unchangeable. For M. Poincaré, on the contrary, all this adjustment of our interpretations of experience to the needs of our intellect is something far less rigid and unalterable and is constantly subject to the suggestions of experience. We must indeed interpret in our own way; but our way is itself only relatively determinate; it is essentially more or less plastic; other interpretations of experience are conceivable. Those that we use are merely the ones found to be most convenient. But this convenience is not absolute necessity. Unverifiable and irrefutable hypotheses in science are indeed, in general, indispensable aids to the organization and to the guidance of our interpretation of experience. But it is experience itself which points out to us what lines of interpretation will prove most convenient. Instead of Kant's rigid list of *a priori* "forms," we consequently have in M. Poincaré's account a set of conventions, neither wholly subjective and arbitrary, nor yet imposed upon us unambiguously by the external compulsion of experience. The organization of science, so far as this organization is due to hypotheses of the kind here in question, thus resembles that of a constitutional government—neither absolutely necessary, nor yet determined apart from the will of the subjects, nor yet accidental—a free, yet not a capricious establishment of good order, in conformity with empirical needs.

Characteristic remains, however, for our author, as, in his decidedly contrasting way, for Kant, the thought that *without principles which at every stage transcend precise confirmation through such experience as is then accessible the organization of experience is impossible.* Whether one views these principles as conventions or as *a priori* "forms," they may therefore be described as hypotheses, but as hypotheses that, while lying at the basis of our actual physical sciences, at once refer to experience and help us in dealing with experience, and are yet neither confirmed nor refuted by the experiences which we possess or which we can hope to attain.

Three special instances or classes of instances, according to our author's account, may be used as illustrations of this general type of hypotheses. They are: (1) The hypothesis of the existence of continuous extensive *quanta* in nature; (2) The principles of geometry; (3) The principles of mechanics and of the general theory of energy. In case of each of these special types of hypotheses we are at first disposed, apart from reflection, to say that we *find* the world to be thus or thus, so that, for instance, we can confirm the thesis according to which nature contains continuous magnitudes; or can prove or disprove the physical truth of the postulates of Euclidean geometry; or can confirm by definite experience the objective validity of the principles of mechanics. A closer examination reveals, according to our author, the incorrectness of all such opinions. Hypotheses of these various special types are needed; and their usefulness can be empirically shown. They are in touch with experience; and that they are not merely arbitrary conventions is also verifiable. They are not *a priori* necessities; and we can easily conceive intelligent beings whose experience could be best interpreted without using these hypotheses. Yet these hypotheses are *not* subject to direct confirmation or refutation by experience. They stand then in sharp contrast to the scientific hypotheses of the other, and more frequently recognized, type, i.e., to the hypotheses which *can* be tested by a definite appeal to experience. To these other hypotheses our author attaches, of course, great importance. His treatment of them is full of a living appreciation of the significance of empirical investigation. But the central problem of the logic of science thus becomes the problem of the relation between the two fundamentally distinct types of hypotheses, i.e., between those which can not be verified or refuted through experience, and those which can be empirically tested.

IV

The detailed treatment which M. Poincaré gives to the problem thus defined must be learned from his text. It is no part of my purpose to expound, to defend, or to traverse any of his special conclusions regarding this matter. Yet I can not avoid observing that, while M. Poincaré strictly confines his illustrations and his expressions of opinion to those regions of science wherein, as special investigator, he is himself most at home, the issues which he thus raises regarding the logic of science are of even more critical importance and of more impressive interest when one applies M. Poincaré's methods to the study of the concepts and presuppositions of the organic and of the historical and social sciences, than when one confines one's attention, as our author here does, to the physical sciences. It belongs to the province of an introduction like the present to point out, however briefly and inadequately, that the significance of our author's ideas extends far beyond the scope to which he chooses to confine their discussion.

The historical sciences, and in fact all those sciences such as geology, and such as the evolutionary sciences in general, undertake theoretical constructions which relate to past time. Hypotheses relating to the more or less remote past stand, however, in a position which is very interesting from the point of view of the logic of science. Directly speaking, no such hypothesis is capable of confirmation or of refutation, because we can not return into the past to verify by our own experience what then happened. Yet indirectly, such hypotheses may lead to predictions of coming experience. These latter will be subject to control. Thus, Schliemann's confidence that the legend of Troy had a definite historical foundation led to predictions regarding what certain excavations would reveal. In a sense somewhat different from that which filled Schliemann's enthusiastic mind, these predictions proved verifiable. The result has been a considerable change in the attitude of historians toward the legend of Troy. Geological investigation leads to predictions regarding the order of the strata or the course of mineral veins in a district, regarding the fossils which may be discovered in given formations, and so on. These hypotheses are subject to the control of experience. The various theories of evolutionary doctrine include many hypotheses capable of confirmation and of refutation by empirical texts. Yet, despite all such empirical control, it still remains true that whenever a science is mainly concerned with the remote past, whether this science be archaeology, or geology, or anthropology, or Old Testament history, the principal theoret-

ical constructions always include features which no appeal to present or to accessible future experience can ever definitely test. Hence the suspicion with which students of experimental science often regard the theoretical constructions of their confrères of the sciences that deal with the past. The origin of the races of men, of man himself, of life, of species, of the planet; the hypotheses of anthropologists, of archaeologists, of students of "higher criticism"—all these are matters which the men of the laboratory often regard with a general incredulity as belonging not at all to the domain of true science. Yet no one can doubt the importance and the inevitableness of endeavoring to apply scientific method to these regions also. Science needs theories regarding the past history of the world. And no one who looks closer into the methods of these sciences of past time can doubt that verifiable and unverifiable hypotheses are in all these regions inevitably interwoven; so that, while experience is always the guide, the attitude of the investigator toward experience is determined by interests which have to be partially due to what I should call that "internal meaning," that human interest in rational theoretical construction which inspires the scientific inquiry; and the theoretical constructions which prevail in such sciences are neither unbiased reports of the actual constitution of an external reality, nor yet arbitrary constructions of fancy. These constructions in fact resemble in a measure those which M. Poincaré in this book has analyzed in the case of geometry. They are constructions molded, but *not* predetermined in their details, by experience. We report facts; we let the facts speak; but we, as we investigate, in the popular phrase, "talk back" to the facts. We interpret as well as report. Man is not merely made for science, but science is made for man. It expresses his deepest intellectual needs, as well as his careful observations. It is an effort to bring internal meanings into harmony with external verifications. It attempts therefore to control, as well as to submit, to conceive with rational unity, as well as to accept data. Its arts are those directed toward self-possession as well as toward an imitation of the outer reality which we find. It seeks therefore a disciplined freedom of thought. The discipline is as essential as the freedom; but the latter has also its place. The theories of science are human, as well as objective, internally rational, as well as (when that is possible) subject to external texts.

In a field very different from that of the historical sciences, namely, in a science of observation and of experiment, which is at the same time an organic science, I have been led in the course of some study of the history of certain researches to notice the existence of a theoretical conception which has proved extremely fruitful in guiding research, but which apparently resembles in a measure the type of hypotheses of which M. Poincaré speaks when he characterizes the principles of mechanics and of the theory of energy. I venture to call attention here to this conception, which seems to me to illustrate M. Poincaré's view of the functions of hypothesis in scientific work.

The modern science of pathology is usually regarded as dating from the earlier researches of Virchow, whose *Cellular Pathology* was the outcome of a very careful and elaborate induction. Virchow, himself, felt a strong aversion to mere speculation. He endeavored to keep close to observation, and to relieve medical science from the control of fantastic theories, such as those of the *Naturphilosophen* had been. Yet Virchow's researches were, as early as 1847, or still earlier, already under the guidance of a theoretical presupposition which he himself states as follows: "We have learned to recognize," he says, "that diseases are not autonomous organisms, that they are no entities that have entered into the body, that they are no parasites which take root in the body, but *that they merely*

show us the course of the vital processes under altered conditions" ("dass sie nur Ablauf der Lebenserscheinungen unter veränderten Bedingungen darstellen").

The enormous importance of this theoretical presupposition for all the early successes of modern pathological investigation is generally recognized by the experts. I do not doubt this opinion. It appears to be a commonplace of the history of this science. But in Virchow's later years this very presupposition seemed to some of his contemporaries to be called in question by the successes of recent bacteriology. The question arose whether the theoretical foundations of Virchow's pathology had not been set aside. And in fact the theory of the parasitical origin of a vast number of diseased conditions has indeed come upon an empirical basis to be generally recognized. Yet to the end of his own career Virchow stoutly maintained that in all its essential significance his own fundamental principle remained quite untouched by the newer discoveries. And, as a fact, this view could indeed be maintained. For if diseases proved to be the consequences of the presence of parasites, the diseases themselves, so far as they belonged to the diseased organism, were still not the parasites but were, as before, the reaction of the organism to the *veränderte Bedingungen* which the presence of the parasites entailed. So Virchow could well insist. And if the famous principle in question is only stated with sufficient generality, it amounts simply to saying that if a disease involves a change in an organism, and if this change is subject to law at all, then the nature of the organism and the reaction of the organism to whatever it is which causes the disease must be understood in case the disease is to be understood.

For this very reason, however, Virchow's theoretical principle in its most general form *could be neither confirmed nor refuted by experience*. It would remain empirically irrefutable, so far as I can see, even if we should learn that the devil was the true cause of all diseases. For the devil himself would then simply predetermine the *veränderte Bedingungen* to which the diseased organism would be reacting. Let bullets or bacteria, poisons or compressed air, or the devil be the *Bedingungen* to which a diseased organism reacts, the postulate that Virchow states in the passage just quoted will remain irrefutable, if only this postulate be interpreted to meet the case. For the principle in question merely says that whatever entity it may be, bullet, or poison, or devil, that affects the organism, the disease is not that entity, but is the resulting alteration in the process of the organism.

I insist, then, that this principle of Virchow's is no trial supposition, no scientific hypothesis in the narrower sense—capable of being submitted to precise empirical tests. It is, on the contrary, a very precious *leading idea,* a theoretical interpretation of phenomena, in the light of which observations are to be made—"a regulative principle" of research. It is equivalent to a resolution to search for those detailed connections which link the processes of disease to the normal process of the organism. Such a search undertakes to find the true unity, whatever that may prove to be, wherein the pathological and the normal processes are linked. Now without some such leading idea, the cellular pathology itself could never have been reached, because the empirical facts in question would never have been observed. Hence this principle of Virchow's was indispensable to the growth of his science. Yet it was not a verifiable and not a refutable hypothesis. One value of unverifiable and irrefutable hypotheses of this type lies, then, in the sort of empirical inquiries which they initiate, inspire, organize, and guide. In these inquiries hypotheses in the narrower sense, that is, trial propositions which are to be submitted to definite empirical control, are indeed everywhere present. And the use of the other sort of principles lies

wholly in their application to experience. Yet without what I have just proposed to call the "leading ideas" of a science, that is, its principles of an unverifiable and irrefutable character, suggested, but not to be finally tested, by experience, the hypotheses in the narrower sense would lack that guidance which, as M. Poincaré has shown, the larger ideas of science give to empirical investigation.

V

I have dwelt, no doubt, at too great length upon one aspect only of our author's varied and well-balanced discussion of the problems and concepts of scientific theory. Of the hypotheses in the narrower sense and of the value of direct empirical control, he has also spoken with the authority and the originality which belong to his position. And in dealing with the foundations of mathematics he has raised one or two questions of great philosophical import into which I have no time, even if I had the right, to enter here. In particular, in speaking of the essence of mathematical reasoning, and of the difficult problem of what makes possible novel results in the field of pure mathematics, M. Poincaré defends a thesis regarding the office of "demonstration by recurrence"—a thesis which is indeed disputable, which has been disputed, and which I myself should be disposed, so far as I at present understand the matter, to modify in some respects, even in accepting the spirit of our author's assertion. Yet there can be no doubt of the importance of this thesis, and of the fact that it defines a characteristic that is indeed fundamental in a wide range of mathematical research. The philosophical problems that lie at the basis of recurrent proofs and processes are, as I have elsewhere argued, of the most fundamental importance.

These, then, are a few hints relating to the significance of our author's discussion, and a few reasons for hoping that our own students will profit by the reading of the book as those of other nations have already done.

Of the person and of the lifework of our author a few words are here, in conclusion, still in place, addressed, not to the students of his own science, to whom his position is well known, but to the general reader who may seek guidance in these pages.

Jules Henri Poincaré was born at Nancy, in 1854, the son of a professor in the Faculty of Medicine at Nancy. He studied at the École Polytechnique and at the École des Mines and later received his doctorate in mathematics in 1879. In 1883 he began courses of instruction in mathematics at the École Polytechnique; in 1886 received a professorship of mathematical physics in the Faculty of Sciences at Paris; then became member of the Academy of Sciences at Paris, in 1887, and devoted his life to instruction and investigation in the regions of pure mathematics, of mathematical physics, and of celestial mechanics. His list of published treatises relating to various branches of his chosen sciences is long; and his original memoirs have included several momentous investigations, which have gone far to transform more than one branch of research. His presence at the International Congress of Arts and Science in St. Louis was one of the most noticeable features of that remarkable gathering of distinguished foreign guests. In Poincaré the reader meets, then, not one who is primarily a speculative student of general problems for their own sake, but an original investigator of the highest rank in several distinct, although interrelated, branches of modern research. The theory of functions—a highly recondite region of pure mathematics—owes to him advances of the first importance, for instance, the definition of a new type of functions. The "problem of the three bodies," a famous and fundamental problem of celestial mechanics, has received from his studies a treatment whose significance has been recognized by the highest authorities. His international reputation has been confirmed by the conferring of more than one important prize for his researches. His membership in the most eminent learned societies of various nations is widely extended; his volumes bearing upon various branches of mathematics and of mathematical physics are used by special students in all parts of the learned world; in brief, he is, as geometer, as analyst and as a theoretical physicist, a leader of his age.

Meanwhile, as contributor to the philosophical discussion of the bases and methods of science, M. Poincaré has long been active. When, in 1893, the admirable *Revue de Métaphysique et de Morale* began to appear, M. Poincaré was soon found amongst the most satisfactory of the contributors to the work of that journal, whose office it has especially been to bring philosophy and the various special sciences (both natural and moral) into a closer mutual understanding. The discussions brought together in the present volume are in large part the outcome of M. Poincaré's contributions to the *Revue de Métaphysique et de Morale*. The reader of M. Poincaré's book is in presence, then, of a great special investigator who is also a philosopher.

William James and the Philosophy of Life

Fifty years since, if competent judges were asked to name the American thinkers from whom there had come novel and notable and typical contributions to general philosophy, they could in reply mention only two men—Jonathan Edwards and Ralph Waldo Emerson. For the conditions that determine a fair answer to the question, "Who are your representative American philosophers?" are obvious. The philosopher who can fitly represent the contribution of his nation to the world's treasury of philosophical ideas must first be one who thinks for himself, fruitfully, with true independence, and with successful inventiveness, about problems of philosophy. And, secondly, he must be a man who gives utterance to philosophical ideas which are characteristic of some stage and of some aspect of the spiritual life of his own people. In Edwards and in Emerson, and only in these men, had these two conditions found their fulfillment, so far as our American civilization had yet expressed itself in the years that had preceded our civil war. Edwards, in his day, made articulate some of the great interests that had molded our early religious life. The thoughts which he most discussed were indeed, in a sense, old, since they largely concerned a traditional theology. Yet both in theology and general philosophy, Edwards was an originator. For he actually rediscovered some of the world's profoundest ideas regarding God and humanity simply by reading for himself the meaning of his own religious experience. With a mysterious power of philosophical intuition, even in his early youth, he observed what, upon the basis of what we know to have been his range

of philosophical reading, we could not possibly have expected him to observe. If the sectarian theological creed that he defended was to our minds narrow, what he himself saw was very far-reaching and profound. For he viewed religious problems with synoptic vision that enabled him to reconcile, in his own personal way, some of the greatest and most tragic conflicts of the spiritual world, and what he had to say consequently far transcended the interests of the special theological issues which he discussed. Meanwhile, he spoke not merely as a thinker, but as one who gave voice to some of the central motives and interests of our colonial religious life. Therefore he was, in order of time, the first of our nationally representative philosophers.

Another stage of our civilization—a later phase of our national ideals—found its representative in Emerson. He too was in close touch with many of the world's deepest thoughts concerning ultimate problems. Some of the ideas that most influenced him have their far-off historical origins in oriental as well as in Greek thought, and also their nearer foreign sources in modern European philosophy. But he transformed whatever he assimilated. He invented upon the basis of his personal experience, and so he was himself no disciple of the orient, or of Greece, still less of England and of Germany. He thought, felt, and spoke as an American.

Fifty years ago, I say, our nation had so far found these two men to express each his own stage of the philosophy of our national civilization. The essence of a philosophy, in case you look at it solely from a historical point of view, always appears to you thus: A great philosophy expresses an interpretation of the life of man and a view of the universe, which is at once personal and, if the thinker is representative of his people, national in its significance. Edwards and Emerson had given tongue to the meaning of two different stages of our American culture. And these were thus far our only philosophical voices.

Today, if we ask any competent foreign critic of our philosophy whether there is any other name to be added to these two classic American philosophers, we shall receive the unanimous answer: "There is today a third representative American philosopher. His name is William James." For James meets the two conditions just mentioned. He has thought for himself, fruitfully, with true independence, and with successful inventiveness. And he has given utterance to ideas which are characteristic of a stage and of an aspect of the spiritual life of this people. He, too, has been widely and deeply affected by the history of thought. But he has reinterpreted all these historical influences in his own personal way. He has transformed whatever he has assimilated. He has rediscovered whatever he has received from without; because he never could teach what he had not himself experienced. And, in addition, he has indeed invented effectively and richly. Moreover, in him certain characteristic aspects of our national civilization have found their voice. He is thus the third in the order of time among our representative American philosophers. Already, within a year of his death, he has begun to acquire something of a classic rank and dignity. In future this rank and dignity will long increase. In one of James's latest utterances he indeed expressed, with characteristic energy, a certain abhorrence of what he called classical tendencies in philosophical thought. But I must repeat the word: Fortune not unjustly replies, and will reply to James's vigorous protest against every form of classicism, by making him a classic.

Thus, then, from the point of view of the competent foreign students of our philosophy, the representative American philosophers are now three and only three— Edwards, Emerson, James.

And of these three there can be little question that, at the present time, the most widely known abroad is James. Emerson has indeed found a secure place in the minds of the English-speaking lovers of his type of thought everywhere, and has had an important part in the growth of some modern German tendencies. But James has already won, in the minds of French, of German, of Italian, and of still other groups of foreign readers, a position which gives him a much more extended range of present influence than Emerson has ever possessed.

It is my purpose, upon the present occasion, to make a few comments upon the significance of William James's philosophy. This is no place for the discussion of technical matters. Least of all have I any wish to undertake to decide, upon this occasion, any controversial issues. My intentions as I address you are determined by very simple and obvious considerations. William James was my friend from my youth to the end of his beneficent life. I was once for a brief time his pupil. I long loved to think of myself as his disciple; although perhaps I was always a very bad disciple. But now he has just left us. And as I address you I remember that he was your friend also. Since the last annual meeting of this assembly he has been lost to us all. It is fitting that we should recall his memory today. Of personal reminiscences, of biographical sketches, and of discussions relating to many details of his philosophy, the literature that has gathered about his name during the few months since we lost him has been very full. But just as this is no occasion for technical discussion of his philosophy, so too I think this is no place to add new items to the literature of purely personal reminiscence and estimate of James. What I shall try to do is this: I have said that James is an American philosopher of classic rank, because he stands for a stage in our national self-consciousness—for a stage with which historians of our national mind must always reckon. This statement, if you will permit, shall be my text. I shall devote myself to expounding this text as well as I can in my brief time, and to estimating the significance of the stage in question, and of James's thought insofar as it seems to me to express the ideas and the ideals characteristic of this phase of our national life.

I

In defining the historical position which William James, as a thinker, occupies, we have of course to take account, not only of national tendencies, but also of the general interests of the world's thought in his time. William James began his work as a philosopher, during the seventies of the last century, in years which were, for our present purpose, characterized by two notable movements of worldwide significance. These two movements were at once scientific in the more special sense of that term, and philosophical in the broad meaning of that word. The first of the movements was concerned with the elaboration—the widening and the deepening—of the newer doctrines about evolution. This movement had indeed been preceded by another. The recent forms of evolutionary doctrine, those associated with the names of Darwin and of Spencer, had begun rapidly to come into prominence about 1860. And the decade from 1860 to 1870, taken together with the opening years of the next decade, had constituted what you may call the storm-and-stress period of Darwinism, and of its allied tendencies, such as those which Spencer represented. In those years the younger defenders of the new doctrines, so far as they appealed to the general public, fought their battles, declared their faith, out of weakness were made

strong, and put to flight the armies of the theologians. You might name, as a closing event of that storm-and-stress period, Tyndall's famous Belfast address of 1874, and the warfare waged about that address. Haeckel's early works, some of Huxley's most noted polemic essays, Lange's *History of Materialism,* the first eight or nine editions of Von Hartmann's *Philosophy of the Unconscious,* are documents characteristic of the more general philosophical interests of that time. In our country, Fiske's *Outlines of Cosmic Philosophy* reflected some of the notable features that belonged to these years of the early conquests of evolutionary opinion.

Now in that storm-and-stress period, James had not yet been before the public. But his published philosophical work began with the outset of the second and more important period of evolutionary thought—the period of the widening and deepening of the new ideas. The leaders of thought who are characteristic of this second period no longer spend their best efforts in polemic in favor of the main ideas of the newer forms of the doctrine of evolution. In certain of its main outlines—outlines now extremely familiar to the public—they simply accept the notion of the natural origin of organic forms and of the general continuity of the processes of development. But they are concerned, more and more, as time goes on, with the deeper meaning of evolution, with the study of its factors, with the application of the new ideas to more and more fields of inquiry, and, in case they are philosophers, with the reinterpretation of philosophical traditions in the light of what had resulted from that time of storm and stress.

James belongs to this great second stage of the evolutionary movement, to the movement of the elaboration, of the widening and deepening of evolutionary thought, as opposed to that early period of the storm and stress. We still live in this second stage of evolutionary movement. James is one of

its most inventive philosophical representatives. He hardly ever took part in the
polemic in favor of the general evolutionary ideas. Accepting them, he undertook
to interpret and apply them.

And now, secondly, the period of James's
activity is the period of the rise of the new
psychology. The new psychology has stood
for many other interests besides those of
a technical study of the special sciences of
the human and of the animal mind. What
is technical about psychology is indeed important enough. But the special scientific
study of mind by the modern methods
used in such study has been a phase and
a symptom of a very much larger movement—a movement closely connected with
all that is most vital in recent civilization,
with all the modern forms of nationalism,
of internationalism, of socialism, and of individualism. Human life has been complicated by so many new personal and social
problems, that man has needed to aim,
by whatever means are possible, toward
a much more elaborate knowledge of his
fellow man than was ever possible before.
The results of this disposition appear in
the most widely diverse sciences and arts.
Archaeology and ethnology, history and
the various social sciences, dramatic art,
the novel, as well as what has been called
psychical research—in a word, all means,
good and bad, that have promised either
a better knowledge of what man is or a
better way of portraying what knowledge
of man one may possess—have been tried
and molded in recent times by the spirit of
which recent technical psychology is also an
expression. The psychological movement
means then something that far transcends
the interests of the group of sciences to
which the name psychology now applies.
And this movement assumed some of its
most important recent forms during the
decade in which James began to publish his
work. His own contributions to psychology
reflect something of the manifoldness and
of the breadth of the general psychological

movement itself. If he published the two
great volumes entitled *Psychology*,* he also
wrote *The Varieties of Religious Experience,*
and he played his part in what is called
"psychical research."

These then are James's two principal offices when you consider him merely in his
most general relations to the thought of the
world at large in his time. He helped in the
work of elaborating and interpreting evolutionary thought. He took a commanding
part in the psychological movement.

II

But now it is not of these aspects of
James's work, significant as they are, that
I have here especially to speak. I must indeed thus name and emphasize these wider
relations of his thought to the world's contemporary thought. But I do so in order to
give the fitting frame to our picture. I now
have to call attention to the features about
James which make him, with all his universality of interest, a representative American thinker. Viewed as an American, he
belongs to the movement which has been
the consequence, first, of our civil war, and
secondly, of the recent expansion, enrich-
ment, and entanglement of our social life.
He belongs to the age in which our nation,
rapidly transformed by the occupation of
new territory, by economic growth, by
immigration, and by education, has been
attempting to find itself anew, to redefine
its ideals, to retain its moral integrity, and
yet to become a world power. In this stage
of our national consciousness we still live
and shall plainly have to live for a long
time in the future. The problems involved
in such a civilization we none of us well
understand; least of all do I myself understand them. And James, scholar, thinker,
teacher, scientific and philosophical writer
as he was, has of course only such relation

---

*[*GBWW*, Vol. 53.]

to our national movement as is implied by the office that he thus fulfills. Although he followed with keen interest a great variety of political and social controversies, he avoided public life. Hence, he was not absorbed by the world of affairs, although he was always ready to engage generously in the discussion of practical reforms. His main office with regard to such matters was therefore that of philosophical interpreter. He helped to enlighten his fellows as to the relations between the practical problems of our civilization and those two worldwide movements of thought of which I have just spoken.

Let me call attention to some of the results of James's work as interpreter of the problems of the American people. I need not say that this work was, to his own mind, mainly incidental to his interest in those problems of evolutionary thought and of psychology to which I just directed your attention. I am sure that James himself was very little conscious that he was indeed an especially representative American philosopher. He certainly had no ambition to vaunt himself as such. He worked with a beautiful and hearty sincerity upon the problems that as a fact interested him. He knew that he loved these problems because of their intense human interest. He knew, then, that he was indeed laboring in the service of mankind. But he so loved what he called the concrete, the particular, the individual, that he naturally made little attempt to define his office in terms of any social organism, or of any such objects as our national life, viewed as an entity. And he especially disliked to talk of causes in the abstract, or of social movements as I am here characterizing them. His world seemed to him to be made up of individuals—men, events, experiences, and deeds. And he always very little knew how important he himself was, or what vast inarticulate social forces were finding in him their voice. But we are now viewing James from without, in a way that is of course as imperfect as it is inevitable. We therefore

have a right at this point to attribute to him an office that, as I believe, he never attributed to himself.

And here we have to speak first of James's treatment of religious problems, and then of his attitude toward ethics.

Our nation since the civil war has largely lost touch with the older forms of its own religious life. It has been seeking for new embodiments of the religious consciousness, for creeds that shall not be in conflict with the modern man's view of life. It was James's office, as psychologist and as philosopher, to give a novel expression to this our own national variety of the spirit of religious unrest. And his volume *The Varieties of Religious Experience* is one that, indeed, with all its wealth of illustration, and in its courageous enterprise, has a certain classic beauty. Some men preach new ways of salvation. James simply portrayed the meaning that the old ways of salvation had possessed, or still do possess, in the inner and personal experience of those individuals whom he has called the religious geniuses. And then he undertook to suggest an hypothesis as to what the whole religious process might mean. The hypothesis is on the one hand in touch with certain tendencies of recent psychology. And insofar it seems in harmony with the modern consciousness. On the other hand it expresses, in a way, James's whole philosophy of life. And in this respect it comes into touch with all the central problems of humanity.

The result of this portrayal was indeed magical. The psychologists were aided toward a new tolerance in their study of religion. The evolution of religion appeared in a new light. And meanwhile many of the faithful, who had long been disheartened by the later forms of evolutionary naturalism, took heart anew when they read James's vigorous appeal to the religious experience of the individual as to the most authoritative evidence for religion. "The most modern of thinkers, the evolutionist, the psychologist," they said, "the heir of all the ages, has thus vindicated anew the witness of the spirit in the heart—the very source of inspiration in which we ourselves have always believed." And such readers went away rejoicing, and some of them even began to write christologies based upon the doctrine of James as they understood it. The new gospel, the glad tidings of the subconscious, began to be preached in many lands. It has even received the signal honor of an official papal condemnation.

For my own part, I have ventured to say elsewhere that the new doctrine, viewed in one aspect, seems to leave religion in the comparatively trivial position of a play with whimsical powers—a prey to endless psychological caprices. But James's own robust faith was that the very caprices of the spirit are the opportunity for the building up of the highest forms of the spiritual life; that the unconventional and the individual in religious experience are the means whereby the truth of a superhuman world may become most manifest. And this robust faith of James, I say, whatever you may think of its merits, is as American in type as it has already proved effective in the expression which James gave to it. It is the spirit of the frontiersman, of the gold seeker, or the home builder, transferred to the metaphysical and to the religious realm. There is our far-off home, our long-lost spiritual fortune. Experience alone can guide us toward the place where these things are; hence you indeed need experience. You can only win your way on the frontier in case you are willing to live there. Be, therefore, concrete, be fearless, be experimental. But, above all, let not your abstract conceptions, even if you call them scientific conceptions, pretend to set any limits to the richness of spiritual grace, to the glories of spiritual possession, that, in case you are duly favored, your personal experience may reveal to you. James reckons that the tribulations with which abstract scientific theories have beset our present age are not to be compared with the glory that perchance shall be, if only

we open our eyes to what experience itself has to reveal to us.

In the quest for the witness to whom James appeals when he tests his religious doctrine, he indeed searches the most varied literature; and of course most of the records that he consults belong to foreign lands. But the book called *The Varieties of Religious Experience* is full of the spirit that, in our country, has long been effective in the formation of new religious sects; and this volume expresses, better than any sectarian could express, the recent efforts of this spirit to come to an understanding with modern naturalism, and with the new psychology. James's view of religious experience is meanwhile at once deliberately unconventional and intensely democratic. The old-world types of reverence for the external forms of the church find no place in his pages; but equally foreign to his mind is that barren hostility of the typical European freethinkers for the church with whose traditions they have broken. In James's eyes, the forms, the external organizations of the religious world simply wither; it is the individual that is more and more. And James, with a democratic contempt for social appearances, seeks his religious geniuses everywhere. World-renowned saints of the historic church receive his hearty sympathy; but they stand upon an equal footing, in his esteem, with many an obscure and ignorant revivalist, with faith healers, with poets, with sages, with heretics, with men that wander about in all sorts of sheepskins and goatskins, with chance correspondents of his own, with whomsoever you will of whom the world was not and is not worthy, but who, by inner experience, have obtained the substance of things hoped for, the evidence of things not seen.

You see, of course, that I do not believe James's resulting philosophy of religion to be adequate. For as it stands it is indeed chaotic. But I am sure that it can only be amended by taking it up into a larger view, and not by rejecting it. The spirit

373

triumphs, not by destroying the chaos that James describes, but by brooding upon the face of the deep until the light comes, and with light, order. But I am sure also that we shall always have to reckon with James's view. And I am sure also that only an American thinker could have written this survey, with all its unconventional ardor of appreciation, with all its democratic catholicity of sympathy, with all its freedom both from ecclesiastical formality and from barren freethinking. I am sure also that no book has better expressed the whole spirit of hopeful unrest, of eagerness to be just to the modern view of life, of longing for new experience, which characterizes the recent American religious movement. In James's book, then, the deeper spirit of our national religious life has found its most manifold and characteristic expression.

III

I must next turn to the other of the two aspects of James's work as a thinker that I mentioned above; namely, to his ethical influence. Since the war, our transformed and restless people has been seeking not only for religious, but for moral guidance. What are the principles that can show us the course to follow in the often pathless wilderness of the new democracy? It frequently seems as if, in every crisis of our greater social affairs, we needed somebody to tell us both our dream and the interpretation thereof. We are eager to have life, and that abundantly. But what life? And by what test shall we know the way of life?

The ethical maxims that most readily meet the popular demand for guidance in such a country, and at such a time, are maxims that combine attractive vagueness with an equally winning pungency. They must seem obviously practical but must not appear excessively rigorous. They must arouse a large enthusiasm for action, without baffling us with the sense of restraint, or of wearisome self-control. They must

not call for extended reflection. Despite their vagueness they must not appear abstract, nor yet hard to grasp. The wayfaring man, though a fool, must be sure that he at least will not err in applying our moral law. Moral blunders must be natural only to opponents, not to ourselves. We must be self-confident. Moreover, our moral law must have an athletic sound. Its first office is to make us "good sports." Only upon such a law can we meditate day and night, in case the "game" leaves us indeed any time for meditation at all. Nevertheless, these popular maxims will of course not be meant as mere expressions of blind impulse. On the contrary, they will appeal to highly intelligent minds, but to minds anxious for relief from the responsibility of being too thoughtful. In order to be easily popular they must be maxims that stir the heart, not precisely indeed like the sound of a trumpet, but more like the call of the horn of an automobile. You will have in mind the watchwords that express some of the popular ethical counsels thus suggested. One of these watchwords has of late enabled us to abbreviate a well-known and surely a highly intelligent maxim, to something that is today used almost as a mere interjection. It is the watchword, "Efficiency"! Another expression of the same motive takes shape in the equally familiar advice, "Play the game."

Now I do not mean to make light of the real significance of just such moral maxims, for awakening and inspiring just our people in this day. The true value of these maxims lies for us in three of their characteristic features. First, they give us counsel that is in any case opposed to sloth. And sloth on every level of our development remains one of the most treacherous and mortal enemies of the moral will. Secondly, they teach us to avoid the dangers to which the souls of Hamlet's type fall a prey. That is, they discourage the spirit that reflectively divides the inner self, and that leaves it divided. They warn us that the divided self is indeed, unless it can heal its deadly wound, by fitting action, a lost soul. And thirdly, they emphasize courage. And courage—not, to be sure, so much the courage that faces one's rivals in the marketplace, or one's foes on the battlefield, as the courage that fits us to meet our true spiritual enemies—the courage that arises anew from despair and that undertakes, despite all tribulations, to overcome the world—such courage is one of the central treasures of the moral life.

Because of these three features, the maxims to which I refer are, in all their vagueness, vehicles of wisdom. But they express themselves in their most popular forms with a willfulness that is often more or less comic, and that is sometimes tragic. For what they do not emphasize is the significance of self-possession, of lifting up our eyes to the hills whence cometh our help, of testing the life that now is by the vision of the largest life that we can in ideal appreciate. These popular maxims also emphasize results rather than ideals, strength rather than cultivation, temporary success rather than wholeness of life, the greatness of "Him that taketh a city," rather than of "Him that ruleth his spirit." They are the maxims of unrest, of impatience, and of a certain humane and generous unscrupulousness, as fascinating as it is dangerous. They characterize a people that is indeed earnestly determined to find itself, but that so far has not found itself.

Now one of the most momentous problems regarding the influence of James is presented by the question: How did he stand related to these recent ethical tendencies of our nation? I may say at once that, in my opinion, he has just here proved himself to be most of all and in the best sense our national philosopher. For the philosopher must not be an echo. He must interpret. He must know us better than we know ourselves, and this is what indeed James has done for our American moral consciousness. For, first, while he really made very little of the formal office of an ethical teacher and seldom wrote upon technical ethical controversies, he was, as a fact, profoundly ethical in his whole influence. And next, he fully understood, yet shared in a rich measure, the motives to which the ethical maxims just summarized have given expression. Was not he himself restlessly active in his whole temperament? Did he not love individual enterprise and its free expression? Did he not loathe what seemed to him abstractions? Did he not insist that the moralist must be in close touch with concrete life? As psychologist did he not emphasize the fact that the very essence of conscious life lies in its active, yes, in its creative relation to experience? Did he not counsel the strenuous attitude toward our tasks? And are not all these features in harmony with the spirit from which the athletic type of morality just sketched seems to have sprung?

Not only is all this true of James, but, in the popular opinion of the moment, the doctrine called pragmatism, as he expounded it in his Lowell lectures, seems, to many of his foreign critics, and to some of those who think themselves his best followers here at home, a doctrine primarily ethical in its force, while, to some minds, pragmatism seems also to be a sort of philosophical generalization of the efficiency doctrine just mentioned. To be sure, any closer reader of James's *Pragmatism* ought to see that his true interests in the philosophy of life are far deeper than those which the maxims "Be efficient" and "Play the game" mostly emphasize. And, for the rest, the book on pragmatism is explicitly the portrayal of a method of philosophical inquiry and is only incidentally a discourse upon ethically interesting matters. James himself used to protest vigorously against the readers who ventured to require of the pragmatist, viewed simply as such, any one ethical doctrine whatever. In his book on pragmatism he had expounded, as he often said, a method of philosophizing, a definition of truth, a criterion for interpreting and testing theories. He was not there concerned with ethics. A pragmatist was free to decide moral issues as he chose, so long as he used the pragmatic method in doing so; that is, so long as he tested ethical doctrines by their concrete results, when they were applied to life.

Inevitably, however, the pragmatic doctrine, that both the meaning and the truth of ideas shall be tested by the empirical consequences of these ideas and by the practical results of acting them out in life, has seemed both to many of James's original hearers, and to some of the foreign critics just mentioned, a doctrine that is simply a characteristic Americanism in philosophy—a tendency to judge all ideals by their practical efficiency, by their visible results, by their so-called cash values.

James, as I have said, earnestly protested against this cruder interpretation of his teaching. The author of *The Varieties of Religious Experience* and of *The Pluralistic Universe* was indeed an empiricist, a lover of the concrete, and a man who looked forward to the future rather than backward to the past; but despite his own use, in his "pragmatism," of the famous metaphor of the "cash values" of ideas, he was certainly not a thinker who had set his affections upon things below rather than upon things above. And the "consequences" upon which he laid stress when he talked of the pragmatic test for ideas were certainly not the merely worldly consequences of such ideas in the usual sense of the word *worldly*. He appealed always to experience; but then for him experience might be, and sometimes was, religious experience—experience of the unseen and of the superhuman. And so James was right in his protest against these critics of his later doctrine. His form of pragmatism was indeed a form of Americanism in philosophy. And he too had his fondness for what he regarded as efficiency, and for those who "play the game," whenever the game was one that he honored. But he also loved too much those who are weak in the eyes of this present world—the religious geniuses, the unpopular inquirers,

the noble outcasts. He loved them, I say, too much to be the dupe of the cruder forms of our now popular efficiency doctrine. In order to win James's most enthusiastic support, ideas and men needed to express an intense inner experience along with a certain unpopularity which showed that they deserved sympathy. Too much worldly success, on the part of men or of ideas, easily alienated him. Unworldliness was one of the surest marks, in his eyes, of spiritual power, if only such unworldliness seemed to him to be joined with interests that, using his favorite words, he could call "concrete" and "important."

In the light of such facts, all that he said about judging ideas by their "consequences" must be interpreted, and therefore it is indeed unjust to confound pragmatism with the cruder worship of efficiency.

IV

Yet, I repeat, James's philosophy of life was indeed, in its ethical aspects, an expression of the better spirit of our people. He understood, he shared, and he also transcended the American spirit. And just that is what most marks him as our national philosopher. If you want to estimate his philosophy of life in its best form, you must read or reread, not the *Pragmatism,* but the essays contained in the volume entitled *The Will to Believe.*

May I still venture, as I close, to mention a few features of the doctrine that is embodied in that volume? The main question repeatedly considered in these essays of James is explicitly the question of an empiricist, of a man averse to abstractions, and of an essentially democratic thinker, who does not believe that any final formulation of an ideal of human life is possible until the last man has had his experience of life and has uttered his word. But this empiricism of the author is meanwhile the empiricism of one who especially emphasizes the central importance of the active life as the basis of our interpretation of experience. Herein James differs from all traditional positivists. Experience is never yours merely as it comes to you. Facts are never mere data. They are data to which you respond. Your experience is constantly transformed by your deeds. That this should be the case is determined by the most essential characteristics of your consciousness. James asserts this latter thesis as psychologist, and has behind him, as he writes, the vast mass of evidence that his two psychological volumes present. The simplest perception, the most elaborate scientific theory, illustrate how man never merely finds but also always cooperates in creating his world.

No doubt then life must be estimated and guided with constant reference to experience, to consequences, to actual accomplishments, to what we Americans now call efficiency. But on the other hand efficiency itself is not to be estimated in terms of mere data. Our estimate of our world is not to be forced upon us by any mere inspection of consequences. What makes life worth living is not what you find in it, but what you are ready to put into it by your ideal interpretation of the meaning that, as you insist, it shall possess for you. This ideal meaning is always for you a matter of faith not to be imposed coercively upon another, but also never to be discovered by watching who it is that wins, or by merely feeling your present worldly strength as a player of the game. Your deeper ideals always depend upon viewing life in the light of larger unities than now appear, upon viewing yourself as a coworker with the universe for the attainment of what no present human game of action can now reveal. For this "radical empiricist" then present experience always points beyond itself to a realm that no human eye has yet seen—an empirical realm of course, but one that you have a right to interpret in terms of a faith that is itself active, but that is not merely worldly and athletic. The philosophy of action thus so

imperfectly suggested by the few phrases that I have time to use can best be interpreted, for the moment, by observing that the influence of Carlyle in many passages of this volume is as obvious as it is by our author independently reinterpreted and transformed. Imagine Carlyle transformed into a representative American thinker, trained as a naturalist, deeply versed in psychology, deprived of his disposition to hatred, open-minded toward the interests of all sorts and conditions of men, still a hero-worshiper, but one whose heroes could be found in the obscurest lovers of the ideal as easily as in the most renowned historical characters; let this transformed Carlyle preach the doctrine of the resolute spirit triumphant through creative action, defiant of every degree of mortal suffering. Let him proclaim "The Everlasting Yea" in the face of all the doubts of erring human opinion; and herewith you gain some general impression of the relations that exist between *Sartor Resartus* and *The Will to Believe*.

The ethical maxims which are scattered through these pages voluntarily share much of the vagueness of our age of tentative ethical effort. But they certainly are not the maxims of an impressionist, of a romanticist, or of a partisan of merely worldly efficiency. They win their way through all such attitudes to something beyond—to a resolute interpretation of human life as an opportunity to cooperate with the superhuman and the divine. And they do this, in the author's opinion, not by destroying, but by fulfilling the purposes and methods of the sciences of experience themselves. Is not every scientific theory a conceptual reinterpretation of our fragmentary perceptions, an active reconstruction, to be tried in the service of a larger life? Is not our trust in a scientific theory itself an act of faith? Moreover, these ethical maxims are here governed, in James's exposition, by the repeated recognition of certain essentially absolute truths, truths that, despite his natural horror of absolutism, he here expounds with a finished dialectic skill that he himself, especially in his later polemic period, never seemed to prize at its full value. The need of active faith in the unseen and the superhuman he founds upon these simple and yet absolutely true principles, principles of the true dialectics of life: First, every great decision of practical life requires faith, and has irrevocable consequences, consequences that belong to the whole great world, and that therefore have endless possible importance. Secondly, since action and belief are thus inseparably bound together, our right to believe depends upon our right, as active beings, to make decisions. Thirdly, our duty to decide life's greater issues is determined by the absolute truth that, in critical cases, the will to be doubtful and not to decide is itself a decision and is hence no escape from our responsible moral position. And this our responsible position is a position that gives us our place in and for all future life. The world needs our deeds. We need to interpret the world in order to act. We have a right to interpret the universe so as to enable us to act at once decisively, courageously, and with the sense of the inestimable preciousness and responsibility of the power to act.

In consequence of all these features of his ethical doctrine a wonderful sense of the deep seriousness and of the possibly divine significance of every deed is felt in James's every ethical counsel. Thus it is that, while fully comprehending the American spirit which we have sketched, he at once expresses it and transforms it. He never loved Fichte; but there is much of the best of the ethical idealism of Fichte in *The Will to Believe*. Many of you have enjoyed James's delightfully skillful polemic against Hegel, and against the external forms, phrases, and appearances of the later constructive idealists. I have no wish here to attempt to comment upon that polemic; but I can assure you that I myself learned a great part of my own form of absolute idealism from the earliest expressions that James

gave to the thoughts contained in *The Will to Believe*. As one of his latest works, *The Pluralistic Universe*, still further showed, he himself was in spirit an ethical idealist to the core. Nor was he nearly so far in spirit even from Hegel as he supposed, guiltless as he was of Hegel's categories. Let a careful reading of *The Pluralistic Universe* make this fact manifest.

Meanwhile, what interests us is that, in *The Will to Believe*, as well as in *The Pluralistic Universe*, this beautifully manifold, appreciative, and humane mind, at once adequately expressed, and, with true moral idealism, transcended the caprices of recent American ethics. To this end he lavishly used the resources of the naturalist, of the humanist, and of the ethical dialectician. He saw the facts of human life as they are, and he resolutely lived beyond them into the realm of the spirit. He loved the concrete, but he looked above toward the larger realm of universal life. He often made light of the abstract reason, but in his own plastic and active way he uttered some of the great words of the universal reason, and he has helped his people to understand and to put into practice these words.

I ask you to remember him then, not only as the great psychologist, the radical empiricist, the pragmatist, but as the interpreter of the ethical spirit of his time and of his people—the interpreter who has pointed the way beyond the trivialities which he so well understood and transcended toward that "Rule of Reason" which the prophetic maxim of our supreme court has just brought afresh to the attention of our people. That "Rule of Reason," when it comes, will not be a mere collection of abstractions. It will be, as James demanded, something concrete and practical. And it will indeed appeal to our faith as well as to our discursive logical processes. But it will express the transformed and enlightened American spirit as James already began to express it. Let him too be viewed as a prophet of the nation that is to be.

Laocoon

Gotthold Ephraim Lessing

Editor's Introduction

Gotthold Ephraim Lessing, who spent most of his life in one or another of the towns and cities of what is now East Germany, where he was born (1729) and died (1781), was nevertheless the sort of man who could exist until the French Revolution made nationality important—one who was not so much a German as a European. He was also what he could be before science created specialization—not just a dramatist, a critic, or a philosopher (in fact he was all of those), but a representative of the Enlightenment, a citizen of the world.

His numerous writings, some of which date from his student days at the University of Leipzig, and which made an edition of more than twenty volumes after his relatively early death, testify to his energy and also his need. For he relied on his pen for a living, and yet, despite considerable success as a dramatist and the high critical reputation he gained during his lifetime, was never well off; indeed, when he died he was recognized as a pauper and buried at public expense.

Among his many works were plays, most of them comedies of a serious kind (Lessing did much to establish the genre which has come to be known as tragicomedy), literary criticism, essays on the drama and other subjects, and even a quasi-religious treatise on human perfectibility. All of them remain in print, though few perhaps are now widely read. And Lessing's critical reputation—as the author, especially, of the *Hamburg Dramaturgy* (1767–69), a collection of essays that is now part of the canon of early dramatic criticism—is still high, if not as high as it seemed to Matthew Arnold, who cited him routinely, in his own essays, as "the great Lessing." Moreover, of the plays, at least one, *Minna von Barnhelm*, as well as the dramatic poem called "Nathan the Wise," have achieved what appears to be permanent place in the literature of their time.

The book by which Lessing will probably always be known is, of course, *Laocoon; or, On the Limits of Painting and Poetry* (1766). It is a classic work in its field, which should probably be called aesthetics, though that term had only about then begun to be used. This is so despite the fact that Lessing was not otherwise an art critic (the "Laocoon" is a sculpture group now in the Vatican Museum, dating from the first century B.C.), his interest being poetry, which he sought to distinguish from the graphic arts. Nor is it fatal that the aesthetic distinction his essay makes is one that has been harder to maintain since the Romantic revolution in sensibility, when all the fine arts came to be thought of in terms of expression rather than form, expression being conceived as a product of the imagination, and thus as indivisible. For Lessing's argument, whether one concedes its application or not in this case, is clearly applicable in others and, in its simplest sense, which is that poetry does some things better than painting, and vice versa, is so plainly true that one cannot believe it was not said before.

Lessing's occasion for saying it was the publication by Johann Winckelmann of a book called *Reflections on the Poetry and Sculpture of the Greeks* (1755). Winckelmann interpreted the Laocoon group as evidence of Greek composure in the face of suffering, the pain of which does not show (he maintained) in the figures of the group, who are the Trojan priest Laocoon and his two sons, shown being strangled by the god Poseidon in the form of a serpent to prevent them from warning Troy of its impending fall by the device of the Trojan Horse—this *contra* Virgil, who speaks of Laocoon's "heart-piercing shrieks" (*Aeneid,* II, 222; *GBWW,* Vol. 13, p. 130a). Such an interpretation carried considerable authority. Winckelmann (1717–68) *was* an art critic, and the first art historian, perhaps, in the modern sense of the term. But Lessing took him on all the same, agreeing with his perception of the sculpture, but attributing its correctness to a different cause, and moved, at least in part (so he acknowledged in the first chapter of his own book), to defend Virgil's poetry from the imputation that it was uncomprehending of the Greek spirit—something that no one of Lessing's profession could easily accept.

It should perhaps be noted in this connection that many observers of the Laocoon group have concluded that both Winckelmann and Lessing were wrong in their observation of it; have insisted that the faces do show anguish, or at least very probably did, the sculpture as we know it being but a copy of the earlier original, done at a period when technique alone was celebrated, and lacking the perfection of detail which the original may be supposed to have had. To this may be added that Lessing himself, at least, had never seen even this copy, since he was never in Rome, but knew of it only in a casting (that is, a copy of the copy), or possibly by no more than an engraved reproduction. That does not affect his position, however, though the arguably inferior quality of the sculpture as we have it would seem to bear somewhat on Winckelmann's.

Laocoon is printed (in translation) as Lessing wrote it, save that long passages of Greek, Latin, Italian, etc., in the notes have been replaced by English equivalents, some of them supplied editorially, and that most of the scholarly references have been deleted, the works cited being now for the most part of merely antiquarian interest.

Preface

The first who compared painting with poetry was a man of fine feeling, who was conscious of a similar effect produced on himself by both arts. Both, he perceived, represent absent things as present, give us the appearance as the reality. Both produce illusion, and the illusion of both is pleasing.

A second sought to analyze the nature of this pleasure and found its source to be in both cases the same. Beauty, our first idea of which is derived from corporeal objects, has universal laws which admit of wide application. They may be extended to actions and thoughts as well as to forms.

A third, pondering upon the value and distribution of these laws, found that some obtained more in painting, others in poetry: that in regard to the latter, therefore, poetry can come to the aid of painting; in regard to the former, painting to the aid of poetry, by illustration and example.

The first was the amateur; the second, the philosopher; the third, the critic.

The first two could not well make a false use of their feeling or their conclusions, whereas with the critic all depends on the right application of his principles in particular cases. And, since there are fifty ingenious critics to one of penetration, it would be a wonder if the application were, in every case, made with the caution indispensable to an exact adjustment of the scales between the two arts.

If Apelles and Protogenes, in their lost works on painting, fixed and illustrated its rules from the already established laws of poetry, we may be sure they did so with the same moderation and exactness with which Aristotle, Cicero, Horace, and Quintilian, in their still existing writings, apply the principles and experiences of painting to eloquence and poetry. It is the prerogative of the ancients in nothing either to exceed or fall short.

But we moderns have in many cases thought to surpass the ancients by transforming their pleasure-paths into highways, though at the risk of reducing the shorter and safer highways to such paths as lead through deserts.

The dazzling antithesis of the Greek Voltaire, that painting is dumb poetry, and poetry speaking painting, stood in no textbook. It was one of those conceits, occurring frequently in Simonides, the inexactness and falsity of which we feel constrained to overlook for the sake of the evident truth they contain.

The ancients, however, did not overlook them. They confined the saying of Simonides to the effect produced by the two arts, not failing to lay stress upon the fact that, notwithstanding the perfect similarity of their effects, the arts themselves differ both in the objects and in the methods of their imitation, ὕλη καὶ τρόποις μιμήσεως.

But, as if no such difference existed, many modern critics have drawn the crudest conclusions possible from this agreement between painting and poetry. At one time they confine poetry within the narrower limits of painting, and at another allow painting to fill the whole wide sphere of poetry. Whatever is right in one must be permitted to the other; whatever pleases or displeases in one is necessarily pleasing or displeasing in the other. Full of this idea they, with great assurance, give utterance to the shallowest judgments, whenever they find that poet and painter have treated the same subject in a different way. Such variations they take to be faults, and charge them on painter or poet, according as their taste more inclines to the one art or the other.

This fault-finding criticism has partially misled the virtuosos themselves. In poetry, a fondness for description, and in painting, a fancy for allegory, has arisen from the desire to make the one a speaking picture without really knowing what it can and ought to paint, and the other a dumb poem, without having considered in how far painting can express universal ideas without abandoning its proper sphere and degenerating into an arbitrary method of writing.

To combat that false taste and those ill-grounded criticisms is the chief object of the following chapters. Their origin was accidental, and in their growth they have rather followed the course of my reading than been systematically developed from general principles. They are, therefore, not so much a book as irregular *collectanea* for one.

Yet I flatter myself that, even in this form, they will not be wholly without value. We Germans suffer from no lack of systematic books. No nation in the world surpasses us in the faculty of deducing from a couple of definitions whatever conclusions we please, in most fair and logical order.

Baumgarten acknowledged that he was indebted to Gesner's dictionary for a large proportion of the examples in his "Aesthetics." If my reasoning be less close than that of Baumgarten, my examples will, at least, savor more of the fountain.

Since I made the Laocoon my point of departure, and return to it more than once in the course of my essay, I wished him to have a share in the title page. Other slight digressions on various points in the history of ancient art, contribute less to the general design of my work, and have been retained only because I never can hope to find a better place for them.

Further, I would state that, under the name of painting, I include the plastic arts generally; as, under that of poetry, I may have allowed myself sometimes to embrace those other arts, whose imitation is progressive.

Laocoon

I.

The chief and universal characteristic of the Greek masterpieces in painting and sculpture consists, according to Winckelmann, in a noble simplicity and quiet grandeur, both of attitude and expression. "As the depths of the sea," he says, "remain always at rest, however the surface may be agitated, so the expression in the figures of the Greeks reveals in the midst of passion a great and steadfast soul."

"Such a soul is depicted in the countenance of the Laocoon, under sufferings the most intense. Nor is it depicted in the countenance only: the agony betrayed in every nerve and muscle—we almost fancy we could detect it in the painful contraction of the abdomen alone, without looking at the face and other parts of the body—this agony, I say, is yet expressed with no violence in the face and attitude. He raises no terrible cry, as Virgil sings of his Laocoon. This would not be possible, from the opening of the mouth, which denotes rather an anxious and oppressed sigh, as described by Sadolet. Bodily anguish and moral greatness are diffused in equal measure through the whole structure of the figure; being, as it were, balanced against each other. Laocoon suffers, but he suffers like the Philoctetes of Sophocles. His sufferings pierce us to the soul, but we are tempted to envy the great man his power of endurance."

The Greek statue Laocoon now stands in the Vatican Museum. " 'Bodily anguish and moral greatness are diffused in equal measure through the whole structure of the figure. . . .' "

"To express so noble a soul far out-runs the constructive art of natural beauty. The artist must have felt within himself the mental greatness which he has impressed upon his marble. Greece united in one person artist and philosopher, and had more than one Metrodorus. Wisdom joined hands with art and inspired its figures with more than ordinary souls."

The remark which lies at the root of this criticism—that suffering is not expressed in the countenance of Laocoon with the intensity which its violence would lead us to expect—is perfectly just. That this very point, where a shallow observer would judge the artist to have fallen short of nature and not to have attained the true pathos of suffering, furnishes the clearest proof of his wisdom, is also unquestionable. But in the reason which Winckelmann assigns for this wisdom, and the universality of the rule which he deduces from it, I venture to differ from him.

His depreciatory allusion to Virgil was, I confess, the first thing that aroused my doubts, and the second was his comparison of Laocoon with Philoctetes. Using these as my starting points, I shall proceed to write down my thoughts in the order in which they have occurred to me.

"Laocoon suffers like the Philoctetes of Sophocles." How does Philoctetes suffer? Strange that his sufferings have left such different impressions upon our minds. The complaints, the screams, the wild imprecations with which his pain filled the camp, interrupting the sacrifices and all offices of religion, resounded not less terribly through the desert island to which they had been the cause of his banishment. Nor did the poet hesitate to make the theatre ring with the imitation of these tones of rage, pain, and despair.

The third act of this play has been regarded as much shorter than the others. A proof, say the critics, that the ancients attached little importance to the equal length of the acts. I agree with their conclusion but should choose some other example in support of it. The cries of pain, the moans, the broken exclamations, $\dot{\alpha}, \dot{\alpha}! \varphi\varepsilon\tilde{v}! \dot{\alpha}\tau\tau\alpha\tau\alpha\tilde{\iota}! \ddot{\omega} \mu o\hat{\iota}, \mu o\hat{\iota}!$ the $\pi\alpha\pi\alpha\tilde{\iota}, \pi\alpha\pi\alpha\tilde{\iota}!$* filling whole lines, of which this act is made up, would naturally require to be prolonged in the delivery and interrupted by more frequent pauses than a connected discourse. In the representation, therefore, this third act must have occupied about as much time as the others. It seems shorter on paper to the reader than it did to the spectator in the theatre.

A cry is the natural expression of bodily pain. Homer's wounded heroes not infrequently fall with a cry to the ground. Venus screams aloud at a scratch [*GBWW*, Vol. 4, p. 33c], not as being the tender goddess of love, but because suffering nature will have its rights. Even the iron Mars, on feeling the lance of Diomedes, bellows as frightfully as if ten thousand raging warriors were roaring at once and fills both armies with terror [*GBWW*, Vol. 4, p. 38d].

High as Homer exalts his heroes in other respects above human nature, they yet remain true to it in their sensitiveness to pain and injuries and in the expression of their feelings by cries or tears or revilings. Judged by their deeds they are creatures of a higher order; in their feelings they are genuine human beings.

We finer Europeans of a wiser posterity have, I know, more control over our lips and eyes. Courtesy and decency forbid cries and tears. We have exchanged the active bravery of the first rude ages for a passive courage. Yet even our ancestors were greater in the latter than the former. But our ancestors were barbarians. To stifle all signs of pain, to meet the stroke of death with unaverted eye, to die laughing under the adder's sting, to weep neither over our own sins nor at the loss of the dearest of friends, are traits of the old northern heroism. The law given by

_____

*[Oh! oh! oh me! pain! pain!]

Detail of the Laocoon. " 'The expression . . . of the Greeks reveals in the midst of passion a great and steadfast soul. . . . Such a soul is depicted in the countenance of the Laocoon.' "

Palnatoko to the Jomsburghers was to fear nothing, nor even to name the word fear.

Not so the Greek. He felt and feared. He expressed his pain and his grief. He was ashamed of no human weakness, yet allowed none to hold him back from the pursuit of honor or the performance of a duty. Principle wrought in him what savageness and hardness developed in the barbarian. Greek heroism was like the spark hidden in the pebble, which sleeps till roused by some outward force, and takes from the stone neither clearness nor coldness. The heroism of the barbarian was a bright, devouring flame, ever raging, and blackening, if not consuming, every other good quality.

When Homer makes the Trojans advance to battle with wild cries, while the Greeks march in resolute silence, the commentators very justly observe that the poet means by this distinction to characterize the one as an army of barbarians, the other of civilized men. I am surprised they have not perceived a similar characteristic difference in another passage [*GBWW*, Vol. 4, p. 50b].

The opposing armies have agreed upon an armistice, and are occupied, not without hot tears on both sides (δάκρυα θερμὰ χέοντες), with the burning of their dead. But Priam forbids his Trojans to weep (οὐδ' εἴα κλαίειν Πρίαμος μέγας), "and for this reason," says Madame Dacier; "he feared they might become too tenderhearted, and return with less spirit to the morrow's fight." Good; but I would ask why Priam alone should apprehend this. Why does not Agamemmon issue the same command to his Greeks? The poet has a deeper meaning. He would show us that only the civilized Greek can weep and yet be brave, while the uncivilized Trojan, to be brave, must stifle all humanity. I am in no wise ashamed to weep (Νεμεσσῶμαί γε μὲν οὐδὲν κλάιειν), he elsewhere makes the prudent son of wise Nestor say [*GBWW*, Vol. 4, p. 201a].

It is worthy of notice that, among the few tragedies which have come down to us from antiquity, there should be two in which bodily pain constitutes not the least part of the hero's misfortunes. Besides Philoctetes we have the dying Hercules, whom also Sophocles represents as wailing, moaning, weeping, and screaming. Thanks to our well-mannered neighbors, those masters of propriety, a whimpering Philoctetes or a screaming Hercules would now be ridiculous and not tolerated upon the stage. One of their latest poets, indeed, has ventured upon a Philoctetes, but he seems not to have dared to show him in his true character.

Among the lost works of Sophocles was a Laocoon. If fate had but spared it to us! From the slight references to the piece in some of the old grammarians, we cannot determine how the poet treated his subject. Of one thing I am convinced— that he would not have made his Laocoon

more of a Stoic than Philoctetes and Hercules. Everything stoical is untheatrical. Our sympathy is always proportionate with the suffering expressed by the object of our interest. If we behold him bearing his misery with magnanimity, our admiration is excited; but admiration is a cold sentiment, wherein barren wonder excludes not only every warmer emotion but all vivid personal conception of the suffering.

I come now to my conclusion. If it be true that a cry, as an expression of bodily pain, is not inconsistent with nobility of soul, especially according to the views of the ancient Greeks, then the desire to represent such a soul cannot be the reason why the artist has refused to imitate this cry in his marble. He must have had some other reason for deviating in this respect from his rival, the poet, who expresses it with deliberate intention.

II.

Be it truth or fable that Love made the first attempt in the imitative arts, thus much is certain: that she never tired of guiding the hand of the great masters of antiquity. For although painting, as the art which reproduces objects upon flat surfaces, is now practised in the broadest sense of that definition, yet the wise Greek set much narrower bounds to it. He confined it strictly to the imitation of beauty. The Greek artist represented nothing that was not beautiful. Even the vulgarly beautiful, the beauty of inferior types, he copied only incidentally for practice or recreation. The perfection of the subject must charm in his work. He was too great to require the beholders to be satisfied with the mere barren pleasure arising from a successful likeness or from consideration of the artist's skill. Nothing in his art was dearer to him or seemed to him more noble than the ends of art.

"Who would want to paint you when no one wants to look at you?" says an old epigrammatist to a misshapen man. Many a modern artist would say, "No matter how misshapen you are, I will paint you. Though people may not like to look at you, they will be glad to look at my picture; not as a portrait of you, but as a proof of my skill in making so close a copy of such a monster."

The fondness for making a display with mere manual dexterity, ennobled by no worth in the subject, is too natural not to have produced among the Greeks a Pauson and a Pyreicus. They had such painters but meted out to them strict justice. Pauson, who confined himself to the beauties of ordinary nature, and whose depraved taste liked best to represent the imperfections and deformities of humanity,[1] lived in the most abandoned poverty; and Pyreicus, who painted barbers' rooms, dirty workshops, donkeys, and kitchen herbs, with all the diligence of a Dutch painter, as if such things were rare or attractive in nature, acquired the surname of Rhyparographer, the dirt-painter. The rich voluptuaries, indeed, paid for his works their weight in gold as if by this fictitious valuation to atone for their insignificance.

Even the magistrates considered this subject a matter worthy their attention and confined the artist by force within his proper sphere. The law of the Thebans commanding him to make his copies more beautiful than the originals, and never under pain of punishment less so, is well known. This was no law against bunglers, as has been supposed by critics generally, and even by Junius himself, but was aimed against the Greek Ghezzi and condemned the unworthy artifice of obtaining a likeness by exaggerating the deformities of the model. It was, in fact, a law against caricature.

From this same conception of the beautiful came the law of the Olympic judges. Every conqueror in the Olympic games received a statue, but a portrait-statue was erected only to him who had been thrice victor. Too many indifferent portraits were

not allowed among works of art. For although a portrait admits of being idealized, yet the likeness should predominate. It is the ideal of a particular person, not the ideal of humanity.

We laugh when we read that the very arts among the ancients were subject to the control of civil law; but we have no right to laugh. Laws should unquestionably usurp no sway over science, for the object of science is truth. Truth is a necessity of the soul, and to put any restraint upon the gratification of this essential want is tyranny. The object of art, on the contrary, is pleasure, and pleasure is not indispensable. What kind and what degree of pleasure shall be permitted may justly depend on the lawgiver.

The plastic arts especially, besides the inevitable influence which they exercise on the character of a nation, have power to work one effect which demands the careful attention of the law. Beautiful statues fashioned from beautiful men reacted upon their creators, and the state was indebted for its beautiful men to beautiful statues. With us the susceptible imagination of the mother seems to express itself only in monsters.

From this point of view I think I detect a truth in certain old stories which have been rejected as fables. The mothers of Aristomenes, of Aristodamas, of Alexander the Great, Scipio, Augustus, and Galerius, each dreamed during pregnancy that she was visited by a serpent. The serpent was an emblem of divinity. Without it Bacchus, Apollo, Mercury, and Hercules were seldom represented in their beautiful pictures and statues. These honorable women had been feasting their eyes upon the god during the day, and the bewildering dream suggested to them the image of the snake. Thus I vindicate the dream and show up the explanation given by the pride of their sons and by unblushing flattery. For there must have been some reason for the adulterous fancy always taking the form of a serpent.

389

But I am wandering from my purpose, which was simply to prove that among the ancients beauty was the supreme law of the imitative arts. This being established, it follows necessarily that whatever else these arts may aim at must give way completely if incompatible with beauty, and, if compatible, must at least be secondary to it.

I will confine myself wholly to expression. There are passions and degrees of passion whose expression produces the most hideous contortions of the face and throws the whole body into such unnatural positions as to destroy all the beautiful lines that mark it when in a state of greater repose. These passions the old artists either refrained altogether from representing or softened into emotions which were capable of being expressed with some degree of beauty.

Rage and despair disfigured none of their works. I venture to maintain that they never represented a fury. Wrath they tempered into severity. In poetry we have the wrathful Jupiter, who hurls the thunderbolt; in art he is simply the austere.

Anguish was softened into sadness. Where that was impossible, and where the representation of intense grief would belittle as well as disfigure, how did Timanthes manage? There is a well-known picture by him of the sacrifice of Iphigenia, wherein he gives to the countenance of every spectator a fitting degree of sadness but veils the face of the father, on which should have been depicted the most intense suffering. This has been the subject of many petty criticisms. "The artist," says one, "had so exhausted himself in representations of sadness that he despaired of depicting the father's face worthily." "He hereby confessed," says another, "that the bitterness of extreme grief cannot be expressed by art." I, for my part, see in this no proof of incapacity in the artist or his art. In proportion to the intensity of feeling, the expression of the features is intensified, and nothing is easier than to express extremes. But Timanthes knew the limits which the

graces have imposed upon his art. He knew that the grief befitting Agamemnon, as father, produces contortions which are essentially ugly. He carried expression as far as was consistent with beauty and dignity. Ugliness he would gladly have passed over, or have softened, but since his subject admitted of neither, there was nothing left him but to veil it. What he might not paint he left to be imagined. That concealment was in short a sacrifice to beauty; an example to show, not how expression can be carried beyond the limits of art, but how it should be subjected to the first law of art, the law of beauty.

Apply this to the Laocoon and we have the cause we were seeking. The master was striving to attain the greatest beauty under the given conditions of bodily pain. Pain, in its disfiguring extreme, was not compatible with beauty and must therefore be softened. Screams must be reduced to sighs, not because screams would betray weakness, but because they would deform the countenance to a repulsive degree. Imagine Laocoon's mouth open, and judge. Let him scream, and see. It was, before, a figure to inspire compassion in its beauty and suffering. Now it is ugly, abhorrent, and we gladly avert our eyes from a painful spectacle, destitute of the beauty which alone could turn our pain into the sweet feeling of pity for the suffering object.

The simple opening of the mouth, apart from the violent and repulsive contortions it causes in the other parts of the face, is a blot on a painting and a cavity in a statue productive of the worst possible effect. Montfaucon showed little taste when he pronounced the bearded face of an old man with wide open mouth to be a Jupiter delivering an oracle. Cannot a god foretell the future without screaming? Would a more becoming posture of the lips cast suspicion upon his prophecies? Valerius cannot make me believe that Ajax was painted screaming in the above-mentioned picture of Timanthes. Far inferior masters, after the decline of art, do not in a single in-

A Gaul, having killed his wife, turns the sword upon himself. *"There are passions and degrees of passion,* [that] . . . *the old artists either refrained altogether from representing or softened into emotions which were capable of being expressed with some degree of beauty."*
National Museum, Rome.

stance make the wildest barbarian open his mouth to scream, even though in mortal terror of his enemy's sword.

This softening of the extremity of bodily suffering into a lesser degree of pain is apparent in the works of many of the old artists. Hercules, writhing in his poisoned robe, from the hand of an unknown master, was not the Hercules of Sophocles, who made the Locrian rocks and the Euboean promontory ring with his horrid cries. He was gloomy rather than wild. The Philoctetes of Pythagoras Leontinus seemed to communicate his pain to the beholder, an effect which would have been destroyed by the slightest disfigurement of the features. It may be asked how I know that this master made a statue of Philoctetes. From a passage in Pliny, which ought not to have waited for my emendation, so evident is the alteration or mutilation it has undergone.

III.

But, as already observed, the realm of art has in modern times been greatly enlarged. Its imitations are allowed to extend over all visible nature, of which beauty constitutes but a small part. Truth and expression are taken as its first law. As nature always sacrifices beauty to higher ends, so should the artist subordinate it to his general purpose, and not pursue it further than truth and expression allow. Enough that truth and expression convert what is unsightly in nature into a beauty of art.

Allowing this idea to pass unchallenged at present for whatever it is worth, are there not other independent considerations which should set bounds to expression and prevent the artist from choosing for his imitation the culminating point of any action?

The single moment of time to which art must confine itself will lead us, I think, to such considerations. Since the artist can use but a single moment of ever-changing nature, and the painter must further confine his study of this one moment to a single point of view, while their works are made not simply to be looked at, but to be contemplated long and often, evidently the most fruitful moment and the most fruitful aspect of that moment must be chosen. Now that only is fruitful which allows free play to the imagination. The more we see the more we must be able to imagine; and the more we imagine, the more we must think we see. But no moment in the whole course of an action is so disadvantageous in this respect as that of its culmination. There is nothing beyond, and to present the uttermost to the eye is to bind the wings of Fancy and compel her, since she cannot soar beyond the impression made on the senses, to employ herself with feebler images, shunning as her limit the visible fullness already expressed. When, for instance, Laocoon sighs, imagination can hear him cry; but if he cry, imagination can neither mount a step higher, nor fall a step lower, without seeing him in a more endurable, and therefore less interesting, condition. We hear him merely groaning, or we see him already dead.

Again, since this single moment receives from art an unchanging duration, it should express nothing essentially transitory. All phenomena, whose nature it is suddenly to break out and as suddenly to disappear, which can remain as they are but for a moment; all such phenomena, whether agreeable or otherwise, acquire through the perpetuity conferred upon them by art such an unnatural appearance, that the impression they produce becomes weaker with every fresh observation, till the whole subject at last wearies or disgusts us. La Mettrie, who had himself painted and engraved as a second Democritus, laughs only the first time we look at him. Looked at again, the philosopher becomes a buffoon, and his laugh a grimace. So it is with a cry. Pain, which is so violent as to extort a scream, either soon abates or it must destroy the sufferer. Again, if a man of firmness and endurance cry, he does not do so unceasingly, and only this apparent continuity in art makes the cry degenerate into womanish weakness or childish impatience. This, at least, the sculptor of the Laocoon had to guard against, even had a cry not been an offense against beauty, and were suffering without beauty a legitimate subject of art.

Among the old painters Timomachus seems to have been the one most fond of choosing extremes for his subject. His raving Ajax and infanticide Medea were famous. But from the descriptions we have of them it is clear that he had rare skill in selecting that point which leads the observer to imagine the crisis without actually showing it, and in uniting with this an appearance not so essentially transitory as to become offensive through the continuity conferred by art. He did not paint Medea at the moment of her actually murdering her children, but just before, when motherly love is still struggling with jealousy. We anticipate the result and tremble at the idea of soon seeing Medea in her unmitigated ferocity, our imagination far outstripping anything the painter could have shown us of that terrible moment. For that reason her prolonged indecision, so far from displeasing us, makes us wish it had been continued in reality. We wish this conflict of passions had never been decided or had lasted at least till time and reflection had weakened her fury and secured the victory to the maternal sentiments. This wisdom on the part of Timomachus won for him great and frequent praise, and raised him far above another artist unknown, who was foolish enough to paint Medea at the height of her madness, thus giving to this transient access of passion a duration that outrages nature. The poet censures him for this and says very justly, apostrophizing the picture, "Art thou then forever thirsting for the blood of thy children? Is there always a new Jason and a new Creusa to inflame thy rage? To the devil with the very picture of thee!" he adds angrily.

Of Timomachus's treatment of the rav-ing Ajax, we can judge by what Philostratus tells us. Ajax was not represented at the moment when, raging among the herds, he captures and slays goats and oxen, mistaking them for men. The master showed him sitting weary after these crazy deeds of heroism, and meditating self-destruction. That was really the raving Ajax, not because he is raving at the moment, but because we see that he has been raving, and with what violence his present reaction of shame and despair vividly portrays. We see the force of the tempest in the wrecks and corpses with which it has strewn the beach.

IV.

A review of the reasons here alleged for the moderation observed by the sculptor of the Laocoon in the expression of bodily pain, shows them to lie wholly in the peculiar object of his art and its necessary limitations. Scarce one of them would be applicable to poetry.

Without inquiring here how far the poet can succeed in describing physical beauty, so much at least is clear, that since the whole infinite realm of perfection lies open for his imitation, this visible covering under which perfection becomes beauty will be one of his least significant means of interesting us in his characters. Indeed, he often neglects it altogether, feeling sure that if his hero have gained our favor, his nobler qualities will either so engross us that we shall not think of his body, or have so won us that, if we think of it, we shall naturally attribute to him a beautiful, or, at least, no unsightly one. Least of all will we have reference to the eye in every detail not especially addressed to the sense of sight. When Virgil's Laocoon screams, who stops to think that a scream necessitates an open mouth, and that an open mouth is ugly? Enough that *"clamores horrendos ad sidera tollit"* is fine to the ear, no matter what its effect on the eye. Whoever

After Jason deserts her for another woman, Medea prepares to murder the children she bore him. The Pompeian wall painting shown here is a duplicate of the scene originally painted by Timomachus. *"[Timomachus] did not paint Medea . . . actually murdering her children, but just before, when motherly love is still struggling with jealousy."*

requires a beautful picture has missed the whole intention of the poet.

Further, nothing obliges the poet to concentrate his picture into a single moment. He can take up every action, if he will, from its origin and carry it through all possible changes to its issue. Every change, which would require from the painter a separate picture, costs him but a single touch; a touch, perhaps, which, taken by itself, might offend the imagination, but which, anticipated, as it has been, by what preceded, and softened and atoned for by what follows, loses its individual effect in the admirable result of the whole. Thus were it really unbecoming in a man to cry out in the extremity of bodily pain, how can this momentary weakness lower in our estimation a character whose virtues have previously won our regard? Virgil's Laocoon cries; but this screaming Laocoon is the same we know and love as the most farseeing of patriots and the tenderest of fathers. We do not attribute the cry to his character but solely to his intolerable sufferings. We hear in it only those, nor could they have been made sensible to us in any other way.

Who blames the poet, then? Rather must we acknowledge that he was right in introducing the cry, as the sculptor was in omitting it.

But Virgil's is a narrative poem. Would the dramatic poet be included in this justification? A very different impression is made by the mention of a cry and the cry itself. The drama, being meant for a living picture to the spectator, should therefore perhaps conform more strictly to the laws of material painting. In the drama we not only fancy we see and hear a crying Philoctetes, we actually do see and hear him. The more nearly the actor approaches nature, the more sensibly must our eyes and ears be offended, as in nature they undoubtedly are when we hear such loud and violent expressions of pain. Besides, physical suffering in general possesses in a less degree than other evils the power of arousing sympathy. The imagination cannot take hold of it sufficiently for the mere sight to arouse in us any corresponding emotion. Sophocles, therefore, might easily have overstepped the bounds not only of conventional propriety, but of a propriety grounded in the very nature of our sensibilities, in letting Philoctetes and Hercules moan and weep, scream and roar. The bystanders cannot possibly feel such concern for their suffering as these excessive outbreaks seem to demand. To us spectators the lookers-on will seem comparatively cold; and yet we cannot but regard their sympathy as the measure of our own. Add to this that the actor can rarely or never carry the representation of bodily pain to the point of illusion, and perhaps the modern dramatic poets are rather to be praised than blamed for either avoiding this danger altogether or skirting it at a safe distance.

Much would in theory appear unanswerable if the achievements of genius had not proved the contrary. These observations are not without good foundation, yet in spite of them *Philoctetes* [*GBWW,* Vol. 5, pp. 182–95] remains one of the masterpieces of the stage. For a portion of our strictures do not apply to Sophocles, and by a disregard of others he has attained to beauties which the timid critic, but for this example, would never have dreamed of. The following remarks will make this apparent:

1. The poet has contrived wonderfully to intensify and ennoble the idea of physical pain. He chose a wound—for we may consider the details of the story dependent upon his choice, insofar as he chose the subject for their sake—he chose, I say, a wound and not an inward distemper, because the most painful sickness fails to impress us as vividly as an outward hurt. The inward sympathetic fire which consumed Meleager when his mother sacrificed him in the brand to her sisterly fury, would therefore be less dramatic than a wound. This wound, moreover, was a divine pun-

ishment. In it a fiercer than any natural poison raged unceasingly, and at appointed intervals an access of intenser pain occurred, always followed by a heavy sleep, wherein exhausted nature acquired the needed strength for entering again upon the same course of pain. Chateaubrun represents him as wounded simply by the poisoned arrow of a Trojan. But so common an accident gives small scope for extraordinary results. Everyone was exposed to it in the old wars; why were the consequences so terrible only in the case of Philoctetes? A natural poison that should work for nine years without destroying life is far more improbable than all the fabulous miraculous elements with which the Greek decked out his tale.

2. But great and terrible as he made the physical sufferings of his hero, he was well aware that these alone would not suffice to excite any sensible degree of sympathy. He joined with them, therefore, other evils, also insufficient of themselves to move us greatly, but receiving from this connection a darker hue of tragedy, which in turn reacted upon the bodily pain. These evils were complete loss of human companionship, hunger, and all the discomforts attendant on exposure to an inclement sky when thus bereft. Imagine a man under these circumstances, but in possession of health, strength, and industry, and we have a Robinson Crusoe, who has little claim to our compassion, though we are by no means indifferent to his fate. For we are seldom so thoroughly content with human society as not to find a certain charm in thinking of the repose to be enjoyed without its pale; more particularly as every one flatters himself with the idea of being able gradually to dispense altogether with the help of others. Again, imagine a man suffering from the most painful of incurable maladies, but surrounded by kind friends who let him want for nothing, who relieve his pain by all the means in their power, and are always ready to listen to his groans and complaints; we should pity him un-

doubtedly, but our compassion would soon be exhausted. We should presently shrug our shoulders and counsel patience. Only when all these ills unite in one person, when to solitude is added physical infirmity, when the sick man not only cannot help himself, but has no one to help him, and his groans die away on the desert air—then we see a wretch afflicted by all the ills to which human nature is exposed, and the very thought of putting ourselves in his place for a moment fills us with horror. We see before us despair in its most dreadful shape, and no compassion is stronger or more melting than that connected with the idea of despair. Such we feel for Philoctetes, especially at the moment when, robbed of his bow, he loses the only means left him of supporting his miserable existence. Alas for the Frenchman who had not the sense to perceive this nor the heart to feel it! or, if he had, was petty enough to sacrifice it all to the pitiful taste of his nation! Chateaubrun gives Philoctetes companionship by introducing a princess into his desert island. Neither is she alone, but has with her a lady of honor: a thing apparently as much needed by the poet as by the princess. All the admirable play with the bow he has left out and introduced in its stead the play of bright eyes. The heroic youth of France would in truth have made themselves very merry over a bow and arrows, whereas nothing is more serious to them than the displeasure of bright eyes. The Greek harrows us with fear lest the wretched Philoctetes should be forced to remain on the island without his bow and there miserably perish. The Frenchman found a surer way to our hearts by making us fear that the son of Achilles would have to depart without his princess. And this is called by the Parisian critics triumphing over the ancients. One of them even proposed to name Chateaubrun's piece *"La difficulté vaincue."*

3. Turning now from the effect of the whole, let us examine the separate scenes wherein Philoctetes is no longer the for-

saken sufferer but has hope of leaving the dreary island and returning to his kingdom. His ills are therefore now confined entirely to his painful wound. He moans, he cries, he goes through the most hideous contortions. Against this scene objections on the score of offended propriety may with most reason be brought. They come from an Englishman, a man, therefore, not readily to be suspected of false delicacy. As already hinted, he supports his objections by very good arguments. "All feelings and passions," he says, "with which others can have little sympathy, become offensive if too violently expressed." "It is for the same reason that to cry out bodily pain, how intolerable soever, appears always unmanly and unbecoming. There is, however, a good deal of sympathy even with bodily pain. If I see a stroke aimed and just ready to fall upon the leg or arm of another person, I naturally shriek and draw back my own leg or my own arm; and when it does fall, I feel it in some measure and am hurt by it as well as the sufferer. My hurt, however, is no doubt excessively slight, and, upon that account, if he makes any violent outcry, as I cannot go along with him, I never fail to despise him."

Nothing is more deceptive than the laying down of general laws for our emotions. Their web is so fine and intricate that the most cautious speculation is hardly able to take up a single thread and trace it through all its interlacings. And if it could, what should we gain? There is in nature no single, unmixed emotion. With every one spring up a thousand others, the most insignificant of which essentially modifies the original one, so that exception after exception arises until our supposed universal law shrinks into a mere personal experience in a few individual cases. We despise a man, says the Englishman, whom we hear crying out under bodily pain. But not always; not the first time; not when we see that the sufferer does all in his power to suppress expressions of pain; not when we know

him to be otherwise a man of resolution, still less when we see him giving proof of firmness in the midst of his suffering; when we see that pain, though it extort a cry, can extort nothing further; that he submits to a continuance of the anguish rather than yield a jot of his opinions or resolves, although such a concession would end his woes. All this we find in Philoctetes. To the old Greek mind moral greatness consisted in unchanging love of friends as well as unfaltering hatred of enemies. This greatness Philoctetes preserves through all his tortures. His own griefs have not so exhausted his tears that he has none to shed over the fate of his old friends. His sufferings have not so enervated him that, to be free from them, he would forgive his enemies and lend himself to their selfish ends. And did this man of rock deserve to be despised by the Athenians, because the waves, that could not shake him, wrung from him a moan?

I confess to having little taste for the philosophy of Cicero in general, but particularly distasteful to me are his views with regard to the endurance of bodily pain set forth in the the second book of his *Tusculan Disputations*. One would suppose, from his abhorrence of all expressions of bodily pain, that he was training a gladiator. He seems to see in such expressions only impatience, not considering that they are often wholly involuntary, and that true courage can be shown in none but voluntary actions. In the play of Sophocles he hears only the cries and complaints of Philoctetes and overlooks altogether his otherwise resolute bearing. Else what excuse for his rhetorical outbreak against the poets? "They would make us effeminate by introducing the bravest of their warriors as complaining." They should complain, for the theatre is no arena. The condemned or hired gladiator was bound to do and bear with grace. No sound of lamentation must be heard, no painful contortion seen. His wounds and death were to amuse the spectators, and art must therefore teach the suppression of all feeling. The least manifestation of it might have aroused compassion, and compassion often excited would soon have put an end to the cruel shows. But what is to be avoided in the arena is the very object of the tragic stage, and here, therefore, demeanor of exactly the opposite kind is required. The heroes on the stage must show feeling, must express their sufferings, and give free course to nature. Any appearance of art and constraint represses sympathy. Boxers in buskin can at most excite our admiration. This term may fitly be applied to the so-called Senecan tragedies. I am convinced that the gladiatorial shows were the chief reason why the Romans never attained even to mediocrity in their tragedies. In the bloody amphitheatre the spectators lost all acquaintance with nature. A Ctesias might have studied his art there, never a Sophocles. The greatest tragic genius, accustomed to these artificial death scenes, could not help degenerating into bombast and rodomontade. But as these were incapable of inspiring true heroism, so were the complaints of Philoctetes incapable of producing effeminacy. The complaints are human, while the deeds are heroic. Both together make the human hero, who is neither effeminate nor callous, but appears first the one and then the other, as now Nature sways him, and now principle and duty triumph. This is the highest type that wisdom can create and art imitate.

4. Sophocles, not content with securing his suffering Philoctetes against contempt, has even shielded him beforehand from such hostile criticism as that employed by the Englishman. Though we may not always despise a man who cries out under bodily pain, we certainly do not feel that degree of sympathy with him which his cry seems to demand. How then should those comport themselves who are about this screaming Philoctetes? Should they appear to be greatly moved? That were contrary to nature. Should they seem as cold and embarrassed as the bystander on such occasions is apt actually to be? Such a want

of harmony would offend the spectator. Sophocles, as I have said, anticipated this and guarded against it in the following way—he gave to each of the bystanders a subject of personal interest. They are not solely occupied with Philoctetes and his cries. The attention of the spectator, therefore, is directed to the change wrought in each person's own views and designs by the sympathy excited in him, whether strong or weak, not to the disproportion between the sympathy itself and its exciting cause. Neoptolemus and the chorus have deceived the unhappy Philoctetes, and while perceiving the despair they are bringing upon him they behold him overpowered by one of his accesses of pain. Even should this arouse no great degree of sympathy in them, it must at least lead them to self-examination and prevent their increasing by treachery a misery which they cannot but respect. This the spectator looks for; nor is his expectation disappointed by the magnanimous Neoptolemus. Had Philoctetes been master of his suffering, Neoptolemus would have persevered in his deceit. Philoctetes, deprived by pain of all power of dissimulation, necessary as that seems to prevent his future traveling companion from repenting too soon of his promise to take him with him, Philoctetes, by his naturalness, recalls Neoptolemus to nature. The conversion is admirable, and all the more affecting for being brought about by unaided human nature. The Frenchman had recourse again here to the bright eyes. "De mes déguisemens que penserait Sophie?" says the son of Achilles. But I will think no more of this parody.

Sophocles, in the *Trachiniae* [GBWW, Vol. 5, pp. 170–81], makes use of this same expedient of combining in the bystanders another emotion with the compassion excited by a cry of physical pain. The pain of Hercules has no enervating effect but drives him to madness. He thirsts for vengeance and, in his frenzy, has already seized upon Lichas and dashed him in pieces against the rock. The chorus is composed of women who are naturally overpowered with fear and horror. Their terror, and the doubt whether a god will hasten to Hercules' relief, or whether he will fall a victim to his misfortune, make the chief interest of the piece with but a slight tinge of compassion. As soon as the issue has been decided by the oracle, Hercules grows calm, and all other feelings are lost in our admiration of his final decision. But we must not forget, when comparing the suffering Hercules with the suffering Philoctetes, that one is a demigod, the other but a man. The man is never ashamed to complain; but the demigod feels shame that his mortal part has so far triumphed over his immortal, that he should weep and groan like a girl [*GBWW*, Vol. 5, p. 179b]. We moderns do not believe in demigods but require our most insignificant hero to feel and act like one.

That an actor can imitate the cries and convulsions of pain so closely as to produce illusion, I neither deny nor affirm. If our actors cannot, I should want to know whether Garrick found it equally impossible; and, if he could not succeed, I should still have the right to assume a degree of perfection in the acting and declamation of the ancients of which we of today can form no idea.

V.

Some critics of antiquity argue that the Laocoon, though a work of Greek art, must date from the time of the emperors, because it was copied from the Laocoon of Virgil. Of the older scholars who have held this opinion I will mention only Bartolomaeus Martiani, and of the moderns, Montfaucon. They doubtless found such remarkable agreement between the work of art and the poem that they could not believe the same circumstances, by no means self-suggesting ones, should have occurred by accident to both sculptor and poet. The question then arose to whom the honor of invention belonged, and they assumed the probabilities to be decidedly in favor of the poet.

They appear, however, to have forgotten that a third alternative is possible. The artist may not have copied the poet any more than the poet the artist; but both perhaps drew their material from some older source, which, Macrobius suggests, might have been Pisander.[2] For, while the works of this Greek writer were still in existence, the fact was familiar to every schoolboy that the Roman poet's whole second book, the entire conquest and destruction of Troy, was not so much imitated as literally translated from the older writer. If then Pisander was Virgil's predecessor in the history of Laocoon also, the Greek artists did not need to draw their material from a Latin poet, and this theory of the date of the group loses its support.

If I were forced to maintain the opinion of Martiani and Montfaucon, I should escape from the difficulty in this way. Pisander's poems are lost, and we can never know with certainty how he told the story of Laocoon. Probably, however, he narrated it with the same attendant circumstances of which we still find traces in the Greek authors. Now these do not in the least agree with the version of Virgil, who must have recast the Greek tradition to suit himself. The fate of Laocoon, as he tells it, is quite his own invention, so that the artists, if their representation harmonize with his, may fairly be supposed to have lived after his time and to have used his description as their model.

Quintus Calaber indeed, like Virgil, makes Laocoon express suspicion of the wooden horse; but the wrath of Minerva, which he thereby incurs, is very differently manifested. As the Trojan utters his warning, the earth trembles beneath him, pain and terror fall upon him; a burning pain rages in his eyes; his brain gives way; he raves, he becomes blind. After his blindness, since he still continues to advise the burning of the wooden horse, Minerva sends two terrible dragons, which, however, attack only Laocoon's children. In vain they stretch out their hands to their father. The poor blind man cannot help them. They are torn and mangled, and the serpents glide away into the ground, doing no injury to Laocoon himself. That this was not peculiar to Quintus, but must have been generally accepted, appears from a passage in Lycophron, where these serpents receive the name of "child-eaters."

But if this circumstance were generally accepted among the Greeks, Greek artists would hardly have ventured to depart from it. Or, if they made variations, these would not be likely to be the same as those of a Roman poet, had they not known him and perhaps been especially commissioned to use him as their model. We must insist on this point, I think, if we would uphold Martiani and Montfaucon. Virgil is the first and only one who represents both father and children as devoured by the serpents; the sculptors have done this also, although, as Greeks, they should not; probably, therefore, they did it in consequence of Virgil's example.[3]

I am well aware that this probability falls far short of historical certainty. But since I mean to draw no historical conclusions from it, we may be allowed to use it as an hypothesis on which to base our remarks. Let us suppose, then, that the sculptors used Virgil as their model, and see in what way they would have copied him. The cry has been already discussed. A further comparison may perhaps lead to not less instructive results.

The idea of coiling the murderous serpents about both father and sons, tying them thus into one knot, is certainly a very happy one, and betrays great picturesqueness of fancy. Whose was it? the poet's or the artist's? Montfaucon thinks it is not to be found in the poem;[4] but, in my opinion, he has not read the passage with sufficient care.

Illi agmine certo
Laocoonta petunt, et primum parva duorum
Corpora natorum serpens amplexus uterque
Implicat et miseros morsu depascitur artus.
Post ipsum, auxilio subeuntem et tela ferentem,
Corripiunt spirisque ligant ingentibus. *

The poet has described the serpents as being of a wonderful length. They have wound their coils about the boys and seize the father also (*corripiunt*) as he comes to their aid. Owing to their great length they could not in an instant have disengaged themselves from the boys. There must therefore have been a moment when the heads and forward parts of the bodies had attacked the father while the boys were still held imprisoned in the hindmost coils. Such a moment is unavoidable in the progress of the poetic picture; and the poet makes it abundantly manifest, though that was not the time to describe it in detail. A passage in Donatus[5] seems to prove that the old commentators were conscious of it; and there was still less likelihood of its escaping the notice of artists whose trained eye was quick to perceive anything that could be turned to their advantage.

The poet carefully leaves Laocoon's arms free that he may have the full use of his hands.

Ille simul manibus tendit divellere nodos.†

---

*Their destined way they take,
And to Laocoon and his children make;
And first around the tender boys they wind,
Then with their sharpened fangs their limbs and bodies grind.
The wretched father, running to their aid
With pious haste, but vain, they next invade.
—Dryden.
[Cf. translation given in note 3.]
†With both his hands he labors at the knots.

In this point the artist must necessarily have followed him; for nothing contributes more to the expression of life and motion than the action of the hands. In representations of passion, especially, the most speaking countenance is ineffective without it. Arms fastened close to the body by the serpents' coils would have made the whole group cold and dead. We consequently see them in full activity, both in the main figure and the lesser ones, and most active where for the moment the pain is sharpest.

With the exception of this freedom of the arms, there was, however, nothing in the poet's manner of coiling the serpents which could be turned to account by the artists. Virgil winds them twice round the body and twice round the neck of Laocoon, and lets their heads tower high above him.

> *Bis medium amplexi, bis collo squamea circum*
> *Terga dati, superant capite et cervicibus altis.**

This description satisfies our imagination completely. The noblest parts of the body are compressed to suffocation, and the poison is aimed directly at the face. It furnished, however, no picture for the artist, who would show the physical effects of the poison and the pain. To render these conspicuous, the nobler parts of the body must be left as free as possible, subjected to no outward pressure which would change and weaken the play of the suffering nerves and laboring muscles. The double coils would have concealed the whole trunk and rendered invisible that most expressive contraction of the abdomen. What of the body would be distinguishable above or below or between the coils would have been swollen and compressed, not by inward pain but by outward violence. So many rings about the neck would have destroyed the pyramidal shape of the group which is now pleasing to the eye, while the pointed heads of the serpents projecting far above this huge mass would have been such a violation of the rules of proportion that the effect of the whole would have been made repulsive in the extreme. There have been designers so devoid of perception as to follow the poet implicitly. One example of the hideous result may be found among the illustrations by Francis Cleyn.[6] The old sculptors saw at a glance that their art required a totally different treatment. They transferred all the coils from the trunk and neck to the thighs and feet, parts which might be concealed and compressed without injury to the expression. By this means they also conveyed the idea of arrested flight, and a certain immobility very favorable to the arbitrary continuance of one posture.

I know not how it happens that the critics have passed over in silence this marked difference between the coils in the marble and in the poem. It reveals the wisdom of the artist quite as much as another difference which they all comment upon, though rather by way of excuse than of praise— the difference in the dress. Virgil's Laocoon is in his priestly robes, while in the group he, as well as his two sons, appears completely naked. Some persons, it is said, find a great incongruity in the fact that a king's son, a priest, should be represented naked when offering a sacrifice. To this the critics answer in all seriousness that it is, to be sure, a violation of usage but that the artists were driven to it from inability to give their figures suitable clothing. Sculpture, they say, cannot imitate stuffs. Thick folds produce a bad effect. Of two evils they have therefore chosen the lesser, and preferred to offend against truth rather than be necessarily faulty in drapery.[7] The

---

*Twice round his waist their winding
  volumes rolled,
And twice about his gasping throat they fold.
The priest thus doubly choked—their
  crests divide,
And towering o'er his head in triumph ride.
  —DRYDEN.
  [Cf. translation given in note 3.]

old artists might have laughed at the objection, but I know not what they would have said to this manner of answering it. No greater insult could be paid to art. Suppose sculpture could imitate different textures as well as painting, would Laocoon necessarily have been draped? Should we lose nothing by drapery? Has a garment, the work of slavish hands, as much beauty as an organized body, the work of eternal wisdom? Does the imitation of the one require the same skill, involve the same merit, bring the same honor as the imitation of the other? Do our eyes require but to be deceived, and is it a matter of indifference to them with what they are deceived?

In poetry a robe is no robe. It conceals nothing. Our imagination sees through it in every part. Whether Virgil's Laocoon be clothed or not, the agony in every fibre of his body is equally visible. The brow is bound with the priestly fillet, but not concealed. Nay, so far from being a hindrance, the fillet rather strengthens our impression of the sufferer's agony.

*Perfusus sanie vittas atroque veneno.**

His priestly dignity avails him nothing. The very badge of it, which wins him universal consideration and respect, is saturated and desecrated with the poisonous slaver.

But this subordinate idea the artist had to sacrifice to the general effect. Had he retained even the fillet, his work would have lost in expression from the partial concealment of the brow which is the seat of expression. As in the case of the cry he sacrificed expression to beauty, he here sacrificed conventionality to expression. Conventionality, indeed, was held of small account among the ancients. They felt that art, in the attainment of beauty, its true end, could dispense with conventionalities altogether. Necessity invented clothes, but what has art to do with necessity? There is a beauty of drapery, I admit; but it is nothing as compared with the beauty of the human form. Will he who can attain to the greater rest content with the lesser? I fear that the most accomplished master in drapery, by his very dexterity, proves his weakness.

VI.

My supposition that the artists imitated the poet is no disparagement to them. On the contrary the manner of their imitation reflects the greatest credit on their wisdom. They followed the poet without suffering him in the smallest particular to mislead them. A model was set them, but the task of transferring it from one art into another gave them abundant opportunity for independent thought. The originality manifested in their deviations from the model proves them to have been no less great in their art than the poet was in his.

Now, reversing the matter, I will suppose the poet to be working after the model set him by the artists. This is a supposition maintained by various scholars. I know of no historical arguments in favor of their opinion. The work appeared to them of such exceeding beauty that they could not believe it to be of comparatively recent date. It must have been made when art was at its perfection, because it was worthy of that period.

We have seen that, admirable as Virgil's picture is, there are yet traits in it unavailable for the artist. The saying therefore requires some modification, that a good poetical description must make a good picture, and that a poet describes well only insofar as his details may be used by the artist. Even without the proof furnished by examples, we should be inclined to predicate such limitation from a consideration of the wider sphere of poetry, the infinite range of our imagination, and the intangibility of its images. These may stand side by side in the greatest number and variety

---

*His holy fillets the blue venom blots.
—DRYDEN.   [Cf. note 3.]

Nike of Samothrace. De Piles observed that the ancient sculptors gave light clothing only to female figures and avoided clothing figures of males, believing that the great folds of drapery gave sculpture a bad effect. *"Necessity invented clothes, but what has art to do with necessity?"*

without concealment or detriment to any, just as the objects themselves or their natural symbols would in the narrow limits of time or space.

But if the smaller cannot contain the greater it can be contained in the greater. In other words, if not every trait employed by the descriptive poet can produce an equally good effect on canvas or in marble, can every trait of the artist be equally effective in the work of the poet? Undoubtedly; for what pleases us in a work of art pleases not the eye, but the imagination through the eye. The same picture, whether presented to the imagination by arbitrary or natural signs, must always give us a similar pleasure, though not always in the same degree.

But even granting this, I confess that the idea of Virgil's having imitated the artists is more inconceivable to me than the contrary hypothesis. If the artists copied the poet, I can account for all their deviations. Differences would necessarily have arisen, because many traits employed by him with good effect would in their work have been objectionable. But why such deviations in the poet? Would he not have given us an admirable picture by copying the group faithfully in every particular?[8]

I can perfectly understand how his fancy, working independently, should have suggested to him this and that feature, but I see no reason why his judgment should have thought it necessary to transform the beauties that were before his eyes into these differing ones.

It even seems to me that, had Virgil used this group as his model, he could hardly have contented himself with leaving the general embrace of the three bodies within the serpents' folds to be thus guessed at. The impression upon his eye would have been so vivid and admirable, that he could not have failed to give the position greater prominence in his description. As I have said, that was not the time to dwell upon its details; but the addition of a single word might have put a decisive emphasis upon

it, even in the shadow in which the poet was constrained to leave it. What the artist could present without that word, the poet would not have failed to express by it, had the work of art been before him.

The artist had imperative reasons for not allowing the sufferings of his Laocoon to break out into cries. But if the poet had had before him in the marble this touching union of pain with beauty, he would certainly have been under no necessity of disregarding the idea of manly dignity and magnanimous patience arising from it and making his Laocoon suddenly startle us with that terrible cry. Richardson says that Virgil's Laocoon needed to scream, because the poet's object was not so much to excite compassion for him as to arouse fear and horror among the Trojans. This I am ready to grant, although Richardson appears not to have considered that the poet is not giving the description in his own person but puts it into the mouth of Aeneas, who, in his narration to Dido, spared no pains to arouse her compassion. The cry, however, is not what surprises me, but the absence of all intermediate stages of emotion, which the marble could not have failed to suggest to the poet if, as we are supposing, he had used that as his model. Richardson goes on to say that the story of Laocoon was meant only as an introduction to the pathetic description of the final destruction of Troy, and that the poet was therefore anxious not to divert to the misfortunes of a private citizen the attention which should be concentrated on the last dreadful night of a great city. But this is a painter's point of view, and here inadmissible. In the poem, the fate of Laocoon and the destruction of the city do not stand side by side as in a picture. They form no single whole to be embraced at one glance, in which case alone there would have been danger of having the eye more attracted by the Laocoon than by the burning city. The two descriptions succeed each other, and I fail to see how the deepest emotion produced by the first could prejudice the one that follows. Any want of effect in the second must be owing to its inherent want of pathos.

Still less reason would the poet have had for altering the serpents' coils. In the marble they occupy the hands and encumber the feet, an arrangement not less impressive to the imagination than satisfactory to the eye. The picture is so distinct and clear that words can scarcely make it plainer than natural signs.

> *Micat alter et ipsum*
> *Laocoonta petit, totumque infraque*
>   *supraque*
> *Implicat et rabido tandem ferit ilia morsu.*
>
> .   .   .   .   .
>
> *At serpens lapsu crebro redeunte*
>   *subintrat*
> *Lubricus, intortoque ligat genua infima*
>   *nodo.**

These lines are by Sadolet. They would doubtless have come with greater picturesqueness from Virgil, had his fancy been fired by the visible model. Under those circumstances he would certainly have written better lines than those we now have of him.

> *Bis medium amplexi, bis collo squamea*
>   *circum*
> *Terga dati, superant capite et cervicibus*
>   *altis.*†

These details satisfy the imagination, it is true; but not if we dwell upon them and try to bring them distinctly before us. We must look now at the serpents, and now at Laocoon. The moment we try to combine them into one picture, the grouping begins to displease and appear in the highest degree unpicturesque.

But these deviations from his supposed model, even if not unfortunate, were entirely arbitrary. Imitation is intended to produce likeness, but how can likeness result from needless changes? Such changes rather show that the intention was not to produce likeness, consequently that there has been no imitation.

Perhaps not of the whole, some may urge, but of certain parts. Good; but what are the parts so exactly corresponding in the marble and in the poem, that the poet might seem to have borrowed them from the sculptor? The father, the children, and the serpents, both poet and sculptor received from history. Except what is traditional in both, they agree in nothing but the single circumstance that father and sons are bound by the serpents' coils into a single knot. But this arose from the new version, according to which father and sons were involved in a common destruction—a version, as already shown, to be attributed rather to Virgil, since the Greek traditions tell the story differently. If, then, there should have been any imitation here, it is more likely to have been on the side of the artist than of the poet. In all other respects their representations differ, but in such a way that the deviations, if made by the artist, are perfectly consistent with an intention to copy the poet, being such as the sphere and limitations of his art would impose on him. They are, on the contrary, so many arguments against the supposed imitation of the sculptor by the poet. Those who, in the face of these objections, still maintain this supposition, can only mean that the group is older than the poem.

VII.

When we speak of an artist as imitating a poet or a poet an artist, we may mean

---

*[One gleaming seeks Laocoon himself, winding him all about, above, below, and attacks his groins at last with poisonous bite. . . . But the slippery snake glides down with frequent folds, and binds his leg below the knee with twisted knot.—*See* note 8.]

†[Their scaly length twice wreathed about his waist, twice round his neck—with heads o'ertop him and high-towering throats.—*See* note 3, Virgil quote.]

one of two things—either that one makes the work of the other his actual model, or that the same original is before them both, and one borrows from the other the manner of copying it.

When Virgil describes the shield of Aeneas, his imitation of the artist who made the shield is of the former kind. The work of art, not what it represents, is his model. Even if he describe the devices upon it they are described as part of the shield, not as independently existing objects. Had Virgil, on the other hand, copied the group of the Laocoon, this would have been an imitation of the second kind. He would then have been copying, not the actual group, but what the group represents, and would have borrowed from the marble only the details of his copy.

In imitations of the first kind the poet is an originator, in those of the second a copyist. The first is part of the universal imitation which constitutes the very essence of his art, and his work is that of a genius, whether his model be nature or the product of other arts. The second degrades him utterly. Instead of the thing itself, he imitates its imitations and gives us a lifeless reflection of another's genius for original touches of his own.

In the by no means rare cases where poet and artist must study their common original from the same point of view, their copies cannot but coincide in many respects, although there may have been no manner of imitation or emulation between them. These coincidences among contemporaneous artists and poets may lead to mutual illustrations of things no longer present to us. But to try to help out these illustrations by tracing design where was only chance, and especially by attributing to the poet at every detail a reference to this statue or that picture, is doing him very doubtful service. Nor is the reader a gainer by a process which renders the beautiful passages perfectly intelligible, no doubt, but at the sacrifice of all their life. This is the design and the mistake of a fa-

mous English work by the Rev. Mr. Spence, entitled, "Polymetis; or, An inquiry concerning the agreement between the works of the Roman poets and the remains of the ancient artists, being an attempt to illustrate them mutually from one another." Spence has brought to his work great classical learning and a thorough knowledge of the surviving works of ancient art. His design of using these as means to explain the Roman poets, and making the poets in turn throw light on works of art hitherto imperfectly understood, has been in many instances happily accomplished. But I nevertheless maintain that to every reader of taste his book must be intolerable.

When Valerius Flaccus describes the winged thunderbolts on the shields of the Roman soldiers,

*Nec primus radios, miles Romane, corusci
Fulminis et rutilas scutis diffuderis alas,* *

the description is naturally made more intelligible to me by seeing the representation of such a shield on an ancient monument. It is possible that the old armorers represented Mars upon helmets and shields in the same hovering attitude that Addison thought he saw him in with Rhea on an ancient coin,[9] and that Juvenal had such a helmet or shield in mind in that allusion of his which, till Addison, had been a puzzle to all commentators.

The passage in Ovid where the wearied Cephalus invokes Aura, the cooling zephyr,

*Aura . . . . . .venias . . . . .
Meque juves, intresque sinus, gratissima,
    nostros,*†

and his Procris takes this Aura for the name of a rival, this passage, I confess, seems

---

*[Nor were you the first, Roman soldier, to spread on your shields the rays and glittering wings of flashing lightning.]

†[Come, Aura, soothe me and come onto my breast, most welcome one.]

to me more natural when I see that the ancients in their works of art personified the gentle breezes, and, under the name Aurae, worshipped certain female sylphs.

I acknowledge that when Juvenal compares an idle patrician to a Hermes-column, we should hardly perceive the point of the comparison unless we had seen such a column and knew it to be a poorly cut pillar, bearing the head, or at most the trunk, of the god, and, owing to the want of the hands and feet, suggesting the idea of inactivity.[10]

Illustrations of this kind are not to be despised, though neither always necessary nor always conclusive. Either the poet regarded the work of art not as a copy but as an independent original, or both artist and poet were embodying certain accepted ideas. Their representations would necessarily have many points of resemblance, which serve as so many proofs of the universality of the ideas.

But when Tibullus describes Apollo as he appeared to him in a dream—the fairest of youths, his temples wreathed with the chaste laurel, Syrian odors breathing from his golden hair that falls in ripples over his long neck, his whole body as pink and white as the cheek of the bride when led to her bridegroom—why need these traits have been borrowed from famous old pictures? Echion's *"nova nupta verecundia notabilis"* may have been in Rome and been copied thousands of times: did that prove virgin modesty itself to have vanished from the world? Since the painter saw it, was no poet to see it more save in the painter's imitation? Or when another poet speaks of Vulcan as wearied and his face reddened by the forge, did he need a picture to teach him that labor wearies and heat reddens? Or when Lucretius describes the alternations of the seasons and brings them before us in the order of nature, with their whole train of effects on earth and air, was Lucretius the creature of a day? Had he lived through no entire year and seen its changes, that he must needs have

taken his description from a procession of statues representing the seasons? Did he need to learn from statues the old poetic device of making actual beings out of such abstractions?[11] Or Virgil's *"pontem indignatus Araxes,"* that admirable poetic picture of a river overflowing its banks and tearing down the bridge that spans it—do we not destroy all its beauty by making it simply a reference to some work of art, wherein the river god was represented as actually demolishing a bridge? [*GBWW*, Vol. 13, p. 278b] What do we want of such illustrations which banish the poet from his own clearest lines to give us in his place the reflection of some artist's fancy?

I regret that this tasteless conceit of substituting for the creations of the poet's own imagination a familiarity with those of others should have rendered a book, so useful as the Polymetis might have been made, as offensive as the feeblest commentaries of the shallowest quibblers, and far more derogatory to the classic authors. Still more do I regret that Addison should in this respect have been the predecessor of Spence and, in his praiseworthy desire to make the old works of art serve as interpreters, have failed to discriminate between those cases where imitation of the artist would be becoming in the poet, and those where it would be degrading to him.

VIII.

Spence has the strangest notions of the resemblance between painting and poetry. He believes the two arts to have been so closely connected among the ancients that they always went hand in hand, the poet never losing sight of the painter, nor the painter of the poet. That poetry has the wider sphere, that beauties are within her reach which painting can never attain, that she may often see reason to prefer unpicturesque beauties to picturesque ones—these things seem never to have occurred to him. The slightest difference, therefore, between the old poets and artists throws him into an embarrassment from which it taxes all his ingenuity to escape.

The poets generally gave Bacchus horns. Spence is therefore surprised that we seldom see these appendages on his statues. He suggests one reason and another; now the ignorance of the antiquarians, and again "the smallness of the horns themselves, which were very likely to be hid under the crown of grapes or ivy which is almost a constant ornament of the head of Bacchus." He goes all round the true cause without ever suspecting it. The horns of Bacchus were not a natural growth like those of fauns and satyrs. They were ornaments which he could assume or lay aside at pleasure.

> Tibi, cum sine cornibus adstas,
> Virgineum caput est, . . .*

says Ovid in his solemn invocation to Bacchus. He could therefore show himself without horns and did, in fact, thus show himself when he wished to appear in his virgin beauty. In this form artists would choose to represent him and necessarily omitted all disagreeable accompaniments. Horns fastened to the diadem, as we see them on a head in the royal museum in Berlin, would have been a cumbersome appendage, as would also the diadem itself, concealing the beautiful brow. For this reason the diadem appears as rarely as the horns on the statues of Bacchus, although, as its inventor, he is often crowned with it by the poets. In poetry both horns and diadem served as subtle allusions to the deeds and character of the god: in a picture or statue they would have stood in the way of greater beauties. If Bacchus, as I believe, received the name of Biformis, Δίμορφος, from having an aspect of beauty as well as of terror, the artists would naturally have chosen the shape best adapted to the object of their art.

In the Roman poets Minerva and Juno often hurl the thunderbolt. Why are they not so represented in art? asks Spence. He answers, "This power was the privilege of these two goddesses, the reason of which was, perhaps, first learnt in the Samothracian mysteries. But since, among the ancient Romans, artists were considered as of inferior rank, and therefore rarely initiated into them, they would doubtless know nothing of them; and what they knew not of they clearly could not represent." I should like to ask Spence whether these common people were working independently, or under the orders of superiors who might be initiated into the mysteries; whether the artists occupied such a degraded position among the Greeks; whether the Roman artists were not for the most part Greeks by birth; and so on.

Statius and Valerius Flaccus describe an angry Venus with such terrible features that we should take her at the moment for a fury rather than for the goddess of love. Spence searches in vain for such a Venus among the works of ancient art. What is his conclusion? That more is allowed to the poet than to the sculptor and painter? That should have been his inference. But he has once for all established as a general rule that "scarce any thing can be good in a poetical description which would appear absurd if represented in a statue or picture." Consequently the poets must be wrong. "Statius and Valerius Flaccus belong to an age when Roman poetry was already in its decline. In this very passage they display their bad judgment and corrupted taste. Among the poets of a better age such a repudiation of the laws of artistic expression will never be found."

Such criticism shows small power of discrimination. I do not propose to undertake the defense of either Statius or Valerius but will simply make a general remark. The gods and other spiritual beings represented by the artist are not precisely the same as those introduced by the poet. To

---

*When thou appearest unhorned, thy head is as the head of a virgin.

the artist they are personified abstractions which must always be characterized in the same way, or we fail to recognize them. In poetry, on the contrary, they are real beings, acting and working, and possessing, besides their general character, qualities and passions which may upon occasion take precedence. Venus is to the sculptor simply love. He must therefore endow her with all the modest beauty, all the tender charms, which, as delighting us in the beloved object, go to make up our abstract idea of love. The least departure from this ideal prevents our recognizing her image. Beauty distinguished more by majesty than modesty is no longer Venus but Juno. Charms commanding and manly rather than tender, give us, instead of a Venus, a Minerva. A Venus all wrath, a Venus urged by revenge and rage, is to the sculptor a contradiction in terms. For love, as love, never is angry, never avenges itself. To the poet, Venus is love also, but she is the goddess of love, who has her own individuality outside of this one characteristic, and can therefore be actuated by aversion as well as affection. What wonder, then, that in poetry she blazes into anger and rage, especially under the provocation of insulted love?

The artist, indeed, like the poet, may, in works composed of several figures, introduce Venus or any other deity, not simply by her one characteristic, but as a living, acting being. But the actions, if not the direct results of her character, must not be at variance with it. Venus delivering to her son the armor of the gods is a subject equally suitable to artist and poet. For here she can be endowed with all the grace and beauty befitting the goddess of love. Such treatment will be of advantage as helping us the more easily to recognize her. But when Venus, intent on revenging herself on her contemners, the men of Lemnos, wild, in colossal shape, with cheeks inflamed and dishevelled hair, seizes the torch, and, wrapping a black robe about her, flies downward on the storm-cloud, that is no moment for the painter, because

he has no means of making us recognize her. The poet alone has the privilege of availing himself of it. He can unite it so closely with some other moment when the goddess is the true Venus, that we do not in the fury forget the goddess of love. Flaccus does this,

> *Neque enim alma videri*
> *Jam tumet; aut tereti crinem subnectitur*
> *auro,*
> *Sidereos diffusa sinus. Eadem effera*
> *et ingens*
> *Et maculis suffecta genas; pinumque*
> *sonantem*
> *Virginibus Stygiis, nigramque simillima*
> *pallam.**

And Statius also,

> *Illa Paphon veterem centumque altaria*
> *linquens,*
> *Nec vultu nec crine prior, solvisse jugalem*
> *Ceston, et Idalias procul ablegasse volucres*
> *Fertur. Erant certe, media qui noctis*
> *in umbra*
> *Divam, alios ignes majoraque tela*
> *gerentem,*
> *Tartarias inter thalamis volitasse sorores*
> *Vulgarent: utque implicitis arcana*
> *domorum*
> *Anguibus, et saeva formidine cuncta*
> *replerit*
> *Limina.†*

---

*Gracious the goddess is not emulous to appear, nor does she bind her hair with the burnished gold, letting her starry tresses float about her. Wild she is and huge, her cheeks suffused with spots; most like to the Stygian virgins with crackling torch and black mantle.

†Leaving ancient Paphos and the hundred altars, not like her former self in countenance or the fashion of her hair, she is said to have loosened the nuptial girdle and have sent away her doves. Some report that in the dead of night, bearing other fires and mightier arms, she had hasted with the Tartarean sisters to bed-chambers, and filled the secret places of homes with twining snakes, and all thresholds with cruel fear.

Or, we may say, the poet alone possesses the art of so combining negative with positive traits as to unite two appearances in one. No longer now the tender Venus, her hair no more confined with golden clasps, no azure draperies floating about her, without her girdle, armed with other flames and larger arrows, the goddess hastes downward, attended by furies of like aspect with herself. Must the poet abstain from the use of this device because artists are debarred from it? If painting claim to be the sister of poetry, let the younger at least not be jealous of the elder, nor seek to deprive her of ornaments unbecoming to herself.

IX.

When we compare poet and painter in particular instances, we should be careful to inquire whether both have had entire freedom, and been allowed to labor for the highest results of their art without the exercise of any constraint from without.

Religion often exercised such constraint upon the old artists. A work, devotional in character, must often be less perfect than one intended solely to produce pleasure. Superstition loaded the gods with symbols which were not always reverenced in proportion to their beauty.

In the temple of Bacchus at Lemnos, from which the pious Hypsipyle rescued her father under the guise of the deity, the god was represented horned.[12] So he doubtless appeared in all his temples, the horns being symbols typical of his nature and functions. The unfettered artist, whose Bacchus was not designed for a temple, omitted the symbol. If, among the statues of the god that remain to us, we find none with horns, that circumstance perhaps proves that none of them were sacred statues, representing the god in the shape under which he was worshipped.[13] We should naturally expect, too, that against such the fury of the pious iconoclasts in the first centuries of Christianity would have

been especially directed. Only here and there a work of art was spared, because it had never been desecrated by being made an object of worship.

But since, among the antiques that have been unburied, there are specimens of both kinds, we should discriminate and call only those works of art which are the handiwork of the artist, purely as artist, those where he has been able to make beauty his first and last object. All the rest, all that show an evident religious tendency, are unworthy to be called works of art. In them Art was not working for her own sake but was simply the tool of Religion, having symbolic representations forced upon her with more regard to their significance than their beauty. By this I do not mean to deny that religion often sacrificed meaning to beauty, or so far ceased to emphasize it, out of regard for art and the finer taste of the age, that beauty seemed to have been the sole end in view.

If we make no such distinction, there will be perpetual strife between connoisseurs and antiquarians from their failure to understand each other. When the connoisseur maintains, according to his conception of the end and aim of art, that certain things never could have been made by one of the old artists, meaning never by one working as artist from his own impulse, the antiquarian will understand him to say that they could never have been fashioned by the artist, as workman, under the influence of religion or any other power outside the domain of art. He will therefore think to confute his antagonist by showing some figure which the connoisseur, without hesitation, but to the great vexation of the learned world, will condemn back to the rubbish from which it had been dug.

But there is danger, on the other hand, of exaggerating the influence of religion on art. Spence furnishes a remarkable instance of this. He found in Ovid that Vesta was not worshipped in her temple under any human image, and he thence drew the conclusion that there had never been any statues of the goddess. What had passed for such must be statues, not of Vesta, but of a vestal virgin. An extraordinary conclusion! Because the goddess was worshipped in one of her temples under the symbol of fire, did artists therefore lose all right to personify after their fashion a being to whom the poets give distinct personality, making her the daughter of Saturn and Ops, bringing her into danger of falling under the ill treatment of Priapus, and narrating yet other things in regard to her? For Spence commits the further error of applying to all the temples of Vesta and to her worship generally what Ovid says only of a certain temple at Rome. She was not everywhere worshipped as in this temple at Rome. Until Numa erected this particular sanctuary, she was not so worshipped even in Italy. Numa allowed no deity to be represented in the shape of man or beast. In this prohibition of all personal representations of Vesta consisted, doubtless, the reformation which he introduced into her rites. Ovid himself tells us that, before the time of Numa, there were statues of Vesta in her temple, which, when her priestess Sylvia became a mother, covered their eyes with their virgin hands. Yet further proof that in the temples of the goddess outside the city, in the Roman provinces, her worship was not conducted in the manner prescribed by Numa, is furnished by various old inscriptions, where mention is made of a priest of Vesta (Pontificis Vestae). At Corinth, again, was a temple of Vesta without statues, having only an altar whereon sacrifices were offered to the goddess. But did the Greeks, therefore, have no statues of Vesta? There was one at Athens in the Prytaneum, next to the statue of Peace. The people of Iasos boasted of having one in the open air, upon which snow and rain never fell. Pliny mentions one in a sitting posture, from the chisel of Scopas, in the Servilian gardens at Rome, in his day. Granting that it is difficult for us now to distinguish between a vestal virgin and the goddess herself, does that prove that the ancients were not able or did not care to make the distinction? Certain attributes point evidently more to one than the other. The scepter, the torch, and the palladium would seem to belong exclusively to the goddess. The tympanum, attributed to her by Codinus, belongs to her, perhaps, only as the Earth. Or perhaps Codinus himself did not know exactly what it was he saw.

X.

Spence's surprise is again aroused in a way that shows how little he has reflected on the limits of poetry and painting.

"As to the muses in general," he says, "it is remarkable that the poets say but little of them in a descriptive way; much less than might indeed be expected for deities to whom they were so particularly obliged."

What is this but expressing surprise that the poets, when they speak of the muses, do not use the dumb language of the painter? In poetry, Urania is the muse of astronomy. Her name and her employment reveal her office. In art she can be recognized only by the wand with which she points to a globe of the heavens. The wand, the globe, and the attitude are the letters with which the artist spells out for us the name Urania. But when the poet wants to say that Urania had long read her death in the stars—

Ipsa diu positis lethum praedixerat astris Urania—

why should he add, out of regard to the artist—Urania, wand in hand, with the heavenly globe before her? Would that not be as if a man, with the power and privilege of speech, were to employ the signs which the mutes in a Turkish seraglio had invented to supply the want of a voice?

Spence expresses the same surprise in regard to the moral beings, or those divinities who, among the ancients, presided over the virtues and undertook the guidance of human life. "It is observable," he says, "that the Roman poets say less of the best of these moral beings than might be expected. The artists are much fuller on this head; and one who would know how they were each set off must go to the medals of the Roman emperors. The poets, in fact, speak of them very often as persons; but of their attributes, their dress, and the rest of their figure they generally say but little."

When a poet personifies abstractions he sufficiently indicates their character by their name and employment.

These means are wanting to the artist, who must therefore give to his personified abstractions certain symbols by which they may be recognized. These symbols, because they are something else and mean something else, constitute them allegorical figures.

A female figure holding a bridle in her hand, another leaning against a column, are allegorical beings. But in poetry Temperance and Constancy are not allegorical beings, but personified abstractions.

Necessity invented these symbols for the artist, who could not otherwise indicate the significance of this or that figure. But why should the poet, for whom no such necessity exists, be obliged to accept the conditions imposed upon the artist?

What excites Spence's surprise should, in fact, be prescribed as a law to all poets. They should not regard the limitations of painting as beauties in their own art, nor consider the expedients which painting has invented in order to keep pace with poetry, as graces which they have any reason to envy her. By the use of symbols the artist exalts a mere figure into a being of a higher order. Should the poet employ the same artistic machinery he would convert a superior being into a doll.

Conformity to this rule was as persistently observed by the ancients as its studious violation is by the viciousness of modern poets. All their imaginary beings go masked, and the writers who have most skill in this masquerade generally understand least the real object of their work, which is to let their personages act, and by their actions reveal their character.

Among the attributes by which the artist individualizes his abstractions, there is one class, however, better adapted to the poet than those we have been considering, and more worthy of his use. I refer to such as are not strictly allegorical, but may be regarded as instruments which the beings bearing them would or could use, should they ever come to act as real persons. The bridle in the hand of Temperance, the pillar which supports Constancy are purely allegorical and cannot therefore be used by the poet. The scales in the hand of Justice are less so, because the right use of the scales is one of the duties of Justice. The lyre or flute in the hand of a muse, the lance in the hand of Mars, hammer and tongs in the hands of Vulcan, are not symbols at all, but simply instruments without which none of the actions characteristic of these beings could be performed. To this class belong the attributes sometimes woven by the old poets into their descriptions, and which, in distinction from those that are allegorical, I would call the poetical. These signify the thing itself, while the others denote only some thing similar.[14]

XI.

Count Caylus also seems to require that the poet should deck out the creatures of his imagination with allegorical attributes.[15] The Count understood painting better than poetry.

But other points more worthy of remark have struck me in the same work of his, some of the most important of which I shall mention here for closer consideration.

The artist, in the Count's opinion, should make himself better acquainted with Homer, that greatest of all word painters—that second nature, in fact. He calls attention to the rich and fresh material furnished by the narrative of the great Greek and assures the painter that the more closely he follows the poet in every detail, the nearer his work will approach to perfection.

This is confounding the two kinds of imitation mentioned above. The painter is not only to copy the same thing that the poet has copied, but he is to copy it with the same touches. He is to use the poet not only as narrator, but as poet.

But why is not this second kind of imitation, which we have found to be degrading to the poet, equally so to the artist? If there had existed previous to Homer such a series of pictures as he suggests to Count Caylus, and we knew that the poet had composed his work from them, would he not lose greatly in our estimation? Why should we not in like manner cease to admire the artist who should do no more than translate the words of the poet into form and color?

The reason I suppose to be this. In art the difficulty appears to lie more in the execution than in the invention, while with poetry the contrary is the case. There the execution seems easy in comparison with the invention. Had Virgil copied the twining of the serpents about Laocoon and his sons from the marble, then his description would lose its chief merit; for what we consider the more difficult part had been done for him. The first conception of this grouping in the imagination is a far greater achievement than the expression of it in words. But if the sculptor have borrowed the grouping from the poet, we still consider him deserving of great praise, although he have not the merit of the first conception. For to give expression in marble is incalculably more difficult than to give it in words. We weigh invention and execution in opposite scales, and are inclined to require from the master as much less of one as he has given us more of the other.

There are even cases where the artist deserves more credit for copying Nature through the medium of the poet's imitation than directly from herself. The painter who makes a beautiful landscape from the description of a Thomson, does more than one who takes his picture at first hand from nature. The latter sees his model before him; the former must, by an effort of imagination, think he sees it. One makes a beautiful picture from vivid, sensible impressions, the other from the feeble, uncertain representations of arbitrary signs.

From this natural readiness to excuse the artist from the merit of invention, has arisen on his part an equally natural indifference to it. Perceiving that invention could never be his strong point, but that his fame must rest chiefly on execution, he ceased to care whether his theme were new or old, whether it had been used once or a hundred times, belonged to himself or another. He kept within the narrow range of a few subjects, grown familiar to himself and the public, and directed all his invention to the introducing of some change in the treatment, some new combination of the old objects. That is actually the meaning attached to the word *invention* in the old textbooks on painting. For although they divide it into the artistic and the poetic, yet even the poetic does not extend to the originating of a subject, but solely to the arrangement or expression. It is invention, not of the whole, but of the individual parts and their connection with one another; invention of that inferior kind which Horace recommended to his tragic poet:

Tuque
Rectius Iliacum carmen deducis in actus,
Quam si proferres ignota indictaque primus.*

Recommended, I say, but not commanded. He recommended it as easier for him,

---

*"Thou wilt do better to write out in acts the story of Troy, than to tell of things not yet known nor sung."

more convenient, more advantageous; he did not command it as intrinsically nobler and better.

The poet, indeed, has a great advantage when he treats of familiar historical facts and well-known characters. He can omit a hundred tiresome details otherwise indispensable to an understanding of the piece. And the sooner he is understood, the sooner he can interest his readers. The same advantage is possessed by the painter when his subject is so familiar to us that we take in at a glance the meaning and design of his whole composition, and can not only see that his characters are speaking, but can even hear what they say. On that first glance the chief effect depends. If that necessitate a tiresome guessing and pondering, our readiness to be touched is chilled. We take revenge upon the unwise artist by hardening ourselves against his expression; and alas for him, if to that expression he have sacrificed beauty! No inducement remains for us to linger before his work. What we see does not please us, and what it means we do not understand.

Considering now these two points: first, that invention and novelty in the subject are by no means what we chiefly require from the painter; and secondly, that a familiar subject helps and quickens the effect of his art, I think we shall find a deeper reason for his avoidance of new subjects than indolence or ignorance or absorption of his whole industry and time in the mechanical difficulties of his art, which are the causes assigned for it by Count Caylus. We may even be inclined to praise as a wise and, as far as we are concerned, a beneficent forbearance on the part of the artist, what seemed to us at first a deficiency in art and a curtailment of our enjoyment.

I have no fear that experience will contradict me. Painters will be grateful to the Count for his good intentions but will hardly make as general use of his advice as he expects. Should such, however, be the case, a new Caylus would be needed at the end of a hundred years to remind us of the old themes and recall the artist to a field where others before him have reaped undying laurels. Or shall we expect the public to be as learned as the connoisseur with his books, and familiar with all the scenes of history and fable that offer fit subjects for art? I grant that artists, since the time of Raphael, would have done better to take Homer for their manual than Ovid. But since, once for all, they have not done so, let us leave the public in its old ruts and not throw more difficulties in the way of its pleasure than are necessary to make the pleasure worth having.

Protogenes had painted the mother of Aristotle. I know not how much the philosopher paid for the picture, but instead of the full payment, or perhaps over and above it, he gave the painter a piece of advice which was of more value than the money. Not, as I believe, in the way of flattery, but because he knew that art needed to make itself universally intelligible, he advised him to paint the exploits of Alexander. The whole world was ringing with the fame of them, and he could foresee that their memory would remain to all posterity. But Protogenes was not wise enough to follow this counsel. *"Impetus animi,"* says Pliny, *"et quaedam artis libido,"* a certain presumption in art, and a craving after something new and strange, led him to the choice of other subjects. He preferred the story of Ialysus, of Cydippe, and others of like kind, whose meaning we can now scarce even conjecture.

XII.

Homer treats of two different classes of beings and actions—the visible and the invisible. This distinction cannot be made on canvas, where every thing is visible, and visible in precisely the same way.

When Count Caylus, therefore, makes pictures of invisible actions follow immediately upon pictures of visible ones; and in scenes of mixed actions, participated in

The Battle of Alexander. *"The whole world was ringing with the fame of* [the exploits of Alexander], *and* [Aristotle] *could foresee that their memory would remain to all posterity."* Mosaic from the House of the Faun, Pompeii. National Museum, Naples.

by beings of both kinds, does not, and perhaps cannot, indicate how those figures which only we who look at the picture are supposed to see, shall be so represented that the characters in the picture shall not see them, or at least shall not look as if they could not help seeing them, he makes the whole series, as well as many separate pictures, in the highest degree confused, unintelligible, and self-contradictory.

With the book before us this difficulty might finally be overcome. The great objection would be that, with the loss of all distinction to the eye between the visible and the invisible beings, all the characteristic traits must likewise disappear, which serve to elevate the higher order of beings above the lower.

When, for instance, the gods who take different sides in the Trojan war come at last to actual blows, the contest goes on in the poem unseen. This invisibility leaves the imagination free play to enlarge the scene at will and picture the gods and their movements on a scale far grander than the measure of common humanity. But painting must accept a visible theatre, whose various fixed parts become a scale of measurement for the persons acting upon it. This scale is always before the eye, and the disproportionate size of any superhuman figures makes beings that were grand in the poem monstrous on canvas.

Minerva, on whom Mars had made the first attack, steps backward and with mighty hand lifts from the ground an enormous stone, black and rough, which, in old times, had required the strength of many men to be rolled into its place and set up as a landmark.

ἡ δ᾿ ἀναχασσαμένη λίθον εἵλετο χειρὶ παχείη
κείμενον ἐν πεδίῳ, μέλανα, τρηχύν τε μέγαν τε,
τόν ῥ᾿ ἄνδρες πρότεροι θέσαν ἔμμεναι οὖρον
ἀρούρης.*

To obtain an adequate idea of the size of this stone, we must remember that Homer makes his heroes twice as strong as the mightiest men of his day, yet says they were far surpassed in strength by the men whom Nestor had known in his youth. Now if Minerva is to hurl at Mars a stone which it had required, not one man, but many men of the time of Nestor's youth to set up as a landmark, what, I ask, should be the stature of the goddess? If her size be proportioned to that of the stone, all marvel ceases. A being of thrice my size can, of course, throw three times as large a stone. But if the stature of the goddess be not proportioned to the size of the stone, the result is a palpable improbability in the picture which cannot be atoned for by the cold consideration that a goddess is necessarily of supernatural strength.

Mars, overthrown by this enormous stone, covered seven hides,

$$\textit{ἑπτὰ δ᾿ ἐπέσχε πέλεθρα πεσών.}$$

It is impossible for the painter to give the god this extraordinary size. Yet if he do not, we have no Homeric Mars lying on the ground, but an ordinary warrior.[16]

Longinus says it has often seemed to him that Homer's design was to raise his men to gods and degrade his deities to men. Painting accomplishes this. On canvas we lose everything which in poetry exalts the gods above mere godlike men. Size, strength, speed—qualities which Homer has always in store for his gods in miraculous measure, far surpassing any thing he attributes to his most famous heroes[17]—are necessarily reduced in the picture to the common scale of humanity. Jupiter and Agamemnon, Apollo and Achilles, Ajax and Mars, are all kindred beings, only to be

---

Iliad xxi. 385.

           She only stepped
Backward a space, and with her powerful hand
Lifted a stone that lay upon the plain,
Black, huge, and jagged, which the men of old
Had placed there for a landmark.—BRYANT.
           [Cf. *GBWW*, Vol. 4, p. 152b.]

distinguished by some arbitrary outward sign.

The expedient to which painters have recourse to indicate that a certain character is supposed to be invisible, is a thin cloud veiling the side of the figure that is turned toward the other actors on the scene. This cloud seems at first to be borrowed from Homer himself. For, when in the confusion of battle one of the chief heroes becomes exposed to a danger from which nothing short of divine aid can save him, the poet makes his guardian deity veil him in a thick cloud or in darkness, and so lead him from the field. Paris is thus delivered by Venus, Idaeus by Neptune, Hector by Apollo [*GBWW*, Vol. 4, pp. 22c, 30b, 146d]. Caylus never omits strongly to recommend to the artist this mist or cloud, whenever he is to paint pictures of such occurrences. But who does not perceive that this veiling in mist and darkness is only the poet's way of saying that the hero became invisible? It always seems strange to me, therefore, to find this poetical expression embodied in a picture, and an actual cloud introduced, behind which, as behind a screen, the hero stands hidden from his enemy. This was not the poet's meaning. The artist in this exceeds the limits of painting. His cloud is a hieroglyphic, a purely symbolic sign, which does not make the rescued hero invisible, but simply says to the observers, "You are to suppose this man to be invisible." It is no better than the rolls of paper with sentences upon them, which issue from the mouth of personages in the old Gothic pictures.

Homer, to be sure, makes Achilles give three thrusts with his lance at the thick cloud while Apollo is carrying off Hector— τρὶς δ' ἠέρα τύψε βαθεῖαν [*GBWW*, Vol. 4, p. 146d]. But that, in the language of poetry, only means that Achilles was so enraged that he thrust three times with his lance before perceiving that his enemy was no longer before him. Achilles saw no actual cloud. The whole secret of this invisibility lay not in the cloud, but in the god's swift withdrawal of the imperiled hero. In order to indicate that the withdrawal took place so instantaneously that no human eye could follow the retreating form, the poet begins by throwing over his hero a cloud, not because the bystanders saw the cloud in the place of the vanished shape, but because to our mind things in a cloud are invisible.

The opposite device is sometimes used, and, instead of the object being made invisible, the subject is smitten with blindness. Thus Neptune blinds the eyes of Achilles when he rescues Aeneas from his murderous hands by transporting him from the thick of the contest to the rear [*GBWW*, Vol. 4, p. 145b]. In reality, the eyes of Achilles were no more blinded in the one case than in the other the rescued heroes were veiled in a cloud. Both are mere expressions employed by the poet to impress more vividly on our minds the extreme rapidity of the removal; the disappearance, as we should call it.

But artists have appropriated the Homeric mist not only in those cases of concealment or disappearance where Homer himself employed or would have employed it, but in cases where the spectator was to perceive something which the characters on the canvas, or some of them at least, were not to be conscious of. Minerva was visible to Achilles only, when she restrained him from committing violence against Agamemnon. "I know no other way of expressing this," says Caylus, "than to interpose a cloud between the goddess and the other members of the council." This is entirely contrary to the spirit of the poet. Invisibility was the natural condition of his deities. So far from any stroke of blindness or intercepting of the rays of light being necessary to render them invisible, a special illumination, an increased power of human vision was needed to see them. [18] Not only, therefore, is this cloud an arbitrary and not a natural symbol in painting, but it does not possess the clearness which, as an arbitrary sign, it should. It has a double meaning, being employed as well to make the invisible visible as to render the visible invisible.

XIII.

If Homer's works were completely destroyed, and nothing remained of the *Iliad* and *Odyssey* but this series of pictures proposed by Caylus, should we from these—even supposing them to be executed by the best masters—form the same idea that we now have of the poet's descriptive talent alone, setting aside all his other qualities as a poet?

Let us take the first piece that comes to hand—the picture of the plague. What do we see on the canvas? Dead bodies, the flame of funeral pyres, the dying busied with the dead, the angry god upon a cloud discharging his arrows. The profuse wealth of the picture becomes poverty in the poet. Should we attempt to restore the text of Homer from this picture, what can we make him say? "Thereupon the wrath of Apollo was kindled, and he shot his arrows among the Grecian army. Many Greeks died, and their bodies were burned." Now let us turn to Homer himself:

Ὥς ἔφατ' εὐχόμενος, τοῦ δ' ἔκλυε Φοῖβος
   Ἀπόλλων,
βῆ δὲ κατ' Οὐλύμποιο καρήνων χωόμενος
   κῆρ,
τόξ' ὤμοισιν ἔχων ἀμφηρεφέα τε φαρέτρην.
ἐκλαγξαν δ' ἄρ' ὀϊστοὶ ἐπ' ὤμων
   χωομένοιο,
αὐτοῦ κινηθέντος· ὁ δ' ἤϊε νυκτὶ ἐοικώς.
ἕζετ' ἔπειτ' ἀπάνευθε νεῶν, μετὰ δ' ἰὸν
   ἕηκεν·
δεινὴ δὲ κλαγγὴ γένετ' ἀργυρέοιο βιοῖο.
οὐρῆας μὲν πρῶτον ἐπῴχετο καὶ κύνας
   ἀργούς,
αὐτὰρ ἔπειτ' αὐτοῖσι βέλος ἐχεπευκὲς ἐφιείς
βάλλ'· αἰεὶ δὲ πυραὶ νεκύων καίοντο
   θαμειαί.*

The poet here is as far beyond the painter, as life is better than a picture. Wrathful, with bow and quiver, Apollo descends from the Olympian towers. I not only see him, but hear him. At every step the arrows rattle on the shoulders of the angry god. He enters among the host like the night. Now he seats himself over against the ships, and, with a terrible clang of the silver bow, sends his first shaft against the mules and dogs. Next he turns his poisoned darts upon the warriors themselves, and unceasing blaze on every side the corpse-laden pyres. It is impossible to translate into any other language the musical painting heard in the poet's words. Equally impossible would it be to infer it from the canvas. Yet this is the least of the advantages possessed by the poetical picture. Its chief superiority is that it leads us through a whole gallery of pictures up to the point depicted by the artist.

But the plague is perhaps not a favorable subject for a picture. Take the council of the gods, which is more particularly addressed to the eye. An open palace of gold, groups of the fairest and most majestic forms, goblet in hand, served by eternal youth in the person of Hebe. What architecture! what masses of light and shade! what contrasts! what variety of expression! Where shall I begin, where cease, to feast my eyes? If the painter thus enchant me, how much more will the poet! I open the book and find myself deceived. I read four

---

*Iliad i. 44–53.
Down he came,

Down from the summit of the Olympian
   mount,
Wrathful in heart; his shoulders bore the bow
And hollow quiver; there the arrows rang
Upon the shoulders of the angry god,
As on he moved. He came as comes the night,
And, seated from the ships aloof, sent forth
An arrow; terrible was heard the clang
Of that resplendent bow. At first he smote
The mules and the swift dogs, and
   then on man
He turned the deadly arrow. All around
Glared evermore the frequent funeral piles.
   —BRYANT.   [Cf. *GBWW*, Vol. 4, p. 3c.]

good, plain lines, which might very appropriately be written under the painting. They contain material for a picture, but are in themselves none.

Οἱ δὲ θεοὶ πὰρ Ζηνὶ καθήμενοι ἠγορόωντο
χρυσέῳ ἐν δαπέδῳ, μετὰ δέ σφισι πότνια "Ηβη
νέκταρ ἐῳνοχόει· τοὶ δὲ χρυσέοις δεπάεσσιν
δειδέχατ᾽ ἀλλήλους, Τρώων πόλιν
*εἰσορόωντες.**

Apollonius, or a more indifferent poet still, would not have said it worse. Here Homer is as far behind the artist as, in the former instance, he surpassed him.

Yet, except in these four lines, Caylus finds no single picture in the whole fourth book of the *Iliad*. "Rich as this book is," he says, "in its manifold exhortations to battle, in the abundance of its conspicuous and contrasting characters, in the skill with which the masses to be set in motion are brought before us, it is yet entirely unavailable for painting." "Rich as it otherwise is," he might have added, "in what are called poetic pictures." For surely in this fourth book we find as many such pictures, and as perfect, as in any of the whole poem. Where is there a more detailed, a more striking picture than that of Pandarus breaking the truce at the instigation of Minerva, and discharging his arrow at Menelaus? than that of the advance of the Grecian army? or of the mutual attack? or of the deed of Ulysses, whereby he avenges the death of his friend Leucus?

What must we conclude, except that not a few of the finest pictures in Homer are no pictures for the artist? that the artist can extract pictures from him where he himself has none? that such of his as the artist can use would be poor indeed did they show us no more than we see on the canvas? what, in short, but a negative answer to my question? Painted pictures drawn from the poems of Homer, however numerous and however admirable they may be, can give us no idea of the descriptive talent of the poet.

XIV.

If it, then, be true that a poem not in itself picturesque may yet be rich in subjects for an artist, while another in a high degree picturesque may yield him nothing, this puts an end to the theory of Count Caylus, that the test of a poem is its availability for the artist, and that a poet's rank should depend upon the number of pictures he supplies to the painter.[19]

Far be it from us to give this theory even the sanction of our silence. Milton would be the first to fall an innocent victim. Indeed, the contemptuous judgment which Caylus passes upon the English poet would seem to be the result not so much of national taste as of this assumed rule. Milton resembles Homer, he says, in little excepting loss of sight. Milton, it is true, can fill no picture galleries. But if, so long as I retained my bodily eye, its sphere must be the measure of my inward vision, then I should esteem its loss a gain, as freeing me from such limitations.

The fact that *Paradise Lost* furnishes few subjects for a painter no more prevents it from being the greatest epic since Homer, than the story of the passion of Christ becomes a poem, because you can hardly insert the head of a pin in any part of the narrative without touching some passage which has employed a crowd of the greatest artists. The evangelists state their facts with the dryest possible simplicity, and the painter uses their various details while the narrators themselves manifested not the smallest spark of genius for the picturesque. There are picturesque and unpicturesque facts, and the historian may relate the most picturesque without picturesque-

---

*Iliad iv. 1–4.
Meantime the immortal gods with Jupiter
Upon his golden pavement sat and held
A council. Hebe, honored of them all,
Ministered nectar, and from cups of gold
They pledged each other, looking down on
   Troy.—BRYANT.
[Cf. *GBWW*, Vol. 4, p. 24a.]

ness, as the poet can make a picture of those least adapted to the painter's use.

To regard the matter otherwise is to allow ourselves to be misled by the double meaning of a word. A picture in poetry is not necessarily one which can be transferred to canvas. But every touch, or every combination of touches, by means of which the poet brings his subject so vividly before us that we are more conscious of the subject than of his words, is picturesque, and makes what we call a picture; that is, it produces that degree of illusion which a painted picture is peculiarly qualified to excite, and which we in fact most frequently and naturally experience in the contemplation of the painted canvas.[20]

XV.

Experience shows that the poet can produce this degree of illusion by the representation of other than visible objects. He therefore has at his command whole classes of subjects which elude the artist. Dryden's "Ode on Cecilia's Day" is full of musical pictures but gives no employment to the brush. But I will not lose myself in examples of this kind, for they after all teach us little more than that colors are not tones, and ears not eyes.

I will confine myself to pictures of visible objects, available alike to poet and painter. What is the reason that many poetical pictures of this class are unsuitable for the painter, while many painted pictures lose their chief effect in the hands of the poet?

Examples may help us. I revert to the picture of Pandarus in the fourth book of the *Iliad,* as one of the most detailed and graphic in all Homer. From the seizing of the bow to the flight of the arrow every incident is painted; and each one follows its predecessor so closely, and yet is so distinct from it, that a person who knew nothing of the use of a bow could learn it

from this picture alone.[21] Pandarus brings forth his bow, attaches the string, opens the quiver, selects a well-feathered arrow never before used, adjusts the notch of the arrow to the string, and draws back both string and arrow; the string approaches his breast, the iron point of the arrow nears the bow, the great arched bow springs back with a mighty twang, the cord rings, and away leaps the eager arrow speeding toward the mark.

Caylus cannot have overlooked this admirable picture. What, then, did he find which made him judge it no fitting subject for an artist? And what in the council and carousal of the gods made that seem more adapted to his purpose? The subjects are visible in one case as in the other, and what more does the painter need for his canvas?

The difficulty must be this. Although both themes, as representing visible objects, are equally adapted to painting, there is this essential difference between them: one is a visible progressive action, the various parts of which follow one another in time; the other is a visible stationary action, the development of whose various parts takes place in space. Since painting, because its signs or means of imitation can be combined only in space, must relinquish all representations of time, therefore progressive actions, as such, cannot come within its range. It must content itself with actions in space; in other words, with mere bodies, whose attitude lets us infer their action. Poetry, on the contrary—

XVI.

But I will try to prove my conclusions by starting from first principles.

I argue thus. If it be true that painting employs wholly different signs or means of imitation from poetry—the one using forms and colors in space, the other articulate sounds in time—and if signs must unquestionably stand in convenient relation with the thing signified, then signs arranged side by side can represent only objects existing side by side, or whose parts so exist, while consecutive signs can express only objects which succeed each other, or whose parts succeed each other, in time.

Objects which exist side by side, or whose parts so exist, are called bodies. Consequently bodies with their visible properties are the peculiar subjects of painting.

Objects which succeed each other, or whose parts succeed each other in time, are actions. Consequently actions are the peculiar subjects of poetry.

All bodies, however, exist not only in space, but also in time. They continue, and, at any moment of their continuance, may assume a different appearance and stand in different relations. Every one of these momentary appearances and groupings was the result of a preceding, may become the cause of a following, and is therefore the center of a present, action. Consequently painting can imitate actions also, but only as they are suggested through forms.

Actions, on the other hand, cannot exist independently but must always be joined to certain agents. Insofar as those agents are bodies or are regarded as such, poetry describes also bodies, but only indirectly through actions.

Painting, in its coexistent compositions, can use but a single moment of an action and must therefore choose the most pregnant one, the one most suggestive of what has gone before and what is to follow.

Poetry, in its progressive imitations, can use but a single attribute of bodies and must choose that one which gives the most vivid picture of the body as exercised in this particular action.

Hence the rule for the employment of a single descriptive epithet, and the cause of the rare occurrence of descriptions of physical objects.

I should place less confidence in this dry chain of conclusions, did I not find them fully confirmed by Homer, or, rather, had they not been first suggested to me by Homer's method. These principles alone furnish a key to the noble style of the Greek and enable us to pass just judgment on the opposite method of many modern poets who insist upon emulating the artist in a point where they must of necessity remain inferior to him.

I find that Homer paints nothing but progressive actions. All bodies, all separate objects, are painted only as they take part in such actions, and generally with a single touch. No wonder, then, that artists find in Homer's pictures little or nothing to their purpose, and that their only harvest is where the narration brings together in a space favorable to art a number of beautiful shapes in graceful attitudes, however little the poet himself may have painted shapes, attitudes, or space. If we study one by one the whole series of pictures proposed by Caylus, we shall in every case find proof of the justness of these conclusions.

Here, then, I leave the Count with his desire to make the painter's color-stone the touchstone of the poet, and proceed to examine more closely the style of Homer.

For a single thing, as I have said, Homer has commonly but a single epithet. A ship is to him at one time the black ship, at another the hollow ship, and again the swift ship. At most it is the well-manned black ship. Further painting of the ship he does not attempt. But of the ship's sailing, its departure and arrival, he makes so detailed a picture, that the artist would have to paint five or six, to put the whole upon his canvas.

If circumstances compel Homer to fix our attention for a length of time on any one object, he still makes no picture of it which an artist can follow with his brush. By countless devices he presents this single object in a series of moments, in every one of which it assumes a different form. Only in the final one can the painter seize it, and show us ready made what the artist has been showing us in the making. If Homer, for instance, wants us to see the chariot of Juno, Hebe must put it together piece by piece before our eyes. We see the wheels, the axle, the seat, the pole, the traces and straps, not already in place, but as they come together under Hebe's hands. The wheels are the only part on which the poet bestows more than a single epithet. He shows us separately the eight brazen spokes, the golden fellies, the tires of brass, and the silver nave. It would almost seem that, as there was more than one wheel, he wished to spend as much more time in the description as the putting on would require in reality.

῞Ηβη δ᾽ ἀμφ᾽ ὀχέεσσι θοῶς βάλε καμπύλα
    κύκλα,
χάλκεα ὀκτάκνημα, σιδηρέῳ ἄξονι ἀμφίς.
τῶν ἤτοι χρυσέη ἴτυς ἄφθιτος, αὐτὰρ
    ὕπερθεν
χάλκε᾽ ἐπίσσωτρα προσαρηρότα, θαῦμα
    ἰδέσθαι·
πλῆμναι δ᾽ ἀργύρου εἰσὶ περίδρομοι
    ἀμφοτέρωθεν.
δίφρος δὲ χρυσέοισι καὶ ἀργυρέοισιν ἱμᾶσιν
ἐντέταται, δοιαὶ δὲ περίδρομοι ἄντυγές
    εἰσιν.
τοῦ δ᾽ ἐξ ἀργυρεος ῥυμὸς πέλεν· αὐτὰρ ἐπ᾽
    ἄκρῳ
δῆσε χρύσειον καλὸν ζυγὸν, ἐν δὲ λέπαδνα
κάλ᾽ ἔβαλε, χρύσει᾽·*

When Homer wishes to tell us how Agamemnon was dressed, he makes the king put on every article of raiment in our presence: the soft tunic, the great mantle, the beautiful sandals, and the sword. When he is thus fully equipped he grasps his scepter. We see the clothes while the poet is describing the act of dressing. An inferior writer would have described the clothes down to the minutest fringe, and of the action we should have seen nothing.

μαλακὸν δ᾽ ἔνδυνε χιτῶνα,
καλὸν νηγάτεον, περὶ δὲ μέγα βάλλετο φᾶρος·
ποσσὶ δ᾽ ὑπὸ λιπαροῖσιν ἐδήσατο καλὰ πέδιλα,
ἀμφὶ δ᾽ ἄρ ὤμοισιν βάλετο ξίφος ἀργυρόηλον.
εἵλετο δὲ σκῆπτρον πατρώϊον, ἄφθιτον αἰεί·†

How does he manage when he desires to give a more full and minute picture of the scepter, which is here called only ancestral and undecaying, as a similar one in another place is only χρυσέοις ἥλοισι πεπάρμενον— golden-studded? Does he paint for us, besides the golden nails, the wood, and the carved head? He might have done so, had he been writing a description for a book of heraldry, from which at some later day an exact copy was to be made. Yet I have no doubt that many a modern poet would have given such heraldic description in the honest belief that he was really making a picture himself, because he was giving the painter material for one. But what does Homer care how far he outstrips the painter? Instead of a copy, he gives us the history of the scepter. First we see it in the workship of Vulcan; then it shines in the hands of Jupiter; now it betokens the dignity of Mercury; now it is the baton of warlike Pelops; and again the shepherd's staff of peace-loving Atreus.

---

*Iliad v. 722.
        Hebe rolled the wheels,
Each with eight spokes, and joined them
    to the ends
Of the steel axle—fellies wrought of gold,
Bound with a brazen rim to last for ages—
A wonder to behold. The hollow naves
Were silver, and on gold and silver cords
Was slung the chariot's seat; in silver hooks
Rested the reins; and silver was the pole
Where the fair yoke and poitrels, all of gold,
She fastened.—BRYANT.
        [Cf. GBWW, Vol. 4, p. 37c.]
†Iliad ii. 43–47.
He sat upright and put his tunic on,
Soft, fair, and new, and over that he cast
His ample cloak, and round his shapely feet
Laced the becoming sandals. Next, he hung
Upon his shoulders and his side the sword
With silver studs, and took into his hand
The ancestral scepter, old but undecayed.
—BRYANT. [Cf. GBWW, Vol. 4, p. 10b–c.]

σκῆπτρον, τὸ μὲν ″Ηφαιστος κάμε τεύχων·
″Ηφαιστος μὲν δῶκε Διὶ Κρονίωνι ἄνακτι,
αὐτὰρ ἄρα Ζεὺς δῶκε διακτόρῳ ᾿Αργειφόντῃ·
᾿Ερμείας δὲ ἄναξ δῶκεν Πέλοπι πληξίππῳ,
αὐτὰρ ὁ αὖτε Πέλοψ δῶκ᾿ ᾿Ατρέϊ, ποιμένι
λαων·
᾿Ατρεὺς δὲ θνήσκων ἔλιπεν πολύαρνι Θυέστῃ,
αὐτὰρ ὁ αὖτε Θυέστ᾿ ᾿Αγαμέμνον·ι λ᾿εἶπε
φορῆναι,
πολλῆσιν νήσοισι καὶ ″Αργεϊ παντὶ ἀνάσσειν.*

And so at last I know this scepter better than if a painter should put it before my eyes, or a second Vulcan give it into my hands.

It would not surprise me to find that some one of Homer's old commentators had admired this passage as a perfect allegory of the origin, progress, establishment, and final inheritance of monarchical power among men. I should smile indeed were I to read that the maker of the scepter, Vulcan, as fire, as that which is of supreme importance to the maintenance of mankind, typified the removal of the necessities which induced the early races of men to subject themselves to a single ruler; that the first king was a son of Time (Ζεὺς Κρονίων), revered and venerable, who desired to share his power with a wise and eloquent man, a Mercury (Διακτόρῳ ᾿Αργειφόντῃ), or to resign it wholly to him; that the wise speaker, at the time when the young state was threatened by foreign enemies, delivered his supreme authority to the bravest warrior (Πέλοπι πληξίππῳ); that the brave warrior, after having subdued the enemies and secured the safety of the realm, let this power play into the hands of his son, who, as a peace-loving ruler, a beneficent shepherd of his people (ποιμὴν λαῶν), introduced comfort and luxury; that thus the way was opened, after his death, for the richest of his relations (πολύαρνι Θυέστῃ) to obtain by gifts and bribery, and finally to secure to his family forever, as a piece of property obtained by purchase, that authority which had originally been conferred as a mark of confidence, and had been regarded by merit rather as a burden than an honor. I should smile at all this, but it would increase my respect for a poet to whom so much could be attributed.

But this is a digression. I am now considering the history of the scepter as a device for making us linger over a single object, without entering into a tiresome description of its various parts. Again, when Achilles swears by his scepter to be revenged on Agamemnon for his contemptuous treatment, Homer gives us the history of this scepter. We see it still green upon the mountains, the axe severs it from the parent trunk, strips it of leaves and bark, and makes it ready to serve the judges of the people, as the token of their godlike office.

ναὶ μὰ τόδε σκῆπτρον, τὸ μὲν οὔποτε φύλλα
καὶ ὄζους
φύσει, ἐπειδὴ πρῶτα τομὴν ἐν ὄρεσσι λέλοιπεν,
οὐδ᾿ ἀναθηλήσει· περὶ γάρ ῥά ἑ χαλκὸς ἔλεψεν
φύλλα τε καὶ φλοιόν· νῦν αὐτέ μιν υἶες ᾿Αχαιῶν
ἐν παλάμῃς φορέουσι δικασπόλοι, οἶτε
θέμιστας
πρὸς Διὸς εἰρύαται.†

---

*Iliad ii. 101–8.

              He held
The scepter; Vulcan's skill had fashioned it,
And Vulcan gave it to Saturnian Jove,
And Jove bestowed it on his messenger,
The Argus-queller Hermes. He in turn
Gave it to Pelops, great in horsemanship;
And Pelops passed the gift to Atreus next,
The people's shepherd. Atreus, when he died,
Bequeathed it to Thyestes, rich in flocks;
And last, Thyestes left it to be borne
By Agamemnon, symbol of his rule
O'er many isles and all the Argive realm.
     —BRYANT. [Cf. *GBWW*, Vol. 4, p. 11a.]
   †*Iliad* i. 234–39.
By this my scepter, which can never bear
A leaf or twig, since first it left its stem
Among the mountains—for the steel has pared
Its boughs and bark away—to sprout no more,
And now the Achaian judges bear it—they
Who guard the laws received from Jupiter.
     —BRYANT.   [Cf. *GBWW*, Vol. 4, p. 5c.]

Homer's object was not so much to describe two staves of different shape and material, as to give us a graphic picture of the different degrees of power which these staves represented. One the work of Vulcan, the other cut upon the hills by an unknown hand; one the old possession of a noble house, the other destined to be grasped by the first comer; one extended by a monarch over many islands and over all Argos, the other borne by one from among the Greeks, who, in connection with others, had been intrusted with the duty of upholding the laws. This was in fact the difference between Agamemnon and Achilles; and Achilles, even in the blindness of his passion, could not but admit it.

Not only when Homer's descriptions have these higher aims in view, but even when his sole object is the picture, he will yet break this up into a sort of history of the object in order that the various parts, which we see side by side in nature, may just as naturally follow each other in his picture, and, as it were, keep pace with the flow of the narrative.

He wants, for instance, to paint us the bow of Pandarus. It is of horn, of a certain length, well polished, and tipped at both ends with gold. What does he do? Does he enumerate these details thus drily one after another? By no means. That would be telling off such a bow, setting it as a copy, but not painting it. He begins with the hunting of the wild goat from whose horns the bow was made. Pandarus had lain in wait for him among the rocks and slain him. Owing to the extraordinary size of the horns, he decided to use them for a bow. They come under the workman's hands, who joins them together, polishes, and tips them. And thus, as I have said, the poet shows us in the process of creation, what the painter can only show us as already existing.

τόξον ἐύξοον ἰξάλου αἰγὸς
ἀγρίου, ὅν ῥά ποτ᾽ αὐτὸς ἐπὶ στέρνοιο τυχήσας

πέτρης ἐκβαίνοντα, δεδεγμένος ἐν προδοκῇσιν,
βεβλήκει πρὸς στῆθος· ὁ δ᾽ ὕπτιος ἔμπεσε
πέτρῃ.
τοῦ κέρα ἐκ κεφαλῆς ἑκκαιδεκάδωρα πεφύκει·
καὶ τὰ μὲν ἀσκήσας κεραοξόος ἤραρε τέκτων,
πᾶν δ᾽ εὖ λειήνας, χρυσέην ἐπέθηκε κορώνην.*

I should never have done, were I to try to write out all the examples of this kind. They will occur in numbers to everyone familiar with Homer.

XVII.

But, it may be urged, the signs employed in poetry not only follow each other but are also arbitrary; and, as arbitrary signs, they are certainly capable of expressing things as they exist in space. Homer himself furnishes examples of this. We have but to call to mind his shield of Achilles to have an instance of how circumstantially and yet poetically a single object can be described according to its coexistent parts.

I will proceed to answer this double objection. I call it double, because a just conclusion must hold, though unsupported by examples, and on the other hand the example of Homer has great weight with me, even when I am unable to justify it by rules.

It is true that since the signs of speech are arbitrary, the parts of a body can by their means be made to follow each other as readily as in nature they exist side by

---

Iliad iv. 105–11.
        He uncovered straight
His polished bow made of the elastic horns
Of a wild goat, which, from his lurking-place,
As once it left its cavern lair, he smote,
And pierced its breast, and stretched it
        on the rock.
Full sixteen palms in length the horns
        had grown
From the goat's forehead. These an artisan
Had smoothed, and, aptly fitting each to each,
Polished the whole and tipped the work with
        gold.—BRYANT.
        [Cf. *GBWW*, Vol. 4, p. 25a.]

side. But this is a property of the signs of language in general, not of those peculiar to poetry. The prose writer is satisfied with being intelligible and making his representations plain and clear. But this is not enough for the poet. He desires to present us with images so vivid, that we fancy we have the things themselves before us, and cease for the moment to be conscious of his words, the instruments with which he effects his purpose. That was the point made in the definition given above of a poetical picture. But the poet must always paint; and now let us see in how far bodies, considered in relation to their parts lying together in space, are fit subjects for this painting.

How do we obtain a clear idea of a thing in space? First we observe its separate parts, then the union of these parts, and finally the whole. Our senses perform these various operations with such amazing rapidity as to make them seem but one. This rapidity is absolutely essential to our obtaining an idea of the whole, which is nothing more than the result of the conception of the parts and of their connection with each other. Suppose now that the poet should lead us in proper order from one part of the object to the other; suppose he should succeed in making the connection of these parts perfectly clear to us; how much time will he have consumed?

The details, which the eye takes in at a glance, he enumerates slowly one by one, and it often happens that, by the time he has brought us to the last, we have forgotten the first. Yet from these details we are to form a picture. When we look at an object the various parts are always present to the eye. It can run over them again and again. The ear, however, loses the details it has heard, unless memory retain them. And if they be so retained, what pains and effort it costs to recall their impressions in the proper order and with even the moderate degree of rapidity necessary to the obtaining of a tolerable idea of the whole.

Let us take an example which may be called a masterpiece of its kind.

*Dort ragt das hohe Haupt vom edeln
   Enziane*
*Weit übern niedern Chor der Pöbelkräuter
   hin,*
*Ein ganzes Blumenvolk dient unter seiner
   Fahne,*
*Sein blauer Bruder selbst bückt sich und ehret
   ihn.*
*Der Blumen helles Gold, in Strahlen
   umgebogen,*
*Thürmt sich am Stengel auf, und krönt sein
   grau Gewand,*
*Der Blätter glattes Weiss mit tiefem Grün
   durchzogen,*
*Strahlt von dem bunten Blitz von feuchtem
   Diamant.*
*Gerechtestes Gesetz! dass Kraft sich Zier
   vermähle,*
*In einem schönen Leib wohnt eine schön're
   Seele.*

*Hier kriecht ein niedrig Kraut, gleich
   einem grauen Nebel*
Dem die Natur sein Blatt im Kreuze hingelegt,
*Die holde Blume zeigt die zwei vergöldten
   Schnäbel,*
Die ein von Amethyst gebildter Vogel trägt.
*Dort wirft ein glänzend Blatt, in Finger
   ausgekerbet,*
*Auf einen hellen Bach den grünen
   Wiederschein;*
*Der Blumen zarten Schnee, den matter Purpur
   färbet,*
*Schliesst ein gestreifter Stern in weisse Strahlen
   ein.*
*Smaragd und Rosen blühn auch auf zertretner
   Heide,*
*Und Felsen decken sich mit einem
   Purpurkleide.**

---

*Von Haller's Alps.
The lofty gentian's head in stately grandeur
   towers
Far o'er the common herd of vulgar weeds and
   low;
Beneath his banners serve communities
   of flowers;

The learned poet is here painting plants and flowers with great art and in strict accordance with nature, but there is no illusion in his picture. I do not mean that a person who had never seen these plants and flowers could form little or no idea of them from his description. Perhaps all poetical pictures require a previous knowledge of their subject. Neither would I deny that a person possessing such knowledge might derive from the poet a more vivid idea of certain details. I only ask how it is with a conception of the whole. If that is to become more vivid, none of the separate details must stand in undue prominence, but the new illumination must be equally shared by all. Our imagination must be able to embrace them all with equal rapidity in order to form from them in an instant that one harmonious whole which the eye takes in at a glance. Is that the case here? If not, how can it be said, "that the most exact copy produced by a painter is dull and faint compared with this poetical description"? It is far inferior to what lines and colors can produce on canvas. The critic who bestowed upon it this exaggerated praise must have regarded it from an entirely false point of view. He must have looked at the foreign graces which the poet has woven into his description, at his idealization of vegetable life, and his development of inward perfections, to which outward beauty serves but as the shell. These he was considering, and not beauty itself or the degree of resemblance and vividness of the image, which painter and poet respectively can give us. Upon this last point everything depends, and whoever maintains that the lines,

Der Blumen helles Gold in Strahlen
    umgebogen,
Thürmt sich am Stengel auf, und krönt sein
    grau Gewand,
Der Blätter glattes Weiss, mit tiefem Grün
    durchzogen,
Strahlt von dem bunten Blitz von feuchtem
    Diamant,

can vie in vividness of impression with a flower-piece by a Huysum, must either never have analyzed his own sensations or must wilfully ignore them. It might be very pleasant to hear the lines read if we had the flowers in our hand; but, taken by themselves, they say little or nothing. I hear in every word the laborious poet, but the thing itself I am unable to see.

Once more, then, I do not deny that language has the power of describing a corporeal whole according to its parts. It certainly has, because its signs, although consecutive, are nevertheless arbitrary. But I deny that this power exists in language as the instrument of poetry. For illusion, which is the special aim of poetry, is not produced by these verbal descriptions of objects, nor can it ever be so produced. The coexistence of the body comes into collision with the sequence of the words, and although while the former is getting resolved into the latter, the dismember-

---

His azure brethren, too, in rev'rence
    to him bow.
The blossom's purest gold in curving radiations
Erect upon the stalk, above its gray
    robe gleams;
The leaflets' pearly white with deep green
    variegations
With flashes many-hued of the moist diamond
    beams.
O Law beneficent! which strength to beauty
    plighteth,
And to a shape so fair a fairer soul uniteth.

Here on the ground a plant like a gray mist
    is twining,
In fashion of a cross its leaves by Nature laid;
Part of the beauteous flower, the gilded beak
    is shining,
Of a fair bird whose shape of amethyst
    seems made.
There into fingers cleft a polished leaf reposes,
And o'er a limpid brook its green reflection
    throws;
With rays of white a striped star encloses
The floweret's disk, where pink flushes its
    tender snows.
Thus on the trodden heath are rose and
    emerald glowing,
And e'en the rugged rocks are purple
    banners showing.

ment of the whole into its parts is a help to us, yet the reunion of these parts into a whole is made extremely difficult, and not infrequently impossible.

Where the writer does not aim at illusion, but is simply addressing the understanding of his readers with the desire of awakening distinct and, as far as possible, complete ideas, then these descriptions of corporeal objects, inadmissible as they are in poetry, are perfectly appropriate. Not only the prose writer, but the didactic poet (for in as far as he is didactic he is no poet) may use them with good effect. Thus Virgil, in his *Georgics*, describes a cow fit for breeding:

Optima torvae
Forma bovis, cui turpe caput, cui plurima
cervix,
Et crurum tenus a mento palearia pendent.
Tum longo nullus lateri modus: omnia magna:
Pes etiam, et camuris hirtae sub cornibus
aures.
Nec mihi displiceat maculis insignis et albo,
Aut juga detractans interdumque aspera
cornu,
Et faciem tauro propior; quaeque ardua tota,
*Et gradiens ima verrit vestigia cauda.**

Or a handsome colt:

Illi ardua cervix,
Argutumque caput, brevis alvus, obesaque
terga,
Luxuriatque toris animosum pectus, &c.†

Here the poet is plainly concerned more with the setting forth of the separate parts than with the effect of the whole. His object is to tell us the characteristics of a handsome colt and a good cow, so that we may judge of their excellence according to the number of these characteristics which they possess. Whether or not all these can be united into a vivid picture was a matter of indifference to him.

Except for this purpose, elaborate pictures of bodily objects, unless helped out

by the above-mentioned Homeric device of making an actual series out of their coexistent parts, have always been considered by the best critics as ineffective trifles, requiring little or no genius. "When a poetaster," says Horace, "can do nothing else, he falls to describing a grove, an altar, a brook winding through pleasant meadows, a rushing river, or a rainbow."

Lucus et ara Dianae,
Et properantis aquae per amoenos ambitus
agros,
Aut flumen Rhenum, aut pluvius describitur
arcus.

Pope, when a man, looked back with contempt on the descriptive efforts of his poetic childhood. He expressly enjoined upon everyone, who would not prove himself unworthy the name of poet, to abandon as early as possible this fondness for description. A merely descriptive poem he declared to be a feast made up of sauces.[22] Herr Von Kleist, I know, prided himself very little on his "Spring." Had he lived, he would have refashioned it altogether. He wanted to introduce into it some plan and was meditating how he could best make the crowd of pictures, which seemed

---

*Georg. lib. iii. 51 and 79.
If her large front and neck vast strength
   denote;
If on her knee the pendulous dewlap float;
If curling horns their crescent inward bend,
And bristly hairs beneath the ear defend;
If lengthening flanks to bounding measure
   spread;
If broad her foot and bold her bull-like head;
If snowy spots her mottled body stain,
And her indignant brow the yoke disdain,
With tail wide-sweeping as she stalks the dews,
Thus, lofty, large, and long, the mother
   choose.—DRYDEN.
        [Cf. *GBWW*, Vol. 13, p. 68b.]
†Ibid.
Light on his airy crest his slender head,
His belly short, his loins luxuriant spread;
Muscle on muscle knots his brawny breast,
   &c.—DRYDEN.
        [Cf. *GBWW*, Vol. 13, p. 69a.]

to have been drawn at random from the whole vast range of fresh creation, rise in some natural order and follow each other in fitting sequence. He would, at the same time, have done what Marmontel, doubtless with reference to his *Eclogues,* recommended to several German poets. He would have converted a series of pictures scantily interwoven with mental emotions, into a series of emotions sparingly interspersed with images.

XVIII.

And shall Homer nevertheless have fallen into those barren descriptions of material objects?

Let us hope that only a few such passages can be cited. And even those few, I venture to assert, will be found really to confirm the rule, to which they appear to form an exception.

The rule is this, that succession in time is the province of the poet, coexistence in space that of the artist.

To bring together into one and the same picture two points of time necessarily remote, as Mazzuoli does the rape of the Sabine women and the reconciliation effected by them between their husbands and relations; or as Titian does, representing in one piece the whole story of the Prodigal Son—his dissolute life, his misery, and repentance—is an encroachment of the painter on the domain of the poet, which good taste can never sanction.

To try to present a complete picture to the reader by enumerating in succession several parts or things which in nature the eye necessarily takes in at a glance, is an encroachment of the poet on the domain of the painter, involving a great effort of the imagination to very little purpose.

Painting and poetry should be like two just and friendly neighbors, neither of whom indeed is allowed to take unseemly liberties in the heart of the other's domain, but who exercise mutual forbearance on the borders and effect a peaceful settlement for all the petty encroachments which circumstances may compel either to make in haste on the rights of the other.

I will not bring forward in support of this the fact that, in large historical pictures the single moment of time is always somewhat extended, and that perhaps no piece, very rich in figures, can be found, in which every character has exactly the motion and attitude proper to him at that particular moment. The position of some belongs to a preceding point of time, that of others to a later. This is a liberty which the painter must justify by certain subtleties of arrangement, such as placing his figures more in the foreground or background, and thus making them take a more or less immediate interest in what is going on. I will merely quote, in favor of my view, a criticism of Mengs on Raphael's drapery. "There is a reason for all his folds, either in the weight of the material or the tension of the limbs. We can often infer from their present condition what they had been previously. Raphael indeed aimed at giving them significance in this way. We can judge from the folds whether, previously to the present posture, a leg or an arm had been more in front or more behind, whether a limb had been bent and is now straightening itself, or whether it had been outstretched and is now bending." Here unquestionably the artist unites into one two distinct points of time. For, since the foot in its motion forward is immediately followed by that portion of the garment which rests upon it—unless indeed the garment be of exceedingly stiff material, in which case it is ill adapted to painting— there can be no moment at which the drapery assumes in the least degree any other fold than the present posture of the limb demands. If any other be represented, then the fold is that of the preceding moment while the position of the foot is that of the present. Few, however, will be inclined to deal thus strictly with the artist who finds it for his interest to bring these two moments of time before us at once. Who will not rather praise him for having had the wisdom and the courage to commit a slight fault for the sake of greater fullness of expression?

A similar indulgence is due to the poet. The continuity of his imitation permits him, strictly speaking, to touch at one moment on only a single side, a single property of his corporeal objects. But if the happy construction of his language enables him to do this with a single word, why should he not sometimes be allowed to add a second such word? why not a third, if it be worth his while, or even a fourth? As I have said, a ship in Homer is either simply the black ship, or the hollow ship, or the swift ship; at most the well-manned black ship. That is true of his style in general. Occasionally a passage occurs where he adds a third descriptive epithet: Καμπύλα κύκλα, χάλκεα, ὀκτάκνημα, "round, brazen, eight-spoked wheels" [cf. GBWW, Vol. 4, p. 37c]. Even a fourth: ἀσπίδα πάντοσε εἴσην, καλὴν, χαλκείην, ἐξήλατον, "a uniformly smooth, beautiful, brazen, wrought shield" [cf. GBWW, Vol. 4, p. 85b]. Who will not rather thank than blame him for this little luxuriance, when we perceive its good effect in a few suitable passages?

The true justification of both poet and painter shall not, however, be left to rest upon this analogy of two friendly neighbors. A mere analogy furnishes neither proof nor justification. I justify them in this way. As in the picture the two moments of time follow each other so immediately that we can without effort consider them as one, so in the poem the several touches answering to the different parts and properties in space are so condensed, and succeed each other so rapidly, that we seem to catch them all at once.

Here, as I have said, Homer is greatly aided by his admirable language. It not only allows him all possible freedom in multiplying and combining his epithets, but enables him to arrange them so happily that we are relieved of all awkward suspense with regard to the subject. Some of the modern languages are destitute of one or more of those advantages. Those which, like the French, must have recourse to paraphrase, and convert the καμπύλα κύκλα, χάλκεα, ὀκτάκνημα of Homer into "the round wheels which were of brass and had eight spokes," give the meaning, but destroy the picture. The sense is here, however, nothing; the picture everything. The one without the other turns the most graphic of poets into a tiresome tattler. This fate has often befallen Homer under the pen of the conscientious Madame Dacier. The German language can generally render the Homeric adjectives by equally short equivalents, but it cannot follow the happy arrangement of the Greek. It can say, indeed, "the round, brazen, eight-spoked," but "wheels" comes dragging after. Three distinct predicates before any subject make but a confused, uncertain picture. The Greek joins the subject with the first predicate and lets the others follow. He says, "round wheels, brazen, eight-spoked." Thus we know at once of what he is speaking and learn first the thing and then its accidents, which is the natural order of our thoughts. The German language does not possess this advantage. Or shall I say, what really amounts to the same thing, that, although possessing it, the language can seldom use it without ambiguity? For if adjectives be placed after the subject (runde Räder, ehern und achtspeichigt) they are indeclinable, differing in nothing from adverbs, and if referred, as adverbs, to the first verb that is predicated of the subject, the meaning of the whole sentence becomes always distorted, and sometimes entirely falsified.

But I am lingering over trifles and seem to have forgotten the shield of Achilles, that famous picture, which, more than all else, caused Homer to be regarded among the ancients as a master of painting. But surely a shield, it may be said, is a single corporeal object, the description of which according to its coexistent parts cannot come within the province of poetry. Yet this shield, its material, its form, and all the figures which occupied its enormous surface, Homer has described, in more than a hundred magnificent lines, so circumstantially and precisely that modern artists have found no difficulty in making a drawing of it exact in every detail.

My answer to this particular objection is, that I have already answered it. Homer does not paint the shield finished, but in the process of creation. Here again he has made use of the happy device of substituting progression for coexistence, and thus converted the tiresome description of an object into a graphic picture of an action. We see not the shield, but the divine master-workman employed upon it. Hammer and tongs in hand he approaches the anvil; and, after having forged the plates from the rough metal, he makes the pictures designed for its decoration rise from the brass, one by one, under his finer blows. Not till the whole is finished do we lose sight of him. At last it is done; and we wonder at the work, but with the believing wonder of an eyewitness who has seen it a-making.

The same cannot be said of the shield of Aeneas in Virgil. The Roman poet either failed to see the fineness of his model, or the things which he wished to present upon his shield seemed to him not of such a kind as to allow of their being executed before our eyes. They were prophecies, which the god certainly could not with propriety have uttered in our presence as distinctly as the poet explains them in his work. Prophecies, as such, require a darker speech, in which the names of those persons to come, whose fortunes are predicted, cannot well be spoken. In these actual names, however, lay, it would seem, the chief point of interest to the poet and courtier. But this, though

it excuse him, does not do away with the disagreeable effect of his departure from the Homeric method, as all readers of taste will admit. The preparations made by Vulcan are nearly the same in Homer as in Virgil. But while in Homer we see, besides the preparations for the work, the work itself, Virgil, after showing us the god at work with his Cyclops,

Ingentum clypeum informant . . .
. . . Alii ventosis follibus auras
Accipiunt, redduntque; alii stridentia tingunt
Aera lacu. Gemit impositis incudibus antrum.
Illi inter sese multa vi brachia tollunt
In numerum, versantque tenaci forcipe
    *massam.**

suddenly drops the curtain and transports us to a wholly different scene. We are gradually led into the valley where Venus appears, bringing Aeneas the arms that in the meanwhile have been finished. She places them against the trunk of an oak; and, after the hero has sufficiently stared at them, and wondered over them, and handled them, and tried them, the description or picture of the shield begins, which grows so cold and tedious from the constantly recurring "here is," and "there is," and "near by stands," and "not far from there is seen," that all Virgil's poetic grace is needed to prevent it from becoming intolerable. Since, moreover, this description is not given by Aeneas, who delights in the mere figures without any knowledge of their import,

---

*Aeneid lib. viii. 447.
    Their artful hands a shield prepare.
One stirs the fire, and one the bellows blows;
The hissing steel is in the smithy drowned;
The grot with beaten anvils groans around.
By turns their arms advance in equal time,
By turns their hands descend and hammers
    chime;
They turn the glowing mass with crooked
    tongs.—DRYDEN.
[Cf. *GBWW,* Vol. 13, p. 271a.]

. . . rerumque ignarus imagine gaudet,

nor by Venus, although she might be supposed to know as much about the fortunes of her dear grandson as her good-natured husband, but by the poet himself, the action meanwhile necessarily remains at a standstill. Not a single one of the characters takes part; nor is what follows in the least affected by the representations on the shield. The subtle courtier, helping out his material with every manner of flattering allusion, is apparent throughout; but no trace do we see of the great genius, who trusts to the intrinsic merit of his work and despises all extraneous means of awakening interest. The shield of Aeneas is therefore, in fact, an interpolation, intended solely to flatter the pride of the Romans; a foreign brook with which the poet seeks to give fresh movement to his stream. The shield of Achilles, on the contrary, is the outgrowth of its own fruitful soil. For a shield was needed; and, since even what is necessary never comes from the hands of deity devoid of beauty, the shield had to be ornamented. The art was in treating these ornamentations as such, and nothing more; in so weaving them into the material that when we look at that we cannot but see them. This could be accomplished only by the method which Homer adopted. Homer makes Vulcan devise decorations, because he is to make a shield worthy of a divine workman. Virgil seems to make him fashion the shield for the sake of the decorations, since he deems these of sufficient importance to deserve a special description long after the shield is finished.

XIX.

The objections brought against Homer's shield by the elder Scaliger, Perrault, Terrasson, and others, are well known, as are also the answers of Madame Dacier, Boivin, and Pope. But these latter, it seems to me, have gone somewhat too far, and confiding in the justness of their cause have asserted things incorrect in themselves and contributing little to the poet's justification.

In answer to the chief objection, that Homer had burdened his shield with more figures than there could possibly have been room for, Boivin undertook to show in a drawing how the necessary space might be obtained. His idea of the various concentric circles was very ingenious, although there is no foundation for it in the poet's words and nothing anywhere to indicate that shields divided in this way were known to the ancients. Since Homer calls it (σάκος πάντοσε δεδαιλωμένον) a shield, artistically wrought on all sides, I should prefer to gain the required space by turning to account the concave surface. A proof that the old artists did not leave this empty is furnished in the shield of Minerva by Phidias. But not only does Boivin fail to seize this advantage, but, by separating into two or three pictures what the poet evidently meant for one, he unnecessarily multiplies the representations while diminishing the space by one-half. I know the motive which led him to this, but it was one by which he should not have allowed himself to be influenced. He should have shown his opponents the unreasonableness of their demands, instead of trying to satisfy them.

An example will make my meaning clear. When Homer says of one of the two cities:

λαοὶ δ᾽ εἰν ἀγορῇ ἔσαν ἀθρόοι· ἔνθα δὲ νεῖκος
ὠρώρει δύο δ᾽ ἄνδρες ἐνείκεον εἵνεκα ποινῆς
ἀνδρὸς ἀποφθιμένου· ὁ μὲν εὔχετο πάντ᾽
    ἀποδοῦναι,
δήμῳ πιφαύσκων, ὁ δ᾽ ἀναίνετο μηδὲν ἑλέσθαι·
ἄμφω δ᾽ ἱέσθην ἐπὶ ἴστορι πεῖραρ ἑλέσθαι.
δ᾽λαοὶ δ᾽ ἀμφοτέροισιν ἐπήπυον, ἀμφὶς ἀρωγοί.
κήρυκες δ᾽ ἄρα λαὸν ἐρήτυον· οἱ δὲ γέροντες
εἵατ᾽ ἐπὶ ξεστοῖσι λίθοις ἱερῷ ἐνὶ κύκλῳ,
σκῆπτρα δὲ κηρύκων ἐν χέρσ᾽ ἔχον
    ἠεροφώνων·
τοῖσιν ἔπειτ᾽ ἤϊσσον, ἀμοιβηδὶς δὲ δίκαζον.

κεῖτο δ' ἄρ' ἐν μέσσοισι δύω χρυσοῖο
  τάλαντα,*

he refers, as I understand him, to but a single picture, that of a public lawsuit about the contested payment of a considerable fine for the committal of a murder. The artist, who is to execute this design, can use but a single moment of the action— that of the accusation, of the examination of witnesses, of the pronouncing of the sentence, or any other preceding or following or intervening moment which may seem to him most fitting. This single moment he makes as pregnant as possible and reproduces it with all that power of illusion which in the presentation of visible objects art possesses above poetry. Left far behind in this respect, what remains to the poet, if his words are to paint the same design with any degree of success, but to avail himself of his peculiar advantages? These are the liberty of extending his representation over what preceded, as well as what was to follow, the artist's single point of time, and the power of showing not only what the artist shows, but what he has to leave to our imagination. Only by using these advantages can the poet raise himself to a level with the artist. Their works most resemble each other when their effect is equally vivid; not when one brings before the imagination through the ear neither more nor less than the other presents to the eye. Had Boivin defended the passage in Homer according to this principle, he would not have divided it into as many separate pictures as he thought he detected distinct points of time. All that Homer relates could not, indeed, be united in a single picture. The accusation and the denial, the summoning of the witnesses and the shouts of the divided populace, the efforts of the heralds to quiet the tumult and the sentence of the judges, are things successive in time, not coexistent in space. But what is not actually in the picture is there virtually, and the only true way of representing an actual picture in words is to combine what virtually exists in it with what is absolutely visible. The poet who allows himself to be bound by the limits of art may furnish data for a picture, but can never create one of his own.

The picture of the beleaguered city Boivin divides likewise into three. He might as well have made twelve out of it as three. For since he has once for all failed to grasp the spirit of the poet, and requires him to be bound by the unities of a material picture, he might have discovered many more violations of these unities. In fact he ought almost to have devoted a separate space on the shield to every separate touch of the poet. In my opinion Homer has but ten different pictures on the whole shield, every one of which he introduces with ἐν μὲν ἔτευξε, or ἐν δὲ ποίησε, or ἐν δ' ἐτίθει, or ἐν δὲ πόικιλλε Ἀμφιγυήεις, "on it he wrought," "on it he placed," "on it he formed," "on it Vulcan skillfully fashioned" [cf. GBWW, Vol. 4, p. 135b]. In the absence of these introductory words we have no right to suppose a distinct picture. On the contrary everything which they cover must be regarded as a single whole, wanting in nothing but the arbitrary concentration into one moment of time, which the poet was in no way bound to observe. Had he observed this, and, by strictly limiting himself to it, excluded every little feature which

---

*Iliad xviii. 497–508.
              Meanwhile a multitude
Was in the forum where a strife went on—
Two men contending for a fine, the price
Of one who had been slain. Before the crowd
One claimed that he had paid the fine, and one
Denied that aught had been received, and both
Called for the sentence which should end
      the strife.
The people clamored for both sides, for both
Had eager friends; the herald held the crowd
In check; the elders, upon polished stones,
Sat in a sacred circle. Each one took
In turn a herald's scepter in his hand,
And rising gave his sentence. In the midst
Two talents lay in gold, to be the meed
Of him whose juster judgment should
      prevail.—BRYANT.
          [Cf. GBWW, Vol. 4, p. 135b.]

in the material representation would have been inconsistent with this unity of time; had he in fact done what his cavillers require, these gentlemen would indeed have had no fault to find with him, but neither would any person of taste have found aught to admire.

Pope not only accepted Boivin's drawing but thought he was doing a special service by showing that every one of these mutilated pieces was in accordance with the strictest rules of painting, as laid down at the present day. Contrast, perspective, the three unities, he found, were all observed in the best possible manner. And although well aware that, according to the testimony of good and trustworthy witnesses, painting at the time of the Trojan war was still in its cradle, he supposes either that Homer, instead of being bound by the achievements of painting at that time or in his own day, must in virtue of his godlike genius have anticipated all that art should in future be able to accomplish, or else that the witnesses could not have been so entirely worthy of faith that the direct testimony of this artistic shield should not be preferred to theirs. Whoever will, may accept the former supposition; the latter, surely, no one will be persuaded to adopt who knows anything more of the history of art than the date of the historians. That painting in the time of Homer was still in its infancy he believes, not merely on the authority of Pliny, or some other writer, but chiefly because, judging from the works of art mentioned by the ancients, he sees that even centuries later no great progress had been made. The pictures of Polygnotus, for instance, by no means stand the test which Pope thinks can be successfully applied to Homer's shield. The two great works by this master at Delphi, of which Pausanias has left a circumstantial description, were evidently wholly wanting in perspective. The ancients had no knowledge of this branch of art, and what Pope adduces as proof that Homer understood it, only proves that he has a very

imperfect understanding of it himself.

"That Homer," he says, "was not a stranger to aerial perspective appears in his expressly marking the distance of object from object. He tells us, for instance, that the two spies lay a little remote from the other figures, and that the oak under which was spread the banquet of the reapers stood apart. What he says of the valley sprinkled all over with cottages and flocks appears to be a description of a large country in perspective. And, indeed, a general argument for this may be drawn from the number of figures on the shield, which could not be all expressed in their full size; and this is therefore a sort of proof that the art of lessening them according to perspective was known at that time." The mere representing of an object at a distance as smaller than it would be if nearer the eye, by no means constitutes perspective in a picture. Perspective requires a single point of view; a definite, natural horizon; and this was wanting in the old pictures. In the paintings of Polygnotus the ground, instead of being level, rose so decidedly at the back that the figures which were meant to stand behind seemed to be standing above one another. If this was the usual position of the various figures and groups—and that it was so may fairly be concluded from the old bas-reliefs, where those behind always stand higher than those in front, and look over their heads—then we may reasonably take it for granted in Homer and should not unnecessarily dismember those representations of his, which according to this treatment might be united in a single picture. The double scene in the peaceful city, through whose streets a joyous marriage train was moving at the same time that an important trial was going on in the marketplace, requires thus no double picture. Homer could very well think of it as one, since he imagined himself to be overlooking the city from such a height as to command at once a view of the streets and the market.

My opinion is that perspective in pictures came incidentally from scene-painting, which was already in its perfection. But the applications of its rules to a single smooth surface was evidently no easy matter; for, even in the later paintings found among the antiquities of Herculaneum, there are many and various offenses against perspective, which would now hardly be excusable even in a beginner.

But I will spare myself the labor of collecting my desultory observations on a point whereon I may hope to receive complete satisfaction from Winckelmann's promised *History of Art*.

XX.

To return, then, to my road, if a saunterer can be said to have a road.

What I have been saying of bodily objects in general applies with even more force to those which are beautiful.

Physical beauty results from the harmonious action of various parts which can be taken in at a glance. It therefore requires that these parts should lie near together; and, since things whose parts lie near together are the proper subjects of painting, this art and this alone can imitate physical beauty.

The poet, who must necessarily detail in succession the elements of beauty, should therefore desist entirely from the description of physical beauty as such. He must feel that these elements arranged in a series cannot possibly produce the same effect as in juxtaposition; that the concentrating glance which we try to cast back over them immediately after their enumeration, gives us no harmonious picture; and that to conceive the effect of certain eyes, a certain mouth and nose taken together, unless we can recall a similar combination of such parts in nature or art, surpasses the power of human imagination.

Here again Homer is the model of all models. He says, Nireus was fair; Achilles was fairer; Helen was of godlike beauty.

But he is nowhere betrayed into a more detailed description of these beauties. Yet the whole poem is based upon the loveliness of Helen. How a modern poet would have reveled in descriptions of it!

Even Constantinus Manasses sought to adorn his bald chronicle with a picture of Helen. I must thank him for the attempt, for I really should not know where else to turn for so striking an example of the folly of venturing on what Homer's wisdom forbore to undertake. When I read in him:

ἦν ἡ γυνὴ περικαλλής, εὔοφρυς, εὐχρουστάτη,
εὐπάρειος, εὐπρόσωπος, βοῶπις, χιονόχρους,
ἑλικοβλέφαρος, ἁβρά, χαρίτων γέμον ἄλσος,
λευκοβραχίων, τρυφερά, κάλλος ἀντικρὺς
    ἔμπνουν,
τὸ πρόσωπον καταλευκὸν, ἡ παρειὰ
    ῥοδόχρους,
τὸ πρόσωπον ἐπίχαρι, τὸ βλέφαρον ὡραῖον,
κάλλος ἀνεπιτήδευτον, ἀβάπτιστον,
    αὐτόχρουν,
ἔβαπτε τὴν λευκότητα ῥοδοχρία πυρινή.
ὡς εἴ τις τὸν ἐλέφαντα βάψει λαμπρᾷ πορφύρᾳ.
δειρὴ μακρά, καταλευκός, ὅθεν ἐμυθουργήθη
κυκνογενῆ τὴν εὔοπτον Ἑλένην χρηματίζειν,*

it is like seeing stones rolled up a mountain, on whose summit they are to be built into a gorgeous edifice; but which all roll down of themselves on the other side. What picture does this crowd of words leave behind? How did Helen look? No two readers out of a thousand would receive the same impression of her.

---

*"She was a woman right beautiful, with fine eyebrows, of clearest complexion, beautiful cheeks; comely, with large, full eyes, with snow-white skin, quick-glancing, graceful; a grove filled with graces, fair-armed, voluptuous, breathing beauty undisguised. The complexion fair, the cheek rosy, the countenance pleasing, the eye blooming; a beauty unartificial, untinted, of its natural color, adding brightness to the brightest cherry, as if one should dye ivory with resplendent purple. Her neck long, of dazzling whiteness; whence she was called the swan-born, beautiful Helen."

But political verses by a monk are, it is true, no poetry. Let us hear Ariosto describe his enchantress Alcina:

Di persona era tanto ben formata,
Quanto mai finger san pittori industri.
Con bionda chioma, lunga e annodata,
Oro non è, che piu risplenda e lustri.
Spargeasi per la guancia delicata
Misto color di rose e di ligustri.
Di terso avorio era la fronte lieta,
Che lo spazio finia con giusta meta.

Sotto due negri, e sottilissimi archi
Son due negri, occhi, anzi due chiari soli
Pietosi a riguardar, a mover parchi,
Intorno a cui par ch' Amor scherzi, e voli,
E ch' indi tutta la faretra scarchi,
E che visibilmente i cori involi.
Quindi il naso per mezzo il viso scende
Che non trova l' invidia ove l' emende.

Scotto quel sta, quasi fra due vallette,
La bocca sparsa di natio cinabro,
Quivi due filze son di perle elette,
Che chiude, ed apre un bello e dolce labro;
Quindi escon le cortesi parolette,
Da render molle ogni cor rozzo e scabro;
Quivi si forma quel soave riso,
Ch' apre a sua posta in terra il paradiso.

Bianca neve è il pel collo, e 'l petto latte,
Ill collo è tondo, il petto colmo e largo;
Due pome acerbe, e pur d' avorio fatte,
Vengono e van, come onda al primo margo,
Quando piacevole aura il mar combatte.
Non potria l' altre parti veder Argo,
Ben si può giudicar, che corrisponde,
A quel ch' appar di fuor, quel che s' asconde.

Mostran le braccia sua misura giusta,
Et la candida man spesso si vede,
Lunghetta alquanto, e di larghezza
   angusta,
Dove nè nodo appar, nè vena eccede.
Si vede al fin de la persona augusta
Il breve, asciutto, e ritondetto piede.
Gli angelici sembianti nati in cielo
Non si ponno celar sotto alcun velo.*

**Orlando Furioso,* canto vii. st. 11–15.
Her shape is of such perfect symmetry,
   As best to feign the industrious painter
      knows;
   With long and knotted tresses; to the eye
   Not yellow gold with brighter lustre glows.
   Upon her tender cheek the mingled dye
   Is scattered of the lily and the rose.
   Like ivory smooth, the forehead gay and
      round
   Fills up the space and forms a fitting bound.

Two black and slender arches rise above
   Two clear black eyes, say suns of radiant
      light,
   Which ever softly beam and slowly move;
   Round these appears to sport in frolic flight,
   Hence scattering all his shafts, the
      little Love,
   And seems to plunder hearts in open sight.
   Thence, through 'mid visage, does the
      nose descend,
   Where envy finds not blemish to amend.

As if between two vales, which softly curl,
   The mouth with vermeil tint is seen to glow;
   Within are strung two rows of orient pearl,
   Which her delicious lips shut up or show,
   Of force to melt the heart of any churl,
   However rude, hence courteous accents
      flow;
   And here that gentle smile receives its birth,
   Which opes at will a paradise on earth.

Like milk the bosom, and the neck of snow;
   Round is the neck, and full and round
      the breast;
   Where, fresh and firm, two ivory apples
      grow,
   Which rise and fall, as, to the margin
      pressed
   By pleasant breeze, the billows come and go.
   Not prying Argus could discern the rest.
   Yet might the observing eye of things
      concealed
   Conjecture safely from the charms revealed.

To all her arms a just proportion bear,
   And a white hand is oftentimes descried,
   Which narrow is and somedeal long,
      and where
   No knot appears nor vein is signified.
   For finish of that stately shape and rare,
   A foot, neat, short, and round beneath is
      spied.
   Angelic visions, creatures of the sky,
   Concealed beneath no covering veil can lie.
                    —WILLIAM STEWART ROSE.

Milton, speaking of Pandemonium, says:

The work some praise, and some the architect.

Praise of one, then, is not always praise of the other. A work of art may merit great approbation without redounding much to the credit of the artist; and, again, an artist may justly claim our admiration, even when his work does not entirely satisfy us. By bearing this in mind we can often reconcile contradictory judgments, as in the present case. Dolce, in his dialogues on painting, makes Aretino speak in terms of the highest praise of the above-quoted stanzas,[23] while I select them as an instance of painting without picture. We are both right. Dolce admires the knowledge of physical beauty which the poet shows; I consider only the effect which this knowledge, conveyed in words, produces on my imagination. Dolce concludes from this knowledge that good poets are no less good painters; I, judging from the effect, conclude that what painters can best express by lines and colors is least capable of expression in words. Dolce recommends Ariosto's description to all painters as a perfect model of a beautiful woman; I recommend it to all poets as the most instructive of warnings not to attempt, with still greater want of success, what could not but fail when tried by an Ariosto.

It may be that when the poet says,

Di persona era tanto ben formata,
Quanto mai finger san pittori industri,

he proves himself to have had a complete knowledge of the laws of perspective, such as only the most industrious artist can acquire from a study of nature and of ancient art.[24]

In the words,

Spargeasi per la guancia delicata
Misto color di rose e di ligustri,

he may show himself to be a perfect master of color—a very Titian. His comparing Alcina's hair to gold, instead of calling it golden hair, may be taken as proof that he objected to the use of actual gold in coloring.[25] We may even discover in the descending nose the profile of those old Greek noses, afterward borrowed by Roman artists from the Greek masterpieces. Of what use is all this insight and learning to us readers who want to fancy we are looking at a beautiful woman, and desire to feel that gentle quickening of the pulses which accompanies the sight of actual beauty? The poet may know the relations from which beauty springs, but does that make us know them? Or, if we know them, does he show them to us here? or does he help us in the least to call up a vivid image of them?

A brow that forms a fitting bound,
*   Che lo spazio finia con giusta meta;*
A nose where envy itself finds nothing to
*   amend,*
*   Che non trova l' invidia, ove l' emende;*
A hand, narrow, and somewhat long,
*   Lunghetta alquanto, e di larghezza*
*   angusta;*

what sort of a picture do these general formulae give us? In the mouth of a drawing-master, directing his pupils' attention to the beauties of the academic model, they might have some meaning. For the students would have but to look at the model to see the fitting bounds of the gay forehead, the fine cut of the nose, and the slenderness of the pretty hand. But in the poem I see nothing and am only tormented by the futility of all my attempts to see anything.

In this respect Virgil, by imitating Homer's reticence, has achieved tolerable success. His Dido is only the most beautiful (*pulcherrima*) Dido. Any further details which he may give, have reference to her rich ornaments and magnificent dress.

Tandem progreditur . . .
Sidoniam picto chlamydem circumdata limbo:
Cui pharetra ex auro, crines nodantur in
    aurum,
Aurea purpuream subnectit fibula vestem.*

If, on this account, any should apply to him what the old artist said to one of his pupils who had painted a gayly decked Helen—"Since you could not paint her beautiful, you have painted her rich"—Virgil would answer: "I am not to blame that I could not paint her beautiful. The fault lies in the limits of my art, within which it is my merit to have kept."

I must not forget here the two odes of Anacreon wherein he analyzes the beauty of his mistress and of Bathyllus. The device which he uses entirely justifies the analysis. He imagines that he has before him a painter who is working from his description. "Thus paint me the hair," he says; "thus the brow, the eyes, the mouth; thus the neck and bosom, the thighs and hands." As the artist could execute but one detail at a time, the poet was obliged to give them to him thus piecemeal. His object is not to make us see and feel, in these spoken directions to the painter, the whole beauty of the beloved object. He is conscious of the inadequacy of all verbal expression; and for that reason summons to his aid the expression of art, whose power of illusion he so extols, that the whole song seems rather a eulogium of art than of his lady. He sees not the picture but herself, and fancies she is about to open her mouth to speak.

    ἀπέχει· βλέπω γὰρ ἀυτήν.
    τάχα, κηρέ, καὶ λαλήσεις.

So, too, in his ode to Bathyllus, the praises of the beautiful boy are so mingled with praises of art and the artist, that we are in doubt in whose honor the song was really written. He selects the most beautiful parts from various pictures, the parts for which the pictures were remarkable. He

takes the neck from an Adonis, breast and hands from a Mercury, the thighs from a Pollux, the belly from a Bacchus, until he has the whole Bathyllus as a finished Apollo from the artist's hand.

    μετὰ δὲ πρόσωπον ἔστω,
    τὸν 'Αδώνιδος παρελθὼν,
    ἐλεφάντινος τράχηλος·
    μεταμάζιον δὲ ποίει
    διδύμας τε χεῖρας 'Ερμου,
    Πολυδεύκεος δὲ μηρούς,
    Διονυσίην δὲ νηδύν.

    .   .   .   .

    τὸν 'Απόλλωνα δὲ τοῦτον
    καθελών, ποίει Βάθυλλου.

Thus Lucian, to give an idea of the beauty of Panthea, points to the most beautiful female statues by the old sculptors. What is this but a confession that here language of itself is powerless; that poetry stammers, and eloquence grows dumb, unless art serve as interpreter.

XXI.

But are we not robbing poetry of too much by taking from her all pictures of physical beauty?

Who seeks to take them from her? We are only warning her against trying to arrive at them by a particular road, where she will blindly grope her way in the footsteps of a sister art without ever reaching the goal. We are not closing against her other roads whereon art can follow only with her eyes.

Homer himself, who so persistently refrains from all detailed descriptions of

---

*Aeneid iv. 136.
The queen at length appears;
A flowered cymar with golden fringe she wore,
And at her back a golden quiver bore;
Her flowing hair a golden caul restrains;
A golden clasp the Tyrian robe sustains.
    —DRYDEN. [Cf. *GBWW*, Vol. 13, p. 170b.]

physical beauty, that we barely learn, from a passing mention, that Helen had white arms and beautiful hair, even he manages nevertheless to give us an idea of her beauty, which far surpasses anything that art could do. Recall the passage where Helen enters the assembly of the Trojan elders. The venerable men see her coming, and one says to the others:

Οὐ νέμεσις Τρῶας καὶ ἐϋκνήμιδας Ἀχαιοὺς
τοιῇδ' ἀμφὶ γυναικὶ πολὺν χρόνον ἄλγεα
    πάσχειν·
αἰνῶς ἀθανάτῃσι θεῆς εἰς ὦπα ἔοικεν.*

What can give a more vivid idea of her beauty than that cold-blooded age should deem it well worth the war which had cost so much blood and so many tears?

What Homer could not describe in its details, he shows us by its effect. Paint us, ye poets, the delight, the attraction, the love, the enchantment of beauty, and you have painted beauty itself. Who can think of Sappho's beloved, the sight of whom, as she confesses, robs her of sense and thought, as ugly? We seem to be gazing on a beautiful and perfect form, when we sympathize with the emotions which only such a form can produce. It is not Ovid's minute description of the beauties of his Lesbia,

Quos humeros, quales vidi tetigique lacertos!
   Forma papillarum quam fuit apta premi!
Quam castigato planus sub pectore venter!
    Quantum et quale latus! quam juvenile
    femur! †

that makes us fancy we are enjoying the same sight which he enjoyed; but because he gives the details with a sensuousness which stirs the passions.

Yet another way in which poetry surpasses art in the description of physical beauty, is by turning beauty into charm. Charm is beauty in motion, and therefore less adapted to the painter than the poet. The painter can suggest motion, but his figures are really destitute of it. Charm therefore in a picture becomes grimace, while in poetry it remains what it is, a transitory beauty, which we would fain see repeated. It comes and goes, and since we can recall a motion more vividly and easily than mere forms and colors, charm must affect us more strongly than beauty under the same conditions. All that touches and pleases in the picture of Alcina is charm. Her eyes impress us not from their blackness and fire, but because they are—

Pietosi a riguardar, a mover parchi,

they move slowly and with gracious glances, because Cupid sports around them and shoots from them his arrows. Her mouth pleases, not because vermilion lips enclose two rows of orient pearls, but because of the gentle smile, which opens a paradise on earth, and of the courteous accents that melt the rudest heart. The enchantment of her bosom lies not so much in the milk and ivory and apples, that typify its whiteness and graceful form, as in its gentle heavings, like the rise and fall of waves under a pleasant breeze.

Due pome acerbe, e pur d' avorio fatte,
Vengono e van, come onda al primo
   margo,
Quando piacevole aura il mar
   combatte.

I am convinced that such traits as these, compressed into one or two stanzas, would

---

*Iliad iii. 156–58.
Small blame is theirs if both the Trojan
  knights
And brazen-mailed Achaians have endured
So long so many evils for the sake
Of that one woman. She is wholly like
In feature to the deathless goddesses.
—BRYANT. [Cf. *GBWW*, Vol. 4, p. 20c.]
†["What shoulders, such arms, I saw and touched! The form of her breasts how apt for grasping! How flat her belly under the blameless bosom! Such a side and how much of it! What a youthful thigh!"]

be far more effective than the five over which Ariosto has spread them, interspersed with cold descriptions of form much too learned for our sensibilities.

Anacreon preferred the apparent absurdity of requiring impossibilities of the artist, to leaving the image of his mistress unenlivened with these mobile charms.

> τρυφεροῦ δ' ἔσω γενέιου
> περὶ λυγδίνῳ τραχήλῳ
> Χάριτες πέτοιντο πᾶσαι.

He bids the artist let all the graces hover about her tender chin and marble neck. How so? literally? But that is beyond the power of art. The painter could give the chin the most graceful curve and the prettiest dimple, *Amoris digitulo impressum* (for the ἔσω here seems to me to mean dimple); he could give the neck the softest pink, but that is all. The motion of that beautiful neck, the play of the muscles, now deepening and now half concealing the dimple, the essential charm exceeded his powers. The poet went to the limits of his art in the attempt to give us a vivid picture of beauty, in order that the painter might seek the highest expression in his. Here we have, therefore, a fresh illustration of what was urged above, that the poet, even when speaking of a painting or statue, is not bound to confine his description within the limits of art.

XXII.

Zeuxis painted a Helen and had the courage to write beneath his picture those famous lines of Homer wherein the elders express their admiration of her beauty. Never did painting and poetry engage in closer rivalry. Victory remained undecided, and both deserved to be crowned.

For as the wise poet showed us only in its effects the beauty which he felt the impossibility of describing in detail, so the equally wise painter exhibited beauty solely through its details, deeming it unworthy of his art to have recourse to any outward aids. His whole picture was the naked figure of Helen. For it was probably the same that he painted for the people of Cortona.

Let us, for curiosity's sake, compare with this Caylus's picture as sketched for modern artists from the same lines of Homer.

"Helen, covered with a white veil, appears in the midst of several old men, Priam among the number, who should be at once recognizable by the emblems of his royal dignity. The artist must especially exert his skill to make us feel the triumph of beauty in the eager glances and expressions of astonished admiration on the countenances of the old men. The scene is over one of the gates of the town. The background of the painting may be lost either in the open sky or against the higher buildings of the town. The first would be the bolder, but the one would be as suitable as the other."

Imagine this picture, executed by the greatest master of our time, and compare it with the work of Zeuxis. Which will show the real triumph of beauty? This, where I feel it myself, or that, where I am to infer it from the grimaces of admiring graybeards? "*Turpe senilis amor!*" Looks of desire make the most reverend face ridiculous, and an old man who shows the cravings of youth is an object of disgust. This reproach cannot be brought against the Homeric elders. Theirs is but a passing spark of feeling which wisdom instantly stifles; an emotion which does honor to Helen without disgracing themselves. They acknowledge their admiration, but add at once,

> ἀλλὰ καὶ ὣς, τοίη περ ἐοῦσ', ἐν νηυσὶ νεέσθω,
> μηδ' ἡμῖν τεκέεσσί τ' ὀπίσσω πῆμα λίποιτο.*

This decision saves them from being the old coxcombs which they look like in Cay-

---

*So be it; let her, peerless as she is,
Return on board the fleet, nor stay to bring
Disaster upon us and all our race.—BRYANT.
[Cf. *GBWW*, Vol. 4, p. 20c.]

lus's picture. And what is the sight that fixes their eager looks? A veiled, muffled figure. Is that Helen? I cannot conceive what induced Caylus to make her wear a veil. Homer, to be sure, expressly gives her one,

αὐτίκα δ' ἀργεννῇσι καλυψαμένη ὀθόνῃσιν
ὡρμᾶτ' ἐκ θαλάμοιο,

"She left her chamber, robed and veiled in white,"

but only to cross the street in. And although he makes the elders express their admiration before she could have had time to take it off or throw it back, yet they were not seeing her then for the first time. Their confession need not therefore have been caused by the present hasty glance. They might often have felt what, on this occasion, they first acknowledged. There is nothing of this in the picture. When I behold the ecstasy of those old men, I want to see the cause and, as I say, am exceedingly surprised to perceive nothing but a veiled, muffled figure, at which they are staring with such devotion. What of Helen is there? Her white veil and something of her outline, as far as outline can be traced beneath drapery. But perhaps the Count did not mean that her face should be covered. In that case, although his words—"Hélène couverte d'un voile blanc"—hardly admit of such an interpretation, another point excites my surprise. He recommends to the artist great care in the expression of the old men's faces and wastes not a word upon the beauty of Helen's. This modest beauty, approaching timidly, her eyes moist with repentant tears—is, then, the highest beauty so much a matter of course to our artists, that they need not be reminded of it? or is expression more than beauty? or is it with pictures as with the stage, where we are accustomed to accept the ugliest of actresses for a ravishing princess, if her prince only express the proper degree of passion for her.

Truly this picture of Caylus would be to that of Zeuxis as pantomime to the most sublime of poetry.

Homer was unquestionably more read formerly than now, yet we do not find mention of many pictures drawn from him even by the old artists. They seem diligently to have availed themselves of any individual physical beauties which he may have pointed out. They painted these, well knowing that in this department alone they could vie with the poet with any chance of success. Zeuxis painted besides Helen a Penelope, and the Diana of Apelles was the goddess of Homer attended by her nymphs.

I will take this opportunity of saying that the passage in Pliny referring to this picture of Apelles needs correcting. But to paint scenes from Homer merely because they afforded a rich composition, striking contrasts, and artistic shading, seems not to have been to the taste of the old artists; nor could it be, so long as art kept within the narrow limits of its own high calling. They fed upon the spirit of the poet and filled their imagination with his noblest traits. The fire of his enthusiasm kindled theirs. They saw and felt with him. Thus their works became copies of the Homeric, not in the relation of portrait to original, but in the relation of a son to a father—like, but different. The whole resemblance often lies in a single trait, the other parts being alike in nothing but in their harmony with that.

Since, moreover, the Homeric masterpieces of poetry were older than any masterpiece of art, for Homer had observed nature with the eye of an artist before either Phidias or Apelles, the artists naturally found ready made in his poems many valuable observations, which they had not yet had time to make for themselves. These they eagerly seized upon, in order that, through Homer, they might copy nature. Phidias acknowledged that the lines,

ᾟ καὶ κυανέῃσιν ἐπ' ὀφρύσι νεῦσε Κρονίων·
ἀμβρόσιαι δ' ἄρα χαῖται ἐπερρώσαντο ἄνακτος

κρατὸς ἀπ' ἀθανάτοιο· μέγαν δ' ἐλέλιξεν
Ὀλυμπον,*

served him as the model of his Olympian Jupiter, and that only through their help had he succeeded in making a godlike countenance, *"propemodum ex ipso coelo petitum."†* Whoever understands by this merely that the imagination of the artist was fired by the poet's sublime picture, and thus made capable of equally sublime representations, overlooks, I think, the chief point and contents himself with a general statement where something very special and much more satisfactory is meant. Phidias here acknowledges also, as I understand him, that this passage first led him to notice how much expression lies in the eyebrows, *"quanta pars animi"‡* is shown in them. Perhaps it further induced him to bestow more attention upon the hair, in order to express in some degree what Homer calls ambrosial curls. For it is certain that the old artists before Phidias had very little idea of the language and significance of the features, and particularly neglected the hair. Even Myron was faulty in both these respects, as Pliny observes, and, according to the same authority, Pythagoras Leontinus was the first who distinguished himself by the beauty of his hair. Other artists learned from the works of Phidias what Phidias had learned from Homer.

I will mention another example of the same kind which has always given me particular pleasure. Hogarth passes the following criticism on the Apollo Belvidere. "These two masterpieces of art, the Apollo and the Antinous, are seen together in the same palace at Rome, where the Antinous fills the spectator with admiration only, whilst the Apollo strikes him with surprise, and, as travellers express themselves, with an appearance of something more than human, which they of course are always at a loss to describe; and this effect, they say, is the more astonishing, as, upon examination, its disproportion is evident even to a common eye. One of the best sculptors we

have in England, who lately went to see them, confirmed to me what has been now said, particularly as to the legs and thighs being too long and too large for the upper parts. And Andrea Sacchi, one of the great Italian painters, seems to have been of the same opinion, or he would hardly have given his Apollo, crowning Pasquilini the musician, the exact proportion of the Antinous (in a famous picture of his now in England), as otherwise it seems to be a direct copy from the Apollo.

"Although in very great works we often see an inferior part neglected, yet here this cannot be the case, because in a fine statue, just proportion is one of its essential beauties; therefore it stands to reason, that these limbs must have been lengthened on purpose, otherwise it might easily have been avoided.

"So that if we examine the beauties of this figure thoroughly, we may reasonably conclude, that what has been hitherto thought so unaccountably excellent in its general appearance, hath been owing to what hath seemed a blemish in a part of it."

All this is very suggestive. Homer also, I would add, had already felt and noticed the same thing—that an appearance of nobility is produced by a disproportionate size of the foot and thigh. For, when Antenor is comparing the figure of Ulysses with that of Menelaus, he says,

στάντων μὲν Μενέλαος ὑπείρεχεν εὐρέας
ὤμους,
ἄμφω δ' ἑζομένω, γεραρώτερος ἦεν
Ὀδυσσεύς.

---

*Iliad i. 528.
As thus he spoke the son of Saturn gave
The nod with his dark brows. The ambrosial
curls
Upon the Sovereign One's immortal head
Were shaken, and with them the mighty mount
Olympus trembled.—BRYANT.
[Cf. *GBWW*, Vol. 4, p. 8c.]
†["as brought almost from heaven itself"]
‡["how much of the mind"]

Hogarth said about the Apollo Belvedere that it " . . . *strikes* [spectators] *with surprise, . . . with an appearance of something more than human, which they of course are . . . at a loss to describe.*"

"When both were standing Menelaus over-topped him by his broad shoulders; but when both were sitting, Ulysses was the more majestic" [cf. *GBWW,* Vol. 4, p. 21a]. Since, when seated, Ulysses gained in dignity what Menelaus lost, we can easily tell the proportion which the upper part of the body in each bore to the feet and thighs. In Ulysses the upper part was large in proportion to the lower; in Menelaus the size of the lower parts was large in proportion to that of the upper.

XXIII.

A single incongruous part may destroy the harmonious effect of many beauties, without, however, making the object ugly. Ugliness requires the presence of several incongruous parts which we must be able to take in at a glance if the effect produced is to be the opposite of that which we call beauty.

Accordingly ugliness in itself can be no subject for poetry. Yet Homer has described its extreme in Thersites, and described it by its coexistent parts. Why did he allow himself in the case of ugliness what he wisely refrained from as regards beauty? Will not the effect of ugliness be as much hindered by the successive enumeration of its elements, as the effect of beauty is neutralized by a similar treatment?

Certainly it will, and therein lies Homer's justification. The poet can make ugliness his theme only because it acquires through his description a less repulsive aspect and ceases in a measure to produce the effect of ugliness. What he cannot employ by itself, he uses as an ingredient to excite and strengthen certain mixed impressions, with which he must entertain us in the absence of those purely agreeable.

These mixed sensations are those of the ridiculous and the horrible.

Homer makes Thersites ugly in order to make him ridiculous. Mere ugliness, how-ever, would not have this effect. Ugliness is imperfection, and the ridiculous requires a contrast between perfections and imperfections. This is the explanation of my friend, to which I would add that this contrast must not be too sharp and decided, but that the opposites must be such as admit of being blended into each other. All the ugliness of Thersites has not made the wise and virtuous Aesop ridiculous. A silly, monkish conceit sought to transfer to the writer the γέλοιον [comicalness] of his instructive fables by representing his person as deformed. But a misshapen body and a beautiful soul are like oil and vinegar, which, however much they may be stirred together, will always remain distinct to the taste. They give rise to no third. Each one produces its own effect—the body distaste, the soul delight. The two emotions blend into one only when the misshapen body is at the same time frail and sickly, a hindrance and source of injury to the mind. The result, however, is not laughter, but compassion; and the object, which before we had simply respected, now excites our interest. The frail, misshapen Pope must have been more interesting to his friends than the strong, handsome Wycherley.

But although Thersites is not ridiculous on account of his ugliness alone, he would not be ridiculous without it. Many elements work together to produce this result; the ugliness of his person corresponding with that of his character, and both contrasting with the idea he entertains of his own importance, together with the harmlessness, except to himself, of his malicious tongue. The last point is the οὐ φθαρτικόν (the undeadly), which Aristotle takes to be an indispensable element of the ridiculous [*GBWW,* Vol. 9, p. 683c]. My friend also makes it a necessary condition that the contrast should be unimportant and not interest us greatly. For, suppose that Thersites had had to pay dearly for his spiteful detraction of Agamemnon, that it had cost him his life instead of a couple of bloody wales, then we should cease to laugh at him. To test the justice of this, let us read his death in Quintus Calaber. Achilles regrets having slain Penthesilea. Her noble blood, so bravely shed, claims the hero's respect and compassion, feelings which soon grow into love. The slanderous Thersites turns this love into a crime. He inveighs against the sensuality which betrays even the bravest of men into follies:

> ἥτ' ἄφρονα φῶτα τίθησι
> καὶ πινυτόν περ ἐόντα.

Achilles' wrath is kindled. Without a word he deals him such a blow between cheek and ear that teeth, blood, and life gush from the wound. This is too barbarous. The angry, murderous Achilles becomes more an object of hate to me than the tricky, snarling Thersites. The shout of delight raised by the Greeks at the deed offends me. My sympathies are with Diomedes, whose sword is drawn on the instant to take vengeance on the murderer of his kinsman. For Thersites as a man is of my kin also.

But suppose that the attempts of Thersites had resulted in open mutiny; that the rebellious people had actually taken to the ships, and treacherously abandoned their commanders, who thereupon had fallen into the hands of a vindictive enemy; and that the judgment of the gods had decreed total destruction to fleet and nation: how should we then view the ugliness of Thersites? Although harmless ugliness may be ridiculous, hurtful ugliness is always horrible.

I cannot better illustrate this than by a couple of admirable passages from Shakespeare. Edmund, bastard son of the Earl of Gloucester in *King Lear*, is no less a villain than Richard, duke of Gloucester, who, by the most hideous crimes, paved his way to the throne, which he ascended under the title of Richard the Third. Why does he excite in us far less disgust and horror? When the bastard says,

> *Thou, nature, art my goddess; to thy law*
> *My services are bound; wherefore should I*
> *Stand in the plague of custom, and permit*
> *The curiosity of nations to deprive me,*
> *For that I am some twelve or fourteen*
> *   moonshines*
> *Lag of a brother? Why bastard? wherefore*
> *   base?*
> *When my dimensions are as well compact,*
> *My mind as generous, and my shape as true*
> *As honest Madam's issue? why brand they*
> *   thus*
> *With base? with baseness? bastardy?*
> *   base, base?*
> *Who, in the lusty stealth of nature, take*
> *More composition and fierce quality,*
> *Than doth, within a dull, stale, tired bed,*
> *Go to creating a whole tribe of fops*
> *Got 'tween asleep and wake?*
> [*GBWW*, Vol. 27, pp. 247d–48a]

I hear a devil speaking, but in the form of an angel of light.

When, on the contrary, the Earl of Gloucester says,

> *But I, that am not shaped for sportive tricks,*
> *Nor made to court an amorous looking-glass;*
> *I, that am rudely stamped, and want*
> *   love's majesty;*
> *To strut before a wanton, ambling nymph;*
> *I, that am curtailed of this fair proportion,*
> *Cheated of feature by dissembling nature,*
> *Deformed, unfinished, sent before my time*
> *Into this breathing world, scarce half*
> *   made up,*
> *And that so lamely and unfashionably,*
> *That dogs bark at me as I halt by them;*
> *Why I, in this weak piping time of peace,*
> *Have no delight to pass away the time;*
> *Unless to spy my shadow in the sun,*
> *And descant on mine own deformity;*
> *And, therefore, since I cannot prove a lover,*
> *To entertain these fair, well-spoken days,*
> *I am determined to prove a villain.*
> [*GBWW*, Vol. 26, p. 105d]

I hear a devil and see a devil, in a shape which only the devil should wear.

XXIV.

Such is the use which the poet makes of ugliness of form. How can the painter legitimately employ it?

Painting as imitative skill can express ugliness; painting as a fine art will not express it. In the former capacity its sphere extends over all visible objects; in the latter it confines itself to those which produce agreeable impressions.

But do not disagreeable impressions please in the imitation? Not all. An acute critic has already remarked this in respect of disgust. "Representations of fear," he says, "of sadness, horror, compassion, &c., arouse painful emotions only insofar as we believe the evil to be actual. The consideration that it is but an illusion of art may resolve these disagreeable sensations into those of pleasure. But, according to the laws of imagination, the disagreeable sensation of disgust arises from the mere representation in the mind, whether the object be thought actually to exist or not. No matter how apparent the art of the imitation, our wounded sensibilities are not relieved. Our discomfort arose not from the belief that the evil was actual, but from the mere representation which is actually present. The feeling of disgust, therefore, comes always from nature, never from imitation."

The same criticism is applicable to physical ugliness. This also wounds our sight, offends our taste for order and harmony, and excites aversion without regard to the actual existence of the object in which we perceive it. We wish to see neither Thersites himself nor his image. If his image be the less displeasing, the reason is not that ugliness of shape ceases to be ugly in the imitation, but that we possess the power of diverting our minds from this ugliness by admiration of the artist's skill. But this satisfaction is constantly disturbed by the thought of the unworthy use to which art has been put, and our esteem for the artist is thereby greatly diminished.

Aristotle adduces another reason for the pleasure we take in even the most faithful copy of what in nature is disagreeable. He attributes this pleasure to man's universal desire for knowledge [*GBWW*, Vol. 9, p. 682c]. We are pleased when we can learn from a copy τί ἕκαστον, what each and every thing is, or when we can conclude from it ὅτι οὗτος ἐκεῖνος, that it is the very thing we already know. But this is no argument in favor of the imitation of ugliness. The pleasure which arises from the gratification of our desire for knowledge is momentary and only incidental to the object with regard to which it has been satisfied, whereas the discomfort which accompanies the sight of ugliness is permanent, and essential to the object causing it. How, then, can one counterbalance the other? Still less can the trifling entertainment of tracing a likeness overcome the unpleasant impression produced by ugliness. The more closely I compare the ugly copy with the ugly original, the more I expose myself to this influence, so that the pleasure of the comparison soon disappears, leaving nothing behind but the painful impression of this twofold ugliness.

From the examples given by Aristotle he appears not to include ugliness of form among the disagreeable things which may give pleasure in the imitation. His examples are wild beasts and dead bodies. Wild beasts excite terror even when they are not ugly; and this terror, not their ugliness, may be made to produce sensations of pleasure through imitation. So also of dead bodies. Keenness of sympathy, the dreadful thought of our own annihilation, make a dead body in nature an object of aversion. In the imitation the sense of illusion robs sympathy of its sharpness, and, by the addition of various palliating circumstances, that disturbing element may be either entirely banished or so inseparably interwoven with these softening features, that terror is almost lost in desire.

Since, then, ugliness of form, from its exciting sensations of pain of a kind incapable of being converted by imitation into pleasurable emotions, cannot in itself be a fitting subject for painting as a fine art, the question arises whether it may not be employed in painting as in poetry as an ingredient for strengthening other sensations.

May painting make use of deformity in the attainment of the ridiculous and horrible?

I will not venture to answer this question absolutely in the negative. Unquestionably, harmless ugliness can be ridiculous in painting also, especially when united with an affectation of grace and dignity. Equally beyond question is it that hurtful ugliness excites terror in a picture as well as in nature, and that the ridiculous and the terrible, in themselves mixed sensations, acquire through imitation an added degree of fascination.

But I must call attention to the fact that painting and poetry do not stand upon the same footing in this respect. In poetry, as I have observed, ugliness of form loses its disagreeable effect almost entirely by the successive enumeration of its coexistent parts. As far as effect is concerned it almost ceases to be ugliness and can thus more closely combine with other appearances to produce new and different impressions. But in painting ugliness is before our eyes in all its strength and affects us scarcely less powerfully than in nature itself. Harmless ugliness cannot, therefore, long remain ridiculous. The disagreeable impression gains the mastery, and what was at first amusing becomes at last repulsive. Nor is the case different with hurtful ugliness. The element of terror gradually disappears, leaving the deformity unchanging and unrelieved.

Count Caylus was therefore right in omitting the episode of Thersites from his series of Homeric pictures. But are we justified in wishing it out of Homer? I perceive with regret that this is done by one critic whose taste is otherwise unerring. I postpone further discussion of the subject to a future occasion.

XXV.

The second distinction mentioned by the critic just quoted, between disgust and other disagreeable emotions, appears in the distaste which deformity excites in us.

"Other disagreeable passions," he says, "may sometimes, in nature as well as in art, produce gratification, because they never arouse pure pain. Their bitterness is always mixed with satisfaction. Our fear is seldom devoid of hope; terror rouses all our powers to escape the danger; anger is mixed with a desire for vengeance; sadness, with the pleasant recollection of former happiness; and compassion is inseparable from the tender sentiments of love and goodwill. The mind is at liberty to dwell now on the agreeable, and now on the disagreeable side, and thus to obtain a mingling of pleasure and pain, more delightful than the purest pleasure. Very little study of ourselves will furnish us with abundant instances. Why else is his anger dearer to an angry man and his sadness to a melancholy one, than all the cheerful images by which we strive to soothe him? Quite different is the case with disgust and its kindred sensations. Here the mind is conscious of no perceptible admixture of pleasure. A feeling of uneasiness gains the mastery, and under no imaginable conditions in nature or art would the mind fail to recoil with aversion from representations of this nature."

Very true; but, since the critic acknowledges the existence of other sensations nearly akin to that of disgust, and producing, like that, nothing but pain, what answers more nearly to this description than emotions excited by the sight of physical deformity? These are not only kindred to that of disgust, but they resemble it in being destitute of all admixture of pleasure in art as well as in nature. Under no imaginable conditions, therefore, would the mind fail to recoil with aversion from such representations.

This aversion, if I have analyzed my feelings with sufficient care, is altogether of the nature of disgust. The sensation which accompanies the sight of physical deformity is disgust, though a low degree of it. This, indeed, is at variance with another remark of our critic, according to which only our more occult senses—those of taste, smell, and touch—are capable of receiving impressions of disgust. "The first two," he says, "from an excessive sweetness, and the latter from an extreme softness of bodies which offer too slight resistance to the fibers coming in contact with them. Such objects, then, become intolerable to the sight, but solely through the association of ideas, because we remember how disagreeable they were to our sense of taste, smell, or touch. For, strictly speaking, there are no objects of disgust to the eyes." I think, however, that some might be mentioned. A mole on the face, a harelip, a flattened nose with prominent nostrils, are deformities which offend neither taste, smell, nor touch. Yet the sight of them excites in us something much more nearly resembling disgust than we feel at sight of other malformations, such as a clubfoot or a hump on the back. The more susceptible the temperament, the more distinctly are we conscious, when looking at such objects, of those motions in the body which precede nausea. That these motions soon subside, and rarely if ever result in actual sickness, is to be explained by the fact that the eye receives in and with the objects causing them such a number of pleasing images that the disagreeable impressions are too much weakened and obscured to exert any marked influence on the body. The more occult senses of taste, smell, and touch, on the contrary, cannot receive other impressions when in contact with the repulsive object. The element of disgust operates in full force and necessarily produces much more violent effects upon the body.

The same rules hold of things loathsome as of things ugly, in respect of imitation. Indeed, since the disagreeable effect of the former is the more violent, they are still less suitable subjects of painting or poetry.

Only because the effect is softened by verbal expression, did I venture to assert that the poet might employ certain loathsome traits as an ingredient in such mixed sensations as can with good effect be strengthened by the use of ugliness.

The ridiculous may be heightened by an element of disgust; representations of dignity and propriety likewise become ludicrous when brought into contrast with the disgusting. Examples of this abound in Aristophanes. I am reminded of the weasel that interrupted the worthy Socrates in his astronomical observations.

ΜΑΘ. πρώην δέ γε γνώμην μεγάλην ἀφηρέθη
ὑπ' ἀσκαλαβώτον. ΣΤΡ. τίνα τρόπον;
κάτειπέ μοι.
ΜΑΘ. ζητοῦντος αὐτοῦ τῆς σελήνης
τὰς ὁδοὺς
καὶ τὰς περιφοράς, εἶτ' ἄνω κεχηνότος
ἀπὸ τῆς ὀροφῆς νύκτωρ γαλεώτης
κατέχεσεν.
ΣΤΡ. ἥσθην γαλεώτῃ καταχέσαντι
Σωκράτους.*

If what fell into the open mouth had not been disgusting, there would be nothing ludicrous in the story.

An amusing instance of this occurs in the Hottentot story of Tquassouw and Knonmquaiha, attributed to Lord Chesterfield, which appeared in the *Connoisseur*, an English weekly, full of wit and humor. The filthiness of the Hottentots is well known, as also the fact of their regarding as beautiful and holy what excites our disgust and aversion. The pressed gristle of a nose, flaccid breasts descending to the navel, the whole body anointed with a varnish of goat's fat and soot, melted in by the

---

Nubes, 170–74.
Disciple. But he was lately deprived of a great idea by a weasel. *Strepsiades.* In what way? tell me. *Disciple.* He was studying the courses of the moon and her revolutions, and, while gazing upward open-mouthed, a weasel in the dark dunged upon him from the roof.
[Cf. *GBWW,* Vol. 5, pp. 489d–90a.]

sun, hair dripping with grease, arms and legs entwined with fresh entrails—imagine all this the object of an ardent, respectful, tender love; listen to expressions of this love in the noble language of sincerity and admiration, and keep from laughing if you can.[26]

The disgusting seems to admit of being still more closely united with the terrible. What we call the horrible is nothing more than a mixture of the elements of terror and disgust. Longinus takes offense at the *"Τῆς ἐκ μὲν ρινῶν μύξαι ρεόν* (mucus flowing from the nostrils) in Hesiod's picture of Sorrow; but not, I think, so much on account of the loathsomeness of the trait, as from its being simply loathsome with no element of terror. For he does not seem inclined to find fault with the *μακροὶ δ' ὄνυχες χείρεσσιν ὑπῆσαν*, the long nails projecting beyond the fingers. Long nails are not less disgusting than a running nose, but they are at the same time terrible. It is they that tear the cheeks till the blood runs to the ground:

> . . . ἐκ δὲ παρειῶν
> αἷμ' ἀπελείβετ' ἔραζε . . .

The other feature is simply disgusting, and I should advise Sorrow to cease her crying.

Read Sophocles' description of the desert cave of his wretched Philoctetes. There are no provisions to be seen, no comforts beyond a trampled litter of dried leaves, an unshapely wooden bowl, and a tinderbox. These constitute the whole wealth of the sick, forsaken man. How does the poet complete the sad and frightful picture? By introducing the element of disgust. "Ha!" Neoptolemus draws back of a sudden, "here are rags drying full of blood and matter" [cf. *GBWW*, Vol. 5, p. 182b–c].

ΝΕ. ὁρῶ κενὴν οἴκησιν ἀνθρώπων δίχα.
ΟΔ. οὐδ' ἔνδον οἰκοποιός ἐστί τις τροφή;
ΝΕ. στειπτή γε φυλλὰς ὡς ἐναυλίζοντί τῳ.
ΟΔ. τὰ δ' ἄλλ' ἔρημα κοὐδέν ἐσθ' ὑπόστεγον;

ΝΕ. αὐτόξυλόν γ' ἔκπωμα φαυλουργοῦ τινὸς
τεχνήματ' ἀνδρὸς, καὶ πυρεῖ' ὁμοῦ τάδε.
ΟΔ. κείνου τὸ θησαύρισμα σημαίνεις τόδε.
ΝΕ. ἰοὺ, ἰού· καὶ ταῦτά γ' ἄλλα θάλπεται
ῥάκη, βαρείας του νοσηλείας πλέα.

So in Homer, Hector dragged on the ground, his face foul with dust, his hair matted with blood,

> *Squalentem barbam et concretos sanguine crines,*

(as Virgil expresses it) is a disgusting object, but all the more terrible and touching [*GBWW*, Vol. 13, p. 131b].

Who can recall the punishment of Marsyas, in Ovid, without a feeling of disgust?

> *Clamanti cutis est summos direpta per artus:*
> *Nec quidquam, nisi vulnus erat; cruor undique manat:*
> *Detectique patent nervi: trepidaeque sine ulla*
> *Pelle micant venae: salientia viscera possis,*
> *Et perlucentes numerare in pectore fibras.* *

But the loathsome details are here appropriate. They make the terrible horrible, which in fiction is far from displeasing to us; since, even in nature, where our compassion is enlisted, things horrible are not wholly devoid of charm.

I do not wish to multiply examples, but this one thing I must further observe. There is one form of the horrible, the road to which lies almost exclusively through the disgusting, and that is the horror of famine. Even in ordinary life we can convey no idea of extreme hunger save by enumerating all the innutritious, unwholesome, and particularly disgusting things with which the

---

*Metamorph. vi. 387. "The skin is torn from the upper limbs of the shrieking Marsyas, till he is nought but one great wound: thick blood oozes on every side; the bared sinews are visible; and the palpitating veins quiver, stripped of the covering of skin; you can count the protruding entrails, and the muscles shining in the breast."

stomach would fain appease its cravings. Since imitation can excite nothing of the feeling of actual hunger, it has recourse to another disagreeable sensation which, in cases of extreme hunger, is felt to be a lesser evil. We may thus infer how intense that other suffering must be which makes the present discomfort in comparison of small account.

Ovid says [*The Metamorphoses, GIT* 1966, pp. 380–82] of the Oread whom Ceres sent to meet Famine,

Hanc (Famem) procul ut vidit. . . .
. . . refert mandata deae; paulumque morata
Quanquam aberat longe, quanquam modo
      venerat illuc,
Visa tamen sensisse famem . . . *

This is an unnatural exaggeration. The sight of a hungry person, even of Hunger herself, has no such power of contagion. Compassion and horror and loathing may be aroused, but not hunger. Ovid has not been sparing of this element of the horrible in the picture of Famine; while both he and Callimachus, in their description of Erisichthon's starvation, have laid chief emphasis upon the loathsome traits. After Erisichthon has devoured everything, not sparing even the sacrificial cow, which his mother had been fattening for Vesta, Callimachus makes him fall on horses and cats, and beg in the streets for crumbs and filthy refuse from other men's tables.

Καὶ τὰν βῶν ἔφαγεν, τὰν Ἑστίᾳ ἔτρεφε
    μάτηρ,
Καὶ τὸν ἀεθλόφορον καὶ τὸν πολεμήιον ι
    ππον,
Καὶ τὰν αἴλουρον, τὰν ἔτρεμε θήρια μικκά—
Καὶ τόθ' ὁ τῶ βασιλῆος ἔνι τριόδοισι
    καθῆστο
αἰτίζων ἀκόλως τε καὶ ἔκβολα λύματα
    δαιτός.

Ovid represents him finally as biting into his own flesh, that his body might thus furnish nourishment for itself.

Vis tamen illa mali postquam consumserat
    omnem
Materiam . . .
Ipse suos artus lacero divellere morsu
Coepit · et infelix minuendo corpus alebat.

The hideous harpies were made loathsome and obscene in order that the hunger occasioned by their carrying off of the food might be the more horrible. Hear the complaints of Phineus in Apollonius:

τυτθὸν δ' ἦν ἄρα δή ποτ' ἐδητύος
    ἄμμι λίπωσι,
πνεῖ τόδε μυδαλέον τε καὶ οὐ τλητὸν
    μένος ὀδμῆς.
οὔ κέ τις οὐδὲ μίνυνθα βρότων ἀνσχοιτο
    πελάσσας,
οὐδ' εἰ οἱ ἀδάμαντος ἐληλαμένον κέαρ εἴη.
ἀλλά με πικρὴ δῆτά κε δαιτὸς ἐπίσχει
    ἀνάγκη
μίμνειν, καὶ μίμνοντα κακῇ ἐν γαστέρι
    θέσθαι. †

I would gladly excuse in this way, if I could, Virgil's disgusting introduction of the harpies. They, however, instead of occasioning an actual present hunger, only prophesy an inward craving; and this prophecy, moreover, is resolved finally into a mere play upon words.

Dante not only prepares us for the starvation of Ugolino by a most loathsome, horrible description of him together with his former persecutor in hell, but the slow starvation itself is not free from disgusting features, as where the sons offer them-

---

**Metamorph.* lib. viii. 809. "Seeing Famine afar off, she delivers the message of the goddess. And after a little while, although she was yet at a distance and was but approaching, yet the mere sight produced hunger."

†*Argonaut.* lib. ii. 228–33. "Scarcely have they left us any food that smells not moldy, and the stench is unendurable. No one for a time could bear the foul food, though his stomach were beaten of adamant. But bitter necessity compels me to bethink me of the meal, and, so remembering, put it into my wretched belly."

selves as food for the father. I give in a note a passage from a play by Beaumont and Fletcher, which might have served me in the stead of all other examples, were it not somewhat too highly drawn.[27]

I come now to objects of disgust in painting. Even could we prove that there are no objects directly disgusting to the eye, which painting as a fine art would naturally avoid, it would still be obliged to refrain from loathsome objects in general, because they become through the association of ideas disgusting also to the sense of sight. Pordenone, in a picture of the entombment, makes one of the bystanders hold his nose. Richardson objects to this on the ground that Christ had not been long enough dead for corruption to set in. In the raising of Lazarus, however, he would allow the painter to represent some of the lookers-on in that attitude, because the narrative expressly states that the body was already offensive. But I consider the representation in both cases as insufferable, for not only the actual smell, but the very idea of it is nauseous. We shun bad-smelling places even when we have a cold in the head. But painting does not employ loathsomeness for its own sake, but, like poetry, to give emphasis to the ludicrous and the terrible. At its peril! What I have already said of ugliness in this connection applies with greater force to loathsomeness. This also loses much less of its effect in a visible representation than in a description addressed to the ear and can therefore unite less closely with the elements of the ludicrous and terrible in painting than in poetry. As soon as the surprise passes and the first curious glance is satisfied, the elements separate and loathsomeness appears in all its crudity.

XXVI.

Winckelmann's *History of Ancient Art* has appeared, and I cannot venture a step further until I have read it. Criticism based solely upon general principles may lead to conceits which sooner or later we find to our shame refuted in works on art.

The ancients well understood the connection between painting and poetry and are sure not to have drawn the two arts more closely together than the good of both would warrant. What their artists have done will teach me what artists in general should do; and where such a man precedes with the torch of history, speculation may boldly follow.

We are apt to turn over the leaves of an important work before seriously setting ourselves to read it. My chief curiosity was to know the author's opinion of the Laocoon; not of its merit as a work of art, for that he had already given, but merely of its antiquity. Would he agree with those who think that Virgil had the group before him, or with those who suppose the sculptors to have followed the poet?

I am pleased to find that he says nothing of imitation on either side. What need is there, indeed, of supposing imitation?

Very possibly the resemblances which I have been considering between the poetic picture and the marble group were not intentional but accidental, and, so far from one having served as a model for the other, the two may not even have had a common model. Had he, however, been misled by an appearance of imitation, he must have declared in favor of those who make Virgil the imitator. For he supposes the Laocoon to date from the period when Greek art was in its perfection: to be, therefore, of the time of Alexander the Great.

"Kind fortune," he says, "watching over the arts even in their extinction, has preserved for the admiration of the world a work of this period of art, which proves the truth of what history tells concerning the glory of the many lost masterpieces. The Laocoon with his two sons, the work of Agesander, Apollodorus [Polydorus], and Athenodorus, of Rhodes, dates in all probability from this period, although we cannot determine the exact time, nor give, as some have done, the Olympiad in which these artists flourished."

In a note he adds: "Pliny says not a word with regard to the time when Agesander and his assistants lived. But Maffei, in his explanation of the ancient statues, professes to know that these artists flourished in the eighty-eighth Olympiad; and others, like Richardson, have maintained the same on his authority. He must, I think, have mistaken an Athenodorus, a pupil of Polycletus, for one of our artists. Polycletus flourished in the eighty-seventh Olympiad, and his supposed pupil was therefore referred to the Olympaid following. Maffei can have no other grounds for his opinion."

Certainly he can have no other. But why does Winckelmann content himself with the mere mention of this supposed argument of Maffei? Does it refute itself? Not altogether. For although not otherwise supported, it yet carries with it a certain degree of probability unless we can prove that Athenodorus, the pupil of Polycletus, and Athenodorus, the assistant of Agesander and Polydorus, could not possibly have been one and the same person. Happily this is proved by the fact that the two were natives of different countries. We have the express testimony of Pausanias that the first Athenodorus was from Clitor in Arcadia, while the second, on the authority of Pliny, was born at Rhodes.

Winckelmann can have had no object in refraining from a direct refutation of Maffei by the statement of this circumstance. Probably the arguments which his undoubted critical knowledge derived from the skill of the workmanship seemed to him of such great weight, that he deemed any slight probability which Maffei's opinion might have on its side a matter of no importance. He doubtless recognized in the Laocoon too many of those *argutiae* (traits of animation) peculiar to Lysippus, to suppose it to be of earlier date than that master who was the first

to enrich art with this semblance of life.

But, granting the fact to be proved that the Laocoon cannot be older than Lysippus, have we thereby proved that it must be contemporaneous with him or nearly so? May it not be a work of much later date? Passing in review those periods previous to the rise of the Roman monarchy, when art in Greece alternately rose and sank, why, I ask, might not Laocoon have been the happy fruit of that emulation which the extravagant luxury of the first emperors must have kindled among artists? Why might not Agesander and his assistants have been the contemporaries of Strongylion, Arcesilaus, Pasiteles, Posidonius, or Diogenes? Were not some of the works of those masters counted among the greatest treasures ever produced by art? And if undoubted works from the hand of these men were still in existence, but the time in which they lived was unknown and left to be determined by the style of their art, would not some inspiration from heaven be needed to prevent the critic from referring them to that period which to Winckelmann seemed the only one worthy of producing the Laocoon?

Pliny, it is true, does not expressly mention the time when the sculptors of the Laocoon lived. But were I to conclude from a study of the whole passage whether he would have them reckoned among the old or the new artists, I confess the probability seems to me in favor of the latter inference. Let the reader judge.

After speaking at some length of the oldest and greatest masters of sculpture—Phidias, Praxiteles, and Scopas—and then giving, without chronological order, the names of the rest, especially of those who were represented in Rome by any of their works, Pliny proceeds as follows:

Nec multo plurium fama est, quorundam claritati in operibus eximiis obstante numero artificum, quoniam nec unus occupat gloriam, nec plures pariter nuncupari possunt, sicut *in Laocoonte, qui est in Titi Imperatoris domo, opus omnibus et picturae et statuariae artis praeponendum. Ex uno lapide eum et liberos draconumque mirabiles nexus de consilii sententia fecere summi artifices, Agesander et Polydorus et Athenodorus Rhodii. Similiter Palatinas domus Caesarum replevere probatissimis signis Craterus cum Pythodoro, Polydectes cum Hermolao, Pythodorus alius cum Artemone, et singularis Aphrodisius Trallianus. Agrippae Pantheum decoravit Diogenes Atheniensis; et Caryatides in columnis templi ejus probantur inter pauca operum: sicut in fastigio posita signa, sed propter altitudinem loci minus celebrata.**

Of all the artists mentioned in this passage, Diogenes of Athens is the one whose date is fixed with the greatest precision. He adorned the Pantheon of Agrippa and therefore lived under Augustus. But a close examination of Pliny's words will, I think, determine with equal certainty the date of Craterus and Pythodorus, Polydectes and Hermolaus, the second Pythodorus and Artemon, as also of Aphrodisius of Tralles. He says of them: *"Palatinas domus Caesarum replevere probatissimis signis."* Can this mean only that the palaces were filled with admirable works by these artists, which the emperors had collected from various places and brought to their dwellings in Rome? Surely not. The sculptors must have executed their works expressly for the imperial palaces, and must, therefore, have lived at the time of these emperors. That they were artists of comparatively late date, who worked only in Italy, is plain from our finding no mention of them elsewhere. Had they worked in Greece at an earlier day, Pausanias would have seen some work of theirs and recorded it. He mentions, indeed, a Pythodorus, but Hardouin is wrong in supposing him to be the same referred to by Pliny. For Pausanias calls the statue of Juno at Coronaea, in Boeotia, the work of the former, ἄγαλμα ἀρχαῖον (an ancient idol), a term which he applies only to the works of those artists

who lived in the first rude days of art, long before Phidias and Praxiteles. With such works the emperors would certainly not have adorned their palaces. Of still less value is another suggestion of Hardouin, that Artemon may be the painter of the same name elsewhere mentioned by Pliny. Identity of name is a slight argument and by no means authorizes us to do violence to the natural interpretation of an uncorrupted passage.

If it be proved beyond a doubt that Craterus and Pythodorus, Polydectes and Hermolaus, with the rest, lived at the time of the emperors whose palaces they adorned with their admirable works, then I think we can assign no other date to those artists, the sculptors of the Laocoon, whose names Pliny connects with these by the word *similiter*. For if Agesander, Polydorus, and Athenodorus were really such old masters as Winckelmann supposes, it would be the height of impropriety for an author, who makes great account of precision of expression, to leap from them to the most modern artists, merely with the words "in like manner."

But it may be urged that this *similiter*

**Lib.* xxxvi. sect. 4. "Nor are there many of great repute the number of artists engaged on celebrated works preventing the distinction of individuals; since no one could have all the credit, nor could the names of many be rehearsed at once: as in the Laocoon, which is in the palace of the emperor Titus, a work surpassing all the results of painting or statuary. From one stone he and his sons and the wondrous coils of the serpents were sculptured by consummate artists, working in concert: Agesander, Polydorus, and Athenodorus, all of Rhodes. In like manner Craterus with Pythodorus, Polydectes with Hermolaus, another Pythodorus with Artemon, and Aphrodisius of Tralles by himself, filled the palaces of the Caesars on the Palatine with admirable statuary. Diogenes, the Athenian, decorated the Pantheon of Agrippa, and the Caryatides on the columns of that temple rank among the choicest works, as do also the statues on the pediment, though these, from the height of their position, are less celebrated."

has no reference to a common date, but to some other circumstance common to all these masters, who yet in age were widely different. Pliny, it may be said, is speaking of artists who had worked in partnership and on this account had not obtained the fame they merited. The names of all had been left in neglect, because no one artist could appropriate the honor of the common work, and to mention the names of all the participators would require too much time (*quoniam nec unus occupat gloriam, nec plures pariter nuncupari possunt*). This had been the fate of the sculptors of the Laocoon, as well as of the many other masters whom the emperors had employed in the decoration of their palaces.

But, granting all this, the probabilities are still in favor of the supposition that Pliny meant to refer only to the later artists whose labors had been in common. If he had meant to include older ones, why confine himself to the sculptors of the Laocoon?

Why not mention others, as Onatas and Calliteles, Timocles and Timarchides, or the sons of this Timarchides, who together had made a statue of Jupiter at Rome? Winckelmann himself says that a long list might be made of older works which had more than one father. And would Pliny have thought but of the single example of Agesander, Polydorus, and Athendorus, if he had not meant to confine himself strictly to the more modern masters?

If ever a conjecture gained in probability from the number and magnitude of the difficulties solved by it, this one, that the sculptors of the Laocoon flourished under the first emperors, has that advantage in a high degree. For had they lived and worked in Greece at the time which Winckelmann assigns to them, had the Laocoon itself existed earlier in Greece, then the utter silence of the Greeks with regard to such a work, "surpassing all the results of painting or statuary" (*opere omnibus et picturae et statuariae artis praeponendo*), is most surprising. It is hard to believe that

such great masters should have created nothing else, or that the rest of their works should have been, equally with the Laocoon, unknown to Pausanias. In Rome, on the contrary, the greatest masterpiece might have remained long concealed. If the Laocoon had been finished as early as the time of Augustus, there would be nothing surprising in Pliny's being the first, and, indeed, the last, to mention it. For remember what he tells of a Venus by Scopas, which stood in the temple of Mars at Rome:

"... *quemcunque alium locum nobilitatura. Romae quidem magnitudo operum eam obliterat, ac magni officiorum negotiorumque acervi omnes a contemplatione talium abducunt: quoniam otiosorum et in magno loci silentio apta admiratio talis est.*"*

Those who would fain see in the group an imitation of Virgil's Laocoon will readily catch at what I have been saying, nor will they be displeased at another conjecture which just occurs to me. Why should not Asinius Pollio, they may think, have been the patron who had Virgil's Laocoon put into marble by Greek artists? Pollio was a particular friend of the poet, survived him, and appears to have written an original work on the *Aeneid*. For whence but from such a work could the various comments have been drawn which Servius quotes from that author? Pollio was, moreover, a lover of art and a connoisseur, possessed a valuable collection of the best of the old masterpieces, ordered new works from the artists of his day, and showed in his choice a taste quite likely to be pleased by so daring a piece as the Laocoon, "*ut fuit acris*

---

*Plinius, xxxvi. sect. 4. "... which would make the glory of any other place. But at Rome the greatness of other works overshadows it, and the great press of business and engagements turns the crowd from the contemplation of such things; for the admiration of works of art belongs to those who have leisure and great quiet."

*vehementiae, sic quoque spectari monumenta sua voluit."**

Since, however, the cabinet of Pollio in Pliny's day, when the Laocoon was standing in the palace of Titus, seems to have existed entire in a separate building, this supposition again loses something of its probability. Why might not Titus himself have done what we are trying to ascribe to Pollio?

XXVII.

A little item first brought to my notice by Winckelmann himself confirms me in my opinion that the sculptors of the Laocoon lived at the time of the emperors, or at least could not date from so early a period as he assigns them. It is this: "In Nettuno, the ancient Antium, Cardinal Alexander Albani discovered in 1717 in a deep vault, which lay buried under the sea, a vase of the grayish black marble now called *bigio*, wherein the Laocoon was inlaid. Upon this vase is the following inscription:

ΑΘΑΝΟΔΩΡΟΣ ΑΓΗΣΑΝΔΡΟΥ
ΡΟΔΙΟΣ ΕΠΟΙΗΣΕ.

"Athanodorus of Rhodes, son of Agesander, made it." We learn from this inscription that father and son worked on the Laocoon; and probably Apollodorus (Polydorus) was also a son of Agesander, for this Athanodorus can be no other than the one mentioned by Pliny. The inscription also proves that more than three works of art have been found—the number stated by Pliny—on which the artists have set the word *made*, in definite past time, ἐποίησε, *fecit*. Other artists, he says, from modesty, made use of indefinite time, "was making," ἐποίει, *faciebat*.

Few will contradict Winckelmann in his conclusion that the Athanodorus of this inscription can be no other than the Athenodorus whom Pliny mentions as among the sculptors of the Laocoon. Athanodorus and

Athenodorus are entirely synonymous; for the Rhodians used the Doric dialect. But the other conclusions which he draws from the inscription require further comment.

The first, that Athenodorus was a son of Agesander, may pass. It is highly probable, though by no means certain. Some of the old artists, we know, called themselves after their teachers instead of taking their fathers' names. What Pliny says of the brothers Apollonius and Tauriscus cannot well be explained in any other way.

But shall we say that this inscription contradicts the statement of Pliny that there were only three works of art to which their masters had set their names in definite past time (ἐποίησε instead of ἐποίει)? This inscription! What need of this to teach us what we might have learned long ago from a multitude of others? On the statue of Germanicus was there not the inscription Κλεομένης—ἐποίησε, Cleomenes made? on the so-called Apotheosis of Homer, Ἀρχέλαος ἐποίησε, Archelaus made? on the well-known vase at Gaeta, Σαλπίων ἐποίησε, Salpion made? nor are other instances wanting.

Winckelmann may answer: "No one knows that better than I. So much the worse for Pliny. His statement has been so much the oftener contradicted, and is so much the more surely refuted."

By no means. How if Winckelmann has made Pliny say more than he meant to say? How if these examples contradict, not Pliny's statement, but only something which Winckelmann supposes him to have stated? And this is actually the case. I must quote the whole passage. Pliny, in the dedication of his work to Titus, speaks with the modesty of a man who knows better than any one else how far what he has accomplished falls short of perfection. He finds a noteworthy example of such modesty among the Greeks, on the ambitious and boastful titles of whose books (*inscriptiones, propter*

---

*["Being shrewd and fervent, he wanted his monuments to be seen."]

quas vadimonium deseri possit*) he dwells at some length, and then says:

Et ne in totum videar Graecos insectari, ex illis nos velim intelligi pingendi fingendique conditoribus, quos in libellis his invenies, absoluta opera, et illa quoque quae mirando non satiamur, pendenti titulo inscripsisse: ut APELLES FACIEBAT, aut POLYCLETUS: tanquam inchoata semper arte et imperfecta: ut contra judiciorum varietates superesset artifici regressus ad veniam, velut emendaturo quidquid desideraretur, si non esset interceptus. Quare plenum verecundiae illud est, quod omnia opera tanquam novissima inscripsere, et tanquam singulis fato adempti. Tria non amplius, ut opinor, absolute traduntur inscripta, ILLE FECIT, quae suis locis reddam: quo apparuit, summam artis securitatem auctori placuisse, et ob id magna invidia fuere omnia ea.†

I desire to call particular attention to the words of Pliny, *"pingendi fingendique conditoribus"* (the creators of the imitative arts). Pliny does not say that it was the habit of all artists of every date to affix their names to their works in indefinite past time. He says explicitly that only the first of the old masters—those creators of the imitative arts, Apelles, Polycletus, and their contemporaries—possessed this wise modesty, and, by his mention of these alone, he gives plainly to be understood, though he does not actually say it in words, that their successors, particularly those of a late date, expressed themselves with greater assurance.

With this interpretation, which is the only true one, we may fully accept the inscription from the hand of one of the three sculptors of the Laocoon without impugning the truth of what Pliny says, that but three works existed whereon their creators had cut the inscription in the finished past time; only three, that is, among all the older works, of the time of Apelles, Polycletus, Nicias, and Lysippus. But then we cannot accept the conclusion that Athen-

odorus and his assistants were contemporaries of Apelles and Lysippus, as Winckelmann would make them. We should reason thus. If it be true that among the works of the old masters, Apelles, Polycletus, and others of that class, there were but three whose inscriptions stood in definite past time, and if it be further true that Pliny has mentioned these three by name, then Athenodorus, who had made neither of these three works, and who nevertheless employs the definite past time in his inscriptions, cannot belong among those old masters; he cannot be a contemporary of Apelles and Lysippus but must have a later date assigned him.

In short, we may, I think, take it as a safe criterion that all artists who employed the ἐποίησε, the definite past tense, flourished long after the time of Alexander the Great, either under the empire or shortly before. Of Cleomenes this is unquestionably true; highly probable of Archelaus; and of Salpion the contrary, at least, cannot be proved. So also of the rest, not excepting Athenodorus.

Let Winckelmann himself decide. But I protest beforehand against the converse of the proposition. If all who employed the ἐποίησε belong among the later artists, not all who have used the ἐποίει are to be

---

*[Inscriptions because of which a right might be lost]

†*Prefatio* Edit. Sillig. "Lest I should seem to find too much fault with the Greeks, I would be classed with those founders of the art of painting and sculpture, recorded in these little volumes, whose works, although complete and such as cannot be sufficiently admired, yet bear a suspended title, as Apelles or Polycletus 'was making'; as if the work were always only begun and still incomplete, so that the artist might appeal from criticism as if himself desirous of improving, had he not been interrupted. Wherefore from modesty they inscribed every work as if it had been their last, and in hand at their death. I think there are but three with the inscription, 'He made it,' and these I shall speak of in their place. From this it appeared that the artists felt fully satisfied with their work, and these excited the envy of all."

reckoned among the earliest. Some of the more recent artists also may have really possessed this becoming modesty, and by others it may have been assumed.

XXVIII.

Next to his judgment of the Laocoon, I was curious to know what Winckelmann would say of the so-called Borghese Gladiator. I think I have made a discovery with regard to this statue, and I rejoice in it with all a discoverer's delight.

I feared lest Winckelmann should have anticipated me, but there is nothing of the kind in his work. If aught could make me doubt the correctness of my conjecture, it would be the fact that my alarm was uncalled for.

"Some critics," says Winckelmann, "take this statue for that of a discobolus, that is, of a person throwing a disc or plate of metal. This opinion was expressed by the famous Herr von Stosch in a paper addressed to me. But he cannot have sufficiently studied the position which such a figure would assume. A person in the act of throwing must incline his body backward, with the weight upon the right thigh, while the left leg is idle. Here the contrary is the case. The whole figure is thrown forward, and rests on the left thigh while the right leg is stretched backward to its full extent. The right arm is new, and a piece of a lance has been placed in the hand. On the left can be seen the strap that held the shield. The fact that the head and eyes are turned upward and that the figure seems to be protecting himself with the shield against some danger from above would rather lead us to consider this statue as representing a soldier who had especially distinguished himself in some position of peril. The Greeks probably never paid their gladiators the honor of erecting them a statue; and this work, moreover, seems to have been made previous to the introduction of gladiators into Greece."

The criticism is perfectly just. The statue is no more a gladiator than it is a discobolus but really represents a soldier who distinguished himself in this position on occasion of some great danger. After this happy guess, how could Winckelmann help going a step further? Why did he not think of that warrior who in this very attitude averted the destruction of a whole army, and to whom his grateful country erected a statue in the same posture?

The statue, in short, is Chabrias.

This is proved by the following passage from Nepos's life of that commander:

Hic quoque in summis habitus est ducibus; resque multas memoria dignas gessit. Sed ex his elucet maxime inventum ejus in proelio, quod apud Thebas fecit, quum Boeotiis subsidio venisset. Namque in eo victoriae fidente summo duce Agesilao, fugatis jam ab eo conductitiis catervis, reliquam phalangem loco vetuit cedere, obnixoque genu scuto, projectaque hasta impetum excipere hostium docuit. Id novum Agesilaus contuens, progredi non est ausus suosque jam incurrentes tuba revocavit. Hoc usque eo tota Graecia fama celebratum est, ut illo statu Chabrias sibi statuam fieri voluerit, quae publice ei ab Atheniensibus in foro constituta est. Ex quo factum est, ut postea athletae, ceterique artifices his statibus in statuis ponendis uterentur in quibus victoriam essent adepti.*

The reader will hesitate a moment, I know, before yielding his assent; but, I

**Cap.* i. "He was also reckoned among their greatest leaders, and did many things worthy of being remembered. Among his most brilliant achievements was his device in the battle which took place near Thebes, when he had come to the aid of the Boeotians. For when the great leader Agesilaus was now confident of victory, and his own hired troops had fled, he would not surrender the remainder of the phalanx, but with knee braced against his shield and lance thrust forward, he taught his men to hope, only for a moment. The attitude of Chabrias appears to be not exactly that of the Borghese statue. The thrusting forward of the lance, *"projecta hasta,"* is common to both; but commentators explain the *"obnixo genu scuto"* to be *"obnixo genu in scutum," "obfirmato genu ad scutum."* Chabrias is supposed to have showed his men how to brace the knee against the shield and await the enemy behind this bulwark, whereas the statue holds the shield aloft. But what if the commentators are wrong, and instead of *"obnixo genu scuto"* belonging together, *"obnixo genu"* were meant to be read by itself and *"scuto"* alone, or in connection with the *"projectaque hasta,"* which follows? The insertion of a single comma makes the correspondence perfect. The statue is a soldier, *"qui obnixo genu, scuto projectaque hasta impetum hostis excipit,"* who, with firmly set knee, and shield and lance advanced, awaits the approach of the enemy. It shows what Chabrias did and is the statue of Chabrias. That a comma belongs here is proved by the *"que"* affixed to the *"projecta,"* which would be superfluous if *"obnixo genu scuto"* belonged together, and has, therefore, been actually omitted in some editions.

The great antiquity which this interpretation assigns to the statue is confirmed by the shape of the letters in the inscription. These led Winckelmann himself to the conclusion that this was the oldest of the statues at present existing in Rome on which the master had written his name. I leave it to his critical eye to detect, if possible, in the style of the workmanship

---

receive the attack of the enemy. At sight of this new spectacle, Agesilaus feared to advance, and ordered the trumpet to recall his men who were already advancing. This became famous through all Greece, and Chabrias wished that a statue should be erected to him in this position, which was set up at the public cost in the forum at Athens. Whence it happened that afterwards athletes and other artists [or persons versed in some art] had statues erected to them in the same position in which they had obtained victory."

any thing which conflicts with my opinion. Should he bestow his approval, I may flatter myself on having furnished a better example than is to be found in Spence's whole folio of the happy manner in which the classic authors can be explained by the old masterpieces, and in turn throw light upon them.

XXIX.

Winckelmann has brought to his work, together with immense reading and an extensive and subtle knowledge of art, that noble confidence of the old masters which led them to devote all their attention to the main object, treating all secondary matters with what seems like studied neglect, or abandoning them altogether to any chance hand.

A man may take no little credit to himself for having committed only such errors as anybody might have avoided. They force themselves upon our notice at the first hasty reading; and my only excuse for commenting on them is that I would remind a certain class of persons, who seem to think no one has eyes but themselves, that they are trifles not worthy of comment.

In his writings on the imitation of the Greek works of art, Winckelmann had before allowed himself to be misled by Junius, who is, indeed, a very deceptive author. His whole work is a cento, and since his rule is to quote the ancients in their very words, he not infrequently applies to painting passages which in their original connection had no bearing whatever on the subject. When, for instance, Winckelmann would tell us that the highest effect in art, as in poetry, cannot be attained by the mere imitation of nature, and that poet as well as painter should choose an impossibility which carries probability with it rather than what is simply possible, he adds: "This is perfectly consistent with Longinus' requirement of possibility and truth from the painter in opposition to the incredibility which he requires from the poet." Yet the addition was unfortunate, for it shows a seeming contradiction between the two great art critics which really does not exist. Longinus never said what is here attributed to him. Something similar he does say with regard to eloquence and poetry, but by no means of poetry and painting. *'Ως δ' ἕτερόν τι ἡ ῥητορικὴ φαντασία βούλεται, καὶ ἕτερον ἡ παρὰ ποιηταῖς, οὐκ ἂν λάθοι σε, οὐδ' ὅτι τῆς μὲν ἐν ποιήσει τέλος ἐστὶν ἔκπληξις, τῆς δ' ἐν λόγοις ἐνάργεια,** he writes to his friend Terentian; and again, *'Ου μὴν ἀλλὰ τὰ μὲν παρὰ τοῖς ποιηταῖς μυθικωτέραν ἔχει τὴν ὑπερέκπτωσιν, καὶ παντῇ τὸ πῖστὸν ὑπεραίρουσαν· τῆς δὲ ῥητορικῆς φαντασίας, κάλλιστον ἀεὶ ἔμπρακτον καὶ ἐναληθές.†*

But Junius interpolates here painting instead of oratory, and it was in his writings, not in those of Longinus, that Winckelmann read: *"Praesertim cum poeticae phantasiae finis sit ἔκπληξις, pictoriae vero, ἐνάργεια, καὶ τὰ μὲν παρὰ τοῖς ποιηταῖς, ut loquitur idem Longinus,"* &c.‡ The words of Longinus, to be sure, but not his meaning.

The same must have been the case with the following remark: "All motions and attitudes of Greek figures which were too wild and fiery to be in accordance with the character of wisdom, were accounted as faults by the old masters and classed by them under the general name of *parenthyrsus*." The old masters? There can be no authority for that except Junius. *Parenthyrsus* was a word used in rhetoric, and, as a passage in Longinus would seem to show, even there peculiar to Theodorus. *Τούτῳ παρακεῖται τρίτον τι κακίας εἶδος ἐν τοῖς παθητικοῖς, ὅπερ ὁ Θεόδωρος παρένθυρσον ἐκάλει· ἔστι δὲ πάθος ἄκαιρον και κενόν, ἔνθα μὴ δεῖ πάθους· ἢ ἄμετρον, ἔνθα μετρίου δεῖ.§*

I doubt, indeed, whether this word can be translated into the language of painting. For in oratory and poetry pathos can be carried to extreme without becoming *parenthyrsus*, which is only the extreme of pathos in the wrong place. But in painting the extreme of pathos would always be *parenthyrsus*, whatever its excuse in the circumstances of the persons concerned.

So, also, various errors in the *History of Art* have arisen solely from Winckelmann's haste in accepting Junius instead of consulting the original authors. When, for instance, he is citing examples to show that excellence in all departments of art and labor was so highly prized by the Greeks, that the best workman, even on an insignificant thing, might immortalize his name, he brings forward this among others: "We know the name of a maker of very exact balances or scales; he was called Parthenius." Winckelmann must have read the words of Juvenal, *"lances Parthenio factas,"* which he here appeals to, only in Junius's catalogue. Had he looked up the original passage in Juvenal, he would not have been misled by the double meaning of the word *"lanx,"* but would at once have seen from the connection that the poet was not speaking of balances or scales, but of plates and dishes. Juvenal is praising Catullus for throwing overboard his treasures during a violent storm at sea, in order to save the ship and himself. In his description of these treasures, he says:

Ille nec argentum dubitabat mittere, lances
Parthenio factas, urnae cratera capacem
Et dignum sitiente Pholo, vel conjuge Fusci.

---

*"But so it is that rhetorical figures aim at one thing, poetical figures at quite another; since in poetry emphasis is the main object, in rhetoric distinctness."

†"So with the poets, legends and exaggeration obtain and in all transcend belief; but in rhetorical figures the best is always the practicable and the true."

‡["Especially since the end of the poetic imagination is astonishment while that of painting is vividness, and that too among the poets, as the same Lucretius says, etc."]

§"Next to this is a third form of faultiness in pathos, which Theodorus calls *parenthyrsus;* it is a pathos unseasonable and empty, where pathos is not necessary; or immoderate, where it should be moderate."

*Adde et bascaudas et mille escaria, multum
Caelati, biberet quo callidus emtor Olynthi.**

What can the "lances" be which are
here standing among drinking-cups and
bowls, but plates and dishes? And what
does Juvenal mean, except that Catullus
threw overboard his whole silver table-
service, including plates made by Parthenius. *"Parthenius,"* says the old scholiast,
"coelatoris nomen" (the name of the engraver). But when Grangäus, in his anno-
tations, appends to this name, *"sculptor, de
quo Plinius"* (sculptor spoken of by Pliny),
he must have been writing at random, for
Pliny speaks of no artist of that name.

"Yes," continues Winckelmann, "even
the name of the saddler, as we should call
him, has been preserved, who made the
leather shield of Ajax," This he cannot
have derived from the source to which he
refers his readers—the life of Homer, by
Herodotus. Here, indeed, the lines from
the *Iliad* are quoted wherein the poet applies to this worker in leather the name
Tychius. But it is at the same time expressly
stated that this was the name of a worker
in leather of Homer's acquaintance, whose
name he thus introduced in token of his
friendship and gratitude.

'Απέδωκε δὲ χάριν καὶ Τυχίῳ τῷ σκύτει. ὃς
ἐδέξατο αὐτὸν ἐν τῷ Νέῳ τείχει, προσελθόντα
πσὸς τὸ σκύτειον, ἐν τοῖς ἔπεσι καταζεύξας
ἐν τῇ 'Ιλιάδι τοῖς δε:

'Αίας δ' ἐγγύθεν ἦλθε, φέρων σάκος
   ἠύτε πύργον,
χάλκεον, ἑπταβόειον· ὅ οἱ Τυχιος κάμε
   τεύχων

σκυτοτόμων ὄχ' ἄριστος, "Τλῃ ἔνι
οἴκια νάιων·†

Here we have exactly the opposite of
what Winckelmann asserts. So utterly forgotten, even in Homer's time, was the
name of the saddler who made the shield
of Ajax, that the poet was at liberty to
substitute that of a perfect stranger.

Various other little errors I have found
which are mere slips of memory, or concern things introduced merely as incidental
illustrations.

For instance, it was Hercules, not Bacchus, who, as Parrhasius boasts, appeared
to him in the same shape he had given him
on the canvas.

Tauriscus was not from Rhodes, but
from Tralles, in Lydia.

The *Antigone* was not the first tragedy
of Sophocles.[28]

But I refrain from multiplying such
trifles.

Censoriousness it could not be taken for;
but to those who know my great respect
for Winckelmann it might seem trifling.

["Nor did he hesitate to throw away the
silver, plates made by Parthenius, a bowl capable
of holding an urnful and worthy a thirsty Pholos
or the wife of Fuscus. Add to that the basins
and thousands of dishes much engraved such as
would have served the wily buyer of Olynthus."]

†["But he showed favor also to Tychios, the
worker in leather, who received him when he
came to his shop, by inserting the following
passage in the *Iliad:* 'Ajax approached, bearing
as a tower his mighty shield, seven-fold,
brass-bound, the work of Tychios, best worker
of those in leather, who dwelt in Hyla'." (Cf.
GBWW, Vol. 4, p. 48b.)]

[1]For this reason Aristotle commanded that his pictures should not be shown to young persons, in order that their imagination might be kept as free as possible from all disagreeable images [*GBWW*, Vol. 9, p. 545d]. . . . As if we needed a philosophic lawgiver to teach us the necessity of keeping from youth such incentives to wantonness! . . . There are commentators . . . who suppose the difference mentioned by Aristotle as existing between Polygnotus, Dionysius, and Pauson to consist in this: that Polygnotus painted gods and heroes; Dionysius, men; and Pauson, animals. They all painted human figures; and the fact that Pauson once painted a horse, does not prove him to have been a painter of animals as Boden supposes him to have been. Their rank was determined by the degree of beauty they gave their human figures; and the reason that Dionysius could paint nothing but men, and was therefore called preeminently the anthropographist, was that he copied too slavishly, and could not rise into the domain of the ideal beneath which it would have been blasphemy to represent gods and heroes.

[2]*Saturnal.* lib. v. cap. 2. "Not a few other things were brought by Virgil from the Greeks and inserted in his poem as original. Do you think I would speak of what is known to all the world? how he took his pastoral poem from Theocritus, his rural from Hesiod? and how, in his Georgics, he took from the Phenomena of Aratus the signs of winter and summer? or that he translated almost word for word from Pisander the destruction of Troy, with his Simon and wooden horse and the rest? For he is famous among Greek poets for a work in which, beginning his universal history with the nuptials of Jupiter and Juno, he collected into one series whatever had happened in all ages, to the time of himself, Pisander. In which work the destruction of Troy, among other things, is related in the same way. By faithfully interpreting these things, Maro made his ruin of Ilium. But these, and others like them, I pass over as familiar to every schoolboy."

[3]I do not forget that a picture mentioned by Eumolpus in Petronius may be cited in contradiction of this. It represented the destruction of Troy, and particularly the history of Laocoon exactly as narrated by Virgil. And since, in the same gallery at Naples were other old pictures by Zeuxis, Protogenes, and Apelles, it was inferred that this was also an old Greek picture. But permit me to say that a novelist is no historian. This gallery and picture, and Eumolpus himself, apparently existed only in the imagination of Petronius. That the whole was fiction appears from the evident traces of an almost schoolboyish imitation of Virgil. Thus Virgil (*Aeneid* lib. ii. 199–224):

A mightier portent and more fearful far,
Poor souls! here bursts upon them, and confounds
Their blinded senses. For Laocoon,
The Priest of Neptune, as by lot assigned,
Was sacrificing at the wonted shrine
A mighty bull, when, lo! from Tenedos,
Over the tranquil ocean serpents twain—
I shudder to recount it—with huge coils
Cumbering the deep, ply shoreward side by side;
Reared on the surge their breasts and blood-red manes
O'ertop the billows; the remaining bulk
Skims ocean aft in labyrinthine folds:
Hark! how the brine seethes audibly! and now,
Their glowing eyes with blood suffused and fire,
The shore-fields they were gaining, and their chaps
Hissed, as with flickering tongues they licked them; we
Pale at the sight fly scattered; they with line
Unwavering at Laocoon aim, and first
His two sons' slender bodies either snake
Embraces and enfolds, and gnawing feeds
Upon the hapless limbs; then him they seize
Up-hurrying armed to aid them, and bind fast
With mighty spires, and now—their scaly length
Twice wreathed about his waist, twice round his neck—
With heads o'ertop him and high-towering throats.
He, while to rend their knots he strives amain,
His fillets with black venom drenched and gore,
Uplifts to heaven heart-piercing shrieks; as when,
'Scaped from the altar, bellows a maimed bull,
that from his neck shakes off the erring axe.
[*GBWW*, Vol. 13, pp. 129b–30a]

And thus Eumolpus, in whose lines, as is usually the case with improvisators, memory has had as large a share as imagination:

But other monsters there inform our eyes,
What mighty seas from Tenedos arise!
The frightened Neptune seems to seek the shore,

With such a noise, with such a dreadful
    roar:
As in a silent night, when from afar
The dismal sound of wrecks invades the ear:
When rolling on the waves two mighty
    snakes,
Unhappy Troy descried; whose circling
    strokes
Had drove the swelling surges on the rocks.
Like lofty ships they on the billows ride,
And with raised breasts the foaming flood
    divide:
Their crests they brandish and red eyeballs
    raise,
That all around dispense a sulphurous
    blaze.
To shore advancing, now the waves
    appear
All fire; unwonted ratlings fill the air.
The ocean trembles at their dreadful hiss;
All are amazed: When in a trojan dress,
and holy wreaths their sacred temples bind,
Laocoon's sons were by the snakes
    entwined:
Now towards heaven their little hands are
    thrown
Each for his brother, not himself does moan,
    and prays to save his ruin by his own.
Both die at last, through fear each other
    should;
And to give death a greater pomp, the
    good
Laocoon to their rescue vainly run,
Now gorged with death, they drag him on
    the ground
Up to the altar, where devoted lies
The priest himself, a panting sacrifice.
             [trans. Wm. Burnaby, 1694]

    The main points are the same in both, and
in many places the same words are used. But
those are trifles, and too evident to require
mention. There are other signs of imitation,
more subtle, but not less sure. If the imitator
be a man with confidence in his own powers, he
seldom imitates without trying to improve upon
the original; and, if he fancy himself to have
succeeded, he is enough of a fox to brush over
with his tail the footprints which might betray
his course. But he betrays himself by this very
vanity of wishing to introduce embellishments,
and his desire to appear original. For his
embellishments are nothing but exaggerations
and excessive refinements. . . . So the imitator
goes on exaggerating greatness into monstrosity,
wonders into impossibilities. The boys are
secondary in Virgil. He passes them over with
a few insignificant words, indicative simply of
their helplessness and distress. Petronius makes a

great point of them, converting the two children
into a couple of heroes. . . . Who expects
from human beings, and children especially,
such self-sacrifice? The Greek understood nature
better, when he made even mothers forget
their children at the appearance of the terrible
serpents, so intent was every one on securing his
own safety.

$$\ldots\ \text{ἔνθα γυναῖκες}$$
Οἰμώζον, καὶ πού τις ἑὸν ἐπελήσατο τέκνων
Αὐτὴ ἀλευομένη στυγερὸν μόρον . . .

    The usual method of trying to conceal an
imitation is to alter the shading, bringing forward
what was in shadow, and obscuring what was in
relief. Virgil lays great stress upon the size of the
serpents, because the probability of the whole
subsequent scene depends upon it. The noise
occasioned by their coming is a secondary idea,
intended to make more vivid the impression
of their size. Petronius raises this secondary
idea into chief prominence, describing the noise
with all possible wealth of diction, and so far
forgetting to describe the size of the monsters
that we are almost left to infer it from the noise
they make. He hardly would have fallen into
this error, had he been drawing solely from his
imagination, with no model before him which
he wished to imitate without the appearance
of imitation. We can always recognize a poetic
picture as an unsuccessful imitation when we find
minor details exaggerated and important ones
neglected, however many incidental beauties the
poem may possess, and however difficult, or even
impossible, it may be to discover the original.
    [4]*Suppl. aux Antiq. Expl. T.* i. p. 243. "*Il y
a quelque petite différence entre ce que dit Virgile,
et ce que le marbre représente. Il semble, selon ce
que dit le poëte, que les serpens quittèrent les deux
enfans pour venir entortiller le père, au lieu que
dans ce marbre ils lient en même temps les enfans
et leur père.*"
    ["There is a small difference between what
Virgil says and what the marble represents. It
seems, according to the poet, that the serpents
leave the two children to twine about the father,
whereas in the marble they bind at the same
time both children and father."]
    [5]*Donatus ad. v. 227, lib. ii. Aeneid. "Mirandum
non est, clypeo et simulacri vestigiis tegi potuisse, quos
supra et longos et validos dixit, et multiplici ambitu
circumdedisse Laocoontis corpus ac liberorum, et
fuisse superfluam partem.* . . ."
    ["It is not to be wondered that the shield and
images of her feet could be covered, since above
he called the snakes long and mighty that could
encircle with many folds both Laocoon and the
children with some left over."]

[6]In the handsome edition of Dryden's Virgil (London, 1697). Yet here the serpents are wound but once about the body, and hardly at all about the neck. So indifferent an artist scarcely deserves an excuse, but the only one that could be made for him would be that prints are merely illustrations, and by no means to be regarded as independent works of art.

[7]This is the judgment of De Piles in his remarks upon Du Fresnoy: "Remark if you will that soft and light clothing was given only to female figures, since the ancient sculptors wanted to avoid as much as possible clothing the figures of men; because, as we have already said, they thought that sculpture could not imitate draperies and that great folds would make a bad effect. There are almost as many examples of this truth as there are among the ancients figures of nude men. I cite only that of the Laocoon who to be plausible should have been clothed. In fact, what kind of appearance would a son of a king and a priest of Apollo make if entirely nude during the very ceremony of a sacrifice? For the serpents proceed from the isle of Tenedos to the shore of Troy and surprise Laocoon and his sons at the very time that they are sacrificing to Neptune on the edge of the sea, as Virgil notes in the second book of his *Aeneid*. Nevertheless the artists who were the authors of this fine work thought they could not provide garments suitable to the occasion without using a mass of rocks, the mass of which would resemble a boulder, instead of the three admirable figures who have always been the admiration of centuries. So of the two evils they judged that providing garments was worse than going against the truth itself."

[8]I can adduce no better argument in support of my view than this poem [prose trans.] of Sadolet. It is worthy of one of the old poets, and, since it may well take the place of an engraving, I venture to introduce it here entire.

Laocoon, by James Sadolet

So, from the depths of earth and the bowels of mighty ruins, the long-deferred day has brought back the returning Laocoon, who stood of old in thy royal halls and graced thy penates, Titus. The image of divine art, a work as noble as any produced by the learning of antiquity, now freed from darkness, beholds again the lofty walls of renovated Rome. With what part shall I begin as the greatest? the unhappy father and his two sons? the sinuous coils of the terrible serpents? the tails and the fierceness of the dragons? the wounds and real pains of the dying stone? These chill the mind with horror, and pity, mingled with no slight fear, drives our hearts back from the dumb image. Two gleaming snakes cover a vast space with their gathered coils, and move in sinuous rings, and hold three bodies bound in a many-twisted knot. Eyes scarce can bear to behold the cruel death and fierce sufferings. One gleaming seeks Laocoon himself, winding him all about, above, below, and attacks his groins at last with poisonous bite. The imprisoned body recoils, and you see the limbs writhe and the side shrink back from the wound. Forced by the sharp pain and bitter anguish, he groans; and, trying to tear out the cruel teeth, throws his left hand upon the serpent's back. The nerves strain, and the whole body in vain collects its strength for the supreme effort. He cannot endure the fierce torture, and pants from the wound. But the slippery snake glides down with frequent folds, and binds his leg below the knee with twisted knot. The calves fall in, the tight-bound leg swells between the pressing coils, and the vitals grow tumid from the stopping of the pulses, and black blood distends the livid veins. The same cruel violence attacks the children no less fiercely, tortures them with many encircling folds, and lacerates their suffering limbs. Now satiated upon the bloody breast of one, who, with his last breath, calls upon his father, the serpent supports the lifeless body with the mighty circles thrown around it. The other, whose body has as yet been hurt by no sting, while preparing to pluck out the tail from his foot, is filled with horror at sight of his wretched father, and clings to him. A double fear restrains his great sobs and falling tears. Therefore ye enjoy perpetual fame, ye great artificers who made the mighty work, although an immortal name may be sought by better deeds, and nobler talents may be handed down to future fame. Yet any power employed to snatch this praise and reach the heights of fame is excellent. Ye have excelled in animating the rigid stone with living forms, and inserting living senses within the breathing marble. We see the movement, the wrath and pain, and almost hear the groans. Illustrious Rhodes begot you of old. Long the glories of your art lay hid, but Rome beholds them again in a second dawn, and celebrates them with many voices, in fresh acknowledgment of the old labor. How much nobler, then, to extend our fates by art or toil than to swell pride and wealth and empty luxury.

[9]I say it is possible, but I would wager ten against one that it is not so. . . . What are the marbles and coins on which Addison saw Mars in this hovering attitude? The old bas-relief to which he appeals is said to be in Bellori, but we shall look for it in vain in the Admiranda, his collection of finest old bas-reliefs. Spence cannot have found it there or elsewhere, for he makes

no mention of it. Nothing remains, therefore, but the coins, which we will study from Addison himself. I see a recumbent figure of Rhea, and Mars standing on a somewhat higher plane, because there was not room for him on the same level. That is all: there is no sign of his being suspended. . . . But I have another objection to make to this supposed hovering attitude of Mars. A body thus suspended, without any visible cause for the law of gravitation not acting upon it, is an absurdity of which no example can be found in the old works of art. It is not allowable even in modern painting. If a body is to be suspended in the air, it must either have wings or appear to rest upon something, if only a cloud. When Homer makes Thetis rise on foot from the sea-shore to Olympus, *Τὴν μὲν ἄρ᾽ Οὔλυμπόνδε πόδες φέρον* [GBWW, Vol. 4, p. 131c], Count Caylus is too well aware of the limitations of art to counsel the painter to represent her as walking unsupported through the air. She must pursue her way upon a cloud, as in another place he puts her into a chariot, although exactly the opposite is stated by the poet. How can it be otherwise? Although the poet represents the goddess with a human body, he yet removes from her every trace of coarse and heavy materiality and animates her with a power which raises her beyond the influence of our laws of motion. How could painting so distinguish the bodily shape of a deity from the bodily shape of a human being, that our eyes should not be offended by observing it acted upon by different laws of motion, weight, and equilibrium? How but by conventional signs, such as a pair of wings or a cloud? But more of this elsewhere; here it is enough to require the defenders of the Addison theory to show on the old monuments a second figure floating thus unsupported in the air. . . .

[10]*Satyr.* viii. v. 52–55.

> . . . *At tu*
> *Nil nisi Cecropides; truncoque simillimus*
> *Hermae!*
> *Nullo quippe alio vincis discrimine, quam*
> *quod*
> *Illi marmoreum caput est, tua vivit imago.*

"But thou art nothing if not a descendant of Cecrops; in body most like a Hermes; forsooth the only thing in which you surpass that, is that your head is a living image, while the Hermes is marble." If Spence had embraced the old Greek writers in his work, a fable of Aesop might perhaps—and yet perhaps not—have occurred to him, which throws still clearer light upon this passage in Juvenal. "Mercury," Aesop tells us, "wishing to know in what repute he stood among men, concealed his divinity, and entered a sculptor's studio. Here he beheld a statue of Jupiter, and asked its value. 'A drachm,' was the answer. Mercury smiled. 'And this Juno?' he asked again. 'About the same.' The god meanwhile had caught sight of his own image, and thought to himself, 'I, as the messenger of the gods, from whom come all gains, must be much more highly prized by men.' 'And this god,' he asked, pointing to his own image, 'how dear might that be?' 'That?' replied the artist, 'buy the other two, and I will throw that in.' " Mercury went away sadly crestfallen. But the artist did not recognize him and could therefore have had no intention of wounding his self-love. The reason for his setting so small a value on the statue must have lain in its workmanship. The less degree of reverence due to the god whom it represented could have had nothing to do with the matter, for the artist values his works according to the skill, industry, and labor bestowed upon them, not according to the rank and dignity of the persons represented. If a statue of Mercury cost less than one of Jupiter or Juno, it was because less skill, industry, and labor had been expended upon it. And such was the case here. The statues of Jupiter and Juno were full-length figures, while that of Mercury was a miserable square post, with only the head and shoulders of the god upon it. What wonder, then, that it might be thrown in without extra charge? Mercury overlooked this circumstance, from having in mind only his own fancied superiority, and his humiliation was therefore as natural as it was merited. We look in vain among the commentators, translators, and imitators of Aesop's fables for any trace of this explanation. I could mention the names of many, were it worth the trouble, who have understood the story literally; that is, have not understood it at all. On the supposition that the workmanship of all the statues was of the same degree of excellence, there is an absurdity in the fable which these scholars have either failed to perceive or have very much exaggerated. . . .

[11]*de Rerum Natura.* lib. v. 736–47.

> *It Ver, et Venus, et Veneris praenuntius ante*
> *Pinnatus graditur Zephyrus; vestigia propter*
> *Flora quibus mater praespargens ante viai*
> *Cuncta coloribus egregiis et odoribus opplet,*
> *Inde loci sequitur Calor aridus, et comes una*
> *Pulverulenta Ceres; et Etesia flabra Aquilonum.*
> *Inde Autumnus adit; graditur simul Evius*
> *Evan;*
> *Inde aliae tempestates ventique sequuntur,*
> *Altitonans Vulturnus et Auster fulmine pollens.*
> *Tandem Bruma nives adfert, pigrumque rigorem*
> *Reddit, Hyems sequitur, crepitans ac dentibus*
> *Algus.*

"Spring advances and Venus and winged Zephyrus, the herald of Venus, precedes, whose path mother Flora fills with wondrous flowers and odors. Then follow in order dry Heat and his companion dusty Ceres, and the Etesian blasts of the Northwind. Then Autumn approaches, and Evian Bacchus. Then other tempests and winds, deep-thundering Volturnus and Auster (south and southeast winds), mighty with lightnings. At length, the solstice brings snow, and slothful numbness returns; Winter follows, and cold with chattering teeth." [Cf. *GBWW*, Vol. 12, p. 70d.]

Spence regards this passage as one of the most beautiful in the whole poem, and it is certainly one on which the fame of Lucretius as a poet chiefly rests. But, surely, to say that the whole description was probably taken from a procession of statues representing the seasons as gods, is to detract very much from his merit, if not to destroy it altogether. And what reason have we for the supposition? This, says the Englishman: "Such processions of their detities in general were as common among the Romans of old, as those in honor of the saints are in the same country to this day. All the expressions used by Lucretius here come in very aptly, if applied to a procession."

Excellent reasons! Against the last, particularly, we might make many objections. The very epithets applied to the various personified abstractions—"*Calor aridus*," "*Ceres pulverulenta*," "*Volturnus altitonans*," "*fulmine pollens Auster*," "*Algus dentibus crepitans*"—show that they received their characteristics from the poet and not from the artist. He would certainly have treated them very differently. Spence seems to have derived his idea of a procession from Abraham Preigern, who, in his remarks on this passage, says, "*Ordo est quasi Pompae cujusdam. Ver et Venus, Zephyrus et Flora*," &c. But Spence should have been content to stop there. To say that the poet makes his seasons move as in a procession, is all very well; but to say that he learned their sequences from a procession, is nonsense.

[12]Valerius Flaccus, from his epic poem *Argonautica*, v. 265–73.

Serta patri, juvenisque comam vestisque Lyaei
Induit, et medium curru locat; aeraque circum
Tympanaque et plenas tacita formidine cistas.
Ipsa sinus hederisque ligat famularibus artus;
Pampineamque quatit ventosis icibus hastam,
Respiciens; teneat virides velatus habenas
Ut pater, et nivea tumeant ut cornua mitra,
Et sacer ut Bacchum referat scyphus.

"The maid clothes her father with the garlands, the locks and the garments of Bacchus, and places him in the centre of the chariot; around him the brazen drums and the boxes filled with nameless terror; herself, looking back, binds his hair and limbs with ivy and strikes windy blows with the vine-wreathed spear; veiled like the father she holds the green reins; the horns project under the white turban, and the sacred goblet tells of Bacchus."

The word *tumeant*, in the last line but one, would seem to imply that the horns were not so small as Spence fancies.

[13]The so-called Bacchus in the garden of the Medicis at Rome has little horns growing from the brow. But for this very reason some critics suppose it to be a faun. And indeed such natural horns are an insult to the human countenance, and can only be becoming in beings supposed to occupy a middle station between men and beasts. The attitude also and the longing looks the figure casts upward at the grapes belong more properly to a follower of the god than to the god himself. I am reminded here of what Clemens Alexandrinus says of Alexander the Great. Ἐβούλετο δὲ καὶ Ἀλέξανδρος Ἄμμωνος υἱὸς εἶναι δοκεῖν, καὶ κεράσφορος ἀναπλάττεσθαι πρὸς τῶν ἀγαλματοποιῶν, τὸ καλὸν ἀνθρώπου ὑβρίσαι σπεύδων κέρατι. It was Alexander's express desire to be represented in his statue with horns. He was well content with the insult thus done to human beauty, if only a divine origin might be imputed to him.

[14]Lib. i. Od. 35.

Te semper anteit saeva Necessitas:
Clavos trabales et cuneos manu
Gestans ahenea; nec severus
Uncus abest liquidumque plumbum.

["Cruel Necessity goes before you (Fortune), carrying spikes and wedges in her brazen hand, nor are the stout clamp and the molten lead missing."]

In this picture of Necessity drawn by Horace, perhaps the richest in attributes of any to be found in the old poets, the nails, the clamps, and the liquid lead, whether regarded as means of confinement or implements of punishment, still belong to the class of poetical, rather than allegorical, attributes. But, even so, they are too crowded; and the passage is one of the least effective in Horace. Sanadon says: "*J'ose dire que ce tableau, pris dans le détail, serait plus beau sur la toile que dans une ode héroïque. Je ne puis souffrir cet attirail patibulaire de clous, de coins, de crocs, et de plomb fondu. J'ai cru en devoir décharger la traduction, en substituant les idées générales aux idées singulières. C'est dommage que le poëte ait eu besoin de ce correctif.*" ["I dare say that this picture taken in detail would be more beautiful on a canvas than in an heroic ode. I cannot stand this apparatus of the gallows with its nails, wedges, hooks, and molten lead. I believe the translation should unburden itself by substituting general ideas for the particulars. It is a pity the poet needs such a correction."] Sanadon's sentiment was fine and true, but he does not give the right ground for it. The objection is not that these attributes are the paraphernalia of the gallows, for he had but to interpret them in their other sense to make them the firmest supports of architecture. Their fault is in being addressed to the eye and not to the ear. For all impressions meant for the eye, but presented to us through the ear, are received with effort, and produce no great degree of vividness. . . .

[15]Apollo delivers the washed and embalmed body of Sarpedon to Death and Sleep, that they may bring him to his native country [GBWW, Vol. 4, p. 119c].

πέμπε δέ μιν πομποῖσιν ἅμα κραιπνοῖσι
φέρεσθαι,
Ὕπνῳ καὶ Θανάτῳ διδυμάοσιν.

Caylus recommends this idea to the painter, but adds: "It is a pity that Homer has given us no account of the attributes under which Sleep was represented in his day. We recognize the god only by his act, and we crown him with poppies. These ideas are modern. The first is of service, but cannot be employed in the present case, where even the flowers would be out of keeping in connection with the figure of Death." That is requiring of Homer ornamentations of that petty kind most at variance with the nobility of his style. The most ingenious attributes he could have bestowed on Sleep would not have characterized him so perfectly, nor have brought so vivid a picture of him before us, as the single touch which makes him the twin brother of Death. Let the artist seek to express this, and he may dispense with all attributes. The old artists did, in fact, make Sleep and Death resemble each other, like twin brothers. On a chest of cedar, in the Temple of Juno at Elis, they both lay as boys in the arms of Night. One was white, the other black; one slept, the other only seemed to sleep; the feet of both were crossed. For so I should prefer to translate the words of Pausanias, ἀμφοτέρους διεστραμμένους τοὺς πόδας, rather than by "crooked feet," as Gedoyn does, "les pieds contrefaits." What would be the meaning of crooked feet? To lie with crossed feet is customary with sleepers. Sleep is thus represented by Maffei. Modern artists have entirely abandoned this resemblance between Sleep and Death, which we find among the ancients, and always represent Death as a skeleton, or at best a skeleton covered with skin. Caylus should have been careful to tell the artists whether they had better follow the custom of the ancients or the moderns in this respect. He seems to declare in favor of the modern view, since he regards Death as a figure that would not harmonize well with a flower-crowned companion. Has he further considered how inappropriate this modern idea would be in a Homeric picture? How could its loathsome character have failed to shock him? I cannot bring myself to believe that the little metal figure in the ducal gallery at Florence, representing a skeleton sitting on the ground, with one arm on an urn of ashes, is a veritable antique. It cannot possibly represent Death, because the ancients represented him very differently. Even their poets never thought of him under this repulsive shape.

[16]This invisible battle of the gods has been imitated by Quintus Calaber in his Twelfth Book, with the evident design of improving on his model. The grammarian seems to have held it unbecoming in a god to be thrown to the ground by a stone. He therefore makes the gods hurl at one another huge masses of rock, torn up from Mount Ida, which, however, are shattered against the limbs of the immortals and fly like sand about them.

. . . οἱ δὲ κολώνας
χερσὶν ἀπορρήξαντες ἀπ' οὔδεος Ἰδαίοιο
βάλλον ἐπ' ἀλλήλους· αἱ δὲ ψαμάθοισι ὅμοιαι
ῥεῖα διεσκίδναντο θεῶν περὶ δ' ἄσχετα γυῖα
ῥηγνύμενα διὰ τυτθά. . . .

A conceit which destroys the effect by marring our idea of the size of the gods, and throwing contempt on their weapons. If gods throw stones at one another, the stones must be able to hurt them, or they are like silly boys pelting each other with earth. So old Homer remains still the wiser, and all the fault-finding of cold criticism, and the attempts of men of inferior genius to vie with him, serve but to set forth his wisdom in clearer light. I do not deny that Quintus's imitation has excellent and original points; but they are less in harmony with the modest greatness of Homer than calculated to do honor to the stormy fire of a more modern poet. That the cry of the gods, which rang to the heights of heaven and the depths of hell, should not be heard by mortals, seems to me a most expressive touch. The cry was too mighty to be grasped by the imperfect organs of human hearing.

[17]No one who has read Homer once through, ever so hastily, will differ from this statement as far as regards strength and speed; but he will not perhaps at once recall examples where

the poet attaches superhuman size to his gods. I would therefore refer him, in addition to the description of Mars just quoted, whose body covered seven hides, to the helmet of Minerva, κυνέην ἑκατὸν πολίων πρυλέεσσ' ἀραρυῖαν [GBWW, Vol. 4, p. 37d], under which could be concealed as many warriors as a hundred cities could bring into the field; to the stride of Neptune [GBWW, Vol. 4, p. 88b]; and especially to the lines from the description of the shield, where Mars and Minerva lead the troops of the beleaguered city. (Iliad, xviii. 516–19.)

ἦωχε δ' ἄρα σφῖν ᾽Αρης καὶ Παλλὰς Αθηνη,
ἄμφω χρυσείω, χρύσεια δὲ εἴματα ἑσθην,
καλω καὶ μεγάλω σὺν τεύχεσιν, ὥστε θεώ
ερ,
ἀμφὶς ἀριζήλω· λαοὶ δ' ὑπ' ὀλίζονες ἦσαν.

. . . While the youths
Marched on, with Mars and Pallas at their head,
Both wrought in gold, with golden garments on,
Stately and large in form, and over all
Conspicuous in bright armor, as became
The gods; the rest were of an humbler size.—BRYANT.
[Cf. GBWW, Vol. 4, p. 135c.]
Judging from the explanations they feel called upon to give of the great helmet of Minerva, Homer's commentators, old as well as new, seem not always sufficiently to have borne in mind this wonderful size of the gods. But we lose much in majesty by thinking of the Homeric deities as of ordinary size, as we are accustomed to see them on canvas in the company of mortals. Although painting is unable to represent these superhuman dimensions, sculpture to a certain extent may, and I am convinced that the old masters borrowed from Homer their conception of the gods in general as well as the colossal size which they not infrequently gave them. Further remarks upon the use of the colossal, its excellent effect in sculpture and its want of effect in painting, I reserve for another place.

[18]Homer, I acknowledge, sometimes veils his deities in a cloud, but only when they are not to be seen by other deities. In the fourteenth book of the Iliad, for instance, where Juno and Sleep, ἠέρα ἑσσαμένω, betake themselves to Mount Ida, the crafty goddess's chief care was not to be discovered by Venus, whose girdle she had borrowed under pretense of a very different journey. In the same book the love-drunken Jupiter is obliged to surround himself and his spouse with a golden cloud to overcome her chaste reluctance.

πῶς κ' ἔοι, εἴ τις νῶϊ θεῶν αἰειγενετάων
εὕδονι ἀθρήσειε. . . .

She did not fear to be seen by men, but by the gods. And although Homer makes Jupiter say a few lines further on—

῝Ηρη, μήτε θεῶν τόγε δείδιθι μήτε τιν' ἀνδρῶν
ὄψεσθαι· τοῖόν τοι ἐγὼ νέφος ἀμφικαλύψω,
χρύσεον.

"Fear thou not that any god or man will look upon us"—that does not prove that the cloud was needed to conceal them from the eyes of mortals, but that in this cloud they would be as invisible to the gods as they always were to men. So, when Minerva puts on the helmet of Pluto, which has the same effect of concealment that a cloud would have, it is not that she may be concealed from the Trojans, who either see her not at all or under the form of Sthenelus, but simply that she may not be recognized by Mars.

[19]Tableaux tirés de l'Iliade, Avert. p. 5. "On est toujours convenu, que plus un poëme fournissait d'images et d'actions, plus il avait de supériorité en poésie. Cette réflexion m'avait conduit à penser que le calcul des différens tableaux, qu' offrent les poëmes, pouvait servir à comparer le mérite respectif des poëmes et des poëtes. Le nombre et le genre des tableaux que présentent ces grands ouvrages, auraient été une espèce de pierre de touche, ou, plutôt, une balance certaine du mérite de ces poëmes et du génie de leurs auteurs."
["It has always been admitted that the more images and actions a poem provides the greater it is as poetry. This reflection leads me to think that the number of different pictures poems provide can serve to measure the respective merits of poems and poets. The number and kind of pictures that these great works have is thus a kind of touchstone, or rather, a certain scale for determining the merits of the poems and the genius of their authors."]

[20]What we call poetic pictures, the ancients, as we learn from Longinus, called "phantasiae"; and what we call illusion in such pictures, they named "enargia." It was therefore said by some one, as Plutarch tells us, that poetic "phantasiae" were, on account of their "enargia," waking dreams: Αἱ ποιητικαὶ φαντασδίαι διὰ τὴν ἐνάργειαν ἐγρηγορότων ἐνύπνια εἰσίν. I could wish that our modern books upon poetry had used this nomenclature, and avoided the word picture altogether. We should thus have been spared a multitude of doubtful rules, whose chief foundation is the coincidence of an arbitrary term. No one would then have thought of confining poetic conceptions within the limits of a material picture. But the moment

these conceptions were called a poetic picture, the foundation for the error was laid.

[21]*Iliad*, iv. 105.

αὐτίκ' ἐσύλα τόξον ἐΰξοον
καὶ τὸ μὲν εὖ κατέθηκε τανυσσάμενος, ποτὶ
    γαίς
ἀγκλίνας' . . .

αὐτὰρ ὁ σύλα πῶμα φαρέτρης, ἐκ δ' ἕλετ' ἰὸν
ἀβλῆτα πτερόεντα, μελαινέων ἕρμ' ὀδυνάων·
αἶψα δ' ἐπὶ νευρῇ κατεκόσμει πικρὸν ὀϊστόν,
ἕλκε δ' ὁμοῦ γλυφίδας τε λαβὼν καὶ νεῦρα
    βόεια·
νευρὴν μὲν μαζῷ πέλασεν, τόξον δὲ σίδηρον.
αὐτὰρ ἐπειδὴ κυκλοτερὲς μέγα τόξον ἔτεινεν,
λίγξε βιός, νευρὴ δὲ μέγ' ἴαχεν ἇλτο δ' ὀϊστὸς
ὀξυβελής, καθ' ὅμιλον ἐπιπτέσθαι μενεαίνων.

To bend that bow the warrior lowered it
And pressed an end against the earth. . . .
Then the Lycian drew aside
The cover from his quiver, taking out
A well-fledged arrow that had never flown,
A cause of future sorrows. On the string
He laid that fatal arrow. . . .
Grasping the bowstring and the arrow's
    notch
He drew them back and forced the string
    to meet
His breast, the arrow-head to meet the
    bow,
Till the bow formed a circle. Then it
    twanged;
The cord gave out a shrilly sound; the
    shaft
Leaped forth in eager haste to reach the
    host.—BRYANT.
                    [Cf. *GBWW*, Vol. 4, p. 25a–b.]

[22]*Prologue to the Satires*, 340.

That not in Fancy's maze he wandered
    long,
But stooped to Truth and moralized his
    song

Ibid. 148.

        . . . Who could take offense
While pure description held the place of
    sense?

Warburton's remark on this last line may have the force of an explanation by the poet himself. "He uses *pure* equivocally, to signify either chaste or empty; and has given in this line what he esteemed the true character of descriptive poetry, as it is called—a composition, in his opinion, as absurd as a feast made up of sauces. The use of a picturesque imagination is to brighten and adorn good sense: so that to employ it only in description is like children's delighting in a prism for the sake of its gaudy colors, which, when frugally managed and artfully disposed,

might be made to represent and illustrate the noblest objects in nature."

Both poet and commentator seem to have regarded the matter rather from a moral than an artistic point of view. But so much the better that this style of poetry seems equally worthless from whichever point it be viewed.

[23]*"Se vogliono i Pittori senza fatica trovare un perfetto esempio di bella Donna, legiano quelle Stanze dell' Ariosto, nelle quali egli discrive mirabilmente le belezze della Fata Alcina; e vedranno parimente, quanto i buoni Poeti siano ancora essi Pittori."*

["If painters would find without any trouble a perfect example of the beautiful woman, they should read those stanzas of Ariosto in which he described wonderfully the beauty of the enchantress Alcina; and they will see also how good poets are also good painters."]

[24]Dolce, *Dialogo della Pittura*. *"Ecco, che, quanto alla proporzione, l' ingeniosissimo Ariosto assegna la migliore, che sappiano formar le mani de' più eccellenti Pittori, usando questa voce industri, per dinotar la diligenza, che conviene al buono artefice."*

["Note that with respect to proportion the ingenious Ariosto gives greater credit to the hands of the more excellent painters by using the word 'industrious' to denote the care that the good artist takes."]

[25]Ibid. *"Poteva l' Ariosto nella guisa, che ha detto chioma bionda, dir chioma d' oro: ma gli parve forse, che havrebbe havuto troppo del Poetico. Da che si può ritrar, che 'l Pittore dee imitar l' oro, e non metterlo (come fanno i Miniatori) nelle sue Pitture, in modo, che si possa dire, que capelli non sono d' oro, ma par che risplendano, come l' oro."*

["Ariosto instead of saying 'blond hair' could have said 'hair of gold', but that would have been too poetical. From this one can deduce that the painter should imitate gold and not put it into their pictures (as the Miniaturists), so that one can say that the hair is not gold but glows as if it were gold."]

[26]*The Connoisseur*, vol. i. no. 21. The beauty of Knonmquaiha is thus described. "He was struck with the glossy hue of her complexion, which shone like the jetty down on the black hogs of Hessaqua; he was ravished with the prest gristle of her nose; and his eyes dwelt with admiration on the flaccid beauties of her breasts, which descended to her navel." And how were these charms set off by art? "She made a varnish of the fat of goats mixed with soot, with which she anointed her whole body as she stood beneath the rays of the sun; her locks were clotted with melted grease, and powdered with the yellow dust of Buchu; her face, which shone like the polished ebony, was beautifully varied with spots

of red earth and appeared like the sable curtain of the night bespangled with stars; she sprinkled her limbs with wood-ashes and perfumed them with the dung of Stinkbingsem. Her arms and legs were entwined with the shining entrails of an heifer; from her neck there hung a pouch composed of the stomach of a kid; the wings of an ostrich overshadowed the fleshy promontories behind; and before she wore an apron formed of the shaggy ears of a lion."

Here is further the marriage ceremony of the loving pair, "The Surri, or Chief Priest, approached them, and, in a deep voice, chanted the nuptial rites to the melodious grumbling of the Gom-Gom; and, at the same time (according to the manner of Caffraria), bedewed them plentifully with the urinary benediction. The bride and bridegroom rubbed in the precious stream with ecstasy, while the briny drops trickled from their bodies, like the oozy surge from the rocks of Chirigriqua."

[27]*The Sea-Voyage,* act iii, scene I. A French pirate ship is thrown upon a desert island. Avarice and envy cause quarrels among the men, and a couple of wretches, who had long suffered extreme want on the island, seize a favorable opportunity to put to sea in the ship. Robbed thus of their whole stock of provisions, the miserable men see death, in its worst forms, staring them in the face, and express to each other their hunger and despair as follows:

Lamure. Oh, what a tempest have I in my
    stomach!
How my empty guts cry out! My wounds ache,
Would they would bleed again, that I
    might get
Something to quench my thirst!
    Franville. O Lamure, the happiness my
    dogs had
When I kept house at home! They had a
    storehouse,
A storehouse of most blessed bones and crusts.
Happy crusts! Oh how sharp hunger
    pinches me!
    Lamure. How now, what news?
    Morillar. Hast any meat yet?
    Franville. Not a bit that I can see.
Here be goodly quarries, but they be cruel
    hard
To gnaw. I ha' got some mud, we'll eat it
    with spoons;
Very good thick mud; but it stinks
    damnably.
There's old rotten trunks of trees, too,
But not a leaf nor blossom in all the island.
    Lamure. How it looks!
    Morillar. It stinks too.
    Lamure. It may be poison.

Franville. Let it be any thing.
So, I can get it down. Why, man,
Poison's a princely dish!
    Morillar. Hast thou no biscuit?
No crumbs left in thy pocket? Here is
    my doublet,
Give me but three small crumbs.
    Franville. Not for three kingdoms,
If it were master of 'em. Oh, Lamure,
But one poor joint of mutton we ha'
    scorned, man!
    Lamure. Thou speak'st of paradise;
Or but the snuffs of those healths,
We have lewdly at midnight flung away.
    Morillar. Ah, but to lick the glasses!

But this is nothing, compared with the next scene, when the ship's surgeon enters.

    Franville. Here comes the surgeon. What
Hast thou discovered? Smile, smile, and
    comfort us.
    Surgeon. I am expiring,
Smile they that can. I can find nothing,
    gentlemen,
Here's nothing can be meat without a
    miracle.
Oh, that I had my boxes and my lints now,
My stupes, my tents, and those sweet helps
    of nature!
What dainty dishes could I make of them!
    Morillar. Hast ne'er an old suppository?
    Surgeon. Oh, would I had, sir!
    Lamure. Or but the paper where such
    a cordial,
Potion, or pills hath been entombed!
    Franville. Or the best bladder, where a
    cooling glister?
    Morillar. 'Hast thou no searcloths left?
Nor any old poultices?
    Franville. We care not to what it hath
    been ministered.
    Surgeon. Sure I have none of these dainties,
    gentlemen.
    Franville. Where's the great wen
Thou cut'st from Hugh the sailor's
    shoulder?
That would serve now for a most princely
    banquet.
    Surgeon. Ay, if we had it, gentlemen.
I flung it overboard, slave that I was.
    Lamure. A most improvident villain!
[28] . . . This reminds me that Winckelmann, in his first work on the imitation of Greek art, allowed an error to creep in with regard to Sophocles. "The most beautiful of the youths danced naked in the theatre, and Sophocles, the great Sophocles, was in his youth the first to show himself thus to his fellow-citizens."

Sophocles never danced naked on the stage. He danced around the trophies after the victory of Salamis, according to some authorities naked, but according to others clothed. Sophocles was one of the boys who was brought for safety to Salamis, and on this island it pleased the tragic muse to assemble her three favorites in a gradation typical of their future career. The bold Aeschylus helped gain the victory; the blooming Sophocles danced around the trophies; and on the same happy island, on the very day of the victory, Euripides was born.

PICTURE CREDITS

—**FRONTISPIECE** Christopher Springmann —**6** Boris De Rachewiltz/ * New Directions Publishing Corp. —**7** AP/Wide World —**8, 9, 12, 16, 17, 22, 29, 35** Thomas Victor —**56** Adapted from *Understanding Biology,* by Philip Applewhite and Sam Wilson, New York: Holt, Rinehart and Winston, 1978 —**67** Huntington Potter and David Dressler, *Life Magazine* © 1980 Time Inc. —**80** Julia Bennett Studios, London —**83 (l.)** Culver Pictures —**83 (r.)** The Granger Collection —**93, 98, 101** The Bettmann Archive —**123** Culver Pictures —**125, 133** The Bettmann Archive —**150** Vivian T. R. Barry —**233 (t., b.)** Hitachi Central Research Lab/Cameramann, International —**234** * Cray Research of Minneapolis —**238** Sidney Harris —**241** From "Operating Systems," by Peter J. Denning and Robert L. Brown, *Scientific American,* vol. 251, no. 3 —**243, 245** Cameramann, International —**248 (l.)** The Bettmann Archive —**248 (r.)** National Portrait Gallery, London —**249** The Bettmann Archive —**251** Roger Ressmeyer/Wheeler Pictures —**255** Joe McNally/Wheeler Pictures —**258** Maurice F. X. Donahue —**290** Victoria and Albert Museum —**338, 380** The Bettmann Archive —**387** The Bettmann Archive —**391** Alinari/Art Resource —**394, 403, 415, 442** Art Resource

N ow there's a way to identify all your fine books with flair and style. As part of our continuing service to you, Britannica Home Library Service, Inc. is proud to be able to offer you the fine quality item shown on the next page.

B ooklovers will love the heavy-duty personalized embosser. Now you can personalize all your fine books with the mark of distinction, just the way all the fine libraries of the world do.

T o order this item, please type or print your name, address and zip code on a plain sheet of paper. (Note special instructions for ordering the embosser). Please send a check or money order only (your money will be refunded in full if you are not delighted) for the full amount of purchase, including postage and handling, to:

Britannica Home Library Service, Inc.
Attn: Yearbook Department
Post Office Box 6137
Chicago, Illinois 60680

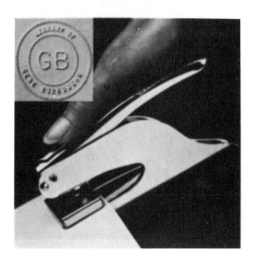

Authors

in Great Books of the Western World

Homer	Nicomachus
Aeschylus	Ptolemy
Sophocles	Marcus Aurelius
Herodotus	Galen
Euripides	Plotinus
Thucydides	Augustine
Hippocrates	Thomas Aquinas
Aristophanes	Dante
Plato	Chaucer
Aristotle	Machiavelli
Euclid	Copernicus
Archimedes	Rabelais
Apollonius	Montaigne
Lucretius	Gilbert
Virgil	Cervantes
Plutarch	Francis Bacon
Tacitus	Galileo
Epictetus	Shakespeare
	Kepler